Street Law

A Course in Practical Law

Fifth Edition

Lee P. Arbetman, M.Ed., J.D.
Adjunct Professor of Law
Georgetown University Law Center

Edward T. McMahon, M.Ed., J.D.

Edward L. O'Brien, J.D.
Adjunct Professor of Law
Georgetown University Law Center

A Publication of the National Institute for Citizen Education in the Law

Minneapolis/St. Paul • New York • Los Angeles • San Francisco

Copyediting: Beverly Peavler, Mary Berry
Composition: American Composition & Graphics, Inc.
Art: Precision Graphics
Indexing: Maggie Jarpey
Cover Image: Superstock
Credits for text photos (continued on page 647): **2** ©Don Milici; **4 (top)** ©Don Milici; **4 (bottom)** ©Mark Richards/PhotoEdit; **5** Los Angeles Daily News ©1993; **8** ©Don Milici; **9** ©Robert W. Ginn/PhotoEdit; **13** ©Bettmann; **16** ©Paul Conklin/PhotoEdit; **17** ©The Bettmann Archive; **18** ©Don Milici; **19** ©Don Milici; **22** ©Don Milici; **23** ©UPI/Bettmann; **27** ©Dennis Brack/Black Star; **29** ©Don Milici; **32** ©Don Milici; **34 (top)** ©Supreme Court Historical Society; **34 (bottom)** Larry Downing/Sygma; **40**

WEST'S COMMITMENT TO THE ENVIRONMENT

In 1906, West Publishing Company began recycling materials left over from the production of books. This began a tradition of efficient and responsible use of resources. Today, up to 95 percent of our legal books and 70 percent of our college and school texts are printed on recycled, acid-free stock. West also recycles nearly 22 million pounds of scrap paper annually—the equivalent of 181,717 trees. Since the 1960s, West has devised ways to capture and recycle waste inks, solvents, oils, and vapors created in the printing process. We also recycle plastics of all kinds, wood, glass, corrugated cardboard, and batteries, and have eliminated the use of Styrofoam book packaging. We at West are proud of the longevity and the scope of our commitment to the environment.

Production, Prepress, Printing and Binding by West Publishing Company.

610 Opperman Drive
P.O. Box 64526
St. Paul, MN 55164-0526

Printed in the United States of America
01 00 99 98 8
Library of Congress Cataloging-in-Publication Data
Arbetman, Lee.
Street law : a course in practical law / Lee P. Arbetman, Edward T. McMahon, Edward O'Brien.—5th ed.
p. cm.
Includes index.
ISBN 0-314-02713-0 (hard)
ISBN 0-314-02935-4 (soft)

1. Law—United States—Popular works. [1. Law. 2. Life skills. 3. Consumer education.] I. McMahon, Edward, 1947–
II. O'Brien, Edward L. III. Title.
KF387.A73 1994
349.73—dc20
[347.3] 93-44422
CIP
AC

Contents

KEEP
RIGHT
DO NOT
ENTER
WRONG
WAY
KEEP
RIGHT
ONE WAY
MUSEU
ONE WAY

Chapter 2

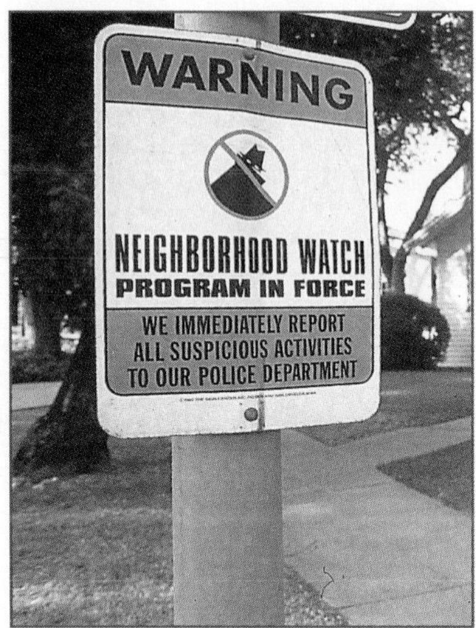

Criminal Law and Juvenile Justice—59

Chapter 3

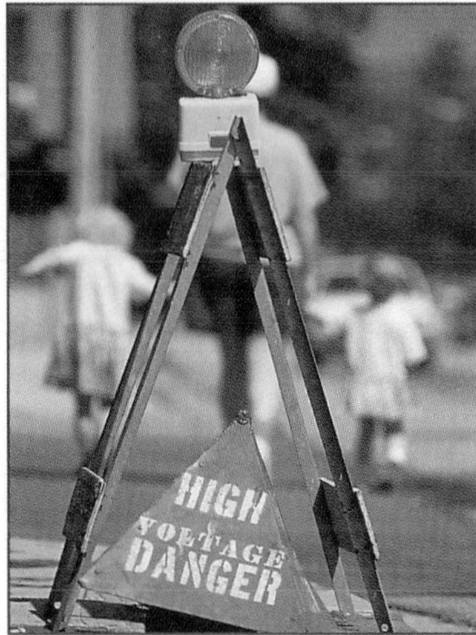

Torts—185

Chapter 4

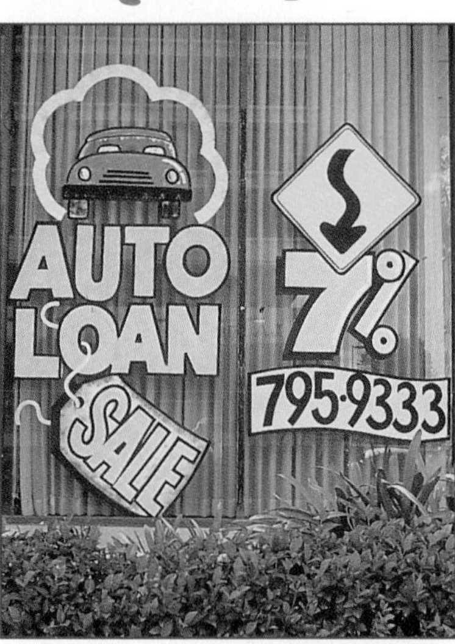

Consumer Law—249

Chapter 5

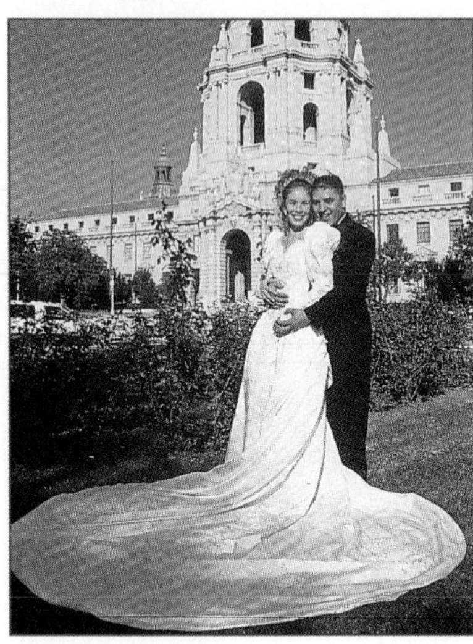

Family Law—319

Chapter 6

Housing Law—383

Chapter 7

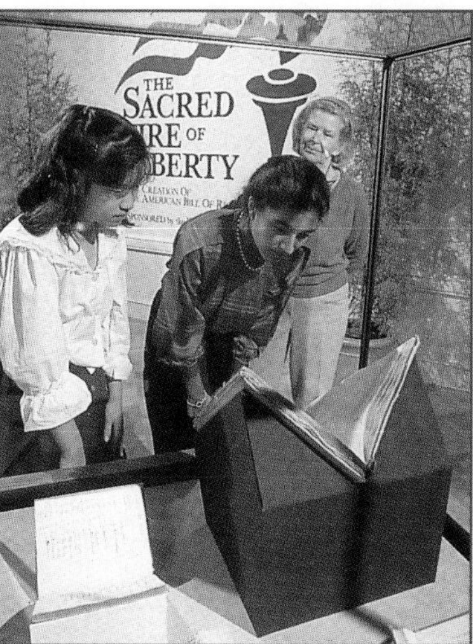

Individual Rights and Liberties—429

Preface

The fifth edition of *Street Law: A Course in Practical Law* builds upon the success and popularity of earlier editions. Incorporating their best features, this edition provides new information, practical advice, and competency-building activities designed to provide students with the ability to analyze, evaluate, and, in some situations, resolve legal disputes. The fifth edition also incorporates a colorful new design.

The text reflects the changes in law and legal procedure that have taken place at the national level since the publication of the fourth edition. Throughout the book, we have added text and problems dealing with the most current law-related public issues, including gangs, guns, and substance abuse. We have continued to expand our emphasis on promoting alternative (nonjudicial) forms of dispute resolution. In addition, we have added to each chapter a new feature called Law Around the World. This material encourages students to analyze how other countries (and their legal systems) handle certain basic legal problems.

Street Law's approach to law-related education is to provide practical information and problem solving opportunities that develop in students the knowledge and skills necessary for survival in our law-saturated society. The curriculum includes case studies, mock trials, role-plays, small group exercises, and visual analysis activities. For optimal results, *Street Law* requires the use of community resource people such as lawyers and police officers. It also requires community experiences such as court tours and police ride-alongs. This methodology allows students to be active participants in their own education. In this way, we hope to promote in students a willingness and capability to participate effectively in the legal and political systems.

Properly used, *Street Law* has been found to contribute to programs that reduce juvenile delinquency, including the devastating problem of juvenile substance abuse. Teachers should note that a separate, comprehensive *Teacher's Manual*, supplemental *Test Bank*, *Work Book*, *Service Learning Video,* and *Street Law: Student Scenes* are available from the publisher.

ADVICE TO READERS: Law varies from state to state and is constantly changing. Therefore, someone confronted with a legal problem should not use this text as a substitute for legal advice from an attorney.

The National Institute for Citizen Education in the Law

Street Law is a product of the National Institute for Citizen Education in the Law (NICEL). The Institute grew out of a Georgetown University Law Center program, launched in 1971, in which law students teach practical law courses in District of Columbia high schools, juvenile and adult correctional institutions, and a number of community-based settings.

NICEL was created to promote increased opportunities for citizen education in the law. It develops curricula, trains teachers, and replicates programs. It also provides technical assistance and curriculum materials to law schools, school systems, departments of corrections, juvenile justice agencies, bar associations, legal service and community organizations, state and local governments, and other groups and individuals interested in establishing law-related education programs. Through its national clearinghouse, NICEL distributes lists of its materials and services as well as technical assistance papers that guide practitioners in the replication of its program models. NICEL also provides assistance for programs at the elementary school level.

Some NICEL programs have also been replicated in South Africa, Hungary, Chile, Bolivia, Ecuador, and the Philippines.

In addition to *Street Law*, the Institute's publications include

Democracy for All (1994)
We Can Work It Out: Problem Solving through Mediation (1993)
Human Rights for All (1993)
Teens, Crime, and the Community (1992)
Practical Law for Jail and Prison Personnel (1987)
Great Trials in American History: Civil War to the Present (1985)
Current Legal Issues Filmstrip Series (1985)
Family Law: Competencies in Law and Citizenship (1984)
Street Law: Mock Trial Manual (1984)
Current Legal Issues Filmstrip Series (1984)

Street Law Filmstrip Series (1983)
Consumer Law: Competencies in Law and Citizenship (1982)
Law and the Consumer (1982)

For further information or assistance, please contact

National Institute for Citizen Education in the Law
711 G Street, S.E.
Washington, D.C. 20003
(202) 546-6644
FAX (202) 546-6649
TT (202) 546-7591

Acknowledgments

Development of this fifth edition of *Street Law* was funded in part under grant #85-JS-CX-004 from the Office of Juvenile Justice and Delinquency Prevention, Office of Justice Programs, U.S. Department of Justice. Points of view or opinions in this document are those of the authors and do no necessarily represent the official position or policies of the U.S. Department of Justice.

The authors gratefully acknowledge the many teachers, law students, law professors, and other attorneys who have assisted in the development of our curriculum materials. Over the years, many people have provided valuable field-testing, research, editorial assistance, encouragement, and support. We can name only a few in the space below, but we appreciate the efforts of all who have worked with us.

In 1987, our coauthor Ed McMahon left NICEL's staff. His work was part of the core of earlier editions of the book, and his writing skill, legal scholarship, and educational expertise are missed by all of us. We appreciate his editorial work on this edition and want to acknowledge that parts of this edition are based on his earlier writing.

In working on the fifth edition, we were particularly fortunate to have the assistance of several people who joined our staff on a temporary basis. Georgetown law student Audrey Kraus provided research and writing assistance on the consumer, housing, and tort law chapters. Hamline law student Lindsey Dodson spent the summer of 1993 with us making a substantial contribution to the revisions of the criminal and individual rights law chapters. Also that summer, Washington University senior Beth Landes helped revise the list of Organizations to Know in Appendix F.

Early in 1994, attorneys Amy L. Strain and Alan Korn (both of whom had taught *Street Law* while in law school) joined the staff and assumed major responsibilities for the completion of the teacher's manual and the glossary. They were instrumental in helping us with the final phases of this project.

There is no question that this project could not have been completed without the enormous contributions of our colleague and friend, Margaret

Fisher. Professor Fisher, formerly a member of our staff at NICEL, now coordinates law-related education programs for the state of Washington while also conducting a *Street Law* clinical program at the University of Puget Sound Law School. She took the lead in developing the new *Work Book* and also made the revisions in the *Test Bank*.

The new edition is also supplemented by a unique video. This video is the work of an extraordinarily dedicated lawyer, Beverly Reeves, and a talented group of high school students from Austin, Texàs. Further information about this project is available with the teaching materials (also developed by Margaret Fisher) that accompany the video, but we hope this is just the first of many contributions that Beverly Reeves makes to the *Street Law* program.

Another new feature of the fifth edition is an appendix in the student text with information on law-related careers. For this excellent idea, and for the draft materials for the appendix, we want to thank Don Morris, a *Street Law* teacher in Cheyenne, Wyoming, who also coordinates his state's law-related education program.

Professor Grayfred B. Gray of the University of Tennessee College of Law provided us with a thorough edit of virtually the entire student manuscript. We benefitted from his recognized expertise in "plain language for lawyers and nonlawyers," as well as his broad-based legal scholarship. He also recruited colleagues from his faculty to review various chapters in their substantive areas of expertise.

NICEL's staff provided important encouragement and assistance during the lengthy process of developing the fifth edition. Praise should certainly go to NICEL's director, Jason Newman, who played a substantial role in the organization's founding and in the original conceptualization and design of the text. Support staff members Karla Williams, Pamela Dennis, Hellene Burnette, Sherri Singleton, and James Rohloff provided assistance that ranged from typing and photocopying draft chapters to proofreading, editing, and providing real-life examples for some of the problems in the text.

Program staff members Aggie Alvez, Rebecca Bond, Jeff Chinn, Bebs Chorak, Erin Donovan, Ruth Gutstein, Maria Hopkins, Caroline Kulczycki, Mary Larkin, Robert Masciola, Rick Ody, Wanda Routier, Ana Sanchez, Jon Wentzel, and Judy Zimmer provided useful ideas, skillful proofreading and editing, and much-needed encouragement. Thanks to Judy Zimmer for her assistance in strengthening the book's overall focus on alternative dispute resolution, to Mary Larkin and Bebs Chorak for their work reviewing and reworking the juvenile justice section of Chapter 2, and to Wanda Routier for her assistance in adding materials throughout about the *Americans with Disabilities Act* (ADA).

Special thanks to Jeff Chinn for his fine work on Chapters 2 and 7, for his legal research for the new Law Around the World features, and for his tireless efforts to keep the research files and the authors organized.

In creating a new edition, we undertook a review process that involved legal experts from across the country. Because significant portions of the text necessarily deal with state statutes and cases, we tried to obtain a broad-based consensus on the current status of the law. We appreciate the generous volunteer efforts of the following persons who reviewed drafts of the chapters in the student text:

Chapter 1: Professor Richard Roe, Georgetown University Law Center; Professor Louis Fischer, University of Massachusetts; Professor Brenda Desmond, University of Montana Law School; and Professor Grayfred B. Gray, University of Tennessee College of Law. **Chapter 2:** Professor Wallace Mlyniec, Georgetown University Law Center; Professor Justin Brooks, Thomas M. Cooley Law School; Professor Gary Anderson, University of Tennessee Law School; Terry Modglin, National Crime Prevention Council. **Chapter 3:** Professor Carol Mutter, University of Tennessee Law School; and attorney Norman Schneider. **Chapter 4:** Federal Trade Commission attorneys Carole L. Reynolds, Richard Donahue, Carole Danielson, Gary Laden, and Robert Doyle; Professor L. Scott Gould, Rutgers Law School; Professor Phyllis C. Wimberly, University of Tennessee College of Law; and attorney Lucy Weisz. **Chapter 5:** Professor Joan Meier, George Washington University Law School; Professor Grayfred B. Gray, University of Tennessee College of Law; and attorney Charles Mwalimu. **Chapter 6:** Attorney Jack Scheuerman. **Chapter 7:** Professor Tom Krattenmaker, Georgetown University Law Center; Professor Eric Neisser, Rutgers Law School; and Diana Hess.

Over the years many agencies and organizations have helped to make possible the work of the National Institute for Citizen Education in the Law. We appreciate their support and acknowledge their assistance. We particularly wish to thank the following for their contributions:

Akin, Gump, Strauss, Hauer & Feld
Ms. Jacqueline Allee
Allegheny Beverage Corporation
The Allstate Foundation
American Security Bank
American Telephone & Telegraph Company Foundation
April Trust Foundation
Arent, Fox, Kintner, Plotkin & Kahn
Arnold & Porter
C. Clyde Atkins
Mary Reynolds Babcock Foundation
Dewey Ballantine
Ms. Eleanor S. Barnard
Mr. George Batchelor
Mr. Lowell Beck
Mr. Bob Belair
Mr. William Bell
Best Products Foundation
Dr. Lee Roy Black
Ms. Jennifer D. Bloom
Mr. Bruce Bonar
Mr. Kevin Boyle
Mr. David Brink
C&P Telephone Company
Mr. A. Gus Cleveland
Mr. Thomas Cobb
Ms. Alice Collopy
Commission on the Bicentennial of the U.S. Constitution
Covington & Burling Foundation
John J. Creedon Foundation
Crowell & Moring
Cypen & Cypen
Dade Community Foundation
Mr. Lawrence Dark
Cora and John H. Davis Foundation
Dechert, Price & Rhoads
Mr. Thomas K. Diemer
District of Columbia Department of Corrections
District of Columbia Natural Gas
District of Columbia Public Schools
Mr. Chuck G. Douglas
Max and Victoria Dreyfus Foundation
Ms. Gretchen Dykstra
Mr. Bert Early
Edlavitch and Tyser Foundation
Mr. David Ellwanger
Justice William Erickson
Mr. Robert M. Ervin
The Exxon Corporation
Mr. William W. Falsgraf
Ms. Beth Farnbach
Federal National Mortgage Association
Mr. John Feerick
Field Foundation

Florida Power Corporation
Mr. Robert L. Floyd
Foundation for the Improvement of Justice
Lazard Freres & Company
Friday, Eldredge & Clark
Fried, Frank, Harris, Shriver & Jacobson
Mr. Mark Gelber
General Mills Foundation
Georgetown University Law Center
Ms. Brenda M. Girton
Philip L. Graham Fund
Judge Thomas Greene
Ms. Katherine Hagen
Mr. Dean Hansell
Ms. Julia Hardin
Mr. Geoffrey C. Hazard, Jr.
The Hechinger Foundation
Mr. William O.E. Henry
Mr. Roger S. Hewitt
Ms. Ruth Hinerfeld
Holland & Knight Foundation
Mr. A.P. Hollingsworth
Mr. Mark Hulsey
IBM Corporation
International Paper Company Foundation
Mr. Leonard Janofsky
Mr. Doug Jobes
Honorable Norma H. Johnson
Judge Sam D. Johnson
Kellogg Foundation
Mr. T. Paine Kelly
Robert F. Kennedy Memorial
Knight-Ridder Newspapers
Mr. John Kramer
Mr. John Krsul
Ms. Liane Levetan
Eli Lilly & Company Foundation
Mr. R. Stanley Lowe
Anthony Lucas-Spindeltop Foundation
Chief Justice Vincent L. McKusick
Mead Data Central
Mr. Abelardo Menendez
Mr. Robert W. Meserve
Eugene and Agnes E. Meyer Foundation
Microsoft Corporation
Ms. Vivian Mills
Mintz, Levin, Cohn, Ferris, Glovsky & Popeo, P.C.
Mobil Foundation
Montgomery Ward
Morrison & Foerster
Mr. Mark Murphy
New World Foundation
O'Connor & Hannan
Olin Corporation Charitable Trust
Mr. Alan C. Page
Mr. Richard Parker
Mr. Richard Pettigrew
Justice Lewis Powell
Mr. E. Barrett Prettyman
Prudential Foundation
Honorable William C. Pryor
Public Welfare Foundation
Publix Supermarkets (through G.W. Jenkins Foundation)
Mr. Ramon Rasco
Ms. Janet Reno
Research Foundation of the Bar Association of D.C.
Ms. Linda J. Riekes
Mr. David Robinson
Ruden, Barnett, McCloskey, Smith Schuester & Russell, P.A.
Mr. Jack Lee Sammons
Satellite Business Systems
Sears, Roebuck & Co.
Mr. Bernard G. Segal
Ms. Debra L. Smith
Mr. Justin A. Stanley
Ms. Linda Start
Sterling Drug, Inc.
Philip M. Stern Family Fund
Hattie M. Strong Foundation
Student Loan Marketing Association
Ms. Janet R. Studley
Mr. Theodore Tetzlaff
Texaco Philanthropic Foundation
Times Publishing Company
Ms. Sabrina Toma
Mr. Lyman M. Tondel, Jr.
Mr. Jerrol Tostrud
Ms. Mary Pat Toups
Mr. Sidney Tuchman
United States Department of Education
United States Trust Company of New York
Mr. Dan Walbolt
Warner-Lambert Company
The Washington Post
West Publishing Company
Weyerhauser Foundation, Inc.
Ms. Fay H. Williams
Wilmer, Cutler & Pickering

Windom Fund (anonymous donor)
The Women's Bar Association Foundation
Xerox Corporation
Mr. Jamil Zainaldin
Mr. Howard A. Zipser

We also thank the following reviewers and teachers who provided valuable comments based on their experience using *Street Law*.

Dr. Edgar Bravo
Edison/Miami High School
Florida

Larry Compton
Northwest High School
Indiana

Rich Fatzinger
Tackland School District
Pennsylvania

Peter Greene
Reading Memorial High School
Massachusetts

Leonne Lizotte
Easthampton High School
Massachusetts

Philip McFarland
East Hampton High School
Missouri

Donald Morris
Cheyenne Central High School
Wyoming

Jim Riddiford
Lincoln Park High School
Illinois

Allen Shapiro
Swampscott High School
Massachusetts

Ron Smith
Lincoln Park High School
Illinois

We owe a special debt of gratitude to our parent organization, the Consortium of Universities of the Washington Metropolitan Area and to its president, Dr. Monte Shepler.

One special group of individuals has helped NICEL to grow and prosper. These dedicated individuals sit on our National Advisory Committee. They are listed separately at the back of the book, but we want to thank them here for their guidance and encouragement. And we want to single out for thanks our chairperson, Mark Gelber, under whose leadership we eagerly anticipate new challenges.

Lee Arbetman
Ed O'Brien
Washington, D.C.
April, 1994

Dedication

TO THE ROBERT F. KENNEDY MEMORIAL, which funded RFK fellowships beginning in 1973 that enabled the authors to work with Jason Newman, Nancy Harrison, Vincent Reed, and others to found the first *Street Law* project in the District of Columbia.

The Memorial then helped establish the National Institute for Citizen Education in the Law, which has expanded *Street Law* nationally and internationally. This book is also dedicated to Robert F. Kennedy's ideals and the people he served.

Lee Arbetman, Ed O'Brien, and Ed McMahon
April, 1994

TO MY PARENTS, William and Elizabeth O'Brien, who taught me how to respect and critically examine the law and TO MY CHILDREN, John and Beth, who every day reaffirm my optimism about our society's future.

Ed O'Brien
April, 1994

Chapter 1

Introduction to Law and the Legal System

Street law is law that is of practical use in everyday life (on the streets). Every purchase, lease, contract, marriage, divorce, crime, or traffic violation places the citizen face-to-face with the law. *Street Law* is designed to provide you with an understanding of your legal rights and responsibilities, a knowledge of everyday legal problems, and the ability to analyze, evaluate, and, in some situations, resolve legal disputes.

Many people believe that only those with power and money can win in our legal system. They see the law as a body of confusing, technical rules that work against them. Some people don't believe, for example, that a tenant can get a landlord to fix up a rundown apartment or that a consumer can convince a merchant to repair, replace, or give a refund for poor-quality merchandise. These things don't always happen, but they are possible, especially when you are aware of your rights and take action to exercise those rights.

Street Law addresses general problems in the areas of criminal and juvenile justice; torts; and consumer, family, housing, and individual rights and liberties law. The text also discusses what to do if you are the victim of crime, when and how to select an attorney, the legal rights and responsibilities of parents and children, how to register to vote, what to do about discrimination or other violations of your constitutional rights, and many other situations.

These and all the topics in *Street Law* provide specific information to help you survive in your everyday life on the street. You will also learn general information about the structure, function, and actual operation of the legal system.

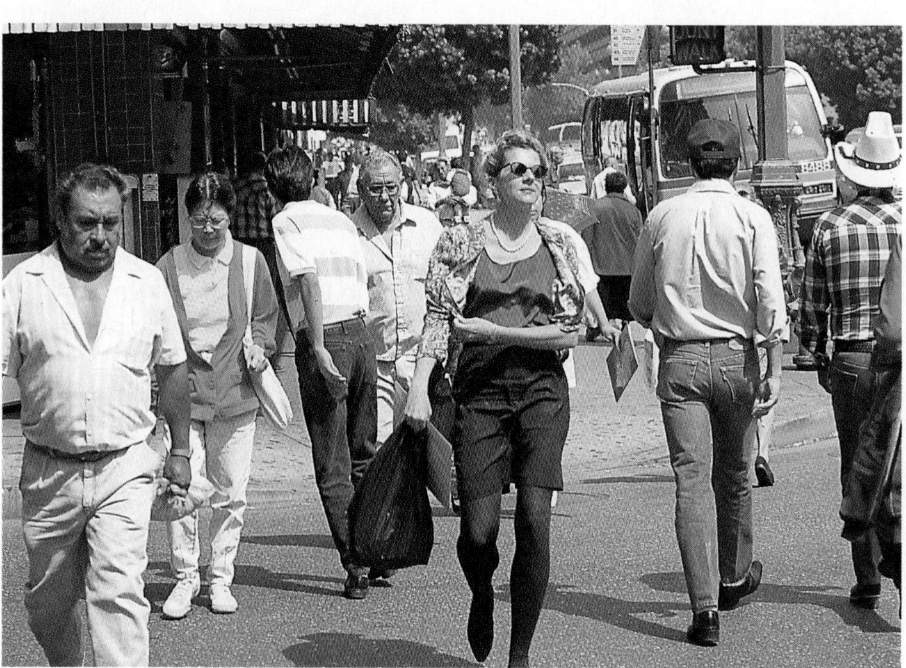

What laws do these people need to know?

Knowledge is most valuable when you can use it. *Street Law* will help you learn how to use the law to improve your life. Throughout the text, you will be given practical legal information and then asked to apply it to real life situations.

Finally, *Street Law* is designed to help you become a better and more active citizen. Involved citizens are law-abiding, are committed to upholding basic rights and freedoms, and work together to oppose unfair laws and improve the legal system. They do this because they understand that democracy is not a spectator sport!

WHAT IS LAW?

The question "What is law?" has troubled people for many years. An entire field of study known as **jurisprudence** (the study of law and legal philosophy) is devoted to answering this question. Many definitions of law exist. For our purposes, however, law can be defined as the rules and regulations made and enforced by government that regulate the conduct of people within a society.

As a child, you learned about rules first at home and later at school. At home, your parents made and enforced rules concerning issues like chores and bedtimes. Rules made and enforced by the government are called laws. The government makes laws that affect almost every aspect of daily life.

One thing is certain: Every society that has ever existed has recognized the need for laws. These laws may have been unwritten, but even pre-industrial societies had rules to regulate people's conduct. Native American societies, for example, were governed by unwritten laws. When Europeans first arrived on the North American continent, each of the Native American nations (or tribes, as they are commonly called today) maintained order through a system of unwritten rules. Because many non-Native American government officials and others did not see or understand these traditional mechanisms, many non-Native Americans held the erroneous view that the societies were lawless. Today, some Native American groups are still governed, at least in part, by traditional unwritten law.

Without laws, there would be confusion and disorder. This does not mean that all laws are fair or even good, but imagine how people might take advantage of one another without a set of rules.

PROBLEM 1

Make a list of all your daily activities (for example, waking up, eating, going to school). Next to each item, list any laws that affect that activity. What is the purpose of each law that you identified? Would you change any of these laws? Why?

Law and Values

What values are placed in conflict by laws protecting the environment?

Laws generally reflect and promote a society's values. Our legal system is influenced by our society's traditional ideas of right and wrong. For example, laws against murder reflect the moral belief that killing another person is wrong. Most people would condemn murder regardless of what the law said. However, not everything that is immoral is also illegal. For example, lying to a friend may be immoral but is seldom illegal.

We expect our legal system to achieve many goals. These include (1) protecting basic human rights, (2) promoting fairness, (3) helping resolve conflicts, (4) promoting order and stability, (5) protecting the environment, (6) representing the will of the majority, and (7) protecting the rights of minorities.

Many of society's most difficult problems involve conflicts among these goals. For example, in trying to make up for past discrimination, some laws give preference to minorities over whites or to women over men. Laws must balance rights with responsibilities, the will of the majority with the rights of the minority, the need for

How does the law encourage people to buy homes?

How does this photo reflect society's changing laws and values?

order with the need for basic freedom. Reasonable people sometimes disagree over how the law can protect the rights of some without violating the rights of others.

Laws can be based on moral, economic, political, or social values. As values change, so can laws. Moral values deal with fundamental questions of right and wrong. For example, laws against killing promote society's primary moral value—the protection of life. However, as already noted, some things that are considered immoral may not violate the law. In limited circumstances, such as in self-defense or during a time of war, even an intentional killing may be legal.

Economic values deal with the accumulation, preservation, use, and distribution of wealth. Many laws promote economic values by encouraging certain economic decisions and discouraging others. The law encourages home ownership by giving tax benefits to people who borrow money to pay for a home, for example. Laws against shoplifting protect property and discourage stealing by providing a criminal penalty.

Political values reflect the relationship between government and individuals. Laws making it easier to vote promote citizen participation in the political process, a basic American political value.

Social values concern issues that are important to society. For example, it is an American social value that all students be provided with free public education through high school. Consequently, all states have laws providing such education. Like other values, social values can change. In the past, for example, society believed that school sports were not as important for girls as for boys. This value has changed. Today, laws require schools to provide females with sports opportunities similar to those offered to males.

Many laws combine moral, economic, political, and social values. For example, laws against theft deal with the moral issue of stealing, the economic issue of protection of property, the political issue of how government punishes those who violate criminal statutes, and the social issue of respecting the property of others.

The Shipwrecked Sailors

Three sailors on an ocean-going freighter were cast adrift in a life raft after their ship sank during a storm in the Atlantic Ocean. The ship went down so suddenly that there was no time to send out an SOS. As far as the three sailors knew, they were the only survivors. In the raft, they had no food or water. They had no fishing gear or other equipment that might be used to get food from the ocean.

After recovering from the shock of the shipwreck, the three sailors began to discuss their situation. Dudley, the ship's navigator, figured that they were at least one thousand miles from land and that the storm had blown them far from where any ships would normally pass. Stephens, the ship's doctor, indicated that without food they could not live longer than thirty days. The only nourishment they could expect was from any rain that might fall from time to time. He noted, however, that if one of the three died before the others, the other two could live awhile longer by eating the body of the third.

On the twenty-fifth day, the third sailor, Brooks, who by this time was extremely weak, suggested that they all draw lots and that the loser be killed and eaten by the other two. Both Dudley and Stephens agreed. The next day, lots were drawn and Brooks lost. At this point, Brooks objected and refused to consent. However, Dudley and Stephens decided that Brooks would die soon anyway, so they might as well get it over with. After thus agreeing, they killed and ate Brooks.

Five days later, Dudley and Stephens were rescued by a passing ship and brought to port. They explained to authorities what had happened to Brooks. After recovering from their ordeal, they were placed on trial for murder.

The state in which they were tried had the following law: Any person who deliberately takes the life of another is guilty of murder.

PROBLEM 2

a. Should Dudley and Stephens be tried for murder?

b. As an attorney for Dudley and Stephens, what arguments would you make on their behalf? As an attorney for the state, what arguments would you make on the state's behalf?

c. If they are convicted, what should their punishment be?

d. What purpose would be served by convicting Dudley and Stephens?

e. What is the relationship between law and morality in this case? Was it morally wrong for Dudley and Stephens to kill Brooks? Explain your answer.

f. Can an act be legal but immoral? Can an act be morally right but unlawful?

PROBLEM 3

For each of the following laws, indicate whether moral, economic, political, or social values are involved. Explain your responses.

a. All drivers must stop at stop signs.

b. It is a crime to cheat on your tax return.

c. All citizens may vote at age eighteen.

d. Special government programs lend money to minority-owned businesses at low interest rates.

e. Government officials may not accept gifts from people who want them to pass certain laws.

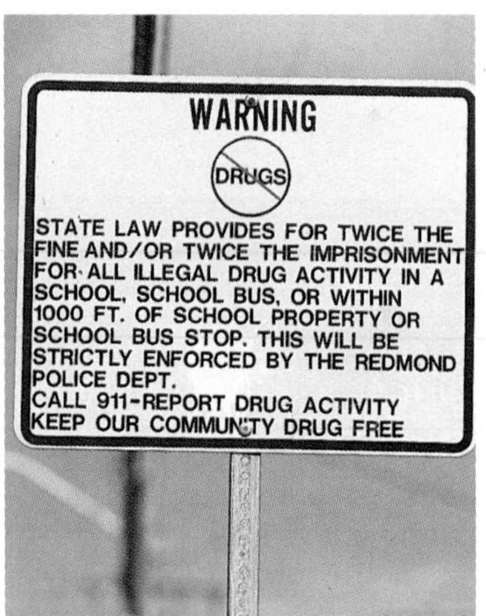

What is the purpose of this law? Will it achieve its goal?

Limits of the Law

You will learn more about lawmaking later in this chapter, but for now you should know that not all laws work equally well. For a law to be fully effective, it must be fair and enforceable. Citizens must also be able to know and understand it.

Americans tend to think that laws can be passed to solve all of their problems. In 1919, the U.S. Constitution was amended to prohibit the manufacture or sale of alcoholic beverages in this country. This law was passed in response to a significant national problem. However, prohibition was extremely difficult to enforce, and fourteen years later it was repealed by another constitutional amendment. Even today, legislators try to deal with the nation's devastating drug problem by passing a wide variety of laws. People disagree on what role the law can play in solving this problem. We know from experience, however, that there is a limit to what laws can reasonably be expected to do.

PROBLEM 4

a. Choose a law that your community has passed to deal with a local problem. Does the law work? If so, why? If not, how could it be improved?

b. Identify a problem in your community for which a new law is needed. Draft the law.

c. Do you think new laws are needed to solve the drug problem in America today? Give your reasons.

Law and Human Rights

A democratic system of government cannot function effectively unless its laws are respected. In other words, society must be based on the "rule of law." This means that all members of society—average citizens and government officials such as senators, judges, and even the president—are required to support the legal system and obey its laws. No one is above the law.

Another important democratic principle is that all people should have basic **human rights**. These are rights that each of us possesses as a human being. There are four categories of human rights: political, social, economic, and environmental. Our political rights include the freedoms of speech, religion, and press, and the right to

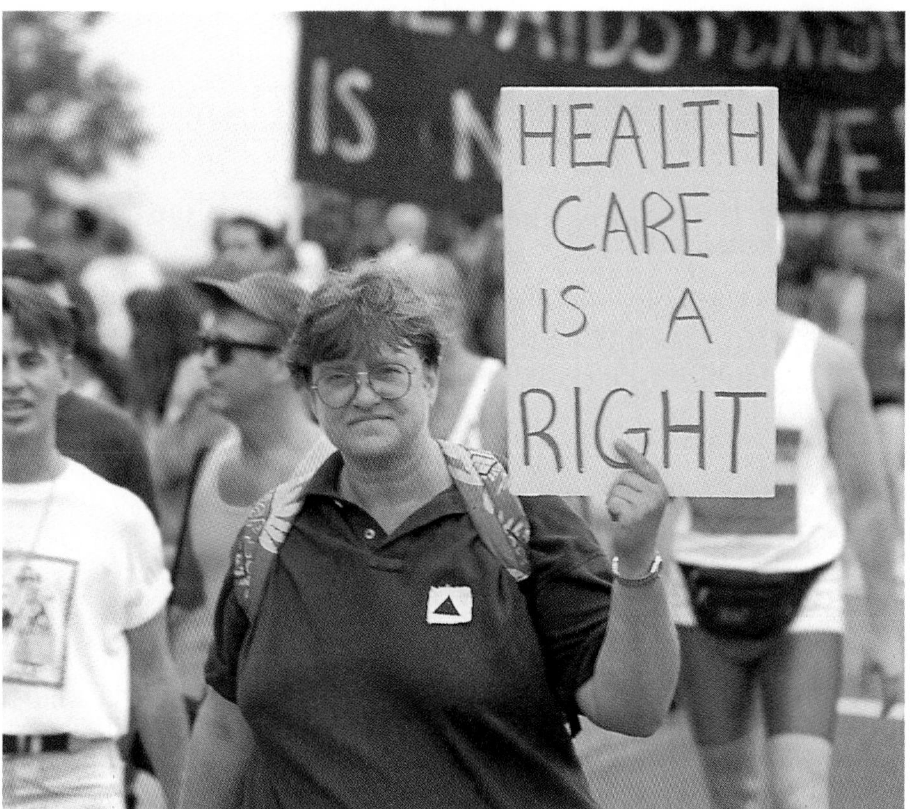

Should the government guarantee a basic level of health care for all citizens?

participate in government. Social rights include the rights to adequate education, food, housing, and health care. Economic rights include the right to hold a job with fair and safe working conditions and the right to own property. Finally, environmental rights include the right to live in a clean and safe environment.

To protect human rights, the United States has signed a number of international documents, including the Universal Declaration of Human Rights and the Covenant on Political and Civil Rights. In addition, the United States has been considering ratifying the International Declaration on the Rights of the Child. Many human rights have become part of our laws and can be found in the U.S., tribal, and state constitutions, in statutes, and in the decisions of our courts. There is, however, an ongoing debate as to whether it is government's role to provide all these human rights.

PROBLEM 5

You have been selected to join a group of space pioneers who will establish a colony on a distant planet. In order to create the best possible society, you and your group decide to make a list of the rights that all space colonists should have.

a. List the three most important rights that should be guaranteed.

b. Compare your list with those of others. Explain the reasons for your selections.

c. Are some of the listed rights more important than others? Why?

d. Do any of the listed rights clash with one another? If so, which ones? Why?

Balancing Rights with Responsibilities

The emphasis on rights in the United States has led some people to criticize America for being too concerned with citizens' rights while neglecting their responsibilities. Some say that "with every right there goes a responsibility" and urge citizens to act more responsibly toward one another, their families, and their communities.

Critics cite America's emphasis on individual rights as evidence of "radical individualism," which has resulted in a self-centered focus and the loss of a sense of community. While individual rights are important, they must be matched by social responsibilities, these critics say. For example, if people wish to be tried by juries of their peers, they must be willing to serve on such juries. If they want to be governed by elected officials who respond to their values and needs, they must not only vote but also get involved in other ways: attend election forums, work for candidates, and run for positions on school boards, county councils, and community associations, for example.

Americans justifiably have great respect for laws extending rights to citizens, including women, minorities, and persons with disabilities, who were previously excluded from full participation in society. Many laws, however, also require citizens to act responsibly: Parents must provide their children with adequate food, shelter, and clothing; drivers must obey traffic laws; and all workers must pay taxes.

Other critics of the emphasis on rights in America point out that "because you have a legal right to do (or not to do) something does not mean it is the right thing to do." For example, people have the right not to call the police to report a crime, but almost everyone would agree that failing to report a crime is not the "right" thing to do. Similarly, the First Amendment guarantee of freedom of speech sometimes gives people the right to say hateful and abusive things to others, but it does not make such speech "right." Summarizing the situation, one critic said, "Rights do not automatically make for rightness."

KINDS OF LAWS

Laws fall into two major groups: criminal and civil. **Criminal laws** regulate public conduct and set out duties owed to society. A criminal case is a legal action brought by the government against a person charged with committing a crime. Criminal laws have penalties, and offenders are imprisoned, fined, placed under supervision, or punished in some other way. Criminal offenses are divided into **felonies** and **misdemeanors**. The penalty for a felony is a term of more than one year in prison. For a misdemeanor, the penalty is a prison term of one year or less. Felonies are more serious crimes such as murder or robbery. Misdemeanors are less serious crimes such as simple assault or minor theft.

Civil laws regulate relations between individuals or groups of individuals. A **civil action** (lawsuit) can be brought by a person who feels wronged or injured by another person. Courts may award the injured person money for the loss, or they may order the person who committed the wrong to make amends in some other way. An example of a civil action is a lawsuit for recovery of damages suffered in an automobile accident. Civil laws regulate many everyday situations, such as marriage, divorce, contracts, real estate, insurance, consumer protection, and negligence.

Sometimes one action can violate both civil and criminal law. For example, if Joe beats up Bob, he may have to pay Bob's medical bills under civil law and may be charged with the crime of assault under criminal law.

PROBLEM 6

Matt and Luther decide to skip school. They take Luther's brother's car without telling him and drive to a local shopping center. Ignoring the sign *Parking for Handicapped Persons Only*, they leave the car and enter a radio and TV shop.

After looking around, they buy a portable AM-FM radio. Then they buy some sandwiches from a street vendor and walk to a nearby park. While eating, they discover that the radio does not work. In their hurry to return it, they leave their trash on the park bench.

When Matt and Luther get back to the shopping center, they notice a large dent in one side of their car. The dent appears to be the result of a driver's carelessly backing out of the next space. They also notice that the car has been broken into and that the tape deck has been removed.

They call the police to report the accident and theft. When the police arrive, they seize a small clear bag containing illegal drugs from behind the car's back seat. Matt and Luther are arrested.

a. List what you think Matt and Luther did wrong.

b. What laws are involved in this story?

c. Which of these are criminal laws? Which are civil laws?

LAWMAKING

Ours is a government of laws, not men.

—John Adams, 1779

The laws that we, as U.S. citizens, are expected to obey come from many sources. Constitutions set forth laws and also establish the structures of governments. Legislatures, of course, make laws; and in some situations, voters can act as lawmakers. Lobbying is a way to influence the lawmaking process. Administrative agencies make many laws. Finally, laws are made by the courts.

Constitutions

To understand lawmaking, it is necessary first to understand the U.S. Constitution, which is the highest law of the land. Drafted over two hundred years ago, this remarkable document is the longest-lasting written constitution in the world. It sets forth the basic framework of our government. It also lists the government's powers, the limits on those powers, and the people's freedoms that cannot be taken away by the government. (The text of the entire Constitution is given in Appendix A.)

Perhaps nothing is more important in the Constitution than the division of lawmaking power among the three branches of government: the executive (the president and federal agencies), the legislative (Congress), and the judiciary (the courts). This division is known as the **separation of powers**. The executive branch is a lawmaker when it issues rules and executive orders, which often have the force of law. The legislative branch uses lawmaking power when it passes laws (also called **statutes**). The judicial branch establishes laws

What is the purpose of a constitution?

through its rulings, which may interpret a provision of the Constitution, a statute, or a rule issued by an executive agency.

The three branches are independent, but each has the power to restrain the other branches in a system of **checks and balances**. The system was designed to prevent one branch from becoming too powerful and abusing its power. Examples of checks and balances include congressional investigations of actions by the president or other executive officials and the prosecution in court of members of Congress or the executive branch for violating the law. Another check is the president's power to **veto** (refuse to approve) laws passed by Congress.

Perhaps the most visible and important check of one branch on another is the courts' power of **judicial review**. Judicial review enables a court to void any law passed by Congress or a state legislature that conflicts with the nation's highest law, the Constitution. For example, Congress might pass a law prohibiting media criticism of elected officials. If challenged in court, this law would be declared invalid and **unconstitutional** because it violates the freedom of press guaranteed in the First Amendment.

Integral to the Constitution is the principle of **limited government**. Just as the Constitution restricts the power of the branches, it also reflects the view that the federal government as a whole should be limited by the power of the states. This division of power between the states and the federal government is known as **federalism**. The federal government's powers to make laws are listed in the Constitution, and the remaining powers are reserved for the states. This is why most civil and criminal laws are passed by state legislatures or local governments. Consequently, many legal differences exist among the states. For example, a sixteen-year-old can obtain a license to drive a car in some states but not in others.

The principle of limited government is also reflected in the **Bill of Rights**, the first ten amendments to the Constitution. The Bill of Rights defines and guarantees the fundamental rights and liberties of all Americans, including the freedoms of religion, speech, and press; the freedom from unreasonable search and seizure; and other rights. Courts have decided that the Bill of Rights limits the power of state and local governments as well as the federal government.

Every state has a constitution, and most state constitutions reflect the major principles of the federal Constitution. Most Native American tribes also have constitutions. All provide for different branches of government, separation of powers, checks and balances, and judicial review. Some state constitutions provide greater protection of rights than the federal Constitution. Our federal system allows states to do this if they wish. For example, some state constitutions have equal rights amendments guaranteeing women greater rights than they have under the U.S. Constitution.

The U.S. Constitution and most state constitutions are difficult to change. This is because they were drafted with the belief that they should not be changed without careful thought, discussion, and debate. The idea was to make these documents as permanent as possible. The U.S. Constitution may be changed in two ways. A proposed amendment must be approved either by two-thirds of both houses of Congress or at a convention called by two-thirds of the states. In either case, it must then be ratified, or approved, by three-fourths of the states.

People try to change the Constitution for many reasons. One of the most common has been to extend rights that were not originally written into the Constitution. Although ratification is difficult, twenty-seven amendments have been added to the Constitution.

These extensions of rights often reflect the changing viewpoints of citizens and their elected representatives. For example, when the original Constitution was ratified in 1789, most states restricted voting to white males who owned property. Since then, various amendments have extended voting rights to minorities, women, and persons aged eighteen to twenty.

A proposed constitutional amendment would extend statehood to the District of Columbia. Another proposed amendment would require the federal government to adopt a balanced budget. The Equal Rights Amendment passed Congress in 1972. It prohibited discrimination on the basis of sex. However, it failed to be ratified by the required thirty-eight states, so it did not become a part of the U.S. Constitution.

In 1993, the Twenty-Seventh Amendment became part of the Constitution. This amendment, first proposed by James Madison in 1789, bans mid-term Congressional pay raises. In recent years, amendments passed by Congress—such as the Equal Rights Amendment—have included deadlines for ratification by the states. However, no such deadline had been included with the ban on mid-term Congressional pay raises.

PROBLEM 7

Examine each of the following situations and attempt to determine whether it involves the principle of separation of powers, checks and balances, judicial review, federalism, or some combination of these principles. Specify the principle or principles involved and explain your answer.

a. A state law requires that a prayer be said each day in public schools. The courts rule that the law violates a First Amendment clause that prohibits the government from establishing a religion.

b. An official in the U.S. Department of Housing and Urban Development is accused of receiving kickbacks of money for making government contracts with certain private corporations. She is required to testify about this before a congressional committee and is prosecuted in court.

c. The U.S. Congress passes a law that restricts imports of handguns from other countries. The legislature in one state allows the sale of handguns to anyone over age eighteen.

d. Because a prison is very old and overcrowded, a state court orders the state legislature to spend $10 million on a new prison.

Legislatures

The citizenry should never rest as long as the legislature is in session.

—Thomas Jefferson

As you have seen, the U.S. Constitution divides the power to make laws between the federal government and the state governments. At

Why does the United States have a federal Congress, shown here, as well as state legislatures?

both the federal and the state levels, legislatures are the primary lawmaking bodies. The U.S. Congress—the federal legislature—is made up of two houses: the Senate (100 members, two from each state) and the House of Representatives (435 members, each state represented according to the size of its population). The U.S. Constitution gives Congress the power to pass laws that are binding on the citizens of every state. States have the power to pass laws that apply within their boundaries.

The lawmaking authority of Congress is exercised through the passage of laws known as federal statutes. When Congress passes a federal statute, it affects citizens of every state. Federal statutes deal with issues of national impact, such as environmental quality, national defense, labor relations, veterans' affairs, public health, civil rights, economic development, postal services, and federal taxes.

The states' lawmaking powers are vested in their legislatures, which pass laws called state statutes. Except for Nebraska, every state has a two-house legislature. Most states' legislatures meet on an annual basis; in a few states, the legislatures meet every two years. States pass laws with statewide impact in such areas as education, traffic, state taxes (including how they will be spent), marriage and divorce, and the powers and duties of state government officials. Although tribal governments vary a great deal, many place legislative authority—and sometimes executive authority as well—in a body known as the tribal council.

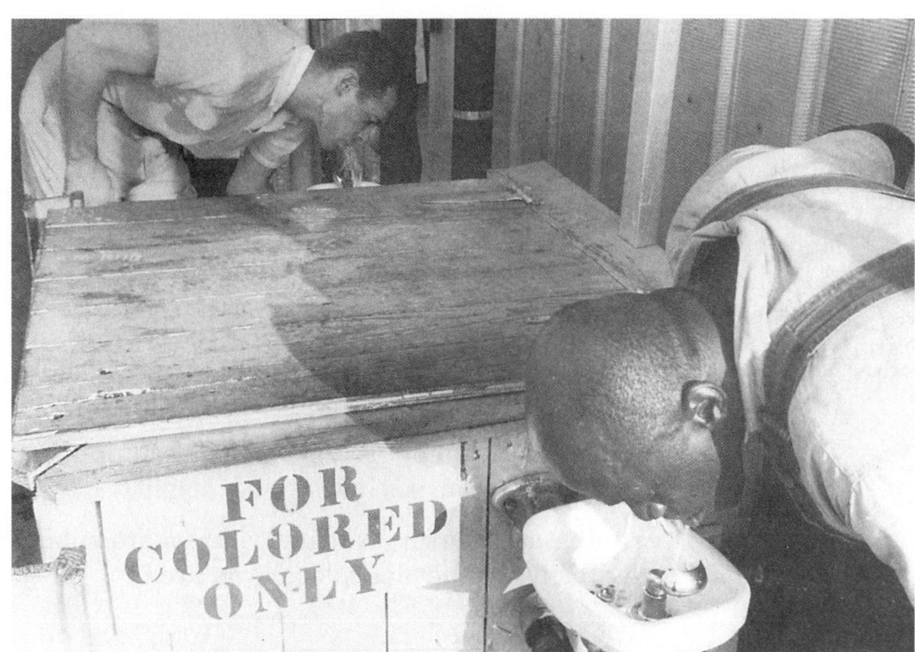

What role did the federal government play in ending racial discrimination?

Sometimes federal laws conflict with state laws. Unless it can be shown that Congress is legislating in an area the Constitution delegated to the states, the courts will usually follow the federal and not the state law. For example, in the 1960s, federal laws against racial segregation in restaurants and hotels came into conflict with laws of some states that required separate accommodations for African Americans and whites. The courts ruled the state laws invalid based on Article VI of the Constitution, the **supremacy clause**, which states that "the Constitution and the Laws of the United States . . . shall be the supreme law of the land."

In addition to the U.S. Congress and state legislatures, cities, towns, and counties have lawmaking bodies. These are called county or city councils, boards of aldermen, local boards of education, or other names. Local governments pass laws known as ordinances or regulations. Legislative issues that concern local governments include land use, parking, schools, and regulation of local business. Laws passed by local governments apply only to a county, city, or town. The local lawmaking body has been given the power to enact ordinances by the state.

What legislatures exist in your state and local area? What are some types of laws that each of these legislatures has enacted?

PROBLEM 8

Decide whether each of the following laws is federal, state, and/or local. Then give one example, not listed among the following, of a federal, a state, and a local law.

a. "No parking on the east side of Main Street between 4:00 P.M. and 6:00 P.M."

b. "All persons between the ages of six and sixteen must attend school."

c. "Whoever enters a bank for purposes of taking by force or violence the property or money in custody of such bank shall be fined not more than $5,000 or imprisoned not more than twenty years or both."

d. "In order to sell any product on a public street, the seller must first apply for and receive a vendor's permit."

e. "No employer of more than fifteen persons may discriminate on the basis of race, color, religion, sex, or national origin."

f. "All persons traveling on interstate airline carriers are subject to search before entering the airplane departure area."

Legislatures and other lawmaking bodies try to respond to the needs of the citizens they represent by introducing legislation in the form of bills. Bills are used to enact new laws or amend or repeal old laws. Ideas for bills can come from legislators, the executive branch, individual citizens, or citizens' groups. The courts also sometimes identify problems that legislatures need to address. If a bill is passed by the legislature and not vetoed by the executive, it becomes a law.

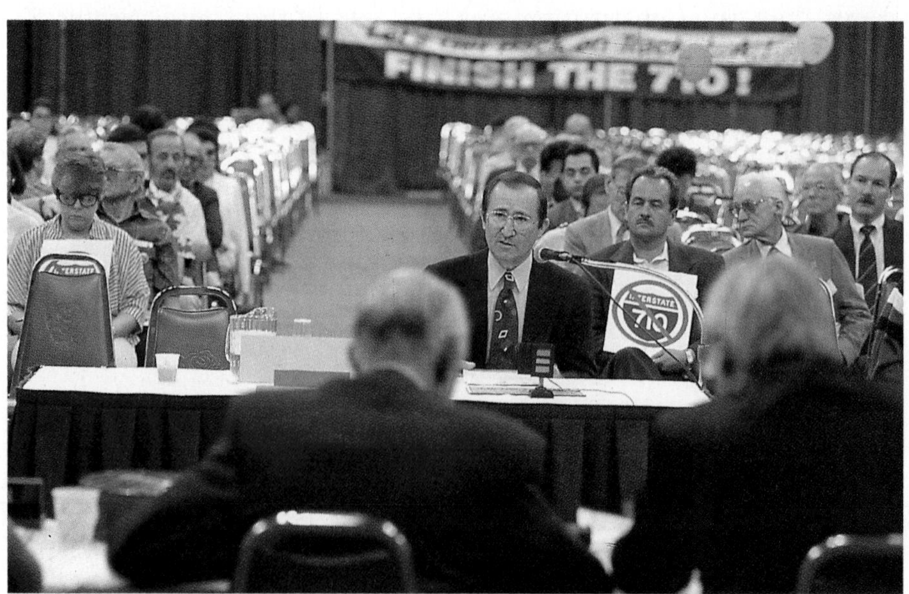

What steps could citizens take either to promote or to stop the building of a highway?

THE CASE OF . . .

The Unclear Law

The town of Beautifica has established a lovely park in the city. The city council wishes to preserve some elements of nature, undisturbed by city noise, traffic, pollution, and crowding. The park is a place where citizens can go and find grass, trees, flowers, and quiet. In addition, there are playgrounds and picnic areas. The city council enacts a law requiring that at all the entrances to the park the following sign is to be posted: *NO VEHICLES IN THE PARK.*

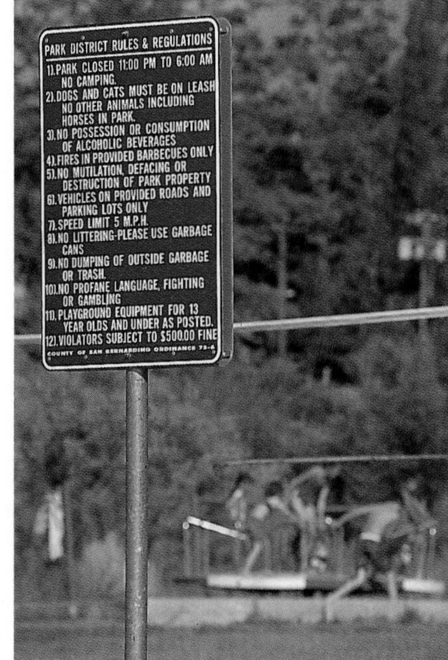

Are any of these park rules unclear?

PROBLEM 9

The law seems clear, but some disputes have arisen over its interpretation. Interpret the law in the following cases, keeping in mind what the law says (the letter of the law) as well as the legislative intent. Examine the following situations and decide whether or not the vehicle described in each case should be allowed in the park. Write down the reasons for your choices.

a. John Smith lives on one side of town and works on the other. He will save ten minutes if he drives through the park.

b. There are many trash barrels in the park for collecting litter, in order to keep the park clean. The sanitation department wants to drive a truck in to collect the trash.

c. Two police cars are chasing a suspected bank robber. If one police car cuts through the park, it can get in front of the suspect's car and trap it between the patrol cars.

d. An ambulance is racing to the hospital with a dying patient. The shortest route is through the park.

e. Some children who visit the park want to ride their bicycles there.

f. Jane Thomas wants to take her baby to the park in a stroller.

g. A monument is being erected to the town's citizens who died in the Vietnam War. A tank, donated by the government, is to be placed beside the monument.

After a bill becomes a law, the people must obey it. Sometimes, though, the language of a law is open to differing interpretations. It is not always easy to know exactly what a law prohibits or allows. Disputes over what a law means frequently end up in court. A judge who interprets what the legislature means is determining **legislative intent**.

Drafting a Bill No matter where the idea for a bill originates, eventually there must come a time when the bill is drafted—that is, when actual language is written. As you can see from the Case of the Unclear Law, sometimes even the simplest language is not clear enough for people to understand what is expected. Legislation is often drafted and redrafted before being introduced and discussed by a legislative body. Despite these efforts, many laws are difficult to read and understand. When this occurs, one of the basic purposes of law—letting citizens know what conduct is expected of them—is lost.

When judges decide what a statute means, they must follow certain rules. One rule is that courts will not enforce laws that are so vague or overbroad that it is unclear exactly what conduct is prohibited. For example, a law that stated "it shall be illegal to gather on a street corner without a good reason" would be ruled too vague or overbroad. Another rule says that if there is doubt as to the meaning of a word in a criminal statute, the word must be strictly interpreted against the government. This usually means that words are given their ordinary everyday meaning by the court. These rules are

Guidelines for Drafting Laws

When drafting laws or other types of rules, it is useful to ask the following questions to evaluate whether problems are likely to result.

- Is the law written in clear language?
- Is the law understandable?
- Does the law contradict any other laws?
- Is the law enforceable?
- Are the penalties for breaking the law clear and reasonable?

Drafting a Law Simulation

Your town has a serious problem. Over the past year, traffic congestion has worsened. One result has been an increase in accidents involving bicycles. Last year, there were nine accidents with serious injuries involving bicycles and cars or bicycles and pedestrians on the streets. The people in the town are not used to so much traffic. A citizens' group asks the city council to draft some bicycle safety legislation. After examining the town ordinances, the council realizes that there is really no law on the books explaining where and how people should ride their bicycles.

PROBLEM 10

You have been appointed to the town's legislative drafting commission. The commission has been asked to draft a new ordinance.

a. What is the problem that the city council will be trying to address with the proposed ordinance?

b. What is the legislative intent of the city council in drafting the ordinance?

c. List all the details you think should be included in the proposed ordinance.

d. Draft four sentences that you think would make a good ordinance to deal with the problem.

e. Role-play a legislative committee meeting at which the members have worked on four-sentence versions of the proposed ordinance and are trying to agree on a final version.

f. After the four-sentence law is drafted, use the guidelines for drafting laws on page 20 to analyze possible problems with the law as drafted. Are there problems? If so, what are they, and how can they be solved?

meant to ensure that citizens are not punished for failing to obey an unclear law.

As you can see, clarity in legal language is important. For that reason, some legislatures now attempt to write in simple, clear English rather than traditional legal language. Those who favor this practice argue that laws have been written in language that is too complex and should instead be written so that a person of ordinary intelligence and education can understand what is expected. However, many laws are still written in language that is difficult to understand.

Voting

The right of citizens of the United States to vote shall not be denied or abridged by the United States or by any State on account of race, color, or previous condition of servitude.

—Fifteenth Amendment of the U.S. Constitution

Voting is a basic constitutional right. Eligible voters may vote for president, vice president, two U.S. senators, and one U.S. representative. They may also vote for governor, state legislators, and numerous other state, tribal, and local officials.

In a representative democracy, laws are usually made by elected legislators acting in the voters' behalf. However, in some situations, citizens can vote directly on proposed laws. Initiatives and referendums allow citizens to circulate petitions and put proposed laws on the ballot. An **initiative** is a procedure that enables a specified number of voters to propose a law by petition. The proposed law is then submitted to either the electorate or the legislature for ap-

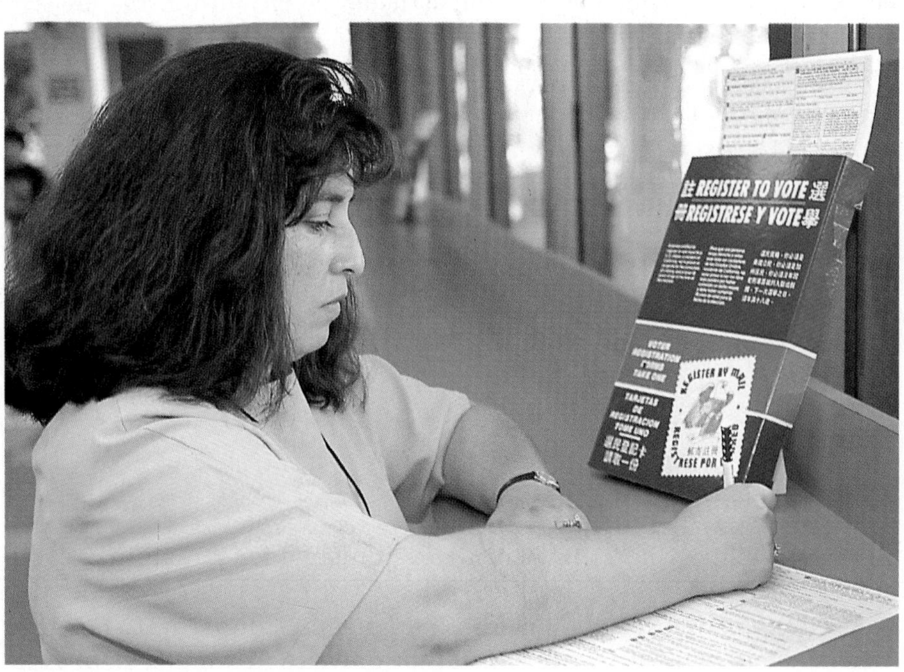

How can voter registration be made easier?

proval. A **referendum** occurs when a legislative act is referred to voters for final approval or rejection. Recent state referendums have been held on issues such as gun control, gay rights, abortion, environmental protection, and funding for schools, parks, roads, and other government programs. Many states also permit **recall** elections, which allow voters to remove elected officials from office. In 1988, for example, the governor of Arizona was removed from office in a recall election.

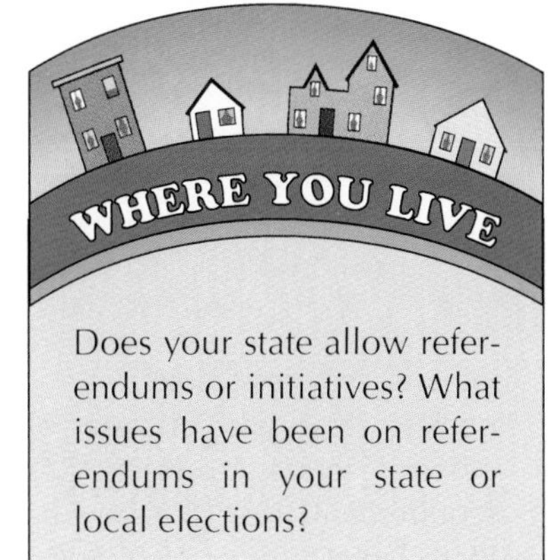

Does your state allow referendums or initiatives? What issues have been on referendums in your state or local elections?

To register to vote, you must be a U.S. citizen, at least eighteen years old, and a resident of the community in which you register. Registering to vote is easy. Applicants usually register by completing an application form in person or by mail. Some states even allow applicants to register automatically when they obtain a driver's license.

Registering to vote was not always easy. African Americans did not receive the right to vote until 1870. Until then, most states allowed only white males with property to vote. Women gained the

Why do some people believe that voting is the most important political right?

Where and how does one register to vote in your area? Is there a residency requirement? If so, for how long? What can people vote for in your area? When and where does one go to vote?

right to vote in 1920. Although some Native Americans had been granted citizenship by special federal legislation before 1924 (for example, veterans of World War I), Congress granted citizenship to all Native Americans in 1924. Until 1965, some states had poll taxes, literacy tests, and character exams that kept millions of people from voting. In 1971, the Twenty-sixth Amendment gave eighteen-year-olds the right to vote. Persons convicted of serious crimes usually lose the right to vote. In some states, convicts may regain the right to vote five years after their sentence is completed.

PROBLEM 11

a. The percentage of eligible voters actually voting declined with each presidential election between 1960 and 1988. In the 1992 presidential election, however, the percentage increased slightly. How do you explain these events?

b. Make two lists: one of all the reasons people give for voting, and another of all the reasons people give for not voting. Are you eligible to vote? If so, have you registered and voted? Why or why not?

c. The following proposals have been made to encourage more people to vote. Do you favor or oppose each proposal? Explain your answers.

1. Levying a $20 fine on a person who is eligible to vote but does not do so and has no good excuse.
2. Allowing people to register and vote on the same day.
3. Lowering the voting age to sixteen so students in high school could vote.
4. Allowing students over the age of fourteen to vote for and serve on the school board that governs their school.
5. Holding all elections on Sundays.
6. Reducing people's taxes by $10 each if they vote.
7. Allowing people to vote not just for representatives but directly for or against issues on the ballot that they care about.
8. Prohibiting the media from reporting poll results or projections until all polls are closed.
9. Automatically registering everyone with a driver's license.

The Screening Law

Electing public officials is an essential part of a democratic system of government. Many countries that have recently moved away from communism and toward democracy, however, have encountered problems with the election process. For example, they have faced the issue of whether or not to allow former communist party members to run for office or otherwise serve the new government.

Assume that the new legislature of one such country, which had been ruled by a communist government for 40 years, passes a law that "bans from holding a senior office in government all those who held management or executive positions in the former communist government or were informants or otherwise assisted the secret police." A list of 140,000 people who were informants for the old government is obtained from the files of the communist regime's secret police.

PROBLEM 12

a. Under the above law, which of the following people might be banned from holding a senior position in the government? Do you think it is in the best interest of the country to impose such restrictions? Explain your answers.

1. A doctor had applied to the communist government to be director of the cancer research institute. She was hired on the condition that she also teach first aid courses to the police.
2. Under the communist government, a university professor was required to join the communist party to qualify for a teaching position.
3. Because of his knowledge and experience, the head of housing under the communist government has been asked to take a senior position in the new government's housing department. In his prior job, he had given better housing to communist party officials.

4. A high-ranking police official in the communist government was known as generally being fair to citizens. He did, however, enforce some of the laws of the old government, including one banning demonstrations against communists. He was also active in the revolution that changed the government.

5. A member of a group that discussed politics and sometimes criticized communists was told by the former government to turn over the names of other members or lose her job. Because she had no other way to support her children, she supplied the names, which the government kept on file although it never acted against the people she listed.

b. What are the reasons for and against having such a screening law? If you were in the legislature of the new government, would you support or oppose the law? Explain.

c. Under the new law, should all the "informers" on the list kept by the secret police be banned from serving in the government? Why or why not?

d. Did the United States ever, or does it now, have any laws restricting eligibility for public office? If so, identify these laws. Do you support them? Why or why not? Does any provision of the U.S. Constitution apply to this situation?

Lobbying

"A president only tells Congress what they should do. Lobbyists tell 'em what they will do."

—Will Rogers

Lobbying is a way to influence the lawmaking process by convincing lawmakers to vote as you want them to. The word *lobbying* comes from the seventeenth century, when interested persons would corner legislators in the outer waiting room of the legislature—the lobby. While the term *lobbying* often has a negative connotation, it is actually a basic right protected by the Constitution.

A lobbyist is someone who tries to convince a lawmaker to vote for or against a particular issue. Anyone can be a lobbyist. As a private citizen, you can lobby elected officials on issues you care about. You can influence elected officials by expressing your opinions individually or as part of a group, either in person or by letter or phone. Lob-

What special interest, pressure, or lobbying groups exist in your state? On behalf of what issues or causes do these groups lobby? What techniques do they use?

byists also use political contributions, ads, favors, letter-writing campaigns, and other techniques to influence legislation.

Today, special interest groups and organizations lobby on behalf of every imaginable cause and issue. Professional lobbyists are hired by businesses and organizations to influence federal, state, and local legislators. For example, the National Rifle Association employs lobbyists to oppose restrictions on gun ownership and use, while Handgun Control, Inc., lobbies for gun control. In 1992, there were more than ten thousand professional lobbyists in Washington, D.C. Those who lobby the federal government must register with Congress and file reports four times a year. In these reports, they must identify their clients and the specific bills on which they are working. They must also indicate how much money they have been paid for their lobbying work and how much they have spent lobbying (for example, the costs of organizing grass-roots letter-writing campaigns).

Professional lobbyists often have an advantage over citizen lobbyists because they have more money behind them and they know legislators and their staffs personally. But citizen lobbyists can be very effective, particularly when they join with others. Demonstration of grass-roots support by large numbers of citizens is a very effective lobbying technique. This is because elected officials know that citizens vote. For example, in 1993, President Bill Clinton nominated a successful corporate lawyer to be U.S. attorney general. Before confirmation, it was revealed that she had broken the law by hiring an illegal alien as a nanny (a child's nursemaid) and then failing to pay required taxes for the nanny. Many legislators dismissed the offense as a minor technical violation of the law. However, an outpouring of

What role does lobbying play in a democracy?

Writing a Public Official

- Write in your own words. Personal letters are far more effective than form letters or petitions. Tell how the issue will affect you and your friends, family, or job.
- Keep your letter short and to the point. Deal with only one issue per letter. If you are writing about some proposed bill or legislation, identify it by name (for example, the National Consumer Protection Act) and by number if you know it (for example, H.R. 343 or S. 675).
- Begin by telling the official why you are writing. Ask the official to state his or her own position on the issue. Always request a reply, and ask the official to take some kind of definite action (for example, vote for or against the bill).
- Always put your return address on the letter, sign and date it, and keep a copy, if possible. Your letter doesn't have to be typed, but it should be legible. Perhaps most importantly, it should reach the official before the issue is voted on.

grass-roots citizen opposition influenced many senators not to support her nomination, and President Clinton withdrew her name.

Many critics of our lobbying system say it enables some people and businesses to "buy legislation." It is true that contributors to political campaigns may have greater access to legislators and greater influence over how they vote on certain issues. However, others argue that lobbying is an integral part of American democracy. They claim that the use of money and influence is a legitimate way for groups to make their views heard.

PROBLEM 13

a. Have you ever lobbied anyone? An elected official? A schoolteacher? Your parents? What issue did you lobby on? What techniques did you use? How effective were you?

b. Select a current issue that concerns you. Draft a letter about it to a public official (for example, your mayor, city council member, state legislator, or federal representative or senator).

c. Send your letter to the elected official and then analyze your letter and any reply you receive by reviewing the advice box on page 28.

d. Do persons with more money have greater influence over legislators than those with less money? If so, is this unavoidable in a society like ours, or should steps be taken to reform the lobbying system? Explain.

Agencies

Many of the laws that affect you are made by government agencies. Legislative bodies usually deal with problems only in a general way. They authorize administrative agencies to develop rules and regulations to make laws more specific. These regulations influence almost every aspect of our daily lives and have the force of law. For example, Congress passed a law requiring safe working conditions in places of employment. To implement the law, Congress established the Occupational Safety and Health Administration (OSHA). This agency develops specific regulations governing health and safety on the job. These regulations dictate specifics such as the height of guardrails in factories, the number of fire exits, and the type of safety equipment to be worn by employees in various occupations.

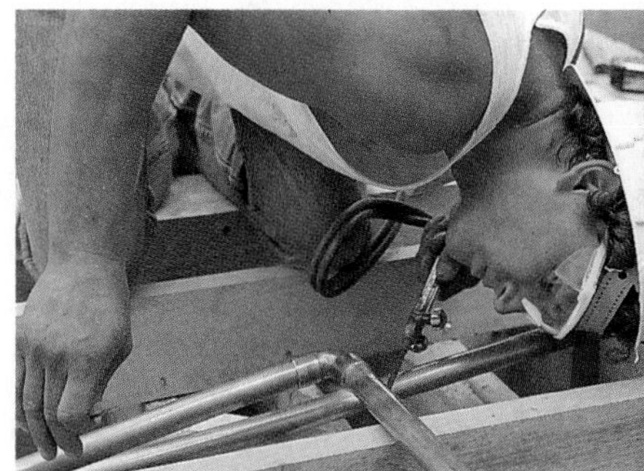

What safety regulations affect this worker?

Administrative agencies, then, are really hidden lawmakers, making numerous rules and regulations that affect business and industry, as well as individuals. For example, regulations govern the amount of pesticide that can be used on produce, the number of animals that can be killed by hunters, the ingredients that can be used in canned food, the costs of phone calls and electricity, the hours of operation for bars and restaurants, the qualifications of people employed in various professions, and hundreds of other subjects. In addition to their lawmaking functions, agencies also administer government programs and provide many services. See Figure 1.1 for a list of major federal agencies.

Not only the federal government but also state, most local, and many tribal governments have administrative agencies. Regulations issued by these agencies become law without going through legislative committees or votes. However, agencies usually hold **public hearings** before issuing proposed regulations. These hearings give individuals or businesses an opportunity to express their views on the proposals. In addition, regulations proposed by the federal government must be published in a special newspaper called the *Feder-*

What are the major departments or agencies of your state government? How are they organized and what do they do?

Figure 1.1 The Government of the United States

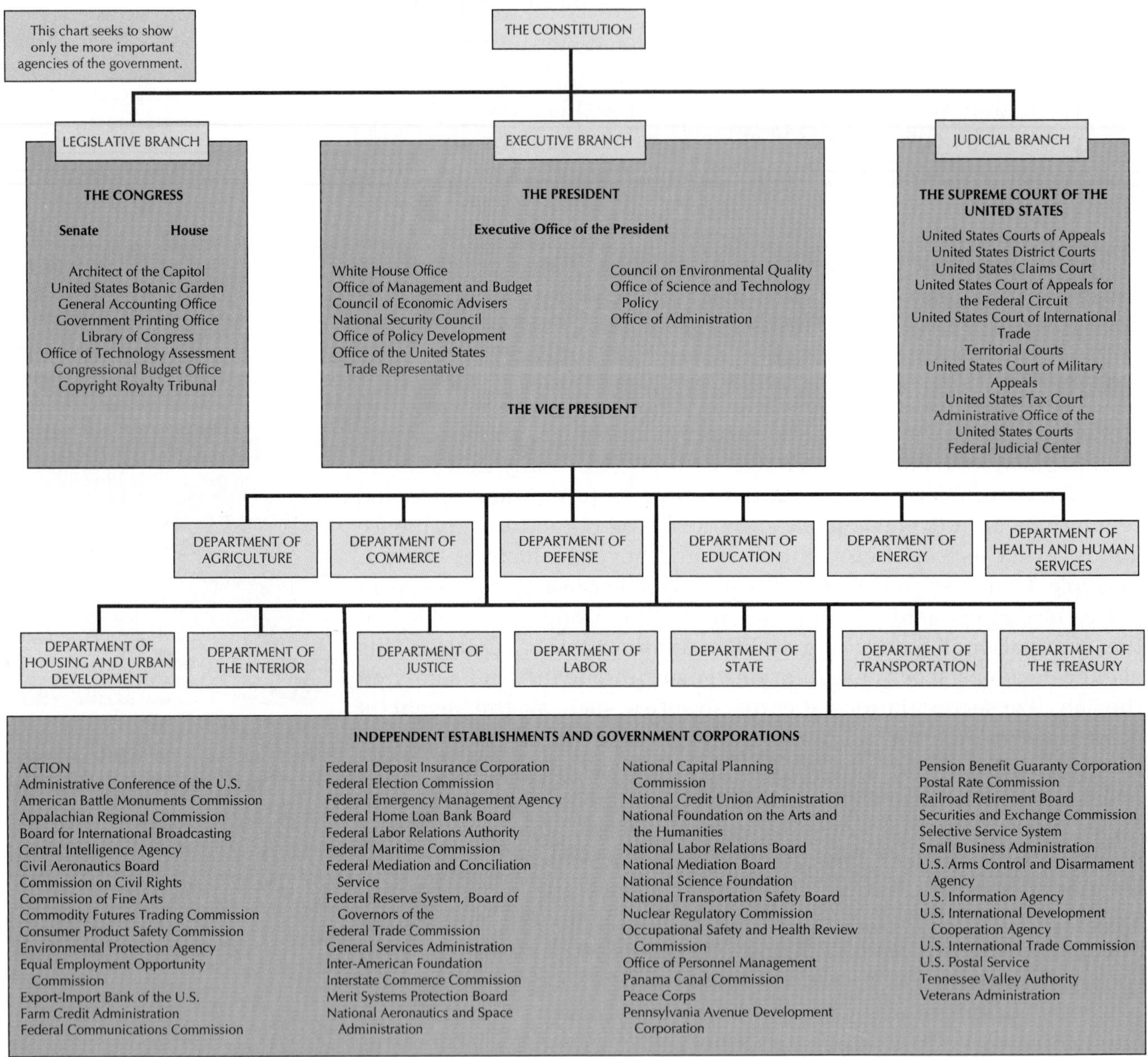

Source: *United States Government Manual*, 1985.

al Register. This allows people to learn about and comment on proposed rules.

In recent years, there has been much criticism of the number of rules and regulations affecting businesses and individuals. Some groups have called for a limit on new regulations or the repeal of regulations they consider too costly and burdensome. Others say administrative regulations are an essential part of modern life.

Changing the Law: Research and Role-play

Divide the class into three groups. Each group should research one of the following proposed laws and answer the questions that follow. The proposed laws would:

- Require everyone under age eighteen to wear a helmet while riding a bicycle.
- Prohibit smoking in restaurants.
- Require a one-week waiting period and a background check for anyone who buys a handgun.

PROBLEM 14

a. What arguments could be presented for and against each law?

b. What groups, organizations, or businesses are likely to lobby for or against the proposed law? What lobbying techniques could they use to influence legislators?

c. If your community held a voter referendum on each of the proposed laws, what would you predict as the outcome? By secret ballot in your classroom, conduct a vote on each proposed law. Analyze and discuss the results.

d. Role-play a meeting between legislators and groups of students who favor and oppose each law. Discuss which citizen lobbyists were effective, which were not, and why.

PROBLEM 15

As a research project, do one of the following exercises:

a. Find an article about an administrative agency in your local newspaper. Then answer the following questions about the agency: What is its name? What does it do? What issues does it regulate? What services does it provide? How is the agency important to people's lives? What does the article say about the agency?

b. Choose an occupation or profession (electrician, physician, lawyer, schoolteacher, beautician, or the like) and answer the following questions: What agency or organization regulates the profession? What are the qualifications for the profession? Are any licenses or tests required? How does the agency decide who gets a license?

Courts

What is the role of courts in a democracy?

Law is also made by courts. Our system of law, which originated in England, gives courts lawmaking power. In this system, court decisions establish legal principles and rules of law known as **common law**.

There are two types of courts in the United States: trial and appeals. **Trial courts** listen to testimony, consider evidence, and decide the facts in disputed situations. In a trial, there are two **parties** (sides) to each case. In a civil trial, the party initiating the legal action is called the **plaintiff**. In a criminal trial, the government (state or federal) initiates the case and serves as the **prosecutor**. In both civil and criminal trials, the party responding to the plaintiff (civil) or prosecution (criminal) is called the **defendant**. Once a trial court has made a decision, the losing party may be able to appeal the decision to an appellate, or appeals, court.

In an **appeals court**, one party presents arguments asking the court to change the decision of the trial court. The other party presents arguments supporting the decision of the trial court. There are no juries or witnesses, and no evidence is presented. Only lawyers appear before the judges to make legal arguments.

Not everyone who loses a trial can appeal. Usually, an appeal is possible only when there is a claim that the trial court has committed an **error of law**. An error of law occurs when the judge makes a mistake as to the law applicable in the case (for example, gives the wrong instructions to the jury or permits evidence that should not have been allowed). A judge's error is considered minor as long as it does not affect the outcome of the trial. In cases involving minor errors of law, the trial court decision will not be reversed.

When an appeals court decides a case, it issues a written opinion or ruling. This opinion sets a **precedent** for similar cases in the future. All lower courts in the place where the decision was made must follow the precedent set in the opinion. This is what is meant by courts "making law." However, a higher court or a court in another area can disagree with this precedent.

THE CASE OF . . .

Taking a Car by Mistake

Joe Harper left the key in his 1990 blue mini-van. When he came back an hour later, he got into someone else's blue mini-van by mistake. This car also had the key in it. Harper, who did not notice it was a different car, started it and drove away. He was arrested for auto theft.

At the trial, the judge told the jury it was not necessary for them to consider whether Harper intended to steal the car. Instead, the judge instructed the jury that to find Harper guilty of auto theft they only had to decide whether he was caught driving a car that was not his. The jury found Joe Harper guilty.

This case illustrates an error of law that could be appealed. Auto theft law requires that the accused person must have intended to steal the car. Harper did not intend to steal the car. The guilty verdict could be reversed.

Appellate court cases are usually heard by more than one judge. Typically, three judges (or justices, as appellate judges are sometimes called) decide such cases. Occasionally there are as many as nine.

When these judges disagree on a decision, two or more written opinions may be issued in the same case. The majority opinion states the decision of the court. Judges who disagree with the majority opinion may issue a separate document called a **dissenting opinion**, which states the reasons for the disagreement. In some instances, judges who agree with the majority opinion, but for reasons different from those used to support the majority opinion, may write a **concurring opinion**.

Dissenting opinions are important because their reasoning may become the basis of future majority opinions. As society and the views of judges on appellate courts change, so can legal opinion. An example is the 1896 case of *Plessy v. Ferguson*, which upheld racial segregation in railroad cars as long as facilities for whites and African Americans were "separate but equal." Justice John Marshall Harlan dissented from the majority opinion because it allowed a state to pass regulations solely based on race, which he believed violated the Constitution. In the 1954 precedent-setting case of *Brown v. Board of Education*, some of the reasoning expressed in Justice

The Justices of the U.S. Supreme Court are, seated left to right, Sandra Day O'Connor, Harry Blackmun (retired in 1994), Chief Justice William H. Rehnquist, John Paul Stevens, and Antonin Scalia; and, standing left to right, Clarence Thomas, Anthony M. Kennedy, David H. Souter, and Ruth Bader Ginsburg.

Harlan's dissent was accepted by the Supreme Court, and the "separate but equal" doctrine was declared unconstitutional.

The U.S. Supreme Court The most important precedents are established by the U.S. Supreme Court, where nine justices hear each case and a majority rules. All United States courts must follow U.S. Supreme Court decisions. Many laws have been changed by the Supreme Court. For example, the Supreme Court has upheld all-male draft registration, ended segregation in public schools, and declared forced prayer in public schools a violation of the Constitution.

What is the purpose of a Senate hearing to confirm a U.S. Supreme Court nominee?

The Supreme Court does not consider all appeals that are brought to it. It rules only on the most important cases. Each year, more than 5,000 cases are appealed to the Supreme Court. The justices rule on about 150.

The nine U.S. Supreme Court justices are nominated by the president and confirmed by the Senate. They have the authority to interpret the meaning of the U.S. Constitution and federal laws. All lower courts must follow these interpretations and other rules of law established by the Supreme Court. The Court's opinions are released in written form and later published in law books.

In recent years, many of society's most controversial issues have ended up before the Court. These include the death penalty, abortion, civil rights, and other issues. Because these issues are so important, the views of persons nominated to become justices have become very important. This is especially true because justices are appointed for life.

Gideon v. Wainwright

In 1963, a case called *Gideon v. Wainwright* came before the U.S. Supreme Court. In this case, a Florida man named Gideon was charged with unlawful breaking and entering into a poolroom. Gideon asked the trial court to provide him with a free lawyer because he was too poor to hire one himself. The state court refused to provide him with an attorney. It said that state law provided free attorneys only to defendants charged with capital offenses (those crimes that carry a penalty of death or life imprisonment).

The Fourteenth Amendment to the Constitution says that no state may deprive a person of life, liberty, or property without **due process of law**. Due process means fair treatment. Gideon argued that to try someone for a felony without providing him with a lawyer violated his right to due process of law. The Supreme Court agreed with Gideon.

PROBLEM 16

a. In the case of *Gideon v. Wainwright*, what was the precedent that the Supreme Court set? Who has to follow this precedent?

b. Who would have had to follow the precedent if the case had been decided by a judge in a state appeals court?

c. Does the *Gideon* case apply if you are charged with a misdemeanor? Does it apply if you are sued in a civil case?

d. Do you know of other precedents established by the U.S. Supreme Court? What are they?

The Supreme Court has the power to reverse rules of law established in prior cases if the same issue comes before it again in a new case. This sometimes occurs when society's prevailing views change and the justices reflect those changes. It also occurs when one or more justices who voted a certain way in an earlier case leave the Court and new justices are appointed who disagree with the prior decision. If this happens, the justices may reverse the precedent by deciding a new case differently. This occurred in the 1980s and early 1990s when Presidents Ronald Reagan and George Bush appointed a number of conservative justices. Many court decisions of the 1960s and 1970s had been viewed by some people as too liberal because they expanded the rights of individuals. The Court cut back or reversed some of the earlier precedents involving the rights of accused criminals, abortion, civil rights, and other issues. This occurred as the more conservative justices formed a new majority on the Court.

Who Should Be on the Supreme Court?

Assume you are an advisor to the president on appointments to the U.S. Supreme Court. The Court has had a five to four conservative majority. One justice, who is conservative on issues like the death penalty, rights of criminal defendants, civil rights, and abortion, has just resigned. The remaining members of the Court are six white males, one African-American male, and one female.

PROBLEM 17

a. Write a description of the background of the type of person you would like the president to nominate. What characteristics did you select? Which three were the most important and why?

b. Assume you interview seven candidates for the Supreme Court. Each has one of the characteristics listed below. How important is each characteristic to you? Would you disqualify any of the candidates? Explain your answers. Assume that in addition to the listed characteristics the person is otherwise qualified to serve on the Court.

1. Seventy years old.
2. Hispanic.
3. Female.
4. Smoked marijuana ten years ago but was never arrested.
5. Allegedly sexually harassed a female law clerk.
6. Believes the Supreme Court should prohibit the use of racial quotas.
7. Strongly favors a woman's right to an abortion.

Some individuals criticize the practice of appointing justices on the basis of their personal or political viewpoints. These critics say court appointees should be above politics because they sit for life and the Court makes its decisions in private. They say that other criteria should be used to select justices, such as demonstrated experience and expertise as a lawyer or a judge, as well as intelligence, integrity, and good moral character.

Others say that the president should be able to appoint whomever he or she wishes. This includes people with political views similar to those of the president.

Court Systems Figure 1.2 illustrates the two separate court systems in the United States—federal and state. Federal courts hear criminal and civil cases involving federal law. They also hear cases involving parties from different states when the amount in dispute is more than $10,000. Federal trial courts are known as U.S. District Courts. If you lose a trial in the U.S. District Court, you may be able to appeal to the U.S. Circuit Court of Appeals in your region. The United States has thirteen circuit courts (shown in Figure 1.3). The court of final appeal is the U.S. Supreme Court.

Most state court systems resemble the federal courts in structure and procedure. All states have trial courts. These are called superior,

Figure 1.2 Federal and State Court Systems

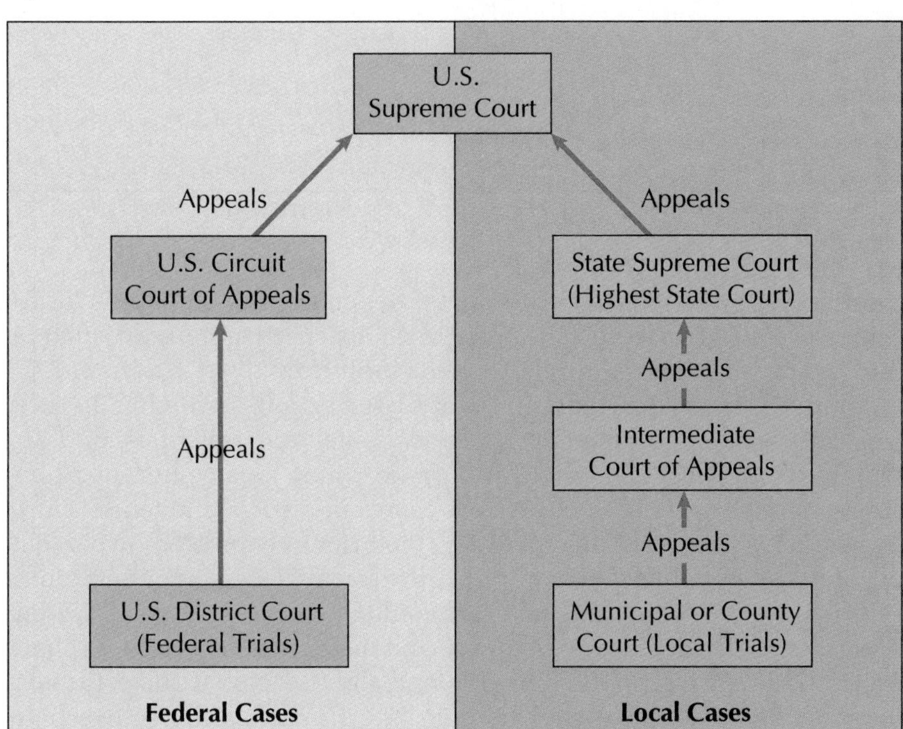

Figure 1.3 The Thirteen Federal Judicial Circuits

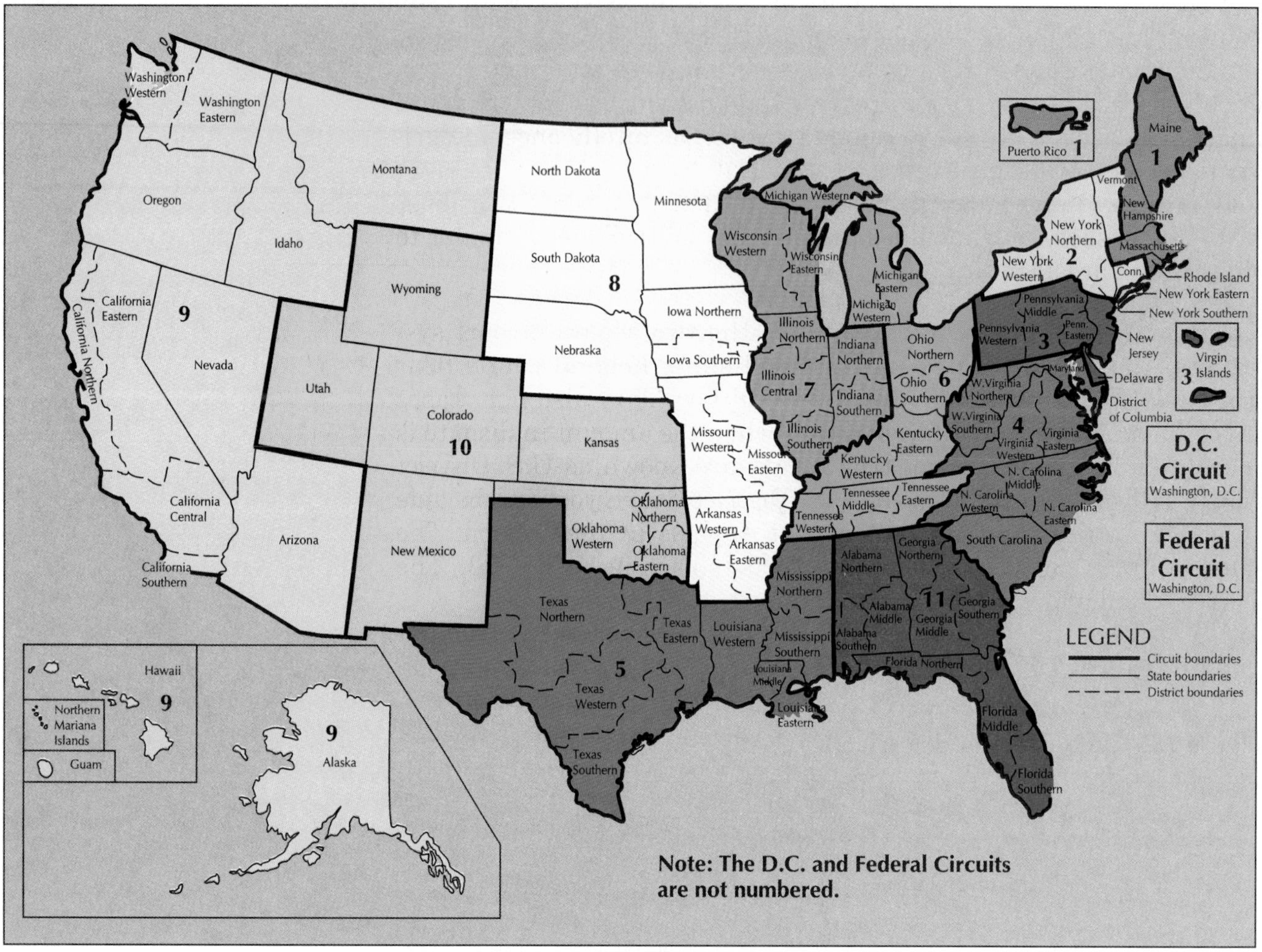

Note: The D.C. and Federal Circuits are not numbered.

Source: Administrative Office of The United States Courts, January, 1993.

county, district, or municipal courts, depending on the state. State courts are often specialized to deal with specific legal areas, such as family, traffic, criminal, probate, and small claims.

Family or domestic relations courts hear actions involving divorce, separation, and child custody. Cases involving juveniles and intrafamily offenses (fights within families) may also be heard. Sometimes, cases involving juveniles are heard in a special juvenile court. Traffic courts hear actions involving violations committed by persons driving motor vehicles. Criminal courts hear cases involving violations of laws for which the violators could go to jail. Frequently, criminal court is divided between felony and misdemeanor cases. Probate courts handle cases involving wills and claims against the estates of persons who die with or without a will. Small claims courts hear cases involving small amounts of money (maximums of $500, $750,

$1,000, or more, depending on the state). Individuals may bring cases here without lawyers—though it is sometimes advised that lawyers be present—and the court fees are low.

If you lose your case in the trial court, you may appeal to an intermediate court of appeals or, in some states, directly to the state supreme court. If a state supreme court decision involves only state law, it can be appealed no further. Each state's highest court has the final say on interpretation of state laws and the state constitution. If a state supreme court decision involves some federal law or constitutional issue, it can then be appealed to the U.S. Supreme Court.

What courts exist in your community? What kinds of cases do they handle? How are appeals handled in your state? What is the highest state court and where is it located?

PROBLEM 18

Consider the following cases. In each, decide whether the case will be tried in a federal or state court. To what court could each case be appealed? Explain your answer. Then give an example, not listed, of a case that could be heard in a state court and a case that could be heard in a federal court.

a. A state sues a neighboring state for dumping waste in a river that borders the two states.

b. A wife sues her husband for divorce.

c. A person is prosecuted for assaulting a neighbor.

d. Two cars collide. One driver sues the other for hospital bills and auto repairs.

e. A group of parents sues the local school board, asking that their children's school be desegregated.

Tribal Courts Many people, especially those who live in states with small Native American populations, do not realize that several hundred Indian tribes govern reservations in the United States today. Native American tribes are no longer independent sovereigns, as they were when Europeans first made contact with North America. As a result of their relationship with the federal government, the tribes no longer possess complete authority over their reservations; they do, however, retain some of their original authority. Sometimes the tribal powers that remain are called inherent powers. These powers include the power to regulate family relationships, tribal membership, and law and order on the reservation. Occasionally Congress grants power to a tribe in a certain area, for example, environmental regulation. This is called a delegated power. Most Native

How does the legal system differ for Native Americans?

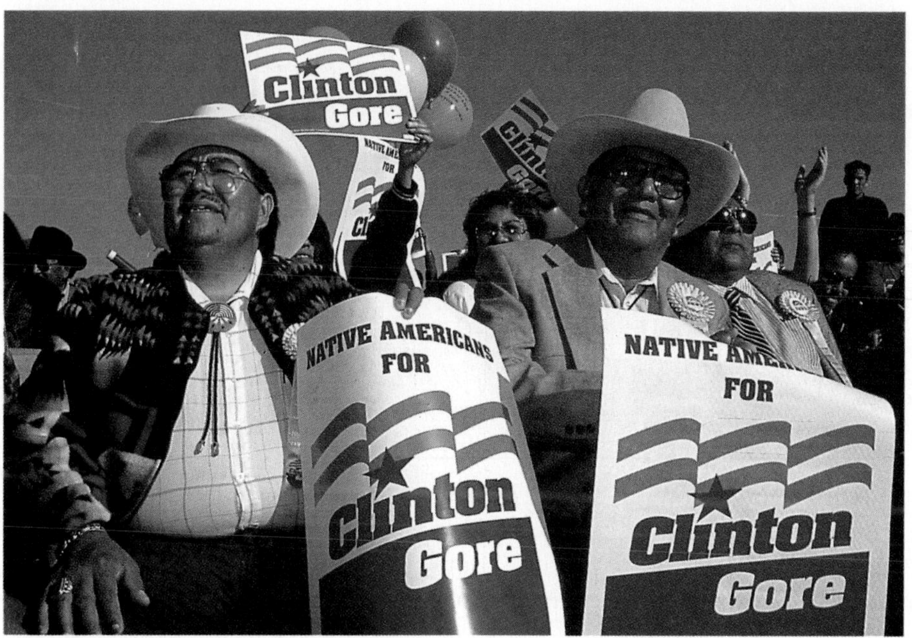

American tribes have justice systems often called tribal court systems. Tribal courts hear a broad range of both criminal and civil cases involving both Native Americans and non-Native Americans.

Some tribal justice systems, for example, those of pueblos in the southwestern United States, are traditional and show little influence by American culture. Many tribal justice systems, however, resemble Anglo-American court systems, primarily because of federal influence and laws such as the *Indian Civil Rights Act*. Still, the work of tribal courts strongly reflects the culture of the tribal people who work in them.

Some confusion and a great deal of controversy surround the power of tribal governments and tribal courts. Both federal law and tribal law determine the jurisdiction of tribal courts. In the criminal area, for example, a federal law gives federal courts jurisdiction over many felonies committed by Native Americans on the reservation. The criminal sentencing authority of tribal courts is limited by the *Indian Civil Rights Act* to imprisonment for no longer than one year and a fine of no more than $5,000. Therefore, some tribes have chosen to criminalize only minor offenses, while others also criminalize more serious offenses. The United States Supreme Court has ruled that inherent tribal authority over the reservation no longer includes the authority to prosecute non-Native Americans for crimes committed on the reservation.

The power of a tribal court to hear civil matters on the reservation appears to be very broad. In recent years, the United States Supreme Court has issued several decisions supporting tribal court

FOCUS ON THE LAW

Indian Civil Rights Act of 1968 (ICRA)

Because Native American societies were established before the U.S. Constitution was adopted, the United States Supreme Court ruled in the 1800s that the U.S. Bill of Rights does not apply to the actions of tribal governments. (Of course the protections of the Bill of Rights do apply to Native Americans, as citizens of the United States, in their relationships with the state and federal governments.)

In 1968, during a time when civil rights were a focus of American politics, Congress passed the *Indian Civil Rights Act*, or ICRA. This law imposed most of the provisions of the Bill of Rights on tribal governments. Out of a recognition that some tribal governments differ from the federal and state governments in their involvement with religion, Congress did not include an establishment clause (see page 466). Similarly, while the *Indian Civil Rights Act* provides that a criminal defendant in a tribal court is entitled to an attorney, the act does not require the tribe to pay for the attorney.

Many tribal officials opposed the enactment of the *Indian Civil Rights Act*. Since the Bill of Rights reflects a culture and tradition that is Anglo-American and not Native American, these tribal leaders saw ICRA as interfering with tribes' inherent, although limited, right to make and be governed by their own laws. Many tribal people remain opposed to the law.

authority and recognizing tribal courts as essential to the preservation of contemporary tribal self-government.

SETTLING DISPUTES OUT OF COURT

The man who strikes first admits that his ideas have run out.

—Chinese proverb

Conflict is a natural part of everyday life, a possibility in every encounter. Since conflict is inevitable, it is important to consider how to handle conflicts in our lives. Courts can help resolve conflicts, but there are other ways to settle many everyday disputes. In reality, only a small number of disputes ever get to court.

Are there any programs in your community that could be used by people who would like to find an alternative to the courts? What types of disputes do these programs handle? How successful are the alternative procedures?

There are sometimes disadvantages in going to court. The court process can be time-consuming and expensive. Going to court can even make some problems worse. For example, in divorces and child custody disputes, going to court often causes extraordinary anger and bitterness. This causes some people to feel that by going to court, they will lose even if they win!

In recent years, alternative forms of dispute resolution have increased in popularity. Among the most common methods for solving disputes out of court are negotiation, arbitration, and mediation.

Negotiation is the process by which people involved in a dispute talk to each other about their problem and try to reach a solution acceptable to all. This informal means of settling disputes should be familiar to everyone. You negotiate when you have a disagreement with your parents, your friends, or your teacher, and you work out an agreement. The informality of negotiation makes it ideal for many types of problems. Sometimes people hire attorneys to negotiate for them. For example, people involved in auto accidents sometimes hire attorneys to negotiate with the insurance company over payments for injuries or damages to their cars. Even if you use an attorney to negotiate, you must approve any agreement before it becomes final. Attorneys sometimes file a case in court and then attempt to work out a **settlement** (agreement) before the case goes to trial. A large number of civil cases are settled this way, saving both time and money.

In **arbitration**, both parties to a dispute agree to have another person listen to their arguments and make a decision for them. The arbitrator is like a judge, but the process is less formal than a trial. Arbitrators, like judges, have the authority to make the final decision, and the parties must follow it (except in what is called nonbinding arbitration). Arbitration is common in contract and labor-management disputes and in some international law cases. Agreements between labor unions and employers include arbitration clauses. This means that the union and the employer agree in advance to submit certain disputes to arbitration and to be bound by the arbitrator's decision. (To learn more about arbitration, see the section on unions in Chapter 7.)

Mediation is another method of alternative dispute resolution. It takes place when a third person helps the disputing parties talk about their problem and settle their differences. Unlike arbitrators, mediators do not impose a decision on the parties. The agreement is the result of the parties' willingness to listen carefully to each other and come up with a reasonable settlement. The mediator acts as a neutral third party by listening carefully to both sides and trying to help the parties understand each other's positions and find ways to resolve the dispute. Mediation is voluntary; therefore, the mediator has no power to impose a decision on the parties. Mediation allows the disputants to air their feelings, avoids placing blame, and concentrates on the future relationship between the parties. The key issue is how the disputants will work or live together when the mediation is over.

Mediation is used to solve a variety of disputes. Community mediation programs help settle disputes between husbands and wives, landlords and tenants, and consumers and businesses. For example, the Better Business Bureau (BBB) often mediates disputes between shoppers and store owners. In other places, neighborhood justice centers help settle disputes between community residents. Government agencies and some universities have **ombudspersons**, who investigate complaints and then help the parties reach some agreement. Even some elementary and secondary schools train students to mediate conflicts and to help settle disputes that occur in and around the school. To locate a mediation program in your community, contact your local court, district attorney's office, or social service agency.

PROBLEM 19

Examine the following situations and list all the methods that could be used to settle each dispute. Then decide the best method for solving each problem. Consider negotiation, arbitration, mediation, going to court, and other methods. Discuss the reasons for your answers.

a. Two sisters share a room. However, they disagree over how the room should be arranged and decorated.

b. A new stereo breaks after two weeks, and the salesperson refuses to fix it.

c. A landlord will not make needed repairs because he believes the tenant caused the damage.

d. A labor union and an employer disagree over the wages and conditions of employment.

e. A married couple wants a divorce.

f. The Internal Revenue Service sends you a letter claiming that you owe another $200 in taxes. You disagree.

g. Carl invites Marlene to the prom, and she agrees to go with him. Then Miguel invites her to the prom. Marlene really wants to go with Miguel and accepts his invitation. Carl finds out about her decision after he has purchased flowers and paid for a limousine to take them to the prom.

Steps in a Typical Mediation Session

Step 1. Explain the Rules.
The mediator sets the parties at ease and explains the ground rules. The mediator's role is not to make a decision but to help the parties reach a mutual agreement. The mediator explains that he or she will not take sides.

Step 2. Tell the Story.
Each party tells what happened. The person bringing the complaint tells his or her side of the story first. No interruptions are allowed. Then the other party explains his or her version of the facts.

Step 3. Identify Facts and Issues.
The mediator attempts to identify agreed-upon facts and issues. This is done by listening to each side, summarizing each party's views, and asking if these are the facts and issues as each party understands them.

Step 4. Identify Alternative Solutions.
Everyone thinks of possible solutions to the problem. The mediator makes a list and asks each party to explain his or her feelings about each possible solution.

Step 5. Revise and Discuss Solutions.
Based on the expressed feelings of the parties, the mediator revises possible solutions and attempts to identify a solution that both parties can agree to.

Step 6. Reach an Agreement.
The mediator helps the parties reach an agreement that both can live with. The agreement should be written down. The parties should also discuss what will happen if either of them breaks the agreement.

PROBLEM 20

Ken Lopez took a $100 sport coat to Ace Dry Cleaners to have it cleaned. The coat was new and had been worn only a few times. When Ken picked it up, he found a large cigarette burn on the lapel. Ken said that the burn had not been there when he brought the coat in and that he didn't smoke. Ken asked the cleaners to pay him $100. Ace denied that it was responsible for the burn and refused to pay. Ace also argued that the coat was used and, as such, was no longer worth $100. Ken countered that he would have to pay at least $100 for a new coat.

a. Examine the situation just described and then role-play a mediation session. Select people to play the roles of each party and the mediator. Follow the steps outlined in the box on this page.

b. Discuss the mediation session. How did the parties act toward each other? What role did the mediator play? Did the parties reach an agreement? What was it? How did the parties feel about the mediation?

c. If this situation had gone to court, what do you think the judge's decision would have been? How would the two parties have felt?

THE ADVERSARY SYSTEM

The trial system in the United States is an **adversary system**. This means it is a contest between opposing sides. The theory is that the trier of fact (the judge or jury) will be able to determine the truth if the opposing parties present their best arguments and show the weaknesses in the other side's case.

How does the adversarial trial system used in the United States differ from the inquisitional trial system used in much of Europe?

If a criminal case goes to trial, the prosecution has the burden of proving the defendant guilty **beyond a reasonable doubt**. In a civil case, the burden is on the plaintiff to prove his or her case by a **preponderance of the evidence** (greater weight of evidence). The standard of proof is more difficult in a criminal case. This is because of a belief that more evidence should be required to take away a person's freedom.

The adversary process is not the only method for handling legal disputes. Many countries have different systems. Some European countries use the **inquisitional system**, in which the judge is active in questioning witnesses and controlling the court process, including the gathering and presenting of evidence. This differs from the adversary process, in which these matters are left to the competing parties and a decision is made by the judge or jury based on the arguments and evidence presented.

The adversary process is often criticized. Critics say that it is not the best method for discovering the truth with respect to the facts of a specific case. They compare the adversary process to a battle in which lawyers act as enemies, making every effort *not* to present *all*

Steps in a Trial

The following is a short explanation of the steps in either a criminal or a civil trial.

Step 1. Opening Statement by Plaintiff or Prosecutor
Plaintiff's attorney (in civil cases) or the prosecutor (in criminal cases) explains to the trier of fact (the judge or jury) the evidence to be presented as proof of the **allegations** (unproven statements) in the written papers filed with the court.

Step 2. Opening Statement by Defense
Defendant's attorney explains evidence to be presented to disprove the allegations made by the plaintiff or prosecutor.

Step 3. Direct Examination by Plaintiff or Prosecutor
Each witness for the plaintiff or prosecution is questioned. Other evidence (such as documents and physical evidence) in favor of the plaintiff or prosecution is presented.

Step 4. Cross-Examination by Defense
The defense has the opportunity to question each witness. Questioning is designed to break down the story or to discredit the witness in the eyes of the jury.

Step 5. Motions
If the prosecution's or plaintiff's basic case has not been established from the evidence introduced, the judge can end the case by granting a **motion** (oral request) made by the defendant's attorney.

Step 6. Direct Examination by Defense
Each defense witness is questioned.

Step 7. Cross-Examination by Plaintiff
Each defense witness is cross-examined.

Step 8. Closing Statement by Plaintiff
Prosecutor or plaintiff's attorney reviews all the evidence presented (noting uncontradicted facts), and asks for a finding of guilty (in criminal cases) or a finding for the plaintiff (in civil cases).

Step 9. Closing Statement by Defense
Same as closing statement by prosecution/plaintiff. The defense asks for a finding of not guilty (in criminal cases) or for a finding for the defendant (in civil cases).

Step 10. Rebuttal Argument
Prosecutor or plaintiff has the right to make additional closing arguments.

Step 11. Jury Instructions
Judge instructs jury as to the law that applies in the case.

Step 12. Verdict
In most states, a unanimous decision is required one way or the other. If the jury cannot reach a unanimous decision, it is said to be a **hung jury**, and the case may be tried again.

the evidence. In this view, the goal of trial is "victory, not truth or justice."

On the other hand, the adversary process is the cornerstone of the American legal system. Most attorneys believe that approaching the same set of facts from totally different perspectives will uncover more truth than would other methods.

PROBLEM 21

a. Do you think the adversary system is the best method for solving disputes? Why or why not?

b. Indicate whether you agree or disagree with the following statement: "It is better that ten guilty persons go free than that one innocent person suffer conviction." Explain your answer.

c. In a criminal case, should a lawyer defend a client he or she knows is guilty? Would you defend someone you knew was guilty? Discuss.

Judges and Juries

Judges and juries are essential parts of our legal system. The judge presides over the trial and has the duty of protecting the rights of those involved. Judges also make sure that attorneys follow the rules of evidence and trial procedure. In nonjury trials, the judge determines the facts of the case and renders a judgment. In jury trials, the judge is required to instruct the jury as to the law involved in the case. Finally, in criminal trials in most states, judges sentence individuals convicted of committing crimes.

The right to trial by jury is guaranteed by the Sixth and Seventh Amendments to the Constitution. This right applies in both federal and state courts. However, a jury is not required in every case. Juries are not used as often as one might think. In civil cases, either the plaintiff or the defendant may request a jury trial. In criminal cases, the defendant decides whether there will be a jury. Many civil cases result in out-of-court settlements or trials by a judge. Most criminal cases are never brought to trial. Instead, they are disposed of by a pre-trial agreement between the government (prosecutor) and the defendant, known as a plea bargain. For additional information on plea bargaining, see page 146.

If a jury trial is requested, a jury is selected and charged with the task of determining the facts and applying the law in a particular case. To serve on a jury, you must be a U.S. citizen, eighteen years old, and a resident of the state. As citizens we have a duty to serve on juries. At one time, people from certain occupations were excluded from jury service. These included members of the clergy, attorneys, physicians, police officers, fire fighters, and persons unable to undertake juror tasks because of mental or physical disability. In many places, these persons are no longer excluded. Convicted felons are usually ineligible for jury service.

How are jurors selected by the courts in your community? How many persons are on the jury in a civil trial? In a criminal trial? Is a unanimous verdict required in a civil trial? In a criminal trial?

Once selected, jurors are assigned to specific cases after being screened through a process known as **voir dire** examination. In this process, opposing lawyers question each prospective juror to discover any prejudices or preconceived opinions concerning the case. After questioning each juror, the opposing attorneys may request the removal of any juror who appears incapable of rendering a fair and impartial verdict. This is called **removal for cause**. In addition, each attorney is allowed a limited number of **peremptory challenges**. This means the attorneys can have prospective jurors removed without stating a cause.

PROBLEM 22

a. Has anyone in your family ever served on a jury? What type of case was involved?

b. Why would someone choose not to have a jury trial in a civil case? In a criminal case?

c. What reasons can you give for the exclusion from jury duty of members of the clergy, attorneys, physicians, police officers, and convicted felons? Should everyone be required to serve on juries? Give your reasons.

d. If you were a defense attorney questioning jurors at the voir dire in a murder trial, what questions would you ask to determine whether the jurors could render a fair and impartial verdict?

e. For what reasons might an attorney use a peremptory challenge?

LAWYERS

There are nearly one million lawyers in the United States. About 65 percent of them are in private practice. Around 15 percent are government lawyers who work for federal, state, or local agencies. Another 15 percent work for corporations, unions, or trade associations. A small number of lawyers work for public interest or legal aid organizations. An even smaller number are law professors, judges, or elected officials.

Contrary to popular belief, most lawyers rarely go to court. Most law practice involves giving advice, drafting legal opinions, negotiating settlements, or otherwise providing out-of-court legal assistance.

Some lawyers do, however, go to court. Such lawyers are called trial attorneys or **litigators**. In civil cases, lawyers act as advocates for their clients' positions. Likewise, in a criminal case, the lawyer for the defendant has a duty to do everything possible (without violating a code of professional ethics) to secure the release and acquittal of his or her client.

When Do You Need a Lawyer?

An important thing to know is when to see a lawyer. Many people think of seeing an attorney only after they get into trouble, but perhaps the best time to consult an attorney is before the problem arises. Preventive advice is an important service that lawyers provide.

You should consider consulting an attorney about a number of common situations. These include:

- buying or selling a home or other real estate.
- organizing a business.
- changing your family status (for example, by divorce or adoption).
- making a will or planning an estate.
- signing a large or important contract.
- handling accidents involving personal injury or property damage.
- defending a criminal charge or bringing a civil suit.

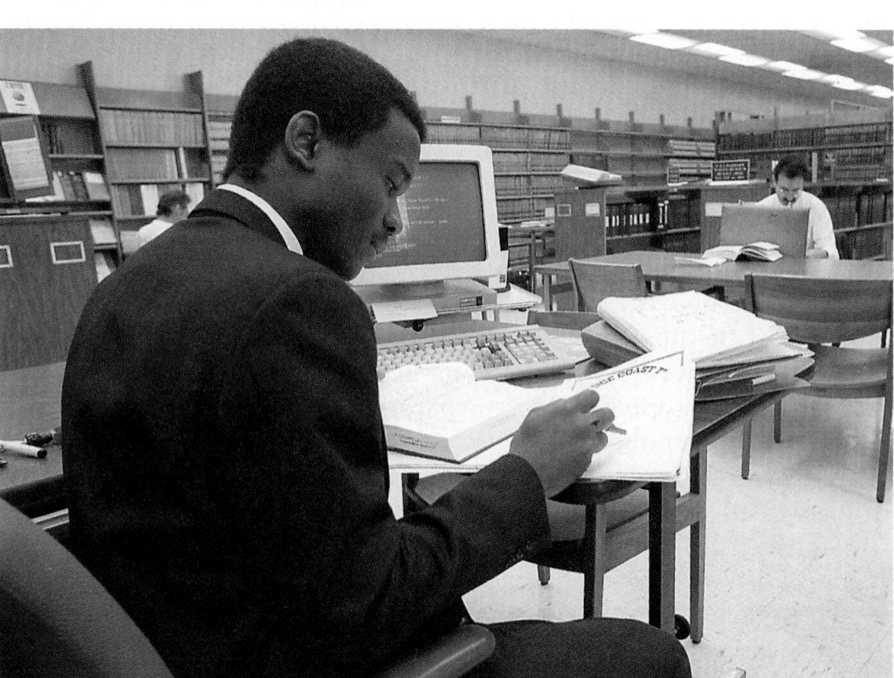

What assistance is this lawyer providing for his client?

How do you decide when you need a lawyer? If a question of law is involved, if a legal document needs to be drawn up or analyzed, or if you are involved in a court case, you will probably need legal help. However, if your problem is minor, you may be able to handle it on your own or with the help of someone other than a lawyer. For example, you can usually sue someone in a small claims court without a lawyer. Likewise, an argument with a spouse may be better handled through a marriage counselor or mediator. Relatives, friends, teachers, members of the clergy, doctors, or accountants may be able to provide the advice that you might have sought from a lawyer.

If you are not sure whether you need a lawyer, it may be advisable to see one to help you decide. Many **bar associations** (organizations that license lawyers) and other groups have services to help you decide if you need a lawyer. These are often provided free or for a small fee.

PROBLEM 23

In each of the following situations, an attorney may or may not be needed. For each situation, discuss the reasons why you may or may not need an attorney.

a. You hit another car in a parking lot. Your insurance agent indicates that the company will pay for bodily injury and property damage.

b. You borrow a friend's car without his knowledge, and he reports it to the police as stolen.

c. You buy a new stereo for $300. One month later, the receiver and speakers blow out. You return to the store, and the salespersons tell you they are sorry but their stereos have only a two-week guarantee.

d. You decide to trade in your old car and buy a new one.

e. Two friends are caught robbing a local store, and they name you as one who helped plan the robbery.

f. The principal suspends you from school for two days because of an article you wrote for the student paper criticizing the school dress code.

g. You are turned down when you apply for a job. You think you were rejected because you are deaf.

h. You do not want your family to inherit the $10,000 you have saved. Told you will die within a year, you want the money to be used for cancer research.

i. You and your spouse find you can no longer get along. You want a divorce.

j. You earn $5,000 working in a restaurant during the year. You want to file your federal income tax return.

How Do You Find a Lawyer?

How do people find lawyers in your area? Does the bar association have a lawyer referral service? Do lawyers advertise? Are there lawyers or legal organizations that will represent you for free if you cannot afford a lawyer or in certain types of cases?

If you need a lawyer, how do you find one who is right for you and your particular problem? Perhaps the best way to find an experienced lawyer is through the recommendation of someone who had a similar legal problem that was resolved to his or her satisfaction. You might also ask your employer, members of the clergy, businesspeople, or other professionals for the name of a lawyer they know and trust.

You can always find a lawyer by looking under "Lawyers" in the Yellow Pages of your phone book. In addition, *Martindale-Hubble Law Directory,* available in your public library, lists most lawyers in the United States. It provides some general information about their education, their professional honors, and the types of cases they handle. Lawyers sometimes advertise their services. In many places, advertisements for lawyers may be found in newspapers and magazines or on radio and television.

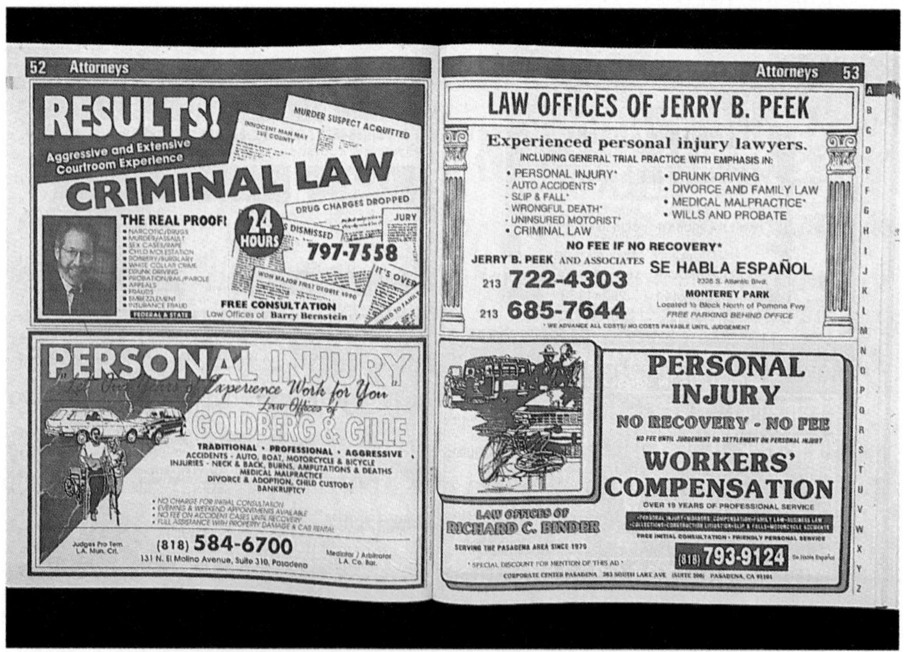

If you were assaulted by a coworker, how would you use these ads to help select an attorney?

Lawyers have not always been allowed to advertise. Until recently, it was considered improper and was forbidden by bar associations and courts. In 1977, the U.S. Supreme Court ruled that advertising by lawyers was protected by the First Amendment's freedom of speech clause. Those in favor of advertising by lawyers think that it helps consumers decide what lawyer to hire. They add that statistics show advertising brings down legal fees through competition. Those against it think that it makes lawyers into salespersons who are likely to make exaggerated claims. They think that lawyers should be hired based on competence and skill and that it is difficult to ascertain those qualities through advertising.

A recent survey found that over 25 percent of lawyers now advertise through various means, including telephone directories, newspapers, radio, and television. Advertising has enabled large, lower-cost law firms, often called legal clinics, to develop, and some have spread nationwide. However, many attorneys and others still consider advertising improper.

PROBLEM 24

a. A television advertisement shows a lawyer in a bathing suit coming out of a lake. He says, "If you're in over your head because of bad debts, let us bail you out. We're the best firm in the state." Should there be any restrictions on ads like this? If so, what? Should there be other restrictions on ads? If so, what should they be?

b. A lawyer hears that many people have been injured as a result of accidents in a particular type of car. He runs a newspaper ad showing a picture of a car crashing. The car's name is clearly visible on its side. The ad reads, "If this happens to you, I may be able to help you recover your losses." Should the lawyer be able to do this?

c. Many people in an area have lost their jobs and are about to lose their homes because they cannot make their monthly payments. Jane, a lawyer, writes to all of these people saying she is willing to represent them to prevent the loss of their homes. Should she be allowed to do this?

Another way to find a lawyer is to contact a local lawyer referral service. Most communities have bar associations that maintain lists

What to Ask Your Lawyer

Once you have found a lawyer who seems interested in your problem, you should get answers to the following questions:

- What is the lawyer's fee? Is the client required to pay a flat fee or by the hour? Is a retainer required? What about a contingency fee, in which the lawyer gets paid only if he or she wins your case?
- Will there be a written fee agreement? What will it say? How often will you be billed? Will the lawyer tell you when the fee is going to exceed a certain limit?
- Has the lawyer ever handled cases like this before? If so, with what results?
- Will the lawyer provide you with copies of all correspondence and documents prepared on your behalf?
- Will the lawyer keep you informed of any new developments in your case and talk to you in "plain English"?

If you are not satisfied with the answers you get, do not hesitate to shop around.

of lawyers who specialize in certain kinds of cases. Many lawyers will meet with and advise clients at a special rate. If you call the referral service, you will be told the amount of the initial consultation fee and will be given a lawyer's name for an appointment. If additional legal service is needed, the fee is subject to agreement between the lawyer and the client.

The Car Crash

On April 1, Al Sundance and his friend Marie Davis were driving along Sixth Street, returning home from a party. Al had stopped at a red light at the corner of Sixth Street and Florida Avenue when a 1989 Buick hit his car in the rear.

Al's 1992 Volvo was smashed in as far as the back seat. Al suffered a severe neck injury, four broken ribs, and many cuts and bruises. As a result, he spent three weeks in the hospital. Al's passenger, Marie, was also severely injured. She suffered a fractured skull, facial and numerous other cuts, a broken right arm and hip, and internal bleeding. Marie, an accountant making $25,000 a year, spent six weeks in the hospital and returned to work after twelve weeks.

The driver of the Buick, Fred Ortego, suffered minor cuts on his face and arm and was released from the hospital after twenty-four hours. As a result of the accident, Fred was given a ticket for speeding and reckless driving.

Fred's insurance company has called Marie and offered her a $4,500 settlement. Marie is uncertain whether she should accept and decides to consult an attorney. After checking with a lawyer referral service, she is referred to a local attorney.

PROBLEM 25

Role-play the initial attorney-client interview between Marie and the attorney. Persons role-playing the attorney should attempt to ask all the questions an attorney should ask at this point. Persons role-playing the client should provide the attorney with all necessary information and ask all those questions that are relevant to Marie's case and that relate to whether she should retain the attorney.

If you are unable to afford the services of a lawyer, you may be eligible for free legal assistance at a legal aid, legal service, or public defender's office. These offices are usually listed in the Yellow Pages under "Legal Services." You may also contact the Legal Services Corporation or a local bar association or law school for the address of the legal aid office nearest you.

It is sometimes wise to interview more than one lawyer before making a selection. You can use these meetings to judge the differences between lawyers' fees, their experience in the type of case in which you are involved, and how you think you will be able to work with each one.

To avoid problems regarding legal fees, ask for an estimate of the total charge. You should also find out who else will be working on the case, what each person charges per hour, and how often you will be billed. Lawyers often require a **retainer**—a down payment on the total fee. In addition, attorneys may charge clients for court costs, filing fees, or other expenses.

Attorneys sometimes take cases on a **contingency fee** basis instead of charging an hourly fee or a lump sum. The fee will be a percentage of what the client wins in the case. However, the client pays nothing except expenses if the case is lost. This fee arrangement is most common in personal injury cases in which money damages are being sought.

A typical contingency fee is one-third of the amount awarded to the client. However, it could be 40 percent or higher in some cases. If a client wins $300,000 in an auto accident case, the lawyer hired on a one-third contingency fee basis would take $100,000, and the client $200,000 minus court costs.

The attorney-client relationship is often based on oral agreements. However, bar associations frequently recommend and sometimes require written fee agreements signed by both the attorney and the client. This can help prevent disagreements later.

Another thing to consider before choosing a lawyer is whether your problem is one that may be of interest to the American Civil Liberties Union (ACLU), Environmental Defense Fund (EDF), National Association for the Advancement of Colored People (NAACP), American Conservative Union (ACU), or some other public interest group. These organizations are usually listed in the phone book and may provide free representation.

Working with Your Attorney

Trust is the foundation of the attorney-client relationship. You must be able to trust your attorney. To help you, your attorney needs

Why should clients speak freely to their lawyers?

to know everything about your problem. To encourage clients to speak freely to their lawyers, the law grants an attorney-client **privilege**. This means that whatever you tell your attorney about your case is secret and confidential. This information cannot be disclosed to anyone without your permission.

Working with an attorney also means making decisions. A good attorney will give you advice, but you must make the final decision (for example, to sue or not to sue or to accept or reject a settlement). So that you can make good decisions, it is the attorney's job to help you understand what is going on. You, in turn, should ask the questions needed to clarify things.

FOCUS ON THE LAW

Code of Professional Responsibility

The Code of Professional Responsibility is a set of rules governing the conduct of lawyers. The code consists of the following nine canons, or principles, which are broken down into ethical considerations and disciplinary rules. Ethical considerations describe goals for the lawyer to keep in mind when facing a moral dilemma. Disciplinary rules are requirements of the profession. An attorney who violates a rule may be fined, suspended, or disbarred.

Canon 1. A lawyer should assist in maintaining the integrity and competence of the legal profession.
Canon 2. A lawyer should assist the legal profession in fulfilling its duty to make legal counsel available.
Canon 3. A lawyer should assist in preventing the unauthorized practice of law.
Canon 4. A lawyer should preserve the confidences and secrets of a client.
Canon 5. A lawyer should exercise independent professional judgment on behalf of a client.
Canon 6. A lawyer should represent a client completely.
Canon 7. A lawyer should represent a client zealously within the bounds of the law.
Canon 8. A lawyer should assist in improving the legal system.
Canon 9. A lawyer should avoid the appearance of professional impropriety.

Source: Adapted from the American Bar Association.

If you are not satisfied, you may discharge your lawyer. Once the case is in court, however, a judge may permit this change only for a very good reason.

Lawyers must follow certain standards of conduct. These standards are set out in a Code of Professional Responsibility and are enforced by the state bar association. In almost every state, a lawyer must pass an examination to become a member of the state bar. Lawyers who violate standards of conduct may be reprimanded, suspended, or **disbarred**. Once disbarred, a lawyer no longer has a license to practice law.

In recent years, there has been a great deal of concern about the conduct of lawyers. A client who has serious complaints that cannot be worked out with his or her attorney can report the problem to the local or state bar association. Like other professionals, lawyers can be sued by clients for serious errors that result in injury or loss. This type of case is known as a **legal malpractice** case. There is additional information on malpractice in the chapter on tort law.

To handle attorney-client disputes, some bar associations have arbitration systems in which panels that consist of lawyers and sometimes include nonlawyers hold hearings and issue opinions. Some disputes deal with the amount charged for the lawyer's services. Panels sometimes order the attorney to return a client's money if they decide the fee was improper.

PROBLEM 26

The following situations present ethical dilemmas faced by attorneys. Examine each case and decide whether the attorney acted ethically or unethically. Explain your answers.

a. Susan, a criminal defense attorney, knows her client is guilty; nevertheless, she tries to convince a jury he is not guilty.

b. Ozzie, a domestic relations attorney handling a divorce, has sexual relations with his female client.

c. Marta, an attorney for the family of a man killed in an auto accident, visits a bar and comes across a juror in the case she is trying. She has a drink with the juror.

d. Mike is a real estate attorney who knows that most attorneys charge only $300 to handle the legal work involved in buying a home. Since his wealthy client is new in town and doesn't know the normal rate, Mike charges him $500.

e. Mohammed, a criminal defense attorney, puts his client on the stand to testify to her innocence even though Mohammed knows she is lying.

f. José, a corporate lawyer, is asked by a wealthy client to recommend her son for admission to the state bar. José says yes.

g. Rosa represents a man injured by a defective lawn mower. The manufacturer's insurance company offers a $100,000 settlement. She accepts the settlement without informing her client.

Chapter 2

Criminal Law and Juvenile Justice

A **crime** is something one does or fails to do in violation of a law. It can also be defined as behavior for which the state has set a penalty.

Crime wears many faces. It may be the teenager snatching a woman's purse or the career criminal planning a kidnapping. It may be the youth who steals a car for a joyride or the car theft ring that takes it for later sale. It may be the professional criminal who profits from organized gambling, extortion, or narcotics traffic, or the politician who takes a bribe. Crime may be committed by the professional person who cheats on tax returns, the businessperson who secretly agrees to fix prices, or the burglar who ransacks homes while the owners are at work.

Criminal law designates certain conduct "criminal" and other conduct "noncriminal." Decisions as to what constitutes a crime are made by legislatures, which try to protect the public based on what most people believe is right and necessary for the orderly conduct of our society. Certain acts are prohibited or commanded to protect life and property, preserve individual freedoms, maintain our system of government, and uphold the morality of society. Ideally, the goal of law is to regulate human conduct so that people can live in harmony.

PROBLEM 1

You are a member of a commission established to evaluate laws. Consider the following acts and in each case decide whether the act should be treated as a crime. Rank the acts from most serious to

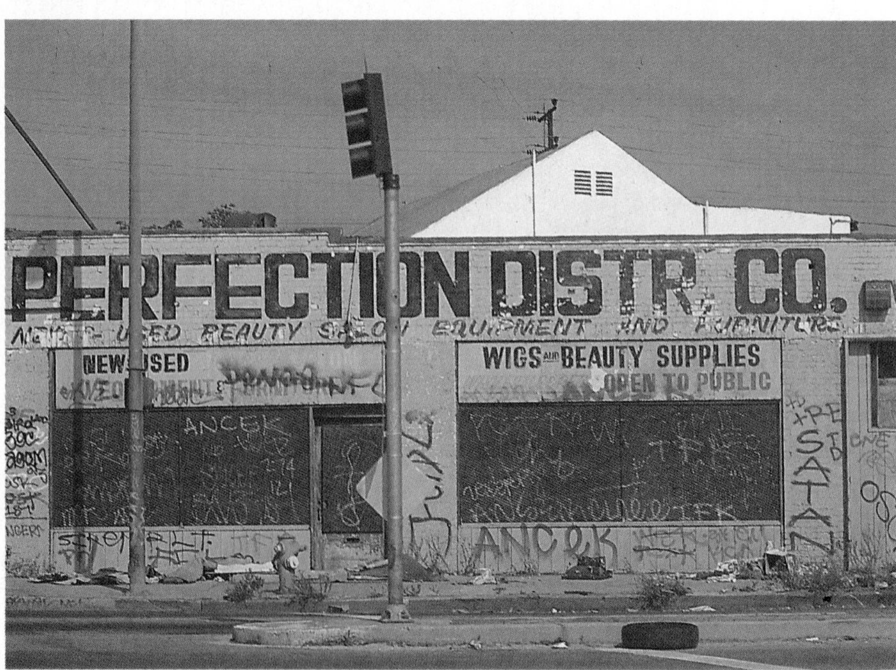

Why do some people vandalize buildings?

least serious. Give reasons for your decisions.

a. Robert pushes crack cocaine and uses the proceeds to support his mother, who is on welfare.

b. Keesha is a passenger in a car she knows is stolen, but she did not participate in the theft of the car.

c. Liz picks an individual's pocket and takes a wallet containing $50.

d. Donald is a used-car dealer who turns back the odometers on cars he sells.

e. Susan is caught with a pound of marijuana.

f. Ted robs a liquor store at gunpoint.

g. Ellen leaves a store with change for a $10 bill after she realizes that she gave the cashier a $5 bill.

h. Lilly approaches a man for purposes of prostitution.

i. Ming refuses to wear a helmet while riding a motorcycle.

j. A company pollutes a river with waste from its automobile factory.

k. Marge gets drunk and hits a child while speeding through a school zone.

l. Burt observes his best friend shoplifting but does not turn him in.

NATURE AND CAUSES OF CRIME

Unfortunately, preventing crime is not an easy task. Crime has long been a major problem in the United States. In 1991, more than 14.8 million serious crimes were reported to the police. (See Figure 2.1 for details.) This is an increase of almost 45% since 1974. Police report that they were able to arrest suspects in nearly 20 percent of these reported cases. However, many crimes are not reported.

Crime rates are generally higher in urban areas. But during the last few years, crime has grown fastest in suburbs and in rural areas. Crime is not confined to any particular group, but youths between the ages of 15 and 24 commit more violent crimes than people in any other age group. Males committed almost four times as many crimes as females, but in recent years the crime rate has grown

Figure 2.1 Crimes Reported and Percentage in Which Arrests Were Made (1991)

Type of Crime	Total Number Reported	Percent Arrested	Type of Crime	Total Number Reported	Percent Arrested
Crime Index[a] Total	14,959,030	19.8%	Aggravated Assault	1,092,739	44.0%
Violent Crime	1,911,767	37.6%	Burglary	3,157,150	13.8%
Property Crime	13,047,263	17.2%	Larceny/Theft	8,142,228	19.5%
Murder and Nonnegligent Manslaughter	24,703	97.3%	Motor Vehicle Theft	1,661,738	12.4%
Forcible Rape	106,593	37.6%	Arson	86,147	18.0%
Robbery	687,732	25.2%			

[a] The crime index is the sum of violent crimes and property crimes.

Source: *Uniform Crime Reports,* 1991.

fastest among women.

One way in which crime affects us all is that it costs everyone money. The cost of lost or damaged lives, or of fear and suffering, cannot be measured solely in dollars and cents, but the total cost of crime in this country has been estimated at over $100 billion per year.

PROBLEM 2

a. According to Figure 2.1, what was the most commonly reported type of crime in 1991?

b. What percentage of reported crimes resulted in arrest?

c. Of the crimes reported, for which crimes were people most likely to be arrested? Least likely to be arrested? Why do you think this is so?

Although authorities agree that crime is a major problem, much disagreement exists over the causes of crime and what can be done about it. Among the reasons suggested for the high crime rate in America are poverty, permissive courts, unemployment, lack of education, abuse of alcohol and drugs, inadequate police protection, rising population, lack of parental guidance, a breakdown in morals, an ineffective correctional system, little chance of being caught or punished, and the influence of television. This lack of agreement on the

Figure 2.2 Crime Clock (1991)

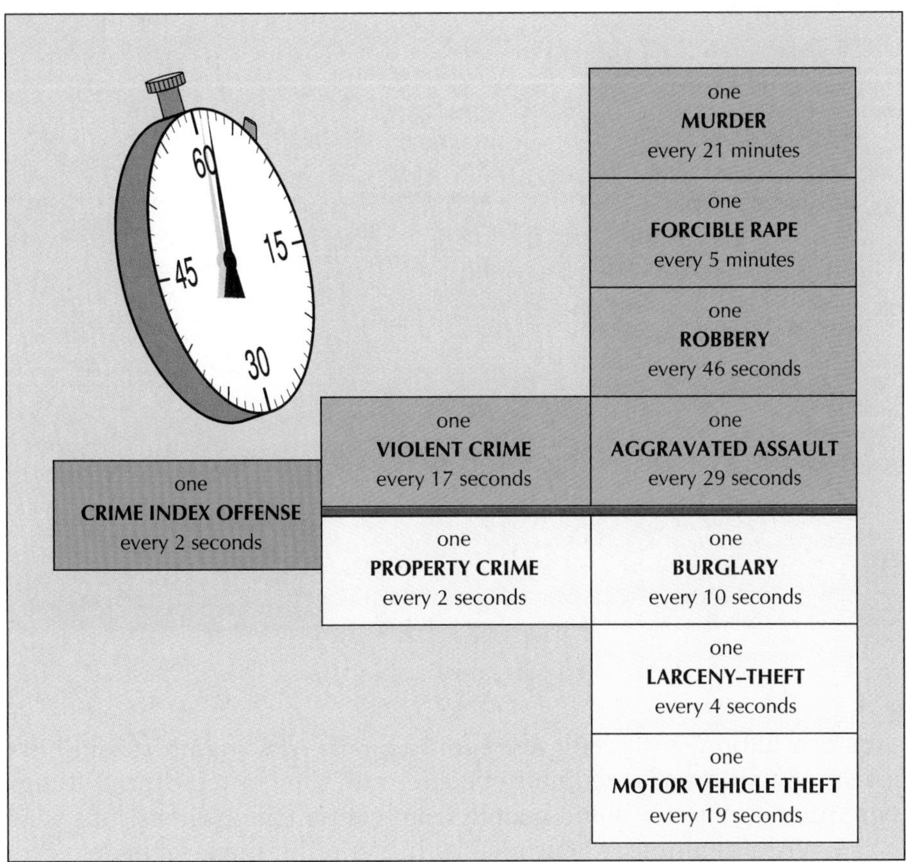

Source: *Uniform Crime Reports,* 1991.

causes of crime indicates that they are many and complex.

Let's examine some proposed causes of crime more closely. Some people point to the economic system with its wide disparity between the rich and the poor in America as a major contributor to the crime rate. However, crime cannot be totally explained in terms of poverty, particularly if one considers that crime rose fastest in this country at a time when the number of people living in poverty was declining. In recent years, crime rates have risen fastest in suburbs and in other affluent areas. Furthermore, if poverty were the sole cause of crime, one could not explain why countries much poorer than the United States have far less crime.

Some people explain increasing crime in terms of rising population. They say there are more people, particularly young people, so there is more crime. While this is true to a degree, the crime rate has risen faster than the population rate.

Will tougher penalties curb crime? Many people think so, but the United States already has some of the toughest criminal laws of any

Should U.S. prisons be operated differently? If so, how?

What is the major crime problem in your community? What crimes have increased most over the last three years? Have any crime rates decreased during this period? Where can you get this information?

Western nation. In recent years, only South Africa and Russia have executed and imprisoned more people than the United States. Tough penalties may deter some people from committing crimes, but compared with the number of crimes, only a small number of people ever go to prison. Thus, some experts say that longer prison terms are not the answer. They say the certainty of punishment is more important than the length of sentence.

Adequate police protection obviously has something to do with the crime rate, but studies show that simply increasing the number of police officers does not necessarily reduce the overall crime rate. Some experts point to peer group pressure, family background, and declining morality as causes of crime. Still others blame crime on the use of drugs or the influence of the mass media, which they claim glamorizes criminal activity, particularly violence. Undoubtedly, family influences, a decline in moral standards, and drugs play a role in crime, but these factors are probably not the only causes.

In recent years, many cities in America have experienced an increase in juvenile gangs and related crime. Most youth gangs are neighborhood gangs and not adult drug organizations. Belonging to a gang may appear to the young person to provide a sense of stability and pride. Some people argue that gangs cause crimes because young people sometimes do things in groups that they would never do alone. Recently incidents have occurred in which gang members of one race have attacked one or more members of another race.

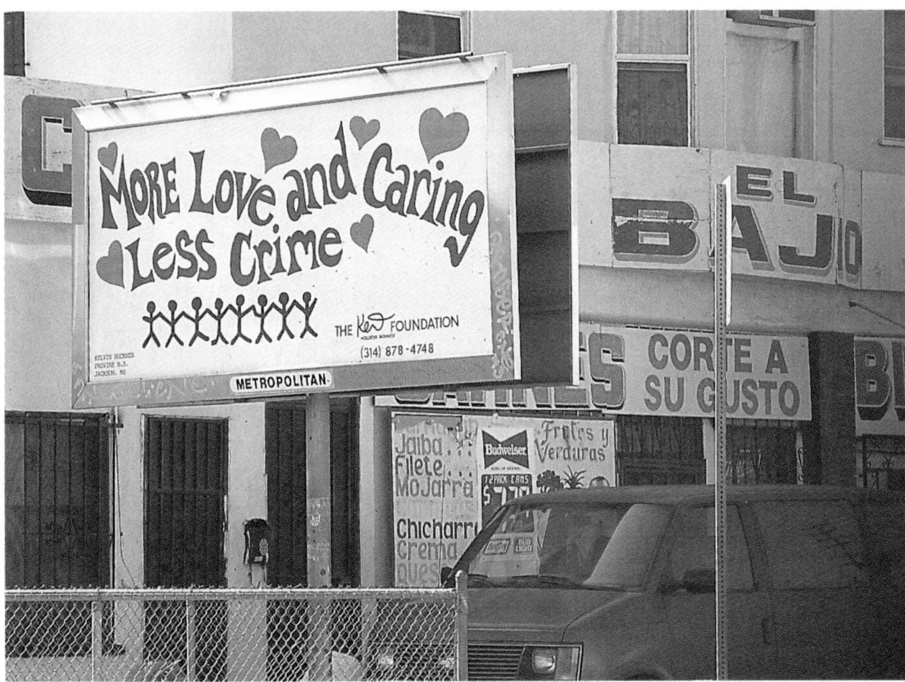

What approaches has your community taken to prevent crime?

Crime on college campuses has risen in recent years. Campus crimes include violent assaults, hate crimes, and property crimes. Many of these crimes are alcohol-related. College students spend over $5 billion yearly on alcohol. Crime statistics from more than 2,400 colleges indicate that 30 murders, nearly 1,000 rapes, over 1,800 robberies, over 32,000 burglaries, and almost 9,000 motor-vehicle thefts were reported in 1992.

Thinking about crime requires us to go beyond slogans and stereotypes. We should carefully consider each of the suggested causes and the possible solutions to the problem. Perhaps the most that can be said is that disagreement exists over the causes of crime and that the solution to the crime problem is not simple.

Is your school safe? If not, what steps should be taken to make it safer?

PROBLEM 3

a. Can you suggest causes of crime not mentioned in the text?

b. Rank the causes of crime from the most important to the least important. Discuss your ranking.

c. Do you think people are more likely to commit crimes if they are members of a gang? Why or why not? What types of crimes are people more likely to commit when they are in groups?

Why? What can be done to reduce violence by gangs or other groups of people?

GANGS AND CRIME

"It takes a village to raise a child."

—African proverb

At one time, violent gangs were thought to operate only in the nation's largest cities. Evidence indicates, however, that gangs are now active in towns and cities of all sizes throughout the country. One reason gangs have spread is the lure of profits from the sale of illegal drugs, an activity in which many gangs participate. Survey information from 1991, furthermore, indicates that gang violence is on the rise. The wide availability of weapons and cars to young people has led, in part, to this increase in violence.

In 1991, the National Youth Gang Information Center estimated that nearly 300,000 young people were members of gangs. Several times that many are estimated to be gang "wanna-bes" (youths who aspire to join gangs).

What Are Gangs?

In this discussion, gangs refer to people who form groups closed to others, for certain common purposes that can include violent, criminal activity. While the media have featured gang activity a great deal in recent years, gangs are not new in the United States. In the 19th century, gangs existed in many American neighborhoods. These gangs were primarily composed of adults and were usually organized along ethnic lines. Even then gangs had names, rules, emblems, initiation rituals, and distinctive ways of dressing. Early gangs were interested in protecting turf, reputation, and cultural heritage. But not all of these gangs engaged in criminal activity; neither do all gangs today. In fact, some gangs have performed pro-social community work and have operated job-training and other government-funded programs.

Today's gang members range in age from 8 to 50. While traditional youth gangs are still concerned with issues of status and turf, many gangs, sometimes called posses or crews, now operate on much more sophisticated organizational structures. Many focus on drug trafficking and other criminal activity. Others use group-oriented violence or other criminal behavior to defend certain beliefs, which may be racist, sexist, or the like.

Who Joins Gangs?

While there are some female gang members, the overwhelming majority are male. In many cases, gang members' relatives or friends are also involved with gangs. Many gang members live under poor conditions at home, where their basic needs are unmet, and lack success in school. They are very pessimistic about their job prospects and other opportunities for the future.

Why Do People Join Gangs?

Some young people join gangs to receive the attention and to experience the sense of belonging that they do not receive or experience at home or at school. Others join because they feel pressure from friends, possibly in the form of threats, or because they believe that once they join they will be protected from police or members of other gangs. To those who see a future without employment, financial, or recreational opportunities, gang membership may appear to be their only alternative. This may account for the fact that many older members, still lacking opportunities, are not "maturing out" of gangs.

How Can the Gang Problem Be Solved?

Most experts agree that the best way to handle the problem of gangs is to prevent young people from getting involved with gangs. Communities that have been successful in dealing with gangs have done the following:

1. Operated outreach and intervention programs in which social workers and trained counselors encouraged gang members to become involved in positive, non-gang activities;
2. Provided greater opportunities for young people, including athletics, clubs, school tutoring, community service work, and job training;
3. Mobilized government agencies, schools, parents, community groups, religious organizations, and other youths to increase awareness of the problem and develop opportunities for young people;

Can the energy of gang members be channelled in positive directions?

4. Organized prevention strategies in which police and probation officers identified gang members (and wanna-bes) and placed them in anti-gang membership programs; and
5. Prosecuted gang members for illegal activity.

PROBLEM 4

a. Is there a gang problem in your community? If not, what steps should be taken now to prevent such a problem? If there already is a problem, how do you know it exists? What steps should be taken to deal with it? Do you agree that police should be able to place gang members (and wanna-bes) in special programs without charging them with specific crimes? Explain your reasons.

b. Why do you think there is such a serious gang problem in the U.S. today? What steps, if any, should be taken on the national level to deal with the problem?

c. To what extent do you think our society encourages violence by presenting so much of it on the nightly news and other television shows, in certain cartoons and movies, and in the lyrics of some popular music? What, if anything, should be done about this?

d. What is the meaning of the African proverb at the beginning of this section? How does it relate to the problem of gangs and crime?

VICTIMS OF CRIME

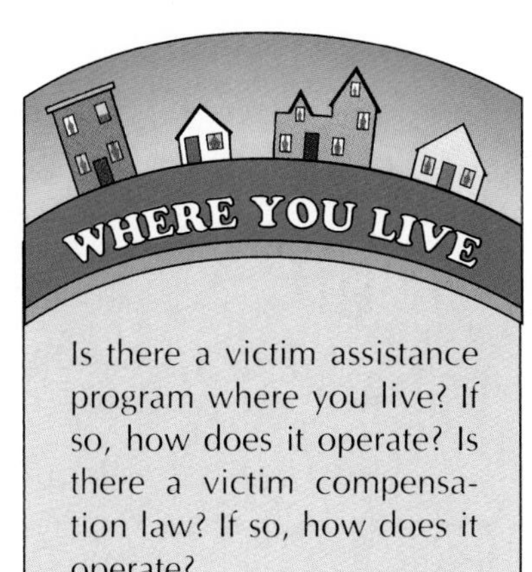

Is there a victim assistance program where you live? If so, how does it operate? Is there a victim compensation law? If so, how does it operate?

Crime affects us all, but victims suffer most. Victims of crime can be found among all segments of society, young and old, rich and poor, and people of all racial and ethnic groups. Each year, more than 36 million Americans are victimized by crime.

Teenagers are more frequently the targets of crime than people in any other age group. Teenagers are victimized by violent crimes (rape, robbery, and assault) at twice the rate for the general adult population and ten times the rate for the elderly.

Males are twice as likely as females to be victims of crime. The poor, along with the unemployed and the separated or divorced, are more likely to be crime victims. Among businesses, it is the owner of the small business, the retailer, who is the hardest hit by crime.

Studies show that African Americans, Hispanics, and other minorities are more likely to be victimized than whites. African-American teens are three to five times more likely than white teens to be murder victims.

PROBLEM 5

a. Why do you think teenagers are more likely than adults to be crime victims?

b. Why do you think the poor, minorities, and small businesses are more likely to be crime victims than the rich, whites, and large businesses?

In recent years, public interest in aiding the victim has grown. Most states now have victim assistance programs. These programs provide victims with counseling, medical care, and other services and benefits. Most states also have victim compensation laws. These laws provide financial help for victims—paying medical bills, mak-

In what ways can a rape crisis center help a rape victim?

ing up lost salary, and in some cases paying funeral costs and death benefits to victims' families. Some states in recent years have begun to allow prosecutors to submit victim impact statements to the court when a person is sentenced for a crime. These impact statements show what effect the defendant's crime has had on the victim's physical and psychological well-being.

In addition, courts sometimes order **restitution**. This means requiring criminals to pay back or otherwise compensate the victims of their crimes. To learn more about victim assistance programs, contact your local police, district attorney, or U.S. attorney's office.

Today, victim advocacy groups are playing a more significant role in the criminal justice system. Their primary function is to help victims through their trauma and also to protect the rights of victims. Most of these groups deal with specific crimes, like rape, spouse abuse, drunk driving, and child abuse. An important victim advocacy group is Mothers Against Drunk Driving (MADD). In recent years, MADD has been instrumental in calling attention to the problem of drunk driving and in lobbying for stricter punishment for people found driving while intoxicated.

If You Become a Victim

There are two different views on what to do if you believe you are about to become the victim of a crime. The first theory is that you

Crime Prevention

Purse snatching! Home burglary! Consumer fraud! Crime is something almost everyone worries about. As a good citizen, you can help fight crime. You can do this by learning how to protect yourself. This means knowing both how to prevent crime and what to do if you are ever a victim of crime. To reduce the risk of crime, follow these rules:

- Report suspicious activity to the police. The police can't help if you don't call them.
- Lock your doors and windows! Many burglaries occur because someone didn't lock up. Police suggest a dead-bolt lock with a one-inch bolt on each outside door.
- Beware of high-crime areas. Dark and deserted streets, parking lots, garages, and bus stops are all high-crime areas.
- Whenever possible, have someone with you at night and in high-risk areas.
- Don't flash money in public.
- When on vacation, cancel newspaper delivery. Stop mail delivery or have a neighbor collect the mail. Consider using a timer to turn lights on at night.
- If you are a woman living alone, list only your last name and first initial on your mailbox and in the phone book.
- If you return to your home and think that someone has broken in, do not enter. Go to a neighbor's home immediately and call the police.
- If someone knocks while you are at home, do not open the door until you are absolutely sure who is outside.

How could this building garage be made safer?

should not fight back. For property crimes, for example, give up the property without objection in order to reduce the risk of injury. The second theory is that you should resist the assailant. Which course should you follow? Every situation is unique, but your safety should always come first.

If you choose to fight back against the assailant, be prepared to risk injury. Know your own limitations. Not everyone has the

ADVICE

How to Report a Crime

If you are ever a victim of or a witness to a crime, you should do the following:

- Stay calm.
- Call the police immediately!
- Always report a crime. If you don't report it, the police can't help. Someone else may become a victim.
- Tell the police who you are, where you are, and what happened.
- If anyone is hurt, ask for an ambulance.
- When the police arrive, tell them exactly what you saw. If possible, write down the following information before the police arrive: what the suspect looked like (age, height, clothing, facial description); if the suspect was driving a car, the make, model, color, license number, and direction of travel.
- You may be asked to make a **complaint** or to **testify** in court. Remember, if you don't help the police, the criminal might commit a crime again.

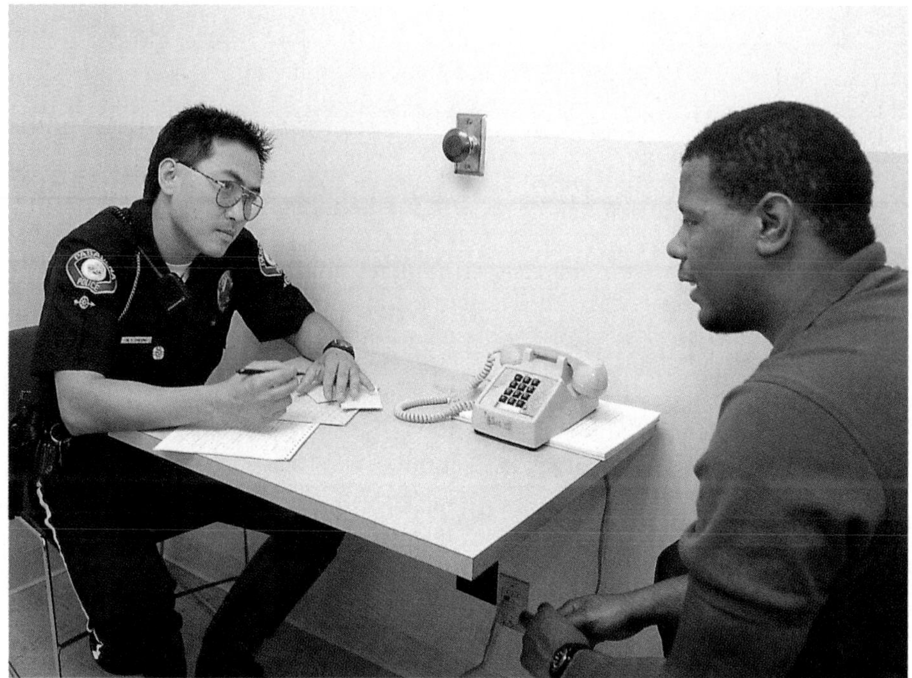

This citizen is reporting a crime, but many victims and witnesses of crime do not. Why?

strength or size to be able to fight back successfully. If the assailant has a weapon, you should assume it is going to be used.

As a general rule, criminals do not want an audience. So if you are able to scream or blow a whistle, do so if you know it will be heard. If you can't run away, sit down so you won't get knocked down.

Finally, call the police as soon as you can. Don't wait! The longer you wait, the more likely it is that the criminal will get away.

PROBLEM 6

a. Do you know anyone who has been the victim of a crime? What was the crime? How did it affect the person?

b. List and discuss at least four things you can do to protect yourself from crime.

c. One afternoon about 2:30 P.M., you see a blue van pull up in front of a neighbor's house. Two strange men get out of the van and walk to the rear of the house. You are suspicious because you know your neighbors are on vacation. What should you do?

d. If you call the police about the incident just described, what will you say? Role-play a phone call between yourself and the police.

e. Have you ever witnessed a crime? What happened? What did you do? If it happened again, would you do the same thing?

f. Suppose you are stopped on a deserted street corner by a man wearing a jacket. He says he has a knife in his pocket and wants your wallet. What will you do?

GENERAL CONSIDERATIONS

Every crime is made up of certain **elements**. Elements are the conditions that make an act a crime. A crime cannot be committed unless all its elements are fulfilled. For example, *robbery* is defined as the unlawful taking of goods or money from someone's person by force or intimidation. Thus, the elements of robbery are (1) the taking of goods or money, (2) the use of force or intimidation, and (3) the lack of consent of the person from whom the goods or money are taken.

If someone picks your pocket without your knowing it, the person cannot be convicted of robbery. This is because the person did not use force or intimidation—one of the elements of robbery. However, the person could be convicted of *larceny*, because the elements of larceny do not include the use of force or violence.

Almost all crimes require an **act** and an **intent**. Criminal intent means that the person intended or meant to commit a crime. Criminal intent usually involves knowing and willful action. If a person acts because of a mistake or some other innocent reason, there is no criminal intent.

A few crimes are **strict liability** offenses. These crimes do not require criminal intent. Strict liability offenses make the act itself a crime regardless of the knowledge of the person committing the act. For example, the law makes it illegal to sell alcoholic beverages to minors. This is true regardless of whether or not the seller knew the buyer was underage.

Intent is different from **motive**. The motive is the reason a person commits a crime. For example, in murder, the motive is the reason a person kills someone (for revenge, to obtain money, or the like.) A good motive seldom justifies a criminal act. Robin Hood had a good motive. He stole from the rich to give to the poor, but his actions were still unlawful.

A single act can be both a criminal and a civil wrong. For example, if Paul purposely sets fire to Floyd's store, the state may file criminal

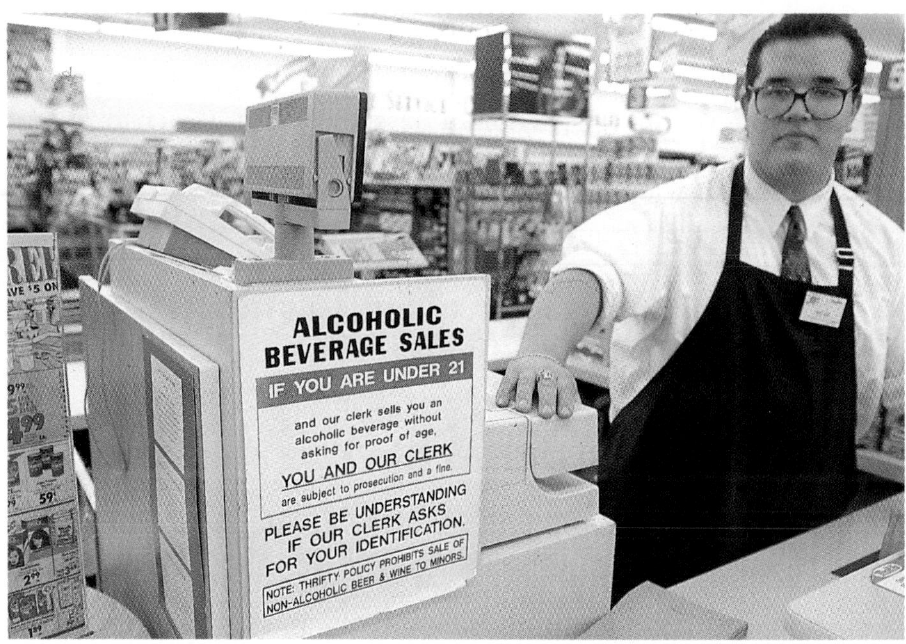

Read this sign regarding the sale of alcoholic beverages. Why does the law punish the buyer and the seller?

charges against Paul for *arson*. Floyd may also bring a separate civil action against Paul to recover for the damage to his store.

PROBLEM 7

Anton is a bully. One night while eating at a local drive-in, he notices Derek selecting a tune on the jukebox. To impress his girlfriend, Anton orders Derek to sing along with the record. When Derek refuses, Anton punches him in the face, breaking Derek's jaw. As a result of the injury, Derek misses several weeks of work and has to pay both medical and dental bills.

a. Has Anton violated civil laws, criminal laws, or both?

b. Who decides whether Anton should be charged criminally? Sued in a civil action?

c. If Anton is charged with a crime and sued in a civil action, would these actions be tried in one case? Why or why not?

d. Would procedures in a criminal trial be the same as those in a civil trial? Why or why not?

e. Is going to court the only way to handle this problem? What alternatives are there, and which do you think would work best?

State and Federal Crimes

There are both state and federal criminal laws. Some acts, such as simple assault, disorderly conduct, drunk driving, and shoplifting, can be prosecuted only in a state court unless they occur on federal property, such as a national park. Other acts, such as failure to pay federal taxes, mail fraud, espionage, and international smuggling, can be prosecuted only in a federal court. Certain crimes, such as illegal possession of dangerous drugs and bank robbery, can violate both state and federal law and can be prosecuted in either state or federal court.

Classes of Crimes

As noted in Chapter 1, crimes are classified as either felonies or misdemeanors. A **felony** is a crime for which the penalty is imprisonment for more than one year. Felonies are usually the more serious crimes. A **misdemeanor** is any crime for which the penalty is imprisonment for one year or less. Minor traffic violations are not considered crimes, although they are punishable by law. This chapter deals primarily with felonies and major misdemeanors.

Parties to Crimes

The person who commits a crime is called the **principal**. For example, the person who fires the gun in a murder is the principal. An

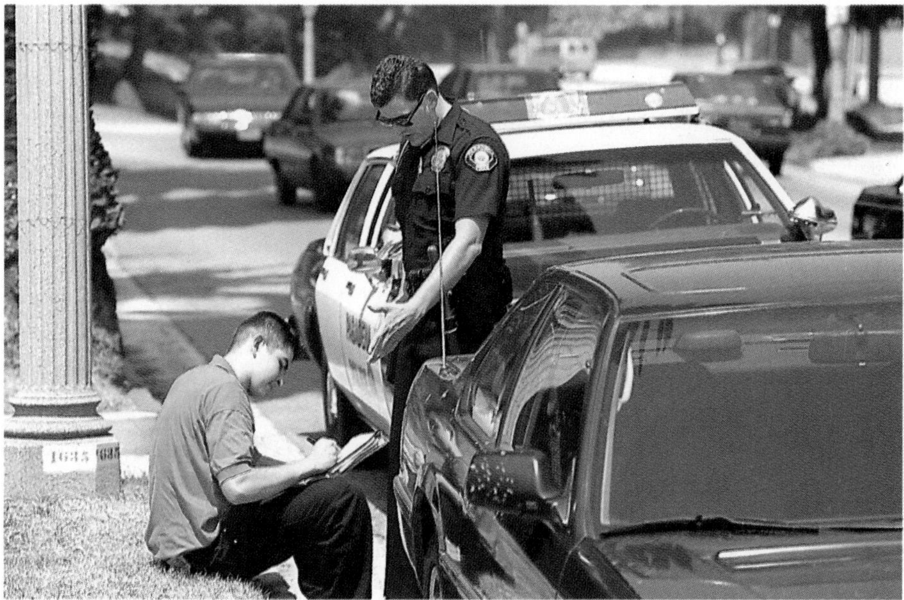

Are traffic offenses considered crimes?

FOCUS ON THE LAW

Good Samaritan Laws

Are witnesses to crimes under any obligation to come to the aid of victims? Until recently, the legal answer, as opposed to the moral answer, was no. Most states have had "Good Samaritan" laws that relieve bystanders from most civil liability when they help people in danger, but they have not required bystanders to help. Now, however, several new state laws *require* witnesses to offer whatever help they can reasonably provide without endangering themselves. In the case of a violent crime, this simply means reporting the crime to the police.

accomplice is someone who helps another person commit a crime. For example, the person who drives the getaway car during a bank robbery is an accomplice. An accomplice may be charged with and convicted of the same crime as the principal. A person who orders a crime or who helps the principal commit the crime but who is not present (for example, the underworld leader who hires a professional killer) is known as an **accessory before the fact**. This person can usually be charged with the same crime, and can receive the same punishment, as the principal. An **accessory after the fact** is a person who, knowing a crime has been committed, helps the principal or an accomplice avoid capture or escape. This person is not charged with the original crime but may be charged with harboring a fugitive, aiding the escape, or obstructing justice (sometimes called aiding and abetting).

PROBLEM 8

Joe and Mary decide to burglarize Superior Jewelers. Their friend Carl, an employee at Superior, helps by telling them the location of the store vault. Mary drives a van to the store and keeps a lookout while Joe goes inside and cracks the safe. Joe later meets a friend, Fred, who was not involved beforehand. Fred is told about the burglary and helps Joe get a train out of town. David, a former classmate of Joe and Mary's, witnesses the crime but doesn't tell the police, even though he recognizes both Joe and Mary. How will each be charged?

Crimes of Omission

Most crimes occur when a person does something or performs some act in violation of a law. However, in a few cases, a person may be criminally liable for an omission or a failure to act. For example, it is a crime for a taxpayer to fail to file a tax return or for a motorist to fail to stop after involvement in an automobile accident. A person is guilty of a *crime of omission* when he or she fails to perform an act required by a criminal law, if he or she is physically able to perform the required act.

The Drowning Girl

Allen, Betty, Chin, and Doris see a girl drowning in a lake, but none of them takes steps to save her. Allen is the girl's father. Betty deliberately pushed the girl into the lake by shoving Chin against her. Doris, a medal-winning swimmer, just stands and watches. Would any of the four be criminally liable for the girl's drowning? Should any of them be liable? Explain your answer.

PRELIMINARY CRIMES

Certain types of behavior take place before the commission of a crime but are nevertheless complete crimes in themselves. These offenses—solicitation, attempt, and conspiracy—give the police the opportunity to prevent the intended crime. Each offense can be punished even if the harm intended never occurred.

Solicitation

A number of states make it a crime for a person to solicit (that is, ask, command, urge, or advise) another person to commit a crime.

For example, Danny wishes to kill his wife, Jean. Lacking the nerve to do the job himself, he asks Wally to kill her. Even if Wally refuses, Danny has committed the crime of **solicitation**.

Attempt

In most states, an **attempt** to commit a crime is in itself a crime. To be guilty of the crime of attempt, the accused must have both intended to commit a crime and taken some substantial step toward committing the crime. Mere preparation to commit a crime is not enough. The difficult problem with the crime of attempt is determining whether the actions of the accused were a step toward the actual commission of a crime or mere acts of preparation. A common example of attempt is the situation in which a person decides to shoot and kill someone but, being a poor shot, misses the intended victim. The person doing the shooting would be guilty of attempted murder.

PROBLEM 9

Examine the following situations and decide whether any of the individuals involved would be guilty of the crime of attempt.

a. Howard, a bank teller, figures out a foolproof method of stealing money from the bank. It takes him some time to get up the nerve to steal any money. Finally, he makes up his mind and tells his girlfriend, Donna, that starting tomorrow he will steal the money. Donna goes to the police, and Howard is arrested an hour later.

b. Gilbert, an accomplished thief, is caught while trying to pick Lewis's pocket. He pleads not guilty and says he can't possibly be convicted, because Lewis didn't have a penny on him.

c. Rita and Anwar decide to rob a liquor store. They meet at a pub and talk over their plans. Rita leaves to buy a revolver, and Anwar leaves to steal a car for use in their getaway. Rita is arrested as she walks out of the gun shop with her new revolver. Anwar is arrested while trying to hot-wire a car.

d. Amy decides to burn down her store to collect the insurance money. She spreads gasoline around the building. She is arrested while leaving the store to get a book of matches.

Conspiracy

A **conspiracy** is an agreement between two or more persons to commit a crime. The designation of conspiracy as a crime is meant to prevent other crimes and to strike against criminal activity by groups. However, it is sometimes criticized as a threat to freedom of speech and association. For example, during the Vietnam War, the government charged several people with conspiracy for speaking publicly to young men on how to avoid the draft. Many critics of conspiracy said the accused were being denied the freedom of speech.

An example of criminal conspiracy is the situation in which Nick, a drug dealer, asks Sunny, his associate, to kill another dealer in his neighborhood. If Sunny agrees to Nick's request and then takes some step to commit the crime, both are guilty of conspiracy to commit murder, even if the murder is never attempted or accomplished.

In most states and in federal law, an **overt** act—that is, an act that is open to view—is required for conviction on a conspiracy charge. In the example of the draft evasion cases, speeches made at an antidraft rally were cited as the overt acts on which the conspiracy charges were based.

CRIMES AGAINST THE PERSON

Crimes against the person include homicide, assault, battery, and rape. All of those crimes are serious offenses. A defendant found guilty of one of them may receive a harsh sentence. However, the law also protects the defendant by defining various levels of these crimes and by considering the circumstances of each offense.

Homicide

Homicide—the killing of one human being by another—is the most serious of all acts. Homicides may be either noncriminal or criminal.

Noncriminal Homicide Some homicides are not crimes at all. Noncriminal homicide is a killing that is justifiable or excusable and for which the killer is deemed faultless. Examples of noncriminal homicide include the killing of an enemy soldier in wartime, the killing of a condemned criminal by an executioner, the killing by a police officer of a person who is committing a serious crime and who poses a threat of death or serious harm, and a killing performed in self-defense or in defense of another.

Has the murder rate changed in your community in recent years? If so, how?

Criminal Homicide Murder, the most serious form of criminal homicide, is a killing that is done with **malice**. Malice means having the intent to kill or seriously harm. At one time, there were no degrees of murder. Any homicide done with malice was considered to be murder and was punishable by death. To reduce the punishment for less grievous homicides, most states now have statutes that classify murder according to the killer's state of mind or the circumstances surrounding the crime.

First-degree murder is a killing that is premeditated (thought about beforehand), deliberate, and done with malice (that is, with intent to kill).

Second-degree murder is a killing that is done with malice but without premeditation. That is, the intent to kill did not exist until just before the murder took place.

Felony murder is a killing that takes place during the commission of certain felonies, such as arson, rape, robbery, or burglary. It is not necessary to prove intent to kill; felony murder includes most killing committed during a felony, even if the killing is accidental. Most states consider felony murder to be first-degree murder.

Voluntary manslaughter is an intentional killing committed under circumstances that mitigate (lessen), but do not justify or excuse, the killing. Manslaughter is based on the idea that even "the reasonable person" may lose self-control and act rashly if sufficiently provoked.

Involuntary manslaughter is an unintentional killing resulting from conduct so reckless that it causes extreme danger of death or bodily injury. An example is a killing that results from playing with a gun known to be loaded.

Negligent homicide is the causing of death through criminal negligence. **Negligence** is the failure to exercise a reasonable or ordinary amount of care in a situation that causes harm to someone. Some states classify death by gross, or extreme, negligence as involuntary manslaughter. The most common form of negligent homicide is vehicular, or automobile, homicide. This is a killing that results from operating a motor vehicle in a reckless and grossly negligent manner. Any death that results from careless driving may lead to a civil suit for damages, but it is usually not considered a crime unless the death results from gross negligence.

PROBLEM 10

Walt decides to shoot Yolanda, whom he blames for all his troubles. As he is driving to her home to carry out the murder, Walt hits a jogger who darts out from behind a tree. Stopping immediately, he rushes to help the jogger, who is already dead. Walt is upset until he discovers that the dead jogger is Yolanda. Assuming Walt was driving at a safe speed and the collision was unavoidable, is he guilty of murder?

PROBLEM 11

Belva is cheated when she buys a car from Fast Eddie's Car Mart. She attempts to return the car, but Eddie just laughs and tells her to go away. Every time Belva has to make a repair on the car, she gets angry. Finally, she decides to wreck Eddie's car to get even. Following Eddie home from work one evening, Belva tries to ram his car, hoping to bend the axle or frame. Instead of bending the frame, the collision smashes Eddie's gas tank, causes an explosion, and kills Eddie.

a. Is Belva guilty of any degree of homicide? If so, which degree and for what reason?

b. What was Belva's motive in acting as she did? Should the motive be considered at any stage in the criminal justice process? Why or why not?

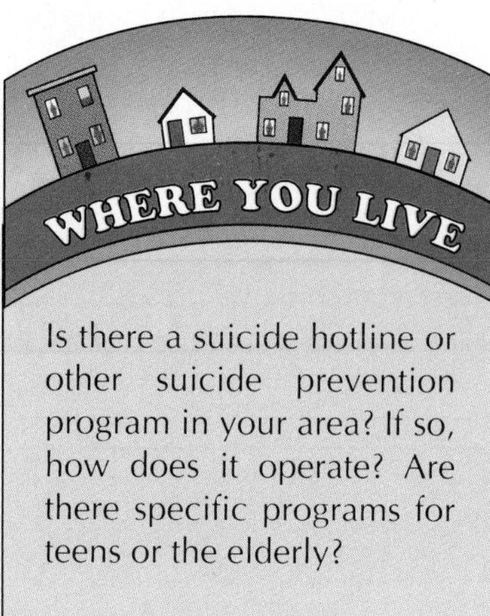

Is there a suicide hotline or other suicide prevention program in your area? If so, how does it operate? Are there specific programs for teens or the elderly?

Suicide, Euthanasia, and the Right to Die

Suicide, the deliberate taking of one's own life, was once considered a crime. States regarding it as criminal today, however, prohibit only attempted suicide. Courts often treat suicide as a plea for help, requiring the person who attempted it to undergo a psychological examination and receive treatment. Someone who helps another commit suicide can, however, be found guilty of the crime of murder or manslaughter.

Suicide is one of the leading causes of death among teenagers. At least 6,000 teenagers take their own lives each year. However, the elderly commit more suicides than any other age group.

Although many people have suicidal thoughts at some point in their lives, most never attempt suicide. Many can be helped by suicide hotlines and other programs for those who may be considering suicide. Despairing individuals most often need a counselor or someone else to talk to who can help them see positive alternatives to suicide.

PROBLEM 12

a. Why do you think so many teenagers commit suicide? What could be done to reduce this number? What would you do if your friend were considering taking his or her life?

b. Why do you think the elderly commit suicide more often than any other age group? What could be done to reduce this number?

How can suicide hotlines help individuals considering killing themselves?

Euthanasia is an act or method of putting someone to death painlessly. It is sometimes called mercy killing, because those who commit this act believe they are acting mercifully by putting an end to the suffering of someone with an incurable or terminal illness. Euthanasia is illegal, however, and people who have committed it have sometimes been prosecuted for murder or manslaughter. It is related to suicide because it is sometimes done at the request of the incurably ill person.

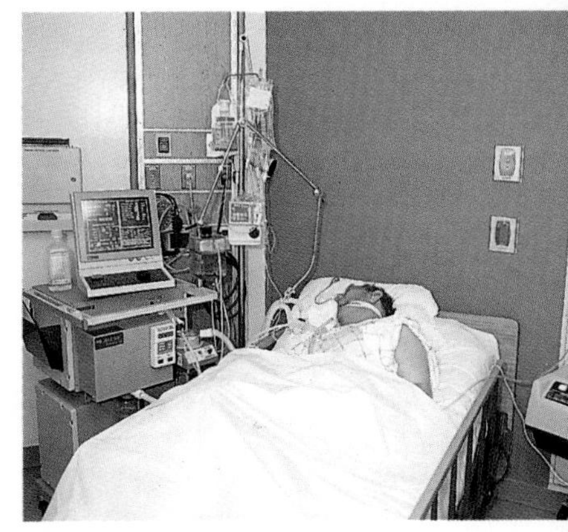

Should the law allow mercy killing in certain situations?

The law generally permits a person to refuse treatment even if this results in the person's death. A person can therefore refuse to have an operation even though he or she will definitely die as a result. This may not apply, however, if the person is mentally ill or incompetent. Refusing treatment for oneself, of course, differs from taking an action that will bring on another person's death, such as disconnecting life-sustaining equipment, which may be a form of euthanasia, or helping to bring about a suicide.

THE CASE OF . . .

The Dying Cancer Patient

Wilfred, age 75, has been suffering from cancer for 10 years, and the pain has become worse and worse. The doctors say there is no treatment to either slow down the cancer's growth or substantially reduce the pain. Wilfred asks his wife, Martha, to relieve him of the terrible pain by bringing him a bottle of pills that would help him end his life. Martha, who cannot stand watching Wilfred suffer anymore, gives him the pills. He swallows them all and dies.

PROBLEM 13

a. If you were the district attorney in the state where Martha lives, would you file charges of murder or manslaughter? Explain.

b. If manslaughter charges were filed and you were on the jury, would you vote to convict Martha? Give your reasons.

c. If Martha were convicted, what sentence should she receive? Why?

d. If the bottle of pills had been given to Wilfred by a physician, instead of by his wife, would your answers have been different? Give your reasons.

The Tube Feeding

Nancy Cruzan lost control of her car. The car overturned, and Cruzan was found lying face down in a ditch. Paramedics were able to restore her breathing and heartbeat at the accident site. She was taken, unconscious, to the hospital, where she was diagnosed as having suffered brain damage caused by a lack of oxygen. Permanent brain damage generally results after approximately 6 minutes without oxygen. Cruzan was without oxygen for approximately 12–14 minutes.

Cruzan remained in a coma for approximately three weeks. She then progressed to an unconscious state in which she was able to receive some nutrition through a feeding tube. For more than seven years, Cruzan has remained in this persistent vegetative state, almost totally unresponsive to the world around her. She cannot ever recover her ability to swallow. Her parents want to remove the feeding tube, which would result in her death.

PROBLEM 14

a. What happened to Nancy Cruzan?

b. What is a persistent vegetative state? Why did Nancy's parents want the hospital to disconnect the feeding tube?

c. What legal and ethical values are at stake in this case?

d. What would you do if you were Nancy's parents? If you were the doctor?

e. How should the court decide this case?

In recent years, the development of medical technology that can sustain people's lives even after the people are considered "brain dead" has helped bring about many controversial cases. The issue of whether doctors, on their own or under the direction of family members, can disconnect life-sustaining equipment has been said by some to involve the "right to die."

Forty-one states have now passed "living will" statutes. These laws state that if the author of the will is ever so ill or badly injured

Figure 2.3 A Living Will

To My Family, My Physician, My Lawyer And All Others Whom It May Concern

Death is as much a reality as birth, growth, and aging—it is the one certainty of life. In anticipation of decisions that may have to be made about my own dying and as an expression of my right to refuse treatment, I ______________________________ (print name), being of sound mind, make this statement of my wishes and instructions concerning treatment.

By means of this document, which I intend to be legally binding, I direct my physician and other care providers, my family, and any surrogate designated by me or appointed by a court, to carry out my wishes. If I become unable, by reason of physical or mental incapacity, to make decisions about my medical care, let this document provide the guidance and authority needed to make any and all such decisions.

If I am permanently unconscious or there is no reasonable expectation of my recovery from a seriously incapacitating or lethal illness or condition, I do not wish to be kept alive by artificial means. I request that I be given all care necessary to keep me comfortable and free of pain, even if pain-relieving medications may hasten my death, and I direct that no life-sustaining treatment be provided except as I or my surrogate specifically authorize.

This request may appear to place a heavy responsibility upon you, but by making this decision according to my strong convictions, I intend to ease that burden. I am acting after careful consideration and with understanding of the consequences of your carrying out my wishes. *List optional specific provisions in the space below. (See other side)*

Durable Power of Attorney for Health Care Decisions (Cross out if you do not wish to use this section)

To effect my wishes, I designate ______________________________, residing at ______________________________ (Phone #) ______________, (or if he or she shall for any reason fail to act, ______________________ (Phone #) ______________, residing at ______________________________) as my health care surrogate—that is, my attorney-in-fact regarding any and all health care decisions to be made for me, including the decision to refuse life-sustaining treatment—if I am unable to make such decisions myself. This power shall remain effective during and not be affected by my subsequent illness, disability or incapacity. My surrogate shall have authority to interpret my Living Will, and shall make decisions about my health care as specified in my instructions or, when my wishes are not clear, as the surrogate believes to be in my best interests. I release and agree to hold harmless my health care surrogate from any and all claims whatsoever arising from decisions made in good faith in the exercise of this power.

I sign this document knowingly, voluntarily, and after careful deliberation, this _____ day of __________, 19_____.

____
(signature)

Address ______________________________

____

I do hereby certify that the within document was executed and acknowledged before me by the principal this_______ day of _____________, 19 _______.

____
Notary Public

Witness______________________________

Printed Name ______________________________

Address ______________________________

____

Witness______________________________

Printed Name ______________________________

Address ______________________________

____

Copies of this document have been given to:

(Optional) My Living Will is registered with Concern for Dying (No. ________)
Distributed by Concern for Dying, 250 West 57th Street, New York, NY 10107 (212) 246-6962

that there is no reasonable hope of recovery, extraordinary efforts to keep that person alive should be stopped. The purpose of a living will is to clarify what people want done if they are unable to convey their wishes at the time. Figure 2.3 shows an example of a living will.

PROBLEM 15

Read the living will in Figure 2.3 and answer the following questions:

a. What is the purpose of a living will? Do you think it is a good idea to have one? Why or why not?

b. Assume that Nasima has signed a living will similar to the one in the figure and is being kept alive on a respirator even though she is certain not to recover. Her family wishes to have the respirator turned off and let her die with dignity. The doctor refuses even though she is certain Nasima will not recover. If members of Nasima's family follow the directions in the living will and turn off the respirator, could they be charged with a crime? Explain.

Assault and Battery

Assault is any attempt or threat to carry out a physical attack upon another person. An assault occurs when the threatened person reasonably believes that he or she is in real danger. For example, suppose John points an unloaded gun at Maggie. This is an assault if Maggie reasonably believes the gun is loaded. **Battery** is any unlawful physical contact inflicted by one person upon another without consent. Actual injury is not necessary. The only requirement is that the person intended to do bodily harm. Today, there is often not much difference in law or practice between the use of the words *assault* and *battery*.

Just as there are degrees of murder, there are also different classifications for assault and battery. Aggravated assault and battery is an assault or battery with intent to murder, rob, rape, or do serious bodily harm. For example, if John knocks Maggie down while trying to snatch her purse, he is guilty of aggravated assault or battery, as well as the crime of attempted robbery. Many states impose greater punishment when the assault is made with a deadly weapon (a weapon that could cause death). In some states, people who knowingly spread AIDS have been charged with aggravated assault (or even attempted murder). Many states also impose greater punishment for assaults on police officers, prison guards, or other law enforcement officers.

Assaults typically result from arguments between people who knew each other. In such arguments, rage—often stimulated by alcohol or jealousy—leads to violence. Whether the violence leads to serious injury or death often depends on the presence of a weapon.

To deal with the growing problem of harassment, forty states now have "anti-stalking" laws. Stalking occurs when a person repeatedly follows or harasses another person and makes threats, causing the victim to fear death or bodily injury. Women are the targets of most of the 200,000 cases of stalking that are estimated to occur each year.

Guns and the Law

A well regulated Militia, being necessary to the security of a free State, the right of the people to keep and bear Arms, shall not be infringed.

— Second Amendment to the U.S. Constitution

While most Americans who own firearms own them legally and use them lawfully, there has been an increase in the use of firearms in serious crimes in recent years. Some believe that the relatively easy availability of firearms to young persons has aggravated the crime

Guns in America

- There are nearly 200 million guns in circulation in America, divided almost evenly among handguns, rifles, and shotguns. (U.S. Bureau of Alcohol, Tobacco, and Firearms, Department of the Treasury, 1991)
- Each year, 639,000 residents face an offender who is armed with a handgun. In about 13% of the cases, the guns are used to shoot at the victims. (U.S. Bureau of Justice Statistics, Department of Justice, 1990)
- In a national poll, 46% of the people questioned said that they had a gun in their home, and 43% of those with a gun said that it was loaded. (1991 Gallup Survey)
- Handguns were used in the homicides of 12,090 people in the United States in 1991, up 14% from 1990. Nearly 19,000 persons used firearms in 1991 to commit suicide. (FBI Uniform Crime Reports, 1991)
- Firearms are the second leading cause of death for men and women 10–34 years of age, second only to motor vehicle crashes. (National Center for Health Statistics, 1991)

Are guns easy to buy in your community? Are new laws needed to regulate the purchase of guns?

What laws, if any, control gun possession in your area? Are they effective?

problem. Others argue that it is not guns but gun users who cause violence and that law-abiding citizens have a right to own firearms.

Some groups look to the language of the Second Amendment as protection against government attempts to ban or regulate firearms. Other groups argue that the language of the Second Amendment protects a *state's* right to maintain a militia (armed forces) but does not protect citizens against government efforts to legislate in this area. Gun control is an extremely controversial issue.

The U.S. Supreme Court has interpreted the Second Amendment on several occasions, and so have many lower courts. All courts have ruled that the amendment guarantees a state's right to maintain a militia. However, the U.S. Supreme Court has not used the Second Amendment to strike down federal, state, or local legislation to control guns.

A wide range of gun laws exists at the state and local levels. A few states require a person to take a safety training course or a test before purchasing a handgun. About half the states have laws requiring some form of waiting period, background check, or permit for the purchase of a handgun.

In 1993, several states defeated legislative initiatives that would have allowed citizens to carry concealed weapons, a few states banned the sale of all assault weapons, and one state limited handgun purchases to one per month. A controversial new law being discussed in some places would, if enacted, permit victims of crimes involving certain guns to sue the manufacturers of the guns for money damages.

The primary federal gun-control law is the 1968 Gun Control Act, passed after the murders of Dr. Martin Luther King, Jr., and Senator Robert Kennedy. This law has the following provisions: It prohibits certain categories of persons (such as convicted felons, minors, and illegal aliens) from buying or possessing weapons; it requires serial numbers on all guns and establishes a licensing-fee schedule for firearms manufacturers, importers, and dealers; it prohibits the mail-order sales of all firearms and ammunition; it prohibits the interstate sale of handguns; it sets penalties for carrying and using firearms in crimes of violence or drug trafficking; and it sets age guidelines for firearms purchased through dealers (handgun purchasers must be at least 21; long-gun purchasers must be at least 18). More recent federal law bans the importation of certain semiautomatic weapons.

Individuals and groups involved in this controversial public issue generally either support the right to bear arms (and want to limit the power of the government to ban or regulate guns) or support some form of gun control. The proponents of these arguments are active in the courts and in legislatures throughout the country. Both sides have their slogans, and both sides have statistics and publications to support their positions.

PROBLEM 16

a. How much do you think gun control can help reduce crime? Give your reasons.

b. What restrictions, if any, should the government place on the manufacture, sale, and possession of firearms? Explain.

LAW IN ACTION

Lobbying Simulation: For and Against Gun Control

Assume you are a member of your state legislature. A new law has been proposed that would prohibit anyone except law enforcement personnel from buying or possessing a handgun. A recent poll shows that voters in your district are split about evenly for and against handgun control. Two citizens call your office and make appointments to see you to discuss your vote on the proposed law. Their views are as follows:

Dana Harvey (for): "I am tired of attending funerals of people killed with handguns. We must make it more difficult for criminals to get and use these weapons. Most murders are committed with handguns, and most police officers killed in the line of duty die from handgun bullet wounds. Also significant are the many children who find handguns, play with them, and die from handgun bullet wounds. And many spouses are shot dead as a result of arguments in which a handgun was easily accessible. It is too dangerous to allow people to keep handguns around the home, where over 50 percent of accidental murders take place.

"Those who argue against this law based on a constitutional right are misinterpreting the Second Amendment, which was meant to protect the right of a militia, not individuals, to have guns. Those who argue that guns are needed for sport should realize the primary purpose of handguns is to kill people. You should be aware that 60 percent of voters responding to a national poll endorsed handgun control. Allowing gun possession by the general public glorifies violence and results in its increased use in settling disputes. This has been demonstrated in recent years by the dramatic increase in drug-related handgun murders."

Sandy Lopez (against): "If guns are outlawed, only outlaws will have guns. We must be able to protect ourselves against the dangerous criminals all around us. Ninety-nine percent of gun owners are not criminals and have handguns either for their own protection or for use at shooting ranges or in other types of competitions. Their constitutional right to bear arms under the Second Amendment to the U.S. Constitution must be protected. It is a long-standing American tradition, starting with this country's pioneers, that citizens be allowed to possess guns.

"This law will not reduce crime, because handguns will still be sold on the black market or brought in from other states. The answer to the crime problem is not gun control but other measures, such as speedy trials and longer prison terms for criminals. We have laws restricting sales of handguns across state lines, but they don't do any good. Many people living in your district are hunters and see handgun control as a step toward confiscating their rifles. They care about this issue much more than the gun-control group. When you are up for reelection next year and are looking for campaign contributions and votes, they will remember how you voted on this issue."

Role-play your meeting with each of the two citizen lobbyists. After the meetings, decide how you will vote on the proposed law. What are the reasons for your vote? What are some reasons why you might have voted the other way?

Rape

Traditionally, the law has recognized two types of **rape**. Forcible rape is the act of unlawful sexual intercourse committed by a man with a woman by force and without her consent. Statutory rape is sexual intercourse by a male with a female who has not yet reached the legal age of consent.

Under the common-law definition, a rape occurred only when there was sexual penetration of the female by the male. To constitute forcible rape, the intercourse must have occurred without the consent of the female. There is no consent if a woman submits as a result of force or threats of bodily harm. Likewise, there is no consent if a woman is unconscious or mentally incompetent or if her judgment is impaired by drugs or alcohol.

A number of states have recently rewritten their rape laws. The new laws classify the offense as sexual assault and make it applicable to both men and women. States that have not adopted new sexual assault laws continue to use the common-law definition.

In statutory rape cases, consent is not an issue. Sexual intercourse with an underage female is rape *whether she consents or not*. A mistake by a male as to the female's age is not a defense, even if the male reasonably believed the female was over the age of consent.

Should all women participate in anti-rape, self-defense classes?

The age at which a young person can legally agree to have sex varies by state from 11 to 18; most states, however, put it at 16. Only males can commit statutory rape; and contrary to popular belief, an underage male can be prosecuted for having sex with an underage female.

A woman's lack of chastity is *not* a defense to rape. This means anyone, including a prostitute, can be raped. However, some states allow evidence of prior sexual conduct to be considered in regard to the issue of consent. Moreover, to convict a person of rape, some states require independent proof that the act took place. This means confirmation or support for the story of the victim, including testimony of a witness, a doctor's report that sexual intercourse took place, or a prompt report to the police.

In recent years, the term *acquaintance rape* (also known as *date rape*) has been used to describe a sexual assault by someone known to the victim—a date, steady boyfriend, neighbor, or friend. Many victims of acquaintance rape do not report the assault. This may be because they did not realize an attack that occurs on a date can in fact constitute a rape.

PROBLEM 17

For each case below, assume that (1) the man and the woman have sexual intercourse, (2) the woman later reports the activity to the police, and (3) the man contends that the woman consented. Should the man be prosecuted? Give your reasons.

a. At midnight, a man breaks into the home of a woman he does not know. He goes to her bedroom, awakens her, pulls out a knife, and threatens to stab her unless she has sex with him. She tells him that she does not want to have sex. But then she says, "If you are going to do this, you'd better use a condom." He agrees.

b. A famous boxer serves as a judge at a beauty contest. After the contest, he invites an 18-year-old contestant to his room. She meets him there. Later, she says he forced her to have sex.

c. A male high-school student, aged 17, and a female high-school student, aged 14, go out on a date. After attending a party, they agree to have intercourse in his car. The next day, he brags about this at school, and she goes to the police. There is some evidence that he is part of an informal organization of high-school seniors who are involved in a competition to have sex with as many girls as possible.

d. Lydia and Alex, both 27, have been living together for two years. After a particularly severe fight over finances, they make

Date Rape Information

How to Protect Yourself

- When going on a date with someone you don't know well, try to get information on the person from others you know and trust. Plan to meet in a place where there are lots of people.
- Be sure to let your date know your limits in advance. Be assertive about how you feel and what you expect.
- Be prepared to find your own transportation home. Carry enough money to make a phone call or take a cab.
- Don't leave an event with someone you just met, and don't ride in a car with someone you don't know and trust.
- Don't get high on either drugs or alcohol, as this reduces your ability to take care of yourself and make sensible decisions.

What If It Happens to You?

- Call the police. Date rape is a crime, and it may be more difficult to prosecute the person if the crime is not reported immediately.
- Don't shower or bathe before going to the hospital, and don't destroy any clothing you were wearing, as it may be important evidence. Get medical attention for any injuries, along with testing for venereal disease, AIDS, and pregnancy.
- Tell your parents, a school counselor, the family doctor, or any adult you trust. Consider calling your local rape hotline or rape crisis center. Seek counseling; don't bury your emotions.

Do you think date rape is a problem at your school? If so, what should be done?

up and begin to kiss. She later claims that he then forced her to have sex with him against her wishes.

e. Scott and Sherri are college juniors who have had three dates. On these dates, they have never engaged in any sexual activity beyond a brief good-night kiss. On their fourth date, he invites her to an all-night drinking party at his fraternity house. She drinks too much, goes up to his room alone around 1 A.M., and falls asleep. In the morning, she wakes up to discover that they had intercourse during the night.

CRIMES AGAINST PROPERTY

The category of crimes against property includes crimes in which property is destroyed (such as **arson** and **vandalism**) and crimes in which property is stolen or otherwise taken against the will of the owner (such as **robbery** and **embezzlement**).

Arson

Why do people sometimes burn their own property?

Arson is the willful and malicious burning of another person's property. In most states, it is a crime to burn any building or structure, even if the person who burns the structure owns it. Moreover, burning property with the intent to defraud an insurance company is usually a separate crime, regardless of the type of property burned or who owned the property.

Vandalism

Vandalism, also known as malicious mischief, is willful destruction of, or damage to, the property of another. Vandalism causes millions of dollars in damage each year. It includes such things as breaking windows, ripping down fences, flooding basements, and breaking off car aerials. Depending on the extent of the damage, vandalism can be either a felony or a misdemeanor.

Do you think graffiti is art or visual pollution? Explain.

PROBLEM 18

a. Why do young people sometimes commit acts of vandalism?

b. What, if anything, can be done to reduce vandalism?

c. Should parents be held liable for willful damage caused by their children? Why or why not?

d. If you saw two youths throwing rocks through the windows of a school at night, would you report the youths to the police? Why or why not? Suppose you saw two friends throwing rocks through the windows of a neighbor's home. Would you report your friends to the police? Why or why not? Did you answer both questions the same way? If not, explain why.

Larceny

Larceny is the unlawful taking and carrying away of the property of another with intent to steal it. In most states, larceny is divided into two classes, grand and petty, depending on the value of the stolen item. Grand larceny involves the theft of anything above a certain value (often $100 or more) and is a felony. Petty larceny is the theft of anything of small value (usually less than $100) and is a misdemeanor.

The crime of larceny also includes keeping lost property when a reasonable method exists for finding the owner. For example, if you find a wallet that contains the identification of its owner but nevertheless decide to keep it, you have committed larceny. Likewise, you may be guilty of larceny if you keep property delivered to you by mistake.

Shoplifting is a form of larceny. It is the crime of taking items from a store without paying or intending to pay for them. Some states have a separate crime called concealment. This is the crime of attempted shoplifting.

Shoplifting results in businesses' losing billions of dollars each year. The costs are usually passed on to consumers in the form of higher prices. Consequently, all of us pay for shoplifting.

PROBLEM 19

a. Why do you think people shoplift?

b. What could be done to address each of the reasons for shoplifting you listed? Which would be most effective? Why?

c. If you saw a stranger shoplifting in a store, what would you do? Would your answer be different if you knew the person? If the person were a good friend of yours?

Embezzlement

Embezzlement is the unlawful taking of property by someone to whom it was entrusted. For example, the bank teller who takes money from the cash drawer or the stockbroker who takes money that should have been invested are both guilty of embezzlement. In recent years, a number of states have merged the crimes of embezzlement, larceny, and obtaining property by false pretenses (intentional misstatement of fact) into the statutory crime of theft.

Robbery

Robbery is the unlawful taking of property from a person's immediate possession by force or intimidation. Though included here as a crime against property, robbery, unlike other theft offenses, involves two harms: theft of property and actual or potential physical harm to the victim. In most states, the element of force is the difference between robbery and larceny. Hence, a pickpocket who takes your wallet unnoticed is liable for the crime of larceny. A mugger who knocks you down and takes your wallet by force is guilty of the crime of robbery. Robbery is almost always a felony, but many states impose stricter penalties for armed robberies—that is, thefts committed with a gun or other weapon.

Extortion

Extortion, popularly called blackmail, is the use of threats to obtain the property of another. Extortion statutes generally cover threats to do future physical harm, destroy property (for example, "I'll burn down your barn unless you pay me $500"), or injure someone's character or reputation.

Burglary

Burglary was originally defined as breaking and entering the dwelling of another during the night with intent to commit a felony. Modern laws have broadened the definition to include the unauthorized entry into any structure with the intent to commit a crime, regardless of the time of day. Many states have stiffer penalties for burglaries committed at night, burglaries of inhabited dwellings, and burglaries committed with weapons.

Forgery

Forgery is a crime in which a person falsely makes or alters a writing or document with intent to defraud. This usually means signing, without permission, the name of another person to a check or some other document. It can also mean changing or erasing part of a previously signed document. **Uttering**, which in many states is a separate crime, is offering to someone as genuine a document (such as a check) known to be a fake.

Receiving Stolen Property

If you receive or buy property that you know or have reason to believe is stolen, you have committed the crime of **receiving stolen property**. Knowledge that the property is stolen may be implied by the circumstances. In most states, receiving stolen property is a felony if the value of the property received is more than $100 and a misdemeanor if the value is $100 or less.

Unauthorized Use of a Vehicle

Several crimes may occur when a person unlawfully takes a motor vehicle without the owner's consent. The crime of unauthorized use of a vehicle (UUV) is committed if the person only intends to take the vehicle temporarily. This crime, which includes joyriding, is usually punished as a misdemeanor. However, if the person intends to take the car permanently, then the crime may be larceny or auto theft. These crimes usually have stiffer penalties than UUV. The crime of carjacking occurs if a person uses force or intimidation to steal a car from a driver. Carjacking is a federal crime and is punishable by a sentence of up to life in prison.

PROBLEM 20

Ivan met his friend Anthony, who was driving a flashy new red convertible. Ivan knew that neither Anthony nor his family owned this car, but it looked good, so he got in and let Anthony take him for a ride. Ivan knew Anthony used drugs and sometimes took other people's things and sold them to get money to buy cocaine. Anthony offered to sell Ivan a walkman he had in the back seat of the car for $10. Ivan agreed to pay him the money.

a. Have any crimes been committed in the example? If so, which crimes and by whom?

b. Why does society make receiving stolen property a crime? Should it be a crime?

c. Would you ever buy something for an extremely low price from a friend? How would you know for sure it was not stolen?

Computer Crime

Computer crime is broadly defined as unauthorized access to, use of, alteration of, or taking of another person's computer systems or files. This activity is illegal even if the person does not intend to do any harm.

Corporate and government computer systems are the most popular targets of computer crime. Some people who work for corporations or the government may try to sell information to business rivals or foreign governments. Others may use computers to embezzle money.

Most of those who gain unauthorized access to computer systems are "hackers." Hackers, sometimes high-school or college-age persons, intentionally try to break into computer systems. Once hackers

Should computer hackers be punished as criminals?

enter a system, they usually look at confidential or classified files. Occasionally, a hacker may copy a file and distribute it. Hackers annually cause an estimated $1 billion worth of damage to computer files. There is disagreement on how hackers should be punished. Many persons feel that hackers are dangerous and should receive jail terms and pay large fines like other white-collar criminals. Others argue that hackers break into systems as a hobby, do not intend any harm, and can be rehabilitated.

Some hackers release "viruses" or "worms" into computer systems. Viruses are computer programs designed to play practical jokes or destroy data and damage computer files. Worms are designed to slow down computer systems but not to destroy data. Both viruses and worms are prohibited by computer crime laws.

Throughout the early 1980s, federal legislation related to computer crime, as well as traditional criminal statutes, were used to prosecute computer criminals. However, the laws proved to be vague and ineffective. In response, Congress passed the Computer Fraud and Abuse Act of 1986, which provided the government with a specific law to prosecute hackers. The law made it a crime to modify, destroy, or disclose information gained from unauthorized entry into a computer. This law is jointly enforced by the United States Secret Service and the FBI.

In addition to the federal government, 48 states have laws on computer crime. Law enforcement officials are now applying traditional police procedures against computer criminals.

Despite the attention given to computer crimes, most probably go unreported. Many companies are reluctant to publicize their vulnerability to computer criminals. Also, many are discouraged by the resources and time needed to prosecute individuals.

The federal government has also been carefully watching computer bulletin board systems. Bulletin boards allow users to exchange computer files and messages using computers and modems. Some of these bulletin boards make commercial software programs available to users. However, making the programs available without the publisher's permission is illegal. Many bulletin board operators claim that users upload these programs without the operators' knowledge. However, many states hold the operator responsible for making sure that no illegal copies appear. Furthermore, the person downloading the program is in possession of illegal software.

Another type of computer crime occurs when someone illegally copies software he or she has purchased. Software companies lose over $2 billion each year to illegal copying. A person who opens a software package is agreeing to use the software on one computer only. This person is allowed to make copies of the software only to use as a backup. Placing software on more than one computer without the publisher's permission is illegal and violates federal copy-

Why is it illegal to copy computer software packages without the publisher's permission?

right laws. The violator is subject to a possible jail term and a fine of up to $250,000. Violators can include individuals, businesses, and schools.

Computers have become a way of life for most people. Courts, Congress, and state legislatures will continue to deal with new criminal law problems as computer technology evolves.

PROBLEM 21

Jamahl and Nigel are college freshmen who run a computer bulletin board system. They decide to hack into the computer system of the local telephone company. They enter the system without being asked for a password. While looking through computer files, Jamahl finds a confidential memo written by the company president admitting that the telephone rates are too high. Jamahl copies the file and posts it on the bulletin board for users to read. To get even with the telephone company, Nigel inserts a worm to slow its computer system down and sends the company president the message "You are a crook." However, because of a mistake Nigel made in creating the worm, the system crashes, and telephone service is out for eight hours. Many office buildings and government services are disrupted. The police chief shuts down the bulletin board and the prosecutor charges both youths with trespassing, theft, and the intentional destruction of property.

a. Should Jamahl and Nigel be prosecuted? What purpose would be served?

b. Are Jamahl and Nigel guilty of the charges? Explain your answer.

c. If they are convicted, how should they be punished?

SUBSTANCE ABUSE

The term *substance abuse* has come into general use in recent years. The word *substance* is used to describe all the kinds of chemicals that people abuse, including alcohol, drugs, and tobacco. This type of abuse has always plagued our society. Today, substance abuse is said to contribute to many social problems, including the breakup of family structures, decreased productivity in industry, injuries in the workplace, and automobile crashes. Criminal activity is often the result of substance abuse or the desire for money to purchase drugs.

Alcohol

Alcohol is the most widely abused substance in the United States today. One reason for this is that it is socially acceptable in our society. Alcohol use has been legal for adults over 21 years of age since the birth of the country (with the exception of a 14-year period from 1919 to 1933 known as *prohibition*).

The abuse of alcohol is very detrimental to our society. Alcoholism is seen by many as contributing to the poor functioning of some families, and many people commit spouse and child abuse and other crimes while under the influence of alcohol. According to the Department of Health and Human Services, alcohol is involved in 10 percent of work-related injuries and 40 percent of suicide attempts. The annual cost of alcohol abuse to American society is estimated at more than $100 billion. Approximately two in every five Americans will, at some time in their lives, be involved in an alcohol-related automobile crash.

How does your court system handle drunk drivers? Does it treat adults and juveniles differently? Are there programs in your community designed to help teens and adults with alcohol problems?

The term **drunk driving** is used in a general sense to refer to the legal terms *driving while intoxicated* (DWI) and *driving under the influence* (DUI). Legally, the term has a meaning more precise than its meaning in everyday usage. The legal definition of DWI/DUI refers to a person's blood alcohol concentration (BAC). The BAC indicates the grams per deciliter (g/dl) of alcohol in the blood. A person's BAC can be determined through breath, urine, or blood samples. Alcohol is a mind-altering drug, and tests have shown that thinking

What, if anything, should happen if a driver refuses to take a field sobriety test?

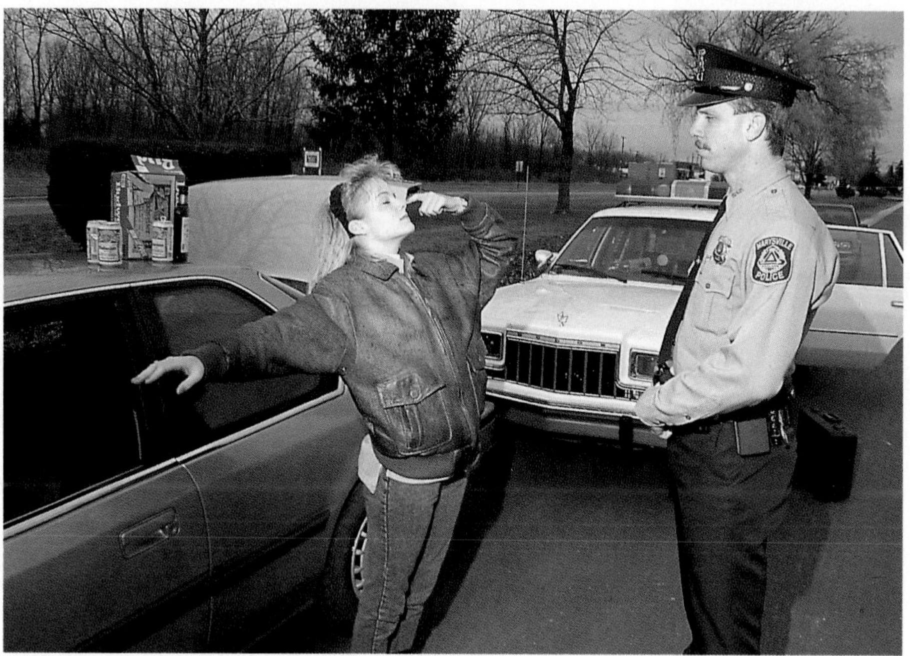

and reaction time are affected in varying degrees by the level of alcohol in the blood system. An individual is considered *intoxicated* when the BAC is 0.10g/dl or greater. An individual is considered *impaired* when the BAC is between 0.01g/dl and 0.09g/dl. These levels may vary somewhat from state to state.

Every state in the country has a DWI/DUI law. More than 1.7 million people were arrested for driving under the influence of alcohol in 1991. Use of drugs, legal or illegal, that impair driving ability is also a violation of DWI/DUI laws.

People can receive a variety of penalties for driving under the influence:

- License suspended (taken away for a period of time)
- License revoked (permanently taken away)
- Jail sentence (some laws require a minimum term)
- Fine
- Enrollment in a DWI school
- Community service

Any combination of these penalties may be imposed on the convicted drunk driver. A repeat offender is likely to receive stiffer penalties, and many states now automatically suspend drivers' licenses for DWI/DUI. In most states, repeat offenders end up in jail; and in some states, even a first offender must serve a brief jail sentence.

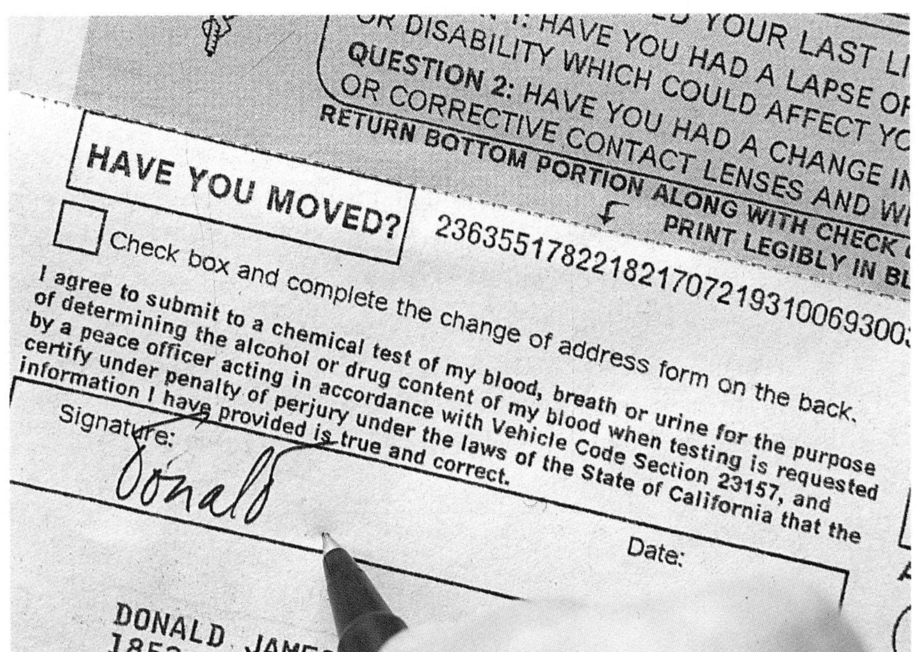

Does your state's driver's license application include this consent provision? Should it?

A driver who has been stopped may choose not to take an alcohol test. However, most states have an **implied consent law** under which the driver agrees to submit to a BAC test in exchange for the privilege of driving. In those states, refusal to take the test could result in immediate and automatic suspension of the driver's license for a certain period of time, even if the driver is not found guilty of DWI.

As drivers or passengers, young people are at a greater risk of being injured or killed in alcohol-related accidents. This is because teens are affected by alcohol faster and to a greater extent than adults and because on the whole teens are less-experienced drivers. Approximately 40% of all highway deaths involve alcohol, and thousands of teens are injured each year in alcohol-related car crashes.

There are both national and local organizations that exist to help reduce the amount of drunk driving and provide assistance to individuals who are victims of drunk-driving crashes. Such organizations include Mothers Against Drunk Driving, Students Against Driving Drunk, Remove Intoxicated Drivers, National Commission Against Impaired Driving, and National Coalition to Prevent Impaired Driving.

PROBLEM 22

Assume your state has recently had a series of crashes, including a number of deaths, caused by people driving under the influence of alcohol. A high percentage of these crashes have been caused by drivers aged 17 to 25. Others have been caused by older drivers who have had drinking problems for years. These drivers have been arrested before for DWI and have been fined or given probation.

a. You are a member of the state legislature, which has the power to change the law to try to solve this problem. Draft such a law.

b. Analyze the law that has been drafted. Will it create any new problems? What can be done to resolve them?

c. What else could be done to reduce alcohol-related crashes? Would these measures work better than the law proposed? Why or why not?

Drugs

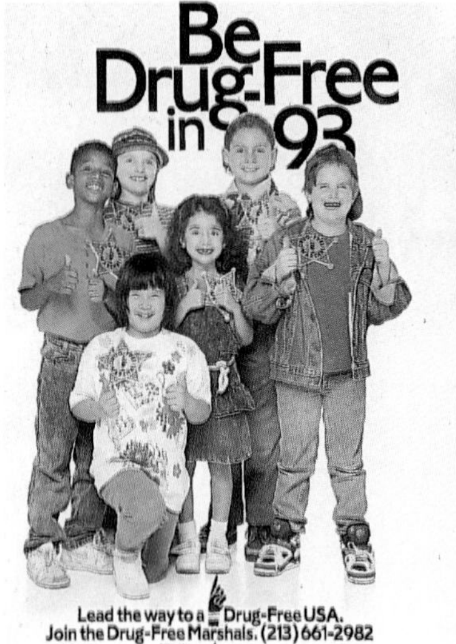

Be Drug-Free in '93
Lead the way to a Drug-Free USA.
Join the Drug-Free Marshals. (213) 661-2982

While illegal drug use is not new, it has become increasingly widespread, and its effects have touched everyone in our society. It is estimated that illegal drug use costs society over $60 billion a year. The flourishing illegal drug industry has led to a dramatic increase in criminal activity ranging from murder to high-level government corruption. This has placed an overwhelming burden on the criminal justice system. Many people are being arrested for selling or possessing drugs. Two-thirds of all inmates in federal prisons today are there because of drug-related offenses. Approximately one-third of all inmates in state prisons are in prison for drug offenses. In addition, thousands of babies across the country are born addicted to drugs as a result of their mothers' addictions.

Possession, distribution, or sale of certain drugs is a crime that may violate federal law, state law, or both. Some drugs, such as heroin, are physically addictive and can cause severe disruption to the personal life of the addict. The federal drug law, known as the *Controlled Substances Act*, classifies drugs into five groups, depending on medical use (if any), potential for abuse, and capability to create physical or psychological addiction. The penalties and criminal sanctions are different for each of the five groups.

Federal laws and most state laws now carry harsher penalties than they once did. Those who sell drugs or possess large amounts with intent to sell often face mandatory jail terms even for their first offense. Under federal law and in some states, those found guilty of being major drug traffickers may face a sentence of "life without parole." Some states treat simple possession of even small amounts of certain types of drugs as felonies. Some states and the federal gov-

Legislative Hearing: Drugs in the City

The city of Southland recently has been plagued by a growing drug epidemic. City officials and citizens are especially outraged that adults are using teenagers to sell drugs for them. The reasons for this are that teenagers often receive lighter sentences than adults do for drug-related offenses and that many teens will take the risk for the substantial amounts of money they are being paid. Southland police are also encountering problems in stopping the influx of drugs and pushers from other cities. The mayor, under intense political pressure from the community, has called a special council meeting to address the problem. Six experts have been asked to testify and present six different approaches to the council to address the problem. The experts and their views are as follows:

Police Chief Anderson: "We cannot be everywhere at once. The police department needs 100 more officers. The best way to combat the drug epidemic, in my opinion, is to put more police officers on the street and arm them with the latest weapons. Let's show the dealers and their customers that we mean business." (Law Enforcement Approach)

District Attorney Fisher: "I think that the city should declare an emergency and clamp down on drug sales on the street. Because of the epidemic, the civil liberties of the citizens of Southland must be limited temporarily. Since teenagers are playing such a predominant role in selling drugs late at night, we need to institute a 9 P.M. curfew for anyone under 18. I also advocate conducting random searches of students in school and establishing checkpoints where all cars will be stopped and searched in areas where drug trafficking is high." (Restrict Civil Liberties Approach)

Terry Blade: "I am an ex–drug addict, and I was cured through being arrested and sent to a good treatment program. I want the city to devote more resources to treating people addicted to drugs. I see drug treatment as the best way to cut the demand for drugs, thereby driving the drug dealers out of business. Many addicts are turned away because treatment spaces are limited in this community." (Drug Treatment Approach)

School Superintendent Alvarez: "I see preventive education as the real answer to the drug problem. We must address the issue of values and the choice every student has to either obey the law or use or sell drugs. I want innovative drug education for every student starting in the first grade. If we attack the drug issue early on, I feel that people will not choose to use drugs when they get older. We must also offer employment training programs so that students can earn money legally." (Preventive Education Approach)

Judge Horton: "I think stiffer penalties are needed. I think the city council should recommend to the state legislature that tougher mandatory sentences be given to drug offenders. Anyone 15 or older who is convicted of selling drugs should be given a mandatory two-year sentence and be treated as an adult. Deterrence through tough sentences is the only way to stop the drug epidemic." (Penalties Approach)

Alana Friday: "We should push for the legalization of drugs. If drugs are made legal, the black market for drugs will be reduced or eliminated. In addition, by legalizing drugs, the government can regulate the price and quality of the product. Drug addicts won't need to commit other crimes in order to obtain money to buy drugs at outrageously high street prices. Drug addicts won't die from using tainted drugs. Finally, our tax dollars won't be wasted chasing after drug traffickers and international cartels. Some of the money we save should be used to fund Superintendent Alvarez's preventive education programs, as well as the treatment programs Terry Blade recommends." (Legalization Approach)

PROBLEM 23

a. Each person has testified. You are a member of the city council, and at a hearing you must now decide which of the approaches will most help the city of Southland. Explain which approach you will choose. Also list the six approaches in order of your preference and give reasons for your rankings.

b. What are the costs and benefits of each approach?

c. What are the problems related to each approach?

d. Could more than one of the approaches be tried at the same time? If so, which ones go together most easily?

ernment have also enacted special drug forfeiture laws, which allow the government to take property such as bank accounts, airplanes, automobiles, and even houses that are being used in or are the proceeds of drug crimes.

As a result of the escalation of the drug problem and drug-related violence, some people, including a few politicians, have proposed that perhaps American society should consider a form of legalization

To win the war on drugs, should the government put greatest emphasis on stopping drugs from entering the country, on prosecuting drug sellers and users, or on educating people about the dangers of drugs?

of some drugs. These people point to the failure of the "war on drugs" and say that as long as all drugs are illegal, we are creating a market for their illegal sale. They believe we will be better able to control the sale and use of drugs if we change our laws from drug prohibition to drug regulation. They say we should treat drugs as a health problem. It is hypocritical, they claim, to restrict the use of drugs while allowing the legal sale of alcohol and cigarettes, which studies show are very harmful to people's health and cause many more deaths than drugs.

Many people are opposed to any sort of drug legalization, however. They believe that making drugs more easily available would lead to greater drug use, cause more deaths, and increase other problems related to drugs. The fact that cigarettes and alcohol are harmful, they argue, does not mean it is a good idea to legalize much more dangerous substances. These people feel that criminal laws deter drug use and that reducing penalties would deliver a message of acceptance. This would result in what some people have called "the addicting of America" and endanger our society as a whole.

Tobacco

Many Americans are unaware that tobacco contains an addictive drug, nicotine. Thus, tobacco can create an addiction, just as drugs and alcohol can. Smoking can cause premature death and crippling disease. According to an organization called the Coalition on Smoking or Health, smoking kills more people yearly than alcohol, car accidents, AIDS, suicides, homicides, fires, and drugs *combined*. Furthermore, the coalition estimates that the use of tobacco products costs society approximately $65 billion in lost work time and

Do cigarettes contain a dangerous drug? Explain.

health costs. Approximately one-fourth of the American adult population currently smoke cigarettes.

The *sale* of cigarettes, cigars, and tobacco to minors is illegal in 47 states and the District of Columbia. However, the easy availability and accessibility of tobacco in vending machines and stores make enforcement of tobacco sale laws extremely difficult. According to a survey conducted by the National Institute on Drug Abuse, almost half of the 8th-graders surveyed had tried cigarettes, and over 5 percent of the 12th-graders smoked approximately one-half pack of cigarettes a day. The use of cigarettes among African-American young people has continuously declined, while the use among whites has remained steady.

The use of tobacco is often glorified in advertising that depicts smoking and smokers as glamorous, sociable, happy, and sexy. Almost $4 billion was spent in 1990 by the tobacco industry for advertising.

Government has banned tobacco advertisements from television and radio in an effort to reduce the number of smokers and to limit the effects of smoking on society. In addition, Congress passed the *Comprehensive Smoking Education Act* in 1984. It requires one of four warnings to be placed on all cigarette packages and in advertisements. These four warnings are rotated quarterly:

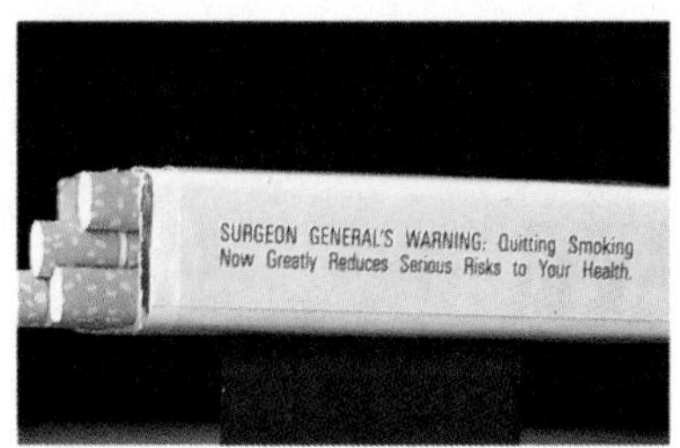

Is the Surgeon General's warning effective?

1. SURGEON GENERAL'S WARNING: Smoking Causes Lung Cancer, Heart Disease, Emphysema, and May Complicate Pregnancy.
2. SURGEON GENERAL'S WARNING: Quitting Smoking Now Greatly Reduces Serious Risks to Your Health.
3. SURGEON GENERAL'S WARNING: Smoking by Pregnant Women May Result in Fetal Injury, Premature Birth, and Low Birth Weight.
4. SURGEON GENERAL'S WARNING: Cigarette Smoke Contains Carbon Monoxide.

In addition to these efforts, many cities and businesses are restricting smoking to specific locations or to outside areas only. Many smokers argue that they have a right to smoke where they choose. Others argue that nonsmokers as well as smokers are affected by cigarette smoke.

Environmental tobacco smoke (ETS), or second-hand smoke, has been defined by the Environmental Protection Agency as a carcinogen, a cancer-causing agent. Environmental tobacco smoke affects both adults and children. It is estimated that ETS causes over 3,000 lung cancer deaths yearly in adult nonsmokers. In children, ETS increases the risk of diseases such as bronchitis and pneumonia.

Smokeless tobacco (chewing tobacco and snuff) is also addictive and poses significant health risks. Smokeless tobacco can cause can-

Do all public buildings in your area have separate, smoke-free areas? Should they?

cer as well as other diseases of the mouth. Warning labels are required on smokeless tobacco products. These labels warn that smokeless tobacco may cause mouth cancer, gum disease, and tooth loss and that smokeless tobacco is not a safe alternative to cigarettes. Nevertheless, between 1972 and 1991, the use of smokeless tobacco tripled. Many youths regularly see athletes using smokeless tobacco and identify it as a popular adult activity in which to participate.

Although the tobacco industry has sometimes come under attack, some people argue that smoking involves some economic benefits for society. The tobacco industry provides employment, international trade, and financial support for sporting and cultural events. In addition, many argue that people in a free society should be able to make the decision to smoke.

PROBLEM 24

a. Why do some people smoke? Why do other people criticize smoking?

b. What actions has government taken against smoking? Have these actions been effective?

c. Should government take additional actions against smoking? Should adults and juveniles be treated the same? Give your reasons.

DEFENSES

For a conviction to occur in a criminal case, the prosecutor must establish beyond a reasonable doubt that the defendant committed the act in question with the required intent. The defendant is not required to present a defense but can instead simply force the government to prove its case. However, a number of possible defenses are available to defendants in criminal cases.

No Crime Has Been Committed

The defendant may present evidence to show either (1) that no crime was committed or (2) that there was no criminal intent. In the first case, a defendant might attempt to show that she was carrying a gun but had a valid license, or a defendant might attempt to show that he did not commit rape because the woman was of legal age and consented. In the second case, the defendant might attempt to show that he mistakenly took another person's coat when leaving a restaurant. The defendant is innocent of a charge of larceny if it was an honest and reasonable mistake.

Defendant Did Not Commit the Crime

Often, no doubt exists that a crime has been committed. In such cases, the question is, who committed it? In this situation, the defendant may present evidence of a mistake in identity or may offer an **alibi**, which is evidence that the defendant was somewhere else at the time the crime was committed.

Defendant Committed a Criminal Act, but the Act Was Excusable or Justified

Sometimes, a criminal act may be considered excusable or justified. Defenses in this category include self-defense and defense of property and others.

The law recognizes the right of a person unlawfully attacked to use reasonable force in self-defense. It also recognizes the right of one person to use reasonable force to defend another person from an attack that is about to occur. There are, however, a number of limitations to these defenses.

A person who *reasonably* believes there is imminent danger of bodily harm can use a reasonable amount of force in self-defense. However, a person cannot use more force than appears to be necessary. If, after stopping an attacker, the defender continues to use force, the roles reverse, and the defender can no longer claim self-defense. Deadly force can be used only by a person who reasonably believes that there is imminent danger of death or serious bodily harm. A person is also allowed to use deadly or nondeadly force to defend a third person if the person defended is entitled to claim self-defense.

Reasonable nondeadly force may be used to protect property. Some states have enacted controversial "make my day" laws, which give persons the right to use deadly force to defend their property against unwarranted intrusion.

PROBLEM 25

a. Ms. Roe kept a pistol in her home as protection against intruders. One evening, she heard a noise in the den and went to investigate. Upon entering the room, she saw a man stealing her television. The burglar, seeing the gun, ran for the window, but Ms. Roe fired and killed him before he could escape. In a trial for manslaughter, Ms. Roe pleaded self-defense. Would you find her guilty? Why or why not?

b. Mr. Peters has a legal handgun to protect his home against intruders and against the increasing crime in his neighborhood. One night, Takahiro, a 16-year-old Japanese exchange student, walks up Mr. Peters's driveway looking for a party. Takahiro thinks Mr. Peters is hosting the party and begins yelling and waving his arms. Mr. Peters gets scared, retrieves his handgun, and points it at Takahiro while yelling "Freeze!" Takahiro does not understand English and keeps walking toward Mr. Peters. Thinking he is an intruder, Mr. Peters shoots and kills Takahiro. Mr. Peters is charged with first-degree murder. Does he have a defense?

c. The owner of a jewelry store spots a shoplifter stealing an expensive necklace. Can the owner use force to prevent the crime? If so, how much?

Defendant Committed a Criminal Act but Is Not Criminally Responsible for His or Her Actions

Some defenses rest on the defendant's lack of criminal responsibility for his or her criminal act. In this category are the defenses of infancy, intoxication, insanity, entrapment, duress and necessity.

Infancy Traditionally, children of a very young age, usually under 7, were considered legally incapable of committing a crime. Children between the ages of 7 and 14 were generally presumed incapable of committing a crime, but this presumption could be shown to be wrong. Under modern laws, most states simply provide that children under a specified age shall not be tried for their crimes but shall be turned over to the juvenile court. Children under the specified age have the defense of **infancy**.

Intoxication Defendants sometimes claim **intoxication** as a defense—that is, they claim that at the time of a crime, they were so drunk on alcohol or high on drugs that they didn't know what they were doing. As a general rule, voluntary intoxication is *not* a defense to a crime. However, it may sometimes be a valid defense if the crime requires proof of a specific mental state. For example, when Grady is charged with assault with intent to kill, he claims he was drunk. If he can prove this, his intoxication may be a valid defense, because it may negate the specific mental state (the intent to kill) required to prove the crime. Grady can still be convicted of the crime of assault, because specific intent is not required to prove that crime. And if Grady decided to kill someone before he got drunk, or if he got drunk to get up enough nerve to commit the crime, then intoxication would not be a defense. This is because the required mental state (the intent to kill) existed before the drunkenness.

Insanity Over the centuries, the **insanity** defense has evolved as an important legal concept. Ancient Greeks and Romans believed that insane people were not responsible for their actions and should not be punished like ordinary criminals. Since the 14th century, English courts have excused offenders who were mentally unable to control their conduct. The modern standard grew out of an 1843 case involving the attempted murder of the British prime minister.

The basic idea is that people who have a mental disease or defect should not be convicted if they don't know what they are doing or if they don't know the difference between right and wrong. About half the states and the federal government use this standard. The other states hold that accused persons must be acquitted if they lack the "substantial capacity" to appreciate the nature of the act or to conform their conduct to the requirements of law.

During criminal proceedings, the accused's mental state can be an issue in determining (1) whether the defendant is competent to stand trial, (2) whether the defendant was sane at the time of the criminal act, and (3) whether the defendant is sane after the trial. The insanity defense applies only if the accused was insane at the time of the crime. Insanity at the time of trial may delay the proceedings until the accused can understand what is taking place. But insanity during or after the trial does not affect criminal liability.

In most states, there are three possible verdicts: guilty, innocent, or not guilty by reason of insanity. The last verdict results in automatic commitment to a mental institution in some states. In others, the judge or jury exercises discretion, sometimes in a separate hearing, to determine commitment of the accused. In recent years, a number of states have come up with a new verdict: guilty but mentally ill. Defendants found guilty but mentally ill can be sent to a hospital and later transferred to a prison after they've recovered.

To prove insanity, the defense must produce evidence of a mental disease or defect. Psychiatrists usually give testimony in this instance. Both the defense and the prosecution may have psychiatrists examine the defendant, and their testimony is often in conflict. The decision as to whether insanity is a valid defense rests with whoever—judge or jury—decides the facts of the case.

PROBLEM 26

a. What is the insanity defense? How does it work?

b. Should the insanity defense be kept as is, changed in some way, or abolished? Explain your answer.

Entrapment The **entrapment** defense applies when the defendant admits committing a criminal act but claims that he or she was induced, or persuaded, to commit the crime by a law enforcement officer. There is no entrapment when a police officer merely provides the defendant with an opportunity to commit a crime; rather, it must be shown that the defendant would not have committed the crime *but for* the inducement of the police officer. Entrapment is difficult to prove and cannot be claimed as a defense to crimes involving serious physical injury, such as rape or murder.

PROBLEM 27

Can entrapment be claimed as a valid defense in either of the following cases? Explain your answer.

a. Mary, an undercover police officer masquerading as a prostitute, approaches John and tells him that she'll have sex with him in exchange for $50. John hands over the money and is arrested.

b. Marvin, a drug dealer, offers to sell drugs to Walter, an undercover police officer disguised as a drug addict. Walter buys the drugs, and Marvin is arrested.

Duress A person acts under **duress** when he or she does something as a result of coercion or a threat of immediate danger to life or personal safety. Under duress, an individual lacks the ability to exercise free will. For example, suppose someone points a gun at your head and demands that you steal money or be killed. You steal the money. Duress would be a good defense in this case if you were prosecuted for theft. Duress is not a defense to homicide, however.

Necessity An individual acts under **necessity** when he or she is compelled to react to a situation that is unavoidable in order to protect life. Suppose, for example, that a group of people is left adrift in a lifeboat and the lifeboat is so heavy with cargo that it is in danger of sinking. The group throws the cargo overboard to make the lifeboat lighter and more manageable. In this case, necessity would be a good defense to a charge of destruction of property. Necessity is not a defense to homicide.

THE CRIMINAL JUSTICE PROCESS

The criminal justice process includes everything that happens to a person from arrest through prosecution and conviction to release from the control of the state. Freedom may be gained almost immediately—at the station house—or after time has been served in a correctional institution. Freedom may also come at any stage in between. At various points in the process, the prosecutor may drop a case for lack of evidence. A judge can also dismiss a case for lack of evidence or if the jury is unable to reach a verdict. Figure 2.4 diagrams the criminal justice process, and the following sections describe some aspects of the process in detail. The juvenile justice process is somewhat different and is discussed at the end of the chapter.

Make a chart showing the steps in your state's criminal justice system. Who could help you get the information needed to make this chart?

ARREST

An **arrest** takes place when a person suspected of a crime is taken into custody. A person can be taken into custody in one of two ways: by an arrest warrant or by a warrantless arrest based on probable

Figure 2.4 Sequence of Events in the Criminal Justice Process

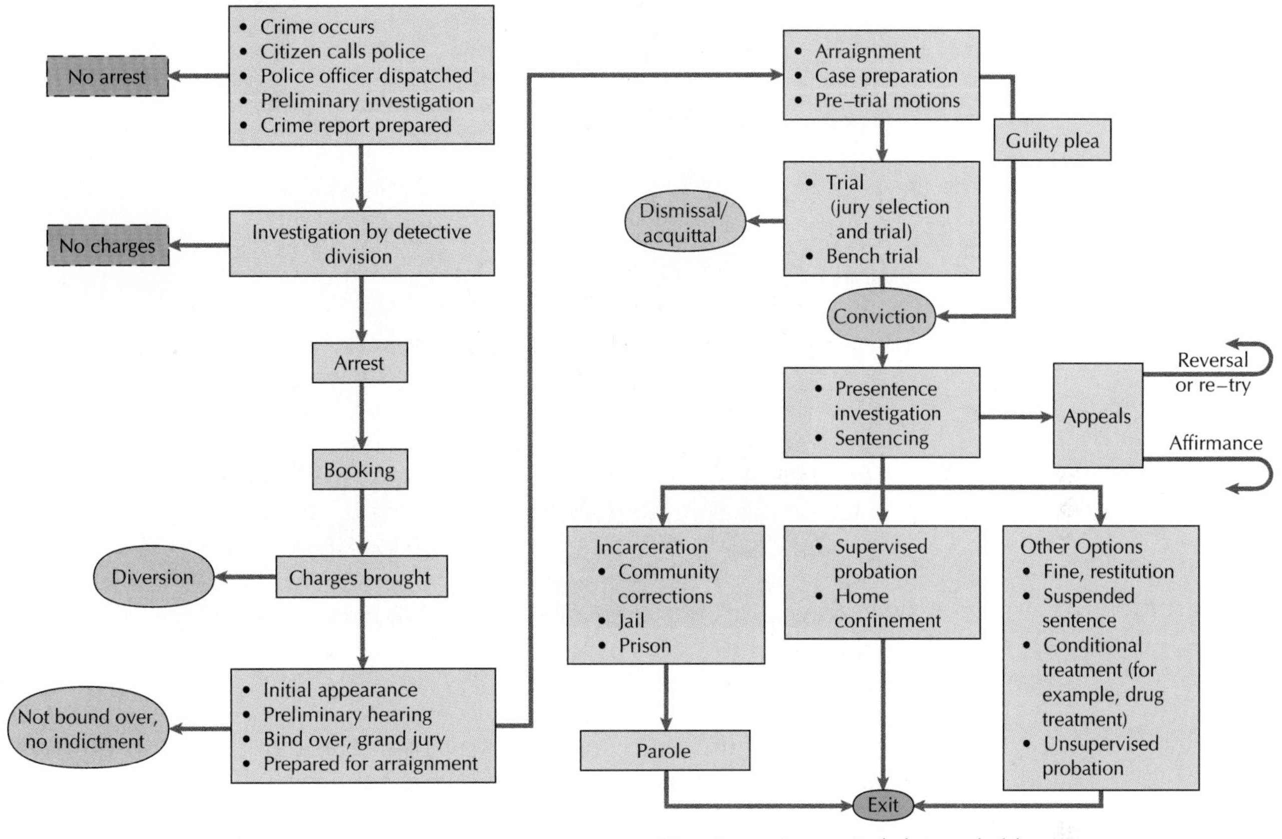

Note: Sentencing may include several of the options (for example, prison *and* a fine). Parole is being eliminated in many places.

cause. A person, once taken into custody and not free to leave, is considered to be under arrest, whether he or she is told that or not.

An **arrest warrant** is a court order commanding that the person named in it be taken into custody. A warrant is obtained by the filing of a complaint before a judge or magistrate. The person filing the complaint is generally a police officer but may be a victim or a witness. The person making the complaint must set out and swear to the facts and circumstances of the alleged crime. If, on the basis of the information provided, the judge finds probable cause to believe that an offense has been committed and that the accused committed it, a warrant will be issued. On many occasions, police don't have time to get a warrant. In felony and certain misdemeanor cases, they may make a warrantless arrest based on probable cause.

Probable cause is defined as a reasonable belief that a person has committed a crime. This reasonable belief may be based on much less evidence than is necessary to prove a person guilty at trial. For example, suppose the police receive a radio report of a bank robbery. An officer sees a man matching the description of the bank robber

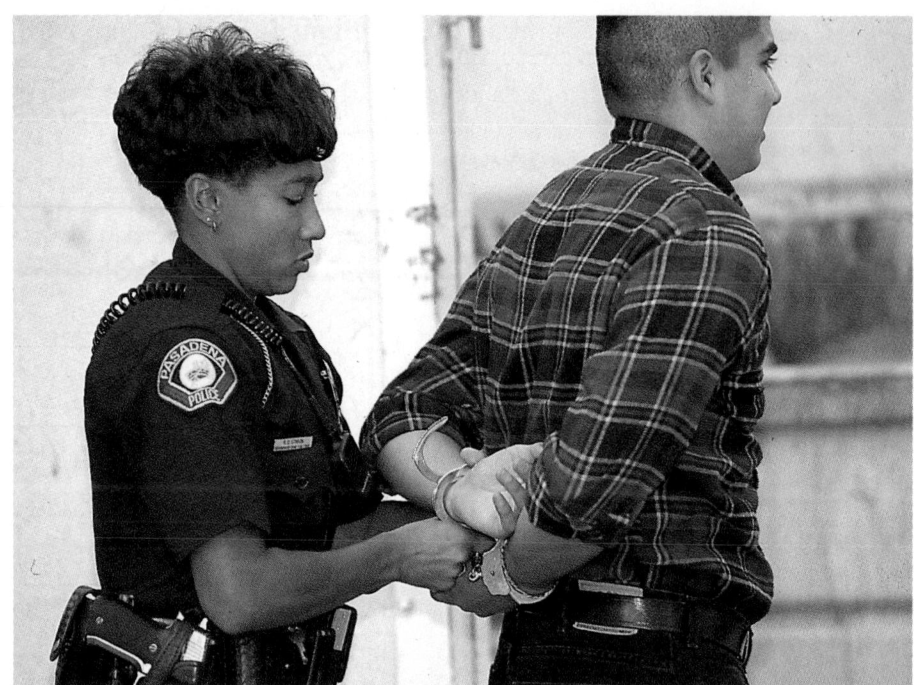

Can this officer make a lawful arrest without a warrant? Explain.

waving a gun and running away from the bank. The officer would have probable cause to stop and arrest the man.

There is no exact formula for determining probable cause. When arresting without a warrant, police must use their own judgment as to what is reasonable under the circumstances of each case. In all cases, probable cause requires more than mere suspicion or a hunch. Some facts must be present that indicate that the person arrested has committed a crime.

In recent years, the courts have allowed drug enforcement officials to use what is known as a *drug courier profile* either to provide a basis to stop a person and question that person or to help establish probable cause for arrest. This profile is often based on commonly held notions concerning the typical age, race, personal appearance, and mannerisms of drug couriers.

Police may establish probable cause from information provided by citizens in the community. Information from victims or witnesses can be used to obtain an arrest warrant. Police also receive information from informants. Police may use informants' tips to establish probable cause, so long as they can convince a judge that the information is reliable. In determining the reliability of an informant's tip, a judge will consider all the circumstances. These include whether the informant has provided accurate information in the past, how the informant obtained the information, and whether the police can corroborate, or confirm, the informant's tip with other information.

PROBLEM 28

The police receive a tip that a drug pusher named Richie will be flying from New York to Washington sometime on the morning of September 8. The informant describes Richie as a tall man with reddish hair and a beard. He also tells police that Richie has a habit of walking fast and that he will be carrying illegal drugs in a brown leather bag. The police have received reliable information from this informant in the past.

On the morning of September 8, the police watch all passengers arriving from New York. When they see a man who fits the description—carrying a brown leather bag and walking fast—they arrest him. A search of the bag reveals a large quantity of cocaine.

a. Based on what you know, do you think the police had probable cause to arrest Richie? Why or why not?

b. Should the police have obtained a warrant before arresting Richie? Why or why not?

c. Assume the police have not received a specific tip but they know that crack cocaine is being brought regularly on trains from one city to another by teenagers hired by older drug dealers. They see a 16-year-old African-American male arriving by train alone with a small canvas bag. Should they be able to stop and question him? Under what circumstances should they be able to search or arrest him?

The police do not need probable cause to stop and question individuals whom they reasonably suspect to be involved in criminal activity. In such cases, the police may ask for identification and for an explanation of the suspicious behavior. When questioned, such individuals do not have to answer. However, a refusal to cooperate may result in further detention. In some cases, it may provide sufficient additional evidence to result in a valid arrest. For example, suppose a police officer has reason to suspect someone of a crime, and the person refuses to answer the police officer's questions or attempts to flee when approached by the officer. This conduct, when considered together with other factors, might provide the probable cause necessary for an arrest. In addition, if a police officer, based on his or her experience, thinks a person is behaving suspiciously and is likely to be armed, the officer may **stop and frisk** (pat down) the suspect for weapons.

What To Do If Arrested

- **Don't struggle with the police.** Be polite. Avoid fighting or swearing, even if you think the police have made a mistake. Resisting arrest and assaulting a police officer are usually separate crimes that you can be charged with even if you've done nothing else wrong.

  Give your name, address, and phone number to the police. Otherwise, *keep quiet* until you have spoken to a lawyer. Don't discuss your case with anyone at this point, and don't sign any statements about your case.

  You may be searched, photographed, and fingerprinted. Notice carefully what is done but don't resist. If any personal property is taken from you, ask for a written receipt.

  As soon as possible after you get to the police station, call *a trusted relative or friend.* Tell this person where you are, what you've been charged with, and what your bail or bond is (if you know).

- **When you're arrested for a minor offense**, you may, in some places, be released without having to put up any money (this is called an unsecured bond or citation release). If you don't qualify for a citation release, you may have to put up some money before release (this is called posting a cash bond or collateral). Ask for a receipt for the money.

- **When you're arrested for a serious misdemeanor or felony**, you won't be released immediately. Ask the friend or relative you have called to get a lawyer for you. If you can't afford a lawyer, one will be appointed by the judge when you are first brought to court.

  Before you leave the police station, be sure to find out when you're due in court. *Never be late or miss a court appearance.* If you don't show up in court at the assigned time, a warrant will be issued for your rearrest.

- **Don't talk about your case with anyone except your lawyer.** Be honest with your lawyer, or he or she will have trouble helping you. Ask that your lawyer be present at all lineups and interrogation sessions.

A police officer may use as much physical force as is reasonably necessary to make an arrest. However, most police departments limit the use of deadly force to incidents involving dangerous or

The Unlucky Couple

After an evening at the movies, Lonnie Howard and his girlfriend, Susan, decide to park in the empty lot behind Briarwood Elementary School. After several beers, they are startled by the sound of breaking glass from the rear of the school.

Unnoticed in their darkened car, Lonnie and Susan observe two men loading office equipment from the school into the back of a van. Quickly concluding that the men must be burglars, Lonnie revs up his engine and roars out of the parking lot onto Main Street.

Meanwhile, unknown to Lonnie and Susan, a silent alarm has also alerted the police to the break-in at the school. Responding to the alarm, Officer Ramos heads for the school and turns onto Main Street just in time to see Lonnie's car speeding away.

PROBLEM 29

a. If you were Officer Ramos, what would you do in this situation? If you were Lonnie, what would you do?

b. If Officer Ramos chases Lonnie, will she have probable cause to stop and arrest him?

c. How do you think Officer Ramos would act after stopping Lonnie? How do you think Lonnie and Susan would act?

d. Role-play this situation. As Officer Ramos, decide what you would say and how you would act toward the occupants of the car. As Lonnie and Susan, decide what you would say and how you would act toward the police.

e. What could Lonnie and Susan do if they were mistakenly arrested for the burglary? What could they do if they were abused or mistreated by Officer Ramos?

f. Assume Lonnie takes a baseball bat from the back of the car and begins to wave it. Would it be legal for Officer Ramos to use deadly force?

threatening suspects. In 1985, the U.S. Supreme Court was asked to decide whether it was lawful for police to shoot an "unarmed fleeing felony suspect." In deciding the case, the Court ruled that deadly force "may not be used unless it is necessary to prevent the escape, *and* the officer has probable cause to believe the suspect poses a significant threat of death or serious physical harm to the officer or others."

If a police officer uses too much force or makes an unlawful arrest, the accused may bring a civil action for a violation of the federal *Civil Rights Act*. The government could also file a criminal action against the police. In addition, many local governments have processes for handling citizen complaints about police misconduct. You should know, however, that a police officer is never liable for false arrest simply because the person arrested did not commit the crime. Rather, it must be shown that the officer acted maliciously or had no reasonable grounds for suspicion of guilt.

SEARCH AND SEIZURE

The right of the people to be secure in their persons, houses, papers, and effects, against unreasonable searches and seizures, shall not be violated, and no Warrants shall issue, but upon probable cause, supported by Oath or affirmation, and particularly describing the place to be searched, and the persons or things to be seized.

—Fourth Amendment to the U.S. Constitution

Americans have always valued their privacy. They expect to be left alone, to be free from unwarranted snooping or spying, and to be secure in their own homes. This expectation of privacy is important and is protected by the U.S. Constitution. The Fourth Amendment sets out the right to be free from "unreasonable searches and seizures" and establishes conditions under which search warrants may be issued. (This right, like others in the Bill of Rights, limits the power of government; it does not apply to actions by private citizens. If an individual violates your privacy, however, you may be able to make a claim under tort law, discussed in Chapter 3.)

Balanced against the individual's right to privacy is the government's need to gather information. In the case of the police, this is the need to collect evidence against criminals and to protect society against crime.

The Fourth Amendment does not give citizens an absolute right to privacy, and it does not prohibit all searches—only those that are unreasonable. In deciding if a search is reasonable, the courts look to the facts and circumstances of each case. As a general rule, courts have found searches and seizures reasonable when authorized by a valid warrant. In addition, courts have recognized that certain searches conducted without a warrant can also be reasonable. These

Can police use trained dogs to establish probable cause? Explain.

exceptions to the warrant requirement are discussed on page 122.

Although the language of the Fourth Amendment is relatively simple, search and seizure law is complex. Courts look at the law on a case-by-case basis, and there are many exceptions to the basic rules. Once an individual is arrested, it is up to the courts to decide whether any evidence found in a search was legally obtained. If a court finds that the search was unreasonable, then evidence found in the search cannot be used at the trial against the defendant. This principle, called the **exclusionary rule**, does not mean that the defendant cannot be tried or convicted, but it does mean that evidence seized in an unlawful search cannot be used at trial. (For a further discussion of the exclusionary rule, see page 141.)

Searches with a Warrant

A **search warrant** is a court order. It is obtained from a judge who is convinced that there is a real need to search a person or place. Before a judge issues a warrant, someone, usually a police officer, must appear in court and testify under oath concerning the facts that provide the probable cause to believe that a search is justified. This sworn statement of facts and circumstances is called an **affidavit**. If a judge issues a search warrant, the warrant must specifically describe the person or place to be searched and the particular things to be seized.

Once the search warrant is issued, the search must be conducted within a certain number of days specified in the warrant. Also, in many states, the search must be conducted only in the daytime, unless the warrant expressly states otherwise. Finally, a search warrant does not usually authorize a general search of everything in the specified place. For example, if the police have a warrant to search a house for stolen 21-inch televisions, it would be unreasonable for the police to look in desk drawers, envelopes, or other small places where such televisions could not possibly be hidden. However, the police *can* seize evidence related to the case and any other illegal items that are in their plain view when they are properly searching the house for the televisions.

PROBLEM 30

a. Examine Figure 2.5, an affidavit for a search warrant. Who is requesting the warrant? What are the searchers looking for? What people or places do they seek to search? What facts and circumstances are given to justify the search?

b. Examine Figure 2.6, a search warrant. Who authorized the search? When may the search be conducted? Considering the affidavit, do you think the judge had sufficient grounds to authorize the warrant? Is there anything missing from the warrant?

c. As a general rule, why do you think the Fourth Amendment requires police to obtain a warrant before conducting a search? Why do you think there is a general requirement that searches be conducted during daylight hours?

d. Under what conditions do you think police should be allowed to search without a warrant?

Searches without a Warrant

Although the police are generally required to get a search warrant before conducting a search, the courts have recognized a number of situations in which searches may be legally conducted without a warrant.

- **Search incident to a lawful arrest.** A search incident to a lawful arrest is the most common exception to the warrant requirement. This exception allows the police to search a lawfully arrested person and the area immediately around that person for hidden weapons or for evidence that might be destroyed. In a recent case, the U.S. Supreme Court also

Figure 2.5 Affidavit for a Search Warrant

Form A.O. 106 (Rev. Apr. 1973) **Affidavit for Search Warrant**

United States District Court

FOR THE

Eastern District of Missouri

Docket No. A

Case No. 11246

UNITED STATES OF AMERICA

vs.

John Doe

AFFIDAVIT FOR SEARCH WARRANT

BEFORE Michael J. Thiel, Federal Courthouse, St. Louis, Missouri
Name of Judge[1] or Federal Magistrate — Address of Judge[1] or Federal Magistrate

The undersigned being duly sworn deposes and says:

That he has reason to believe that (on the person of) Occupants, and (on the premises known as) 935 Bay Street, St. Louis, Missouri, described as a two story, residential dwelling, white in color and of wood frame construction.....

in the Eastern District of Missouri

there is now being concealed certain property, namely
here describe property

Counterfeit bank notes, money orders, and securities, and plates, stones, and other paraphernalia used in counterfeiting and forgery,

which are
here give alleged grounds for search and seizure[2]

in violation of 18 U.S. Code ¶471-474

And that the facts tending to establish the foregoing grounds for issuance of a Search Warrant are as follows:[3] (1) Pursuant to my employment with the Federal Bureau of Investigation, I received information from a reliable informant that a group of persons were conducting an illegal counterfeiting operation out of a house at 935 Bay Street, St. Louis, Missouri. (2) Acting on this information agents of the FBI placed the house at 935 Bay Street under around the clock surveillance. During the course of this surveillance officers observed a number of facts tending to establsh the existence of an illegal counterfeiting operation. These include: observation of torn & defective counterfeit notes discarded in the trash in the alley behind the house at 935 Bay Street, and pick-up & delivery of parcels at irregular hours of the night by persons known to the FBI as having records for distribution of counterfeit money.

Barry J. Cunningham Special Agent
Signature of Affiant.

Federal Bureau of Investigation
Official Title, if any.

Sworn to before me, and subscribed in my presence, December 3rd, 19 94

Michael J. Thiel,
Judge[1] or Federal Magistrate.

Figure 2.6 A Search Warrant

Form A. O. 93 (Rev. Nov. 1972) Search Warrant

United States District Court

FOR THE

Eastern District of Missouri

UNITED STATES OF AMERICA

vs.

John Doe

Docket No. A

Case No. 11246

SEARCH WARRANT

To Any sheriff, constable, marshall, police officer, or investigative officer of the United States of America.

Affidavit (s) having been made before me by

Special Agent, Barry I. Cunningham

that he has reason to believe that { on the person of / on the premises known as }

on the occupants of, and
on the premises known as 935 Bay Street, St. Louis, Missouri described as a two story, residential dwelling, white in color and of wood frame construction .....

in the Eastern District of Missouri

there is now being concealed certain property, namely

Counterfeit bank notes, money orders, and securities, and
Plates, stones, and other paraphernalia used in counterfeiting and forgery

and as I am satisfied that there is probable cause to believe that the property so described is being concealed on the person or premises above described and that the foregoing grounds for application for issuance of the search warrant exist.

You are hereby commanded to search within a period of 10 (not to exceed 10 days) the person or place named for the property specified, serving this warrant and making the search { ~~in the daytime (6:00 a.m. to 10:00 p.m.)~~ / at anytime in the day or night[1] } and if the property be found there to seize it, leaving a copy of this warrant and a receipt for the property taken, and prepare a written inventory of the property seized and promptly return this warrant and bring the property before me as required by law.

Dated this 3rd day of December, 19 94

Michael J. Thiel
Judge or Federal Magistrate.

[1] The Federal Rules of Criminal Procedure provide: "The warrant shall be served in the daytime, unless the issuing authority, by appropriate provision in the warrant, and for reasonable cause shown, authorizes its execution at times other than daytime." (Rule 41(C))

allowed a "protective sweep" through an arrested person's home in search of another potentially armed suspect.

- **Stop and frisk.** A police officer who reasonably thinks a person is behaving suspiciously and is likely to be armed may stop the suspect and frisk him or her for weapons. This exception to the warrant requirement was created to protect the safety of officers and bystanders who might be injured by a person carrying a concealed weapon. In 1993, the U.S. Supreme Court said that seizing an illegal substance (such as drugs) during a valid frisk is reasonable if the officer's sense of touch makes it immediately clear that the object felt is an illegal one (this is the so-called "plain feel" exception).
- **Consent.** When a person voluntarily agrees, the police may conduct a search without a warrant and without probable cause. Normally, a person may grant permission to search only his or her own belongings or property. In some situations, however, one person may legally allow the police to conduct a search of another person's property. For example, a parent may usually allow officers to search a child's property.
- **Plain view.** If an object connected with a crime is in plain view and can be seen by an officer from a place where he or she has a right to be, it can be seized without a warrant. For example, if a person is growing marijuana outside and the police can identify the plants from their cruiser, then the plants can be seized without a warrant.
- **Hot pursuit.** Police in hot pursuit of a suspect are not required to get a search warrant before entering a building that they have seen the suspect enter. It is also lawful to seize evidence found during a search conducted while in hot pursuit of a suspected felon.
- **Vehicle searches.** A police officer who has probable cause to believe that a vehicle contains **contraband**, or illegal items, may conduct a search of the vehicle without a warrant. This does not mean that the police have a right to stop and search any vehicle on the streets. The right to stop and search must be based on a reasonable belief that evidence of a crime will be found.
- **Emergency situations.** In certain emergencies, the police are not required to get a search warrant. These situations include searching a building after a telephoned bomb threat, entering a house after smelling smoke or hearing screams, and other situations in which the police don't have time to get a warrant.
- **Border and airport searches.** Customs agents are authorized to search without warrants and without probable cause. They

Is it reasonable to search all airline passengers using a metal detector, even when there is no probable cause?

may examine the baggage, vehicles, purses, wallets, and similar belongings of people entering the country. Body searches or searches conducted away from the border by customs agents are allowed only where there is reasonable suspicion of criminal activity. In view of the danger of airplane hijacking, courts have also held it reasonable for airlines to search all carry-on luggage and to search all passengers by means of a metal detector.

THE CASE OF . . .

Police Searching the Trash

The police suspected that Bill Greenwood was involved in dealing drugs. They observed many vehicles making brief stops at his house during late-night hours, and one truck was followed from Greenwood's house to another residence that had previously been investigated for drug sales.

Though they did not have enough evidence to obtain a search warrant, the police asked the garbage collector to pick up plastic garbage bags that Greenwood had left on the curb in front of his house and turn them over to police without mixing them with other garbage. Upon opening them, the police found evidence of drug use.

Based on this evidence, they obtained a search warrant for Greenwood's house and discovered quantities of cocaine and hashish. Greenwood was arrested and convicted based on this evidence.

Was the police search of the garbage illegal? Should the evidence from that search have been allowed to be the basis for a search warrant that resulted in Greenwood's conviction? This case was appealed to the U.S. Supreme Court, and the justices split and came up with two different opinions. Read the following two opinions and answer the questions that follow.

Opinion A

The plastic garbage bags were closed containers that one could not see through. Therefore, they are no different from other containers that, in prior cases, the Court has held may only be opened after the police obtain a search warrant.

We believe that allowing the search of trash bags without a warrant would paint a grim picture of our society. It would be a society that says it is unreasonable to expect privacy in personal effects sealed in a container and disposed of in a manner that will commingle it with the trash of others. Consequently, we hold that the search was illegal under the Fourth Amendment and that the items should not have been used to convict Greenwood.

Opinion B

People are protected by the Fourth Amendment's freedom from unreasonable search and seizure only if they have a "reasonable expectation of privacy" with respect to what is being searched. It is common knowledge that plastic garbage bags left on or at the side of a public street are readily accessible to animals, children, scavengers, snoops, and others. They have also been left there so that a third party, a trash collector, can take them and perhaps sort through them.

In prior cases, this Court has held that "a person has no expectation of privacy in information he voluntarily turned over to third parties." For example, in one case, the Court ruled that the police could install a device at phone company offices that recorded the phone numbers a suspect called. In another case, warrantless airplane surveillance of a fenced backyard was allowed for purposes of detecting marijuana cultivation. The police should be allowed to gather evidence that any member of the public could also see and gather. Therefore, we hold that the trash collected may be used as evidence against Greenwood.

PROBLEM 31

a. What are the two strongest arguments in Opinion A? Why?

b. What are the two strongest arguments in Opinion B? Why?

c. Which opinion do you agree with? Give your reasons.

d. Which opinion do you think represents the majority view of the U.S. Supreme Court in the case?

e. What is the importance of allowing the evidence from the search of the garbage to be used in the case against Greenwood? Could he be arrested and convicted without the evidence?

f. Can a private citizen go through someone's trash without violating the law? What if a reporter does it to gather information for a news article?

PROBLEM 32

Examine each of the following situations. Decide whether the search and seizure violates the Fourth Amendment and whether the evidence seized can be used in court. Explain your decisions.

a. Jill's former boyfriend breaks into her apartment and looks through her desk for love letters. Instead he finds drugs, which he turns over to the police.

b. After José checks out of a hotel, the police ask the maid to turn over the contents of the wastebasket, where they find notes planning a murder.

c. A student informs the principal that Bob, another student, is selling drugs on school grounds. The principal opens Bob's locker with a master key, finds drugs, and calls the police.

d. The police see Dell, who has been arrested before for selling drugs, standing at a bus stop on a downtown street. They stop and search him and find drugs in his pocket.

e. Susan is arrested for reckless driving. After stopping her, the police search her purse and find a pistol.

f. Larry is observed shoplifting items in a store. Police chase Larry into his apartment building and arrest him outside the closed door of his apartment. A search of the apartment reveals a large quantity of stolen merchandise.

g. The police receive a tip from an anonymous informant who provides detailed information about the counterfeit money Rudy has in his office. Acting on this information, they get a search warrant and find the money just where the informant told them it would be.

h. Sandy is suspected of receiving stolen goods. The police go to her apartment and ask Claire, her roommate, if they can search the apartment. Claire gives the police permission, and they find stolen items in Sandy's dresser.

Fingers McGee

Officers Yomoto and Jones receive a radio report of a robbery at the Dixie Liquor Store. The report indicates only that the suspect is male, about six feet tall, and wearing old clothes. Meanwhile, Fingers McGee has just seen the owner of the Dixie Liquor Store chasing a man carrying a sack and what appeared to be a knife down the street. McGee thinks the man looks like Bill Johnson, a drug addict, and he thinks the man was running toward Johnson's house at 22 Elm Street. Officers Yomoto and Jones encounter McGee on a street corner.

PROBLEM 33

a. Role-play this encounter. As the officers, decide what questions to ask McGee. As McGee, decide what to tell the officers.

b. Assuming McGee tells the police what he knows, what should the police do then?

c. Should the police get a search warrant before going to Johnson's house? If they go to Johnson's house without a warrant, do they have probable cause to arrest him? Why or why not?

d. If the police decide to enter Johnson's house, what should they do? Should they knock and announce themselves, or should they break in unannounced?

e. If the police enter the house, can they arrest Johnson? Where can they search, and what, if anything, can be seized? Role-play the scene at the house.

THE CASE OF . . .

Drug Testing for Student Athletes

Based on information about possible drug use by athletes on the high-school baseball team, the coach ordered all 16 team members to provide urine samples. Five specimens tested positive for marijuana. Based on these results, other reports of drug use by student athletes, and general concern about the level of drug use among high-school students nationwide, the school board instituted a random urine-testing program for interscholastic athletes and cheerleaders.

All students who wished to participate as athletes or cheerleaders, as well as their parents or guardians, were required to sign a consent form agreeing that the students would submit to urinalysis if chosen on a random basis.

The testing procedure was to work this way. The student selected is accompanied by a school official of the same sex to the bathroom, provided with an empty specimen bottle, and allowed to enter the lavatory and close the door to produce a sample. The monitor stands outside the door and checks the temperature of the sample by hand to assure its genuineness.

The sample is marked with the student's school number (no names are used with the samples) and sent to a private laboratory for evaluation. If it tests positive, it is sent to a second laboratory and put through a more expensive and more accurate test. If it still tests positive, the student and parent are notified and asked to supply any evidence that might provide an innocent explanation for the result (for example, evidence that the student was taking a prescription drug).

If there is no satisfactory explanation, the student is suspended from participation in a portion of the varsity competitions held during the athletic season. A first offense results in suspension from 30% of the remaining contests; a second offense, in suspension from 50% of the remaining games; and a third offense, in a complete suspension from sports for the year. Students who violate the policy are also referred to a drug education course. No other penalties are imposed.

After learning of the drug-testing program at an organizational meeting, two female swimmers decided not to go out for the team. They then brought a lawsuit in federal court claiming that the school's program violated their rights.

PROBLEM 34

a. Why did the school decide to implement the drug-testing program?

b. What legal issue is involved in this case?

c. What arguments could the student athletes make in attacking the school's policy?

d. What arguments could the school make in defense of its policy?

e. Is the school's policy reasonable or unreasonable? Consider the policy, along with policies 2, 3, and 4 below, in terms of their reasonableness. Place the number of each policy on the accompanying continuum where you believe it belongs. What makes some of the policies more reasonable than others?

1. Student athletes are tested for drugs as described in this problem.
2. In a school where there has been some violence, metal detectors are installed at all outside doors. All students and staff members must pass through the detectors each day to enter the school.
3. A large urban school system institutes a policy of random drug testing of all high-school students.
4. A large urban school system only tests a student for drugs when there is a reasonable suspicion that the student is using drugs.

reasonable ———————————————— unreasonable

INTERROGATIONS AND CONFESSIONS

No person . . . shall be compelled in any criminal case to be a witness against himself, nor be deprived of life, liberty, or property, without due process of law.

—Fifth Amendment to the U.S. Constitution

In all criminal prosecutions, the accused shall . . . have the Assistance of Counsel for his defence.

—Sixth Amendment to the U.S. Constitution

Should a suspect ever answer police questions without an attorney present?

After an arrest is made, it is standard police practice to question, or **interrogate**, the accused. These interrogations often result in confessions or admissions, which are later used as evidence at trial.

Balanced against the police's need to question suspects are the constitutional rights of people accused of a crime. The Fifth Amendment to the U.S. Constitution provides citizens with a privilege against **self-incrimination**. This means that a suspect has a right to remain silent and cannot be forced to testify against himself or herself. Under the Sixth Amendment, a person accused of a crime has the right to the assistance of an attorney.

For many years, the Supreme Court has held that a confession is not admissible as evidence if it is not voluntary and trustworthy. This means that using physical force, torture, threats, or other techniques that could force an innocent person to confess is prohibited. In a more recent development, in the case of *Escobedo v. Illinois*, the Supreme Court has said that even a voluntary confession is inadmissible as evidence if it is obtained after the defendant's request to talk with an attorney has been denied.

Although some defendants might ask for an attorney, others might not be aware of or understand their right to remain silent or their right to have a lawyer present during questioning. In 1966, the Supreme Court was presented with such a situation in the case of *Miranda v. Arizona*.

In its decision, the Supreme Court ruled that Miranda's confession could not be used at trial, because officers had obtained it without informing Miranda of his constitutional rights. As a result of this case, police are now required to inform people accused of a crime of the so-called Miranda rights *before questioning begins*.

Suspects sometimes complain that they were not read their Miranda rights and that the entire case should therefore be dropped and charges dismissed. Failure to give Miranda warnings, however, does not affect the validity of an arrest. The police have to give Mi-

Miranda v. Arizona

Ernesto Miranda was accused of kidnapping and raping an 18-year-old girl near Phoenix, Arizona. The girl claimed she was on her way home from work when a man grabbed her, threw her into the back seat of a car, and raped her. Ten days later, Miranda was arrested, placed in a lineup, and identified by the girl as her attacker. The police then took Miranda into an interrogation room and questioned him for two hours. At the end of the two hours, the officers emerged with a written and signed confession. This confession was used as evidence at trial, and Miranda was found guilty.

Miranda later appealed his case to the U.S. Supreme Court, arguing that he had not been told of his right to remain silent or of his right to counsel. Miranda did not suggest that his confession was false or brought about by coercion but rather that he would not have confessed if he had been advised of these rights.

PROBLEM 35

a. What happened in the Miranda case? On what grounds did Miranda appeal his conviction?

b. Do you think Miranda's confession should have been used as evidence against him at trial? Why or why not?

c. Do you think police should be required to tell suspects their rights before questioning them?

d. Do you think suspects would confess after being warned of their rights?

e. Do you think people who are deaf, are mentally retarded, or speak a language other than English should be able to waive their rights and make a confession that can later be used against them? If so, under what circumstances?

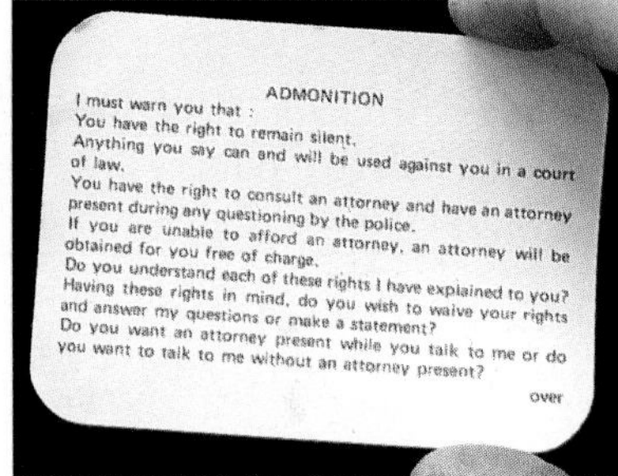

Does reading the Miranda warnings printed on this card adequately inform a defendant who cannot speak English?

What is the practice regarding Miranda warnings in your area? How do the police provide warnings to people who are deaf, are mentally retarded, or speak a language other than English?

randa warnings only if they want to use statements from the accused at the trial. In fact, in his second trial, even though the court could not use his confession as evidence against him, Miranda was convicted based on other evidence.

The *Miranda* case has been controversial. It illustrates the delicate balance between the protection guaranteed to the accused and the protection from crime provided to society. This balance is constantly changing, and the effect of the *Miranda* case has been somewhat altered by more recent cases. In one case, the Supreme Court created a "public safety" exception to the Miranda rule. In this case, a police officer who was arresting a rape suspect in a grocery store asked the suspect where his gun was before advising him of his rights. The suspect then pointed to a nearby grocery counter, where the gun was found. The Court held that police may ask questions related to public safety before advising suspects of their rights.

FOCUS ON THE LAW

The Criminal Justice System and the Americans with Disabilities Act

The Americans with Disabilities Act (ADA), a civil rights act dealing with discrimination against individuals with disabilities, became law in July 1990. Title II of the ADA prohibits discrimination on the basis of disability in state and local government services. The ADA requires that state and local government entities, such as police departments and courts, provide an accommodation to individuals with disabilities. An accommodation may be an auxiliary aid or a service, such as a qualified interpreter, a transcription service, or a videotext display. Individuals with disabilities involved in the criminal justice system may include defendants, jurors, witnesses, and others.

PROCEEDINGS BEFORE TRIAL

Before a criminal case reaches the courtroom, several preliminary proceedings take place. Most of these proceedings are standard for every case and may result in the charges' being dropped or in a plea of guilty by the defendant.

Booking and Initial Appearance

After an arrest, the accused is normally taken to a police station for booking. **Booking** is the formal process of making a police record of the arrest. At this time, the accused is asked for information including name, address, date of birth, place of work, and information

What is happening to the defendant during each of these pretrial proceedings?

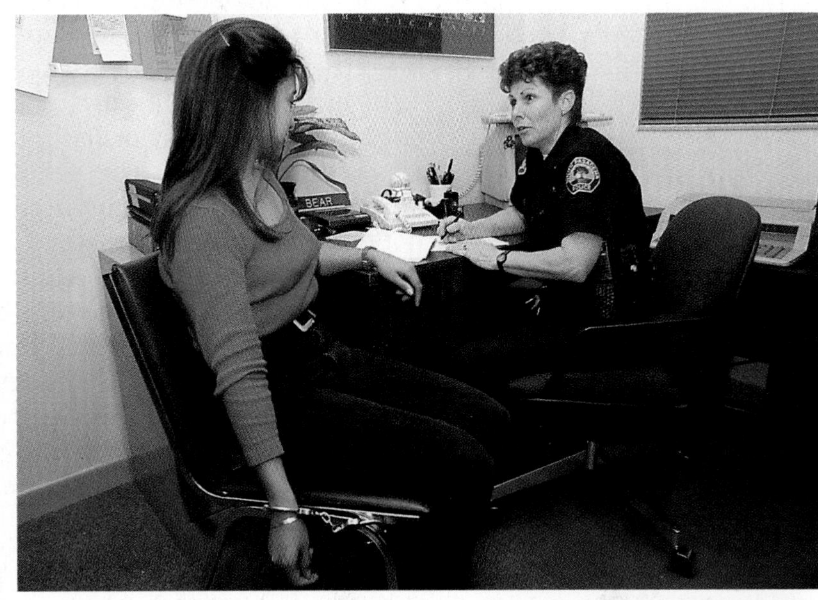

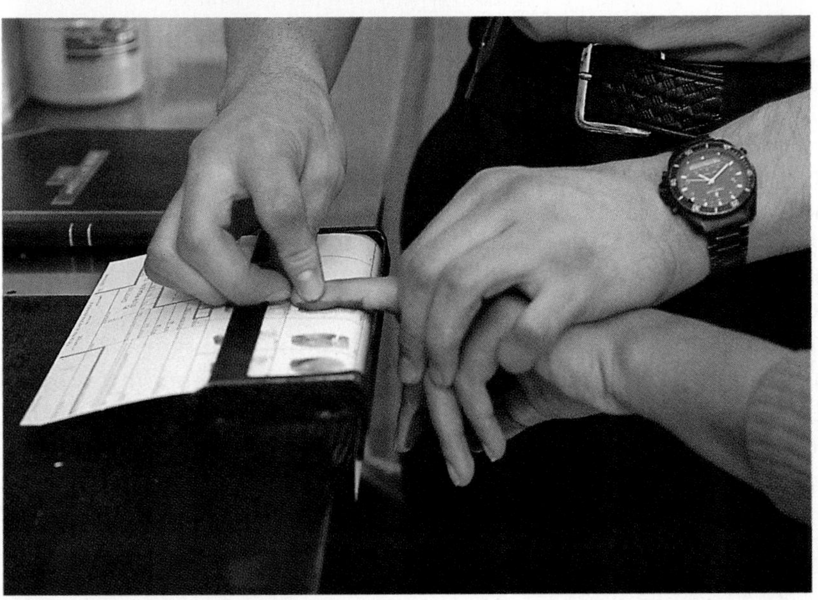

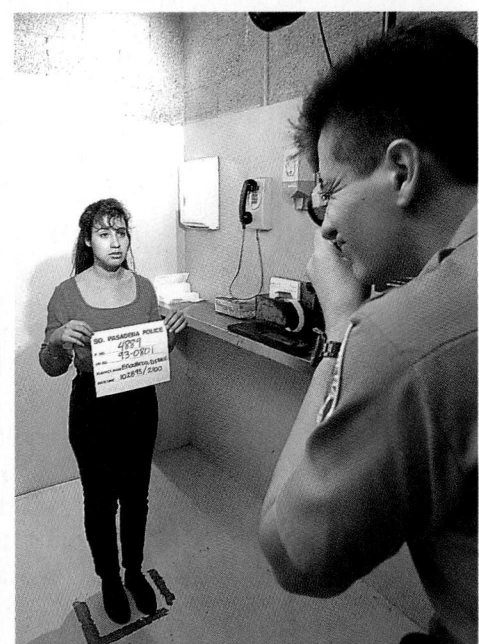

about any previous arrests. Following this, the accused is usually fingerprinted and photographed. In certain circumstances, the police are allowed to take fingernail clippings, handwriting specimens, or blood samples. Required urine tests to ascertain drug use have also become quite common. In some places, these tests show evidence of drugs in the bodies of many of those arrested.

Within a limited period of time following the arrest and booking, the accused must appear before a judicial officer (a judge or magistrate). At this initial appearance, the judge explains the defendant's rights and advises him or her of the exact nature of the charges. The defendant has an attorney appointed for him or her or is given the opportunity to obtain one. The judge may also set bail.

In a misdemeanor case, the defendant is asked at this time to enter a plea of guilty or not guilty. In a felony case, the procedure is somewhat different. The defendant is informed of the charges and advised of his or her rights, as in a misdemeanor case, but a plea is not entered until a later stage in the criminal process, known as the felony **arraignment**. In addition, the defendant is told that he or she is entitled to a preliminary hearing to determine if there is probable cause to believe that a crime was committed and that the defendant committed it. (The arraignment and the preliminary hearing are discussed later in this chapter.)

The most important part of the initial appearance is deciding whether the defendant will be released from custody and, if so, under what conditions.

Bail and Pretrial Release

An arrested person can usually be released after putting up an amount of money known as **bail**. The purpose of bail is to assure the court that the defendant will return for trial. The constitutional right to bail has been recognized in all but the most serious cases, such as murder.

How does the bail system work in your locality? How difficult is it for a defendant to remain free before trial in your area?

Bail may be paid directly to the court. The entire amount may be required; or in some places, the defendant may be released after paying a portion of the total amount (for example, 10 percent). If a person released on bail fails to return, the court will keep the money. If the defendant doesn't have the money, a bonding company may put up a bail bond in exchange for a fee. For example, a defendant with a bond of $2,000 might be released after paying $200 (10 percent of the total) to the bonding company. If a bond is posted, the bonding company will be required to pay the amount of the bond to the court if they can't produce the defendant.

The Eighth Amendment to the U.S. Constitution states that "excessive bail shall not be required." However, a poor person unable to

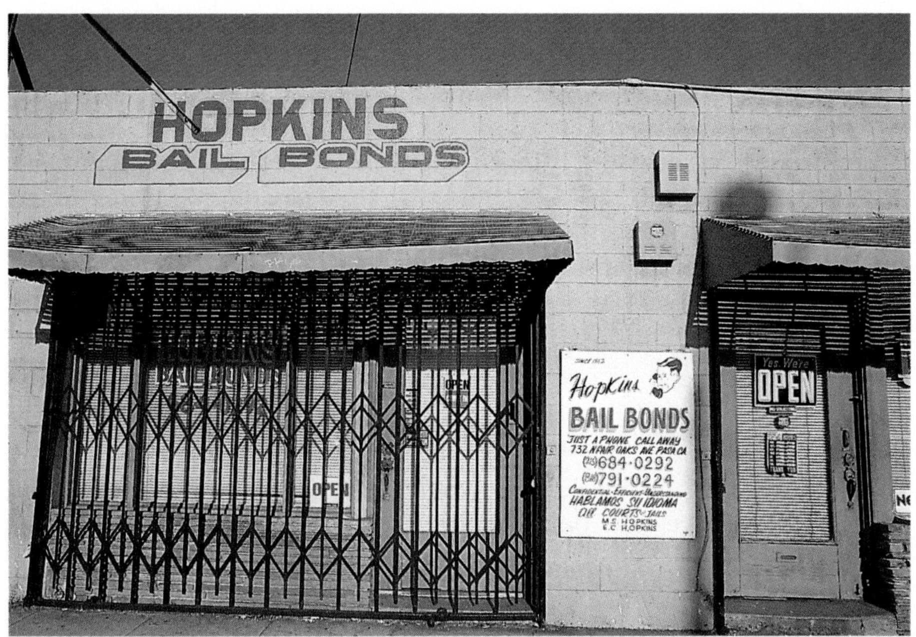

In some places, bail bonding companies have gone out of business. Why might this be?

raise any money could be detained in jail before trial and without conviction. Many people consider this unfair; and in recent years, courts have started programs to release defendants without requiring any money.

To be eligible for release on **personal recognizance**, or personal bond, the defendant must promise to return and must be considered a good risk to show up for trial. In determining the likelihood of the defendant's return, judges consider factors such as the nature and circumstances of the offense and the accused's family and community ties, financial resources, employment background, and prior criminal record.

In addition to personal recognizance programs, courts may set a variety of nonmonetary conditions designed to ensure the return of the defendant. These conditions include placing the defendant in the custody of a third party or requiring the defendant to maintain or get a job, to reside at a certain address, or to report his or her whereabouts on a regular basis.

Despite the advantages of these programs, releasing defendants may involve problems. Statistics indicate that a large number of defendants commit crimes while out on bail. As a result, some people argue that it should be made more difficult to get out on bail. In 1984, Congress passed the *Bail Reform Act*, which can prevent someone from being freed on bail if he or she is charged with a federal felony offense and believed to be dangerous. In order for this to occur, there must be a hearing, and the person being denied bail must have been charged with a violent crime or a drug offense. In addition, the individual must already have been convicted of a felony more than once. While the U.S. Supreme Court has upheld this act as constitutional, most states have not adopted similar legislation.

Supporters of pretrial release say that it prevents punishment prior to conviction and gives defendants the freedom to help prepare their cases. Supporters also claim that our system rests on the presumption that defendants are innocent until proven guilty and that setting high bail or holding a person in jail before trial goes against that presumption.

PROBLEM 36

a. What is the purpose of the constitutional right not to be subjected to excessive bail? Should it apply to all people who are arrested?

b. Can you think of any circumstances in which a person should not have any bail requirements set?

c. Can you think of any circumstances under which a person should not be released on bail of any kind?

d. Does our bail system need reform? If so, how?

YOU BE THE JUDGE

Bail Hearing

The following five people have been arrested and charged with a variety of crimes. In each case, decide whether the person should be released and, if so, under what conditions. Choose from one of the following options and discuss your decision: (1) bail (release after a certain amount of money is paid; set an amount), (2) personal recognizance (release with no money required), (3) conditional release (release under certain conditions; set the conditions), and (4) pretrial detention (no release).

Case 1

Name: Marta Garcia. **Age:** 26.
Charge: Possession of crack cocaine.
Residence: 619 30th Street, lives alone, no family or references.

Employment: Unemployed.
Education: 11th grade.
Criminal record: As a juvenile had five arrests, mostly misdemeanors. As an adult had two arrests for petty larceny and a conviction for possession of dangerous drugs (probation was successfully completed).
Comment: Defendant arrested while leaving a train station carrying a suitcase containing a large quantity of crack cocaine. Urine test indicates defendant presently using narcotics.

Case 2

Name: Gloria Hardy. **Age:** 23.
Charge: Prostitution.
Residence: 130 Riverside Drive, Apt. 10.
Employment: Works for call-girl service; reportedly earns $1,500 per week.
Education: Completed high school.
Criminal record: Five arrests for prostitution, two convictions. Currently on probation.
Comment: Vice detective alleges defendant is involved in prostitution catering to wealthy clients.

Case 3

Name: Stanley A. Wexler. **Age:** 42.
Charge: Possession and sale of crack cocaine.
Residence: 3814 Sunset Drive, lives with wife and two children.
Employment: Self-employed owner of a drugstore chain, net worth $250,000.
Education: Completed college, holds advanced degrees in pharmacology and business administration.
Criminal record: None.
Comment: Arrested at his store by undercover police after attempting to sell a large quantity of crack cocaine. Alleged to be a big-time dealer. No indication of drug usage.

Case 4

Name: Michael D. McKenna. **Age:** 19.
Charge: Assault.
Residence: 412 Pine Street.
Employment: Waiter, Vanguard Restaurant; earns $200 per week.
Education: 10th grade.
Criminal record: Six juvenile arrests (possession of marijuana, illegal possession of firearms, and four burglaries); convicted of firearms charge and two burglaries; spent two years in juvenile facility.
Comment: Arrested after being identified as assailant in a street fight. Alleged leader of a street gang. Police consider him danger-

ous. No indication of drug usage. Lives on his own, and his parents are in prison.

Case 5

Name: Chow Yang. **Age:** 34.
Charge: Possession of stolen mail and forgery.
Residence: 5361 Texas Street, lives with common-law wife and two children by a prior marriage.
Employment: Works 30 hours per week at a service station, earns minimum wage.
Education: Quit school after eighth grade; no vocational skills.
Criminal record: Nine arrests—mostly vagrancy and drunk and disorderly conduct. Two convictions: (1) driving while intoxicated (fined and lost license) and (2) forgery (completed two years' probation).
Comment: Arrested attempting to cash a stolen social security check. Probation officer indicates defendant has a drinking problem.

Preliminary Hearing

A **preliminary hearing** is a screening device. It is used in felony cases to determine if there is enough evidence to require the defendant to stand trial. At a preliminary hearing, the prosecutor is required to establish that a crime probably has been committed and that the defendant probably did it.

In most states, the defendant has the right to be represented by an attorney, to cross-examine prosecution witnesses, and to call favorable witnesses. If the judge finds no probable cause to believe that a crime was committed or that the defendant committed it, the case may be dismissed. However, dismissal of a case at the preliminary hearing does not always mean that the case is over. This is because the prosecution may still submit the case to a grand jury.

Grand Jury

A **grand jury** is a group of 16 to 23 people charged with determining whether there is sufficient cause to believe that a person has committed a crime and should be made to stand trial. The Fifth Amendment to the U.S. Constitution requires that before anyone can be tried for a serious crime in federal court, there must be a grand jury **indictment**.

To secure an indictment, a prosecutor will present evidence designed to convince members of the grand jury that a crime has been committed and that there is probable cause to believe the defendant committed it. Neither the defendant nor his or her attorney has a right to appear before a grand jury. Also, the prosecutor is not required to present all the evidence or call all the witnesses as long as the grand jury is satisfied that the evidence presented amounts to, at least, probable cause.

The U.S. Constitution only requires grand jury indictments in the federal courts. However, many states also use a grand jury indictment process. Other states bring defendants to trial following a preliminary hearing or based on a prosecutor's **information**. This is a formal accusation filed with the court by the prosecutor that details the nature and circumstances of the charge.

Felony Arraignment and Pleas

After an indictment is issued, the defendant will be required to appear in court and enter a plea. If the defendant pleads guilty, the judge will set a date for sentencing. If the defendant pleads not guilty, the judge will set a date for trial and ask the defendant if he or she wants a jury trial or a trial before a judge alone.

Nolo contendere is a plea by the defendant that does not admit guilt but also does not contest the charges. It is equivalent to pleading guilty. The only advantage of this plea to the defendant is that it cannot be used as evidence in a later civil trial for damages based on the same set of facts.

Pretrial Motions

An important preliminary proceeding is the **pretrial motion**. A motion is a formal request that a court make a ruling or take some other action. Prior to trial, a defendant may file motions seeking to have the case dismissed or to obtain some advantage or assistance in preparing the case. Common pretrial motions include motion for discovery of evidence, which is a request by the defendant to examine, before trial, certain evidence in the possession of the prosecutor; motion for a continuance, which seeks more time to prepare the case; and motion for change of venue, which is a request to change the location of the trial to avoid community hostility, for the convenience of witnesses, or for other reasons. Perhaps the most important and controversial pretrial motion is the motion to suppress evidence, which will be discussed next.

The Exclusionary Rule

The Fourth Amendment protects citizens against "unreasonable searches and seizures" by the government. But it doesn't say what happens if the police violate the amendment. To put teeth into the amendment, the U.S. Supreme Court adopted the exclusionary rule. This rule holds that any evidence illegally seized by law enforcement officials cannot be used to convict the accused at trial. It also applies to evidence obtained from illegal questioning of the accused.

The rule is used by criminal defense lawyers when they file a **motion to suppress evidence**. This motion asks the court to exclude any evidence that was illegally obtained. If the judge agrees that the evidence was obtained in violation of the accused's constitutional rights, it will be suppressed. This does not mean the evidence is returned to the defendant. For example, if the police illegally seize contraband, such as marijuana, it cannot be used at trial, but it does not have to be given back to the defendant.

The exclusionary rule has been used in federal courts since 1914. However, the rule was not extended to state courts until the 1961 case of *Mapp v. Ohio*. This famous case made the exclusionary rule binding on the states. Over the years since the *Mapp* decision, the courts have modified and reevaluated the exclusionary rule, but the basic rule remains.

The exclusionary rule does not prevent the arrest or trial of a suspect. However, in some cases, it does mean that guilty people may go free. This is because when an important piece of evidence is excluded from the trial, the case is often dismissed or the defendant is acquitted.

The exclusionary rule is very controversial. Many people claim that it is a legal loophole that allows dangerous criminals to go free. They also point out that many other countries have no such rule; instead, those countries punish the police for violating citizens' rights.

Does a school principal need a warrant to search a student's locker? Explain.

Others say the rule is necessary to safeguard our rights and to prevent police misconduct. The two major arguments in support of the rule are *judicial integrity* and *deterrence*. Judicial integrity is the idea that courts should not be parties to lawbreaking by the police. Deterrence means that police will be less likely to violate a citizen's rights if they know illegally seized evidence will be thrown out of court.

As a practical matter, police are sometimes more concerned with arrests than with convictions. They frequently make arrests to seize contraband, gather information, or disrupt criminal activity. Even when they are seeking a conviction, they sometimes make mistakes.

In 1985, criticism of the rule led to the adoption of a so-called "good faith exception." In the case of *United States v. Leon*, the Supreme Court held that the "exclusionary rule should not apply to bar evidence obtained by police acting in reasonable reliance on a search warrant, issued by a detached and neutral magistrate, that is later found to be invalid."

PROBLEM 37

a. What is the exclusionary rule? How does it work?

b. Why do you think the Supreme Court adopted the exclusionary rule? What are some arguments in favor of the rule? Against the rule? Do you favor or oppose the rule? Explain your answer.

c. What is the good faith exception to the exclusionary rule? What are some arguments in favor of the good faith exception? Should it be extended to warrantless searches?

THE CASE OF . . .

The Purse Search

Ms. Chen, a high school teacher, found two students holding lit cigarettes. Since smoking violated school rules, Chen took the girls to the principal's office. When the principal asked the girls whether they had been smoking, one student, T.L.O., denied it and claimed that she did not smoke.

The principal then asked for her purse, which she handed to him. When he opened it, he saw cigarettes and a pack of rolling papers. T.L.O. denied that these belonged to her. However, on the basis of experience, the principal knew that rolling papers often indicated marijuana. When he looked further into the purse, the principal found marijuana, drug paraphernalia, $40 in $1 bills, and written documentation of T.L.O.'s sales of marijuana to other students.

PROBLEM 38

a. Should the exclusionary rule apply to searches by school officials of students in high school? Why or why not?

b. How much evidence should a school official have before searching a student's purse or locker? Should probable cause or reasonable suspicion be required?

c. Do you believe that the principal had the right to open T.L.O.'s purse? Could the marijuana and drug paraphernalia be used against her in court?

d. Should high school students have more rights, fewer rights, or the same rights as adults in the community? Explain your answer.

YOU BE THE JUDGE

Police Conduct

In each of the following situations, decide whether the police conduct was reasonable or unreasonable. Then decide whether the evidence obtained could be used at the trial of the accused. Be prepared to explain your answers.

1. Police officers see two masked men flee from a jewelry store in an unidentified dark-colored van. The officers approach the store and find the owner shot dead and his store ransacked. There are no witnesses. Several hours later, in a neighboring town, other police alerted to the crime see two men in a dark-colored van. They stop the van and question the occupants. Their answers are unhelpful. With only their intuition to rely on, the police search the van and find the stolen merchandise, the murder weapon, and the masks. Arrested, confronted with the evidence, and told their rights, the suspects confess to robbery and murder.
2. Jail guards routinely conduct body cavity searches of pretrial detainees to deter visitors from smuggling drugs or other contraband to inmates. A rectal search of defendant Odom reveals a quantity of illegal pills.
3. Williams is suspected of kidnapping and murdering a 10-year-old girl. Soon after the girl's disappearance, witnesses see Williams carrying a large bundle with two feet sticking out of it. Williams is later arrested and advised of his Miranda rights. He then talks with an attorney, who advises him to keep quiet. He tells the police that he will not discuss the case until he sees his attorney. Later, during a ride to a jail in another city, one of the officers, knowing the girl's body has not been found, remarks, "I wish we could stop and locate the body because this little girl's parents are entitled to give her a Christian burial." After apparently thinking this over, Williams says, "Turn around. I'll show you where the body is."
4. Dorothy Jackson summoned police officers to her house to report that her daughter, Gail Fischer, had been beaten up by Edward Rodriguez, with whom she had been living. Police asked Fischer if Rodriguez dealt in narcotics. Although she did not answer that question, she did agree to let them into his apartment so they could arrest him for battery. Once in the apartment, the police saw drug paraphernalia and cocaine in plain view. They arrested him in his bedroom, where he had been sleeping, and also discovered two attaché cases full of cocaine.

Fischer had vacated the apartment about a month before the incident. Her name was not on the lease, she paid no rent, and most of her possessions had been removed. However, she continued to possess a key.

5. Two persons robbed a pizza parlor. One of them was wearing a red running suit. The day of the robbery, police obtained arrest warrants for Buie and his suspected accomplice. Buie's house was then placed under police surveillance. Two days later, seven officers executed the warrant.

Once inside the house, the officers fanned out through the first and second floors. Officer Rozen went to the basement door, ordering anyone down there to come out. A few seconds later, Buie emerged with his hands up. Once he was handcuffed, another officer went into the basement to conduct a "protective sweep" in the event that anyone else was down there. While in the basement, this officer saw the red running suit in plain view and seized it.

6. As part of the war on drugs, Broward County (Florida) police routinely boarded interstate buses at scheduled stops and asked persons for permission to search their bags for drugs. Two officers boarded a bus on which Bostick was a passenger and, without any reason to believe that he was carrying drugs, asked him for his ticket and some form of identification. He had been sleeping near the back of the bus before they began questioning him. One officer carried a zipper pouch with a pistol, but it was never drawn during the questioning. Both officers were in uniform.

Bostick's ticket matched his identification, and both items were immediately returned to him. Police then asked him if they could search his luggage for drugs, telling him that he had a right to refuse to cooperate. He gave his permission. In the search, they found cocaine, and Bostick was arrested.

7. The Michigan State Police Department established a highway sobriety checkpoint program with guidelines regulating operation, site selection, and publicity. The day before the operation began, two licensed Michigan drivers filed suit against the state police, asking that the checkpoint system be ordered stopped as a violation of the Fourth Amendment.

The program operated at one location for just over an hour. Nineteen police officers were involved. During the operation, 126 cars passed through the checkpoint, drivers were detained an average of 25 seconds, and two DUI arrests were made. All cars passing through the checkpoint were stopped and briefly detained. Where there was evidence of drinking, cars were pulled off the road for a lengthier detention.

Plea Bargaining

Contrary to popular belief, most criminal cases never go to trial. Rather, most defendants who are convicted plead guilty before trial. In minor cases, such as traffic violations, the procedure for pleading guilty is simple. The defendant signs a form waiving the right to appear and mails the court a check for the amount of the fine. In major cases, guilty pleas result from a process of negotiation among the accused, the defense attorney, and the prosecutor. This process is known as **plea bargaining**. It involves granting certain concessions to the defendant in exchange for a plea of guilty. Typically, the prosecution will allow the defendant to plead guilty to a less serious charge or recommend a lighter sentence on the original charge if a guilty plea is entered. When accepting a guilty plea, the judge must decide if the plea was made freely, voluntarily, and with knowledge of all the facts. Thus, once a defendant pleads guilty, withdrawing the guilty plea is very difficult.

Plea bargaining allows the government to avoid the time and expense of a public trial. It may also benefit the defendant, who often receives a lighter sentence than if the case had resulted in a conviction at trial. Plea bargaining is controversial, however. Critics charge that plea bargaining allows dangerous criminals to get off with light sentences. Others, more concerned with the plight of the defendant, argue that the government should be forced to prove guilt beyond a reasonable doubt at trial. They say that the plea-bargaining system is unfair to the accused, particularly if the prosecution has a weak case.

Do your local courts use plea bargaining? Are there proposals to change the system? Are changes needed?

Some places have abolished or limited plea bargaining. Without plea bargaining, some argue that the criminal justice system will be overwhelmed by the increase in cases coming to trial. Others say that eliminating plea bargaining will provide greater justice because the government will drop (not prosecute) weak cases and defendants will still plead guilty when the government's case is very strong.

PROBLEM 39

a. Should plea bargaining be allowed? Do you think plea bargaining offers greater advantages to the prosecutor or to the defendant? Explain your answer.

b. Marty, who is 22 years old, is arrested and charged with burglarizing a warehouse. He has a criminal record, including a previous conviction for shoplifting and two arrests for auto theft. The prosecution has evidence placing him at the scene of the crime. The defense attorney tells Marty that the prosecution will reduce the charge to petty larceny in exchange for a guilty plea. If you were Marty, would you plead guilty to the lesser charge? Why or why not?

c. Suppose Marty pleads guilty after being promised probation by the prosecutor, but instead he receives a long prison term. Is there anything he can do about this?

d. Do you think anyone accused of a crime would plead guilty if he or she were really innocent? Explain your answer.

Plea Bargaining: United States and Germany

In the United States, most criminal cases—in some places, 90–95%—never go to trial. This is because they are plea bargained. In plea bargaining, the defendant admits guilt and the prosecutor, in return, drops certain charges, reduces them in seriousness, or recommends a lesser sentence to the judge. Many criticize this system as unfair, saying that it forces people to plead guilty and penalizes those who choose to exercise their right to a jury trial. Others maintain that plea bargaining allows accused criminals to get off with reduced sentences.

Germany and most other countries do not allow U.S.-style plea bargaining. In Germany's non-adversarial legal system, the judge controls the investigation and conducts most questioning of witnesses at trial. German trials are simpler and quicker than American trials; attorneys are less aggressive and there is no jury. In Germany, even if the defendant admits guilt, the trial goes forward and proof must be provided that the defendant committed the crime as charged. A study indicated that 41% of defendants made full confessions during trial and another 26% made partial confessions. Furthermore, it appears that the defendant's cooperation is a factor that sometimes results in a lesser sentence.

Defenders of U.S.-style plea bargaining claim that the system is necessary because of the enormous numbers of crimes committed and the large number of criminals arrested in the United States. They also say that, although trials using juries are much more time consuming, they provide those accused of crimes with more rights than they might receive elsewhere. Finally, supporters of plea bargaining say that having a trial after a person pleads guilty is unnecessary because the judge, when accepting the guilty plea, is required to question the defendant to be sure facts exist that support the defendant's guilt.

PROBLEM 40

a. What is plea bargaining? Why do you think it is used so much in the U.S.?

b. What are some of the principle differences between the U.S. and the German criminal justice systems? How do you account for these differences?

c. Does Germany allow plea bargaining or anything like it? What characteristics of the German system might explain why it does not have plea bargaining?

d. Which do you think is better, the American or the German criminal justice system? What are the advantages and disadvantages of each?

PROBLEM 41

Study Figure 2.7, then answer the following questions.

a. In what year were the fewest people convicted and sentenced?

b. In what year were the fewest people imprisoned? Fined?

c. Why do you think the number of defendants increased so dramatically in the 1990s?

THE TRIAL

In all criminal prosecutions, the accused shall enjoy the right to a speedy and public trial, by an impartial jury of the State and district wherein the crime shall have been committed, which district shall

Figure 2.7 Criminal Cases Handled in Federal Trial Courts

Year	Total Defendants	Total Not Convicted	Total Convicted and Sentenced	Total Imprisoned[a]	Probation	Fine	Other
1950	38,835	4,210	34,625	14,998	16,603	3,024	0
1960	31,984	3,828	28,156	14,170	11,081	2,905	0
1970	36,356	8,178	28,178	12,415	11,387	1,935	2,441
1980	36,560	7,962	28,598	13,191	11,053	3,916	438
1990	56,519	9,794	46,725	27,796	14,196	4,176	557

[a] Includes sentences of more than six months that are to be followed by a term of probation (mixed sentences).

Source: *Sourcebook of Criminal Justice Statistics,* 1991.

have been previously ascertained by law, and to be informed of the nature and cause of the accusation; to be confronted with the witnesses against him; to have compulsory process for obtaining witnesses in his favor, and to have the Assistance of Counsel for his defence.

—Sixth Amendment to the U.S. Constitution

Due process of law means little to the average citizen unless and until he or she is arrested and charged with a crime. This is because many of the basic rights set out in the U.S. Constitution apply to people accused of crime. Accused people are entitled to have a jury trial, in public and without undue delay, to be informed of their rights and of the charges against them, to confront and cross-examine witnesses, to refuse to testify against themselves, and to be represented by an attorney. These rights are the essence of due process of law. Taken together, they make up the overall right to a fair trial.

Right to Trial by Jury

The right to a jury trial is guaranteed by the Sixth Amendment to the U.S. Constitution. It is applicable in both federal and state courts. However, a jury is not required in every case. In fact, juries are not used very much. Most criminal cases are resolved by guilty

Should jurors be allowed to take notes during a trial? Give arguments in favor of and against this practice.

pleas before ever reaching trial. Jury trials are not required for certain minor offenses—generally, those punishable by less than six months in prison. Furthermore, defendants can **waive** (give up) their right to a jury trial; in some states, waivers may occur in the majority of cases.

Jury panels are selected from voter registration or tax lists and are supposed to be generally representative of the community. In federal courts, juries consist of 12 persons, who must reach a unanimous verdict before finding a person guilty. While many states do use 12-person juries, they are not required to do this by the Constitution. The U.S. Supreme Court has only required at least six jurors. Similarly, most states require unanimous verdicts in criminal cases, but the U.S. Supreme Court, in interpreting the Constitution, has not required unanimous verdicts.

PROBLEM 42

a. Why is the right to a jury trial guaranteed by the Bill of Rights? Why would someone choose not to have a jury trial?

b. Do you think jury verdicts should be unanimous? Why or why not?

The U.S. Supreme Court has ruled in a number of recent cases that attorneys may not exclude or try to exclude jurors from juries solely because of their race. This ruling applied in one case when an attorney tried to exclude white jurors and in another when an attorney tried to exclude African-American jurors.

Rodney King

Rodney King, a 250-pound African-American male, was stopped by the police for speeding and driving an automobile while under the influence of alcohol. Four white Los Angeles police officers tried to subdue him with a stun gun and then beat him repeatedly with billy clubs.

The officers were charged with the crime of assault. Because of media publicity in Los Angeles, the first trial was moved to a state court in a primarily white suburb. At trial, the police officers argued that they had only used the force needed to get King under control so they could arrest him. King argued that they had used excessive force against him. A videotape of the incident had been made and became an important element of the state's case against the police officers. The trial was held before a jury that did not include any African Americans, who found the police officers not guilty.

Many people protested the verdict. Some marched and demonstrated. Others rioted, burning and looting stores, throwing rocks at cars, and pulling white drivers from automobiles and beating them. Federal government prosecutors, questioning whether there had been a fair trial, decided to bring a new case in federal court charging the officers with violating King's civil rights. The second trial took place in Los Angeles before a jury made up of people of different races. In this second trial, two of the four police officers were found guilty.

According to the law, what amount of force should the police have been able to use when arresting Rodney King?

PROBLEM 43

a. In the first trial, do you think it was a violation of King's right to due process for the case to be tried before a jury that did not include any African Americans? Can a person of one race ever receive a fair trial before a jury made up entirely of people of another race?

b. What if the lawyers defending the police officers at the first trial purposely excluded African-American jurors, believing such jurors would be more sympathetic to King? Would this have been a violation of King's rights? Which rights? Should a defense attorney be able to limit the number of African Americans on the jury in a case in which a white person has assaulted an African American?

c. Do you think the federal government did the best thing in bringing the case again in federal court? Why or why not? Do you think the federal government's prosecutors were influenced by the first jury verdict, the protests, and/or the riots? Should they have been?

d. Do you think the second jury was affected by the riots? Should it have been?

Right to a Speedy and Public Trial

The Sixth Amendment to the U.S. Constitution provides a right to a speedy trial in all criminal cases. The Constitution does not define *speedy*, and courts have had trouble deciding what this term means. To remedy this problem, the federal government and some states have set specific time limits within which a case must be brought to trial.

If a person does not receive a speedy trial, the case may be dismissed. However, defendants often waive the speedy-trial requirement. They may do this because of the unavailability or illness of an important witness or because they need more time to prepare their cases. Before dismissing a case, courts will consider the cause and reasons for the delay and whether the defendant was free or in jail during the pretrial period.

PROBLEM 44

a. Why is the right to a speedy trial important? How soon after arrest should a person be brought to trial? What are some reasons for and against bringing a defendant to trial within a short time after arrest?

b. Do you think that televising criminal trials is a good idea? Why or why not?

Right to Confront Witnesses

The Sixth Amendment provides people accused of a crime with the right to confront (face-to-face) the witnesses against them and to ask them questions by way of cross-examination. Although a defendant has the right to be present in the courtroom during all stages of the trial, the U.S. Supreme Court has said that this right may be restricted if the defendant becomes disorderly or disruptive. In such instances, judges have the power to remove the defendant from the courtroom, to cite him or her for **contempt of court**, or, in extreme circumstances, to have the defendant bound and gagged.

The right to confrontation is sometimes modified for child witnesses, especially in abuse cases. Many courts in these cases install closed-circuit television cameras, thus enabling the child to testify through the camera in a room separate from the one the defendant is in.

PROBLEM 45

a. What are the arguments for and against closed-circuit television in child-abuse cases?

b. Should it be allowed in cases involving rape or any other violent crime?

Freedom from Self-Incrimination

Freedom from self-incrimination means that you cannot be forced to testify against yourself in a criminal trial. This right comes from the Fifth Amendment and can be exercised in all criminal cases. In addition, the prosecutor is forbidden to make any statement drawing the jury's attention to the defendant's failure to testify.

Although a defendant has a right not to testify, this right can be waived. Moreover, a defendant who takes the witness stand in his or her own criminal trial must answer all questions.

Related to the right against self-incrimination is the concept of **immunity**. Immunity laws force a witness to answer all questions—even those that are incriminating. If granted immunity, however, a witness is not prosecuted based on information provided in the testimony. Prosecutors often use these laws to force people to testify against codefendants or others involved in the crime.

PROBLEM 46

a. Suppose you are a defense attorney. What would be the advantages and disadvantages of having a criminal defendant testify at trial?

b. If you were a member of the jury in a criminal trial, what would you think if the defendant failed to testify? Would you be affected by the judge's instruction not to draw any conclusion from the defendant's failure to testify?

c. If a defendant is forced to stand in a lineup, give a handwriting sample, or take an alcohol breath or urine test, does this violate the privilege against self-incrimination?

Right to an Attorney

The Sixth Amendment provides that "In all criminal prosecutions, the accused shall enjoy the right to . . . have the Assistance of Counsel for his defence." At one time, this meant that, except in capital cases, a defendant had the right to an attorney only if he or she could afford one. However, in 1938, the Supreme Court required the federal courts to appoint attorneys for indigent defendants in all federal felony cases. Twenty-five years later, in the case of *Gideon v. Wainwright*, the Supreme Court extended the right to counsel to *all* felony defendants, whether in state or federal court. In 1972, the Supreme

In what ways can an attorney help a defendant prepare for trial?

Court further extended this ruling by requiring that no imprisonment may occur, even in misdemeanor cases, unless the accused is given an opportunity to be represented by an attorney.

As a result of these decisions, criminal defendants who cannot afford an attorney are appointed one by the government free of charge. These attorneys may be either public defenders or private attorneys.

Prosecutors in recent years have begun to use federal racketeering laws called *Racketeer Influenced and Corrupt Organizations* (RICO) statutes to seize the assets (such as bank accounts, cars, and houses) of defendants who they believe possess the "fruit of illegal activity." Critics protest that seizing accused persons' assets not only does away with the presumption of innocence but also may make it difficult for the accused persons to hire lawyers.

PROBLEM 47

a. Do you think court-appointed attorneys are as good as those who are privately paid? Why or why not?

b. Assume a defendant wants to handle his or her own defense. Should this be allowed? Do you think this is a good idea?

c. Assume a lawyer knows that his or her client is guilty. Is it right for the lawyer to try to convince the jury that the person is not guilty? Why or why not?

d. Do you think it is a violation of the Fifth or Sixth Amendment for the government to use the RICO statutes to seize defendants' funds and possessions before they are convicted of a crime? Why or why not?

SENTENCING

The final phase of the criminal justice process begins with the sentence. Once found guilty, the defendant will be sentenced by the judge or, in a few states, by the jury. The sentence is perhaps the most critical decision in the criminal justice process. It can determine a defendant's fate for years or, in some cases, for life.

Most criminal statutes set out a basic sentencing structure, but judges generally have considerable freedom with respect to the actual sentence, including the type, length, and conditions of the sentence. Depending on the state, judges may choose from one or a combination of the following options:

- **Suspended sentence.** The sentence is given but does not have to be served at the time it is imposed. However, the defendant may have to serve the time later if he or she is rearrested on another charge or violates a condition of probation.
- **Probation.** The defendant is released to the supervision of a probation officer after agreeing to follow certain conditions, such as getting a job, avoiding drugs, and not traveling outside of the area.
- **Home confinement.** The defendant is sentenced to serve the term at home. Normally, the only time that this defendant can leave his or her home is for essential purposes such as work, school, or a doctor's appointment. The defendant's activities are sometimes electronically monitored by a probation officer.
- **Fine.** The defendant must pay the government an amount of money set by the court.
- **Restitution.** The defendant is required to pay back or make up for whatever loss or injury was caused to the victim of the crime.
- **Work release.** The defendant is allowed to work in the community but is required to return to prison at night or on weekends.
- **Imprisonment.** The defendant is sentenced to a term in jail or prison. Some states require that a *definite* sentence be given, in which case the judge specifies the exact amount of time to be served (for example, 2 years). Some states provide for an *indeterminate* term, in which case the sentence is stated not as a specific number of years but as a minimum and maximum term (for example, not less than 3 years nor more than 10 years). Some judges allow defendants in misdemeanor cases to serve short jail sentences on weekends.

Many factors go into the sentencing decision. These include the judge's theory of corrections and what he or she thinks is in the best interest of society and the individual. In addition, most states authorize a **presentence report**. This report is prepared by the probation department. It contains a description of the offense and the circumstances surrounding it. The report also sets out the defendant's past criminal record, data on the defendant's social, medical, educational, and employment background, and a recommendation as to sentence. After studying the report and listening to recommendations from the defense attorney and the prosecutor, the judge will impose sentence.

Many people criticize the system of sentencing because it gives too much discretion to the court. Two people who commit the same crime may receive very different sentences.

In 1988, Congress passed federal sentencing guidelines that listed more specifically the sentences judges should impose for specific crimes. These guidelines included mandatory sentences without the opportunity for parole. Critics of the guidelines state that it is a mistake to take away judges' discretion because many outside factors, such as poverty, lack of education, and drug addiction, contribute to criminal behavior. They believe judges should be able to take these factors into consideration when deciding a defendant's sentence. The U.S. Supreme Court has upheld the guidelines as constitutional.

Over the years, the criminal sentence has served a number of different purposes, including retribution, deterrence, rehabilitation, and incapacitation.

At one time, the primary reason for punishing a criminal was **retribution**. This was the idea of "an eye for an eye and a tooth for a tooth." Instead of individuals' seeking revenge, society takes on the role of punishing those who violate its laws.

Can job training programs rehabilitate prison inmates?

Another reason for sentencing criminals is **deterrence**. Many people believe that punishment will discourage the offender from committing another crime in the future. In addition, the punishment will serve as an example to deter other people from committing crimes.

A third goal of sentencing is **rehabilitation**. Rehabilitation means helping convicted persons change their behavior so that they can lead useful and productive lives after release. Rehabilitation is based on the idea that criminals can be helped to overcome the social, educational, or psychological problems that caused them to commit a crime and that they can be helped to become responsible members of society. Educational, vocational, and counselling programs in prisons and jails are supposed to rehabilitate inmates.

PROBLEM 48

Study Figure 2.8, then answer the following questions.

a. For what crime did no individual receive probation?

b. For what crime did fewer than half of the individuals receive imprisonment?

A fourth reason for sentencing is **incapacitation**. This means that the criminal will be physically separated from the community and the community will thus be protected. While locked up in prison, the offender will not pose a threat to the safety of the community.

In most states, the actual length of time a person serves in prison depends on whether **parole** is granted. Parole is the release of a con-

Figure 2.8 Sentences Imposed under the U.S. Sentencing Commission's Guidelines (1991)

	Total Cases	Total Receiving Imprisonment	Total Receiving Probation	Other
Total	32,747	25,036	7,604	107
Murder	27	27	0	0
Manslaughter	59	52	7	0
Assault	291	239	52	0
Robbery	1,357	1,352	5	0
Arson	72	62	10	0
Drug Trafficking	13,365	12,621	740	4
Simple Possession of Drugs	901	459	432	10
Burglary	99	91	8	0
Auto Theft	155	113	42	0
Larceny	2,392	957	1,398	37

Source: *Sourcebook of Criminal Justice Statistics,* 1991.

victed person from prison before his or her entire sentence has been served. Depending on the state, a person might become eligible for parole after serving a minimum sentence specified by the judge or law. In other states, people become eligible after serving a portion of the total sentence (for example, one-third). Eligibility for parole is not a right but, rather, a privilege. Inmates may go before a parole board that makes the decision. Some inmates are never paroled and serve their full sentences in prison. The federal system and some states do not even have a system of parole, and critics of parole say this is better, because it gives certainty to the sentence. Others believe inmates should be evaluated as to whether they have been rehabilitated and released early if there is evidence they have changed.

Does your community have any prisons, jails, or halfway houses? Who is kept there? What are living conditions like in these institutions? What rights do the inmates have?

The Murdered Wife

Marsha was severely beaten by her husband many times during their marriage. She finally reported it to the police, and he was convicted and sentenced to five years in prison. He vowed to kill her when he got out. She was not notified when he was released on parole after 20 months. He murdered her two months later.

PROBLEM 49

a. Should Marsha have been told when her husband was eligible for parole? Should she have been given input into the decision? Should all crime victims have such input?

b. Are the government and the legal system responsible for Marsha's death? Give arguments on both sides.

c. In what way, if any, should the system be changed to prevent future tragedies like this from occurring?

Legislative Hearing: Mandatory Minimum Sentences

You have been asked to present testimony to your legislative committee on criminal justice. The committee is reviewing a proposed state law that would require mandatory minimum sentences for drug offenses. This law, if enacted, would limit the choices that judges currently have in sentencing convicted persons. In some circumstances, the law would require them to send convicted criminals to prison for definite periods of time.

The hearing that follows will provide an opportunity for two spokespersons to give information about the law to the committee. After each statement, the legislators may address questions to the person testifying.

Jocelyn (for): "We want all drug traffic stopped. Now! Drug dealers must be taken off our streets so they will stop ruining our neighborhoods and our children's lives. With the use of mandatory minimum sentences, drug dealers will go to prison and will *stay* in prison until their sentences are finished.

"Drug use is rampant. In 1992, nearly one million drug-use and drug-related crimes were brought in the nation's courts. The 1992 statistics also show that drug-related crimes committed by young people increased about 15% over 1991.

"It is necessary that judges no longer have discretion to pick and choose the sentences for drug dealers, giving lighter sentences to drug dealers from well-off families and stiffer sentences to drug dealers from poor families. If mandatory minimum sentences are used, *everyone* involved with drugs—from possessing to selling to manufacturing—will be sent to prison.

"Mandatory minimum sentences must be utilized until we have won the war on drugs and our streets and schools are safe again and free of drugs."

Livia (against): "Our prisons are overcrowded! In 1992, the prison population hit a new high of over 880,000. Most of the people in federal prisons today are there for drug offenses.

"We must concentrate our efforts on the *violent* offenders. It is the violent offender that must be kept off the streets for a long time. It is unfair for a first-time drug offender to be in prison longer than some murderers. Violent offenders are being released from prison to make room for drug offenders who have been given a specific sentence that must be served in prison.

"A judge must be able to take into consideration individual factors, such as the defendant's attitude, employment background, family history, and education, when sentencing a convicted person. It doesn't make sense that all the judge can consider is the weight of the drugs the person possessed.

"We must not allow the use of mandatory minimum sentences when we can use probation, community service, and education to reduce the number of drug offenders sentenced to overcrowded prisons."

Role-play these presentations to the committee. Which argument do you think is stronger? Why? What additional arguments would you add for each presentation? Why? Are mandatory minimum sentences fair? Explain.

CORRECTIONS

When a person is convicted of a crime, state and federal governments have the right to punish the offender. The system of corrections includes the entire range of treatment and punishment options available to the government. These include community corrections, halfway houses, jails, and prisons.

Life Behind Bars

An inmate's life is controlled by many rules. Inmates are told when to get up and when to go to sleep. Mail is screened. Access to

Should inmates lose all rights once they are sent to prison? If not, which rights should they keep?

radio, television, and books is controlled. Visitors are limited, and inmates are subject to constant surveillance and searches. Some inmates work at prison jobs, which pay almost nothing; others spend all day locked in their cells.

Until the 1960s, courts had a hands-off policy toward prisons. Inmates had few, if any, rights. Prison officials could make almost any rules they wanted. As a result, harsh treatment, solitary confinement, and beatings were all fairly common.

Today, courts have established and enforced many prisoners' rights. The U.S. Supreme Court has said that people who enter prison must give up many of their rights. However, the Court has set out certain rights that inmates retain even after entering prison. These include the right to be free from cruel and unusual punishment, the right to freedom of religion, the right to due process, the right to medical treatment if ill, and the right of access to law libraries and the courts.

Prison Overcrowding

In recent years, the number of people in American jails and prisons has risen considerably. At the beginning of 1992, there were over 880,000 adults in the nation's jails and prisons. This total was a 7.2% increase from 1991. Consequently, jail and prison overcrowding is a problem all across America. Federal, state, and local governments continue to be faced with the need to find funds to expand old facilities or build new ones.

The major reason for the booming prison population is a get-tough attitude toward crime. Legislatures and courts are acting to ensure that more criminals are sentenced to longer terms. In recent years, most states have passed mandatory sentencing laws. At the same time, many states have doubled or tripled the length of minimum prison sentences. The crackdown on drunk driving and tougher bail and parole laws are other reasons for overcrowding. See Figure 2.9.

The growing prison population has created many problems. Overcrowding sparks fights and riots. Drug use, sexual assault, and violence are all common occurrences. Life behind bars is often dangerous and unpleasant. Many prisoners live in tiny cells under uncomfortable conditions.

PROBLEM 50

Study Figure 2.9, then answer the following questions.

a. For what type of crime did the state prison population increase the most from 1986 to 1991?

b. For what type of crime did the state prison population decrease the most from 1986 to 1991?

c. Why do you think this happened?

Many state prisons and local jails are now under court order to alleviate overcrowding and improve conditions. Courts and prison officials are constantly being asked to balance the rights of prisoners against the need to maintain security and order in prison.

Controversy continues as to whether anything can be done to deal with the overcrowding problem besides building more prisons. Those against building more prisons point to the construction cost, which is estimated at $35,000 to $100,000 per cell, and the cost of maintaining a person in prison, which ranges from $15,000 to $50,000 per year. They claim that the many nonviolent offenders who are locked up could serve their sentences in the community or be released earlier. Others say that stern actions must be taken to punish offenders, get criminals off the streets, and reduce crime.

In recent years, the overcrowding problems have led some states to contract with other states or the federal government to send their prisoners elsewhere. Others have looked to private corporations to

Figure 2.9 State Prison Populations, 1986 vs. 1991

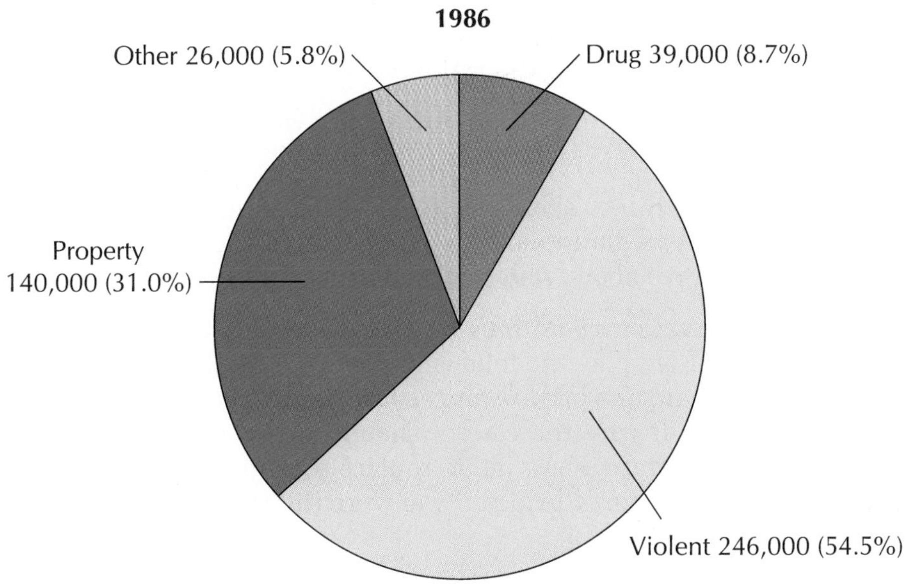

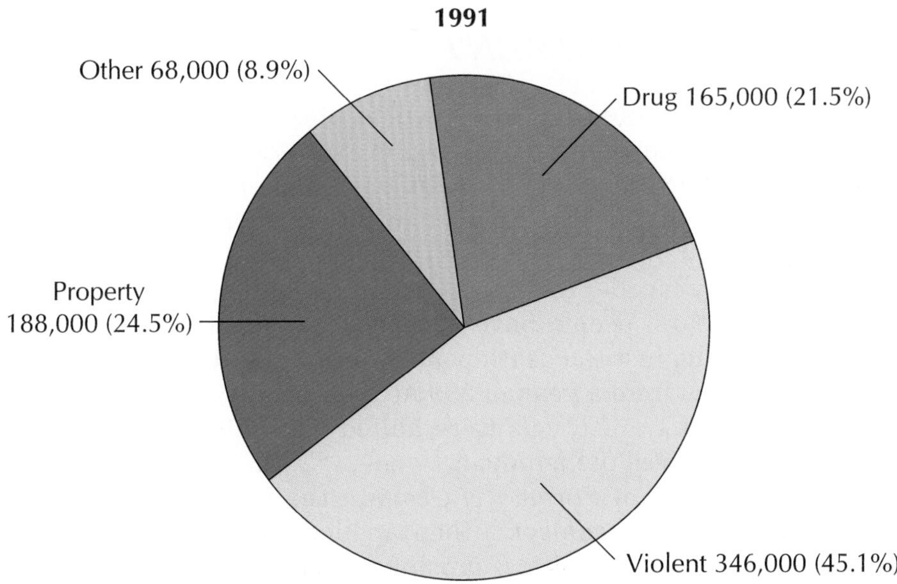

Source: *The State of Criminal Justice: An Annual Report* (American Bar Association), February, 1993.

run their prisons for them, claiming that private prisons can save millions of dollars and lead to better and more efficiently run institutions. Critics worry that private corporations may violate inmates' rights more often, lobby for longer sentences, and be less concerned about rehabilitation.

PROBLEM 51

a. Should prisoners have rights? If so, what rights should they have? Make a list of these rights.

b. If you were a prison warden, what rules would you make to control the prisoners? List these rules.

c. What, if anything, should be done to reduce prison overcrowding? Should we build more and bigger prisons, or should we be more selective about who is locked up?

d. Should private corporations be allowed to run jails and prisons for profit? Role-play the following scenario: As the head of a corporation that runs private homes for the elderly, you explain to a county sheriff why the county should hire your corporation to build and operate a new jail to replace the old, overcrowded one. Would you support the idea if you were the sheriff? Explain.

CAPITAL PUNISHMENT

Does your state have capital punishment?

Capital punishment, also known as the death penalty, has a long history in America. The first person executed for murder among settlers in America was hanged in 1630. In colonial years, the death penalty was imposed for a number of different crimes. Gradually, however, capital punishment was restricted to the most serious crimes—usually murder and rape.

For many years, people have argued about capital punishment. Public protest against the death penalty gradually reduced the number of executions from a peak of 199 in 1935 to only one in 1967. For the next 10 years, executions were halted while the courts studied the legality of capital punishment.

In the 1972 case of *Furman v. Georgia*, the U.S. Supreme Court held that the death penalty as then applied was unconstitutional. States rewrote their capital punishment laws; and in 1976, the Court ruled that the new laws were constitutional as long as certain factors were considered in sentencing. Executions soon resumed. In 1992, 27 executions were carried out; and 2,729 inmates were on death row in 1993.

As of 1992, 36 states had death penalty statutes. To carry out the death penalty, 21 states use lethal injection, 13 states use electrocution, 6 states use lethal gas, 3 states use hanging, and 2 states use firing squads. Some states use more than one method. State-by-state information is presented in Appendix D.

FYI

Prisons and Jails: What's the Difference?

- Prisons are operated by federal or state governments. They are used to incarcerate people convicted of more serious crimes, usually felonies for which the sentence is more than one year.
- The nearly 700 U.S. prisons range in size from small, well-designed facilities to huge, maximum security penitentiaries sprawling over thousands of acres.
- Some U.S. prisons are so big that they resemble small cities. For example, both Louisiana's State Prison at Angola and Michigan's State Penitentiary at Jackson contain over 4,000 inmates and thousands of employees.
- Jails, on the other hand, are operated by cities and counties. They are used to detain people awaiting trial and to hold mental patients, drug addicts, alcoholics, juvenile offenders, and felons on a temporary basis as they await transfer to other facilities. Jails also hold people convicted of minor crimes for which the sentence is a year or less.
- The 3,400 U.S. jails vary in size from big-city facilities holding over 1,000 inmates a day to small rural jails consisting of an office and a few cells.

The United States is the only country in the world to use electrocution, gas, and lethal injection for carrying out the death penalty. Other countries use hanging, shooting, beheading, and stoning. As of 1989, 35 countries had abolished the death penalty, while 100 countries retained its use.

Most capital punishment laws call for two trials, one to decide guilt or innocence and another to set the sentence. They spell out guidelines for determining whether death or life imprisonment is appropriate. Judges and juries are required to consider both aggravating and mitigating circumstances. **Aggravating circumstances** are those factors that tend to make the crime worse, such as a particularly gruesome murder or previous convictions of the accused. **Mitigating circumstances** are those factors that tend to make the crime less severe. Examples could include a history showing that the victim had previously abused the defendant or the defendant's having no prior criminal record.

Does capital punishment deter crime?

The controversy over capital punishment continues. It involves legal, political, and moral issues. Is the death penalty constitutional? If so, for what crimes? Is it a moral punishment for murder? Does it deter crime? Is it applied fairly?

Opponents of capital punishment say that no one who values life can approve the death penalty. They argue that "thou shalt not kill" also applies to those who carry out the death penalty. They say the death penalty does not deter murder. To support this idea, they cite statistics showing that murder rates are the same in states with the death penalty as in those without it. Opponents also argue that the death penalty is applied in an unfair manner, that members of minority groups are more likely to receive it, and that it violates the Eighth Amendment's ban against "cruel and unusual punishment." They even present evidence that some people who were sentenced to death were later found innocent.

Advocates of the death penalty say that killers get what they deserve. They argue that the threat of death does deter crime. They concede that studies on deterrence are inconclusive, but they maintain that people fear nothing more than death. Advocates also point to opinion polls showing that most Americans favor capital punishment. They argue that execution protects society and saves the government money. Finally, they say the death penalty is fairly applied and that the Supreme Court has upheld this view.

PROBLEM 52

a. Do you favor or oppose the use of the death penalty? Explain your answer. If you favor it, to what crimes should it apply?

b. If you oppose the death penalty, what do you think is the strongest argument in favor of it? If you favor the death penalty, what do you think is the strongest argument against it?

The 15-Year-Old Murderer

William Wayne Thompson was found by an Oklahoma jury to have actively participated at the age of 15 in the brutal murder of his former brother-in-law, Charles Keane. There was evidence that Keane had in the past physically abused Thompson and his sister. Thompson and three others kidnapped Keane, beat him, kicked him, cut his throat and chest, shot him in the head, and dumped his body into the river. Photographs of the body were described by the court as "ghastly."

It was determined at a hearing that Thompson, who had been arrested previously for a number of serious assaults, had "no reasonable prospects for rehabilitation within the juvenile justice system." He was then tried as an adult and convicted. The law of Oklahoma did not specify that any minimum age was required before the death penalty could be ordered, and the judge followed the jury's recommendation and ordered the death penalty for Thompson. The sentence was appealed and upheld by Oklahoma's Supreme Court. Thompson's appeal ended up before the U.S. Supreme Court.

PROBLEM 53

a. Are you for or against capital punishment as a possible penalty for those under the age of 16 who commit murder? Write down the two strongest reasons in support of your position. What are the two strongest arguments on the other side?

b. If you were on the U.S. Supreme Court, would you find the imposition of the death penalty on William Wayne Thompson to be "cruel and unusual punishment"? Give reasons for your position.

c. Suppose a mentally retarded person with the IQ of a 7-year-old commits a murder. Would it be cruel and unusual to sentence this person to death? Why or why not?

d. Should some persons convicted of operating a drug ring with many employees who distribute and sell drugs to a large number of people be eligible to receive the death penalty? How about sentencing them to life without parole? Explain your answers.

Race as a Factor in Imposing the Death Penalty

George McDonald, an African-American male, was committing a robbery in a furniture store in Georgia. During the course of the robbery, a silent alarm went off, leading a white police officer, Mike Luster, to the scene of the crime. McDonald fired two shots, killing the officer.

McDonald was found guilty of two counts of armed robbery and one count of murder. The prosecutor in the case asked the jury for the death penalty. The jury, which included 11 whites and 1 African-American, unanimously agreed to sentence McDonald to death for Officer Luster's murder.

McDonald argued on appeal to the U.S. Supreme Court that capital punishment was administered in a discriminatory fashion against African Americans in Georgia. He cited a study showing that in homicide cases involving African-American defendants and white victims, African Americans received the death penalty 21.9 percent of the time. White defendants with African-American victims received the death penalty only 3.1 percent of the time. The study also showed that while 60 percent of homicide victims in Georgia were African-American, more than 84 percent of the total death sentences handed out involved African-American defendants and white victims.

PROBLEM 54

a. What arguments do you think McDonald's attorney might make to try to stop the execution? What arguments could the state of Georgia make in response?

b. If you were a justice on the U.S. Supreme Court, how would you rule?

c. Should steps be taken to try to ensure that African Americans are not given harsher sentences than whites for the same crime? If so, what should be done?

JUVENILE JUSTICE

In the United States, juveniles involved with the law are treated differently from adults. However, this has not always been the case. In earlier times, children were thrown into jails with adults. Long prison terms and **corporal punishment** (involving striking the juvenile's body) were common. Some children were even sentenced to death for some crimes that seem relatively minor by today's standards.

In the mid-19th century, reformers began to argue that the failure of the family was the cause of delinquent behavior. In other words, parents had failed to teach their children proper values and respect for authority. The solution that evolved was for a separate juvenile court to assume the responsibility that had been the parents' job. Instead of punishing young people through the adult system, a separate juvenile court would seek to rehabilitate them by taking a moralistic approach and trying to help them learn community values.

Under this philosophy, the first juvenile court was set up in Cook County, Illinois, in 1899. Juvenile courts were designed to be informal, allowing the court to act as a parent or guardian for the child. The right of the state to intervene in the life of a child is based on the concept of ***parens patriae*** (a Latin term meaning "parent of the country"). The hearings were closed to the public, the youth's identity would remain private, and the juvenile court would use terms different from those used in the adult court.

Today, juvenile courts generally handle three groups of juveniles: delinquent offenders, status offenders, and neglected and abused children. **Delinquent offenders** are youths who have committed acts that would be crimes if committed by adults under federal, state, or local law. **Status offenders** are youths who have committed acts that would not be crimes if committed by adults. Status offenses include running away from home, skipping school, refusing to obey parents, or engaging in certain behaviors such as underage consumption of alcohol. Status offenders are considered unruly or beyond the control of their parents or legal guardians; they are persons or children in need of court supervision (PINS or CHINS).

Neglected or abused children are seeking the court's protection from a parent or guardian. A neglect case occurs when the parent or guardian is charged with failing to provide adequate food, clothing, or shelter for the child. An abuse case occurs when a child has been sexually or physically abused. In either case, a judge must decide whether the child needs the protection of the court. The next step is to determine whether the child should remain with the family while under court protection. The judge has several options to choose from and works closely with social services agencies. Such an agency can provide a range of services, including foster care, counseling, and treatment. The judge will usually set certain conditions for the child's remaining with his or her family, such as participation by the parents in a counseling program or a later hearing to monitor the progress of the case.

Some people believe parents should be held responsible for crimes committed by their children. Those in favor of these **parental responsibility laws** believe they are particularly appropriate in cases in which parents know or should know that their children are using or selling drugs or belong to juvenile gangs. In some states, parents may also be charged with **contributing to the delinquency of a minor**.

Since 1899, the history of the juvenile justice system has continued to be defined in part by the tension between a "humanitarian" philosophy (rehabilitate the offender) and a "control" philosophy (punish the offender). This tension has played a major role in determining the system's practices.

PROBLEM 55

a. Why did reformers want to change the way children were treated?

b. What is *parens patriae*? Do you agree with this idea?

c. What is the difference between a status offender and a delinquent offender?

d. Do you think the treatment of young persons should be a balance between "humanitarian" and "control" philosophies? Why or why not?

e. Are you in favor of or opposed to parental responsibility laws? Explain. If you believe parents should be held criminally responsible, give three examples of situations in which this should apply.

Who Is a Juvenile?

Before the establishment of juvenile courts, children under the age of 7 were never held responsible for criminal acts. The law considered them incapable of forming the necessary criminal intent. The law at that time also assumed that children between the ages of 7 and 14 were incapable of committing a criminal act. However, this belief could be disproved if it was shown that the child knew that the act was a crime or that it would cause harm to another and committed it anyway. Children over the age of 14 could be charged with a crime and handled in the same manner as an adult.

Today, all states set age limits to determine whether a person accused of a crime will be handled in adult or juvenile court. In most states, young people are considered juveniles until age 18. However, some states set the limit at 16 or 17.

In most states, a juvenile charged with a *serious* felony such as robbery, assault, rape, or murder can be tried as an adult. Some states have laws automatically transferring a youth to adult court under certain conditions. Other states allow the prosecutor to make the decision, while some states require a judge to hold a hearing before a youth may be transferred. At the transfer, or waiver, hearing, a judge usually considers: (1) the juvenile's age and past record, (2) the seriousness of the crime, and (3) the likelihood that the juvenile may be rehabilitated before the **age of majority**. As a result of a "get-tough" attitude involving juvenile crime, many states have revised their juvenile codes to make it easier to transfer juveniles to adult court. These revisions include lowering the eligible age, making waiver automatic in certain cases, and making the criteria easier to satisfy. Often gang members involved in violent crime are transferred to adult court.

Does your state have a waiver law for transfer of juveniles to the adult system? At what age may a juvenile be tried as an adult? Who makes the decision? What factors must be considered?

PROBLEM 56

In each of the following situations, decide whether the person should be tried as a juvenile or transferred to criminal court and tried as an adult. Explain the reasons for your decisions and what factors you considered.

a. Eric, age 15, is accused or robbing an 86-year-old woman at gunpoint. He has a long juvenile record, including acts of burglary, and brags about the robbery.

b. Marcia, age 17, is accused of killing a pedestrian while driving a stolen car. She has never been in trouble before, is remorseful about the killing, and claims that she planned to return the car after a short joyride.

c. José, age 14, is accused of selling drugs for his older brother. According to the police, one day a customer stole the money José had collected for his older brother. The police claim that José then stabbed the customer with a knife. He has been arrested twice before, but the charges were dropped.

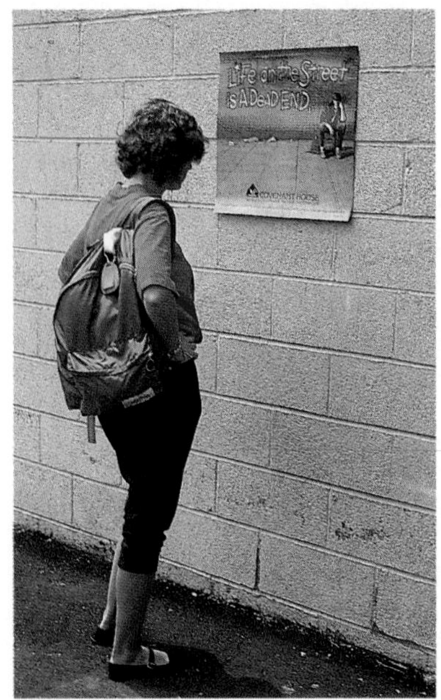

What resources are available in your community to help runaways?

When a juvenile court is confronted with a status offender, special problems arise. As mentioned, juveniles who fall into this category are charged with being "beyond control" or "habitually disobedient" or with truancy from school or other acts that would not be crimes if committed by an adult.

Status offenders may be emotionally troubled juveniles who need help. Many status offenders are runaways or young people with drinking and drug problems. Some are trying to escape from abusive or other difficult home situations. It is estimated that over 170,000 minors run away from home each year. Over 80 percent of them are between the ages of 15 and 17. Although most runaways return home of their own accord, others are picked up by the police and referred to the juvenile court.

In recent years, a number of programs have been set up to help runaways. These include counseling centers, shelters, and a nationwide toll-free phone number that runaways can call for assistance.

As a general rule, a single act of unruly behavior is not enough to support a finding that a juvenile is in need of supervision. Rather, most states require a showing that the young person is habitually disobedient or has repeatedly run away, skipped school, or been out of control.

Because of problems at home, parents sometimes ask the court to file a PINS (person in need of supervision) petition against their own child. Children charged with status offenses may defend their conduct by showing that it was justified or that the parents were unreasonable and at fault. In such cases, the PINS petition might be withdrawn and replaced by a neglect petition against the parents.

PROBLEM 57

a. Do you think courts should interfere in disputes between parents and children? If not, why not? If so, why and under what circumstances?

b. Should attendance at school be mandatory? Why or why not? What should be done about students who are chronically absent from school?

Juvenile Justice Today

In the 1960s, many people argued that the juvenile court was providing harsher treatment than the adult system without procedural safeguards and constitutional rights that would be available in the

Gerald Gault

Gerald Gault, age 15, was taken into custody and accused of making an obscene phone call to a neighbor. At the time Gerald was taken into custody, his parents were at work, and the police did not notify them of what had happened to their son. Gerald was placed in a detention center. When his parents finally learned that he was in custody, they were told that there would be a hearing on the next day, but they were not told the nature of the complaint against him.

Mrs. Cook, the woman who had complained about the phone call, did not show up at the hearing. Instead, a police officer testified to what he had been told by Mrs. Cook. Gerald blamed the call on a friend and denied making the obscene remarks. No lawyers were present, and no record was made of what was said at the hearing.

Since juries were not allowed in juvenile court, the hearing was held before a judge, who found by a preponderance of the evidence that Gerald was delinquent and ordered him sent to a state reform school until age 21. An adult found guilty of the same crime could have been sent to county jail for no longer than 60 days.

PROBLEM 58

a. Make lists of the fair and unfair things that happened to Gerald Gault. Explain your reasoning for each item.

b. How would you change the unfair things on your list? Why is it important to change these things?

adult court. Beginning in 1966, this movement found support in the U.S. Supreme Court, and several decisions were later made that began to change the theory and operation of the juvenile justice system.

In deciding the *Gault* case, the U.S. Supreme Court held that juveniles should receive many of the same due process rights as adults. Specifically, the Court ruled that juveniles charged with delinquent acts are entitled to four rights: (1) the right to notification of the charges against them, (2) the right to an attorney, (3) the right to confront and cross-examine witnesses, and (4) the right to remain silent.

PROBLEM 59

a. What rights that adults have were not granted in the *Gault* decision?

b. Do you agree with the *Gault* decision? Why or why not? Should adults and minors have the same legal rights? Why or why not?

c. Do you think Gerald Gault's hearing would have turned out differently if he had been given the rights the Supreme Court later ruled he was entitled to?

The *Gault* decision gave young people accused of a crime many of the same rights as adults, but it also left many unanswered questions. In the case of *In re Winship* (1970), the Supreme Court decided that juveniles charged with a criminal act must be found "delinquent by proof beyond a reasonable doubt." This is the same standard required in adult court. However, in *McKeiver v. Pennsylvania* (1971), the Supreme Court decided that jury trials were not required in juvenile cases. In reaching this decision, the Supreme Court expressed concern that jury trials could hurt juveniles by destroying the privacy of juvenile hearings. More recently, a series of court decisions and legislative actions have changed the informality of juvenile court proceedings somewhat. Some courts even provide spectators and newspaper reporters with access to juvenile court proceedings. In general, however, although juveniles now possess many of the same rights as adults, the Supreme Court has made it clear that not all of the procedures used in an adult court apply in a juvenile proceeding.

The federal government has also played a major role in guiding the juvenile courts. The Juvenile Justice and Delinquency Prevention Act of 1974 required the Department of Justice to oversee changes ordered by Congress. The juvenile court would now treat both status and delinquent offenders differently. For example, status offenders would be removed from institutions, or "deinstitutionalized." Juvenile offenders remaining in institutions would be separated from incarcerated adults. In addition, the individual states would have responsibility for developing community alternatives to incarceration and improving the juvenile justice system.

PROBLEM 60

Study Figure 2.10, then answer the following questions.

a. What police disposition occurred the least?

b. What happened to 28% of the juvenile offenders?

In the 1980s, communities became concerned with both the rise in crime and a juvenile court system that was seen as being too soft on crime. The public demanded law and order and harsher penalties for adults as well as juveniles. Many proposed sending youthful offenders to military-style "boot camps." Some critics even called for abolishing the juvenile court. The government response resulted in more juveniles' being tried as adults. In addition, juvenile facilities and programs in many states became overcrowded. In the 1990s, some juvenile justice leaders recognized that the "lock-em up" philosophy

Figure 2.10 Police Dispositions of Juvenile Offenders Taken into Custody (1990)

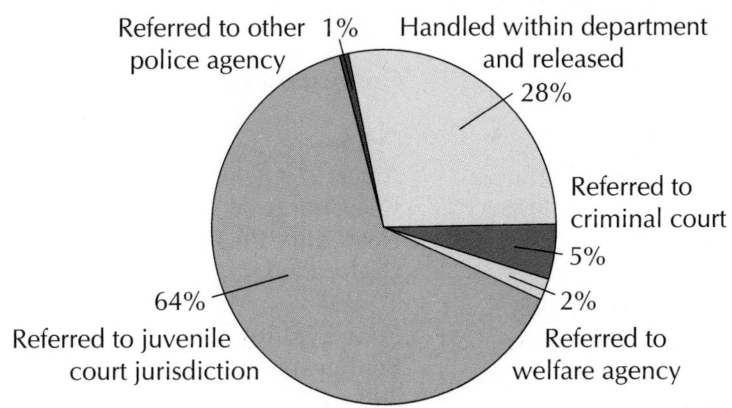

Source: *OJJDP Update on Statistics, Arrests of Youth,* 1990, January 1992.

Will strict, military-style boot camps help reform offenders?

was not working. New programs were developed that balanced community protection and individual accountability with a careful assessment of each juvenile. These programs are designed to reduce the number of young persons who return to the juvenile justice system.

Juvenile Law Terms Compared with Adult Law Terms

Juvenile Law Term	Corresponding Adult Law Term
Offense	Crime
Take into Custody	Arrest
Petition	File Charges
Denial	Not Guilty Plea
Admission	Guilty Plea
Adjudicatory Hearing	Trial
Found Delinquent	Found Guilty
Disposition	Sentencing
Detention	Jail
Aftercare	Parole

Procedures in Juvenile Court

Suppose a young person is accused of a delinquent act. What happens to this person from the time he or she is taken into custody until release from the juvenile justice system? The exact procedures vary from state to state, but the general process is similar throughout the country.

Taking into Custody On the whole, young people may be taken into custody for all the same reasons the police might arrest an adult. In addition, juveniles can be taken into custody for status offenses. These offenses include running away from home, truancy, promiscuity, disobeying one's parents, and other actions suggesting the need for court supervision.

After taking a juvenile into custody, the police have broad authority to release or detain the juvenile. If the offense is minor, the police may give the juvenile a warning, release the juvenile to his or her parents, or refer the case to a social service agency. If the offense is serious or if the young person has a prior record, the police may detain the youth and refer him or her to juvenile court.

Intake is the informal process by which court officials or social workers decide if a complaint against a juvenile should be referred to juvenile court. They usually make this decision after interviewing the youth and considering the seriousness of the offense, the past record of the accused, his or her family situation, and other factors.

It is estimated that as many as one-third of all complaints are disposed of during the intake process by dismissal, diversion, or transfer. Most of the cases are dismissed. Some youths are diverted, which means that they receive educational services (including, in some places, "street law" classes) and treatment services without going through juvenile court. In addition, the prosecutor may decide to charge some of the juveniles as adults and request a waiver hearing. (Waiver hearings were discussed on page 171.)

Initial or Detention Hearing Young people who are taken into custody and formally referred to juvenile court are entitled to an **initial hearing** on the validity of their arrest and detention. At this initial hearing, the state must generally prove two things: that an offense was committed and that there is reasonable cause to believe that the accused committed it. If the state wants to further detain the juvenile, it must prove that the juvenile is a danger to self or others, that he or she is likely to run away if released, or that his or her past record warrants detention. If the juvenile does not have an attorney, the court will usually assign one at this time and set a date for a hearing on the facts.

Figure 2.11 Juvenile Justice System

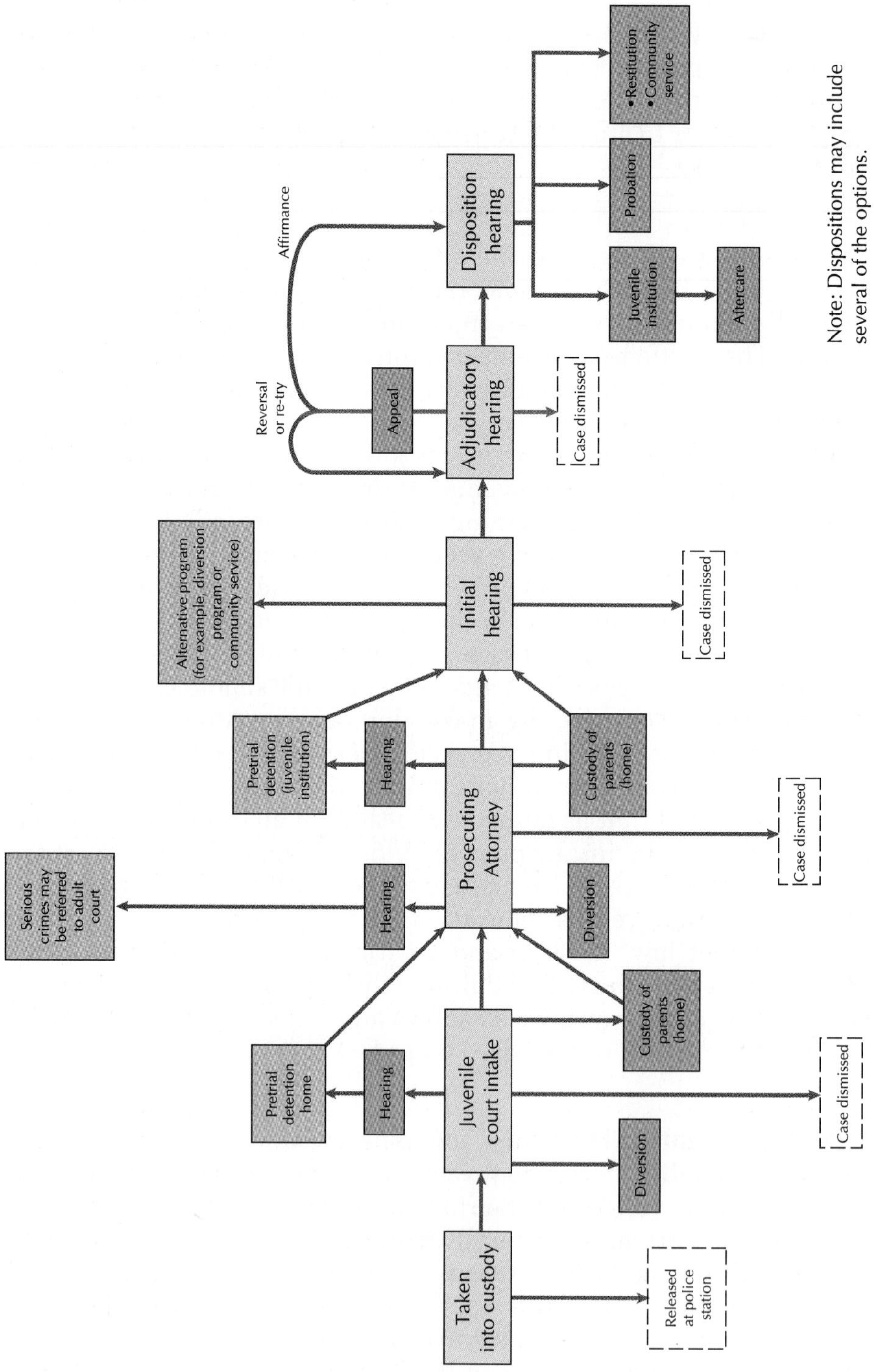

Taken into custody
Released at police station
Juvenile court intake
Diversion
Case dismissed
Hearing
Pretrial detention home
Custody of parents (home)
Prosecuting Attorney
Diversion
Case dismissed
Hearing
Serious crimes may be referred to adult court
Hearing
Pretrial detention (juvenile institution)
Custody of parents (home)
Initial hearing
Alternative program (for example, diversion program or community service)
Case dismissed
Adjudicatory hearing
Case dismissed
Appeal
Reversal or re-try
Affirmance
Disposition hearing
Juvenile institution
Aftercare
Probation
• Restitution
• Community service

Note: Dispositions may include several of the options.

The U.S. Supreme Court has held that juveniles do not have a constitutional right to bail. No money bond is set, and the juvenile court may decide either to release juveniles to their parents or other adults or to detain them before trial. The U.S. Supreme Court justified what is referred to as **preventive detention** of juveniles on the grounds that it serves the legitimate purpose of protecting the community and the juveniles themselves from the consequences of future crime. It is based on a judge's decision that a juvenile is better off in detention than in his or her own home. Federal law requires juveniles who are detained to be held separately from adults who have been accused of crime. However, this is still not the case in a number of places around the country.

PROBLEM 61

a. Should juveniles have the same right to bail as adults? Why or why not? When should they be detained?

b. Should juveniles be detained separately from adults? What if a small town only has one jail, or the juvenile detention center is full?

Adjudicatory Hearing A juvenile charged with a delinquent act is given a hearing. Generally known as an **adjudicatory hearing**, its purpose is the same as that of an adult trial—to determine the facts of the case. Generally, unlike an adult trial, a juvenile hearing is closed to the public, and the names of the accused and the details of the offense are withheld from the press. Although juveniles do not have a constitutional right to a jury trial, some states do provide for juries in juvenile cases.

At the adjudicatory hearing, the juvenile is entitled to be represented by an attorney. The attorney can offer evidence, cross-examine witnesses, and force the prosecution to prove its case beyond a reasonable doubt. If the judge finds the juvenile nondelinquent (not guilty), he or she is free to go. If the judge decides that the facts, as set out in the petition, are true, the court will enter a finding of delinquent. This is similar to a conviction in adult proceedings.

Dispositional Hearing The dispositional hearing is perhaps the most important stage in the system for juveniles who are found delinquent. At the hearing, the judge decides what sentence, or **disposition**, the juvenile offender should receive. The judge's sentence

Should judges in your community change their approach to sentencing juveniles? If so, how?

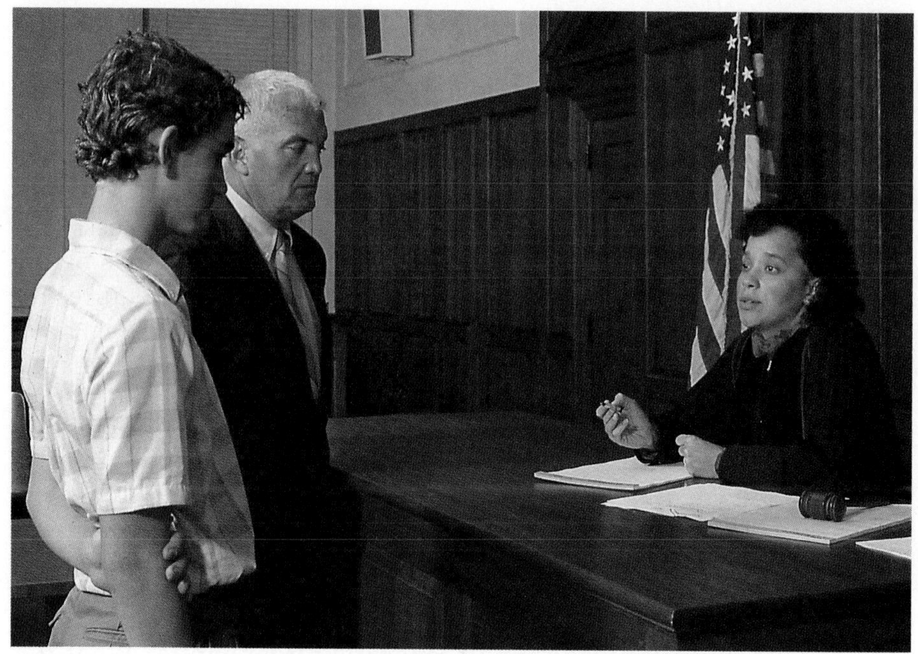

is usually based primarily on the presentence report prepared by the probation department. This report is the result of an investigation of the juvenile's social, psychological, family, and school background.

In theory, in making their disposition, courts are supposed to provide individualized treatment to rehabilitate the juvenile offender. However, in practice, courts often balance the needs of the offender against the obligation to protect the community. Alternatives usually include probation, placement in a group home or community treatment program, or commitment to a state institution for juveniles.

Probation is the most common disposition. The judge can impose a number of conditions on the juvenile on probation. For example, the juvenile might be ordered to attend school regularly, hold a steady job, attend counseling sessions at a treatment center, take weekly drug tests, be home by 8:00 P.M., or stay away from certain people. A juvenile on probation usually has to meet with a probation officer on a regular basis. If the conditions of probation are not met, the youth can be sent back to court for another hearing. At this time, the judge can decide to send the juvenile to a group home or a state institution.

For serious offenses, the juvenile can be committed to a juvenile institution. Most courts have the power to place a juvenile in such an institution for an indeterminate length of time. This means that no matter what the offense, the juvenile offender can be locked up for the maximum period allowed by state law. This generally varies from one to three years. In certain cases, it lasts until the young person reaches the age of majority, and it can continue in some states

What behaviors of juvenile offenders do you think therapy sessions can correct?

until the age of 21. Most juveniles, however, do not serve the maximum sentence. The exact time of release is usually up to the agency that operates the institution.

Although the stated goal of the juvenile correctional institution is rehabilitation, many corrections officials say this is seldom achieved. One of the main problems is overcrowding in juvenile facilities. Up to one-half of the nation's juvenile facilities have more residents than they were designed to hold. In addition, the overrepresentation of minorities has been increasing. Some critics claim that this results from discrimination. They say that more whites than minorities seem to be placed by juvenile courts in private programs to meet their special needs, while more minorities are placed in juvenile facilities. Other concerns include the safety and security of the facilities, due process, and health care. The courts have also seen an increase in claims of abuse of children in training schools and detention centers.

Where are juvenile offenders placed in your state and community? What is the maximum length of time for which a juvenile can be committed to a juvenile institution? What happens to status offenders in your community?

Some juvenile justice reformers call for a new philosophy in which violent offenders would be housed in small facilities where many services would be offered. Most other offenders, especially status offenders, would be placed in well-structured community-based programs. Some states have moved in this direction, and supporters say it works. Some critics counter that the approach won't work and call for tougher measures. Today, many practitioners seek a balanced approach to juvenile corrections and consider the individual in light of community protection, offender accountability, and the development

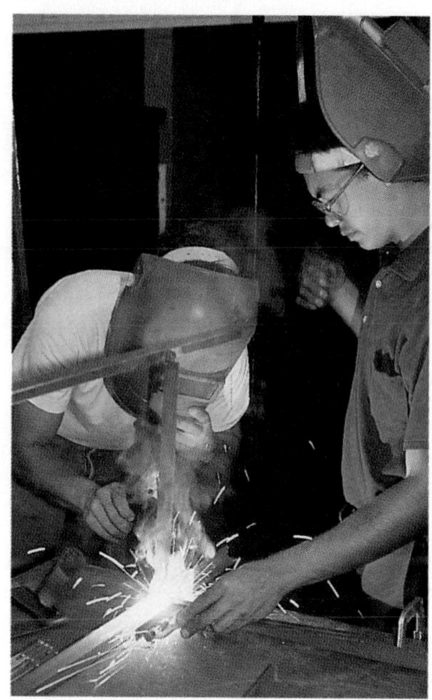
How can job training help juvenile offenders?

of life skills that will enable the offender to experience success once released from the juvenile justice system.

What happens to status offenders presents special problems. Should they be taken out of the home? Should they be committed to institutions? Should they be mixed with delinquents or adult offenders? In response to these concerns, many states have removed status offenders from large institutions and placed them in foster homes, halfway houses, or other community facilities.

PROBLEM 62

a. Do you think juvenile offenders should be treated and rehabilitated, or punished? Explain your answer.

b. Do you think there should be a set penalty for each juvenile offense, or should judges have the discretion to set a different sentence for each offender?

Postdisposition Most states give young people the right to appeal decisions of a juvenile court. However, because the U.S. Supreme

Hearing on a PINS Petition

Assume that a parent, Mr. Jones, goes to the county prosecutor and asks that a PINS petition be filed against his 15-year-old son, Billy. The petition asks the court to take the son out of the home and place him in a county institution because he is beyond control and needs the state's supervision. An attorney appointed to defend the youth says that the father is guilty of neglect.

The PINS statute: "A child may be declared a person in need of supervision (PINS) for continually refusing to obey the lawful orders of his or her parents, being beyond the control of the parents, running away from home on a repeated basis, or being a habitual truant from school."

The neglect statute: "A child may be declared neglected if the child's parents fail to provide necessary support or education required by law, abandon or abuse the child, or fail to provide the supervision and care necessary for the child's well-being."

Statement of Mr. Jones (father): "I give up. There is nothing more I can do with my son. He won't do anything I say. He stays out all night with his friends, and he constantly gets into trouble. He has been arrested three times—once for possession of drugs and twice for burglary. Twice he was released, but he got six months' probation for the second burglary when he was 14. He has run away twice. He is failing in school. His mother died three years ago, and things haven't been the same since. I need him at home to help take care of his two sisters. They are 10 and 12 years old. I may sometimes go out for a drink after work and miss dinner, but I'm not an alcoholic. Now he refuses to be home at dinnertime, and I know he's out using drugs and committing crimes."

Statement of Billy Jones (age 15): "Sure, I've gotten into some trouble, but there is never any food in our house, and my father won't give me any money to go out to eat. I had to get money somehow. Dad is almost never home at dinnertime. He comes home drunk almost every night of the week and gives me a bad time. Sometimes he hits me across the face when he has been drinking. We are always arguing, and he often yells at me. He's acted weird since mom died, and I can't take it. So I run away or stay out all night."

Role-play the hearing. Take the parts of Mr. Jones and his attorney (the county prosecutor), Billy Jones and his attorney, and the judge, following these steps:

1. The judge should announce the case and ask the county attorney to call his or her witness.
2. The father should be questioned by the county attorney as to his reasons for wanting the PINS petition.
3. The father should be cross-examined by Billy's attorney (the judge may interrupt with questions at any time).
4. Billy should be called to the stand and questioned by his attorney.
5. Billy should then be cross-examined by the county prosecutor.
6. At this point, the judge may ask additional questions of anyone involved and should ask the attorneys to make final arguments if they desire.
7. Finally, the judge should decide whether Billy is a PINS or whether he is neglected. Depending on what the judge decides, an order may be issued to remove him from the home, either temporarily or permanently, and place him in a juvenile institution, group home, or foster home; leave him in the home; have a social worker or court psychiatrist provide some follow-up treatment; or place other conditions on the father or the son that the judge believes are appropriate.

In your community, are juvenile records sealed or are they destroyed? What is the procedure?

Court has never ruled on this issue, the provisions for appeal vary greatly from state to state.

Once released from an institution, a juvenile may be placed on **aftercare**. This is the equivalent of parole in the adult system. Aftercare usually involves supervision by a parole officer, who counsels the juvenile on education, jobs, vocational training, or other services.

Unlike an adult criminal, a juvenile delinquent does not lose any of his or her civil rights. Upon reaching adulthood, the juvenile can still register to vote. In addition, all states make juvenile court records confidential and limit public access to them. Despite this confidentiality, a juvenile record can still cause problems. Only certain states have juvenile records permanently sealed or destroyed; and even though juvenile court records are confidential, a number of people and agencies may gain access to them.

Chapter 3

Torts

In criminal law, when someone commits a wrong, we call it a crime. In civil law, when a person commits a wrong, we call it a **tort**. A tort is not a crime. It is a civil wrong committed by one person against another. The rules that govern civil wrongs are called tort law. Tort law deals with basic questions such as (1) who should be responsible, or liable, for harm caused by human activities and (2) how much the responsible person should have to pay. Almost any activity—driving a car, operating a business, speaking, writing, or using property—can be a source of harm and therefore of tort liability. Knowledge of torts can help people resolve their conflicts, often without going to court.

For practical purposes, a tort occurs when one person causes injury to another person or to another's property or reputation. The injured party, the **plaintiff**, can take the alleged wrongdoer, the **defendant**, to court. Tort law provides the injured party with a **remedy**, something to make up for what was lost. This usually takes the form of money **damages**. For example, a person injured in an auto accident might receive $5,000 in damages. Therefore, one purpose of tort law is to compensate people for their injuries. However, not all injuries result in compensation. A person may be injured in an accident through no fault of another person. In such cases, tort law generally provides no remedy.

Tort law also establishes standards of care that society expects from people. Simply put, the law requires us to act with reasonable care toward people and their property. Failure to exercise reasonable care may result in legal **liability**. The person harmed may sue the

Why has this warning been posted by the property owner?

person who acted unreasonably for damages. Through the payment of damages, it is hoped that future injuries and losses will be prevented and that more reasonable behavior will be encouraged.

PROBLEM 1

Read the following descriptions. Each case involves an injury. Assume that a civil suit is brought by the injured person. For each case (1) identify the plaintiff and the defendant or defendants and (2) determine whether the defendant should pay for the plaintiff's damages. Explain your answers.

a. Fourteen-year-old Carrie is babysitting for four-year-old Jill. Carrie leaves Jill in the living room and goes into the kitchen to call her boyfriend. From the kitchen she can hear but not see Jill. While she is away, Jill falls off a chair and is hurt.

b. Ben, a high-school football player, tackles a teammate in practice. When the teammate hits the ground, his shoulder is separated.

c. Mr. Gundy owns a large apartment building. When his janitors wax the lobby floor, they place a 12-inch square sign near the front door that reads: "Caution. Wet Floors." Mrs. Gonzalez is hurrying home from shopping carrying two large bags of groceries. She does not see the sign and slips and falls on the freshly waxed floor, injuring her knee and arm.

d. Consuela leaves a sharp knife on the kitchen table after making a sandwich. A three-year-old neighbor who has been invited over to play with Consuela's daughter climbs up on a chair, grabs the knife, and seriously cuts his finger.

e. Harry, a school bus driver, has a heart attack while driving the bus. The bus slams into a wall, injuring several students. One month earlier Harry's doctor had warned him of his heart condition.

f. Matt and Sara are sitting in the upper deck behind first base at a major league baseball game. A foul ball hit by their team's star player bounces off a railing, smacking Matt in the head and giving him a concussion.

g. Janet, an expert auto mechanic, continues to drive her car even though she knows that the brake linings are badly worn. Driving on a rain-slicked road at night, she skids into a bicyclist who is riding one foot away from the right curb.

Why do some laws require property owners to shovel snow from their sidewalks?

Deciding whether behavior is reasonable or unreasonable is often difficult. Yet it is one of the main questions in tort law. One problem with defining reasonableness is that the meaning of the term changes over time, and it may mean different things in different places. For example, in an African tribal society, it might be considered reasonable to require a male teenager to single-handedly kill a lion. Obviously, requiring such behavior would be considered unreasonable in the United States. We will take a closer look at the concept of reasonableness later in this chapter. For now, remember that a defendant's unreasonable behavior is called a **wrongful act** when it violates his or her duty to others. A violation of one's duty, or a wrongful act, occurs when a person:

- Does something he or she is not supposed to do (for example, hits someone in the face).
- Fails to do something he or she is supposed to do (for example, fails to shovel the snow from the sidewalk in front of his or her house).
- Does something he or she should do, or is allowed to do, but does it in a careless way that endangers others (for example, drives a car above the speed limit).

Duties are created by statute or by court decisions. In addition, individuals have a general duty to exercise reasonable care toward other persons and their property. These duties are an expression of the collective values or generally accepted beliefs of the community. In a way, they are a statement of a society's common sense.

Tort law provides a legal process for injured persons to recover money damages from wrongdoers who cause them harm. The two parties can simply meet and discuss how to compensate the injured person. The agreement they reach is called a **settlement**. If, however, they cannot agree on compensation, or if the noninjured person insists that he or she was acting reasonably when the injury occurred, then the injured party may decide to sue. In such instances, a trial may be conducted to decide the rights and liabilities of the parties.

It is important to note that settlements are *much* more common than trials. Approximately 90% of tort cases filed in court are settled without a trial. For cases that do go to trial, there can be delays of a year or more between the time the case is filed in court and the trial.

The following example illustrates the tort law process. Sally claims that Martha shoved her, causing her to fall down a flight of stairs and break her leg. Sally wants $5,000 from Martha to compensate for her injury. This dispute can be resolved in at least three different ways.

First, Martha could acknowledge that she acted unreasonably and agree to pay the $5,000. This is called a settlement.

Second, Martha could argue that she did not act unreasonably—that Sally ran past her, bumped into her, and then tripped down the stairs—and she could refuse to pay any money damages. If Sally wanted to recover the money, she would have to sue Martha in court.

In a third scenario, Martha might admit nudging Sally a bit but might claim that she should only have to pay $4,000, because the $5,000 Sally wants includes money for a subscription to cable television, a videocassette recorder, and three movie cassettes that Sally bought when she was home in bed for two weeks. Here, the dispute is not about liability but rather is about the amount of damages. In this situation, Sally might accept Martha's $4,000 offer, or she might sue for the full amount. There is risk in not accepting the $4,000, because if a court decides that Martha did not act unreasonably, Sally could recover nothing!

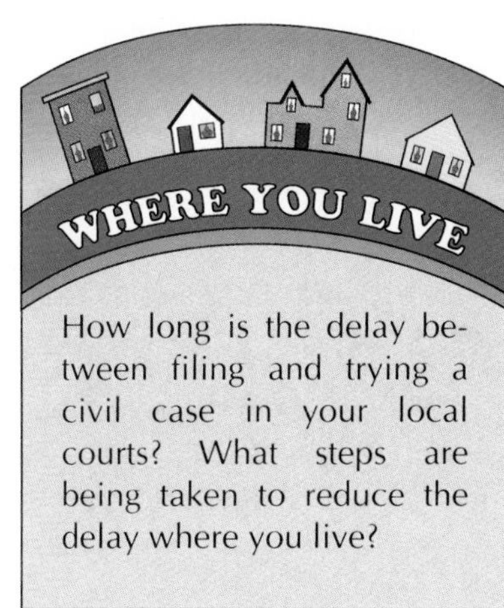

How long is the delay between filing and trying a civil case in your local courts? What steps are being taken to reduce the delay where you live?

THE IDEA OF TORTS: YESTERDAY, TODAY, AND TOMORROW

The concept of a tort is not new. Judges in England were deciding tort cases in the 15th century. Tort law has always tried to balance the usefulness of certain conduct against the harm that conduct might cause.

Tort law is generally based on **common law**. This is law made by judges through court decisions. These decisions become precedents used to decide future cases. Tort law may also be based on statutes, such as a state's motor vehicle code. For example, suppose you make a left turn in front of an approaching car and the two vehicles collide in the intersection. If the state's motor vehicle code requires drivers to yield to oncoming traffic when making a left turn, your conduct will be seen as wrongful. The police could give you a ticket, and the injured driver could sue you for damages.

There are a number of specific torts, which we will describe later in the chapter. There is also a saying that "for every interference with a recognized legal right, the law will provide a remedy." If you can convince a judge that you deserve compensation for some injury, you may be able to recover damages without fitting your case into an existing category of tort protection.

Tort law has evolved over time, reflecting changes in both technology and social values. Lawmakers must often decide whether a particular product is more useful than harmful to society. Imagine, for example, that a 17th-century court was told that a new invention would carry six adults 60 miles in one hour (the usefulness of the

Why does the government require that food be inspected?

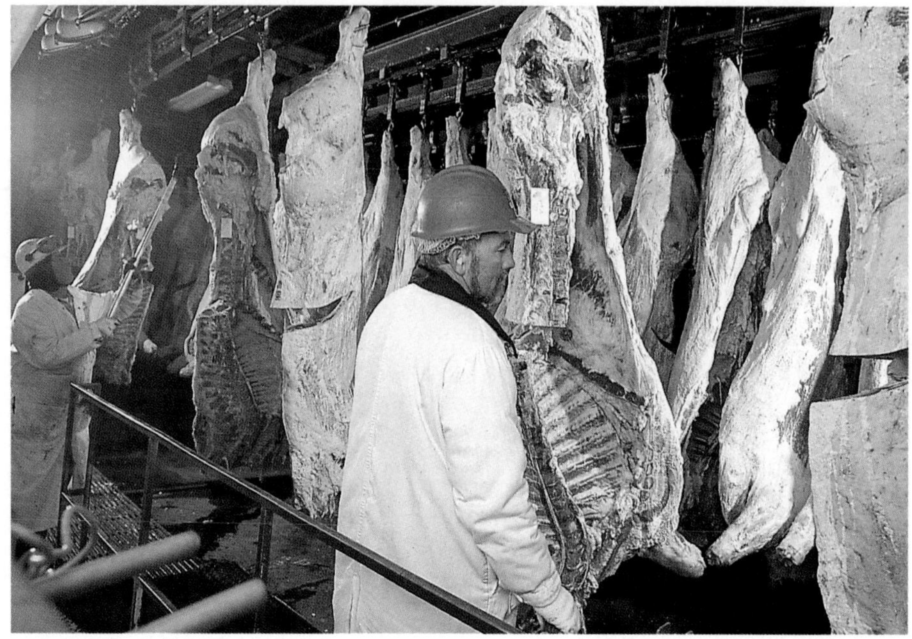

machine). On the other hand, the machine would eventually cause thousands of deaths per year and would significantly harm the air we breathe (the harm caused by the machine). Would you permit the operation of such a machine? The machine, of course, is the automobile. Hundreds of years ago, people might have considered automobiles more dangerous than useful. Technology and values change, however, and today the car—along with the many lawsuits it creates—is a permanent fixture in our lives.

Tort law today continues to balance usefulness against harm. For example, how safe must a new prescription drug be before the government allows its widespread use? If a drug is discovered that saves the lives of many cancer patients but causes some deaths, should its use be permitted?

Tort law also tries to preserve individual choice. With a warning of the dangers of smoking prominently displayed on the package, adults are permitted to purchase cigarettes. This product may be more harmful than useful. However, some people argue that letting adults purchase cigarettes preserves their individual choice and that, in theory, the warning allows the individual to make an informed choice. Others criticize this government decision and argue that the sale of cigarettes should be restricted or banned.

Tort law is often at the forefront of public controversy and is closely related to economic and political, as well as legal, policy decisions. As you will see throughout this chapter, tort cases involve a clash of values and interests. Arriving at fair solutions is rarely easy.

Should the government regulate the sale of cigarettes?

The Lung Cancer Death

Mrs. Garrett dies of lung cancer at the age of 42. Her family brings a civil suit against ABC Tobacco Company, the manufacturer of the cigarettes she had smoked daily for the previous 20 years. Her doctors say that cigarette smoking was the major factor leading to her death.

PROBLEM 2

a. If you were the Garrett family's attorney, what arguments would you make at the trial? What evidence would you want to introduce?

b. If you were ABC's attorney, what arguments would you make for the company? What evidence would you want to introduce?

c. If you were the Garrett family's attorney, would you want a judge or a jury to decide this case? Why?

d. Assume that each package of ABC cigarettes carries the following warning: "Caution: cigarette smoking can be harmful to your health." How should this case be decided? Give reasons for your decision.

TYPES OF TORTS

Tort liability exists for three major categories of conduct: intentional wrongs, negligence, and activities for which strict liability is imposed. An **intentional wrong** occurs when a person acts with the intent of injuring a person, his or her property, or both. For example, Jim is angry at Tom, so he intentionally smashes the windshield of Tom's car. Tom may sue Jim to recover the cost of damage to his windshield. Another example: Lucy writes a letter telling her friends that Andrew is a lazy drunk and a drug addict, when she knows this is not true. Andrew may recover damages from Lucy for harm to his reputation caused by her deliberate lie.

Intentional torts may also be crimes. In these cases, the defendant can be prosecuted by the state as well as sued by the plaintiff. However, punishing a criminal does not usually make up for the harm to the victim. A civil tort action is used to recover monetary damages.

The most common tort is negligence. **Negligence** is an unintentional tort. It occurs when a person's failure to use reasonable care causes harm. If a drunk driver accidentally hits a pedestrian, the driver is negligent. Although the driver did not intend to hurt the pedestrian, he acted unreasonably in driving drunk and will be liable for the harm caused to the pedestrian.

Strict liability differs from both negligence and intentional wrongs. It applies when the defendant is engaged in an activity so dangerous that there is a serious risk of harm even if he or she acts

Why should consumers carefully read the labels on medicines?

with utmost care. In a strict liability case, there is no need to prove that the defendant was either negligent or intended to cause harm in order to recover damages. For example, suppose you are hit by a brick falling from a building being demolished. In this case, you do not have to prove that the contractor was careless in order to recover damages. Demolishing buildings is so dangerous that contractors are automatically responsible if a passerby is injured. Three groups of people face strict liability: (1) owners of dangerous animals, (2) people who engage in highly dangerous activities, and (3) manufacturers and sellers of dangerous products.

Remember that not all injuries to you or your property will lead to a recovery under tort law. In some instances, harmful behavior may not be a tort. In other cases, the person causing the harm may have a legal **defense** to a tort action. In still other cases, the defendant may be liable but may simply be too poor to pay for the harm to the plaintiff.

PROBLEM 3

Carefully examine each of the following situations and determine whether a tort has been committed. If there is a tort, do you think it is an intentional wrong, negligence, or an activity for which strict liability should be imposed? Give your reasons.

a. José trips over his untied shoelace while running to catch a bus, breaking his ankle.

b. Cheryl is caught smoking marijuana in school and is suspended by Ms. Miller, the vice-principal. Although Cheryl's mother knows her daughter sometimes uses this drug, she tells all the parents and teachers at the PTA meeting that Ms. Miller is a liar and a bad administrator.

c. Mr. Garnett buys a strong pain killer at the drugstore and takes the capsules according to the directions on the package. He has an extremely bad reaction to the drug and has to be taken to the hospital.

d. Meilei drinks too much alcohol at the office Christmas party. His supervisor, Ruth, advises him to take a taxi home, but he thinks he will be all right if he drives slowly. Not noticing a stop sign, he strikes and kills a pedestrian.

e. After raking the leaves from their lawn, Skip and his father move the pile of leaves to an open area near the street and light it. A sudden gust of wind blows flaming leaves into a neighbor's garage and sets it on fire.

f. Marsha's mother asks her to run to the corner store to buy a bottle of ginger ale that she needs to make a holiday punch for guests who will be arriving soon. Marsha buys the ginger ale and runs home. When her mother opens the bottle, the glass explodes, cutting her arm and face in several places.

TAKING YOUR CASE TO COURT

Tort law is **civil law**. Civil law deals with disputes between individuals or groups of individuals, and torts involve disputes of this kind. In a civil case, the injured party may sue the party who caused the damage. This differs from criminal law, in which the state brings charges against the accused. Criminal law deals with actions that are defined as crimes against the general public, even if there is an individual victim.

In some situations, an act can be both a tort and a crime. This may lead to two separate actions against the defendant. For example, Meilei (Problem 3d, above) may be sued for driving while intoxicated and killing a pedestrian. Meilei may also be charged with the crime of negligent homicide or manslaughter for his actions.

The criminal case will be brought by the state, which must prove that Meilei was guilty beyond a reasonable doubt. This is called the standard of proof.

The victim's family may also sue Meilei in civil court. In the civil case, the victim's family will attempt to recover damages for the wrongful death. The civil court will use "preponderance of the evidence" as the standard of proof. This standard requires that more than 50% of the weight of the evidence be in favor of the winning party. The civil standard is easier to meet than the criminal standard. This is appropriate, because the penalties for those found liable in a civil action are less severe than the penalties for those found guilty of a crime. A person does not go to jail for committing a tort but instead pays damages to those injured.

Who Can Be Sued?

Almost anyone can be sued, including individuals, groups of individuals, organizations, businesses, and even units of government. Plaintiffs sometimes sue several different defendants at once. Typically, plaintiffs try to sue a defendant who has enough money to pay for the damages. This is called looking for a defendant with "deep pockets." For example, suppose you slip on a wet rag that the janitor left on the floor of a local restaurant. You break your leg as a result

Whom can a customer sue for food poisoning?

of the fall. You will probably sue the restaurant owner rather than the janitor because the owner will usually have "deeper pockets."

People can sue employers for torts committed by employees in the course of their employment. The reason for this rule is that the employer is in a better position than the employee to handle the cost of the suit. The employer may purchase liability insurance or raise prices, for example. In addition, imposing financial responsibility on the employer will encourage that person to be very careful when hiring, training, and supervising employees.

Children commit torts and may be sued for damages. To recover damages from a **minor**, you have to prove that the child acted unreasonably for a person of that age and experience. Because most children do not have very "deep pockets," plaintiffs also sue the child's parents. For example, a child leaves toys on the front step, injuring a visitor who trips on them. The visitor may sue the parents and try to prove that they were negligent in failing to supervise their child.

Sometimes there can be more than one plaintiff or injured party. In some cases, hundreds of people may be injured by one action. When this happens, the injured parties may be able to form a "class" and bring their lawsuit together. This is called a **class action**. For example, if an entire town gets its drinking water from the same source and a company pollutes the water, the townspeople may get together and file a class action suit against the company. The settlement or damage award will be divided among the townspeople who bring the suit.

Are parents responsible for torts committed by their children in your state? Should they be?

The Airline Explosion

A bomb was smuggled onto an international flight from Frankfurt, Germany, to New York City. The flight carried 259 passengers, many of them students returning from a European trip, along with a crew of 11. The bomb exploded over a small town in Scotland, killing everyone on board.

PROBLEM 4

a. Could the families of those who died bring a class action? Explain.

b. Who are the possible defendants in this case?

c. Which defendant would have the "deepest pockets"?

d. Which defendant, if any, should be held liable?

What steps should an airline take to ensure the safety of its passengers?

Individuals wishing to file a tort action should hire an attorney to handle the filing of the legal papers, the negotiations with the other side, and, if necessary, the trial. Many plaintiffs' lawyers will work for a **contingency fee**. This means the lawyer does not charge the client an hourly fee. Rather, the lawyer receives a portion of the recovery (typically between 30% and 40%) if the plaintiff wins. If the plaintiff loses, the attorney does not receive a fee. This arrangement allows a person who might otherwise be unable to hire an attorney to be represented by counsel in a tort action. The contingency fee is, of course, something of a gamble for the attorney. Lawyers rarely agree to this arrangement unless the plaintiff has a winnable case.

The contingency fee may not always be a good arrangement for the plaintiff. For example, a lawyer may be able to negotiate a large settlement with an insurance company without even filing a case in court. In such a case, it may be better for the plaintiff to hire a lawyer on an hourly basis or for an agreed-upon, overall fee (a fixed fee).

The Cut Lip

Seth and Ferman argue over who should have won a basketball game. Ferman insults Seth's favorite team, the Buckets. He calls its players lazy, worthless, and lucky. Seth is outraged. He has been a Bucket fan for years. Losing all control, Seth punches Ferman in the mouth. Ferman suffers two broken teeth, three chipped teeth, and a badly cut lip that requires 10 stitches. His dental bills total $2,000 and he misses five days of work as a result of his injury. He also requires pain medication for a week and is extremely uncomfortable. Seth needs four stitches in his hand.

PROBLEM 5

a. Has Seth committed a crime? Explain.

b. Has either Seth or Ferman committed a civil wrong? Explain.

c. Who could bring a criminal charge in this case?

d. Who could bring a civil action in this case?

e. Exactly what damages could the plaintiff seek to recover?

f. Would the plaintiff want to hire a lawyer on a contingency-fee, hourly, or fixed-fee basis? Why? Which would the lawyer prefer?

g. What method other than a civil trial could the plaintiff use to deal with this situation? How would it work?

The Spilled Peanut Butter

Mr. Grant is in Foodland Supermarket doing the weekly grocery shopping. His four-year old daughter Jenny is seated in the shopping cart. As they pass a large peanut butter display, Jenny reaches out and pulls a jar off the shelf. The display collapses, and a dozen jars come tumbling down. Some of the jars break, spreading peanut butter and glass all over the floor. Mr. Grant scolds Jenny severely as he wheels her down the aisle.

Ten minutes later, Mrs. Hightower slips and falls on the peanut

What responsibility does a market have to protect its customers from harm?

butter. She breaks her hip in the fall and suffers several deep cuts from the broken glass. Because she is elderly, the hip injury turns out to be quite complicated and may never heal properly.

PROBLEM 6

a. Whom should Mrs. Hightower sue for damages? Why?

b. Who, if anyone, was at fault in this case? Give your reasons.

The Steering Wheel Failure

Sarah buys a new car at Town and Country Motors. Just before her first scheduled maintenance visit (at 2,000 miles), she hears an odd noise coming from her steering wheel. She tells the service manager about the sound, and he notes it on the work order. After picking up the car the next day, she has a serious accident when the steering suddenly fails. The car is totalled, and her medical bills from the accident come to more than $30,000.

PROBLEM 7

a. Could Sarah bring a civil action? Who are the potential defendants in this case?

b. Who do you think would win? Why?

c. Should Sarah hire a lawyer on a contingency-fee, hourly, or fixed-fee basis? Why?

RESOLVING TORT CASES OUT OF COURT

In most instances, taking a case to court should be viewed as a remedy of last resort. Lawsuits are expensive and time-consuming, and the outcome is never certain. In addition, drawn-out legal battles can exact a heavy emotional toll.

Informal Dispute Resolution

As we mentioned earlier, most tort cases are resolved without the need for going to court or hiring an attorney. Many are resolved when people accept responsibility for harming someone else and offer to pay for the damages. Punting a football through a neighbor's window may be a tort, but the law is seldom used to settle this problem. The individual responsible for the bad kick apologizes, offers to pay for the window, or does some work for the neighbor to make up

Managing Conflict

To use conflict management skills to help resolve a problem, each party to the dispute should:

- Come to the discussion with a sincere interest in settling the problem.
- Listen carefully to the other person's position. Do not let anger get in the way of listening and solving the problem.
- Listen actively to the other person's position. This means that you must hear what is being said and understand it. Good listeners make eye contact, relax, think carefully about what the other person is saying, and ask good questions.
- Try to think about the problem from the other person's point of view.
- Think about the issue that is causing the problem, not about the personalities of the people involved. What is the real, underlying problem? Sort out the facts from the feelings.
- Think of as many solutions to the problem as possible. Make a list of them and try not to decide right away whether they are good solutions.
- Identify listed solutions that both parties can live with. Be sure these solutions are realistic.
- Repeat the main points of the agreement to be sure that both parties understand it. It is a good idea to write down the agreement.
- Discuss the problem again if the agreement does not seem to be working.

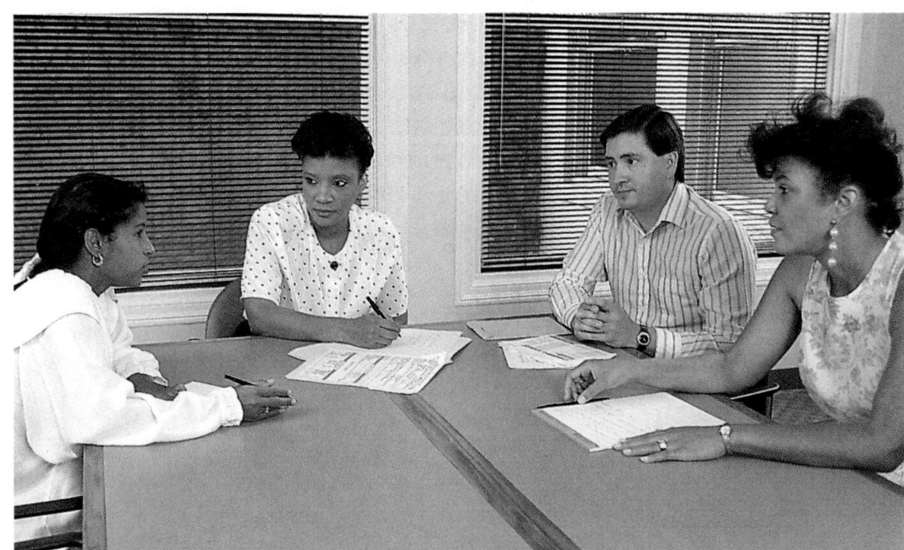

How can disputes be resolved informally, thus reducing the number of trials and lawsuits?

for the damage.

The process of informally working out a solution to a dispute is called **negotiation**. This is a give-and-take process involving one or more discussions in which the parties may make settlement offers and counteroffers until they agree on a solution. Most tort disputes are settled through negotiation.

Sometimes people cannot agree on adequate compensation through negotiation. They may even disagree on who was at fault or whether anyone was at fault. For example, assume that Smith and Lopez are next-door neighbors. The oak tree in Lopez's yard has grown so tall and full that Smith's flower garden no longer gets the direct sunlight it needs. Smith asks Lopez to trim the tree, but Lopez likes the tree as it is. In addition, tree trimming is expensive. How should this dispute be settled? Should the neighbors negotiate or go to court?

Many communities have **mediation** programs like those described in Chapter 1. These programs offer people such as Smith and Lopez an opportunity to settle disputes without going to court. Mediation programs are part of a national movement to avoid costly, time-consuming lawsuits and replace them with a process that allows people to work together to solve their problem. Mediation sessions focus on the future relationship between the people involved. The parties work with a mediator to reach a practical solution to their problem.

Individuals can use mediation skills to resolve a problem without going through a formal mediation program. Whenever difficult problems arise, it helps to have a process that can be used to organize the discussion about the issues. Conflict management skills help individuals discuss problems. A process for managing conflict is described in the box on page 200. Anyone can use the conflict management process to exchange information in attempting to resolve a problem. You should always consider conflict management before contacting a community mediation program or filing a lawsuit.

Many torts can be settled by direct negotiation or with the assistance of a mediator. Other cases are handled through insurance or workers' compensation.

The Barking Dog

Nathan, 16, and his mother, Hilda, have lived in the same house for 15 years. They like the neighborhood and have made many home improvements. Two years ago, Nathan's mother fell and broke her leg. Although she has recovered, she moves much more slowly than she used to. The convenient location of their house is important because she can walk to stores and to the bus stop. Until recently, they have been very happy living in this house.

Their problems began six months ago when Mark and Carla rented the house next door. They own a three-year-old dog named Sadie. Sadie barks constantly throughout the day while Mark and Carla are at work. At first, Nathan and his mother thought the dog would settle down, but as time went on it seemed that the dog just liked to bark.

Recently Hilda talked to Mark about the dog, but he said the dog was not really barking that much. He sees Hilda as a chronic complainer. In addition to her complaint about the dog, she is upset that Mark and Carla park their car so close to her driveway.

Nathan is unhappy because his mother is upset constantly, and he often hears the dog barking when he gets home from school.

PROBLEM 8

a. What are three options available to Nathan and his mother?

b. What will happen if Nathan and Hilda call the police and report the barking dog?

c. Use the conflict management process outlined in the box on page 200 to role-play a possible resolution to the problem.

Insurance

Americans buy billions of dollars of liability insurance every year so that when an accident occurs, the injured party can recover money from the wrongdoer's insurance company, not the wrongdoer. While insured persons must sometimes go to court, most tort cases between insurance companies and injured persons are settled without resorting to such an action.

Liability insurance is a **contract** (agreement). The insured person agrees to make payments (called **premiums**) to the insurance company, and the company agrees to pay for damages caused by the insured person for as long as the contract lasts. Insurance companies set a limit on how much they will pay. Usually the contract also requires the insurance company to defend the insured person in court.

Most doctors, lawyers, and other professionals carry liability insurance to protect them against **malpractice** suits. These are lawsuits brought by clients or patients who claim that a professional person provided services in a negligent manner. Plaintiffs in malpractice cases sometimes win verdicts or settle for large sums of money—sometimes millions of dollars. Without liability insurance, doctors and lawyers would be personally liable for these verdicts.

The Expensive Insurance Premium

Dr. Sam Wong, a surgeon, complains that he must pay $25,000 each year in premiums for adequate malpractice insurance. This insurance protects him against having to pay claims made by a patient or a patient's family in the event that the patient suffers injury or death through a medical error during surgery.

PROBLEM 9

a. What might happen to Dr. Wong if he did not carry malpractice insurance?

b. Why do you think Dr. Wong's insurance premium is so high?

c. Who pays the cost of Dr. Wong's insurance?

d. What action can be taken to lower these premiums?

Manufacturers often carry liability insurance to protect against lawsuits brought by customers injured when using the manufacturers' products. For manufacturers and professionals alike, the cost of insurance is usually added into the price of products or services. This allows them to spread the costs of insurance among all of their customers or clients.

Homeowners and renters may also carry liability insurance. These policies typically provide coverage for loss and damage to the insured person's property. For example, if your property is taken during a burglary, you can ask the insurance company for money to replace the stolen items. This is usually more practical than trying to sue the burglar for the value of the items.

While many different types of liability insurance exist, it is important to note that hardly any insurance policies cover intentional harm caused by the insured person. Therefore, a homeowner who assaults a guest cannot have an insurance company pay the guest's damages.

Insuring a Car Auto insurance is the most important liability insurance for young people. In a typical year, more than six million automobile accidents cause nearly 47,000 deaths (approximately 40% of these involve alcohol) and nearly four million injuries. Losses caused by automobile accidents exceed $70 billion. On a typical day, there are more than 16,000 automobile accidents in the United States. Each day, these accidents kill nearly 130 people, injure almost 11,000, and cause close to $20 million in losses. It is not surprising that most states require drivers to carry insurance and that many drivers purchase even more insurance than their state requires.

What type and amount of auto insurance does your state require? Is there a law dealing with uninsured motorists? What does it provide? How much does auto insurance cost for high-school-age drivers in your state? Is there a discount for taking driver's education? Does the rate differ depending on the driver's age and the type and home location of the car?

Auto insurance protects you by promising to pay for certain possible losses. Insurance can pay for the cost of repairing your car, medical bills, lost wages, and pain and suffering arising from the injury. When you buy insurance, you can choose various coverage combinations. Coverage depends on the kind of protection you want and how much you can afford to pay. Common coverage includes liability, medical, collision, comprehensive, uninsured motorist, and no-fault.

Your liability insurance pays for injuries to other people and property if you are responsible for the accident. It may also include representation in court by the company's attorneys or payment of your legal fees. Liability coverage pays for damages up to (but not more than) the limits listed in your policy. If injuries and property damage are greater than the policy limits, the person at fault will have to pay the difference.

Liability policies generally have three limits on how much a person can collect: (1) a limit on injuries per person, (2) a limit on total injuries to all persons involved in the accident, and (3) a limit on

What steps should this driver take after discovering damage to her parked car?

property damage per accident. For example, a "10/20/5" policy would pay up to $10,000 per person for personal injury, $20,000 per accident for all personal injuries, and $5,000 per accident for property damage. Sometimes an injured person brings a lawsuit against the driver or car owner responsible for the injuries. Because the damages in these cases can be very high, careful consideration should be

THE CASE OF . . .

The Nonstop Car

Pulling left into the outside lane to pass a slow-moving truck, Larry saw the traffic light ahead turn yellow. "If I step on it, I'll make this light," he thought. He speeded up, exceeding the limit slightly. Just then an oncoming car made a left turn in front of him. Larry hit the brakes, but it was too late. Two seconds later, pinned against the steering wheel, he saw the other driver, Charles, stagger out of the car, bleeding and holding his shoulder in pain. Who should be responsible for the medical and car repair bills resulting from this accident? In most cases, who pays for repairs resulting from auto accidents?

given to how much insurance you want to carry. For example, a $50,000 limit on injuries per person might be far less than the damage incurred in a serious accident. If you were negligent, you would be liable for the amount in excess of your insurance policy limit.

Your **medical coverage** pays for your own medical expenses resulting from accidents involving your car or the car you are driving. It also pays for the medical expenses of any passengers in your car, no matter who is at fault. The amount of medical benefits and the kind of medical costs covered (hospital bills, office visits and so on) are limited in the policy. For example, medical coverage may be limited to $1,000 per person injured.

Your **collision coverage** pays for damage to your own car even if the accident was your fault. Collision coverage usually pays up to the actual value of the car (not for its replacement with a new car). You can lower the cost of collision insurance by including a **deductible**. This is an amount that you agree to pay toward repairs before the insurance company pays anything. For example, a $100 deductible means that if your car has $250 in damages, you will pay $100 and the insurance company will pay the remaining $150. The higher the amount of the deductible, the less expensive the collision insurance.

Your **comprehensive coverage** protects you against damage or loss to your car from causes other than collisions. For example, comprehensive coverage includes damages due to vandalism, fire, or theft. Read your policy carefully to determine whether valuables in your car, such as a tape deck, are covered in case of theft. Insurance policies sometimes include (usually at an extra charge) coverage for towing or car rental costs.

Your **uninsured motorist coverage** protects you from other drivers who do not have insurance or do not have enough insurance. It does this by paying you for the personal injuries or damage they cause. Be sure to find out how much your policy pays for personal injuries caused by uninsured motorists and whether it pays for damages to your car. Uninsured motorists coverage is usually an inexpensive and worthwhile addition to your policy.

About half the states have **no-fault insurance**. If you have no-fault insurance, your own insurance company will pay up to a certain amount for injuries you receive in an accident, regardless of fault. Notice the difference between no-fault and liability insurance. With liability insurance, your company pays the other driver only if you were at fault, whereas no-fault laws may allow settlement of such claims without the delay and expense of determining fault in a court case. Some people criticize no-fault benefits because they are limited to a certain amount of money and usually only cover personal injuries. However, when damages are higher than the no-fault limits, the injured person can still sue the other party.

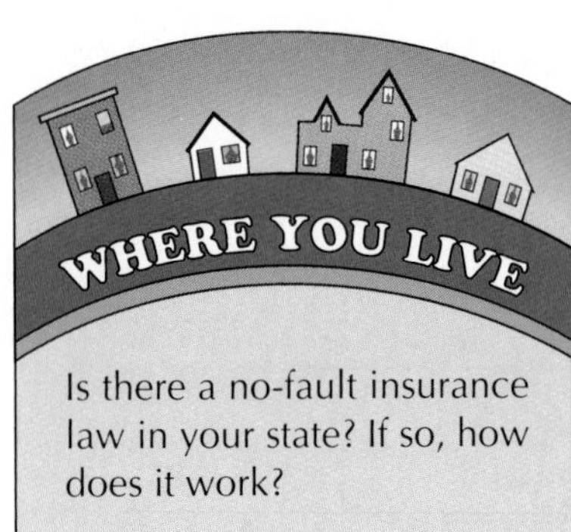

Is there a no-fault insurance law in your state? If so, how does it work?

PROBLEM 10

Reread the Case of the Nonstop Car. Assume that the accident happened in a state without no-fault insurance and that both Larry and Charles had insurance coverage. Each had a policy covering all types of losses and including a $250 deductible for collision insurance. Also assume that Larry was at fault.

a. Whose insurance company would pay for Charles's hospital and car repair bills?

b. Whose insurance company would pay for Larry's hospital and car repair bills?

c. What do you think would happen if the damages to Charles and his car were greater than the limits of Larry's policy?

d. If the damages were less than the policy's limits, would Larry have to pay any money to get his car fixed?

PROBLEM 11

You have an eight-year-old car with a market value of only $900. The annual cost of collision insurance is $350. If the state does not require collision insurance, should you continue to purchase it? Give your reasons.

Workers' Compensation

Every state has a workers' compensation system. The system operates to automatically compensate employees who are injured on the job. Employers make regular contributions to a state fund or buy insurance for this purpose. Workers are compensated for injuries that occur in the course of their employment. They do not have to go to court to prove that their employer was at fault. They also receive a portion of their salary while they are recovering and unable to work. Many states provide employees with two-thirds of their regular salary. In exchange, the injured employee usually gives up the right to sue his or her employer. Accidents that occur while the employee is commuting to or from work are rarely covered.

Does your state have workers' compensation? Are all jobs covered? What are the principal provisions of your state's law? How effectively and fairly does the system work?

Unlike the plaintiffs in typical tort cases, workers can usually recover for their injuries even if they were negligent. However, work-

If a worker not using protective eyewear is injured in this area, should workers' compensation pay for the injury?

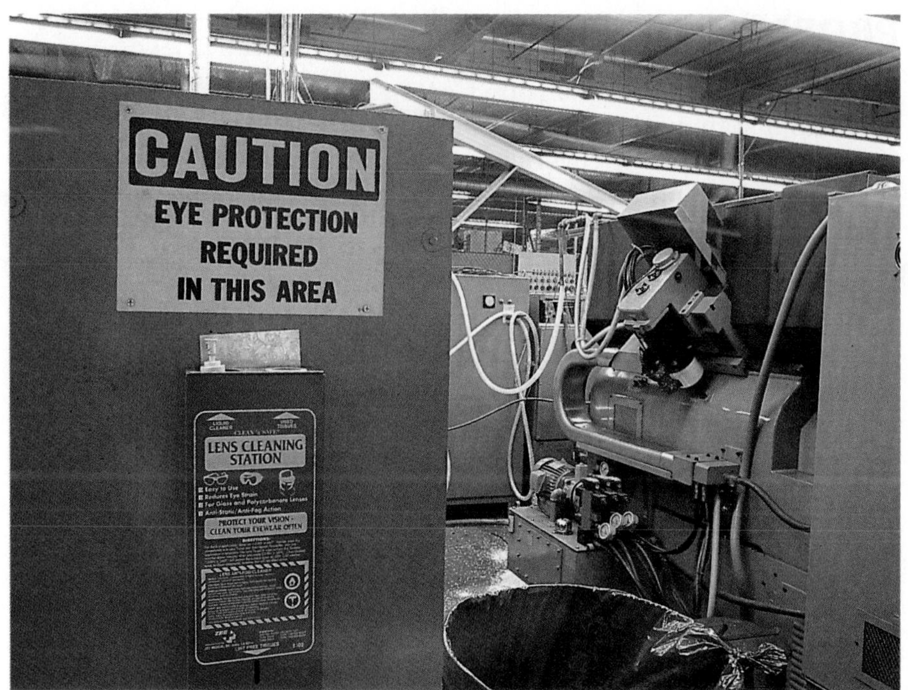

ers' compensation statutes generally deny recovery when the injury was caused by the intoxication of the injured employee. In addition, nearly half of the states either reduce or prohibit recovery when the accident is caused by a worker's refusal to follow safety rules. For example, a welder who is blinded on the job after ignoring repeated warnings to wear safety goggles would not be able to recover money under workers' compensation statutes in some states.

The amount of money awarded for a specific injury is limited according to a schedule set up by the state. The schedule sets the amount that can be recovered based on the seriousness of the injury, the amount of time the worker is expected to be out of work, and the worker's average weekly wage. Workers cannot usually recover additional damages from the employer. This means that workers' compensation is the **exclusive remedy** for on-the-job injuries.

A worker who is injured on the job must notify the employer. Often the employer will ask a doctor to certify the injury. Then either the employer or the injured employee will file a claim. Once the claim is filed, the injured employee will regularly receive a workers' compensation payment, just like a paycheck. The payments will continue until the employee can return to work or recovers from the injury.

Many states have a workers' compensation commission that hears claims and decides how much money will be given to injured workers. If the commission decides that little or no money should be given, the injured person may appeal to a court.

The School Slip and Fall

Mrs. Martinez is the art teacher at Central High School. Dale is a tenth-grade student. One afternoon the maintenance staff forgot to display a warning notice that the floors had been mopped and were wet. The stairway leading to the art studio was so slippery that Dale fell down the stairs, breaking his arm. Mrs. Martinez was teaching an art class at the time. When she heard the noise of his fall, she ran out to see what was wrong. She, too, slipped on the soapy water and broke her ankle.

PROBLEM 12

a. Who is responsible for Dale's injury? For Mrs. Martinez's injury?

b. From whom will Dale recover damages?

c. Is there a limit to the amount that Dale can recover?

d. From whom will Mrs. Martinez recover damages? How will she recover those damages?

e. Is there a limit to the amount that Mrs. Martinez can recover?

f. Why does the law treat these two injured people differently? Is this fair? Explain.

INTENTIONAL TORTS

An intentional tort occurs when an action is taken to deliberately cause harm. There are two general types of intentional torts: those causing injury to persons and those causing harm to property.

A person who proves that someone else committed an intentional tort against him or her can recover damages to make up for the harm caused. These are called **compensatory damages**, because the award compensates for harm caused by the defendant. For example, when Geri is punched by Stan, she receives damages of $6,000 to cover her hospital bills. These are compensatory damages.

Compensatory damages can also include lost wages and pain and suffering. The plaintiff has to prove any future losses (such as medical bills, reduced or lost wages, and pain and suffering) with reasonable certainty. Juries decide how much money will fully compensate the injured person for pain and suffering.

In some cases, the plaintiff can recover **nominal damages** (that is, just a token amount, such as one dollar). These are symbolic awards of money. Nominal damages are awarded to recognize that the defendant was wrong even though he or she did not cause substantial injury or loss. For example, suppose Juan slapped José in an argument. In court, it is shown that even though Juan wrongfully slapped José, José suffered no injury. The court might award one dollar in nominal damages to José.

Punitive damages are amounts of money awarded to the plaintiff to punish the defendant for malicious, willful, or outrageous acts. Punitive damages serve as a warning to others not to engage in such conduct. Nominal and punitive damages can be awarded for intentional torts, but they are not awarded in negligence cases.

It is possible for nominal and punitive damages to be awarded even where there is little or no actual harm that would justify compensatory damages. Suppose that Betty shoots a gun at Mark and misses him. This is an intentional tort. The court could award both nominal damages (because there was no actual harm) and punitive damages (because Betty's act was so outrageous).

Sometimes people sued for intentional torts do not have to pay any damages at all, even though they did exactly what the plaintiff claims. In these instances, the defendant may have a **legal defense**.

Torts That Injure Persons

The following sections will explain the most common intentional torts and the legal defenses to those torts.

Assault and Battery Assault and battery can be both crimes and intentional torts. A **battery** is an act intended to cause a harmful or offensive contact with another person. An **assault** is a threat or attempt to commit a battery that puts the victim in fear of immediate harm. If Jerry raises his fist and threatens to slug Sy, there is an assault if Sy reasonably fears being hit. If Jerry connects, there is also a battery.

Suppose that Tim pulls a chair out from under Jeb as he is getting ready to sit down. This is a battery, even though Tim did not touch Jeb, because there was an act (pulling the chair out) intended to cause a harmful contact (Jeb's hitting the floor). Tim would be liable to Jeb even if he was just playing a joke on his friend.

The intent required for an intentional tort is not a bad motive or even the desire to do harm. It is simply the intent to bring about a result that invades the legal rights of another person. In the case of

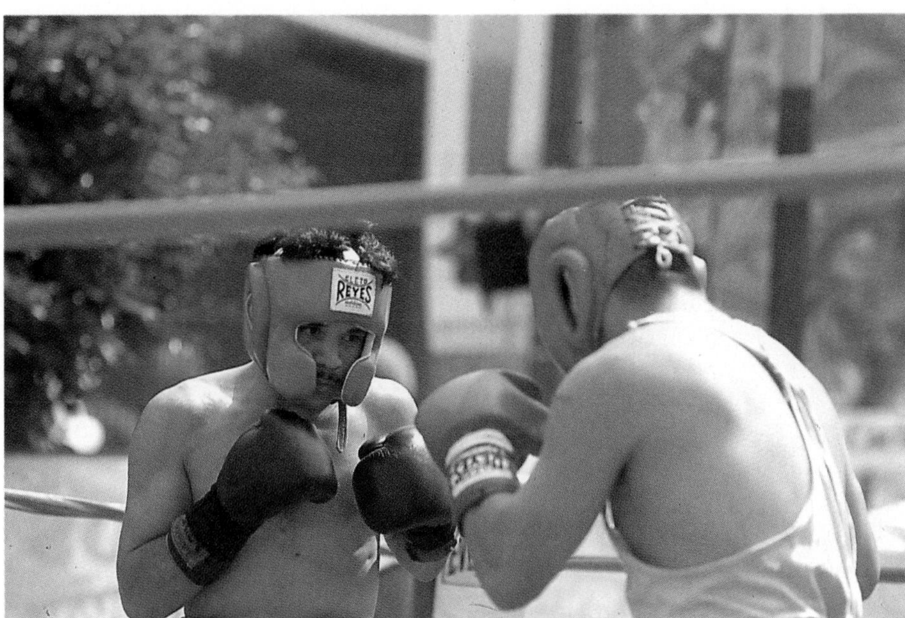

Can a boxer win a suit for an injury suffered during a boxing match?

Tim and Jeb, we are not concerned about whether Tim *meant* to cause Jeb any harm but rather whether Tim acted in a way that was intended to cause Jeb to fall and hence to invade Jeb's rights (his right not to fall when he sat down).

The damage award for an assault or a battery depends on the seriousness of the injury. For an assault, the plaintiff can recover damages for mental disturbance, such as fright or embarrassment, along with any physical illness that directly results from the assault. The damages recoverable from a battery are those for any harm caused by the physical contact.

Consent is the most common defense to a battery. This defense means that the plaintiff consented, or agreed, to the harmful contact and thus gave up the right to sue later. In boxing, punches are thrown that in almost any other situation would be serious batteries. However, boxers sign a contract consenting to be punched. Of course, if one boxer cut another with a knife, this would be a battery, as the consent was limited to punches.

Consent can be written, spoken, or simply assumed based on the situation. For example, children often knock each other down while playing, but this contact does not constitute a battery. In another example, suppose you were seriously injured in an auto accident and taken to the hospital for emergency surgery. Ordinarily you would sign a consent form before the operation, but in an emergency, when it is impossible to sign a form, the law will assume that you consent to surgery that is absolutely necessary.

If one of these women injures an attacker while defending herself, can the attacker recover damages from her?

Privilege is another defense to intentional torts. Privilege justifies conduct that would otherwise be a tort. This group of legal defenses excuses the defendant's behavior because his or her own interests (or those of the public) require it and because public policy is best served by permitting such behavior. Perhaps the best-known privilege is **self-defense**.

Tort law is designed to protect persons and their property from harm. Thus, if Al is attacked by Ed, he can use reasonable force to protect (or defend) himself. If Ed later sues Al for battery, Al will be able to use self-defense to justify his acts as long as the force he used was not excessive. A defender who takes control of a situation and becomes an aggressor may be committing a battery, however.

A person can also come to the rescue of another person and use the same amount of force the victim could have used to repel the attacker. Self-defense allows you to defend yourself against an attacker. It does not mean you can teach the attacker a lesson or gain revenge. These rules are similar to the self-defense rules in criminal law.

PROBLEM 13

Determine whether an assault, a battery, or both have been committed in each of the following situations. Is there legal defense in each situation? Give reasons for your answers.

a. A pitcher in a high-school baseball game loses control of an inside pitch. The ball hits the batter, shattering a bone in his arm.

b. Hal arranges to have an oral surgeon remove a tooth that has been causing him great discomfort. While he is under anesthesia, the surgeon notices that two other teeth are emerging in a crooked position and are likely to cause Hal great pain in the near future, so she removes these teeth as well.

c. Sandy, 17, throws a snowball at a friend on a crowded street corner. The snowball misses the friend but hits an elderly man, who falls to the ground and is injured.

d. As a joke, Annette removes the bullets from her father's revolver, takes the gun outside, and points it at the head of her neighbor, Mrs. Joiner, who is just leaving her house. Mrs. Joiner, who unknown to Annette suffers from serious heart disease, has a stroke and dies instantly.

e. Martha, a prison guard, is attacked by an inmate. The inmate knocks Martha down and kicks her in the head and ribs. Martha gets up, knocks the inmate down, and kicks her in a similar fashion.

Infliction of Mental Distress A relatively new tort is intentional **infliction of mental distress**. Courts have only recognized it since about 1940. A person commits this tort by intentionally using words or actions that are meant to cause someone fright, extreme anxiety, or mental distress. Actual physical injury is not required for the plaintiff to recover. However, courts do require that the defendant's conduct be quite outrageous and that the plaintiff prove extreme distress. Mere insults are not enough to form the basis of a lawsuit for mental distress.

When the actions of bill collectors, insurance adjustors, and landlords have been truly outrageous and excessive, courts have sometimes allowed plaintiffs to recover damages. For example, a young man owed a debt to a store. The store tried to collect the debt from the youth's father by falsely accusing him of guaranteeing the son's debt, making late-night calls to the father and sending letters telling the father that his credit had been revoked. In this case, the court found that the store had intentionally caused the father severe emotional distress.

Extremely outrageous conduct by restaurants, hotels, or transportation companies can also sometimes form the basis for the tort of mental distress. These businesses, and certain others, have a special obligation to deal with the public in a courteous manner.

Recovery for this tort is sharply limited to keep the legal system from being flooded with lawsuits brought by persons suffering from unkind, inconsiderate acts. In addition, there is some value for a free society in letting angry people blow off steam without fear of being sued. Among the legal defenses that can be used are that the defendant's conduct was not outrageous, that the plaintiff is overly sensitive, and that a reasonable person would not suffer extreme distress as a result of the defendant's conduct.

PROBLEM 14

Give a specific example of a situation in which you believe someone should be able to recover for infliction of mental distress. Write the dialogue, showing exactly what was said and done by each party. Determine the amount of damages that should be awarded.

False Imprisonment Being able to sue for **false imprisonment** protects a person's interest in being free from unreasonable restraint. False imprisonment does not mean being kept in jail or even arrested by police. It occurs when someone intentionally and wrongfully confines another person against his or her will.

What actions can storeowners take to protect themselves against shoplifters?

For example, assume that a restaurant manager tells an employee to get out of the walk-in refrigerator so she can lock up and go home. When the employee takes too long, the manager shuts the refrigerator door and leaves for the night. The restaurant manager has committed the tort of false imprisonment.

The Captured Shoplifter

Kathleen, 17, is in a record store. As she passes a rack of compact discs, she quickly slips one under her jacket. Thinking that no one has noticed, she turns to leave the store. The store manager, however, was watching her on a closed-circuit television. As soon as she passes the cash register, he stops her, before she leaves the store.

PROBLEM 15

a. The store manager has several options. Rank the following in order of most reasonable to least reasonable:

1. The manager calls the police and keeps Kathleen in his office until they come.
2. The manager tells an assistant manager to keep Kathleen in the back room until the police arrive. The assistant manager is called away on another task, and he ties Kathleen's hands and feet together so she cannot run away.
3. The manager yells "Stop, you thief" as he runs after Kathleen in the store, and he shouts at her as he walks her back to his office. Then he calls her parents and tells them he is taking her to the police station immediately.
4. The manager locks Kathleen in the storage room for seven hours, until he is ready to close the shop for the evening. Then he takes her to the police station.
5. The store manager tells his security guard to arrest Kathleen. The guard pulls a gun, takes her to the back of the store, and calls the police.

b. Would any of these alternatives qualify as false imprisonment? If so, which ones and why? What should a shopkeeper do if he or she catches a shoplifter?

Suspected shoplifters sometimes sue shopkeepers who detain them. In balancing an individual's right to be free from confinement and a shopkeeper's right to protect his or her property from theft, the law recognizes a shopkeeper's privilege to temporarily detain a person suspected of shoplifting. However, shopkeepers must act reasonably, using no more restraint than is necessary to protect their property.

Shelter for Street People

In order to prevent homeless citizens from freezing during the winter, Big Town passes an ordinance. It requires its social-service workers to pick up homeless street people whenever the nighttime temperature is predicted to fall below 35 degrees. The homeless people are then taken to a city shelter and provided with food, clothing, and a bed. They are not allowed to leave until the next morning.

Mr. Stobbs, a homeless person, believes the shelter is dangerous and unsanitary. He also believes he has a right to live on the street. One night, he is taken to the shelter against his will. He later convinces a public-interest law firm in Big Town to help him sue the city for false imprisonment.

PROBLEM 16

a. What arguments can Mr. Stobbs make?

b. What arguments can Big Town make?

c. How would you decide this case? Explain how your decision best serves the public interest.

d. Would your answer be different if Mr. Stobbs were mentally disturbed? What should happen then?

Torts Related to Reputation and Privacy Tort law also protects your reputation and your privacy. A person's reputation is protected by the law of **defamation**. There are two kinds of defamation. Oral statements that harm reputation are called **slander**; written defamation is called **libel**. Damages are often more difficult to prove for slander than for libel.

Defamation occurs when a person makes a false statement that is communicated to a third party (not just to the person defamed), causing harm to the plaintiff. A patient's telling his doctor "You're a drunken butcher" is not slander if no one else hears the statement. If the patient yells this false statement in the hospital hallway where others can hear it and the doctor's reputation is harmed, a tort has been committed.

Proving that the offensive statement is true is a defense to defamation. For example, Sid brings his car to a garage and yells at the mechanic "You ruined my transmission!" in front of other customers. This statement might be harmful to the mechanic. But if Sid can prove that the mechanic *did* ruin his transmission, he has a good defense to slander charges.

The Malicious Interview

Orange J and Ice Pop were both singers in the group Brain Death. After they argued violently about what to wear during a concert, they decided to pursue solo careers, and the band broke up.

A reporter from *Top Hits* magazine interviewed Orange J about the former band and particularly about Ice Pop's music. The reporter knew that Orange J knew Ice Pop very well. He also knew that Orange J was bitter about the breakup of Brain Death. Based on this interview, *Top Hits* published a story about Ice Pop describing him as a second-rate musician who steals other artists' music.

Although Ice Pop's music may sound similar to that of other performers, he claims that his songs are all original compositions. He wants to sue the magazine.

PROBLEM 17

a. Is Ice Pop a public figure?

b. Should the reporter have relied on Orange J's information?

c. What will Ice Pop have to prove to win a suit against *Top Hits*?

d. What value will be protected if Ice Pop wins? What value will be protected if the magazine wins?

e. How should this case be decided?

The law also protects opinion. Assume that a movie critic attends a new movie and, in her review, is particularly critical of one actor's performance. The movie review may harm the actor's reputation and economic interests, but the statements will usually be protected as opinion.

In the United States, freedom of speech and freedom of the press are very important. Therefore, courts balance a person's right to protect his or her reputation against the public's interest in receiving a wide range of information. For this reason, the U.S. Supreme Court has established rules making it difficult for public figures or public officials to win damage awards against the media. To win a defamation suit against the media, a public figure must prove not only that a statement was false and caused harm but also that the statement was made with actual **malice** (that is, with knowledge of its falsity or with a reckless disregard for whether the statement was true). These rules make it very difficult for famous people to sue the media and win. In a sense, famous people who step into the public's eye sacrifice some protection of their reputations.

Torts That Harm Property

Why does the law protect the rights of property owners?

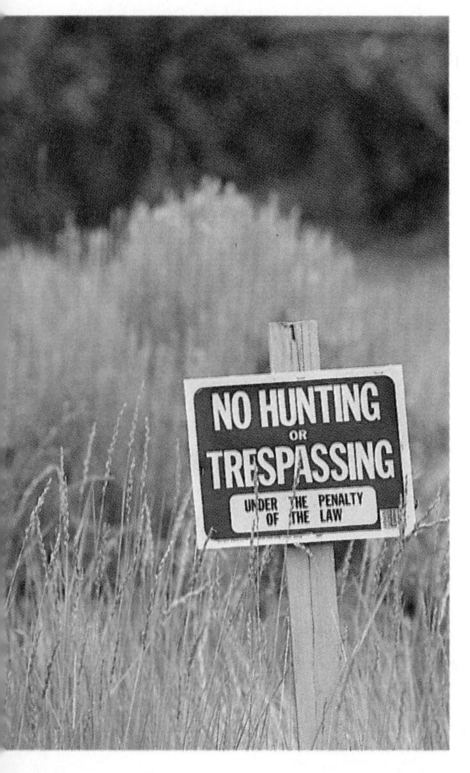

Tort law protects your property in two ways: (1) it protects against interference with the owner's exclusive use of the property, and (2) it protects against the property's being taken or damaged. Two kinds of property are protected: **real property** (land and the items attached to it, such as houses, crops, and fences), and **personal property** (property that can be moved, such as cars, clothing, and appliances).

Real Property Everyone has seen signs that read "Private Property—Keep Out" or "No Trespassing." The tort of **trespass** occurs when a person goes onto another person's property without permission. The owner can recover damages from the trespasser even if there is no harm to the property, because the law protects the owner's *exclusive* right to the property.

In a technical sense, a trespass occurs every time you cut across a neighbor's lawn on the way to the store. Obviously, landowners rarely sue people who merely walk across their property. However, what would you do if someone committed a continuing trespass by going on your property without permission and erecting a sign advertising a nearby restaurant? Our legal system is very protective of private property rights.

In some cases, tort law protects against harm caused by someone who never *physically* enters your property. A **nuisance** occurs when there is an unreasonable interference with the use and enjoyment of your property. Courts will balance the usefulness of the activity complained of against the harm caused.

You do not have a right to be free from all interference with your property, only unreasonable interference. For example, Ari and Brenda are neighbors. One Sunday, Ari has a large barbecue in his backyard, and Brenda is unable to listen to the baseball game on the radio while lying in her hammock. This one-time event is not a nuisance. If Ari were to cut his lawn at six o'clock every Sunday morning, however, that would probably be a nuisance.

You can recover damages if you win a nuisance suit. In some cases, you may also be able to get a court order requiring the defendant to stop the activity complained of. This court order is called an **injunction**. An injunction requires that a person do, or not do, a specific act.

Tort law protects you when others damage your property. In some instances, tort law also requires that you use reasonable care to protect other persons from harm when they are on your property. In general, though, you are not liable if a trespasser is injured on your property. For example, if a trespasser walks across your lawn, trips on a sprinkler, and sprains her ankle, she will not be able to recover damages from you.

An exception to the general rule has developed when the trespasser is a child too young to appreciate a dangerous condition on your land. The law imposes a duty on landowners to use reasonable care to eliminate a dangerous condition on their land or otherwise protect children when the condition presents an unreasonable risk of serious injury where children are likely to trespass. Because of this law,

If teenagers climb over the fence and drown in this pool, should their families be able to recover damages from the property owner?

The Unfenced Swimming Pool

The Garcia family built a large swimming pool in their backyard. The pool was two feet deep in the shallow end and nine feet deep near the diving board. They placed lights around the pool that turned on automatically at dusk. They also placed four large "Danger—Deep Water" signs around all sides of the pool.

One day, a four-year-old who lived a block away wandered onto their property, entered the pool, and drowned. The child's parents sued the Garcia family for not fencing in the pool.

How should this case be decided? Suppose the Garcias had fenced in the pool and the child had climbed the fence and drowned. Should the child's parents be able to recover damages in that situation?

sometimes called the **attractive nuisance** doctrine, construction companies generally fence in excavation sites.

Most people who enter your property are probably not trespassers. Generally, they are either social guests in your home or businesspeople or customers visiting your workplace. In most states, you have a legal duty to warn social guests of any known danger on your property. For example, if your front porch is being repaired, you have a duty to warn your guests to avoid this dangerous situation.

A friend invited to your home trips over items left on your sidewalk and is hurt. Can she recover damages from you?

If you own a store or other business establishment and the public comes to see you for a business purpose, the law imposes an even higher duty. Business owners have a duty to use reasonable care to inspect the property to make it safe for business visitors. For this reason, a restaurant owner is not merely required to warn customers of a slippery sidewalk on a snowy day but is obligated to use reasonable care to make the sidewalk safe (by shoveling the snow, spreading salt or sand, or the like).

YOU BE THE JUDGE

PROBLEM 18

Read each case carefully. Identify the usefulness of the action complained of and the harm caused. Decide whether a nuisance exists. If it does, decide on a fair remedy. Give your reasons.

a. Mr. Iwamoto works the 11:00 P.M. to 7:00 A.M. shift at the factory and then comes home to sleep. On his way to school, Tommy James walks by Mr. Iwamoto's house every weekday at 8:30 A.M. with his "boom box" blaring. The loud music awakens Mr. Iwamoto.

b. An oil tanker runs aground, spilling more than a million barrels of oil. Some of the oil washes up on privately owned beachfront property. The property owners sue the oil company for damage to their beaches. They also ask the judge to prohibit oil tankers from using the port near their property in order to avoid harm from future accidents.

c. Morgan owns a restaurant next to High Penn's oil refinery. The refinery occasionally emits gases and odors that make people feel sick. Morgan, believing that this hurts her restaurant business, brings a suit. High Penn argues that (1) the refinery was properly constructed, (2) there is no way to operate the refinery without these occasional odors, and (3) the refinery was in operation before Morgan opened her restaurant.

d. Gomez owns a house with a view of the ocean. When he built the house, the county owned all the land between the house and the ocean. The land was completely undeveloped. Ten years later, the county rezoned the land and sold it to a seafood restaurant. As the construction started, Gomez sued. He argued that he would lose his unobstructed view of the ocean and that the value of his house would be greatly reduced.

e. In order to earn money to send their children to college, Larry and Meg operate a small auto repair shop in their garage. After returning from their day jobs, they work on cars until 10:00 P.M. The noise produced when they rev up car engines disturbs their neighbors.

f. Adriana Stein is a successful musician who travels extensively to give concerts. She buys a house in the countryside only five miles from the nearest airport. As the metropolitan area grows, traffic at the airport increases. Eventually, the airport needs another runway. Experts report that the runway can be built in only one location at the airport. Planes using this runway would descend directly over Stein's house. She organizes her neighbors into a citizen action group called RAMP (residents against more planes). It sues the airport, seeking an injunction to stop construction of the new runway.

Personal Property Tort law also provides compensation to someone whose personal property is taken, damaged, or interfered with. Suppose a burglar breaks into Laura's house and steals her stereo and television set. If the person is arrested, there will be a criminal prosecution for burglary. Laura could also sue the thief in civil court for a tort. This tort, called **conversion**, occurs when someone unlawfully exercises control over the personal property of another person.

A series of privileges has developed for protecting property. You

The Burglar Who Was Bitten

The Kims own a small store in a crime-ridden section of town. To protect their family and store, they purchase a guard dog. The dog is trained to attack on command. The dog also stays in the store from 11:00 P.M. to 7:00 A.M., while the store is closed. One night, a person breaks into the store and is attacked by the dog. The police catch the person, and he is convicted of burglary. After the judge gives him a suspended sentence, the burglar sues the Kims for the injuries caused by the guard dog. How would you decide this case? Give your reasons.

can always use nonviolent means to protect real property ("please get off my land . . . you are trespassing") or to recover personal property. However, you must use careful judgment in these cases. Telling your lockermate that she has taken the wrong lunch bag may work well; yelling at a fleeing thief to put down your possessions is likely to fail!

Reasonable force can also be used to protect property. Precisely how much force is reasonable depends on the circumstances. Generally, deadly force can never be used to protect property, although the rules of self-defense allow the use of deadly force to protect a person if serious bodily harm is threatened.

NEGLIGENCE

We have already examined intentional torts and their defenses. Another type of tort is called negligence. Tort law establishes standards of care that society expects from people. Negligence is conduct that falls below the standard established by law for protecting others against unreasonable risks of harm. But what does this mean?

The word *negligence* comes from the root word *neglect*. This may lead us to think of negligence as forgetfulness, inattentiveness, or lack of care about others. But tort law requires us to analyze negligence as it relates to a person's *conduct*. Even a person who cares a great deal about others may be negligent if his or her conduct creates an *unreasonable risk of harm*. On the other hand, a person who is totally unconcerned about the safety of others may not be negligent if his or her conduct did not subject the plaintiff to an unreasonable risk of harm.

These are some examples of negligent conduct:

- Dr. D'Angelo, a surgeon, forgets to remove a clamp from a patient's body while operating and stitches the patient up.
- Monica leaves a loaded rifle on the floor where her younger brothers and sisters usually play. A child is shot.
- A city employee working in a manhole forgets to replace the cover when he goes to lunch and a pedestrian falls in and is injured.
- A drug company markets a birth control device for women without conducting much medical testing. It assumes the device is safe because people have used similar devices for years. A woman develops a serious illness from using the device.

When we studied intentional torts, there were names for many of them (such as battery, assault, and false imprisonment). For the most part, *negligence* is a very broad term that deals with many kinds of wrongful conduct. While the different types of wrongful conduct may not have separate names, they do have something in common: for a plaintiff to win a negligence action against the defendant, each of the following **elements** must be proven by a preponderance of the evidence:

1. **Duty:** The defendant, or wrongdoer, owed a duty of care to the plaintiff, or injured person.
2. **Breach of duty:** That duty was violated, or **breached**, by the defendant's conduct.
3. **Causation:** The defendant's conduct caused the plaintiff's harm.
4. **Damages:** The plaintiff suffered actual **damages**.

All of these elements must be proven or the plaintiff will not prevail. For example, in the case of the drug company described above, the woman would have to prove each of the elements of negligence by a preponderance of the evidence against the company. Specifically, she would have to prove that the company had a duty of care to its customers to test any new birth control product before selling it, that the company breached this duty through its failure to test, and that this breach resulted in a defective product that caused actual damage to the woman bringing the lawsuit (ill health, hospital bills, and so on).

As in intentional torts, defendants in negligence cases sometimes have legal defenses. These defenses are different from those used in intentional torts. They are explained below.

Does this sign provide adequate warning of danger to swimmers and divers?

Duty and Breach

Everyone has a general duty to exercise reasonable care toward other persons and their property. Negligence law is primarily concerned with compensating victims who are harmed by a wrongdoer's action or inaction that violates or breaches this standard of reasonable care. If a mechanic fixes the brakes on your car without using reasonable care and skill and this faulty repair causes you to have an accident, you can recover damages from the mechanic.

What if someone is harmed by another person's inaction? For example, Brian is drowning in a lake and Jennifer, an expert swimmer, is passing by in a boat. Does she have a legal duty to rescue Brian? While she may have a moral obligation to help, she generally does

Bartender Liability

Lance is a bartender at the local pub. He sees that Mike and Nancy, two regular customers, are clearly intoxicated. They ask him for one more round of drinks before they leave. Not wanting to offend them, he serves them, saying, "Let's make this the last round." Thirty minutes later the couple leaves the bar to go home. Just after Nancy pulls her car onto the highway, she swerves and hits another car head-on. Mike and the driver of the other car are seriously injured.

PROBLEM 19

a. Who can sue whom in this situation?

b. What duty did Lance have in this situation? Did he violate that duty?

c. Now assume that Lance is hosting a private Christmas party in his home. During the party, Nancy and Mike have a little too much to drink. The rest of the facts are the same as above. Answer Questions a and b using this scenario.

d. Is it fair to hold Lance responsible in either of the situations above? Give your reasons. Is anyone else responsible? If you were at the bar or the party and knew Mike and Nancy, what would you do?

e. Some restaurants and bars have "designated driver" programs. Why have they done this? What else, if anything, should be done?

not have a legal duty to act unless there is some special relationship between them (for example, she is a lifeguard and he is drowning in an area she is supervising).

In some cases, a specific duty of care owed to the plaintiff is set out in a statute (either federal, state, or local). For example, a federal transportation regulation requires all manufacturers of automobiles to provide seat belts in every new car. Car manufacturers have a duty to provide a mechanism (seat belts) that will help keep drivers and their passengers safe from certain foreseeable harm.

Is there a law in your state requiring a person to rescue another from harm if it can be done safely? Should there be such a law?

AIDS Liability

Jim is infected with HIV, the virus that causes AIDS. He is new in town and does not want anyone to know about his condition. He becomes romantically involved with Amy and has sex with her but does not disclose his infection with HIV. Amy contracts the virus.

PROBLEM 20

a. Did Jim have a duty to tell Amy about his condition? Explain.

b. Would it make a difference if AIDS were curable?

c. What, if anything, should Amy be able to recover in damages from Jim? Explain.

d. Could Amy sue Jim if she did not contract the virus but was very upset when she learned that he had not told her about it?

Causation

Once a plaintiff proves that the defendant owes him or her a duty and that this duty was violated, there must be proof that the defendant's acts caused the harm to the plaintiff. While it seems like common sense to require a causal connection between the act complained of and the plaintiff's injury, the concept is sometimes troublesome to apply. For an interesting historical example, see the Case of the Great Chicago Fire on page 227.

When you think about the element of causation, you must consider two separate issues: **cause in fact** and **legal**, or **proximate**, **cause**. Cause in fact is easy to understand. If the harm would not have occurred *without* the wrongful act, the act is the cause in fact. If Mrs. O'Leary had not placed the lantern too close to the cow, it would not have been kicked over, and the Great Chicago Fire would not have occurred. Her act was the cause in fact of the fire.

The more difficult part of causation is establishing legal, or proximate, cause. Would it have been fair to make Mrs. O'Leary pay for all the damage caused in the Chicago fire? A certain amount of damage from her wrongful act was **foreseeable**. At some point, however,

THE CASE OF . . .

The Great Chicago Fire

In 1871, a major fire destroyed much of the city of Chicago. After a thorough investigation, the cause of the fire was determined. It began in Mrs. O'Leary's shed when a cow she had been milking kicked over a kerosene lantern she had placed too close to the cow's rear leg.

Was Mrs. O'Leary negligent in placing the lantern so close to the cow's leg? Should she have had to pay for all the damage caused by the fire? Give reasons for your answer.

the damage to the city of Chicago was greater than what could have been foreseen when she negligently placed the lantern near the cow.

It is often hard to draw the line in legal cause situations. Different judges have different theories about legal cause, and the results of tough cases are difficult to predict. The basic idea behind legal cause is that there must be a close connection between the wrongful act and the harm caused. The harm caused must have been a foreseeable result of the act or acts. Negligence law does not hold people responsible for harm that was completely unforeseeable.

An artist's rendition of how the Great Chicago Fire started.

THE CASE OF . . .

The College Prank

As a freshman college prank, Cynthia decides to remove a stop sign from an intersection and put it in her dormitory room. To avoid being noticed, she chooses a stop sign at the intersection of a little-used country road and a two-lane state highway several miles out of town. The night after her prank, a motorist from out of state drives through this intersection and is struck by a car traveling at 50 miles per hour along the state highway. Both motorists are seriously injured, and their cars are totally demolished. They recover from their injuries after several months. The police suspect a college prank and are able to find out who removed the sign. The injured motorists bring a civil action against Cynthia, claiming extensive damages. Can they prove that her act caused their harm? Explain your answer.

Assume, for example, that your car wrongfully crosses the center line and collides with a truck. It turns out that the truck is carrying dynamite, which explodes and kills a person two blocks away. Your negligent crossing of the yellow line is the cause in fact of the harm to the person two blocks away, but most courts would say that your negligence was not the legal, or proximate, cause of this death. Crossing a yellow line does not usually result in a death two blocks away. The death was not foreseeable. This case would be decided differently, though, if the person who died was a pedestrian on the sidewalk 50 feet from the collision.

Sometimes the negligence of more than one person harms someone. For example, suppose two cars, each negligently driven, collide and injure a pedestrian on a nearby sidewalk. Each driver is responsible for the pedestrian's injuries. If one driver is unable to pay, the other driver may have to pay the entire amount of the damages.

Damages

A plaintiff who proves duty, breach, and both forms of causation still must prove actual damages to recover in a negligence action. The basic idea behind damages is that the plaintiff should be restored to his or her preinjury condition, to the extent that this can be achieved with money.

Courts allow plaintiffs to recover for hospital bills, lost wages, damage to property, reduced future earnings, and other economic harm. Plaintiffs may also recover for noneconomic harm such as pain and suffering, mental distress, and permanent physical losses (for example, loss of a limb or blindness). However, in some states, a plaintiff must first prove economic harm—even if only one dollar—before a judge or jury can make an award for noneconomic harm like pain and suffering.

PROBLEM 21

Reread the Case of the College Prank on page 228. Assume that the plaintiffs can prove duty, breach, and causation. List all the types of damages each plaintiff might have suffered. Could they recover all of these damages? Explain your answer.

The Reasonable Person Standard

To help judge whether certain conduct is negligent, the law has developed an imaginary creature—"the reasonable person of ordinary prudence or carefulness." The reasonably prudent person does not represent the typical, average individual. Rather, this is an idealized version of such a person. This person acts the way a community *expects* its members to act, not exactly as they do in fact act. However,

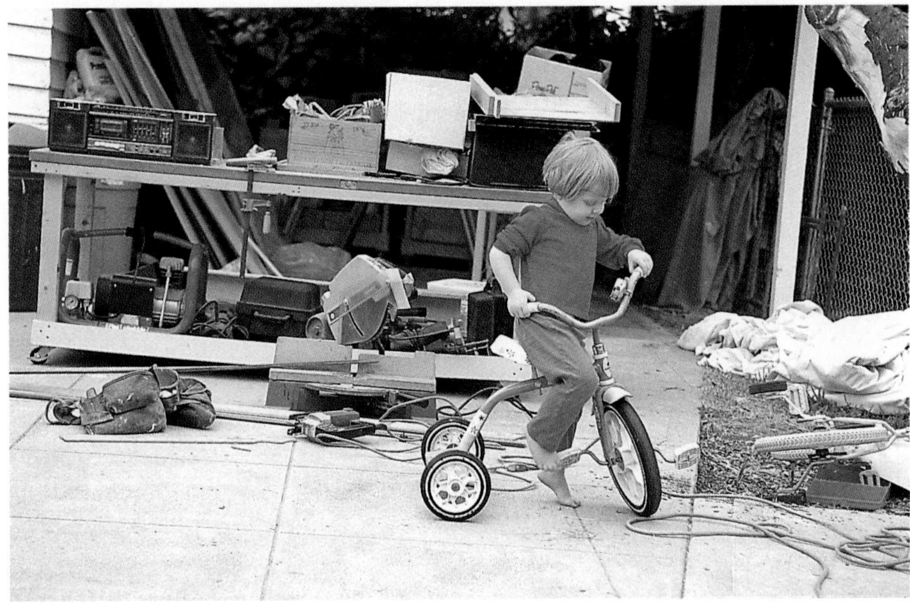

Did the adult who allowed this child to play here act reasonably?

this ordinary, reasonable person is human and therefore not perfect.

How does the reasonable person behave? The reasonable person considers how *likely* a certain harm is to occur, how *serious* the harm would be if it did occur, and the *burden* involved in avoiding the harm. The likelihood and seriousness of the harm are balanced against the burden of avoiding the harm.

For example, assume a pedestrian is about to cross a road where there is very little automobile traffic. The harm to be avoided, of course, is being hit by a vehicle. Our imaginary person asks: How likely is it that such an accident will occur? Not very likely. How serious would the harm be if it did occur? Very serious. How difficult would it be to avoid this harm? Not difficult at all: simply look both ways before crossing. Our reasonably prudent person looks both ways before crossing such a street.

In a second example, the walkway to a secluded home in the woods has a crack in it. The crack is large enough to allow a person to trip

The Blood Transfusion

Highland Hospital has just acquired machinery that can test blood for HIV. Previously it relied on the honesty and knowledge of blood donors to ensure that the blood was safe. Mr. Laden is brought to the emergency room after an accident. He needs emergency surgery and has already lost a lot of blood. The doctors, believing that he will probably need a transfusion, request several units of his blood type, but they do not have time to test the blood with the new machine. Without immediate surgery, Mr. Laden may die.

PROBLEM 22

a. Should the doctors proceed with the surgery even though the blood they need for the transfusion is untested?

b. Assume they use the blood, Mr. Laden recovers from his injuries, and several months later he tests positive for HIV. As Mr. Laden's attorney, what arguments would you make?

c. As the hospital's attorney, what arguments would you make?

d. How should this case be decided? Give your reasons.

and fall. This is the harm to be avoided by the homeowner. In this instance, the likelihood of the harm is small, the harm is probably not very serious, and the cost of avoiding it (fixing the walkway) may be substantial. Even our reasonably prudent person may not have to fix this crack in the walk. However, it may be reasonable to post a sign warning of the danger, because the burden (cost) of the sign would be less than the burden of making the repair.

Certain professionals, such as doctors, plumbers, and pilots, are considered to have the abilities of reasonably skilled persons qualified to be members of their professions. For this reason, a plumber who repairs a kitchen sink that later leaks and damages the floor cannot defend against a tort action by claiming that he completed the job as skillfully as the ordinarily prudent person. The work must be at the level of the ordinarily prudent plumber!

As you know, minors are liable for torts they commit. However, the standard used in negligence cases involving minors is not the same as it is for adults. Instead, the law compares the minor's conduct with reasonable conduct for others of the same age, intelligence, and experience. When a minor reaches the age of majority, the adult standard of care applies. There is one important exception to this rule: when minors engage in what is ordinarily considered an adult activity, such as driving a car, they are held to the adult standard of care.

Does the law hold this teenage driver to the adult standard of care?

The Stolen Car

Alan, 17, lends his car to his friend Esther, 16, so that she can pick up her prom dress. Esther drives to a large shopping center on the outskirts of town. As she hurries into the store to pick up the dress, she leaves the keys in the car and the driver's side door unlocked. When she returns 10 minutes later, the car is gone. Esther calls Alan immediately, and he reports to the police that the car has been stolen. The car cannot be found.

PROBLEM 23

a. Can Alan sue Esther for the value of the car? Give your reasons.

b. Would it make a difference if Esther did not yet have a driver's license and Alan knew this? Explain your answer.

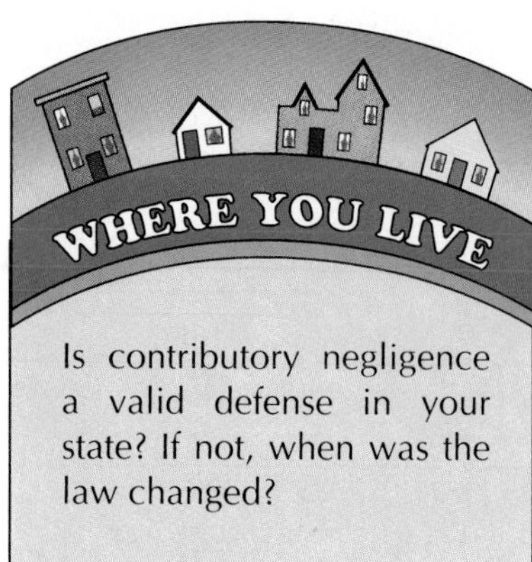

Is contributory negligence a valid defense in your state? If not, when was the law changed?

Defenses to Negligence Suits

We have seen that people can recover for injuries when they are able to prove each of the elements of negligence by a preponderance of the evidence. However, even when all the elements can be proven, the defendant may be able to raise a valid legal defense. One group of legal defenses in negligence cases is based on the plaintiff's conduct.

One traditional legal defense is **contributory negligence**. This means that as a plaintiff, you cannot recover from the defendant if your own negligence contributed in any way to the harm suffered. For example, suppose a train station attendant warns a passenger not to walk in an area where ice has formed on the platform. The passenger walks there anyway, falls, and is hurt. The passenger might sue the railroad for allowing ice to remain on the platform. Applying the contributory negligence defense, the railway would have a legal defense, because the passenger's own negligence in ignoring the warning contributed to the injury.

When both parties are equally at fault, the contributory negligence rule perhaps provides a fair result. Neither party can recover from the other. However, the contributory negligence defense also allows a very slight amount of negligence on the part of the plaintiff to give the defendant a complete legal defense. This is true even when the damage to the plaintiff is great and the defendant has been very negligent. Many people think this produces an unfair result. Therefore, this defense has been eliminated in most states by either state law or judicial decision.

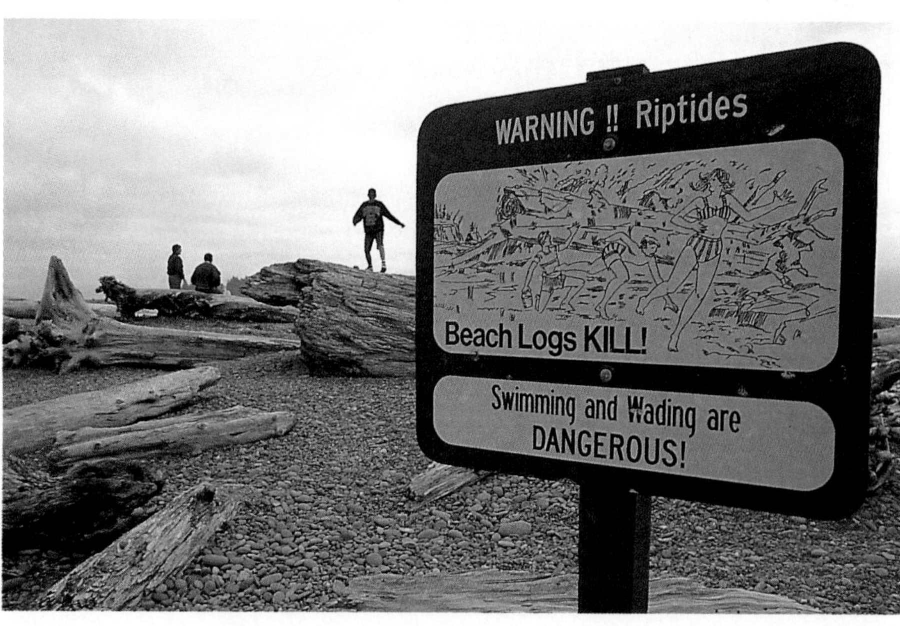

Should a swimmer injured at this beach be able to recover damages from the property owner?

Most states now use a defense called **comparative negligence**. This means dividing the loss according to the degree to which each person is at fault. For example, Al and Bob are in a car accident and Al sues Bob for the $10,000 in damages that he suffers. If the jury finds that Al was somewhat negligent himself, the damages will be reduced. If Al was 10 percent at fault and Bob was 90 percent at fault, Al will receive $9,000 ($10,000 reduced by 10 percent, the amount that was Al's fault). If Al was 30 percent at fault, he will receive only $7,000. But if he was more than 50 percent at fault, he will receive no damages in many states, and Bob might be able to sue Al for some damages. Bob's action against Al is called a **counterclaim**.

Is comparative negligence a defense in your state? How are damages apportioned if more than one person has been negligent?

Sometimes several people commit a negligent act against a third person. If Al and Bob in the example above had negligently collided and injured Charles, who was in another car and was not at fault, Charles could recover from both Al and Bob. Al and Bob might be able to divide their liability to Charles between themselves, according to each one's degree of fault. However, if one of the defendants was unable to pay because he had no money, the other defendant might have to pay all the damages awarded to Charles.

Another legal defense in negligence cases is **assumption of the risk**. This defense is used when a person voluntarily encounters a known danger and decides to accept the risk of that danger. For example, a hockey fan knows that on rare occasions a hockey puck can be deflected off a player's stick, over the glass that surrounds the rink, and into the lower seats. A fan who buys such a seat knows the risk and agrees to accept the danger. If a fan is hit by the puck, assumption of the risk will be a complete defense for the team or the players involved should the injured fan try to sue.

This defense also is used when a warning is posted that gives notice of a certain danger. For example, many hotels operate swimming pools without hiring lifeguards. The hotels post large "Swim at Your Own Risk" signs near the pools.

Can an injured baseball fan sue for damages?

PROBLEM 24

Analyze each case below. Identify the plaintiff and defendant and decide whether the defendant has a legal defense. Assume the state has a comparative negligence law.

a. Caroline and her friends go to an amusement park. She decides to ride the scariest roller coaster. After each rider is seated, the attendant secures that rider with a rollbar. Caroline tells her friends that she does not need the rollbar. After the first large hill, she detaches it. Later in the ride, she is thrown from the roller coaster and is badly hurt.

b. A large sign is posted at the foot of the lifeguard station warning of a very dangerous undertow beyond the first sandbar. There are buoys floating around the sandbar. Howard swims out beyond the sandbar and drowns before the lifeguard is able to reach him.

c. Jerry's car runs out of gas on a railway crossing in a rural area. He puts on his flashers to warn approaching cars and begins walking to the nearest gas station, which is a mile away. A freight train approaches, and the engineer sounds his horn several times, thinking the driver will move off the tracks. By the time the engineer realizes that the car is abandoned, it is too late to stop the train. The car is totally demolished.

A final series of defenses deals with defendants who are **immune** from some kinds of tort suits. In some situations, society has decided that for public policy reasons certain groups of people should not be sued, even though their conduct may have been improper. These immunities involve suits within families and against governments and certain government officials.

Generally, courts do not allow children to sue their parents or vice versa. Historically, courts have also refused to allow husbands and

Should railroad companies have a legal duty to install crossing gates wherever roads cross the track?

wives to sue each other in tort actions. This was because of the traditional idea that the husband and wife were one legal entity! Times change and so do tort laws. Now husbands and wives can sue each other for torts in many states. Even where these immunities remain, brothers and sisters may be able to sue each other in civil actions.

Can a minor child sue a parent in your state? Can spouses sue each other for torts? Should any of these laws be changed in your state? If so, how?

The federal and state governments are also immune from tort liability unless they give up, or **waive**, this immunity. The notion of government immunity comes from England, where there was a tradition that "the king can do no wrong." Today the federal government, through the *Federal Tort Claims Act*, has agreed to be held liable in civil actions for negligent acts or omissions by government employees. However, that act does not allow citizens to sue the federal government for most intentional or strict liability torts. Most states and municipalities also allow for certain tort suits.

The president, federal judges, and members of Congress are totally immune from tort liability for acts carried out within the scope of their duties. Other high-ranking officials, including members of the Cabinet and presidential aides, have qualified immunity, meaning that they can be sued only if they knew or should have known that their acts were violating the legal rights of another person.

STRICT LIABILITY

Up to now, we have examined tort cases in which the defendant was, to some degree, at fault and therefore liable to the plaintiff. In torts, one exception to this requirement of fault is **strict liability**, also known as liability without fault.

Strict liability means that the defendant is liable to the plaintiff regardless of fault. In some situations, even if the defendant acted in a reasonable and prudent manner and took all the precautions necessary, liability is imposed without proof of fault. Strict liability is applied to ultrahazardous activities such as storing or transporting dangerous substances, or blasting; to harm caused by dangerous animals; and, in recent years, to the manufacture and sale of dangerous, defective consumer products.

Remember that proving negligence involves establishing four elements: duty, breach, causation, and damages. To prove strict liability, you must only prove causation and damages. However, you must also convince the court that the activity that caused the harm is the type of unreasonably dangerous activity to which strict liability is applied. Public policy and common sense require people who conduct dangerous activities to accept responsibility for any harm caused, even if they were not negligent. The alternative would be to place the burden of harm on a totally innocent victim.

A bystander crosses the fenced-off area around this building and is injured during the blast. Should the demolition company be liable?

Dangerous Activities

Strict liability applies to activities that are unreasonably dangerous. Activities are considered unreasonably dangerous when they involve a risk of harm that cannot be eliminated even by reasonable care. These activities may be socially useful or necessary, but because of their potential for harm, those who conduct them are held to a higher standard of liability than negligence. They are held to the strict liability standard. Assume that a demolition company has been hired to dynamite an old downtown building. It is dangerous to use dynamite in a populated area, and no amount of care can totally eliminate the risk. Therefore, the law imposes strict liability. The demolition company must assume the risk of any foreseeable harm caused, even if the company is very careful and not negligent at all.

Companies conducting dangerous activities know that they are strictly liable for any harm they cause. Therefore, they build the cost into the price they charge for the work. With strict liability, the company using the dynamite has a financial incentive to be as careful as possible.

PROBLEM 25

In which of the following situations should the plaintiff be able to recover based on strict liability? Give your reasons.

a. Anytown's waste treatment plant develops a leak, and harmful bacteria are released into the town's water supply. Hundreds of families become sick.

b. Anita brings her car to a mechanic for repairs. As she enters the garage, she slips on spilled motor oil and breaks her ankle.

c. Donna drives by a construction site in a downtown shopping district. Following a sudden blast from the site, she is injured by a piece of cement that crashes through her windshield.

d. Choo Lee is eating lunch at a cafeteria. A waiter races by and knocks a pot of coffee into Choo's lap, burning him badly.

In recent years, a concept called toxic torts has been developed to address harm resulting from the use of toxic chemicals and other hazardous materials. Historically, industrial manufacturers disposed of their wastes by dumping them into the nearest river or other convenient location. It wasn't until the 1960s that the public

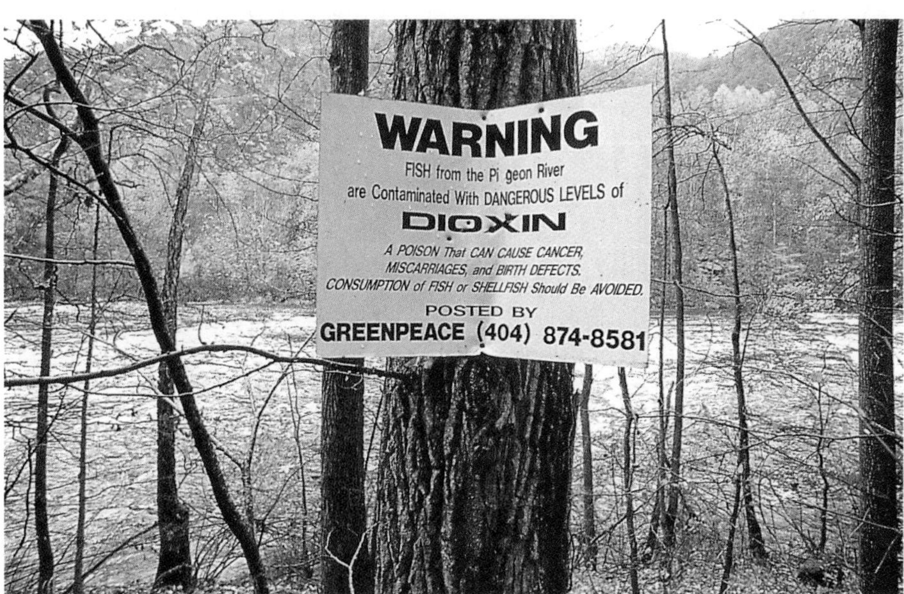

Will a person harmed by eating fish caught in this river be able to recover damages from the polluter?

began to understand that prolonged exposure to toxic chemicals could cause illness and even death!

The toxic tort concept was developed to allow injured parties to recover from industrial polluters if the injured parties could establish causation—that is, if they could establish that the harm resulted from the manufacture or disposal of hazardous materials. For example, when a Massachusetts mother found that her son and a dozen other neighborhood children had leukemia, she successfully sued a local chemical company that had contaminated local drinking water by dumping its waste products.

The Bee-Killing Farmer

Mr. Mattingly, a well-to-do farmer, has a legal right to apply pesticides to his fruit trees. One year, he decided to hire a crop-dusting airplane to spread a pesticide on his orchard. An unexpected gust of wind blew the chemical onto a neighbor's beehives, killing all the bees. The neighbor sued Mattingly for the value of the 60 beehives. Mattingly argued that a good fruit farmer has to apply pesticides and that the crop dusters had exercised extreme caution in applying the chemicals.

PROBLEM 26

a. Was Mattingly negligent? Should strict liability apply to this case? Give your reasons.

b. How should Mattingly defend this case?

c. How would you decide this case? Explain your answer.

Would this woman be liable if her dog attacked and injured someone in a public place?

Animals

The law has traditionally held owners strictly liable for any harm caused by their untamed animals. The situation differs, however, for household pets. In most states, an owner of a pet is strictly liable only if he or she knew or should have known that the pet was dangerous or destructive. There is a saying that "every dog is entitled to one free bite." However, an owner who knows the dog is vicious may be liable for the first bite. There may also be liability if "near misses" have put the owner on notice of the dog's viciousness.

Even the first bite by a pet with no history of bad behavior can result in liability if the owner is negligent. For example, some states and localities have leash laws requiring that pets be kept under the owner's control and on a leash when in public places. If you violate the duty to keep your pet under control, you can be sued based on your negligence.

The Dangerous Dog

Five-year-old Matthew opens a gate and walks into his neighbors' yard to play with their dog. The neighbors' pit bull attacks Matthew, badly mauling his hand. The dog had never attacked anyone before. Matthew's parents sue the dog's owners for not keeping the animal inside or in a pen in the yard. The owners defend themselves by saying that even though there have been reports of attacks by other pit bulls, their dog had been affectionate with family members and had never shown any dangerous or destructive tendencies.

PROBLEM 27

a. What arguments can you make for Matthew's parents?

b. What arguments can you make for the dog's owners?

c. How should this case be decided? Why?

d. Would you have decided this case differently if Matthew had been 15? What if he had been 35?

Dangerous Products

Harm caused by dangerous products is an important social problem. In fact, some lawyers specialize in **product liability** law. In a recent year, more than one million consumers suffered product-related injuries and nearly half of them sued to recover damages. The manufacturer was held strictly liable for the defective product in many of these cases. In some instances, injured consumers brought cases together as a class action against a manufacturer.

The U.S. Consumer Product Safety Commission, created in 1922, is the federal agency that deals with consumer product safety. The commission has the power to force many dangerous products off the market and will advise consumers on product safety.

PROBLEM 28

a. Make a list of five items that are or can be dangerous to use.

b. For each item, decide whether the government should ban it, regulate it (for example, provide warnings), or take no action at all.

c. Explain why you treated each item as you did. Consider in your explanation both the danger(s) and the benefit(s) of each item.

As a matter of public policy, the courts and the legislatures frequently hold manufacturers and sellers strictly liable for harm caused by their products. Strict liability is meant to create a strong incentive for companies to design safe products, test products thoroughly before placing them on the market, and include clear directions and warnings on products. Strict liability has probably caused companies to spend more money on research and development, safety features, and insurance, resulting in higher prices for consumers. Some people criticize these higher prices, while others say that safer products are worth the extra cost.

An unsafe product that causes many lawsuits may become so expensive that it will not be able to compete successfully with safer products in the marketplace. For example, many women were harmed by using a contraceptive called the Dalkon shield. They brought a successful class action against the manufacturer and recovered damages. The Dalkon shield is no longer on the market in the United States, and its maker has been bankrupted. Furthermore, the fear of expensive lawsuits may discourage the development of new and useful but unavoidably dangerous products, such as

Does your state have strict liability laws covering harm caused by defective products? Can the consumer use strict liability to sue everyone from the manufacturer to the seller of the product? Is this fair?

The Exploding Gas Tank

A drunk driver crashes into the side of Gabriel's 1985 United Motors pickup truck, and Gabriel is killed.

His parents sue the manufacturer of the pickup truck. They contend that although Gabriel would have been injured, he would have survived the crash if the pickup truck's fuel tank had not caught fire and exploded. They also contend that the manufacturer was already aware of customer complaints about the fuel tank, which was mounted outside the truck's steel frame.

The company responds that the design of the truck was not defective and that Gabriel died from the collision caused by the drunk driver.

PROBLEM 29

a. Why did Gabriel's parents sue the manufacturer of the truck?

b. What would help Gabriel's parents prove their case?

c. What arguments should United Motors make in court?

d. Should the company be held responsible even though the drunk driver hit Gabriel? Explain.

e. If the placement of the fuel tank is faulty, what should United Motors do to protect other drivers?

f. How would you decide the case? Give your reasons.

vaccines. Some people argue that the government should provide some type of insurance or immunity from lawsuits as an incentive for companies to develop certain new products.

Sometimes the danger caused by a product is so obvious or commonly known to consumers that the courts will not apply strict liability. For example, most courts have not used strict liability in suits brought by smokers against the manufacturers of cigarettes. While cigarettes are harmful, this fact is widely known (and clearly stated in the government-required warning on the package). In a sense, the courts are saying that smokers assume this known risk.

Courts have also been reluctant to apply strict liability to unavoidably unsafe products whose benefits outweigh the dangers. Certain vaccines are unavoidably unsafe. For example, even if the rabies vaccine is properly tested, prepared, and labeled, some people who take it may become sick. However, rabies, if untreated, will lead to death. Because the benefits of the vaccine outweigh the danger, strict liability will not apply. This does not mean that drug manufacturers are automatically protected from liability. If a drug that causes harm has not been properly tested, prepared, or labeled, the plaintiff will be able to recover damages based on negligence (rather than on strict liability).

PROBLEM 30

Kelly is shot during a robbery of his home by a person using a "Saturday night special" handgun. The robber is arrested, convicted, and sent to jail. In a civil suit, Kelly sues the manufacturer of the gun, arguing that the manufacturer produced and sold a product it knew was unreasonably dangerous and that strict liability should be applied. How should this case be decided? Give your reasons.

Should the manufacturers be liable for harm caused by these weapons?

Defenses to Strict Liability

There are very few defenses in strict liability cases. The defendant's best strategy may be to argue that the plaintiff should have to prove negligence in a particular case and that sound public policy does not require the use of a strict liability standard. It will almost always be more difficult for the plaintiff to win a negligence suit, because there must be proof of the defendant's fault—that is, the defendant's breach of duty.

While you do not have to prove fault in a strict liability case, you do have to prove both causation and damages. Therefore, as a de-

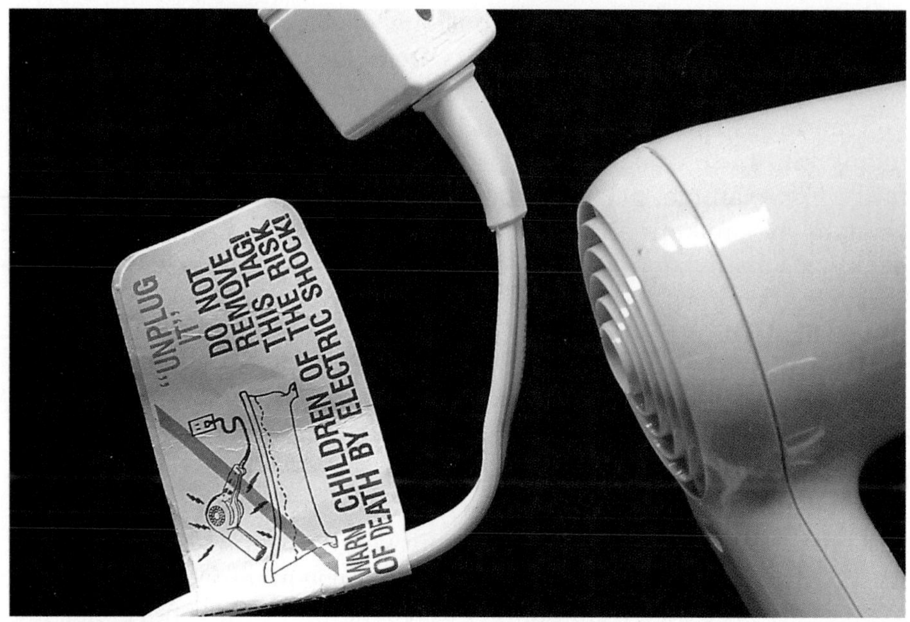

Should a consumer injured by using this product in a bathtub be able to recover damages from the manufacturer?

fense, a defendant could show that there is no causation or there are no damages. For example, assume that a person has a heart attack and dies instantly while driving a car with faulty brakes. That person's family might argue that the car manufacturer is strictly liable. However, if the defect (the faulty brakes) did not cause the harm, the manufacturer would not be liable for the driver's death.

In product liability cases, manufacturers or sellers may have a defense if the consumer *misuses* a product or ignores clear safety warnings. Many courts, however, require manufacturers to anticipate some misuse and to make products safe against any misuse that is foreseeable. For example, a manufacturer should assume that a stool used for eating at a kitchen counter might also be used for a step ladder. The stool should be built to hold a person whether seated or standing.

PROBLEM 31

In each of the following cases, the injured person sues the manufacturer for damages based on strict liability. Does the defendant have a good defense? Give your reasons.

a. Harriet's parents give her a teddy bear on her sixth birthday. While playing with the teddy bear, she pulls out one of the toy's eyes. The sharp pin which had held the eye in place punctures her skin, causing serious injury.

b. Marilyn is rushing to complete her housework so she can go out on a date with Ted. To speed up the defrosting of her freezer, she uses her hair dryer. A melting piece of ice hits the hair dryer, and she receives a serious electric shock. The warning on the dryer says, "Electrocution possible if used or dropped in tub. Unplug after using."

c. Monica, 12, leaves her plastic building blocks out of their box after playing with them. The box says the product is for children aged 10 and older. Her younger brother Micah, 2, swallows one of the small plastic blocks and has to go to the hospital for surgery.

d. In order to change the oil, Jay drives his car up a ramp onto cinder blocks. While he works under the car, a block collapses and he breaks a leg.

TORTS AND PUBLIC POLICY

The tort law system should serve to (1) compensate harmed persons in a prompt and efficient way, (2) fairly allocate benefits to victims and costs to wrongdoers, and (3) deter risky conduct. However, many persons now argue that our tort law system does not always meet these goals. Critics generally claim that:

1. The amount of money awarded to plaintiffs is sometimes unreasonably high.
2. Going to court has become much too expensive.
3. Civil courts take too long to resolve disputes.
4. Tort cases are often complicated, making it difficult to determine who is at fault.
5. The injured party should sometimes receive compensation for a loss, regardless of whether the other party was at fault.

As a result of these concerns, a movement called **tort reform** has developed. The reformers' main focus has been to change the *process* of settling claims. For example, some states now require that parties try to settle a tort case before it is tried in court. Similarly, no-fault insurance laws were developed to eliminate the need for civil suits in some auto accident cases. The growth of community mediation programs (see pages 42–44)—is another outgrowth of the tort reform movement. Mediation programs may allow you to resolve conflicts without using the civil justice system at all.

What tort reform issues are being considered in your state? Has your state legislature passed any laws in recent years to deal with medical malpractice?

England and the U.S.: Who Pays the Attorney Fees?

William Smith stepped off a curb into the street, where he was struck by a car driven by Mary Minow and seriously injured. One witness said Minow was exceeding the speed limit of 25 mph and should have seen Smith and stopped. Another said that Smith should have been more careful when entering the street.

If Smith hires a lawyer and files a lawsuit asking Minow to pay his medical bills, who will pay his attorney fees? The answer to this question is likely to vary depending on the country where the incident occurred. Let's listen to two lawyers describe how England and America differ on the issue of attorney fees:

English lawyer: "In Great Britain (and most European countries), if Smith sues Minow and proves she was at fault, Minow will have to pay Smith's medical bills and attorney fees. Since the idea is to make the injured party whole, it would not be fair if Smith won the case and still had to pay his own attorney fees. If Smith loses, however, he will have to pay both his *and Minow's* attorney fees."

American lawyer: "In the U.S., Smith and Minow are each responsible for their own attorney fees. We believe that going to court is everyone's right, and the English rule would discourage people from filing lawsuits. In the U.S., Smith would be allowed to pay his attorney through a contingency fee, with the attorney receiving one-third of the amount the court orders Minow to pay Smith."

English lawyer: "If Smith wins and is required to pay his attorney one-third of the money awarded to him, either he won't be able to pay his medical bills fully or the jury will recognize his high attorney fees and give him a very high money award, which occurs too often in America. You also encourage frivolous lawsuits by not requiring the loser to pay the winner's attorney fees."

American lawyer: "Smith and Minow's case is a close one in that neither party is totally right or wrong; therefore, to make the loser pay the winner's attorney fees would be unfair. To discourage Smith from bringing the case for fear he will have to pay Minow's attorney fees is also unfair."

English lawyer: "Under your system, people with small claims, for example $2500, won't file cases because their attorney fees may end up being $3000 or more. Also, poor people and others won't file public interest cases."

American lawyer: "On the contrary, we have small claims courts where people can handle small lawsuits without lawyers; free lawyers for poor people; and laws which allow attorney fees to be awarded to the plaintiff in civil rights, environmental, and other public interest cases."

English lawyer: "To us, paying attorney fees should be a necessary part of losing a lawsuit. On what principle can a person wrongfully run down someone on a public highway and have to pay that person's doctor's bills but not his or her lawyer's bills?"

PROBLEM 32

a. Describe the differences between the English and American rules on who pays attorney fees in civil cases.

b. Assuming Smith was injured in England, would he have to pay his own attorney fees? Would he have to pay Minow's? Would your answer change if the incident occurred in the U.S.?"

c. What are the three best arguments for the English rule? What are the three best arguments for the American rule? Do you think one rule is better than the other? Stage a debate.

d. Why do you think America has a different rule on who pays attorney fees? Is it because U.S. society is different from European society? If so, how?

One hotly debated issue is the handling of medical malpractice cases. Various advocates regularly urge state legislatures and Congress to reform medical malpractice laws. During the 1980s, there was a large increase in the number of medical malpractice suits and the size of awards. As awards increased, the insurance premiums paid by doctors and hospitals rose. In one large city, malpractice premiums rose 400 percent from 1981 to 1989. The insurance premiums for obstetricians (doctors who deliver babies) rose nearly 500 percent. At least part of the increased cost of insurance paid by doctors and hospitals is passed along to patients, who pay these higher costs directly or through higher health insurance premiums. As medical costs have skyrocketed, some persons have been unable to afford needed care. In addition, patients with inadequate health insurance are sometimes turned away from hospitals. Some doctors, unable to afford malpractice insurance premiums, have stopped practicing medicine.

If this woman's medical problem is not diagnosed by her doctor, what will she have to prove in order to recover damages?

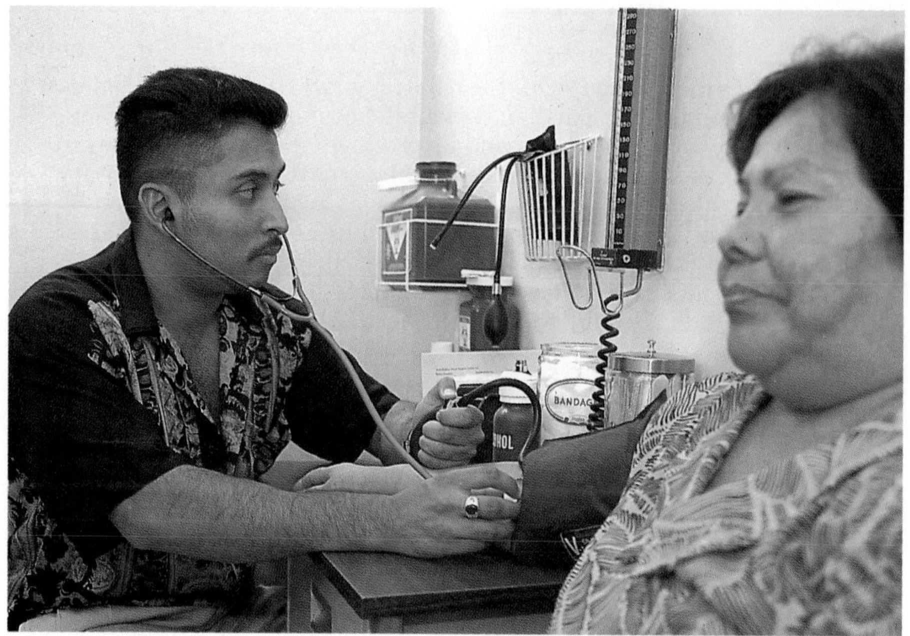

Some people believe that the present system works well and that high damage awards against doctors and hospitals fairly compensate patients for their injuries. They maintain that medical malpractice can result in permanent injuries or even death to patients. Moreover, they argue that relatively few doctors are responsible for a significant number of the malpractice claims and that the medical profession could and should do much more to identify and discipline these doctors. A 1992 study funded by legal, medical, and hospital organizations in one state found that (1) very few plaintiffs ever receive multimillion-dollar payments, (2) few cases are actually settled through jury judgments, and (3) awards for pain and suffering (also called non-economic damages) are *not* a major part of payments made to plaintiffs in these cases. Finally, those who would preserve the present system believe that doctors, hospitals, and their insurance companies should have to live by the same rules as other defendants in tort cases.

Others contend that the system is out of control because juries sometimes award damages completely out of proportion to the harm suffered. Jury awards sometimes exceed $1 million, and much of this money is awarded for punitive damages in addition to pain and suffering and out-of-pocket costs. Reformers believe that opportunistic patients and greedy lawyers drag competent doctors through the legal system, sensing a chance to make some money from a sympathetic jury. This group also argues that there has been a decrease in the number of claims filed in states with new tort reform laws.

Legislative Hearing: Medical Malpractice

Assume that your state has a health care crisis. The cost of medical services has risen 30% in the past 12 months. Malpractice insurance premiums have also risen sharply during this period. The state legislature's Select Committee on Health Care has called for testimony on a new bill.

The bill proposes the following changes in the law. The highest amount of damages that a plaintiff can receive in a medical malpractice suit is $500,000. Damages for pain and suffering are now limited to a maximum of one-fourth of the actual damages proven. Finally, patients filing a medical malpractice case in state courts must attach a letter from at least one state-licensed physician stating that the malpractice claim appears to be valid.

The following witnesses appear at the hearing: (1) a lawyer who regularly represents patients in malpractice suits wants to argue against the bill; (2) a person who has filed a large malpractice suit against a doctor who failed to diagnose his father's lung cancer in time to treat it also opposes the bill; (3) a doctor who has won several awards from the local medical association and has never been sued but is paying very high malpractice premiums favors the bill; and (4) an attorney who represents the insurance company that writes most of the malpractice insurance in the state also supports the bill.

Prepare to role-play the Select Committee hearing. Three senators and three representatives serve on the committee. One member is the chairperson, who should explain why the hearing is being held and give each witness an opportunity to make a statement. After each statement, the legislators should have an opportunity to ask questions.

Each witness should prepare an argument for or against the bill. The first two witnesses will argue against the proposed bill, and the other two will argue in favor of the bill. In your argument, list all the reasons for your position and write a paragraph supporting each reason.

These laws often cap, or limit, the amount of money that can be recovered in a medical malpractice suit. Other tort reform laws require that malpractice claims be supported by a letter from at least one doctor assuring the court that the claim is valid. Tort reformers also note that doctors are moving out of states where there has been no tort reform in order to avoid the extraordinarily high insurance premiums.

Changes in medical malpractice law can affect many people. If there are restrictions on lawsuits and caps on damage awards, people may be less likely to sue. If there are fewer suits and smaller awards, perhaps medical malpractice insurance will cost less and, ultimately, medical services will become less expensive and more readily available. On the other hand, people with legitimate claims may be discouraged from suing or may be unable to recover a fair amount from a negligent doctor. Perhaps if lawsuits are discouraged, people will no longer be able to use the legal system to ensure the safety of medical practices. What is your view? Which view might be preferred by your family doctor? An insurance company? An injured hospital patient?

Chapter 4

Consumer Law

Have you ever bought a meal in a restaurant or a pair of sneakers at a sporting goods store? Have you ever ridden a bus to work or had your car repaired at a service station? If you did any of these things, you were a consumer. A **consumer** is a person who buys goods and services for personal or household purposes from a seller.

When sellers agree to provide and consumers agree to pay for goods or services, the parties have entered into a legal agreement. The agreement is called a **contract**. Every time you order a meal in a restaurant, you promise to pay for it, and the restaurant promises to give you a meal that is fit to eat. If the consumer and the seller have a dispute they can't settle themselves, the law may help determine the outcome.

For many years, consumer law was characterized by the legal expression **caveat emptor**. This means "let the buyer beware." In other words, consumers had to look out for unfair and misleading sales practices before buying or else be prepared to suffer the consequences. Once consumers bought something, they were stuck with the purchase, even if they got less than they bargained for, such as unsafe or poor-quality products.

Today the law is more balanced. Consumers now have a right to be correctly informed of important information, such as quality, price, and credit terms. Sellers must avoid sales and advertising practices that mislead, deceive, or are otherwise unfair to consumers. This increased concern for consumers is based on the fact that sellers are usually better informed about the products or services being offered and are usually in control of the sales transaction.

What information do consumers need in order to make smart purchases at this market?

Even though the law has changed, the best protection is still a careful purchase. Learning about products and services, shopping carefully, and knowing your legal rights and how to enforce them are the best ways to avoid a problem.

You should also recognize that if you receive poor-quality merchandise or fall victim to a deceptive practice, all is not lost. You can often solve the problem yourself. And when you can't, the law may provide a remedy. This chapter will help you become a better consumer—able to recognize, avoid, and, when necessary, resolve consumer problems.

While consumers have many rights, they also have responsibilities. For example, they have a responsibility to sellers to be fair and honest. A consumer who buys an item of clothing, wears it once to a party, and then returns it is not being fair and honest. When this happens, a seller's costs go up, and everyone winds up paying higher prices.

INFLUENCES ON CONSUMERS

Smart consumers understand the factors that influence their shopping habits. They think about whether they need the product, whether they can afford it, and how they can purchase it carefully. They also know the difference between wanting and needing a product. Of course, sometimes all consumers splurge and buy things they really don't need. But smart shoppers don't spend so much on things they want that they can't afford what they really need.

PROBLEM 1

Select an item costing more than $100 that you or your family would like to purchase. What item did you select? Use the library at your school or in your neighborhood to find answers to the following questions:

a. What publications can provide you with information about this product? How else can you get information about it?

b. What specific information is provided about the product?

c. How can this information help you to be a smart consumer?

Consumers often buy things in response to advertising. A great deal of television, radio, newspaper, and magazine advertising is

What message does this jeans ad send to its viewers?

geared toward specific groups of people. For example, sellers know that teenagers are an extremely important market for their goods and services, and so they develop specific ads for this audience. Advertising to teens has been stepped up as studies have shown that today's parents make fewer buying decisions for their children. The ads, which are often purchased for shows or publications that particularly appeal to teens, are designed to increase sales of the products advertised. Many ads provide useful information about products or announce the start of a sale. However, ads may also attempt to influence you to purchase a product that you do not need or want or that you cannot afford.

PROBLEM 2

Identify an ad for a product you would consider buying. If the ad appeared in a newspaper or magazine, cut it out and bring it to class. If it was aired on the radio or television, either tape (or videotape) the ad or write a description of it and bring it to class.

Answer the following questions about your ad:

a. What product or service does the ad promote?

b. Who is the target audience for this product or service?

c. If the ad appeared on radio or television, at what time and during what program did it appear? If it appeared in print, in what publication did it appear? Why do you think the advertiser chose to run the ad in this way?

d. What information provided in this ad would you need to make a decision to purchase the product? Is there information you would need about the product that is not included in the ad? What is that information? How would you obtain it?

e. What makes this ad effective in encouraging you to buy the item advertised?

PROBLEM 3

Create an ad that would encourage a teenager to buy one of the following products: a portable compact disc player, new basketball shoes, a meal at a fast-food restaurant, or toothpaste.

When you designed your ad, what ideas did you use to appeal to your audience? Do professional advertising people use these ideas?

HOW LAWS PROTECT THE CONSUMER

The federal, state, and local governments all have laws that protect the consumer. As you read this section, and whenever you think about consumer protection problems, ask yourself: What are my rights under federal law? Under state law? Under local law?

Federal Law

Congress has passed many consumer protection laws. These laws protect consumers in several ways. First, they prohibit unfair or misleading trade practices, such as false advertising, unfair pricing, and mislabeling. The Federal Trade Commission (FTC) is the federal agency primarily concerned with unfair or deceptive trade practices.

Second, federal laws set standards for the quality, safety, and reliability of many goods and services. Failure to meet these standards can result in legal action against the seller. For example, the *Consumer Product Safety Act* allows the government to ban, seize, or prevent the sale of harmful products.

Third, the federal government has established many agencies that enforce consumer laws and help consumers. For example, as already mentioned, the Federal Trade Commission has the power to prohibit unfair or deceptive trade practices (such as false advertising) and can take legal action to stop such practices.

Fourth, Congress passes laws and agencies issue rules to improve the operation of the marketplace. In many instances, these laws and rules are designed to give consumers better information about products. For example, in 1992, Congress passed the *Nutrition Labelling and Education Act*. This law requires that all food product labels list ingredients and nutritional information in a form that most people will be able to understand. With this information, consumers will be able to make smarter choices.

Fifth, a new federal law, the *Americans with Disabilities Act* (ADA), protects consumers against discrimination on the basis of disability. Under the ADA, consumers who are disabled must have equal access to goods and services. Consumers who are disabled include but are not limited to persons who are blind, are deaf, or have a physical disability requiring them to use a wheelchair. The ADA covers all establishments that are generally open to the public. These include grocery, clothing, and hardware stores, as well as laundromats, hair salons, and gas stations.

What does it mean to say that consumers with disabilities must have equal access? It means that businesses must make reasonable accommodations to ensure that their goods and services are available to persons who are disabled. One accommodation you may have

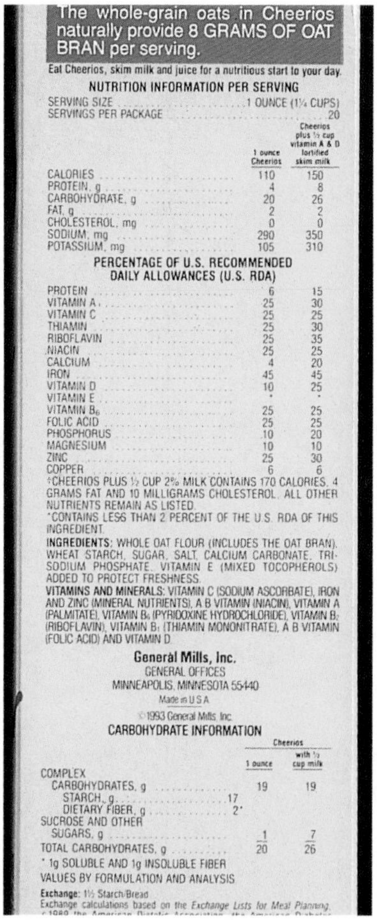

The whole-grain oats in Cheerios naturally provide 8 GRAMS OF OAT BRAN per serving.

Eat Cheerios, skim milk and juice for a nutritious start to your day.

NUTRITION INFORMATION PER SERVING

SERVING SIZE .... 1 OUNCE (1¼ CUPS)
SERVINGS PER PACKAGE 20

	1 ounce Cheerios	Cheerios plus ½ cup vitamin A & D fortified skim milk
CALORIES	110	150
PROTEIN, g	4	8
CARBOHYDRATE, g	20	26
FAT, g	2	2
CHOLESTEROL, mg	0	0
SODIUM, mg	290	350
POTASSIUM, mg	105	310

PERCENTAGE OF U.S. RECOMMENDED DAILY ALLOWANCES (U.S. RDA)

PROTEIN	6	15
VITAMIN A	25	30
VITAMIN C	25	25
THIAMIN	25	30
RIBOFLAVIN	25	35
NIACIN	25	25
CALCIUM	4	20
IRON	45	45
VITAMIN D	10	25
VITAMIN E	*	*
VITAMIN B_6	25	25
FOLIC ACID	25	25
PHOSPHORUS	10	20
MAGNESIUM	10	10
ZINC	25	30
COPPER	6	6

†CHEERIOS PLUS ½ CUP 2% MILK CONTAINS 170 CALORIES, 4 GRAMS FAT AND 10 MILLIGRAMS CHOLESTEROL. ALL OTHER NUTRIENTS REMAIN AS LISTED.
*CONTAINS LESS THAN 2 PERCENT OF THE U.S. RDA OF THIS INGREDIENT.

INGREDIENTS: WHOLE OAT FLOUR (INCLUDES THE OAT BRAN), WHEAT STARCH, SUGAR, SALT, CALCIUM CARBONATE, TRISODIUM PHOSPHATE. VITAMIN E (MIXED TOCOPHEROLS) ADDED TO PROTECT FRESHNESS.

VITAMINS AND MINERALS: VITAMIN C (SODIUM ASCORBATE), IRON AND ZINC (MINERAL NUTRIENTS), A B VITAMIN (NIACIN), VITAMIN A (PALMITATE), VITAMIN B_6 (PYRIDOXINE HYDROCHLORIDE), VITAMIN B_2 (RIBOFLAVIN), VITAMIN B_1 (THIAMIN MONONITRATE), A B VITAMIN (FOLIC ACID) AND VITAMIN D.

General Mills, Inc.
GENERAL OFFICES
MINNEAPOLIS, MINNESOTA 55440
Made in U.S.A.
©1993 General Mills, Inc.

CARBOHYDRATE INFORMATION

		Cheerios 1 ounce	Cheerios with ½ cup milk
COMPLEX CARBOHYDRATES, g		19	19
STARCH, g	17		
DIETARY FIBER, g	2*		
SUCROSE AND OTHER SUGARS, g		1	7
TOTAL CARBOHYDRATES, g		20	26

* 1g SOLUBLE AND 1g INSOLUBLE FIBER
VALUES BY FORMULATION AND ANALYSIS

Exchange: 1½ Starch/Bread
Exchange calculations based on the *Exchange Lists for Meal Planning*,

What information should consumers have about this cereal before deciding whether or not to buy it?

The Baby Milk Boycott

A company had been advertising the sale and use of its baby formula in underdeveloped countries in Africa, Asia, and Latin America. To encourage new mothers to feed their babies formula instead of breast milk, the company had been giving free supplies of its formula to hospitals.

Critics of the company's practices said that breastfeeding at home was difficult once babies had been bottle-fed with formula in the hospital. The critics pointed out that many mothers, after leaving the hospital, discovered that bottled formula was too expensive; as a result, their babies were often underfed. When mothers did use the formula, they often mixed it with polluted water. The critics stated that many of the 3,500 infant deaths occurring daily around the world resulted from inadequate nourishment.

The company denied that its practices caused the deaths of babies. It asserted that its formula was beneficial to babies and that other factors, such as poor health care, caused infant deaths. The company believed it was unfair to criticize the promotion of a safe and useful product, noting that mothers who could not breast-feed needed bottled formula.

Beginning in 1977, citizens of various countries began to organize a boycott of the company's formula and of its other products, which included different types of baby food and chocolate. The boycott attracted attention from the media and other groups. UNICEF (United Nation's International Children's Emergency Fund) and the World Health Organization issued regulations declaring that the company's marketing practices would in the future be considered illegal. In 1988, however, it was discovered that the company was still offering free formula to new mothers in many countries. Because the company was based in Europe, the European Community (EC) was asked to take action. In 1992, the EC set up complaint procedures in 100 countries.

PROBLEM 4

a. Role-play a meeting between "Boycotters to End Infant Formula Deaths" and representatives of the formula manufacturer.

After each side presents its point of view, both should try to reach an agreement to address the problem.

b. With which position in the role-play do you agree? Explain. Was an agreement reached?

c. What does the word *boycott* mean? Do you think the boycott worked in this case?

d. Do you know of other consumer boycotts? Describe them and explain why people were boycotting. Do you think the boycotts were effective? Were any of them waged against someone other than a manufacturer?

e. What alternatives to boycotting do people who dislike the practices of a company or group have? Compare the effectiveness of boycotts with that of alternatives.

noticed is a ramp that would allow persons using wheelchairs to enter a restaurant that has several steps leading to the entrance. The ADA requires businesses to accommodate the needs of persons with disabilities as long as the accommodation is readily achievable. This means that business persons must undertake accommodations that are easy to do and not excessively expensive.

Assume that a group of teens, some of whom are disabled, want to attend a professional baseball game. In order for the teens who are disabled to have equal access to this form of entertainment, the ADA requires that the baseball club make reasonable accommodations at the ballpark. These accommodations could include ramps for wheelchair use, areas in various parts of the park where fans in wheelchairs could sit, messages in print on the scoreboard that would provide a person who is deaf with the information that others are hearing over the public address system, and Braille menus allowing persons who are blind to order food at the concession stands.

State Law

States also have consumer protection laws and agencies. Many of these laws prohibit unfair and deceptive trade practices. Such laws are often similar to the *Federal Trade Commission Act*. State laws allow consumers to bring complaints into state court and before state agencies. They also enable agencies, such as the state attorney general's office or the state office of consumer affairs, to sue on behalf of consumers in order to halt illegal practices. In some cases, consumers can join together to bring **class actions**, which allow one or more persons to bring suit on behalf of a larger group.

Like federal consumer protection laws, state laws give the government power not only to stop unfair and deceptive practices but also to provide consumers with a variety of remedies. A **remedy** makes up for harm that has been done. Remedies include **cease and desist orders**, by which an agency can require a business to stop a forbidden practice; **consent decrees**, which are voluntary agreements to end a practice that is claimed to be illegal; and **restitution**, which is an order to refund or repay any money illegally obtained.

The Cheap Vacation Home

David and Michele Cole were reading the newspaper after dinner one night when the phone rang. A pleasant-sounding person on the other end of the line told them that people in their community had a chance to purchase brand-new vacation homes for only $15,000. The homes were located in a beautiful wooded setting just two hours by car from where the Cole family lived. In order to take advantage of this very low price, the seller said, the Coles had to make a 20% down payment. The rest of the money could be paid over the next 10 years with no interest at all.

The Coles had been thinking about buying a little place away from the city for brief weekend escapes, and this deal seemed too good to be true. They gave the seller their credit card number for the down payment. The seller promised to send literature about the dream home. Unfortunately, the literature never arrived. When the Coles complained to their state's office of consumer affairs, they found that others in their community had been tricked too. Fortunately, a thorough investigation enabled authorities to locate the persons responsible for this fraudulent sales scheme.

PROBLEM 5

a. What remedies could the office of consumer affairs ask for?

b. What steps could the Cole family have taken initially to avoid this problem?

c. Draft a law that would reduce the chances that this situation would happen again.

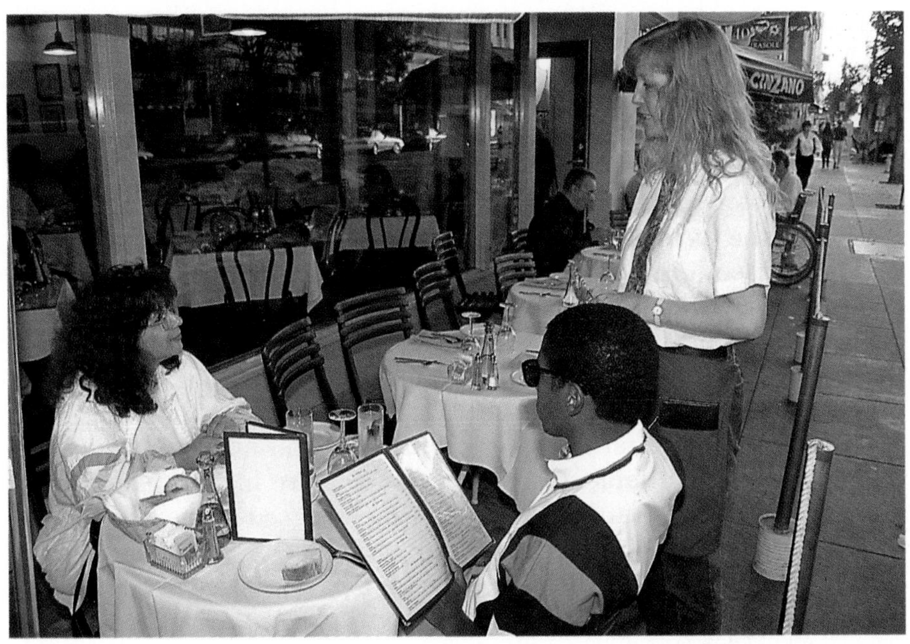

What laws would be important to consumers eating at an outdoor café?

Has your city or county passed any consumer protection laws giving you greater protection than you already had under state and federal laws? If so, what do these laws cover? How are they enforced?

Local Law

Cities and counties may also have consumer protection laws. These laws have been passed to deal with specific consumer issues that have arisen at a local level. For example, some cities have "truth-in-menus" laws. Under these laws, if the menu reads "fresh swordfish," the restaurant cannot serve swordfish that has been frozen.

HOW YOU CAN PROTECT YOUR RIGHTS AS A CONSUMER

Consumers can have a wide variety of problems. The following section will help you avoid some of these problems and will explain how to deal with difficulties that may arise.

Why does a smart consumer comparison shop before buying a bicycle?

PROBLEM 6

You and a friend are planning a summer bicycle trip across your state. You own a very old one-speed bicycle and have decided to shop for a new one to use on this trip. List all the ways you would gather information before making this purchase.

Things to Consider Before Making a Purchase

- Determine exactly what product or service you need.
- Compare brands. Read about various brands and ask friends for recommendations.
- Compare stores. Check out a store's reputation. Find out if there are extra charges. Learn about the store's policy regarding exchanges or refunds.
- Read and compare warranties.
- Read and understand the contract.
- Determine the total purchase price.

What to Do Before Buying

Generally, making large purchases on impulse is not wise. When shopping for products or services, learn as much as possible about them before buying. Careful consumers always compare prices and products before buying. This is called comparison shopping. They purchase the product only after considering other products that could also meet their needs.

For major purchases, careful shoppers go to the library and read about competing brands in consumer publications. Your librarian can point these out to you. You should also speak with your friends to get recommendations about products.

Once you have determined what product you need, you may discover that it is available at more than one store in your community. Especially for important purchases, it makes good sense to buy from a store with a good reputation. Your local Better Business Bureau (BBB), listed in your telephone directory, can tell you if there have been complaints about a particular store. If you are making a purchase from a store that is not in your community, check with the BBB located in the same community as the seller.

Several kinds of policies may differ among stores. For some products, there may be additional charges for delivery, installation, and service. A price that seems lower at one store may really be higher once extra charges have been added on. Also check on the store's return policy. A very low price at a store where all sales are final may not turn out to be such a good deal if you decide that you are unhappy with the product once you have it in your home. Sometimes a shopper may even spend a little more money to purchase an item from a store with an outstanding reputation for service or the ability to deliver the item quickly and install it free of charge.

Before making a purchase, you will want to read the warranty (also known as the guarantee) carefully. Different manufacturers and stores may provide different warranty coverage on very similar products. When studying the warranty, be sure to find out what you must do and what the store or manufacturer must do if you have a problem with the product. A warranty that requires you to ship a broken product to a faraway place for repair at your expense may not be of much value to you. You will learn more about warranties later in this chapter.

If you are required to sign a contract as part of the purchase, be sure that you read and understand the entire contract and that all blanks have been filled in before you sign. If you have trouble understanding the contract, ask the store for permission to take the contract to someone who can help you understand it *before* you sign it. You may not want to deal with a store that will not let you do this.

Finally, do not believe everything you hear from the seller. Later in this chapter, you will learn more about "puffing," or seller's talk. Just because a seller says "This is a real bargain!" does not make it true. You have to determine whether it is a bargain through careful shopping.

What to Do After Buying

Sometimes even careful shoppers have problems. When this happens, it is important to remain calm and be persistent. Often, smart consumers can solve their own problems. When they can't, it is very likely that an agency or organization in their community will be able to provide the needed help.

The first thing to do after buying a product is to inspect it. If you do not receive the exact product you purchased or if some defect reduces its value to you, take it back to the seller and ask for a replacement or refund.

In addition, you should always read and follow the instructions provided and use the product only as recommended by the manufacturer. If the instructions are unclear or seem incomplete, contact the seller. Misuse of a product may be dangerous and may also cancel your legal rights! Be sure to report any problem with a product as soon as possible. Trying to fix the product yourself could cancel the warranty.

If you experience a problem with a product, you should always try to contact the seller first. All contacts should be in writing or documented in a log or journal. Reputable business people are interested in a customer's future business, and most problems and misunderstandings can be cleared up with a face-to-face discussion or a telephone call.

Provide the seller with all the necessary information—identify the item (including model and serial number), give the date and location of purchase, describe when and how the problem arose, and explain what you want done. Be sure to bring along your sales receipt, warranty, or other pertinent information. Be polite but firm. If the seller refuses to help or gives you the runaround, send a written complaint to the owner or store manager. Mention that you will take other measures if you do not receive satisfaction within a reasonable amount of time. Be sure to date the letter and include your name, address, and a phone number where you can be reached during regular working hours. Keep a copy of the letter along with any response for your records. To complete your records, make notes about any conversations you had with the seller. Include promises made, if any, and the date of the conversation.

What information should this consumer present when returning this item?

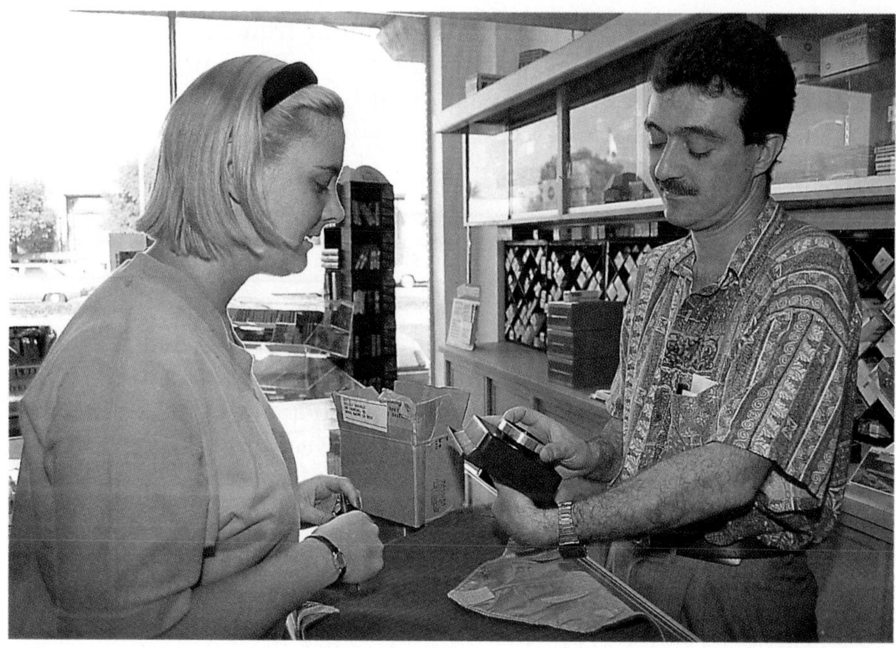

If the seller still refuses to help you, consider contacting the product's manufacturer. If you don't know the name of the manufacturer, ask your librarian for the *Thomas Registry of American Manufacturers*, a volume listing thousands of products and their manufacturers. If the seller is part of a chain store, consider writing to the corporate headquarters of the store. If you don't know the address of the manufacturer or the corporate headquarters, go to your local library and look it up in *Standard and Poor's Register of Corporations*.

ADVICE

Tips on Writing a Consumer Letter of Complaint

- Include your name, address, phone number(s), and account number, if appropriate.
- Be brief and to the point. Don't be sarcastic or angry.
- Include all important facts: date and place of purchase and information identifying the product (for example, model and serial number).

- Explain the problem, what you have done about it, and what you want to have done.
- Include copies of documents relating to your problem (for example, sales receipt). Do not send originals.
- Type the letter if possible. If this is not possible, print it neatly.
- Consider sending copies to your local and state consumer protection organizations.
- Keep a copy of whatever you send.
- Consider mailing the letter from your post office and paying the extra charge for requesting a return receipt. This receipt will be signed by the company when it receives your letter and then returned to you. If you wind up in court with your problem, the receipt is your proof that the company knew of the problem.

Many companies have consumer affairs departments, but you may get faster action by writing directly to the company president. State the facts clearly. Send photocopies of any important documents (such as canceled checks and past letters to the seller). Describe the problem. Explain what you've tried to do about it and what you want the company to do. Consider sending copies of your letter to local and state consumer protection organizations and to your local Better Business Bureau.

If you are still dissatisfied, it may be time to seek outside help. Many agencies and organizations may be able to help you. These groups are discussed in the next section. Above all, don't give up if you feel you have a valid complaint.

Government Consumer Publications

The federal government has hundreds of consumer publications, many of them free. Subjects include automobiles, budgets, children, clothing, consumer education, food, health, housing, insurance, landscaping, recreation, and senior citizens.

A free list of publications is available in both English and Spanish. Write to: Consumer Information Center, Pueblo, CO 81009.

PROBLEM 7

Terry and Martha Tubman saw a newspaper ad for major-brand color TV sets on sale at Tally's Radio & TV Shop. They rushed down to Tally's, where they bought a 21-inch model for $435. Several weeks later, the TV completely lost its picture. A TV service mechanic who came to their home told them that the picture tube had blown and that repairs would cost $200. The next morning, Terry and Martha returned to the store and asked to speak to Mr. Foxx, the salesperson who had sold them the TV.

a. Role-play the meeting between the Tubmans and Mr. Foxx. What should the Tubmans say, and what should Mr. Foxx say?

b. If Mr. Foxx refuses to help, what should the Tubmans do? If they decide to write a letter of complaint, to whom should they send it? Make a checklist of information needed in the letter. Write a letter for the Tubmans.

c. What should the Tubmans do if they get no response to their letter?

How to Make a Complaint

- Gather all the key facts. Save all important documents (such as warranties, bills, canceled checks, and repair estimates).
- Give the seller a chance to correct the problem.
- If this doesn't work, contact the manufacturer of the product or the store's headquarters (if it's a chain).
- If you still aren't satisfied, take your complaint to a consumer protection agency, a media "action line," or a small claims court. You may also wish to contact an attorney at this point.

Consumer Protection Agencies and Organizations

Your telephone directory can save you hours in dealing with consumer protection agencies and organizations. Check the beginning of the white pages of your directory for information about local community resources that can help. Many directories also have a section in the middle of the book that provides a comprehensive listing of government agencies. Look in that section under "Consumer and Regulatory Agencies" to find the phone numbers of organizations that can help you with a consumer problem.

Some places have arbitration programs to help with consumer complaints. These programs arbitrate disputes between buyers and sellers who have not been able to settle a problem. If you choose to use this service, be sure to ask for and read a copy of the rules *before* you file your case. In some instances, the decision of the arbitrators is binding on both the business and the consumer; in others, only on the business; and in still others, on neither party. The party bound by the decision usually agrees not to pursue any other remedy, such as going to court.

Appendix F at the end of this book lists the names, addresses, and phone numbers of many national consumer protection organizations. Many companies not listed in the appendix have established their own consumer affairs departments. Some of them have 800 numbers, which allow you to phone them free of charge. To find out whether a company has such a number, call 800 directory assistance at 1-800-555-1212.

Consumer Groups Many private organizations help consumers. National organizations such as the Consumer Federation of America and the Consumers Union educate consumers and lobby for passage of consumer protection legislation. Private state and local consumer groups may give advice, investigate complaints, contact sellers, try to arrange settlements, and make legal referrals. To find these organizations, contact a local university, your state attorney general's office, or a member of your city council. You should also check the phone book under both "Consumer" and "Public Interest Organizations."

Business and Trade Associations One of the best-known consumer help organizations is the Better Business Bureau (BBB). Better Business Bureaus are supported by private businesses; they are not government agencies. While BBBs have no law enforcement power, they do monitor business activity and try to promote high standards of business ethics. In many places, the BBB investigates consumer complaints, contacts the company involved, and tries to mediate a settlement. Reasonable complaints can often be settled with the BBB's help, but BBBs usually act only as mediators and do not force a business to settle.

In communities that do not have a BBB, you can contact the local Chamber of Commerce. If your problem involves an appliance and both the dealer and the manufacturer have been unhelpful, consider contacting the Major Appliance Consumer Action Panel (MACAP), which can help with complaints. (MACAP's address is listed in Appendix F.)

Media Many local newspapers as well as radio and television stations have special "action line" or "consumer affairs" services that help consumers. Publicity is a powerful weapon, and many consumers find that they can settle problems simply by contacting, or even threatening to contact, the media. To use these services, check with your local newspaper, radio and television stations, or library.

Professional Associations Many business and professional people belong to associations that act on behalf of the entire profession or occupation. While such an association may have no legal enforcement powers over its members, a consumer complaint may result in pressure on, or dismissal of, the offending member. For example, if you have a complaint against an attorney, you can contact the American Bar Association or the bar association for your city or state.

Does your community have a consumer mediation program? Does it have a Better Business Bureau? A media "action line"? If so, what does each of these programs do?

State and Local Government All states and many local governments have consumer protection groups that deal with everything from regulating public utilities to making sure you get a fair deal when you have your car repaired. These groups are often located within the state attorney general's office, consumer affairs bureau, consumer protection agency, public advocate's office, or public utilities commission.

In addition, states and cities have boards or agencies that set minimum standards for health and safety. For example, local public health inspectors routinely inspect restaurants to ensure that they are clean and free of health hazards.

There are also over 1,500 state boards that license or register members of more than 550 professions and service industries. Commonly regulated under these boards are accountants, architects, attorneys, barbers, bill collectors, doctors, electricians, engineers, funeral directors, nurses, plumbers, and real estate agents. Professional and occupational licensing was started by state legislatures to protect the public's health, safety, and welfare. These boards set rules and standards for the occupation, prepare and give exams, issue or deny licenses, and handle complaints from consumers. State boards have the power to revoke (take away) licenses for violations of established standards.

Finally, many places now have mediation centers to help consumers solve problems without going to court. Some of these centers are operated by local governments, while others are sponsored by BBBs or other private organizations.

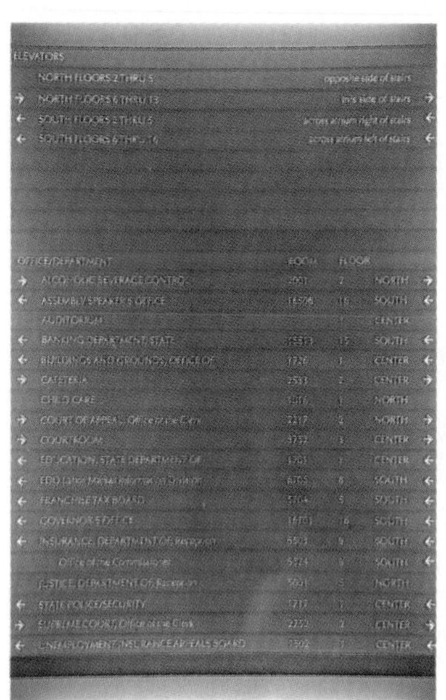

Where is the nearest government agency that can help you solve consumer problems?

PROBLEM 8

Choose a service that you or your family has used (such as medical care, legal aid, or auto repair).

a. Is there a professional association, licensing board, or other agency that could assist you if you had a problem with this service?

b. What steps must a consumer take to register a complaint with this agency or association?

c. What power does this agency have?

Federal Government It is usually best to try to solve your problem on a local level. For certain problems, though, the federal govern-

Federal Consumer Protection Agencies

Office of Consumer Affairs—Conducts consumer education and is a good first contact in the federal system because it can refer you to an agency that can help.
Federal Trade Commission—Is the federal government's main consumer protection agency. It acts to prevent unfair or deceptive trade practices as well as problems with bills, credit, and warranties.
Food and Drug Administration—Regulates the safety of food, drugs, cosmetics, and medical devices through a testing program. It can order unsafe products off the market.
Consumer Product Safety Commission—Makes and enforces safety standards for many consumer products. It can ban, seize, or require warnings for unsafe products.
U.S. Postal Service—Investigates mail fraud.
Department of Transportation—Has various consumer protection offices within the department to set standards for safe air, rail, bus, and auto travel and to handle complaints from passengers.

ment may provide the only remedy. Even if a federal agency can't help, it can often suggest a way to solve your problem. Some of the major federal consumer protection agencies are described in the box above. The address for each of these agencies appears in Appendix F.

PROBLEM 9

A list of consumer problems follows. What federal agency could help with each of the problems? Could a local or state agency be helpful with any of the problems? If so, which agency?

a. Your parents are considering buying an exercise bicycle and are concerned that it might be dangerous to your younger brother.

b. You buy an airline ticket to visit a college campus for an interview. When you arrive at the airport, you find that the plane is already full. You miss your interview.

c. A friend has lost an arm in a serious accident. Her doctor is planning surgery that will involve use of a new type of artificial limb. You want to learn more about the safety of this product.

d. A vocational school in your community runs an advertisement that promises job placement for every graduate. You are suspicious about this claim.

Taking Your Case to Court

Suppose you can't settle your complaint and a consumer agency has been unable to help. Sometimes your complaint may form the basis for a criminal action against the seller. Furthermore, whether or not a crime is involved, you may wish to take your case to civil court. Anyone can go to court. Minors can sue through their parents or guardians.

Criminal Court In some cases, a seller's action may be a crime. Such acts can be prosecuted as criminal **fraud**. Criminal fraud occurs when a salesperson knowingly misstates or misrepresents some important fact, with the intent to defraud you, resulting in harm.

For example, assume you contract with a builder to construct a deck on your home. You pay the builder several thousand dollars to purchase the necessary materials. However, the builder doesn't intend to build the deck. He simply uses the scheme to take your money. In such a case, you're the victim of a crime. You should contact the police or your local prosecutor. Cases like this can be prosecuted by the government in criminal court. State laws not only provide a fine or jail term (or both) for a convicted defendant but may also require that the defendant pay back the defrauded consumer.

Civil Court If a civil dispute involves a large amount of money, the case will be brought in the local civil trial court. Taking a case to court can be costly and time-consuming. In some places, though, free or low-cost legal services may be available to consumers who cannot afford an attorney.

In civil court, you can ask for a number of different remedies. First, you can sue for **damages**, money that a court orders paid to a person who has suffered a loss or an injury. For example, if you are injured by a defective power drill, you can ask for money for a new drill, medical expenses, time lost from your job, and other related costs.

A second remedy is **rescission and restitution**. When you ask the court for this remedy, you ask it to cancel the contract (rescission) and order the person you are suing to give back any money you have already paid (restitution). This releases you from any further performance under the contract, but you will have to return any benefit already received under the contract. Assume, for example, that you sign a contract to purchase a set of pots and pans and that a pan melts the first time it is exposed to a direct flame. In such a case, you might seek rescission and restitution. You would get your money back and would have no further obligations under the contract. However, you would have to return the pots and pans.

The third civil remedy is **specific performance**. Here, you ask the court to order the seller to carry out the specific terms of the agreement. For example, if you ordered goods that were never delivered, the court could order the company to deliver the goods. However, you would still have to pay for them.

A suit for damages or specific performance is designed to place you in approximately the position you would have been in if the contract had been successfully completed. A suit for rescission and restitution is designed to return both the buyer and the seller to the positions they were in before the contract began.

PROBLEM 10

Each of the following consumers has a problem. If the consumer has to go to court in each matter, what is the best remedy? Why? Could any of these situations result in a criminal prosecution? Why?

a. Jeanine takes a floor-length dress that originally belonged to her mother to the dry cleaner. When she picks it up, she finds several holes in it. The store claims the holes were there when the garment was brought in. Jeanine is certain that they are the result of the cleaning.

b. The Gonzales family hires the Weedout Chemical Company to spray their lawn twice a month during May, June, July, and August. Weedout sends a monthly bill. By June 10, Weedout has not yet sprayed, although it sent a bill in May, which the Gonzales family paid. Weedout is behind schedule with its spraying because there is a great demand for its product, a successful new formula not yet available from other local companies.

c. Sergio, a college student, has a summer job selling books door to door. He is paid a commission on every book sold. To make extra money, he uses phony order forms. The top page is a receipt for the sale of one book. The copy beneath, which has its signature line in exactly the same place as the top copy, includes an agreement to purchase another book every month for two additional months.

In June, Mr. and Mrs. Joiner pay $12 for a book. The next month, Sergio returns with another $12 book and asks for payment. The Joiners say they never agreed to buy the second book. Sergio shows them the receipt with their signature. The Joiners have not kept their copy of the receipt. Reluctantly, they pay for the second book. Later, they discover that several neighbors are in the same situation.

Is there a small claims court in your community? If so, where is it located? What is the filing fee? What is the largest amount of money that can be awarded? Are lawyers permitted in this court?

Small Claims Court In the early 20th century, court reformers recognized that the typical civil court was too slow, expensive, and complicated for many minor cases. These reformers proposed a "People's Court" designed to give citizens their day in court for small claims.

Today, every state has a **small claims court**, where you can sue for small amounts of money. The maximum award varies depending on the state. Filing a suit in small claims court is very inexpensive. Attorneys are not required (in some states they are not allowed), and there are few time-consuming delays. Filing a suit in small claims court involves three general steps.

First, call or go to the local courthouse to discuss your case with the court clerk. The clerk will be able to determine if the court can handle your claim. If so, you'll be required to fill out some forms and

How can merchants and consumers use small claims court?

Figure 4.1 A Complaint Form for Small Claims Court

SMALL CLAIMS COURT OF CALIFORNIA
COUNTY OF VENTURA

PLAINTIFF'S STATEMENT

FOR COURT USE ONLY

Trial Date: ______ Case No. ______

Method of Service: ☐ Cert. Mail ☐ Sheriff ☐ Personal

Military Declaration Signed: ☐ Yes ☐ No

PLEASE FOLLOW INSTRUCTIONS CAREFULLY IN FILLING OUT THIS FORM

1. State your name and residence address, and the name and address of any other person joining with you in this action. If this claim arises from a business transaction, give the name and address of your business.

   a. Name ______ Phone No. ______
      Address ______ City ______ State ______ ZIP ______

   b. Name ______ Phone No. ______
      Address ______ City ______ State ______ ZIP ______

   (For additional plaintiff's use reverse side)

2. If you are suing one or more individuals, give full name of each. If you are suing a business owned by an individual, give the name of the owner and the name of the business he/she owns. If you are suing a partnership, give the names of the partners and the name of the partnership. If you are suing a corporation, give its full name. If your claim arises out of a vehicle accident, you must give the name and address of both the driver and registered owner.

   a. Name ______ Phone No. ______
      Address ______ City ______ State ______ ZIP ______

   b. Name ______ Phone No. ______
      Address ______ City ______ State ______ ZIP ______

   (For additional defendants use reverse side)

3. VENUE ☐ In the box at the left, insert one of the letters from the list marked "Venue Table" on the back of this sheet. If you select D, E, or F, specify additional facts in this space. ______

4. ☐ I have filed more than 12 claims in this court, including this claim, during the previous 12 calendar months.

5. Defendant owes me the sum of $______, not including court costs, because (date and brief description of claim): ______

6. If your claim is for rent, complete the following:

   a. Rent is $______ each month/week.

   b. Rent is due on the ______ day of each month/week.

   c. Defendant owes me the sum of $______.

      1. $______ for rent due as of (date) ______ for the months of (specify): ______
         plus $______ per day thereafter.

      2. $______ for (specify) ______.

   d. Notice to Pay Rent or Quit premises was served on (date ______. The notice expired on (date) ______.

(Continued on reverse side)

MC-899 (Rev. 1/85)* **PLAINTIFF'S STATEMENT**

VENUE TABLE

(The plaintiff must file the claim in the proper court and geographical area. This rule is called **venue.** The box on this page describes possible reasons for filing the claim in this court.)

If you are the plaintiff, insert the proper letter from the list below in Item 3 on the reverse side of this sheet and specify additional facts for D, E, or F.

This court is the proper court for the trial of this case because:

A. a defendant lives in this judicial district or a defendant corporation or unincorporated association has its principal place of business in this judicial district.

B. a person was injured or personal property was damaged in this judicial district.

C. a defendant signed or entered into a contract in this judicial district, a defendant lived in this judicial district when the contract was entered into, a contract or obligation was to be performed in this judicial district, or, if the defendant was a corporation, the contract was breached in this judicial district.

D. the claim is on a retail installment account or contract subject to Civil Code section 1812.10. *(Specify facts on the reverse side of this sheet.)*

E. the claim is on a vehicle finance sale subject to Civil Code section 2984.4. *(Specify facts on the reverse side of this sheet.)*

F. other. *(Specify facts on the reverse side of this sheet.)*

ADDITIONAL PLAINTIFF'S

c. Name ______ Phone No. ______
   Address ______ City ______ State ______ ZIP ______

d. Name ______ Phone No. ______
   Address ______ City ______ State ______ ZIP ______

ADDITIONAL DEFENDANT'S

c. Name ______ Phone No. ______
   Address ______ City ______ State ______ ZIP ______

d. Name ______ Phone No. ______
   Address ______ City ______ State ______ ZIP ______

This consumer is preparing to sue a merchant in small claims court because a new product did not work. What evidence should he present?

pay a small filing fee (from $2 to $15). To fill out the forms, known as a complaint or statement of claim, you'll be asked for the name and address of the party you are suing, the reason for your complaint, and the amount you are asking for. The amount you ask for should be based on the loss you incurred.

Second, prepare for your case in advance. In most states, the court will notify the defendant of the date and place of the hearing. In the meantime, you should gather all the evidence necessary to present your case. This includes receipts, letters, canceled checks, sales slips, and estimates of repair. If a defective product is involved, be sure to bring it along, if possible. Contact all witnesses to be sure they come to court. Uncooperative witnesses can be **subpoenaed**. This means they can be ordered to appear in court. If you have time, visit the court before your hearing so you'll know what to expect. Also, practice presenting your case to a friend beforehand.

Third, be on time for court on the date scheduled for the hearing. If for any reason you can't make it, call the court clerk to ask for a postponement called a continuance. Once your hearing begins, the judge will ask you to tell your story. Do this by presenting your facts, witnesses, and any evidence you may have. Don't get emotional. Be prepared for questions from the judge. After both sides have presented their stories, the judge will make a decision.

PROBLEM 11

a. Copy the complaint form in Figure 4.1 (or get a copy of the form used in your local small claims court). Fill out the form with a complaint that you have had or that a friend or a family member has had. Write a short description of the events giving rise to the claim.

b. What would you do if you were notified that you were being sued in small claims court for failing to pay a bill? What would happen if you ignored the notice or did not show up in court?

c. Do you think small claims courts should follow normal court rules? Should lawyers be allowed? Why or why not?

DECEPTIVE SALES PRACTICES

Most sellers are honest, but some are not. A few use deceptive or unfair sales techniques. As a result, consumers must learn to recognize and avoid deceptive sales practices.

Easy Money

Mr. and Mrs. Johnson were struggling to make ends meet and to feed their family of five. They decided that they needed to borrow money to meet their expenses for the month. They considered going to a bank for a loan, but they knew they had poor credit histories, and they didn't want to be paying off interest over a long period of time.

They were very interested when they read the following ad in the newspaper:

> EASY MONEY: Are you having trouble making ends meet? Do you need a short-term loan just to get you through a rough time? We offer quick loans to anyone regardless of credit background. No interest payments. Just a nominal processing fee. CALL TODAY!!

The offer sounded too good to be true. But although the Johnsons were skeptical, they called. The operator said she would be happy to offer them a no-interest loan of $2,000 repayable in six easy monthly installments. All the Johnsons had to do was pay a one-time $200 fee that the company would use to process the paperwork.

The Johnsons did not have to meet anybody from the loan company, and nobody bothered them at their home. They scraped together the $200 and sent Easy Money, Inc., a money order.

When they had not received their money in three weeks, they began to worry. They again called the number listed in the paper, but the line had been disconnected. Finally, after two additional weeks, they realized they were not going to get their loan and would never see the "processing fee" again.

PROBLEM 12

a. Did any unfair or deceptive practices take place in the Johnsons' story? Explain.

b. What could the Johnsons have done to prevent their loss?

c. What can they do now? Can any state or federal agencies help them?

Door-to-Door and Telephone Sales

Most door-to-door salespeople are honest. They offer products and services consumers may need and want. Some, however, use high-pressure tactics and smooth talk to get you to buy things that you otherwise wouldn't buy. Once in the door, this type of salesperson won't take no for an answer and will do almost anything to make the sale.

Some state laws and a Federal Trade Commission rule give consumers a "cooling-off" period of three business days after they have signed a contract for over $25 with a door-to-door salesperson. During this period, consumers can notify door-to-door sellers in writing that they wish to cancel the contract. The FTC rule also requires door-to-door salespeople to tell their customers about the right to cancel and to put this notice in writing. If the seller does not do this, the consumer may be able to cancel the contract by sending a letter or telegram to the seller.

Consumers should be cautious regarding sales offers made by telephone. Many fraudulent schemes are conducted this way. The cooling-off period of three days does not yet apply to telephone sales. Be particularly careful if a telephone salesperson asks for your credit card number. This person may not only fail to send what you order but may also make additional purchases using your credit card number!

Telemarketing Scams

According to the United States House Committee on Government Operations, consumers lose between \$3 billion and \$15 billion annually due to telemarketing fraud. The National Consumers League identifies the following top ten telemarketing scams:

1. Postcard guaranteed prize offers
2. Advance fee loan scams
3. Fraudulent 900 number promotions
4. Precious metal investment schemes
5. Toll call fraud
6. "Free" airfare vacation offers
7. Direct debit from checking accounts
8. Phony Yellow Pages invoices
9. Phone credit card promotions
10. Collectors items

Phony Contests and Referral Sales

A seller may convince consumers that they can save money by referring the seller to other customers. The consumer then enters into a sales contract assuming that the price will be reduced if he or she gives a list of other potential purchasers of the product to the seller. However, the agreement usually provides savings to the consumer only if the potential customers actually buy the product. This selling technique is called a referral sale. Unless deceptive, referral sales are generally legal.

In what unusual places have you seen advertising?

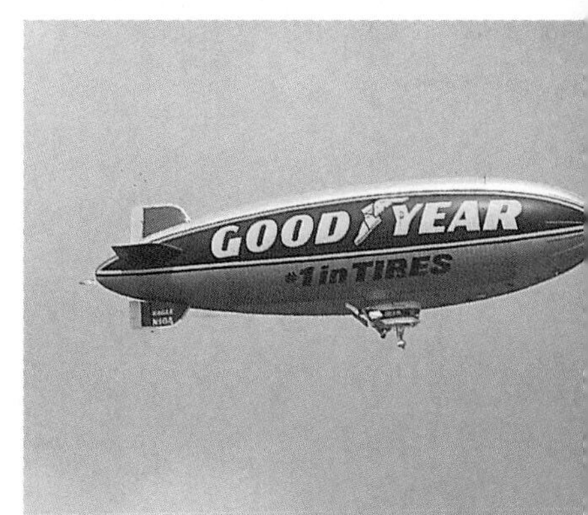

Advertising and the Consumer

Advertising is everywhere. Each day, American consumers are bombarded by ads on radio and television, in newspapers and magazines, on billboards and bus shelters, even on blimps in the air and benches in the park.

THE CASE OF . . .

The Guaranteed Jeep

Janine Gomez received a mailgram addressed to her with the word *URGENT* in bold letters across the front. She opened the envelope and read the letter. It told her she was a guaranteed prizewinner. The two prizes listed in large, bold letters were a brand new jeep and a big-screen color television. In much smaller print, the letter said that there were other valuable prizes that she could win instead. No matter what, she was preselected as a certain winner.

All she had to do to claim her prize was call a direct number: 1-900-NEW-JEEP. In even smaller print, the letter informed her that the call would cost $5 for the first minute and $3 for each additional minute and that it would take from three to five minutes to adequately discuss her prize. Although this was an expensive call, Janine decided that the prize she would get would be worth the cost of the call.

PROBLEM 13

a. Assume that the prize Janine is offered is a kitchen appliance available in grocery stores for less than $2. What should she do?

b. What mistake, if any, did she make in deciding to respond to the mailgram?

c. Have you or has anyone in your family ever received notice of a guaranteed prize in the mail? How did you respond?

d. What, if anything, was deceptive about the mailgram?

e. In what way, if any, should the law regulate situations such as the one encountered by Janine?

The United States has always been a commercial society; but in recent years, advertising has become more widespread. In 1992, over $130 billion was spent on advertising in the mass media, and this doesn't include non–mass-media advertising like direct mail ads. Advertising has also become more persistent and intrusive. As a result, people sometimes try to avoid advertising by flipping the channel during TV commercials or tossing unopened junk mail into the trash can.

The First Amendment to the U.S. Constitution protects advertising as an expression of free speech. However, courts have ruled that government may regulate and even prohibit certain types of advertising. One of the most controversial types of advertising involves tobacco. Tobacco advertising is controversial because smoking is the nation's leading preventable cause of death. More people die from smoking each year than from AIDS, accidents, fires, homicides, suicides, and drunk driving combined. As a result, there have been efforts to eliminate or restrict tobacco advertising. In 1972, tobacco advertising was prohibited on radio and television, but it is still allowed in magazines, in newspapers, and on billboards and other forms of outdoor advertising. Tobacco ads on billboards are particularly controversial. Unlike newspapers and magazines, which can be ignored or thrown away, billboards make the American public a "captive audience" to huge, intrusive ads that can't be avoided. What's more, numerous studies have shown that more billboards are located in neighborhoods where poor people live than elsewhere.

PROBLEM 14

To determine the impact of one form of advertising on you and your community, conduct a survey of outdoor advertising in your neighborhood and around your school. Next time you travel from home to school, note the following:

a. How many billboards do you see? If you don't see any, do you see any other forms of outdoor advertising? Explain.

b. How many advertisements do you see for alcoholic beverages and cigarettes? How many for other products? What percentage of the outdoor ads you see are for alcohol and tobacco?

c. How many billboards are located in inappropriate locations, such as near schools, churches, homes, or parks?

d. What is the character of the neighborhood around your school and home? Are most residents African Americans? Latinos? Asian Americans? Whites? Is the neighborhood racially mixed? Compare your answers with those of other students. Are there any differences in the number of outdoor ads among different types of neighborhoods? (Note: If you don't see any outdoor advertising at all, it is probably because your city or town has an ordinance prohibiting this form of advertising.)

Advertising can, of course, be beneficial. For example, merchants use advertising to tell potential customers about their products. Ads can also help consumers by telling them about new goods and services and by providing other useful information. Although ads can be helpful, they can also mislead, deceive, and confuse.

Ads sometimes mislead consumers through vague claims or, in a few cases, outright lies. Other times, ads try to create a desire for products that consumers don't really need or want. Many ads appeal to emotion rather than provide the kind of factual information needed to make a wise buying decision.

The federal and state governments have laws that prohibit false or deceptive advertising. However, these laws are difficult to enforce, and deception can take many forms.

When the public is widely exposed to a misleading ad, the FTC can order the seller to stop the false advertising. It can also order **corrective advertising**. This means that the advertiser must admit the deception in all future ads for a specified period of time. For example, a well-known mouthwash company advertised that its product cured sore throats and colds. When an investigation proved this claim false, the FTC ordered that all new ads state that the previous claims were untrue.

Although, as a general rule, false or misleading ads are illegal, one type of ad is an exception to this rule. Ads based on the seller's opinion, personal taste, or obvious exaggeration are called **puffing**. While perhaps not literally true, ads that puff are not illegal. For example, a used car dealer that advertises the "World's Best Used

Must this advertisement be true? If not, why not?

Cars" is engaged in puffing. A reasonable person should know better than to rely on the truthfulness of such a statement. Similarly, announcing a sale at a furniture store, an ad reads: "2,750 items of furniture have to disappear *tonight*!" This ad is not literally true; but again, a reasonable consumer should understand that it is just "seller's talk."

In contrast, consider an ad that reads: "Giant Sale—Top-Quality CD Players, formerly $300, now just $225." If the compact disc players were never sold at $300 and could have been purchased anytime for $225, this ad is illegal. It misleads consumers about an important fact concerning the product. The ad is not puffing, because it is not based on the seller's opinion, personal taste, or obvious exaggeration.

The difference between illegal advertising and puffing may be small, so consumers should be on guard. If an ad tends to mislead about an important fact concerning the product, it is illegal; but if the ad is merely an exaggeration or a nonspecific opinion, it is probably puffing and legal.

PROBLEM 15

Study ads that appear in your local newspaper. Bring in three examples of puffing. For each, explain why the ad is *not* illegal, even though it may not be literally true.

For many consumers, the biggest problem is not false advertising. Rather, it is legal advertising that influences them to buy things they really don't want, need, or know much about. Many ads try to sell products by appealing to the emotions. The accompanying box describes some emotional appeals.

Ads that Appeal to Our Emotions

Some ads *associate* products with popular ideas or symbols, such as family, motherhood, wealth, or sex appeal. These ads try to convince you that purchasing the advertised products will associate you with the same ideas or symbols. Nearly all perfume ads in magazines, for example, include photos of beautiful women. The message to consumers: Use this perfume and you will appear to be as beautiful as the woman in our ad.

The *bandwagon approach* is a technique that promotes the idea that everybody's using the product. Automotive manufacturers sometimes claim, for example, that their car, truck, or minivan is "best selling in its class in America . . . three years running." The message: Because others have bought our product, you should, too.

Related to this is *celebrity appeal*. This technique involves having famous athletes or movie stars advertise the product. The best-known celebrity ads show professional athletes promoting sports equipment. These people bring glamour and style to ads, but this does not necessarily mean the products are of high quality.

Still other ads try to convince consumers by resorting to the *claims of authorities*, such as doctors, or by citing test results or studies that appear scientific. Ads for certain medicines include the phrase, "recommended by doctors." Of course, smart consumers would want to know which doctors recommended it, and for what symptoms.

A common television technique is based on the notion that *seeing is believing*. A popular television ad shows a housekeeper cleaning two areas of bathroom tile, one with the recommended product and the other with the product of a leading competitor. After one quick stroke, one area of tile sparkles, and the other is still dirty. Consumers tend to remember this picture when thinking about cleaning products.

Some ads appeal to emotion simply by trying to make us laugh or feel good. One airline ran an ad frequently in winter months showing a tanned, rested couple lounging on a warm, sunny beach. The idea was to make customers feel good and think of that airline first for travel to warm vacation spots in the winter.

Other ads include catchy musical jingles. One cola company contracted with a famous rhythm-and-blues performer to play the piano and sing in its ads. Consumers remembered both the jingle and the product.

Some advertisers have been successful in getting consumers to connect one brand name with a certain product. For example, consumers often say *jello* when they may mean *gelatin* and *kleenex* when they may mean *tissue*. The people who make the ads for these products know that many shoppers select nationally advertised brands even though local or store brands may cost less and be of equal quality.

Whatever technique advertisers use, you should learn to separate the product from the characters and images in its ads.

PROBLEM 16

Read and analyze the following ads. For each, answer the following questions: What technique or appeal is used? Is any important information missing? To whom is the ad trying to appeal—children, adults, women, men, or some other group?

a. "Show your love to a friend and to Mother Earth. Use the greeting card made from recycled products."

b. "Nine out of 10 doctors recommend 'Super Strength' Pain Reliever."

c. A famous actress says: "If you want to get that special man in your life, use AvecMoi Perfume."

d. "Going out of business! Bargains galore! Everything at the Pants Palace is priced to sell, sell, sell."

e. "Your mother used Stuart's Baby Powder; shouldn't you?"

f. "For the time of your life, drink Brewmeister Beer."

g. "You've come a long way, baby. Why not smoke a woman's cigarette?"

PROBLEM 17

Select three effective ads from a newspaper or magazine. Why is each ad effective? What technique or appeal is being used in each ad? (Instead of using print ads, you could tape ads from radio or videotape ads from television.)

Bait and Switch

The bait-and-switch sales technique involves an insincere offer to sell a product on terms that sound almost too good to be true. The seller does not really want to sell the product, or "bait," being offered. The bait is simply used to get the buyer into the store. Once the consumer is in the store, he or she finds that the product is much less appealing than expected. Furthermore, on some occasions, the store may have only a very limited quantity of the "bait," or the product may not be available at all. The seller then tries to "switch" the consumer to a more expensive item. Salespersons who use the bait-and-switch technique are told to "talk down," or disparage, the advertised product and then refer the consumer to a higher-priced item. As encouragement, they may be given a higher commission if they sell the higher-priced item.

The Federal Trade Commission has rules against use of the bait-and-switch selling technique and will take appropriate action when it receives complaints from consumers. Many state and local agencies also handle such complaints. If state law prohibits bait and switch, a consumer may be able to cancel a contract with a seller when the seller has used this technique.

Sellers can legally advertise specials at very low prices to get customers into their stores without violating the bait-and-switch law. The items offered in these specials are sometimes referred to as *loss leaders*, because the seller may lose money or make very little money on them. It is not illegal to advertise a loss leader, so long as the seller has an adequate supply of the item in stock and does not disparage the item in order to switch the buyer to a more expensive product.

PROBLEM 18

Judy and her brother Ralph are shopping for a new motorcycle. They see an ad in the Friday newspaper that says, "Come to Big Wheel for the best deals on the slickest wheels in town! This weekend only, a 250 cc street bike, only $1,395!"

When they arrive at Big Wheel, the salesperson tells them that the street bike is not very powerful, tends to vibrate above 40 miles per hour, and is uncomfortable for long trips. He suggests that they test ride a 500 cc, four-cylinder motorcycle on sale this weekend for $2,795.

a. Role-play this encounter.

b. What is the best way for a customer to handle an aggressive seller?

c. Has the salesperson used the bait-and-switch technique, or was the advertised product a loss leader for Big Wheel? Give reasons for your answer.

d. Assume that Judy and Ralph arrive at the store on Saturday at noon and are told that all the 250 cc cycles have already been sold. Do they have a right to buy one at the advertised price?

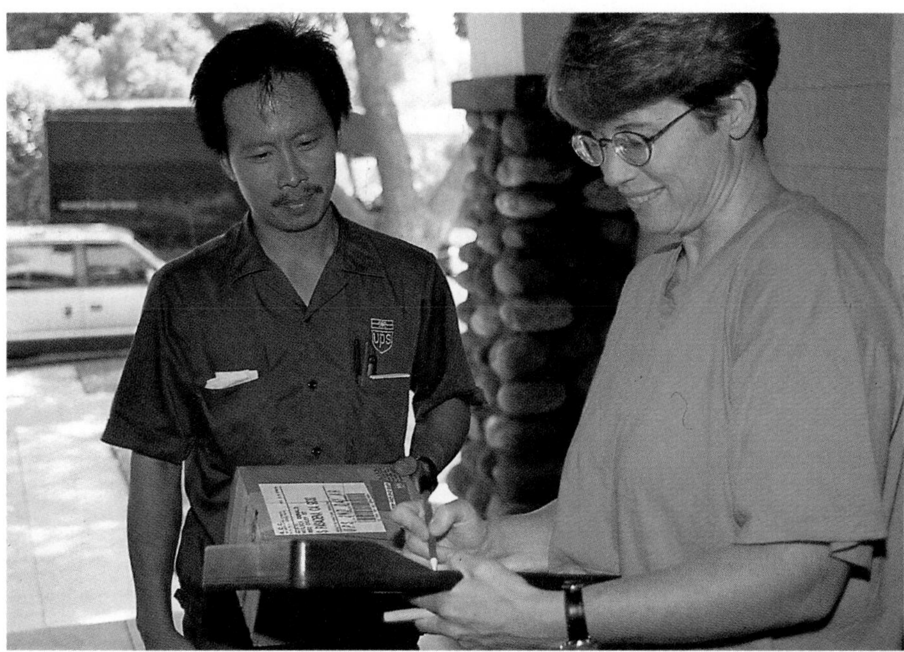

What special laws protect consumers who shop by mail?

Mail-Order Sales

Millions of consumers shop by mail. Mail-order shopping is convenient. Items may cost less, and some items may be available that are not available in local stores. However, mail-order shopping can also cause problems. Mail-order packages can arrive late, broken, or not at all.

According to federal law, you have a right to know when you can expect merchandise to be shipped. Sellers must comply with the promises in their ads (such as "will be rushed to you within a week"). If no shipping date is stated, the merchandise must be shipped within 30 days of the seller's receipt of your order. If the seller does not ship within 30 days, you have the right to cancel the order.

The Federal Trade Commission monitors compliance with the mail-order rule. This rule does not apply, however, to purchases made by telephone. With several cable television channels offering extensive opportunities for telephone shopping, some state legislatures are considering whether additional consumer protection laws are needed regarding home shopping.

Consumers should watch out for ads sent through the mail offering "free" items in exchange for subscriptions or memberships. Offers of free items almost always require a commitment to purchase other items in the future (for example, "four free books now if you purchase four more during the next year at the members' price"). Book and recording clubs often mail catalogs to members on a monthly basis.

ADVICE

Shopping by Mail

- Carefully read the product description.
- Be certain that the order form is filled out correctly and that all required information is provided.
- Pay by check or money order. Never send cash.
- Keep a copy of the order blank, the seller's name and address, and the date you sent in the order.
- Note the promised delivery time.
- Carefully inspect all mail-order packages upon receipt to be sure that nothing is missing.

The Electric Knife

One day, Barry received a package in the mail containing an electric knife from the Super-Knife Corporation. A letter was enclosed that said he was getting the knife for a free 10-day trial. Barry used it once and then forgot about it. Three weeks later, a bill came for $39.95. Must Barry pay?

Barry does not have to pay for the knife, nor does he have to return it. Under federal law, all unordered merchandise received by mail may be kept as a gift. Sending unordered merchandise is unlawful, and such activity should be reported to the U.S. Postal Service or the Federal Trade Commission. It is lawful to send free samples and to ask for charitable contributions, but the receiver of the goods cannot be forced to pay.

The clubs preselect the item that will be sent to you unless you take some action (usually within 10 days) to make another selection or to reject all selections. These plans are legal, but they can be inconvenient. If you are not careful, they can also be expensive.

PROBLEM 19

Shannon receives a mailing announcing a special introductory offer for persons who join a popular music club. As part of the promotion, she can get six cassettes for only $1, plus shipping. In smaller print, the offer says that she will also be required to purchase at least three cassettes per year for two years. The additional cassettes are sold at the club's regular members' price, plus shipping.

The club publishes a catalog of new releases every other month. The catalog is mailed to each member with one cassette preselected. A member who does not want that cassette must return a card to the company within two weeks of receiving the catalog. Otherwise the cassette will automatically be sent.

a. Is this mailing legal?

b. If Shannon takes advantage of this introductory offer, how many cassettes will she have to purchase?

c. What are the advantages and disadvantages of membership in this club?

Repairs and Estimates

The Costly Estimate

Nicole takes her car to Scott's Repair Shop. The mechanic tells her the car needs a tune-up and estimates the cost at $75. Nicole tells the mechanic to go ahead with the tune-up, but when she returns to pick up the car, the bill amounts to $125. Did Nicole do something wrong? What can happen if she refuses to pay?

Is there a repair and estimate law in your community? If so, how does it work?

Nicole is the victim of an "open-ended estimate." Sometimes, service mechanics estimate the cost of the repair but then have you sign a repair agreement that says (usually in small print) that you autho-

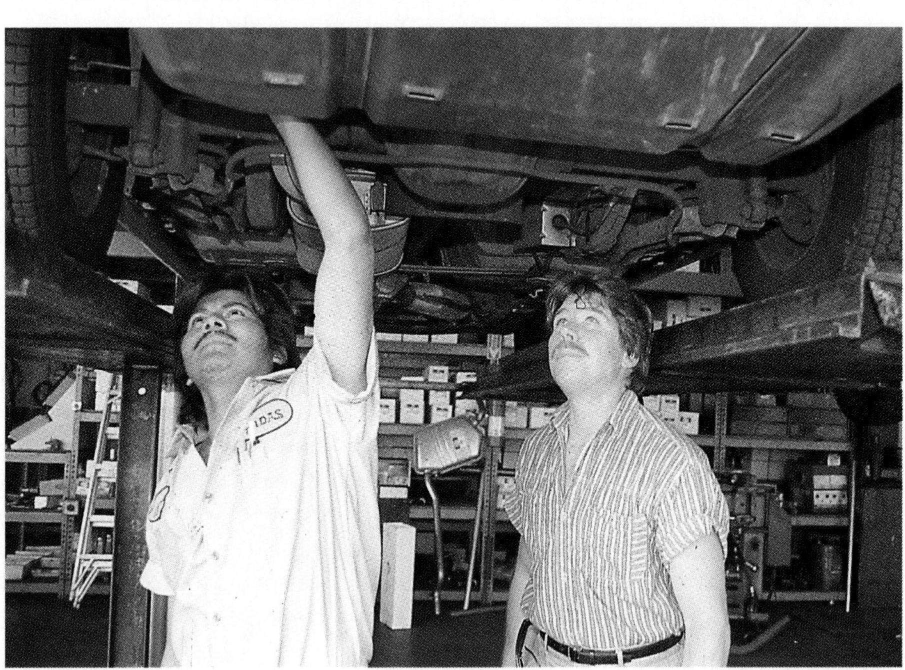

Why do careful consumers ask auto repair shops to save and return used and replaced parts?

rize all repairs deemed necessary. You should always get a written estimate and insist that any repairs not listed on the repair agreement be made only after you give your specific approval.

Some places have laws that require repair shops to give written estimates. Frequently, these laws limit the percentage difference between the estimate and the final bill.

You should also watch out for "free estimates." Sometimes the estimate is free only if you agree to have the shop make the repairs.

Another way to protect yourself when having repairs made on your car or appliance is to ask the repair shop to save and return all used and replaced parts. This identifies you as a careful consumer. Also, if you suspect fraud, you will have the old parts as evidence to make it easier to prove your case.

Being careful ahead of time is particularly important, because if you refuse to pay for repairs after they have been made, the repair shop or garage may be able to place a **lien** on the repaired item. This enables the repair shop to keep the item until you pay the bill.

Repairs

- Become generally familiar with how cars and major appliances operate.
- Get estimates from several repair shops. Find out if there is a charge for each estimate.
- Demand and keep an itemized written estimate.
- Insist that any repairs not listed on the estimate be made only after you give your approval.
- Request that repaired parts be saved and returned to you.

CONTRACTS

A **contract** is an agreement between two or more persons to exchange something of value. In a contract, each person is legally bound to do what is promised. If one party to a contract does not carry out the promise, the other party is entitled to a remedy.

The law of contracts reaches into many aspects of our daily lives. To protect yourself as a consumer, it is important to understand how contracts are formed and how they affect your rights.

Elements of a Contract

A legally binding contract must have certain elements. There must be an **offer** by one party and an **acceptance** by the other. In addition, the two parties must agree exactly to the terms of the contract. This is called **mutual agreement**. To have mutual agreement, the parties do not always have to say "we agree." The law infers agreement from certain actions, such as signing a contract or beginning to carry out the terms of the bargain.

In every valid contract, there must also be an exchange of **consideration**. This means something of value is given for something else of value. For example, when you buy an item at a store, your consideration is the money you pay, and the merchant's consideration is the item you are buying. The values of the items being exchanged do not have to be the same. The law allows consumers to make both good deals and bad deals.

People entering into a contract must be legally competent to make contracts. This means they cannot be mentally ill or intoxicated. Also, agreements to do something illegal or against public policy are not enforceable in court.

If Lorenzo says to Sally, "I will sell you my motorcycle for $150," this is an offer. If Sally says, "OK," if she pays the $150 to Lorenzo, or if she signs an agreement to pay $150, there is an acceptance. They have agreed to the exact terms. The motorcycle being exchanged for the money is the exchange of consideration. Both parties are competent, and the agreement is not illegal or against public policy. Therefore, a contract has been made.

You should not be too quick to enter into a contract. Be sure you understand and agree with all the terms before you accept; otherwise, it may be too late to back out of the deal.

Why is it important to read a contract before signing it?

PROBLEM 20

For each of the following situations, decide whether a contract has been made. Give your reasons.

a. An auctioneer says, "What am I bid for this antique sofa?" Someone in the crowd says, "$300."

b. Adam says to Basil, "I'm going to sell my car for $500." Basil replies, "All right, here is the money. I'll take it."

c. The citizens of a small town collect $1,000 and offer it as a reward for the capture of a suspected criminal. The sheriff captures the suspect and seeks the reward.

d. Sara's father promises to pay her $1,000 when she turns 18. On her 18th birthday, she seeks the money.

e. Standing at one end of a long bridge, Shelly says to Lynn, "I'll give you $5 if you walk across the bridge." Lynn says nothing but starts walking across the bridge.

f. Liz offers Sharon $100 to steal four hubcaps for her sports car. Sharon steals the hubcaps, brings them to Liz, and asks for the money.

Minors and Contracts

A minor is a person under the age of legal majority (18 in most states). Minors may make contracts. However, as a general rule,

The Required Cosigner

Keith, 16, a drummer in a popular band, goes to a local music store to purchase a new set of drums. The drums cost $750. He offers to put down $150 and make monthly payments on the remaining amount. Because Keith is only 16, the manager of the store refuses to sell him the drums. Is this fair? Is this legal?

they cannot be forced to carry out their promises and may cancel or refuse to honor their contracts. Minors who cancel contracts usually must return any goods or consideration still in their possession. This rule is designed to protect minors from being taken advantage of because of their age and lack of experience. However, minors may have a tough time getting credit because of this rule. Many stores require minors to have a parent or other adult **cosign** any major contract. The adult cosigner is responsible for making payments if the minor backs out of the deal.

Minors may, however, be held to contracts that involve necessities, such as food, clothing, shelter, or medical aid. Minors can be required to pay for the reasonable value of such goods and services.

In most states, a minor who continues making payments on a contract after reaching the age of majority is considered to have **ratified** the contract. Once the contract has been ratified, it can no longer be canceled.

Written and Oral Contracts

Most contracts may be either written or oral (spoken). However, certain kinds of contracts must be in writing to be enforceable. These include contracts for the sale of land or real estate, contracts for the sale of goods priced at $500 or more, agreements to pay another person's debt, and agreements that cannot be performed within a year from the date of the agreement.

The law favors written contracts. For your protection, it is always better to have a written contract. Otherwise, it can be difficult to prove that a party promised to do something. If there is a written contract, a court will not listen to evidence of promises made before

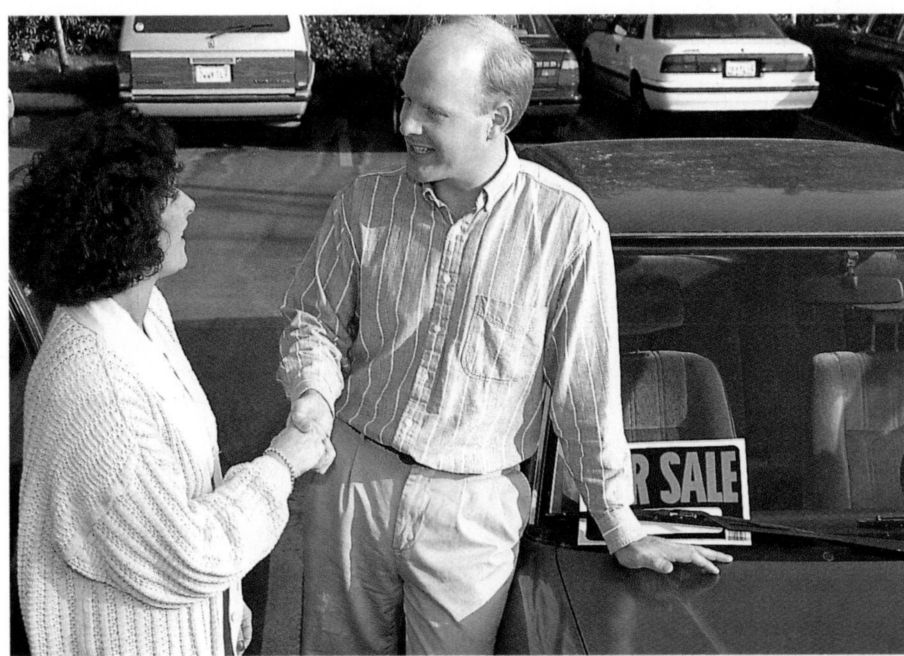

Should courts enforce an oral agreement to buy a car? Give reasons.

the signing of the contract except when the written contract is unclear or one party was tricked into entering the contract.

The Broken Promise

Ruth orally agreed to sell her car to Mike for $2,000. A few days later, she got an offer of $2,300 from Paul. Thereafter, she refused to sell her car to Mike. Can Mike hold her to the agreement? Should he be able to?

Because the car sold for more than $500, a court would not force Ruth to sell her car to Mike unless they had a written contract.

Illegal Contracts

Some contracts are unenforceable in court because they are illegal or against public policy. For example, an agreement between two persons to sell illegal drugs could never be enforced in court.

The Unfair Contract

A furniture store made an unemployed woman on public assistance sign its standard form contract for credit every time she made a purchase at the store. The contract had a term that said the store would own every item the woman purchased until all the items were fully paid for. The woman made several purchases at the store, signing this contract each time.

After several years of making all her payments, she purchased a stereo and missed two payments. The store believed it had the right under the contract to take back *all* the items the woman had ever purchased there.

A court of appeals found a portion of the contract to be unconscionable and did not enforce this unfair term in the agreement. The woman had to return the stereo but was able to keep all the items she had already paid for.

In addition, courts sometimes find that a contract is so unfair, harsh, and oppressive that it should not be enforced. Such a contract is considered to be **unconscionable**.

Courts will usually not refuse to enforce a contract simply because it requires someone to pay a very high price for something. As noted earlier, the law allows for freedom of contract, and consumers are allowed to make bad deals as well as good ones. On rare occasions, though, a court may not enforce an extremely unfair contract (or the unfair clause in a contract).

A court is more likely to find a contract unconscionable when (1) the consumer is presented with a contract on a take-it-or-leave-it basis and (2) there is very uneven bargaining power between the parties (as when an experienced seller is dealing with an uneducated consumer).

WARRANTIES

A **warranty** is a promise or guarantee made by a seller concerning the quality or performance of goods offered for sale. A warranty is also a statement of what the seller will do to remedy the problem if the product doesn't perform as promised. If the seller does not live up to the promises made in the warranty, the warranty is said to be **breached**.

Warranties give consumers very important rights. You should always be aware of the warranties that exist when you make a purchase. There are two types of warranties: express and implied.

Warranties

- Not all warranties are the same. It's worthwhile to compare warranties when shopping.
- When you look at a warranty, consider the duration (how long does it last?), the scope (what parts or problems are covered or excluded?), and the remedy (what do you get under the warranty and what must you do to get the remedy?).
- Check your own state's law. Sometimes it gives you rights that are not in the warranty.

Express Warranties

An **express warranty** is a statement—written, oral, or by demonstration—concerning the quality or performance of goods offered for sale that becomes a part of the bargain between the parties. For example, if a salesperson tells you "This TV will not need any repairs for five years," this salesperson has created an express warranty. Similarly, an express warranty is created if you purchase a vacuum cleaner from an appliance store after seeing a demonstration of the vacuum picking up small particles from a deep shag rug. Since oral warranties and warranties by demonstration are difficult to prove, it is always best to get a written warranty.

Express warranties are created by statements of fact. Not everything a seller says is a warranty. If the seller's statement is merely an opinion or an obvious exaggeration, it is considered puffing, or sales talk, and cannot be relied on. For example, a used car dealer advertising "Fantastic Used Cars" is engaged in puffing. No warranty is created, and no customer should rely on such a statement.

What happens if your TV blows a tube or your watch won't keep time? The first thing to do is check the warranty. One TV may be guaranteed for 90 days, while another may be covered for a full year. Your warranty may provide a remedy when things go wrong. You may be able to return the item for a refund, exchange it for another, or have it repaired.

Sellers do not have to give written warranties. However, if they do, the *Magnuson-Moss Warranty Act* requires that the written warranties (1) disclose all the essential terms and conditions in a single document, (2) be stated in simple and easy-to-read language, and (3) be made available to the consumer before a sale. Written warranties must also tell you exactly what is included and what is not included. For example, the warranty must explain what repairs are covered and who will make them. The warranty act does not apply to products that cost $15 or less.

Under the act, warranties are labeled either full or limited. Under a full warranty:

- A defective product will be fixed or replaced free, including removal and reinstallation, if necessary.
- The consumer will not have to do anything unreasonable (such as shipping a piano to a factory) to get the warranty service.

- The product will be fixed within a reasonable time after the consumer complains.
- If the product can't be fixed after a reasonable number of attempts, the consumer can get a refund or a replacement.
- The warranty applies to anyone who owns the product during the warranty period (not just the first purchaser).

Any protection less than this is called a limited warranty. Such a warranty could cover some defects or problems and not others. For example, the limited warranty on a video recorder might cover the cost of new parts but not labor. Or it might cover some parts but not others. To learn what is covered, read all of the warranty carefully.

PROBLEM 21

Read and evaluate the one-year limited warranty in Figure 4.2 and answer the following questions.

a. Who is making the warranty? Who will make any repairs—dealer, service center, manufacturer, or independent repairer?

b. How long is the warranty in effect? Does the buyer have to do anything to make the warranty effective?

Figure 4.2 One-Year Limited Warranty

ONE-YEAR LIMITED WARRANTY

Electro Toasters fully guarantees this entire product to owner against defects in material or workmanship for one year from purchase date.

Defective product may be brought or mailed to purchase place, authorized service center, or Service Department, Electro Toasters, Inc., 3rd & Maple Streets, Arlington, PA 15616, freight prepaid, for free repair or replacement at our option.

Warranty does not include cost of inconvenience, damage due to product failure, transportation damages, misuse, abuse, accident, or commercial use.

For information, write Consumer Claims Manager at above Arlington address. Send owner's name, address, name of store or service center involved, model, serial number, purchase date, and description of problem.

This warranty gives specific legal rights. You may have other rights that vary from state to state.

This warranty becomes effective upon purchase. Mailing the enclosed registration card is one way of proving purchase date but is not required for warranty coverage.

c. What is covered—the entire product or only certain parts? What is promised—repair, replacement, labor, postage? Are there any limitations or exclusions? Is this a full or a limited warranty? Why?

Implied Warranties

Many consumers believe they have no protection if a new product without express warranties does not work. In many cases, however, consumers are protected—even though they may not realize it—by an implied warranty. An **implied warranty** is an unwritten promise, created by law, that a product will do what it is supposed to do. In other words, the law requires products to meet certain minimum standards of quality and performance, even if no express promise is made. Implied warranties apply only to products sold by dealers; they do not apply to goods sold by casual sellers. For example, if a friend sells you her bike, no implied warranties are involved. The three types of implied warranties are (1) warranty of merchantability, (2) warranty of fitness for a particular purpose, and (3) warranty of title.

A **warranty of merchantability** is an unwritten promise that the item sold is of at least average quality for that type of item. For example, a radio must play, a saw must cut, and a freezer must keep food frozen. This warranty is always implied unless the seller expressly disclaims it. Be especially wary of goods marked with disclaimers such as "as is" or "final sale."

A **warranty of fitness for a particular purpose** exists when a consumer tells a seller before buying an item that it is needed for a specific purpose or will be used in a certain way. A salesperson who sells an item with this knowledge makes an implied promise that the item will fulfill the stated purpose. For example, suppose you tell a salesperson you want a waterproof watch and the salesperson recommends a watch, which you then buy. An implied warranty of fitness has been created. If you go swimming and water leaks into the watch, the warranty has been breached.

A **warranty of title** is a seller's promise that he or she owns the item being offered for sale. Sellers must own the goods and be able to transfer title or ownership to the buyer. If a person sells stolen goods, the warranty of title has been broken.

PROBLEM 22

Is a warranty created in any of the following situations? If so, what type of warranty? Has the warranty been broken?

a. Juan sells Terri his used car. As Terri drives home, the car breaks down. The cost of fixing the car is greater than the sale price.

b. Deitra buys a dress after telling the sales clerk that she plans to wash it in a washing machine. The clerk replies, "That's fine. This material is washable." Deitra washes the dress in her washing machine and the dress shrinks.

c. A salesperson tells Suzanne, "This is the finest camera on the market. It will last for years." Eight months later, the lens breaks.

d. Mike steals a diamond ring from a jewelry store and sells it to Maria after telling her his mother has given it to him.

e. Sandy orders a baseball bat from a catalog. The catalog reads, "31-inch baseball bat, $7.95," and includes a picture of a wooden bat. Two weeks later, Sandy receives an aluminum bat in the mail.

f. Ned buys a new sofa from a furniture store. One of the legs falls off two weeks after delivery.

Consumers who are harmed by products may be able to sue for damages because the manufacturer or seller has breached a warranty. Consumers may also be able to recover damages based either on the negligence of the manufacturer or seller or on a legal theory called strict liability. The topic of harm caused by dangerous products is dealt with more fully in Chapter 3.

You should remember that if you fully examine goods (or have the opportunity to do so) before making a purchase, the implied warranty may not apply to those defects you should have discovered during the inspection. Therefore, *carefully inspect for defects any goods you buy*. Be especially careful with used cars. It is wise to have a mechanic you trust examine the car before you purchase it.

Be sure to carefully read all instructions that come with a product. If you fail to use the product properly, or if you use it for an improper purpose, you may cancel the warranty.

Disclaimers

A **disclaimer** is an attempt to limit the seller's responsibilities should anything go wrong with a product. The clause quoted in the Case of the Guitar That Quit is a disclaimer. It is an attempt by the

The Guitar That Quit

Sherry buys a new guitar for $300. On the sales receipt is a clause that reads, "This writing is the exclusive statement of the terms of agreement between the parties. Seller makes no warranties either express or implied with respect to this product." The third time Sherry plays the guitar, one of the strings snaps. Can she return the guitar?

store to avoid responsibility for anything that goes wrong with the guitar. The quoted clause makes it clear that an express warranty is not being offered. But does the clause disclaim the implied warranty?

Sellers can usually disclaim the implied warranty of merchantability by using such expressions as "with all faults" or "as is." Unless these or other easily understood words are used, the seller must actually use the word *merchantability* in disclaiming the implied warranty of merchantability. In addition, to be effective, the disclaimer must be written so as to be easily seen by the consumer. Because the sales receipt for the guitar did not say "as is," "with all faults," or "merchantability," it is probably *not* effective as a disclaimer of the implied warranty of merchantability. Sherry should be protected if she returns the guitar.

Under the *Magnuson-Moss Warranty Act*, sellers offering a written warranty may not disclaim or modify any implied warranty during the effective period of the written warranty.

Sellers sometimes use disclaimers to limit the consumer's remedy. For example, a contract may read, "It is expressly understood and agreed that the buyer's only remedy shall be repair or replacement of defective parts. The seller is not liable in damages for injury to persons or property." Suppose the warranty limits the remedy to "repair or replacement of defective parts" and this remedy does not work (that is, after repeated attempts at repair, the product still does not work). In such cases, the buyer can usually seek other remedies. But courts will require that the buyer give the seller a reasonable opportunity to repair the product.

CREDIT

Using **credit** means buying goods or services now in exchange for a promise to pay in the future. It also means borrowing money now

LAW IN ACTION

Mock Trial: *James Phillips v. The Radio Shop*

FACTS

In this case, James Phillips purchased a radio/cassette player from The Radio Shop and later attempted to exchange it because it did not work. The date of the sale was November 14; the return was made 10 days later. The sales slip has the following language printed at the bottom: "This product is fully guaranteed for 5 days from the date of the purchase. If defective, return it in the original box for credit toward another purchase."

The store refused to make the exchange, and James brought this action in small claims court.

EVIDENCE

James has (1) the sales slip for $79.95 plus tax paid to The Radio Shop and (2) the broken radio/cassette player. He claims to have thrown away the box.

WITNESSES

For the plaintiff:

1. James Phillips
2. Ruby Phillips, James's sister.

For the defendant:

1. Al Jackson, the salesperson
2. Hattie Babcock, the store manager

COURT

The judge should provide an opportunity for James to make his case and should give the representatives of the store a chance to tell the court why the money should not be returned. Both sides should call their witnesses. At the end, the judge should decide the case and provide the reasons for the decision.

WITNESS STATEMENT: James Phillips

"I went into The Radio Shop to buy a battery-operated, portable radio/cassette player. I looked at a few different models, but the salesperson talked me into buying the Super Electro X-15. I paid the $79.95 price, and he gave me the radio in a cardboard box. When I got home, I found that it didn't work. I went back to the store to get my money back, but the salesperson wouldn't return it. He said I should have brought it back right away. I explained to him that my mother had been sick and I'd been busy. Here are the broken radio/cassette player and the receipt as proof. I want my money back!"

WITNESS STATEMENT: Ruby Phillips

"All I know is that when James got home the other day, he was excited and wanted to show me something. He called me into the kitchen to show me his new radio/cassette player. I said, 'Let's hear how it works.' He turned it on and nothing came out but static. He moved the dials around but couldn't get it to play. Was he ever mad! I told him that he ought to take it back to the store and demand his money back."

WITNESS STATEMENT: Al Jackson

"I sold the kid the radio, but as far as I know it worked OK. All the table models worked well enough, so why shouldn't the one boxed and straight from the factory? I'll bet what really happened is that he dropped it on his way home. Or maybe he broke it during the 10 days he had it. That's not my fault, is it?"

WITNESS STATEMENT: Hattie Babcock

"As Jackson said, all the other X-15s have worked fine. We've never had a single complaint about them. We have a store policy not to make refunds unless the merchandise is returned within 5 days in the box we sold it in. Also, the guarantee on the product says that it must be returned in the original box. That's the reason Jackson didn't give the kid his money back. Otherwise, we'd have been more than happy to give him credit toward a new purchase. After all, pleasing our customers is very important to us. Personally, I agree with Jackson. The kid probably didn't bring back the box because it was all messed up after he dropped it."

in exchange for a promise to repay it in the future. People who lend money or provide credit are called **creditors**. People who borrow money or buy on credit are called **debtors**. Debtors usually pay creditors additional money over the amount borrowed for the privilege of using the credit. This additional money owed to the creditor is called the **finance charge**. It is based on the **interest** charged plus other fees.

General Types of Credit

The two general types of credit are unsecured and secured. **Unsecured credit** is credit extended in exchange for a promise to repay in the future. The buyer is not required to pledge property in order to obtain the credit. Most credit cards and store charge accounts are examples of unsecured credit.

Secured credit is credit for which the consumer must put up some property of value, called **collateral**, as protection in the event the debt is not repaid. A borrower who does not make the required payments is said to **default** on the loan. If a borrower defaults, the lender can take the collateral.

For example, a person who buys an automobile may be required by the lender (often a bank) to post the car as collateral until the debt is paid off. If the buyer fails to pay off the loan, the lender can repossess and sell the car, using the proceeds of this sale to pay off the debt.

We discuss repossession on page 312.

Credit Cards and Charge Accounts

What are the advantages and disadvantages of using a debit card to pay for purchases?

Today, many stores and companies (including banks) issue credit cards and allow their customers to maintain charge accounts. Consumers can use credit cards to buy gasoline, take a vacation, go out to dinner, and buy furniture, clothing, and many other things. Some of these cards can also be used to obtain cash advances from banks and bank machines.

Credit cards are engraved with the holder's name and identification number. They entitle the holder to buy goods or services on credit. Some companies provide these cards free; some charge a yearly fee, typically between $15 and $75. Consumers are usually given a credit limit and can make purchases up to that limit.

Companies issuing credit cards send out monthly statements indicating how much you owe. Most credit card and charge accounts allow you to pay bills over time, making a minimum monthly payment. You then pay interest on the unpaid amount of the bill. Often, if you pay the entire amount on or before the due date indicated on the bill, there is no extra charge. However, some companies impose interest charges from the date of the transaction. A few require full payment of money owed each month.

Companies use slightly different methods to compute interest. However, you can estimate the monthly interest charge by multiplying the balance owed by the monthly rate. For example, if the interest rate is 1.5%, you will multiply by .015. Suppose you owe a balance of $500.00. The monthly interest charge will be about $7.50 ($500.00 x .015), and the total amount owed for the month will be approximately $507.50 ($500.00 + $7.50 interest).

To more easily compare the rates charged by different companies, you can ask what **annual percentage rate (APR)** is charged. This rate is calculated the same way by all lenders. The APR is the percentage cost of credit on a yearly basis.

When deciding which credit cards or charge accounts to maintain, you should find out the annual fee, if any; the annual percentage rate charged on money owed; and whether interest is charged from the date of the transaction or only on balances unpaid at the end of the billing period. Providers of credit compete with each other to get new customers. Some offer credit without a fee or very low interest for a certain period of time. Annual interest rates may vary by as much as 10 percentage points. It pays to shop around for credit.

Credit cards are in such wide use today that certain goods and services may be difficult to obtain without one. For example, some car rental companies will not rent to people without a major credit card.

While credit cards are an important convenience for many consumers, others use their cards to obtain "instant loans." They regularly purchase goods and services with credit cards. Then, at the end of the month, they cannot pay the balance. The interest rate on unpaid credit card balances is almost always higher than the interest on a bank loan, so this is not a smart way to take out a loan.

If your credit card is lost or stolen, you should report it immediately to the credit card company. For protection, any person with credit cards should keep a list of the following information for each card: (1) the name of the company issuing the card, (2) the account number on the card, and (3) the number to call if the card is lost or stolen.

The Lost Credit Cards

Sally lost her wallet, which contained credit cards from a bank and a retail store. By the time Sally realized her wallet was missing, someone had charged $800 on the bank card and $100 on the store account. Does Sally have to pay these bills?

If your credit card is lost or stolen, you are not responsible for any unauthorized charges made after you have notified the issuer that the card is missing. The law limits your liability for charges made before notification to $50 per card. If your card was not used but the thief obtained your credit card number and made unauthorized charges, you are not responsible for any of the charges. In Sally's case, she would probably be liable for $50 on each card. If she had notified the store and the bank before any charges were made, she would have owed nothing.

What steps should you take if your EFT card is lost or stolen?

EFT Cards and Debit Cards In recent years, many banks have offered their customers electronic funds transfer (EFT) cards. These engraved plastic cards look like credit cards but are not credit cards. Instead, they allow you to withdraw money from your account by using an automatic teller machine.

If your EFT card is lost or stolen and you do not notify your bank within two business days after discovering its loss, you may be liable for up to $500 in unauthorized withdrawals. If you notify the bank within two business days, your loss is limited to $50.

Some businesses (such as gas stations and grocery stores) are now issuing **debit cards** to their customers. These cards look like credit cards but work like EFT cards. For example, when a consumer purchases gasoline using a debit card, the amount of the purchase is transferred immediately from his or her account to the gas station's bank account.

Billing Errors Billing errors can be a real headache. It takes time and energy to sort them out, and they can cost you money if you don't discover them. To avoid billing problems, check *all* sales slips carefully, save receipts and canceled checks, and go over each bill or monthly statement carefully.

If you still encounter a problem, the *Fair Credit Billing Act* provides you with a measure of protection. If you complain in writing about your bill, this law requires creditors to acknowledge and respond to your complaint within 90 days. You may withhold payment of the disputed amount pending the investigation; however, undisputed amounts must be paid as normally required. Until your complaint is settled, the law forbids the creditor from reporting the matter to a credit bureau.

If it is determined that the bill is correct, you may have to pay a finance charge on the unpaid amount in dispute. However, a creditor who does not follow the requirements of the law may not collect the first $50 of the disputed amount, even if the bill turns out to be accurate. A consumer can sue such a creditor for damages and can also recover attorney's fees.

If you are to receive the protection of the *Fair Credit Billing Act*, your communication to the creditor must meet certain requirements. As noted, you must complain in writing. Phone calls do not protect your rights under this act. Your notice must be received at the creditor's address for billing error inquiries within 60 days after the statement was first sent to you. In the notice, you must include your name, complete address, and account number. Finally, you must explain why you believe there is a billing error and state the amount of the error.

It is important to follow these requirements when complaining about a bill. Once negative information is reported to a credit bureau, it may be difficult to have it removed.

PROBLEM 23

Examine the billing statement reproduced in Figure 4.3 and answer the following questions.

a. Who is the creditor?

b. Who is the debtor?

c. What is the new balance? How did the creditor arrive at the new balance?

d. How much credit is available? How did the creditor determine the credit available?

e. Assume the debtor had a store receipt from the camera shop for $77.67. Draft a letter to the creditor about this billing error.

When Should You Use Credit?

To make an informed decision about a credit purchase, you must first answer this question: Is it worth having a car, television, vaca-

Figure 4.3 A Billing Statement

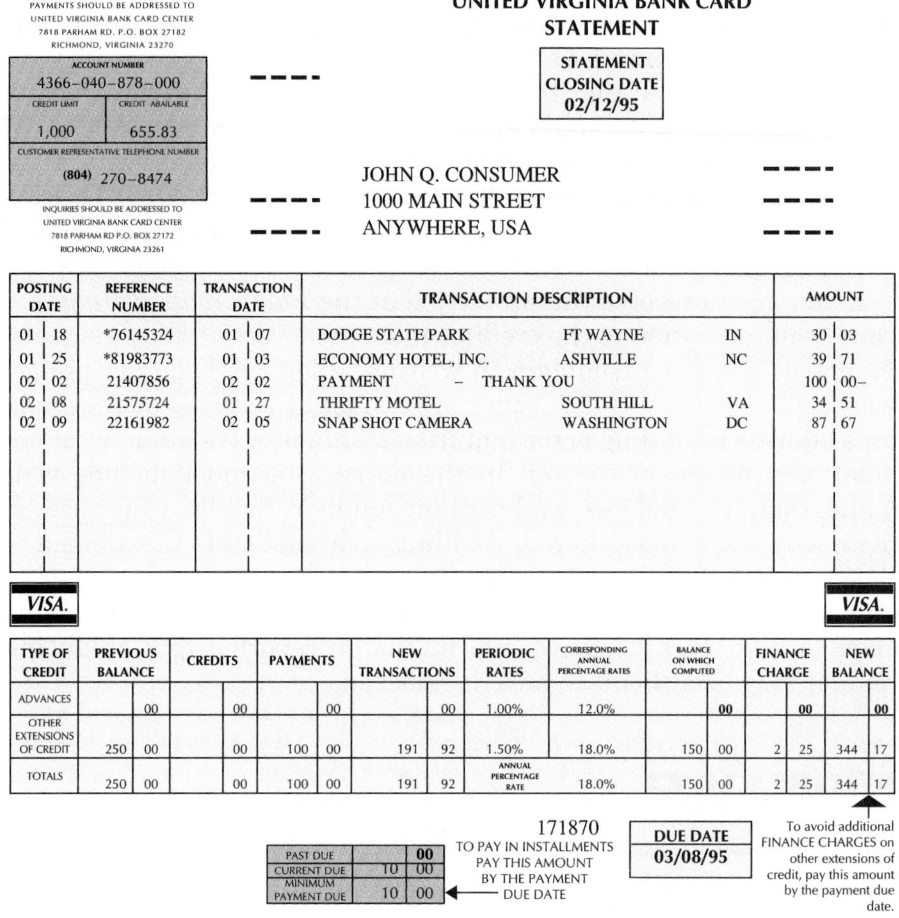

PAYMENTS SHOULD BE ADDRESSED TO
UNITED VIRGINIA BANK CARD CENTER
7818 PARHAM RD. P.O. BOX 27182
RICHMOND, VIRGINIA 23270

UNITED VIRGINIA BANK CARD STATEMENT

ACCOUNT NUMBER	
4366–040–878–000	
CREDIT LIMIT	CREDIT ABAILABLE
1,000	655.83
CUSTOMER REPRESENTATIVE TELEPHONE NUMBER	
(804) 270–8474	

STATEMENT CLOSING DATE 02/12/95

JOHN Q. CONSUMER
1000 MAIN STREET
ANYWHERE, USA

INQUIRIES SHOULD BE ADDRESSED TO
UNITED VIRGINIA BANK CARD CENTER
7818 PARHAM RD P.O. BOX 27172
RICHMOND, VIRGINIA 23261

POSTING DATE	REFERENCE NUMBER	TRANSACTION DATE	TRANSACTION DESCRIPTION			AMOUNT
01 18	*76145324	01 07	DODGE STATE PARK	FT WAYNE	IN	30 03
01 25	*81983773	01 03	ECONOMY HOTEL, INC.	ASHVILLE	NC	39 71
02 02	21407856	02 02	PAYMENT – THANK YOU			100 00–
02 08	21575724	01 27	THRIFTY MOTEL	SOUTH HILL	VA	34 51
02 09	22161982	02 05	SNAP SHOT CAMERA	WASHINGTON	DC	87 67

VISA. VISA.

TYPE OF CREDIT	PREVIOUS BALANCE	CREDITS	PAYMENTS	NEW TRANSACTIONS	PERIODIC RATES	CORRESPONDING ANNUAL PERCENTAGE RATES	BALANCE ON WHICH COMPUTED	FINANCE CHARGE	NEW BALANCE
ADVANCES	00	00	00	00	1.00%	12.0%	00	00	00
OTHER EXTENSIONS OF CREDIT	250 00	00	100 00	191 92	1.50%	18.0%	150 00	2 25	344 17
TOTALS	250 00	00	100 00	191 92	ANNUAL PERCENTAGE RATE	18.0%	150 00	2 25	344 17

PAST DUE	00
CURRENT DUE	10 00
MINIMUM PAYMENT DUE	10 00

171870
TO PAY IN INSTALLMENTS PAY THIS AMOUNT BY THE PAYMENT DUE DATE

DUE DATE 03/08/95

To avoid additional FINANCE CHARGES on other extensions of credit, pay this amount by the payment due date.

NOTICE: SEE REVERSE SIDE FOR IMPORTANT INFORMATION

tion, or other item before you have saved enough money to pay the entire purchase price, even though you'll pay more for the item in the long run?

Most American families answer yes to this question. In recent years, consumer debt has averaged approximately $1,000 for every man, woman, and child in America! And this figure does not include money owed for home mortgages. Many American families are seldom out of debt.

Extensive use of credit is here to stay, but consumers should know that credit purchases may cost more than cash purchases. In addition, studies show that consumers who use credit spend more and buy more often. This is the reason many merchants offer "easy credit."

Furthermore, consumers who buy on credit risk losing their products (and their previous payments) if they fail to make the required payments.

As a general rule, consumers who spend more than 20 percent of their take-home salary to pay off debts (excluding mortgages) are using too much credit. Consumers who skip payments to cover living expenses or who take out new loans to cover old loans are also using too much credit.

PROBLEM 24

a. Make a list of products or services that you, friends, or family members have bought on credit.

b. What are the advantages and disadvantages of using credit to pay for college or vocational school tuition? For a car to get you to work? For a vacation? For clothing to be worn at a formal party?

c. Write some rules that will help you decide when to use credit.

The Cost of Credit

As mentioned earlier, you should shop for credit just as you shop for products and services. The cost of credit includes interest and other finance charges. Because there are different methods for calculating interest rates, always ask lenders for the annual percentage rate (APR). This number is calculated the same way by all lenders, so you can use it to compare rates.

Interest Rates Each state sets limits on the amount of interest that can be charged for various types of credit. Charging any amount

Toll-free Numbers for Credit Card Companies

Many major credit card companies have toll-free 800 telephone numbers. Services offered by the companies differ, but generally you can notify them of a stolen or lost credit card, make inquiries about your bill or your account, apply for a credit card, and register a change of address.

You can obtain toll-free numbers by calling 1-800-555-1212.

The 50/50 Credit Plan

Joy tells Linda, "This washing machine is a good buy—only $500. Now, if you don't have the cash, I can arrange easy credit for you. Only $50 down and $50 a month for 12 months. Just sign here." Linda signs and pays $50. How much interest will she pay if the contract calls for 12 monthly payments of $50 each?

Linda will pay a total of $650 over 12 months ($50 down plus $600 in installment payments). Since the cash price of the washing machine was $500, she paid $150 in interest.

above the legal limit is called **usury**. Lenders who charge interest rates above the legal maximum may be liable for both civil and criminal penalties.

Interest rate ceilings vary from state to state. Generally, however, loans from banks or finance companies carry interest rates of 10 to 30% per year. Credit card companies and department stores often charge 1.5% per month (18% per year), but these rates can vary widely depending on the lender and the economic conditions at the time. Installment contracts for consumer goods such as new cars or furniture also vary widely.

Some companies now offer **variable interest rates**. For example, such a rate may be described as "2% over the prime rate" or a "10% variable annual percentage rate." With a variable rate, the amount of interest you are charged changes from time to time and is computed based on financial market indicators. That means your rate can go up or down with changing economic conditions. Carefully review the information provided by the lender to determine how often the rate can change and how much it can change at each adjustment as well as over the entire term of the loan. When the rate changes, your payments will change. While your payments may start out low, they could increase over time if the rate goes up.

Other Charges Besides the interest paid on a credit sale, there are sometimes other charges that may be added onto the basic price. These include:

- **Credit property insurance**—Insures the purchased item against theft or damage.

- **Credit life/disability insurance**—Guarantees payment of the balance due if the buyer should die or become disabled during the term of the contract.
- **Service charge**—Covers the seller's cost of bookkeeping, billing, and so on.
- **Penalty charge**—Covers the seller's inconvenience in case of late payments. May include court costs, repossession expenses, and attorney's fees.

PROBLEM 25

Choose an item you would like to have but could purchase only by using credit.

a. Where could you shop for this credit?

b. What is the APR for each creditor? What other finance charges are required?

Costly Credit Arrangements Consumers may fall prey to **loan sharking**. Loan sharks lend money at high, often usurious (illegal) rates of interest. They promise "easy" credit and appeal to people who have problems obtaining and keeping good credit standing.

What goods and services can consumers obtain from a pawn shop?

Using Credit

- Credit costs money. Don't buy things you don't need or want. Resist high-pressure sales techniques.
- Determine how much debt you can handle.
- Comparison shop for credit. If you are suspicious about a lender, check to see if the lender is licensed and whether complaints have been filed.
- Before making a credit purchase, read and understand the entire contract. Don't sign contracts with blank spaces.
- If a contract calls for a large final payment, be sure you can afford it.
- Once you've signed a credit agreement, keep a copy in a safe place. Keep receipts for each payment.

Usurious loans are illegal under state laws. There are, however, a variety of legal but costly credit arrangements that consumers may want to avoid.

Some creditors call for **balloon payments** in their agreements. In such agreements, the last payment is much larger than the monthly payments. This may make it difficult for you to make the final payment. Consumers should carefully consider any agreement that calls for a large final payment. Be sure you can save up enough to make this payment.

Another thing to avoid in financing agreements is the **acceleration clause**. This clause permits the creditor to accelerate the loan, making all future payments due immediately in the event a consumer misses a single payment. Most auto sales finance agreements have acceleration clauses. If you miss a payment, you may suddenly owe the creditor the entire amount of the loan. Many cars are repossessed by lenders for this reason.

You should also beware of **bill consolidation**. This means combining all your debts into a single one. Lenders sometimes claim you can wipe out all your bills by making easy monthly payment to them, which they will distribute to your creditors. However, the consolidation loan may require payments over a longer period of time and at a higher rate of interest. Some lenders also charge a substantial fee for these loans. They may subtract the fee from your monthly payment to them before paying off your creditors, so you wind up falling deeper in debt.

Truth in Lending To prevent credit abuses, Congress passed the *Truth in Lending Act*. This law requires creditors to give you certain basic information about the cost of buying on credit. The creditor

The Hidden Charges

Chang buys a new guitar amplifier on an installment plan. When he receives the itemized bill, he discovers that he owes a total of $745, though the price of the amp was only $553. He calls the music store and is told that he is paying more than 20 percent interest. He would never have bought the amp if he'd known it would cost this much. What mistakes did Chang make? What can he do now?

must tell you—*in writing and before you sign a contract*—the finance charge and the annual percentage rate. The finance charge is the total amount you pay to use the credit, including interest charges and any other fees. The APR is the percentage cost of credit on a yearly basis.

The law requires creditors to give you special information about variable-rate loans if you are being offered this plan. Remember that with these plans, your payments may increase over time.

The law also requires that consumers be given a copy of the disclosure form containing the credit information. They must also be told the rules and charges for any late payments. Violators can be subject to both civil and criminal penalties, and consumers who sue creditors under this act may recover damages, court costs, and attorney's fees.

PROBLEM 26

Rafael wants to buy a refrigerator from Melissa's Appliance Store. He cannot afford to pay the entire purchase price, so she suggests that he apply for credit at the store. The credit application and the form agreement between the buyer and seller are reprinted in Figure 4.4. Carefully read this material and then answer the questions below.

a. Why might the seller ask that a second person sign the credit application?

b. What is the annual percentage rate in this agreement?

c. Must the consumer purchase credit insurance according to the agreement?

d. Why has the seller included a paragraph on credit cards?

e. Reread the paragraph of the agreement dealing with default. Is there an acceleration clause in this paragraph? Explain.

f. What action can the seller take if the consumer does not make the required payments?

g. If the consumer misses a payment and the seller takes back the product, is it possible that the consumer would still owe the seller money? Explain.

h. Is this agreement fair to the seller? Is it fair to the buyer? Explain your answer.

i. Much of the information in the credit agreement is required by the federal *Truth in Lending Act*. Do you think most consumers

Figure 4.4 A Typical Credit Application

MELISSA'S APPLIANCES

Please read the following before completing this form: (1) Applicant represents that the information given in this application is complete and accurate and authorizes us to check with credit reporting agencies, credit references and other sources disclosed herein in investigating the information given. (2) Applicant requests a credit card if our current consumer credit plan provides for the issuance of such a card. (3) Married applicants may apply for an individual account. READ AND SIGN THE ATTACHED AGREEMENT BEFORE SUBMITTING YOUR APPLICATION.

1. TELL US ABOUT YOURSELF ***PLEASE PRINT***

First Name | Middle Initial | Last Name

Present Address | City | State | Zip Code

Previous Address (if less than two years at present address) | City | State | Zip Code

Birthdate / / | Social Security No. | Home Phone No. ( ) | Business Phone No. ( )

Employer | How Long (Years) | Annual Income* $ | Occupation: (✓)

No. Dependents | ☐ Own ☐ Board ☐ Rent ☐ Live with Relatives | How Long (Years) | Mortgage/Rent Payment $

1. ☐ Professional/ Technical
2. ☐ Sales
3. ☐ Clerical
4. ☐ Self-Employed
5. ☐ Retired
6. Other

Credit References: (✓)
☐ Checking ☐ Savings ☐ VISA ☐ MasterCard ☐ Sears/ Discover ☐ American Express/ Optima ☐ Dept. Stores

2. PLEASE COMPLETE FOR CO-APPLICANT OR AUTHORIZED USER ***Co-Applicant must sign Section 4 (Acknowledgement Signatures).***

First Name | Middle Initial | Last Name

Present Address | City | State | Zip Code

Annual Income* | Social Security No. | Relationship to Applicant ☐ Spouse ☐ Other | If individual listed above is Co-Applicant, check box ☐

3. INSURANCE OPTIONS
Indicate coverage chosen by signing and completing one of the following options. If insurance is not elected, do not sign or complete the following options.

By signing below, you acknowledge for any insurance elected that: (1) the purchase of such insurance was voluntary and was not required by us in the extension of credit; (2) the decision to purchase such insurance was made after we disclosed the cost of the insurance as set out in the agreement; and (3) you may obtain property insurance from a person of your own choosing other than us.

Single Credit Life, Disability, and Involuntary Unemployment Insurance with Property Insurance: ☐ is elected ☐ is not elected

X

Buyer's Signature | Date | Age | Name of Proposed Insured (Accountholder or Accountholder's Spouse) | Age

4. ACKNOWLEDGEMENT SIGNATURE(S)

NOTICE TO BUYER: DO NOT SIGN BELOW BEFORE YOU HAVE RECEIVED AND READ THE COPY OF THE SELLER'S REVOLVING CREDIT ACCOUNT AGREEMENT.
You acknowledge that you have signed, dated, and kept the copy of the SELLER'S REVOLVING CREDIT ACCOUNT AGREEMENT and you agree to be bound by its terms and conditions.

SIGN HERE ➧ **X** | **X**

Buyer's Signature | Date | Co-Buyer's Signature | Date

*Alimony, child support or separate maintenance payments need not be disclosed unless relied upon for credit.

Seller's Copy

FOR DEALER USE ONLY

Dealer Name | Telephone ( ) | Salesperson

Initial Amount Financed | Special Minimum Monthly Payment (applicable only if appropriate space on agreement is filled in) $ | Approval given by:

Branch No. | Dealer No. | Account No. | Credit Line

MELISSA'S APPLIANCES
REVOLVING CREDIT ACCOUNT AGREEMENT

ACCOUNT: In consideration of the granting of credit on this account by us (the Seller), you (meaning each person signing this account as Buyer) promise to pay us the purchase price for purchases made on this account by you (or anyone authorized by you) from time to time and any finance charges due under the terms of this agreement. You will be billed monthly for credit purchases from us, as shown on a sales invoice signed by you (or completed at your direction), and for any previous unpaid balance. You agree to pay us the amount billed on your account, including the finance charge, in consecutive monthly installments. This account and all purchases made on it are not binding on us until your credit is approved.

FINANCE CHARGE: The **FINANCE CHARGE** will be computed by applying a periodic rate of **1.82%** per month **(ANNUAL PERCENTAGE RATE: 21.84%)** to the balance subject to finance charge.

BALANCE SUBJECT TO FINANCE CHARGE: The balance subject to finance charge is the average daily balance, including new purchases, which is arrived at by adding the daily balances in the account during the billing period and dividing this total by the number of days in the period. The daily balances are determined by taking the beginning balance each day during the billing period and adding any new purchases and subtracting any payments and credits entered on that day.

WHEN CHARGE BEGINS: Since purchases are included in the daily balance from the date you receive the goods or services purchased, they start incurring a finance charge from that date and there is no period in which credit extended may be paid without incurring a finance charge.

MINIMUM MONTHLY PAYMENT: You will pay a minimum monthly payment in an amount (rounded to the next higher dollar) which is the larger of: (1) **1/30** of the highest balance of your account since it last had a **$0** balance, (2) **$25**, or (3) ____________. When your balance is less than **$25**, the minimum monthly payment will be equal to the entire balance. Except as stated, the amount of your minimum monthly payment will remain the same. **You have the right to pay your entire balance in full or more than the minimum monthly payment at any time.**

SECURITY: You are giving us and we are retaining a purchase money security interest in the merchandise purchased under this agreement until the debt for that merchandise is paid in full. This permits us, under certain circumstances as provided for by law, to take back, or repossess, the merchandise if you do not pay for it under the terms of this agreement.

FILING FEES: We may charge and you agree to pay a $6 fee for filing a security interest financing statement with public officials and up to that amount for any required termination of such financing statement.

APPLICATION OF PAYMENTS: Payments, except downpayments, shall be applied first to the unpaid finance charge and then to the payment of the unpaid balance of each item of merchandise in the order of its purchase. Downpayments will be credited in full to the items to which they apply.

DEFAULT: If you do not pay any minimum payment when due, or breach any other terms of this agreement, we may demand, subject to any notice of default and right to cure default required by state law, that the entire unpaid balance be paid immediately and start a lawsuit for collection of this balance. You agree to pay court costs and reasonable attorney's fees not to exceed 15% of the unpaid indebtedness if your account is referred for collection to any attorney who is not our salaried employee. We also reserve our rights and remedies pertaining to repossession and resale of any repossessed merchandise as provided under applicable law. We agree to pay you a surplus, if any, resulting from a resale of any repossessed merchandise, and you agree to pay us a deficiency when permitted by law.

CREDIT CAPACITY AND LIMIT: You give us the right to investigate your credit capacity and credit history. You agree that your outstanding balance on this account will not exceed your credit limit. In addition, you agree that we may change your credit limit from time to time, based on changes in your credit capacity. We are authorized to furnish information about the account and yourself to credit reporting agencies and others who may lawfully receive the information. You also give us the right to rent information (usually only your name and address) to others who may lawfully receive such information and who may solicit you for quality products or services. You can request that such rental be discontinued at any time by notifying us.

CREDIT CARD: You request a credit card from us, if it is our practice to provide one. You further agree to immediately notify us, orally or in writing, of the loss, theft or unauthorized use of your credit card. If notice is given orally, you will confirm it in writing.

CANCELLATION: We and you have the right to cancel this agreement as it relates to future purchases. You agree to return all credit cards to us upon notice of cancellation. You remain obligated to pay for all purchases made prior to cancellation.

ENTIRE AGREEMENT: This is our entire agreement and no oral changes can be made.

INSURANCE OPTIONS: Although insurance is not required under this revolving charge plan, we will provide the following combined insurance coverage for you (also referred to as "Accountholder") if you elect and qualify for such insurance: Single Credit Life, Disability, and Involuntary Unemployment Insurance with Property Insurance.

INSURANCE ELECTIONS: Accountholder has the right to cancel such insurance without charge by notifying Seller.

NOTICE TO THE BUYER: (a) DO NOT SIGN THIS AGREEMENT BEFORE YOU READ IT OR IF IT CONTAINS ANY BLANK SPACES. (b) YOU ARE ENTITLED TO A READABLE COPY OF THE CONTRACT AT THE TIME YOU SIGN IT. KEEP IT TO PROTECT YOUR LEGAL RIGHTS. (c) YOU HAVE THE RIGHT TO PAY IN ADVANCE THE FULL AMOUNT DUE.

NOTICE

ANY HOLDER OF THIS CONSUMER CREDIT CONTRACT IS SUBJECT TO ALL CLAIMS AND DEFENSES WHICH THE DEBTOR COULD ASSERT AGAINST THE SELLER OF GOODS OR SERVICES OBTAINED PURSUANT HERETO OR WITH THE PROCEEDS HEREOF. RECOVERY HEREUNDER BY THE DEBTOR SHALL NOT EXCEED AMOUNTS PAID BY THE DEBTOR HEREUNDER.

Buyer acknowledges that before Buyer signed the REVOLVING CREDIT ACCOUNT AGREEMENT, Seller submitted the REVOLVING CREDIT ACCOUNT AGREEMENT to Buyer with all blank spaces filled in, that Buyer had a reasonable opportunity to examine it, and that thereafter a legible, executed copy thereof was delivered to Buyer.

BUYER(S) SIGN HERE

Signed **X** ______________________________ Date ____________
(BUYER)

Signed **X** ______________________________ Date ____________
(BUYER)

SELLER SIGN HERE

____
(SELLER)

By ______________________________ Date ____________
(AUTHORIZED REPRESENTATIVE — TITLE)

Seller's Address ______________________________

____

read this information before making their decision? What are the benefits of reading the agreement? What are the costs?

What Lenders Want to Know Before Extending Credit

Where can consumers go to comparison shop for a loan?

Any store, bank, or credit card company that extends credit to consumers wants to know that the money will be repaid. Before making a loan, the creditor will want to know several things about the consumer:

- Is the consumer a reliable person? (For example, a person who moves or changes jobs frequently might not be considered reliable.)
- Does the consumer have a steady income that is likely to continue into the future?
- Is the consumer's income high enough to enable him or her to pay for the items to be purchased?
- Does the consumer have a good record in paying off other loans and bills?

Creditors are in business to make money; thus, it is understandable that they would ask questions such as these. However, creditors have sometimes unfairly denied credit for reasons such as the debtor's race, sex, or source of income (such as public assistance or alimony). Today a federal law, the *Equal Credit Opportunity Act*, protects consumers against credit discrimination based on sex, marital status, race, color, religion, national origin, old age, or source of income. The Federal Trade Commission handles credit discrimination complaints against finance companies, retail stores, oil companies, and travel and entertainment credit card companies. Bank regulatory agencies, such as the Federal Reserve Board and the Comptroller of the Currency, handle complaints against banks and bank credit cards. If you think you have been discriminated against, you may complain to one of these agencies or sue the creditor in court.

Many states also have laws that forbid credit discrimination. Complaints should be directed to the state or local consumer affairs office or human rights commission.

PROBLEM 27

You are a loan officer at a local bank. Each of the following people is seeking a loan. Based on the information provided, evaluate each applicant and make a decision regarding each loan request. Discuss your reasons for granting or denying credit.

a. Alice Johnson is the mother of four children. Her only income consists of public assistance payments of $420 per month and $80 per month from the pension of her deceased husband. She wishes to buy a new oven and refrigerator totalling $700. She lives in a public housing development. Her rent and other expenses usually total about $375 a month.

b. Jerry Levitt is a carpenter seeking work wherever he can find it. Depending on the weather and other factors, he is subject to seasonal unemployment. He currently brings home about $650 per month and has car payments of $150 a month, TV payments of $105 a month, rent of $220 a month, and no money in the bank. He would like to borrow $2,500 to buy a motorcycle.

c. Barbara Griego, 22, is in her second year of college. She has excellent grades and plans to attend medical school after graduation. Until recently, her parents paid her bills, but she is now on her own. She is seeking $2,000 for her college tuition and expenses. She has never borrowed money before, but she plans to repay all loans after finishing medical school.

What to Do If You Are Denied Credit

If you ever apply for credit, the creditor will evaluate your application according to certain standards. The creditor may investigate you personally or may pay a credit bureau to check your credit record. Many creditors do both. There are thousands of credit bureaus across the country. Financial and personal information about consumers is often stored in computers and may be passed among the various bureaus. Information about you in a credit bureau's files can be a key factor in determining whether you get loans, credit cards, or other forms of credit in the future.

If a credit report indicates that you are a poor risk, the creditor will probably deny credit. Also, if you are trying to get credit for the first time and have no credit record at all, the creditor may deny credit. Sometimes creditors decide to deny credit based solely on information in the application, without taking the time to order a credit report.

The *Equal Credit Opportunity Act* says that creditors must tell consumers why they were turned down. The reasons given must be specific. For example, "applicant does not meet our standards" is not specific enough. On the other hand, "insufficient income" is a specific reason. It tells you how your circumstances must change to qualify for credit.

Another federal law protects you from inaccurate credit bureau reporting. The *Fair Credit Reporting Act* requires creditors who deny credit based on information received from a credit bureau to tell you that fact. The creditor must also give you the name and address of the credit bureau that supplied the report.

Every consumer has the right to learn the nature of information in his or her credit file. Although credit bureaus are not required to show consumers copies of the actual file, they must disclose the nature and substance of the information it contains.

If you discover false, misleading, incomplete, irrelevant, or out-of-date information in your file, you can require the credit bureau to recheck its information and correct the errors. If the credit bureau does not cooperate in correcting your credit file, you may complain to the Federal Trade Commission or sue the bureau in court. If after reinvestigating the information the bureau still believes that it is correct, you have the right to have your version of the dispute inserted in the file. If the information being reported about you is accurate, the credit bureau can report it for seven years.

DEFAULT AND COLLECTION PRACTICES

What steps should be taken by a consumer who is unable to pay her bills?

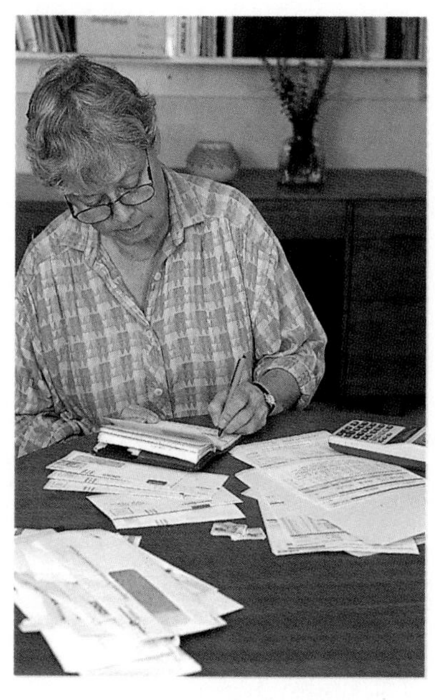

Consumers who use credit sometimes have difficulty making all their payments. Problems can arise because the consumer is overextended or too deeply in debt. Problems can also arise because of unexpected unemployment, family illness, or a variety of other reasons. A consumer who is unable or unwilling to pay a debt goes into default.

What a Consumer Can Do in Case of Default

If you have problems paying your bills, you should consider the following options:

1. Reassess your financial lifestyle to determine where the problem arose. If you are not already on a budget, consider starting one.
2. Notify each creditor of the problem and ask to have the term of debt extended (leading to smaller monthly payments) or to have the amount of the debt reduced or refinanced. Keep in mind that refinancing over a longer period usually results in increased finance charges.

3. Contact a consumer credit counseling service or a family service agency that offers free or low-cost financial counseling (see Appendix F for addresses).
4. Seek assistance from friends or relatives to reduce the debt to a manageable level.

Bankruptcy If these steps do not resolve your problem, you may have to declare **bankruptcy**. This is a procedure through which a person places assets under the control of a federal court in order to be relieved of debt. In recent years, an enormous number of bankruptcies have been filed in the United States. In 1991–1992, more than 70% of the civil cases filed in federal court were bankruptcies.

Under Chapter 13 of the federal bankruptcy law, a wage earner can make an arrangement, supervised by a federal court, to pay off some or all of what is owed to creditors over an extended period of time. A more severe form of bankruptcy is called a Chapter 7 bankruptcy. Under Chapter 7, the federal court takes control of most of the debtor's assets (some states allow the debtor to keep certain items), sells them, and pays off as much debt as possible. Generally, the money received from the sale of the assets is not enough to fully pay all creditors.

What agencies and organizations in your community provide financial counseling services? Do they charge a fee for their services?

A declaration of bankruptcy has serious long-term consequences for the debtor. Records of personal bankruptcy remain in credit reports for 10 years. Even after that time, it may be very difficult to obtain credit or borrow money. In addition, some debts are not wiped out through bankruptcy. Taxes, alimony, child support, and student loans must still be repaid.

Creditor Collection Practices

Creditors have many ways of collecting money from consumers who are unwilling or unable to pay their debts. It is understandable that creditors will take action to recover money or property owed them. However, in the past, some bill collectors engaged in unsavory practices. As a result, some debtors suffered family problems, lost their jobs, and had their privacy invaded.

These practices prompted Congress to pass the *Fair Debt Collection Practices Act* in 1978. This act protects consumers from abusive and unfair collection practices by professional debt collectors. It does not apply to creditors collecting their own bills. Under the act, the debt collector's communications are limited to reasonable times and places. False or misleading statements as well as acts of harassment or abuse are strictly prohibited.

Calls and Letters If you receive unreasonable or harassing phone calls or letters from a debt collector, you should report the collection practice to the Federal Trade Commission or to your local consumer protection agency. Under federal law, you can send bill collectors a notice demanding that all collection contacts cease. You might still owe the money, but the collection contacts would have to stop. You should also consider contacting the phone company, which has the power to remove telephones from anyone using them for harassment.

Repossession As mentioned earlier, consumers sometimes post collateral when they take out a loan or sign credit sales contracts. The creditor can usually **repossess**, or take back, the collateral if the borrower defaults on the loan or obligation. Most states do not permit creditors to repossess if repossession would involve violence or a breach of the peace.

Once the collateral has been repossessed, the creditor can sell it and then apply the proceeds of the sale to the amount owed. Debtors are also charged for any costs incurred in the repossession and sale. After the sale, the debtor is entitled to get back any amount received by the seller that is in excess of the amount owed (plus expenses). However, if the sale brings in less than the amount owed (plus expenses), the debtor must still pay the difference.

Court Action As a last resort, creditors may sue debtors in court for the exact amount owed on the debt. At times, the trouble and expense of suing in court make creditors avoid this method. However, creditors often sue debtors in small claims court.

Just because you are sued does not mean the creditor is entitled to collect the disputed amount. Consumers often have legitimate defenses, such as the fact that the goods were defective. As a result, *if you ever receive a summons to go to court, don't ignore it*. If you cannot appear in court on the date set in the summons, contact the court clerk in advance to arrange for a postponement of the trial. In addition, contact a lawyer immediately. If you are unable to afford one, you may call the local legal services or legal aid office.

The main thing to avoid when being sued is a **default judgment**. This is a judgment entered for the plaintiff (creditor) and against the defendant (debtor). Most default judgments occur because the defendant simply fails to show up in court.

Garnishment and Attachment A creditor who wins a court judgment against a consumer may still have trouble collecting if the consumer does not pay voluntarily. It was once common practice to have people imprisoned for not paying debts; however, this is no longer allowed.

One solution creditors use is to get a court order that forces the debtor's employer to withhold part of the debtor's wages and pay it directly to the creditor. This is called **garnishment**. The federal *Wage Garnishment Act* limits the amount that can be garnished to

25% of the debtor's take-home pay (pay after taxes and social security deductions). Persons who are employed by the federal government or who receive other federal money, such as welfare or unemployment compensation, cannot have their income garnished (unless the money is used to meet court-ordered child support payments). The act also prohibits employers from firing employees who have their wages garnished for a single debt. State laws may further limit and sometimes completely prohibit garnishment.

Creditors can also get possession of a debtor's money or property by **attachment**. This is a court order that forces a bank to pay the creditor out of a consumer's bank account or that allows the court to seize the consumer's property and sell it to satisfy the debt.

The Missed Payment

Orlando buys a used car from Top Value Cars for $1,200 and signs a contract calling for monthly payments for three years. After paying $800, he misses a payment because of large doctor bills. Leaving home one morning, he finds that the car is gone. Top Value has hired someone to repossess the car in the middle of the night.

PROBLEM 28

a. Assume that Top Value sells the car for $500 and incurs expenses of $200 in the repossession and sale. Will Orlando get money back, or will he still owe money to Top Value (even though he no longer has the car)? How much is owed, and to whom?

b. Is the action taken by Top Value legal? Do you think the repossession laws are fair? What arguments could creditors make in support of these laws? What arguments could debtors make against them?

What procedures must you follow to register a car and obtain license plates in your community?

CARS AND THE CONSUMER

One of the most important purchases you will ever make is the purchase of an automobile. Buying, owning, maintaining, and selling

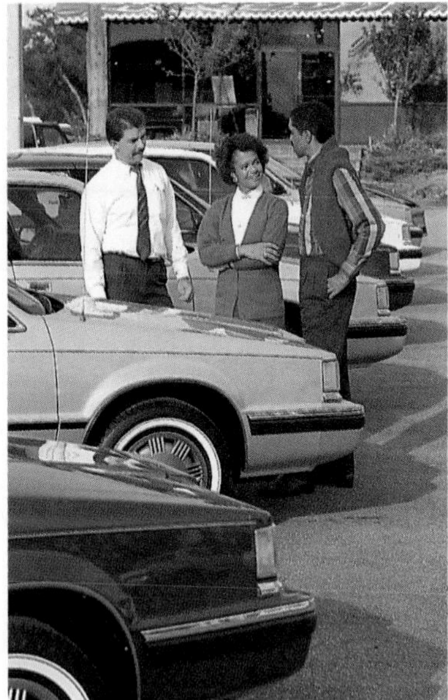
What factors should this couple consider before purchasing a car?

an automobile involve many legal issues. Earlier in this chapter, you learned how the law affects car owners in cases of repair fraud and repossession. Now you will apply some concepts you have already studied (comparison shopping, contracts, warranties, and credit) to automobiles.

Buying a Car

When you shop for a new or used car, you should consider at least five general characteristics: (1) safety, (2) price, (3) quality, (4) warranty, and (5) fuel economy. Many consumers fail to compare safety features when shopping for a car. Safety features are important because in an average year, one out of every three motorists has an automobile accident! Federal law requires car dealers to provide a pamphlet that details safety aspects of new cars. This pamphlet includes information on acceleration and passing ability, stopping distance, and tire load. Besides obtaining this information, you should always check visibility from the driver's seat (check for blind spots, windshield glare in strong sunlight, and positioning of inside and outside mirrors). In addition, you should check whether you can reach all controls while sitting in the driver's seat with the seat belts fastened and what protection is afforded by bumpers and safety belts.

THE CASE OF . . .

The Used-Car Purchase

Having saved $1,000 from her summer job, Sharon responded to an ad for "like-new, one-owner used cars." A salesperson for A-1 Used Cars watched Sharon wander around the lot until she was attracted to a bright red compact car. Sharon told the salesperson that this car looked just right for her. He replied, "You've made a good choice. This is an excellent car. It will give you many years of good service."

Although the sticker price was $3,550, the salesperson thought that he might be able to get Sharon a $50 discount because she was "a nice young kid getting her first car." After conferring with the sales manager, he told her that she could have the car for $3,500 and that the dealer could arrange to finance the car and sell her all necessary insurance.

Sharon knew that she'd need a loan, and her parents had warned her that insurance was required by law. Her excitement increased as it appeared that all her problems could be solved in one stop.

Sharon saw a sticker in the car's window indicating that this car came with a warranty. The salesperson told her that A-1 would make any repairs to the engine for damage not caused by her misuse for 30 days or 10,000 miles, whichever came first. Now she felt confident about using all of her savings as a down payment. After all, what repair bills could she have with such a nice car accompanied by a terrific warranty?

PROBLEM 29

a. Make a list of things Sharon should have done or thought about before going to A-1.

b. Make a list of things she should have done at A-1 before agreeing to buy the car.

c. What promises, if any, did the seller make to her? Did he say anything that could be considered puffing? If so, what?

d. What are the advantages and disadvantages to Sharon of obtaining financing and insurance from the dealer?

e. Taking into account the lists you've made, role-play Sharon's encounter with the salesperson.

In considering price, remember that virtually no one pays the sticker price for a new or used car. Discounts are quite common. The size of the discount depends on the time of year, your negotiating ability, special sales, manufacturer's bonuses, rebates, and other factors.

PROBLEM 30

In addition to the purchase price, what other costs should you consider in deciding to purchase a car? Where is information available about each of these costs?

You should compare fuel economy, warranties, and the dealer's capability to make repairs the same way you compare safety features and price. Many new cars have warranties covering most parts, except batteries and tires, against defects for 12,000 miles or 12

Are there laws in your state requiring that used cars be sold with some warranty protection?

months, whichever comes first. Some manufacturers warrant the engine and drive train for a longer period. A few manufacturers now offer multi-year bumper-to-bumper warranties. Other manufacturers offer a warranty as part of the purchase price but also make available an extended warranty (actually a service contract) for an additional price. Warranties vary, so be certain that you read and fully understand exactly what protections the warranty provides.

In some instances, used cars come with warranties. The Federal Trade Commission now requires used-car dealers to place a large sticker—a "Buyer's Guide"—in the window of every vehicle offered for sale. The sticker must tell you whether the vehicle comes with an express warranty. If so, the sticker must tell you what the warranty includes. If the sticker says the car comes "as is," this means no warranty is provided. However, in some places, state law prohibits a car from being sold "as is." Finally, the sticker will advise you to get all promises in writing and to have the car inspected by a mechanic before you buy it.

Although car warranties are now easier to read and protections have been expanded, there are still time or mileage limits (or both) on warranties. Also, a warranty may become ineffective if you fail to perform proper maintenance or if you misuse the car.

Always be sure the warranty and any additional promises are in writing. Keep these papers in a safe place.

Financing a Car

Most new-car buyers and many used-car buyers make their purchases on credit. Buyers may select the length of the repayment period, which may be as long as five years. The longer the repayment period, the lower the monthly payments will be (but the larger the amount paid in interest). Figure 4.5 shows the total interest charges on a $6,000 loan at a 10% interest rate over various repayment periods. Actual interest rates vary from lender to lender and change with economic conditions.

Figure 4.5 Interest on a $6,000 Loan

Amount Borrowed	APR	Term of Loan (in months)	Monthly Payment	Total Finance Charge
$6,000	10%	24	$276.86	$644.64
$6,000	10%	36	$193.90	$980.40
$6,000	10%	48	$152.17	$1,304.16

PROBLEM 31

Sam is buying a used car for $7,000. He can make a down payment of $1,000 and needs to borrow the remaining $6,000. Assume that credit is available only from the source listed in Figure 4.5.

a. What is the total cost of the car if the term of the loan is 24 months? 36 months? 48 months?

b. If Sam decided to borrow, which credit arrangement would be least expensive? Which would be most desirable? Explain your answers.

Automobile financing is usually available from the following sources: car dealers, banks, credit unions, and finance companies. When comparing finance charges among lenders, make certain that the same down payment and repayment periods are used for each loan. In comparing terms, you'll mostly be concerned with the annual percentage rate. However, you should also read all of the terms carefully so that you can answer such questions as:

1. Will there be a refund of finance charges if the loan is repaid ahead of schedule?
2. Will there be fair warning in the event of a repossession?
3. Is there a penalty for late payments? If so, how much?
4. Will all payments immediately become due if a payment is missed?

If you can't answer all of these questions by reading your loan terms, always ask the questions of your lender or have someone help you read and understand the agreement.

In considering how much you can afford for a car, you must also consider the cost of fuel, repairs, license and registration fees, and auto insurance. Insurance payments can be a major cost. The price will vary based on the type of car you buy, where you live, how much you plan to drive the car, your driving record, your age, and the company that sells you the insurance. A discussion of the various types of insurance can be found in Chapter 3.

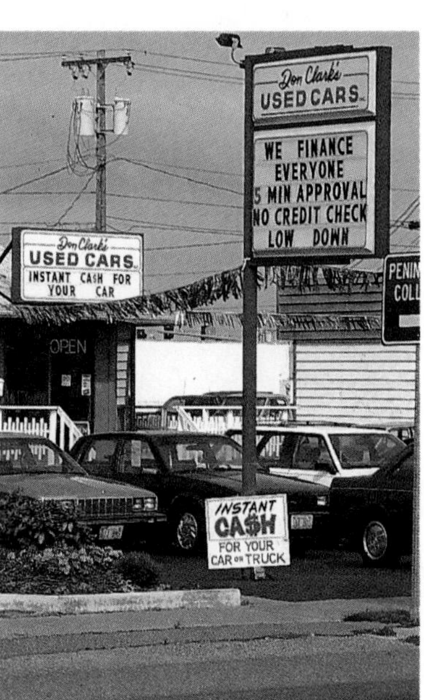

What sources, in addition to dealers, offer financing when you want to purchase a car?

In the Event of an Auto Accident . . .

- Check for injuries. Get medical help if needed.
- Route traffic around the accident.
- Call the police.
- Exchange information with the other driver(s), including: names, addresses, and phone numbers; license and registration numbers; makes, models, and years of cars; names, addresses, and phone numbers of insurance agents; names and phone numbers of witnesses (or their license numbers, so you can locate them later if necessary).
- Do not tell the other driver(s) the extent of your insurance, do not confess guilt, do not indicate that your insurance company will take care of everything, and do not sign any paper indicating you were not injured.
- Note the name and badge number of the police officer if one is called to the scene of the accident. Your state law may require that you file an accident report with the police.
- Make careful notes about the accident while the information is fresh in your mind.
- Contact your insurance agent as soon as possible after the accident and follow his or her instructions carefully.

Chapter 5

Family Law

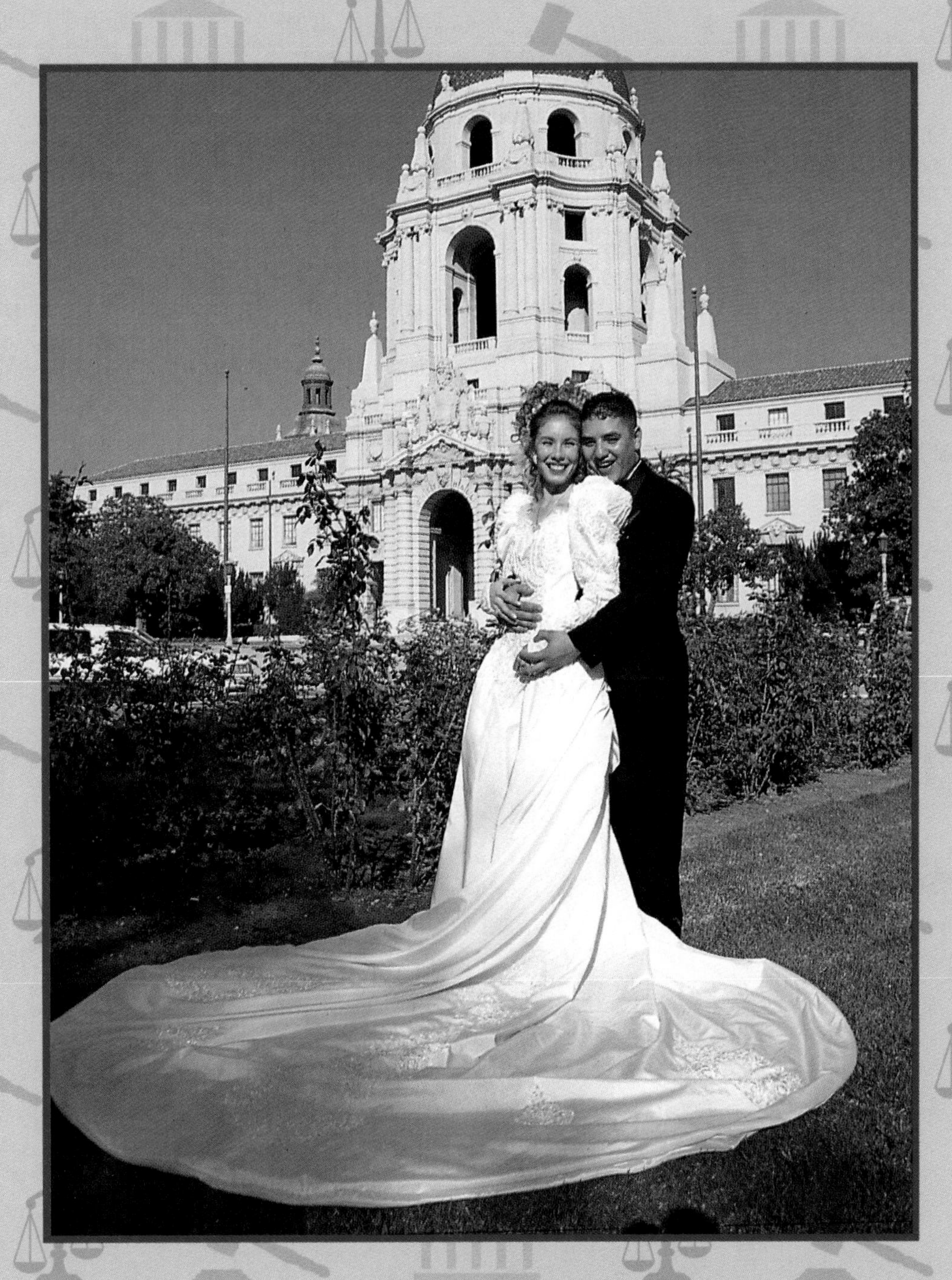

The family is the basic unit of society. It is the most intimate and important of all social groups. Most people consider family life a private matter, and in many ways it is. If you argue with your brother or decide to have 10 children, the law will not interfere. All the same, the law is very much a part of family life.

The law is involved every time a birth, death, marriage, or divorce takes place. Every state has laws affecting the family. For example, state laws set requirements that must be met before anyone can be married. Likewise, every state has laws that outline the basic rights and duties of family members. Other laws govern areas such as adoption, alimony, child care, custody, divorce, and family support.

If asked to identify a family, most of us would say we know one when we see one. We are surrounded by families wherever we go, and most of us live in family settings. However, families come in all shapes and sizes, and defining the term *family* is sometimes difficult.

Legally, the word *family* is used to describe many relationships: parents and children; people related by blood, marriage, or adoption; or a group of people living together in a single household, sharing living space and housekeeping. Since the word *family* does not have a precise meaning, many laws define the term when they use it. For example, zoning laws that set aside certain areas for single-family homes define family one way. Laws involving insurance, social security, or inheritance may define family in other ways.

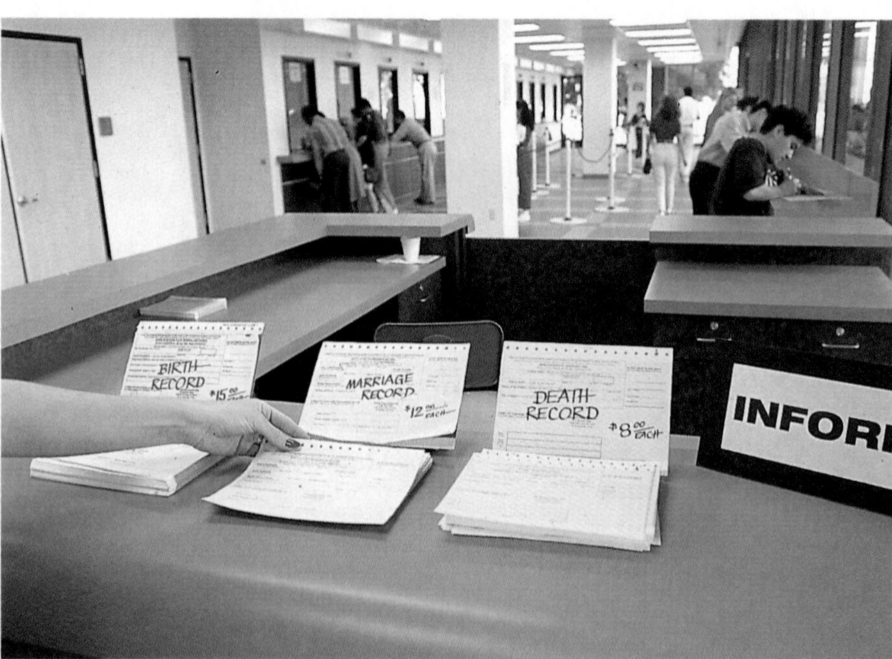

Why do governments maintain records of births, marriages, and deaths?

PROBLEM 1

Examine the group of photos above. For each photo, answer the following questions:

a. Is this a family? Why or why not?

b. Is this living arrangement common where you live?

c. How does the law affect this living arrangement?

Then answer these questions:

d. What are the characteristics of a family? How would you define the term *family*?

e. Are a divorced husband and wife still a family? Would you answer differently depending on whether they have children?

THE CHANGING AMERICAN FAMILY

The American family has undergone dramatic changes during the past 90 years. One of these changes has been a reduction in size. In 1900, the average family size was 5.7 persons. By 1991, the average family had shrunk to 2.63 persons. Today, couples have fewer children or, in some cases, no children at all.

Families have also changed because women's roles have changed. During the early part of this century, most married women did not work outside their homes. Today, however, 55% of all married women hold jobs outside their homes.

The increase in single-parent families also illustrates how families are changing. Although most families still include two parents, the number of one-parent families has doubled in the past decade. There

In what ways have families changed?

Fig. 5.1 Changes in American Families, 1970–1991

	1970	1991	Percentage Increase/ Decrease
Marriages performed	2,159,000	2,448,000	+13
Divorces granted	708,000	1,175,000	+66
Married couples	44,728,000	50,708,000	+13
Married couples with children	25,541,000	24,552,000	–4
Children living with two parents	58,926,000	46,658,000	–21
Children living with one parent	8,230,000	16,624,000	+102
Average size of household	3.3	2.63	–20
Families with both partners working	20,327,000	25,144,000	+24

Source: Bureau of the Census, 1992.

are two reasons for this. First, divorces are at an all-time high. Second, the number of unmarried parents has increased.

These and other changes have caused problems and conflicts, which often involve the law. Nevertheless, the family no doubt will continue to adapt.

PROBLEM 2

a. Look at Figure 5.1. What do you think are the most significant changes in American families since 1970? In your opinion, why have these changes occurred?

b. How many children did your grandparents have? How many children do your parents have? How many children would you like to have?

c. Where did your grandparents live? Where do your parents live? How often did they move during their lives?

d. Did both your grandparents hold jobs outside the home? Do both your parents hold jobs outside the home?

e. What do you think families will be like in the future?

PROBLEM 3

The law reflects the idea that marriage and the family are essential to the strength of society. As a result, the law affects families and family life. Below is a survey that asks for your ideas about law and the family. For each statement, decide whether you strongly agree (SA), agree (A), disagree (D), strongly disagree (SD), or are undecided (U). Discuss your answers.

a. Getting married should be made more difficult.

b. A wife and a husband should have an equal say about all decisions in their marriage.

c. Adopted children have a right to know who their birth parents are.

d. Mothers with small children should not work outside the home.

e. All children should be required to go to school until age 18.

f. Parents should be able to discipline their children in any way they see fit.

g. Getting divorced should be made more difficult.

h. Spouse abuse should be a crime.

i. Grown children should be required to support elderly or disabled parents.

j. When a women gets married, she should keep her own name.

k. Husbands and wives should own everything equally, regardless of who earns it or pays for it.

l. If parents get divorced, their children are better off living part-time with each parent.

MARRIAGE

Marriage is a personal, social, economic, legal, and often religious relationship. More than 90 percent of all Americans will be married at some time during their lives. This section examines the legal aspects of marriage. It describes the steps that one must follow to get married, the requirements for a legal marriage, and the difference between formal and common-law marriage.

PROBLEM 4

a. Marriage involves many considerations. Rank the following considerations in order of importance: money, desire for children, sexual relations, religious beliefs, racial or ethnic backgrounds, common interests, relationships with in-laws, faithfulness, and age differences. Are there any other factors that you consider important to a successful marriage?

b. Make a list of all the questions you would ask yourself before deciding to get married. Do any of these questions involve the law?

c. If you were getting married within the next six months, what social, religious, and legal arrangements would you have to make?

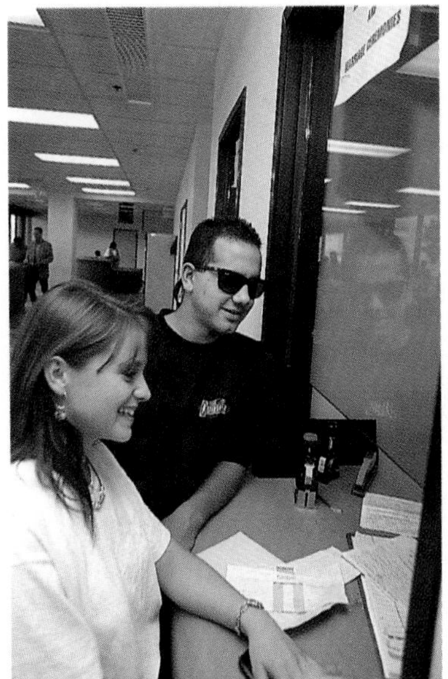
Why do states require a couple intending to marry to apply for a marriage license?

Getting Married

To get legally married, a couple must follow certain steps. These usually include the following:

- **Blood test.** Most states require a couple to have a blood test for venereal disease (VD) before getting married. A few states also require a physical examination. These tests make the couple aware of certain medical problems that may affect their marriage.
- **Marriage license.** All states require a marriage license. When they apply for a marriage license, the couple will be asked to provide certain information, such as proof of age and a copy of their blood test results. They will then have to swear to the truth of the information and pay a small fee.
- **Waiting period.** After applying for a marriage license, a couple must often wait for a short period before they can pick it up. In some states, there is another waiting period between getting the license and participating in the marriage ceremony. Waiting periods help ensure that people are serious about marriage. For example, the waiting period might prevent people from getting married without thinking it over carefully.
- **Wedding ceremony.** A wedding ceremony is required for a valid marriage. It can be either a religious or a civil ceremony. Weddings may be conducted by clergy members or by public officials such as judges or justices of the peace. The law does not require any set form for the wedding ceremony. However, to be legally married, each person must, in the presence of an official and a witness, state that he or she agrees to marry. After the ceremony, the couple will receive a marriage certificate.

Where does a person obtain a marriage license in your community? Is a physical exam or a blood test required? Is there a waiting period? If so, how long is it?

Why does the law require a wedding ceremony?

Legal Aspects of Marriage

In legal terms, marriage is a contract between two persons who agree to live together as husband and wife. It creates legal rights and duties for each party. Anyone who wants to get married must meet certain legal requirements.

In the United States, marriage laws are set by the individual states. The legal rules vary from state to state. However, all states have the following requirements:

- **Age.** A couple must meet certain age requirements. Usually, females must be 16 and males 18. Some states allow younger couples to get married if their parents consent. Some states also allow people under the minimum age to marry if the female is pregnant.
- **Relationship.** Every state forbids marriage between close relatives. It is illegal for a person to marry his or her parent, child, grandparent, grandchild, brother, sister, uncle, aunt, niece, or nephew. Many states also prohibit marriages between first cousins. Marrying or having sexual relations with a close relative is a crime known as **incest**.
- **Two people.** Marriage is between two persons only. Marrying someone who is already married is illegal. Having more than one husband or wife is a crime known as **bigamy**.

- **Man and woman.** Marriage is a relationship between a man and a woman. Marriages between two persons of the same sex have traditionally been considered invalid.
- **Consent.** Both persons must agree to the marriage. No one can be forced to marry someone against his or her will. For example, no one can be forced to marry someone at gunpoint.

As a rule, if a marriage is legal in one state, it will be recognized as legal in all other states. However, if a couple goes through a wedding ceremony without meeting the requirements for a legal marriage, the marriage may be annulled. **Annulment** is a court order saying that the marriage never existed. It is different from a **divorce**, which is a court order that ends a valid marriage. In other words, a divorce means that a man and a woman are no longer husband and wife. An annulment means that a man and a woman were never husband and wife.

The grounds for annulment vary from state to state, but common reasons for annulment include the following:

- **Age.** The couple were too young to get married.
- **Bigamy.** One spouse was already married.
- **Fraud.** One spouse lied to the other about an important matter, such as the desire to have children.
- **Lack of consent.** One spouse was forced to marry against his or her will, was too drunk to understand that a wedding was taking place, or was insane.

Laws place many restrictions on marriage. Laws prescribe who can marry, some of the obligations created by marriage, and how marriage can be ended. However, states cannot prohibit marriage between healthy adults without a good reason.

Most marriages in the United States take place in a church or synagogue. In America, customs and religious traditions play an important role in married life. However, these customs and traditions sometimes run afoul of the law.

In 1878, George Reynolds, a Mormon living in Utah, was arrested and charged with the crime of bigamy. At the time, the Mormon religion regarded plural marriages as a religious obligation. Mormons then believed that refusal to practice polygamy when circumstances permitted would lead to "damnation in the life to come." Reynolds argued that the antibigamy law violated his constitutional right to freedom of religion. After his conviction, he appealed his case to the U.S. Supreme Court.

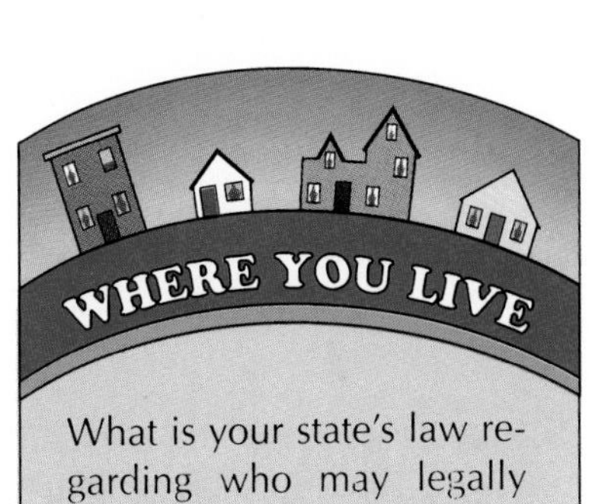

What is your state's law regarding who may legally marry? Are there any restrictions regarding people with disabilities?

In the case of *Reynolds v. United States*, the Supreme Court upheld the antibigamy law. It ruled that religious *belief* cannot justify an

Loving v. Virginia

In 1958, Harvey Loving, a white man, and Diana Jeter, an African-American woman, decided to get married. Legal residents of Virginia, they went to Washington, D.C., to get around a Virginia law forbidding marriage between people of different races. After their marriage, they returned to Virginia, where they were arrested and charged with violating the ban on interracial marriage. The Lovings pleaded guilty and were sentenced to one year in jail. The judge agreed to suspend the sentence if the Lovings would leave Virginia for 25 years. The Lovings moved to Washington, D.C., but appealed their case to the U.S. Supreme Court. They asked that the law against interracial marriages be declared unconstitutional.

PROBLEM 5

a. What happened in the *Loving* case? Why were the Lovings arrested?

b. What arguments do you think the state made in favor of the law? What arguments do you think the Lovings made against the law?

c. How would you decide this case? Explain your answer.

d. Some marriage regulations are appropriate, and others are not. Should the state regulate marriage based on age? Mental capacity? Physical disability? Health? Religious or racial differences? Other factors? Explain your answers.

illegal act. Reynolds could believe anything he wanted, but he could not put into practice a belief that society condemned. (Today, the Mormon church condemns polygamy and excommunicates members who espouse it.)

Common-Law Marriage

Common-law marriage is a marriage without a blood test, a license, or a wedding ceremony. It is created when two people agree to be married, hold themselves out to the public as husband and wife, and live together as if married. Only the District of Columbia and 14 states—Alabama, Colorado, Georgia, Idaho, Iowa, Kansas, Montana, Ohio, Oklahoma, Pennsylvania, Rhode Island, South Carolina, Texas, and Utah—allow common-law marriage.

Some of these states require a couple to live together for a certain number of years before "the knot" is legally tied. In others, people can be married in a matter of days if they actually agree to be married (now, not sometime in the future), live together, and represent themselves as husband and wife. If a couple split up after entering into a common-law marriage, they must get a divorce before either may remarry. If one remarries without first getting a divorce, he or she can be charged with the crime of bigamy.

States that do not allow common-law marriages will still recognize such a marriage if it took place in one of the states listed above. Also, the children of a common-law marriage are **legitimate** and have the same rights and duties as other children.

Does your state allow common-law marriage? If so, how long must a couple live together to make the common-law marriage valid?

THE CASE OF . . .

The Common-Law Marriage

Rick Schwartz and his girlfriend, Sarah, live together in the mountains of Montana. They talk about having a wedding but never get around to it. They are in love and think it is much simpler to tell people that they are married. They buy a house, open a joint bank account, and are known everywhere as Mr. and Mrs. Schwartz. The situation is fine until Sarah gets bored and leaves. She soon finds a new boyfriend, Dennis. Coming from a traditional background, Dennis insists that they get married right away.

PROBLEM 6

a. What are the requirements of a common-law marriage?

b. Do Rick and Sarah have a valid common-law marriage? Why or why not?

c. If Rick and Sarah had lived together in Arizona instead of Montana, would they have a valid common-law marriage?

d. Can Sarah marry Dennis? Why or why not?

e. Should all states allow common-law marriage?

Two African Marriages

In American culture, the idea of a man's being allowed to marry more than one woman at the same time is quite foreign and unacceptable. In the past, however, many African countries allowed this practice; in fact, it is still legal in some countries today. Examine the following case to try to gain an understanding of what probably seems like a very strange marriage practice.

Nape, age 18, wished to marry Pumla, age 16, who lived in his village. Nape asked Pumla's father, Kenneth, how much the latter expected to be paid as part of the marriage arrangement between the two families. Nape's "lobolo" would be one cow and $100 in cash, payable at the rate of $10 per month for ten months. Lobolo is a payment to make up for the loss of the daughter's services to her family (for example, her work inside and outside the home).

After two months of marriage, Nape announced his intention to marry a second wife, Jackie, an 18-year-old from a neighboring village. Pumla and her father Kenneth objected. They doubted that Nape, who only worked occasionally on construction jobs, could afford to support two wives or the children the marriages might produce. Though the laws of both the tribe and the country allowed polygamy, Kenneth opposed the second marriage because he thought it might prevent his being paid the full bride-price from the first marriage. Kenneth also claimed that the proposed second wife was not a virgin, which, according to custom in this country, lowered the amount of lobolo to be paid. Nape countered that this was not her fault, since she had been seduced as a young girl; furthermore, Jackie's lack of virginity reduced the amount of lobolo Nape had to pay her father to $50. Kenneth sued in the local court to try to stop the second marriage. The law allows objections to such marriages based on economic hardship and the personal unsuitability of the proposed second wife.

PROBLEM 7

a. What did Nape and his family have to pay Pumla's father when they got married? Why? Is this different from the practice in western culture of a wife's bringing a **dowry** to a marriage?

b. Was it against the law for Nape to marry Jackie while he was still married to Pumla? What advantages might there be in a society's allowing a man to marry more than one woman? Why have most countries in the world outlawed this practice? What negative effects might polygamy have on women?

c. Why did Nape have to pay a smaller bride-price or lobolo to Jackie's family? How, if at all, might society as a whole benefit from having a rule like this?

d. Role-play the African court hearing to decide this case. Pumla and her father should present their cases, and then Nape should present his. The judge should then make a ruling. What reasons did the judge give for the decision? Do you agree with the reasons? Why or why not?

HUSBANDS AND WIVES

In the past, the law considered the husband to be the head of the household. He had a duty to support his wife and children. In return for this support, he was entitled to his wife's household services and companionship. The law reflected this traditional view by giving husbands the legal right to make decisions such as where the family would live, how money would be spent, and other important matters. Over the past several decades, however, this view of marriage has been challenged by economic and social changes in our society. The law has also changed to reflect the idea that marriage is a partnership between equals.

Financial Responsibilities

Husbands and wives are now required to support one another in accordance with their respective needs and abilities. Many states require both spouses to pay for necessary family items either of them purchase. However, some states retain the traditional rule that the husband has a legal duty to provide his wife with food, clothing, shelter, medical care, and other **necessities**. If the husband fails to provide such essentials, the wife can purchase the necessary items and make her husband pay for them. At the same time, the wife has no legal duty to pay her husband's bills.

In addition to the basic necessities, some courts require the husband to maintain the family in accordance with his economic position. In general, however, a woman cannot obligate her husband to pay for luxury items bought without his knowledge.

Who owns property acquired during a marriage? At one time, the law considered a husband and wife as one person. This meant the

THE CASE OF . . .

The Unpaid Bills

Bryan and Kelly have been married for five years. Both work, and each earns about $30,000 per year. They have problems paying their bills and often fight over money. One day, Kelly goes shopping and charges groceries, clothes for the children, and a VCR costing over $500. Bryan gets angry and tells Kelly that he is not paying for anything.

PROBLEM 8

a. Is Bryan responsible for the debts of his wife?

b. Suppose Bryan was out of work and charged the previously mentioned items without telling his wife. Would she have to pay?

c. Do you agree or disagree with the following statement: "Husbands should be required to support their wives, but wives should not have to support their husbands"? Explain your answer.

wife had no property rights. Any money or property a woman owned before marriage or acquired during marriage became the property of her husband. In 1887, states began to pass married women's property acts that changed the law. These acts gave married women the right to own and control their own property.

Today, any property owned by either spouse before the marriage remains the property of that person throughout the marriage. Under this **separate property** system, whoever earns it, pays for it, is given it, or has title to it is considered to own it. Husbands and wives may make gifts to each other or place bank accounts, real estate, automobiles, or other property in both names. When they do this, the property is the **joint property** of both spouses.

Nine states—Arizona, California, Idaho, Louisiana, Nevada, New Mexico, Texas, Washington, and Wisconsin—and Puerto Rico have **community property** systems. These systems are usually derived from French and Spanish law. In community property states, all property acquired during the marriage belongs equally to the husband and wife. If the marriage breaks up, either by death or divorce, each spouse is entitled to one-half of all the property acquired during the marriage.

Contrast the community property system with the separate property system by considering the case of a married woman who does not work outside the home. In a community property state, the wife owns half of everything the couple acquire during the marriage, including the income of her husband. In a separate property state, the wife owns only property that she herself acquires or that is acquired in the names of both herself and her husband.

PROBLEM 9

a. Lloyd and Gloria were married four months ago. Before they were married, Gloria inherited a piece of land from her grandfather. Now that they are married, to whom does the land belong?

b. Frances and Leon are married and have two children. Frances is an architect making $50,000 a year. Leon is an artist who earns very little. Frances uses some of her income to buy a vacation home. If Frances and Leon split up, who owns the vacation home in a community property state? In a separate property state?

c. Which is fairer, a separate or a community property system? Why?

Decisions in a Marriage

Married life involves many decisions and responsibilities. Couples need to cooperate, share, and make decisions together about their lives. For instance, how will housework be divided? Who will handle the money? Will they have children? How will any children they have be brought up? Today, some couples use prenuptial agreements to put some of these issues in writing. A **prenuptial agreement** is a written document made *before* marriage that sets forth certain rights and responsibilities of the husband and wife (for example, whether any alimony will be paid in the event of a divorce).

In most matters, wives and husbands are free to make their own decisions and work out their own problems. Except in rare cases, the law will not interfere in everyday family life. There are, however, some legal rules you should know:

- **Name change.** Women have traditionally used their husbands' last names as a matter of social custom. However, a woman is

In what ways, if any, have the roles of husbands and wives changed?

not legally required to do so. Legally, a woman can keep her maiden name, take her husband's name in combination with her own (for example, Smith-Larkin), or use her husband's name. Likewise, a man may take his wife's name or use one that is hyphenated. Children may be given any surname the parents choose.

- **Support.** A husband generally has the legal duty to support his wife and children. However, the law is changing to make the duty of support more equal. Today, many states require the husband and wife to pay for necessary family items bought by either of them. For more information about support, see page 344.

Planning a Marriage

Larry Dunn, 25, and Tisha Palo, 27, plan to be married. Larry, a college graduate, earns $35,000 a year as a salesperson. Tisha has an associate (two-year) degree and earns $25,000 a year as a paralegal. Larry rents an apartment and owns a new car and a boat. Tisha recently bought a condominium and has a four-year-old car. They would like to have children, but Tisha first wants to finish college and go on to law school. Both agree that when they have a child, one of them will stay home for the first two or three years after their baby is born.

PROBLEM 10

a. What issues should Larry and Tisha discuss before getting married? Should they put their decisions on those issues in writing? Give reasons for your answers.

b. Tisha would like to keep her maiden name. What does the law require in this regard? Do you think a married woman should keep her maiden name, take her husband's name, or combine her name with her husband's? What last name should the children have? Explain your answer.

c. Role-play a conversation between Larry and Tisha as they plan where to live, how to handle their finances, how to divide the housework, whether to share ownership of their property, when Tisha will return to school, when they will have children, and any other important decisions you believe they should make before their marriage.

- **Privileged communications.** The law considers certain relationships private and confidential. Attorney-client, therapist-patient, and husband-wife relationships are all considered **privileged**. This means that neither person can be forced to disclose information received as part of the relationship. Historically, a spouse who was a witness at a trial could not testify against his or her mate unless the mate consented (agreed). However, in 1980, the Supreme Court decided that one spouse may testify against another in federal criminal prosecutions without the mate's consent. A person also can testify against a spouse under other circumstances, such as when one spouse is accused of abusing the other.
- **Inheritance.** If a husband or wife dies, the other spouse is automatically entitled to a share of the deceased's estate. This amount varies from one-third to one-half depending on state law. One spouse may leave the other more than the statutory share, but not less. Even if a spouse is left out of a will, state law gives the survivor the right to receive a portion of the estate.

PROBLEM 11

a. Kevin is in an auto accident with a delivery truck. At the hospital, he tells his wife, Rita, that the accident was all his fault. Later, in a lawsuit for damages resulting from the accident, the delivery company subpoenas Rita to testify about Kevin's statements at the hospital. Does Rita have to testify against her husband?

b. Roberto has argued with his wife, Jean, for years. In a fit of anger, he rewrites his will, leaving his entire fortune to charity. If Roberto dies, will Jean be left with nothing? Explain your answer.

c. James and his wife, Eleanor, both work for local companies. James's company, however, is experiencing financial difficulties. He is offered a better position with a company 400 miles away. Eleanor is doing very well with her company and would rather not move. How do they decide what to do? Who has the legal right to make the final decision? Who should have that right?

Spouse Abuse

Spouse abuse occurs among families of all backgrounds: rich and poor; African-American and Caucasian; urban, suburban, and rural. Victims suffer injuries ranging from psychological abuse to severe

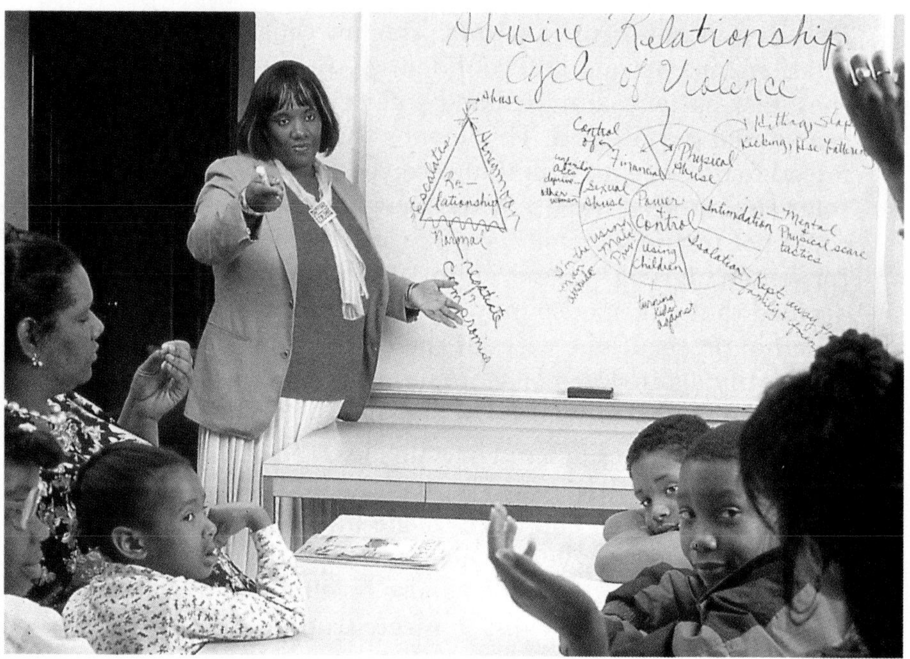

Why is it important for children to learn about abuse that may occur in families?

battering and murder. In fact, spousal assaults are more likely to result in serious injuries than assaults committed by strangers. Approximately one-fourth of all murders in the United States involve people who are related, and many of these are husband-wife killings.

Both women and men can be abusers, but women suffer 95 percent of the injuries inflicted between spouses. An estimated four million women are abused each year.

Abuse is rarely a one-time incident. Batterers typically repeat the act, often with increasing severity. Spouse abuse, however, usually remains behind closed doors and often goes undetected by friends and neighbors.

Historically, the police and the courts have been reluctant to get involved in domestic disputes. Until the late 1800s, it was legal in most states for a man to strike his wife. Even after spousal battering was outlawed, police officers often refused to respond to requests for assistance from battered women or to arrest battering husbands.

In part, police officers hesitated to become involved in domestic disputes because they felt they lacked training in safe, effective methods of intervening. In the past, most police officers were taught to either counsel the abuser and the victim or make the abuser leave the house for several hours.

These practices are changing. Most urban police departments now encourage officers to arrest spouses (or domestic partners) suspected of assault. Several states have enacted statutes that require the arrest of alleged batterers, even if their injured spouses have not

What to Do if Spouse Abuse Occurs

Both victims and their batterers need to seek help to end the cycle of spouse abuse. The first incident of domestic violence is rarely the last. Victims can take the following steps:

- **Call the police.** Assaulting anyone is a crime, and many consider arrest to be the most effective means of halting spouse abuse. Moreover, even if the police do not make an arrest, a police report can support later legal action. For instance, victims can later (1) file charges on their own and testify against their spouses, (2) request protective orders, or (3) file for divorce.
- **Seek counseling.** Crisis "hotline" numbers can be found at local libraries and under "Community Service Numbers" at the front of area phone books. The YWCA, churches and synagogues, and various social service agencies maintain counseling services for battered spouses.
- **Obtain a protective order.** Courts can order an abuser to (1) stop the abuse, (2) cease all contact with his or her spouse, (3) leave the home, (4) get counseling, or (5) do something else. Violating a court order is considered **contempt of court**, and a person found guilty of it can be jailed or fined.
- **Move out.** The law does not require an abuse victim to stay in the family home. Without help, though, it is often difficult for the victim to leave. Many places have protective shelters where a woman and her children can live temporarily. Either the police or crisis hotline personnel can help a victim locate a shelter. She should then notify a friend or relative of her reasons for leaving.
- **Obtain a divorce.** If a couple are legally separated, one spouse has no right to enter the other's home without permission. Local bar associations, legal aid offices, family courts, and women's organizations can give victims information about divorce.

signed complaints against them. Advocates of arrest point to studies that show that arrest is the most effective way to prevent repeated abuse.

However, prosecutors sometimes fail to bring charges against abusive spouses and are often more willing to reduce the charges than in

What programs does your community have to help abused women? Are there facilities where abused women can go if they decide to leave home?

Spouse Abuse

Late one night, you hear screams and the sounds of crashing furniture coming from the apartment next door. You look out in the hall and see your neighbor, Mrs. Darwin, being slapped and punched by her husband. Before she can get away, Mr. Darwin pulls her back in and slams the door. You hear breaking glass and more screams. You know that Mr. Darwin has a drinking problem. You also know that this is not the first time he has beaten his wife.

PROBLEM 12

a. If you were the Darwins' neighbor, what would you do? Would you call the police? If so, what would you tell them? If you would not call the police, explain why not.

b. If you were a police officer, what would you do in this situation? Would you question the couple? Would you arrest the husband? Would you remove the wife from the house?

c. If you were the husband, how would you react to the police in this situation? If you were the wife, how would you react? Would you press charges against your husband? Would you stay in the home? Would you do something else?

d. Suppose you are a judge confronted with the Darwin case. Would you send Mr. Darwin to jail? Would you take some other action? What other information would you want to know?

e. Besides calling the police, what are some things Mrs. Darwin could do about the problem?

cases of assault between two strangers. Some judges merely dismiss spouse abuse cases or give warnings or probation to spouses found guilty. They cite the need to protect family privacy or to promote domestic harmony as the reason for their inaction. However, recent court decisions recognize that there is little "family harmony" to protect when one family member is assaulting another.

Spouse abusers usually need help to change their behavior and to learn effective means of controlling their anger. Abusers are frequently addicted to alcohol or drugs and must deal with their addiction as well as their abusive behavior. Independent men's organizations, as well as services started by battered women's programs, offer men counseling and support. Social service agencies, such as the Red Cross and YMCA, often can refer men to nearby programs. Some states' statutes require counseling for spouse abusers as a condition of their probation. Many women do not want their abusive husbands to go to jail, but the most effective way to ensure that a batterer receives counseling is to prosecute him.

Until recently, men could not be criminally prosecuted for raping their wives. All 50 states and the District of Columbia now recognize marital rape as a crime. In addition, a battered wife can file a civil damage suit against her husband that includes a cause of action for rape.

PROBLEM 13

a. Why do you think that in the past the law did not prosecute husbands for raping their wives?

b. Assume you are a prosecutor. A woman files a complaint against her husband, stating that he forced her at knifepoint to have sexual intercourse with him. She tells you that she and her husband have been arguing violently for years. Knowing that a rape conviction carries a penalty of 20 years in prison, would you file a rape charge against the husband? Explain your answer.

c. Assume that the facts are the same as in Question b, above, except that the husband and wife are legally separated. Should it make any difference in proving rape that the couple is separated rather than living together?

LEGAL RIGHTS OF SINGLE PEOPLE WHO LIVE TOGETHER

Single adults are those who have never been married or who are divorced or widowed. Understanding the legal rights of single people is important because a growing number of unmarried couples live to-

What legal problems can arise when unmarried people live together?

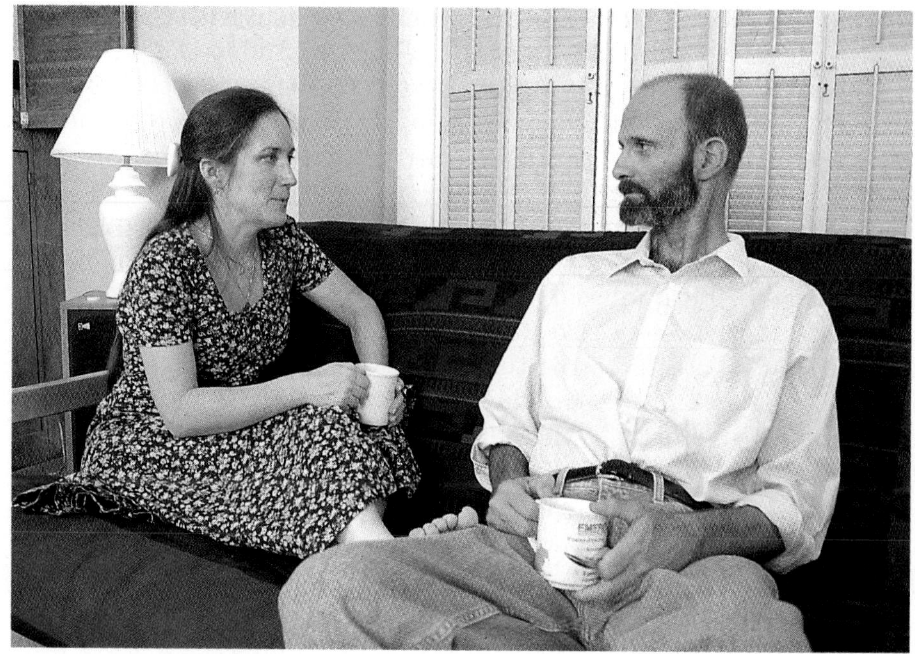

gether. Also, many single people have children. Although many unmarried couples eventually get married, others do not.

In the past, unwed couples had few rights. In most states, if a man and a woman lived together, shared household duties and expenses, and then split up, they could go their separate ways without legal obligation. On the other hand, if the couple had been married, numerous laws would have set out their legal rights and duties concerning divorce, alimony, child support, and other issues.

However, the situation is changing. Unmarried adults may think that their love lives are their own affair, but they should beware. Legal problems can arise when single people live together. Certain legal rights and duties may exist between the partners.

Palimony

Some unmarried couples develop a **cohabitation agreement**—a written or oral contract that outlines how they want to deal with their money, property, or responsibilities, both during and after their relationship. Until recently, courts would not enforce agreements between unwed couples as to support or property ownership. Courts would not require that one member of an unwed couple make payments, sometimes called **palimony**, to the other after the couple split up. Courts said that contracts could not be based on an immoral relationship or be used to enforce an agreement for sex. If an unwed couple split up, any property went to the person who had legal title to it. In relationships in which the man was the wage earner and the woman the homemaker, this meant the man often got all the property. In these situations, the wage earner "owned" any property acquired through his wages.

The rules changed in 1976 with the California Supreme Court's decision in *Marvin v. Marvin*. Since then, some state courts have upheld cohabitation agreements between unwed couples. In *Marvin v. Marvin*, the court ruled that unmarried adults who voluntarily live together can make contracts regarding their earnings and property rights. For the first time, a court said that unmarried persons may acquire property rights similar to those of married couples. Never-

The Model v. The Football Player

After seeing a photograph in a magazine, a professional football player named Bill phoned a modeling agency to arrange a meeting with Heather, one of its models. Bill and Heather began dating. Later, Heather left her career and moved in with Bill. They never married. After three years, Bill left Heather and moved in with an actress. Heather filed a breach of contract and unjust enrichment suit against Bill. She claimed that she had worked without pay as Bill's homemaker, chauffeur, and business and public relations manager and that Bill had received financial benefits from these services. She said he had promised to pay her at least $2,000 per month but had never done so. Her suit demands that he pay her $680,000 plus attorney's fees.

PROBLEM 14

a. Why did Heather sue Bill?

b. Assuming that an unwritten contract is enforceable, should the court enforce the agreement described above?

c. What effect do you think enforcing such unwritten agreements between unmarried couples will have on marriage? What effect will it have on relationships between unmarried couples?

d. Do you think Heather and Bill should have signed a cohabitation agreement? If so, what terms should they have included?

theless, the court said that for this to happen, there must have been some form of contract between the partners. Only Oregon's courts recognize such property rights without the existence of a contract, and some states do not do so under any circumstances.

Paternity

No one can be forced to marry someone against his or her will; such a marriage would be invalid and could be annulled. Nevertheless, all fathers are legally required to support their children. If a man denies being a child's father, the mother may bring a **paternity** action to establish his fatherhood and force him to pay pregnancy expenses and child support. If the mother is a minor, some states allow her parents to bring the suit. The *Family Support Act of 1988* requires all states to assist mothers and children in obtaining paternity testing and to allow paternity suits until the child is 18 years of age.

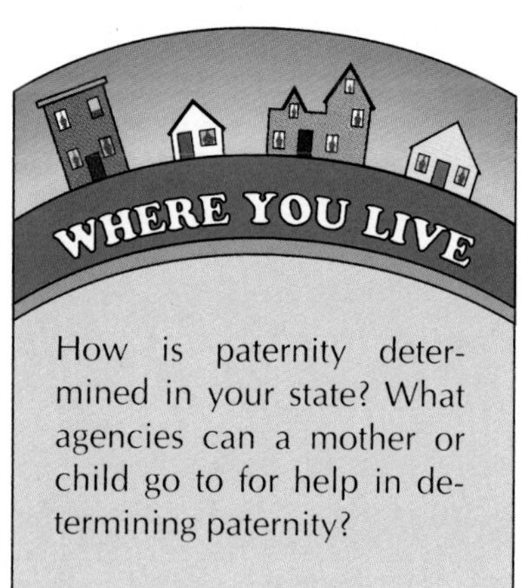

How is paternity determined in your state? What agencies can a mother or child go to for help in determining paternity?

Blood samples can be used to prove that a particular man is *not* a particular child's father. For example, if both the mother and the alleged father have blood type A, and the child has blood type B, the man cannot be the child's father. A child cannot have type B blood unless either the father or the mother has that type.

Blood type alone, however, cannot prove that a man *is* a child's father. Increasingly, courts are using a new technique known as "DNA fingerprinting." This is a method of testing blood for genes that link

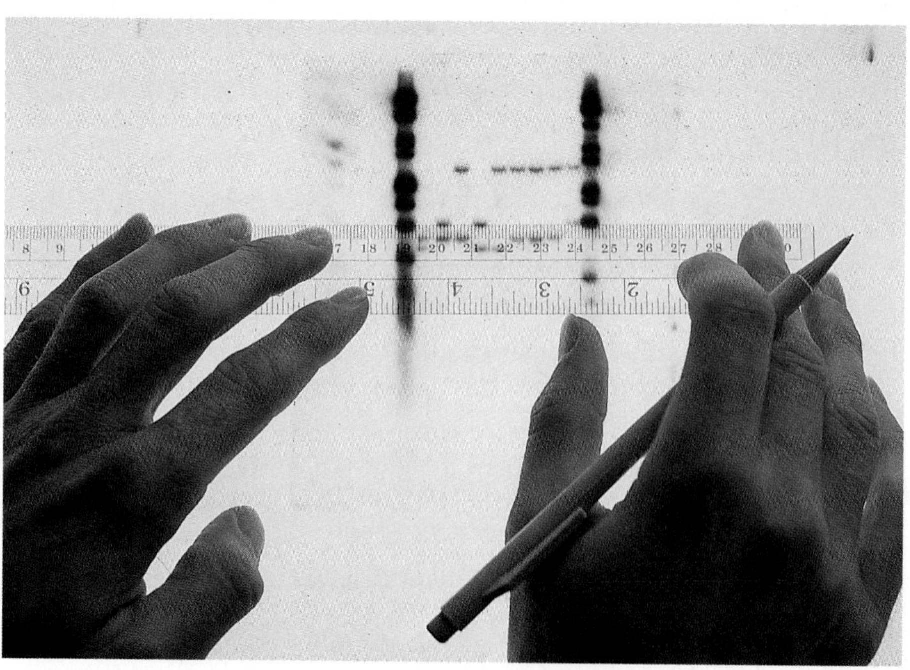

How can DNA fingerprinting be used to prove paternity?

The Unwed Father

Martha, 15, becomes pregnant. She claims that Michael, 17, is the father, but Michael denies it and refuses to marry her or support the child. Does the law require Michael to marry Martha? Does the law require unmarried teenagers to provide support for their children?

a specific parent and child. Test results are 99.9% accurate and promise to greatly reduce the uncertainties that once plagued paternity suits.

PARENTS AND CHILDREN

The relationship between parents and children is very special. Being a parent involves many rewards and many responsibilities. Parents have a legal obligation to care for, support, and control their children. When parents are unable or unwilling to fulfill their responsibilities, the law gets involved. This section explores the legal rights and responsibilities of parents and children. It discusses how the law affects family planning, child rearing, and adoption.

In what ways does the law require parents to support their minor children?

PROBLEM 15

a. What do you think are some of the rewards of being a parent?

b. What do you think are the responsibilities of being a parent?

c. Why do you think so many unmarried teenagers have children?

Responsibilities Between Parents and Children

Parents are legally responsible for their children in many ways. Most importantly, they must provide the necessities of life. They must also provide for their children's social and moral development and must control and supervise their children's behavior.

May teenagers receive health services without their parents' permission in your state? May these services include birth control counseling? At what age may a person legally obtain contraceptives in your state?

THE CASE OF . . .

The School Health Clinic

A study shows that many students in your school district do not receive medical care. In response, the school board decides to open a health clinic in your high school. The County Board of Health staffs the clinic with two full-time registered nurses. A doctor is in attendance two mornings and three afternoons each week.

The clinic offers all students emergency medical care, routine physical exams, and instruction in preventive health and nutrition. Clinic doctors are authorized to prescribe and administer medication. Noting the rise in teen pregnancy, the County Board of Health also suggests that the clinic be authorized to counsel students regarding birth control and to dispense contraceptives.

PROBLEM 16

a. Should teenagers be able to obtain routine health care at the clinic without parental consent? Give your reasons.

b. Should teenagers be able to obtain contraceptives at school without parental consent? Give your reasons.

c. If the clinic does provide contraceptives, what limitations (if any) should it place on who may receive them? What legal issues should you consider in your answer?

d. Should high schools teach sex education? If so, should the classes be required or optional? If the classes are required, and a parent has religious objections or does not want his or her child to take the class, should the student be exempt from the requirement?

Support The most basic parental responsibility is to support minor children. This means that parents must provide the basic necessities of life, including food, clothing, shelter, education, and medical care.

All parents—rich and poor, married and unmarried, teenagers and older parents—are expected to support their minor children. The amount of support a family can give, of course, depends on what it can afford. Poor parents, for example, would not be in a position to provide expensive clothes or fancy meals.

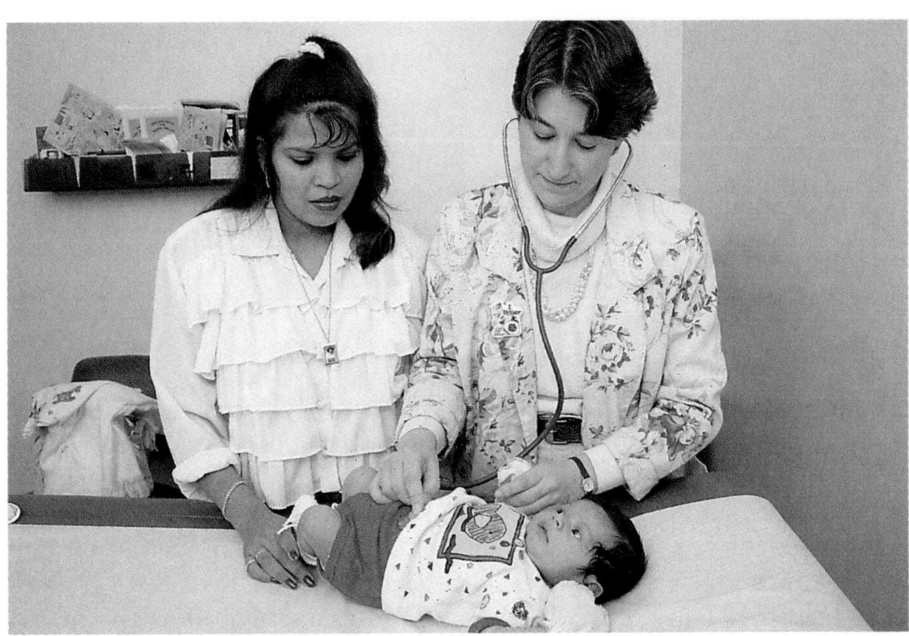

Is medical care a basic necessity for an infant?

Increasingly, the law is making mothers and fathers equally responsible for child support. This does not mean that each parent pays the same amount of money but that each parent provides according to his or her ability. In the event of a divorce, there usually is a support agreement or court order that indicates how much each parent must pay.

In your state, how long must a parent support a child? What if the child is disabled? Does your state have any programs to assist parents of children with disabilities?

The Mentally Disabled Adult

When Diem and Kim divorce, the court orders Diem to pay $100 per month in child support for their six-year-old daughter, Meena, who is mentally disabled and is expected never to function at a level higher than that of a second-grader. She lives with her mother and will probably never be capable of living independently. When Meena reaches 21, Diem files a motion seeking to end his child support payments.

PROBLEM 17

a. How should the court rule in this case?

b. What is the general rule for how long parents must financially support their children? Should that rule be different if the child is mentally or physically disabled?

c. What other conditions might make it reasonable to require that a parent support a child who is no longer a minor?

Emancipation Parents are not required to support an adult child. Parents' legal responsibility ends when their children become emancipated. **Emancipation** means that children are set free from the legal control and custody of their parents. It also means that parents are no longer required to support their children. Emancipation normally takes place when the child reaches adulthood—age 18 in most states. It also can occur when a child gets married, joins the armed forces, or becomes self-supporting. In some states, emancipation can occur by agreement between parent and child, while other states require that a petition for emancipation be approved by a court.

Family Responsibility Laws A long tradition of law and social custom has called upon adult children to support their parents when in need. Some states have **family responsibility laws**. These laws require adult children to care for elderly parents. Other states have abolished these laws, and almost all states limit the support obligation to what a relative can fairly afford.

The Rich Daughter

Rosa, 42, owns a successful business. Her mother, 65, will retire from her job at the end of the year. Her meager savings and social security payments are not enough for her to continue paying rent where she lives. She can move to a publicly supported home for the elderly but would prefer to stay in her own apartment. Does Rosa have a legal obligation to support her mother? Should the law require adult children to support their parents when they are in need? Is there a moral obligation to support needy parents?

Should the law require adults to care for their elderly parents?

Education All children have a right to a free public school education through the 12th grade. The state sets standards for an adequate education, but parents have a right to send children to the school of their choice—public, private, or parochial. School attendance is generally required for children ages 7 to 16, although state laws vary. A child who misses school without justification is considered a **truant**. Parents who fail to send their children to school may be fined or arrested.

Parents are not legally required to pay for college tuition. However, many parents do so, and some separation agreements require support through college for the couple's children.

Does your state permit parents to educate their children at home? If so, what must a home school provide? What reasons must a parent give for wanting to educate his or her children at home?

Medical Care Parents have a duty to protect and supervise their children's health. This means that they must provide proper medical and dental care. Children usually need their parents' permission to obtain medical treatment. For example, suppose a 14-year-old wants cosmetic surgery. Without his parents' permission, a doctor could not perform such surgery. Parents have a right to supervise medical care, but they can be charged with neglect if they ignore their children's health. Also, in life-threatening emergencies, a court may permit a doctor to treat a child without parental consent. Doctors may also act in certain emergencies, such as automobile accidents, without either the parents' or court's permission.

The School at Home

Michelle and Larry Novitzki have four children. Two are of school age. Both parents are high-school graduates, and Michelle has a college degree. They began educating their children at home while living in New York, because they disapproved of the school's sex education classes and believed that the children would learn more in a less structured environment. They obtained the permission of the local board of education and designed lessons that related to activities around their house and community. However, after they moved to North Carolina, a state education official said that their home instruction did not satisfy the compulsory school attendance laws. The North Carolina law reads:

> "Every parent, guardian or other person in this State having charge or control of a child between the ages of 7 and 16 years shall cause such child to attend school continuously for a period equal to the time which the public school to which the child is assigned shall be in session."

The Novitzkis use books and materials obtained in New York and have set aside one room to serve as a classroom. The children receive instruction six hours a day, all months of the year. Both children score above-average on standardized tests and appear to psychologists to be healthy and normal.

PROBLEM 18

a. Reread the North Carolina law. Is the Novitzkis' home classroom a school?

b. Should the court allow the Novitzkis to instruct their children at home? Do you think their reasons for wanting to do so are valid?

c. Why do you think states have compulsory school attendance laws? Should they have such laws?

d. Do you think children can receive as good an education at home as at a school? Give your reasons.

e. Do you think students should be excused from classes when they or their parents disagree with the course content? Why or why not?

Gregory K.

Rachael K. was married in 1979 at age 17. Gregory was born a year later, followed by Jeremy and Zach. When Rachael became pregnant with Zach, Gregory's father moved out. At age 4, Gregory went to live with his father, where he stayed for five years. His mother never visited. In 1988, Rachael moved to Florida. At this point, Gregory returned to live with his mother. But she couldn't make ends meet, and she placed Gregory and Jeremy in foster care. "I was crushed," she said. "They took my boys and that was an awful feeling."

Rachael visited the boys while they were in foster care. After about a year she found a job and convinced the state to return her sons. Two months later, she fell behind on her rent and returned the boys to foster care.

Feeling unloved and neglected, Gregory was placed in the care of a foster couple who had eight children. The Russ family immediately took to Gregory, and within weeks Gregory asked them to adopt him. During this period, the Russes never heard from Rachael. They assumed that adopting Gregory would not be a problem. They then learned that Rachael wanted Gregory back. At this point, Gregory retained a lawyer and sued to break his ties with his natural parents so that he could be adopted by the Russ family.

PROBLEM 19

a. What happened in this case? Why does Gregory want to end the relationship with his mother?

b. What arguments can Rachael make for keeping Gregory? What arguments can Gregory and the Russes make? What social values are involved in this case?

c. Should the law allow children to end their relationship with their parents? If so, under what circumstances? If not, why not?

d. Rachael complained that the state paid foster parents $1,200 a month to take care of her children. She said that if the state had helped her, she would have been able to keep her children. What do you think of this argument?

What responsibilities do parents have for their young children at the beach?

Care and Supervision Parents may decide what is best for their children as long as they do not abuse or neglect their children. There are no minimum requirements for the number of hours parents must spend with their children. Both parents may work, and the children may be "latchkey children"—youngsters left home alone after school or at other times. However, there are laws governing the age at which a child may be left alone in the home, so parents must be sure that someone is caring for their young children at all times. Parents may plan activities for their children and limit the amount of time their children spend outside the home.

Can parents require their children to complete chores around the house?

Discipline Parents have a right and a duty to supervise their children. Likewise, children have a legal duty to obey their parents and to follow reasonable rules. Parents can ask children to do chores around the house and yard. Parents may also decide where their children live, what school they attend, what religion they practice, and other aspects of their lives. However, parental authority is not absolute. Children do not have to obey parents who order them to do something dangerous or illegal. Parents who mistreat their children can be charged with child abuse.

Children who *continually* disobey their parents or run away from home may be charged as status offenders. As we explained in Chapter 2, status offenses are not crimes. They are acts that are not illegal if committed by adults. Status offenses include running away from home, skipping school, refusing to obey parents, or engaging in

FOCUS ON THE LAW

Family and Medical Leave Act

In 1993, Congress passed the *Family and Medical Leave Act* to help parents who want to stay home with their babies, as well as workers who need time off to care for ailing relatives. The legislation guarantees you up to 12 weeks of unpaid leave during any 12-month period for any of the following reasons: (1) because of the health of your child, (2) because you adopt a child or take a foster child into your home, (3) because you must care for a close family member who is suffering from a "serious health condition," or (4) because your own serious health condition makes you unable to perform your job.

The legislation does not apply to everyone. Only firms with 50 or more employees are covered, and there are "key exceptions" for "highly compensated" employees. This means if you are one of the most highly paid employees in your office or region, your employer may deny your request for leave.

immoral or dangerous behavior. A status offender may be placed under court supervision. When this happens, the child is known as a PINS, CHINS, or MINS—a person, child, or minor in need of supervision. Courts may order counseling or special schooling or, in serious cases, may place the child in a juvenile facility or a foster home.

Parental Responsibility for Children's Acts Parents who fail to exercise proper supervision and control over their children may be held legally responsible for their children's acts. This is especially true if they aid or encourage improper conduct. For example, a father who allows his underage son to drink and drive may be held liable if the son has an accident.

Almost all states hold parents civilly liable for certain acts of their minor children, such as property damage, theft, or vandalism. Some states also have the crime of **contributing to the delinquency of a minor**. A parent who encourages a child to sell drugs could be charged with this crime. Some states are passing and trying to enforce laws that make parents criminally responsible for certain delinquent acts committed by their children. Other states see such laws as unworkable and believe they shift responsibility away from the children, who should be held accountable for their actions.

PROBLEM 20

Vanessa, 14, constantly stays out late at night and often misses school. She seems to have a lot of cash and nice clothes. When her parents ask where she gets the money, she says she earns it babysitting at night. Her parents suspect she's involved in drugs—maybe even selling them. One night Vanessa and her boyfriend break into a neighbor's house, steal a television, and sell it for drugs. A neighbor sees them, and Vanessa and her boyfriend are arrested.

a. Have Vanessa's parents adequately supervised their daughter? If not, what should they have done differently? Can parents' actions affect the actions of their children?

b. Should Vanessa's parents have to pay for the neighbor's television? Why or why not?

c. Should parents be held criminally responsible for the actions of their children? If so, under what circumstances?

Historically, parents were not responsible for injuries caused by their children, whether accidental or intentional, unless the parents were somehow to blame. For example, if a parent gave a child a gun to play with, the parent could be liable for any injuries caused by the child.

Today, all states make parents legally responsible for harm caused by their children, up to a certain dollar limit. This amount varies from $200 to $10,000, depending on state law. A special rule known as the **family car doctrine** makes parents responsible for damages caused by any driver in the family. This means that if you cause an accident while driving your parents' car, your parents may have to pay for any damage.

PROBLEM 21

Consider the following situations. In each case, decide whether the parents have the legal authority to make the decision involved. What rights do you think the children have in each situation? What arguments can you make in support of the parents? In support of the children?

a. Mr. McBride disapproved of the lifestyle of his 18-year-old son, Larry, who regularly smoked marijuana. When Larry refused to stop using the drug, Mr. McBride cut off his support, including college tuition.

b. Monica, 17, has a birthmark on her cheek. On the advice of a friend, she decides to have plastic surgery to remove it. Her parents absolutely forbid it.

c. Murray, a high-school senior, does not want to move to a new city with his parents. He wants to finish high school with his friends. His parents insist that he live with them.

d. Mr. and Mrs. Parham think that their 16-year-old daughter is mentally ill and needs psychiatric treatment. The daughter objects, but her parents decide to commit her to a mental institution.

Earnings and Employment In most families, children who work keep and spend their own money. Nevertheless, parents have the legal right to take the earnings of their minor children. Children may keep only the wages that their parents want them to keep. However, parents have no right to use other money that legally belongs to their children. For example, if you receive an inheritance or recover damages in a lawsuit, you have the right to have this money set aside in a bank account until you become an adult.

Child Abuse and Neglect

Child abuse takes many forms. It occurs whenever an adult or other care provider inflicts or threatens to inflict intentional physical, emotional, or sexual harm on a child. Child neglect occurs more frequently than child abuse and involves the failure to properly feed, clothe, shelter, educate, or tend to the medical needs of a child. Abuse and neglect are the leading causes of death for children in some American cities.

Abuse and neglect of children have effects that go far beyond the obvious immediate dangers. Studies have shown that more than 80% of all juveniles who break the law have been victims of abuse. Truan-

Fig. 5.2 Child Abuse Reported, 1962–1992

YEAR	CASES
1962 (prior to reporting laws)	662
1976 (first year data collected)	1.1 million
1984	1.7 million
1988	2.2 million
1992	2.9 million

Source: National Committee to Prevent Child Abuse.

cy and suicide attempts often result from emotional abuse. Moreover, abused children frequently grow up to be abusing adults.

Not surprisingly, most youths who run away from home have suffered physical and emotional abuse and neglect. Nearly three-fourths of all female runaways have been sexually abused, and so have many male runaways. Older teenage runaways are sometimes

What information should a child protective services worker try to get when investigating a reported case of abuse?

How to Report Child Abuse and Neglect

1. **To whom do I make a report?**
   You may call the National Child Abuse Hotline, 1-800-4-A-CHILD. It will tell you how to contact your local child protective service (CPS) agency. You also may want to talk to a teacher, counselor, medical person, or other trusted adult. If you believe the child is in immediate danger, contact the police.
2. **Who must report suspected cases of child abuse?**
   Usually, medical practitioners, teachers, child care professionals, school officials, and social workers.
3. **Who may report?**
   Anyone suspecting that a child is being mistreated, including the child who is being abused.
4. **What conditions should I report?**
   Any situation that suggests abuse or neglect: unexplained bruises or burn marks, constant hunger or inappropriate dress for the weather, major weight gain or loss, or chronic uncleanliness, fatigue, or school absences.
5. **What happens if I report someone?**
   A child protective service worker will ask for all the information you have. Then the worker will visit the family to determine if the child is in immediate danger and whether it is necessary to call in the police or a doctor. Under extreme circumstances, the child may be removed from the home. Otherwise, the worker will interview the parents, observe the physical and emotional conditions of the household, and decide if there is a need for counseling or family support services.
6. **Must I give my name when I make a report?**
   No, although it might assist the social worker in gaining more information and enable the authorities to take legal action against the abuser.

termed "throw-aways." These are children whose parents refuse to care for them.

Abused children often are unable to do anything about their abuse. Accordingly, every state has laws requiring doctors, nurses, teachers, social workers, and others to report suspected cases of abuse or neglect. At least 17 states require *all* citizens to report their reasonable suspicions. Accusing someone of child abuse without having *any* reason to suspect the person of abuse might provide the basis for a civil lawsuit. However, you may not be sued for a mistaken report made in good faith. In fact, *failure* to report suspected abuse can lead to criminal or civil penalties, or both.

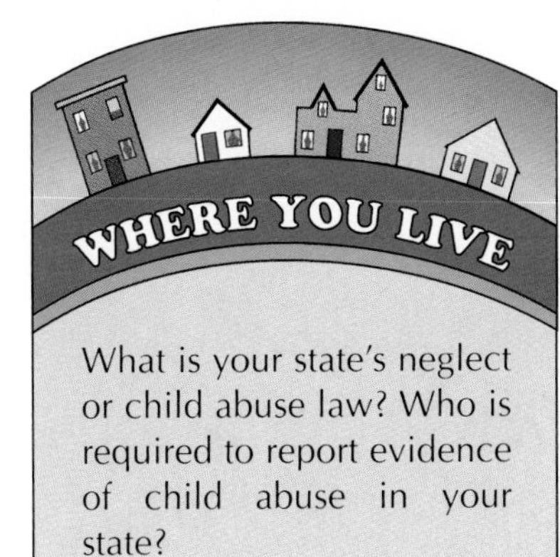

What is your state's neglect or child abuse law? Who is required to report evidence of child abuse in your state?

Sexual Abuse Reported cases of child sexual abuse have increased dramatically in recent years. Sexual fondling, using a child in pornography, and making a child view pornography all may constitute sexual abuse, along with other forms of sexual contact. The sexual offender is usually a person the child knows and trusts, such as a family member, a family friend, a child care worker, or a school employee. The abuser can be an older child or an adult—even a parent. Child sexual abusers prey on a child's obedience, trust, and embarrassment. They often use threats to prevent a child from reporting the abuse.

Increasingly, parents are bringing civil suits against child abusers and their employers. The suits typically charge an employer, such as a day-care center, with negligence for not properly overseeing employees or screening job applicants with a history of child abuse. Therefore, it is now common for organizations that employ adults who work with children to require job applicants to submit fingerprints. The fingerprints go to the FBI, which checks for any past child abuse violations by the applicant.

Some people say that children simply imagine episodes of sexual abuse. However, most psychologists stress that young children lack the sexual experience to make up stories of sexual abuse by themselves. Moreover, while it is possible for an older child to invent such a story, such instances are considered unusual. Therefore, any time a minor reports sexual abuse, his or her story should be taken seriously and investigated.

If a child does report sexual abuse, the police should be notified and, if justified, charges should be brought against the abuser. An investigation will determine whether the child is in immediate, ongoing danger and if the case should go to trial. If the abuser is a parent, the child will be removed from the home. Most states currently allow child victims to testify in court through closed-circuit television or by means of videotaped questioning to save them from the trauma of having to face their attackers.

Drugs and the Unborn Baby

The police arrested a 30-year-old pregnant women for forging checks. This was her first offense. During her trial, the woman testified that she was a cocaine addict. The judge sentenced her to remain in prison until she gave birth to her baby. Normally, the judge said, he would have given her probation. He gave the harsher sentence to protect her fetus from her cocaine use.

PROBLEM 22

a. Assume that the judge's sentencing of this woman was appealed. If you were an appellate judge, how would you rule? Give your reasons.

b. Is it child abuse for a pregnant woman to use illegal drugs? What if she uses alcohol, tobacco, caffeine, or other legal substances that may harm her fetus?

c. Is a pregnant woman guilty of neglect or abuse if she fails to see a doctor and follow his or her orders during her pregnancy?

PROBLEM 23

Consider the following situations. For each situation decide whether or not the action of the parent or parents should be considered child neglect or abuse. Explain your answer.

a. When Emilio misbehaves, his parents make him wear signs such as "I am a liar" or "I hit my little sister" wherever he goes for several days.

b. Parents go away for the weekend and leave their 6-year-old son in the care of their 12-year-old daughter.

c. Sixteen-year-old Theresa returns home late one evening. As punishment, her parents ground her for a week.

d. Although her brother and sister often get new clothes, Vicky only has castoffs. She is the only child in her family not allowed to join a scout troop, and she has to eat her meals standing alone at the kitchen sink while her siblings sit at the table. Vicky cannot figure out what she has done to make her parents unhappy.

e. George's parents refuse to allow him to date or go anywhere without them, even though he is now 16 years old.

f. Thomas finds his four-year-old son taking cookies out of the cupboard, and he spanks him. The boy cries.

g. Mr. Davenport tells his 14-year-old daughter that she can stay out all night or do anything else she wants, as long as she doesn't bother him.

A Parent, Drug Use, and Neglect

Cheryl is the mother of six-year-old Kimberly. The police recently searched their apartment for drugs and found it to be a "shooting gallery" for heroin. Numerous syringes and needles were found, and Cheryl and others present were arrested. Kimberly sat on the living room couch during the raid.

There is no definite evidence that Cheryl is now using drugs, although she has a history of drug use and is currently in a drug rehabilitation program. She claims that her boyfriend comes into her apartment with his friends and they use drugs without her permission. Cheryl has a full-time job as a secretary, and Kimberly is doing well in school. She loves her mother and does not want to be taken from her home.

The state law regarding child neglect reads: "Neglect means the negligent treatment or the maltreatment of a child by a person responsible for the child's welfare under circumstances indicating harm or threatened harm to the child's health or welfare. The term includes both acts and omissions on the part of the responsible person."

PROBLEM 24

a. Assuming the state brings a neglect petition against Cheryl, what are the arguments for and against finding Kimberly to be a neglected child?

b. If you were the judge, would you find neglect in this case? Why or why not?

c. If Kimberly is found to be neglected, would you terminate parental rights and remove her from the home? What other orders might you issue?

d. Do you think a parent who uses drugs is committing neglect? Does it make a difference if the child is aware of the drug use? What other factors should be considered before neglect is found to exist?

FOSTER CARE AND ADOPTION

Neglected or abused children may be removed from the family home, placed in a foster home, or made available for adoption. Sometimes parents simply decide to give up their children for adoption, usually at birth.

Foster parents are people who, at the direction of a court or government agency, care for minors who are not their birth children. Full legal guardianship and custody rights are still held by the birth parents or by a government agency. Foster parents are usually paid for child care, and children can be removed from foster homes at any time by the agency. Though foster parents have few legal rights regarding foster children, they often form close attachments and sometimes adopt the child or children in their care.

How can the law encourage adoption?

Adoption is the legal process by which an adult or adults become the legal parent(s) of another person. Though adults usually adopt children, most states permit adults to adopt another adult. The law places few restrictions on who can adopt another. Therefore, people—regardless of marital status, race, religion, or age—are eligible to adopt anyone else. In practice, however, adoption agencies and courts try to make a child's new family as much like that of the birth parents as possible. This means adoption agencies are sometimes reluctant to place children with a single parent or with parents of a different race or religion. Some states also have restrictions preventing homosexuals from becoming foster or adoptive parents.

Most adoptions are set up through public or private adoption agencies. People wishing to adopt apply to an agency and are investigated to determine whether they will be suitable parents. Public agencies usually charge little or no fee for this service. Private agencies charge much more. Some people work through agencies to adopt children living in foreign countries. Other people turn to go-betweens, who arrange for pregnant women to turn their babies over to adopting parents without going through an adoption agency. Some states allow this practice and license the go-betweens. Other states refer to the practice as "black-market adoption" and make it illegal.

People who wish to adopt must also apply to a court to have the adoption legally approved. An attorney often takes the legal steps to make the adoption final. An adoption agency will submit its report on the adopting parents and will seek written consent from the birth parents. In most states, consent is required, but in some cases, even if the birth parents refuse or cannot be found, courts may still grant adoptions that they decide are in the best interest of the child. A child over a certain age (often 12 or 14) must also consent to the adoption.

In most states, when the court approves an adoption, a temporary order is issued. This means the agency or birth parents remain the legal guardians for a specified waiting period, such as six months or a year. After this, a new birth certificate is issued showing the adopting parents as the parents of the child. The child and the adoptive parents then assume the same rights and responsibilities as children and their birth parents.

PROBLEM 25

Assume that you work for an adoption agency and a Caucasian infant, whose mother is Jewish, has just become available for adoption.

a. What type of parents would you look for to adopt this child? What factors would be most important?

b. Would you allow single people to adopt? What about people of a race, ethnic group, or religion different from that of the child?

c. Would you permit a homosexual couple to adopt the child?

Some couples who have had difficulty having their own biological children turn to surrogate parenting. A **surrogate mother** is a woman, other than the wife, who agrees to be artificially inseminated with the husband's sperm. The surrogate and the couple typically sign a contract in which the surrogate consents to the child's adoption by the couple and releases her parental rights. State laws vary widely on the legality of surrogacy contracts and the terms that may be included in them. At least 16 states have laws regulating surrogate birth. Others are attempting to design guidelines to regulate the practice.

THE CASE OF . . .

Scarpetta v. The Adoption Service

Olga Scarpetta, 32, comes from a wealthy California family. During an affair with a married man, she becomes pregnant. Olga thinks her pregnancy will embarrass her family, so she goes to New York to have the baby. The child is born May 18 and turned over to the Spence-Chapin Adoption Service four days later. On June 1, Olga signs a document giving the agency full authority to find new parents for the child.

The agency places the child with the DeMartino family on June 18. Dr. DeMartino and his wife have already adopted a four-year-old boy from the same agency, and everything worked out fine.

Within two months of the baby's birth, Olga changes her mind and asks for her baby. The agency refuses to help her and will not tell her who has the child. After several weeks of arguing with the agency, Olga goes to court. She tells the judge that she was physically and emotionally upset following childbirth. She is now sure that she wants to keep the child. Her family in California has learned of the birth and also wants Olga to get the baby back.

PROBLEM 26

Read the following opinions and decide which one you agree with. Give reasons for your choice. Note that the adoption agency is the defendant in this case because the DeMartinos had not yet received final legal custody of the child. The court must decide whether to return the child to the birth parent or leave the child with the adoptive parents.

Opinion 1

There are many reasons this court believes it is in the best interest of the child to leave her with her adoptive parents, the DeMartinos.

First, Olga waited six weeks after putting the child up for adoption before requesting the child's return. During this period, the DeMartinos formed a strong attachment to the child and made many sacrifices because they had every reason to believe the child would be their own.

Second, the DeMartinos' situation is much more secure than Olga's. Olga is 32, is unmarried, and, from the evidence before us, appears emotionally unstable. As for the DeMartinos, the agency selected them because they had already adopted a four-year-old boy and proved themselves well able to provide for the child's moral and physical well-being. They can give the attention of two parents to the child. To take the baby away at this point would cause them a great deal of suffering.

Finally, Olga freely gave up the child, and the agency acted in a proper manner in obtaining her consent.

Opinion 2

There is a legal presumption that, unless proven unfit, the birth mother is best suited to provide adequate support and care for the child. This court believes that Olga Scarpetta is a fit birth parent.

First, Olga was under great pressure when she placed the child for adoption. She had just gone through an unwanted pregnancy, labor, and delivery. She was worried about the reaction of her highly religious family. Her decision could not have been freely given under the circumstances.

Second, she now clearly wants the child and is very able to provide for the child's welfare. Her wealthy family also supports her in this decision and will no doubt help her if she needs financial assistance.

Finally, there is no evidence that Olga will be an unfit parent. Even though the DeMartinos may be good or even better parents, this does not mean they should be given rights ahead of the birth mother.

Do you think adopted children should have a right to know who their birth parents are? Traditionally, adoption records have been sealed, and adopted children were not allowed to find out the names or whereabouts of their birth parents. However, adoptive children are often interested in learning about and meeting their birth parents. Some adoptees even spend a great deal of time seeking information on their family history. Today, a few states allow them to look at adoption records. Furthermore, some states have laws that give

Should adopted children be able to find out the names of their birth parents?

Adoption Records Hearing

Assume that your state proposes the following law: "All adopted persons over the age of 18 shall have the right to obtain copies of their original birth certificates and shall be given the names and last known addresses of their birth parents." At a hearing on the proposed law, two people testify.

Mrs. Margaret Jones: "When I was 16, I became pregnant. The father, a soldier at a nearby army base, was transferred and I never saw him again. My parents could not afford to support another child and I didn't want to leave high school. I was also embarrassed, so I went to visit my aunt in another town. I had the baby and then placed him for adoption. I returned to my home town and finished school. I am now happily married and the mother of two children, ages 11 and 14. My husband does not know about my earlier affair or the child I gave up. The adoption agency promised that it would never tell anyone my name. I do not wish to see the child I put up for adoption, and I believe it best that we live our own separate lives."

Michael Franklin: "I am 19 years old. Last year my adoptive parents told me that I was adopted at birth. I love my adoptive parents very much, but I need to find out who my birth parents are and to meet them. I want to know where I came from and a little more about why I am the way I am. Everyone needs to belong somewhere. It's inhuman not to let me know who my birth parents are."

PROBLEM 27

a. If you were a member of the legislature and heard these two witnesses' testimony, how would you vote on the adoption records law? Explain your answer. Would the law be better if it allowed adopted children to look at records only after the birth parents had given their consent?

b. Would fewer people place children for adoption if they knew the children could later find out their names? Would opening adoption records result in more abortions and more black-market adoptions?

c. What problems do you think may arise if the proposed law is passed? Can you rewrite the law to improve it?

d. Do you think Michael's adoptive parents should have told him sooner that he was adopted? If they know, should they tell him who his birth mother is and why he was placed for adoption?

Does your state law allow adopted children to find out who their birth parents are? What does the law provide?

adopted children who have reached the age of majority the right to obtain the names of their birth parents. Many people oppose these laws, believing that the birth parents have a right to privacy and a right not to see children they put up for adoption unless they desire to do so.

FAMILY PROBLEMS

Problems occur in all marriages, even happy ones. Although most problems can be solved, marriages do break down. The hard reality of everyday life and personal problems can wear away a couple's love and compatibility. At times, a husband and wife may consider ending their marriage.

This section discusses resources available to help people with family problems. It also deals with the procedures for ending a valid marriage, namely separation and divorce. It discusses some of the issues that arise when a marriage breaks up. These include child custody, support, alimony, and property division.

Marriage Problems

A national survey found that the most common problems in a marriage are conflicts with in-laws or relatives, job and career pressures, adultery, conflicts about children, sexual problems, a breakdown in communication, alcohol or drug abuse, money problems, and loss of shared goals or interests.

Minor disagreements are usually settled by the couple's working together or with the help of family members or friends. Major differences may require the couple to seek the help of a marriage counselor, psychologist, social worker, or clergy member. A **marriage counselor**, for example, can help them explore the reasons for their

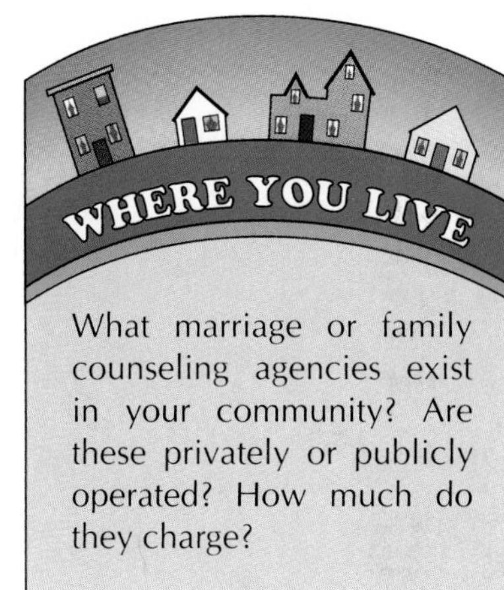

What marriage or family counseling agencies exist in your community? Are these privately or publicly operated? How much do they charge?

For what types of marital problems might a counselor be helpful?

problems and, ideally, work out a solution. The American Association for Marriage and Family Therapy (see Appendix F) can help couples find a qualified marriage counselor. Couples can also ask friends or members of the clergy.

Separation and Divorce

If a married couple decide that the marriage has broken down, the partners have the following legal options:

- **Informal separation.** The couple may decide to live apart. This separation may be for a short cooling-off period, or it may be permanent. In either case, the couple are still legally married and may reunite at any time.
- **Legal separation.** A legal separation is much like an informal separation except that the terms are put into a written separation agreement. This written agreement is approved by a court.
- **Divorce.** A divorce is a court order that legally ends a valid marriage. Once a divorce is final, the partners may legally remarry.

Separation For religious reasons, some couples won't consider divorce. Sometimes, however, a husband and wife need time alone to consider the future. In these situations, a separation rather than a divorce may be the best idea.

If a married couple separate, they still have legal and financial responsibilities to each other and their children. They remain husband and wife, and neither may remarry. For these reasons, having a formal **separation agreement** is a good idea. This is a written document that sets out the couple's understanding on alimony, child custody, support, division of property, and so forth.

Once a separation agreement is signed by both the husband and the wife, it becomes a legally enforceable contract. For example, if the husband or wife refuses to pay promised support money or will not leave home as agreed, he or she can be taken to court by the other.

A separation agreement can say anything the husband and wife want it to. However, once signed, it cannot be changed unless a court changes it or both spouses agree to a change. If a couple later seek a divorce, the terms of the separation agreement are usually made part of the divorce decree (court order).

Divorce Each year, more than one million couples are divorced in the United States. Today, about half of all marriages end in divorce.

Many people see divorce as a way to end forever a relationship that has become unbearable. Yet this is not always what happens. It almost never happens if children are involved. Children can tie a couple together for many years after the divorce. Divorce may change the relationship between spouses, but it won't necessarily end it.

Anyone thinking about divorce or separation should also know that splitting up can be expensive. Major costs include legal fees, alimony, and child support payments. The couple will also have to divide their property, including their house, car, furniture, life insurance, cash, bank accounts, and everything else they own. In addition, they will incur the cost of maintaining two homes rather than one.

Second or third marriages present additional difficulties. Each partner will carry the problems left over from any previous marriage. There may be alimony, child support payments, or debts to resolve. Children and parents from previous marriages must form a "blended family." Children will gain stepparents, spouses will acquire stepchildren, and all must learn to live with new persons in the household.

For all these reasons, a couple should never rush into a divorce. Divorce is a serious step that will affect them and their children for the rest of their lives. A couple should not seek a divorce in the heat of anger or without at least trying to work out their problems.

Once a couple have decided to seek a divorce, they can proceed in several ways. Until recently, most divorcing couples hired lawyers

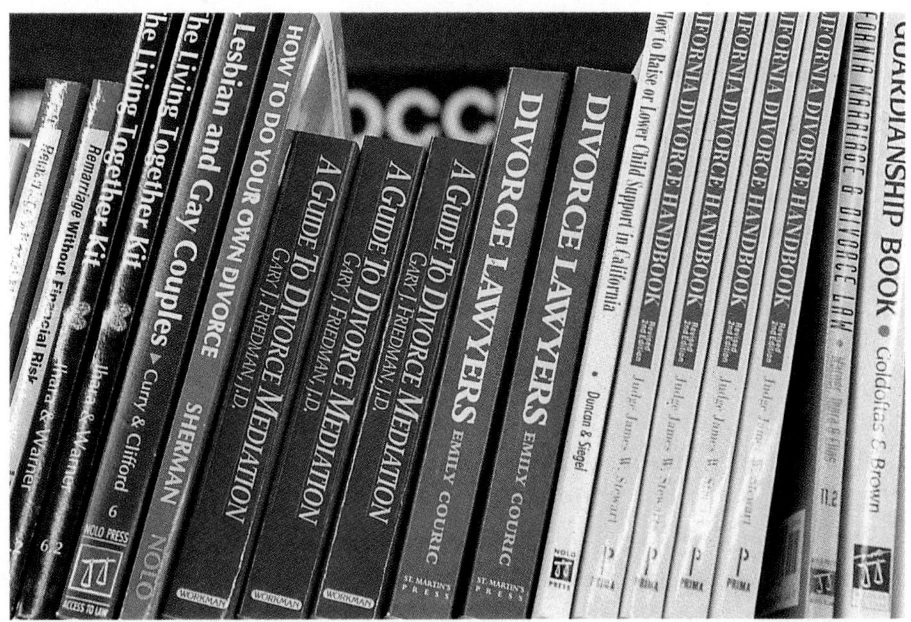

What are the advantages and disadvantages of using an attorney when divorcing?

and prepared for battle. However, it is not absolutely necessary to have attorneys involved in every aspect of a divorce.

Pro se (or do-it-yourself) divorce kits and classes are available in many places. To learn more about this, check with your local court, library, bookstore, or legal aid office.

If the divorce involves disagreement over children, large sums of money, property, or anything else substantial, then each spouse should have an attorney or consult a family mediation service.

A family mediator works with a couple, guiding them through a series of negotiations designed to achieve an agreement with which both can live. The agreement is usually then reviewed by lawyers before being filed in court. Mediators can help divorcing couples reach a settlement without the time, expense, or hard feelings of the traditional adversary process.

PROBLEM 28

Bill and Rachel married when both were 21. One year later, they had a baby. After two years of marriage, they fight constantly and are generally miserable. They are unsure about a divorce, but both think it might be better to live apart for awhile. Bill works as an auto mechanic making $1,500 a month. Rachel works as a teller in a local bank, also making $1,500 a month. Bill and Rachel rent an apartment for $750 a month and spend $500 a month on child care. They own the following assets: $750 in a savings account, a car worth $6,000, and furniture and appliances.

a. Do Bill and Rachel have any choices besides divorce? Explain.

b. Do Bill and Rachel need a lawyer to help them? How could a mediator help them? Who else could help them?

c. List the things that Bill and Rachel must decide before agreeing to a separation. Then role-play a meeting in which they try to work out a separation agreement. Be sure to deal with financial issues.

d. Explain the differences between an informal separation, a legal separation, and a divorce.

At one time, most states allowed divorce only if one spouse could show that the other spouse had done something wrong or was at fault. Typical "faults," or grounds for divorce, include the following:

- **Adultery.** Sexual intercourse between a married person and someone other than his or her spouse.

- **Desertion.** Leaving one's spouse with no intention of returning.
- **Mental cruelty.** Behavior that makes normal married life impossible.
- **Physical cruelty.** Acts of violence or physical abuse against one's spouse.
- **Insanity.** Mental illness.

Proving that one spouse was at fault was often hard. Divorce was also embarrassing. Many couples went to a foreign country or to another state to get a divorce.

In recent years, the laws have changed. Most states now permit **no-fault divorce**. To obtain a no-fault divorce, a spouse does not have to prove the other spouse did something wrong. Instead, the husband or wife has to show only there are **irreconcilable differences**. This means that the marriage has completely broken down. Many states also allow divorces when a couple can show that they voluntarily lived apart for a certain period of time, usually one year or more. Despite the easier divorce laws in most places, a few states still require that one of the fault grounds be proved before a divorce will be granted.

What are the grounds for divorce in your state? Does your state allow no-fault divorce or divorce by consent? How long does it take to obtain a divorce in your state?

PROBLEM 29

a. The divorce rate is now much higher than it was 30 years ago. Why do you think this is so?

b. Explain the difference between a fault divorce and a no-fault divorce.

c. Do you think states should make it harder or easier to get a divorce? Why?

d. Some courts require that couples see a marriage counselor before obtaining a divorce. Do you think this is a good idea?

Child Custody

If a couple with children separate or divorce, important questions arise: Who will take care of the children? With whom will the children live? In legal terms, the question is: Who will have **custody** of the children? The importance of the custody issue is illustrated by the fact that in 1991, over 11 million minor children in the United States were living with divorced or separated parents.

Custody decisions are important because the parent with custody decides most aspects of the child's life, such as where the child will live and go to school. Custody may be temporary, or it may be permanently awarded to one parent. Once custody is awarded, it is rarely changed. However, courts can change custody if circumstances change. For example, if the custodial parent (the one who has custody) became addicted to drugs, the court might order a change of custody.

The noncustodial parent is usually given visitation rights. This means that he or she can visit the child on certain days and at certain times of the year. The noncustodial parent is also usually required to contribute money for the child's support.

Sometimes courts award custody to both parents. This is known as **joint custody**. Both parents have full responsibility for the child's supervision, and both have an equal say in important issues, such as schooling and religion. The child may live with both parents, part-time with the father and part-time with the mother. The child need not spend the same amount of time with one parent as with the other. For example, a child who attends school near his or her father might spend school nights with him and weekends with the mother.

Joint custody is becoming more common, but courts have not favored it. There is concern that parents who cannot cooperate during marriage may not be able to cooperate after a divorce. Therefore, judges are reluctant to approve a joint custody arrangement unless the parents can demonstrate an ability to work well together. Mediation is often helpful for couples trying to make joint custody work.

PROBLEM 30

Wilma and Robert are getting divorced. They have a four-year-old child. Both are employed full-time, and they plan to live 10 miles apart after the divorce.

a. What are the advantages and disadvantages of joint and sole custody arrangements for Wilma and Robert?

b. What other information would you want to know before deciding the best arrangement?

c. If they choose joint custody, will both have to agree to the arrangement? What will happen if they cannot agree?

d. Role-play a meeting between Wilma and Robert to decide how the custody arrangement will work. What items must they agree on?

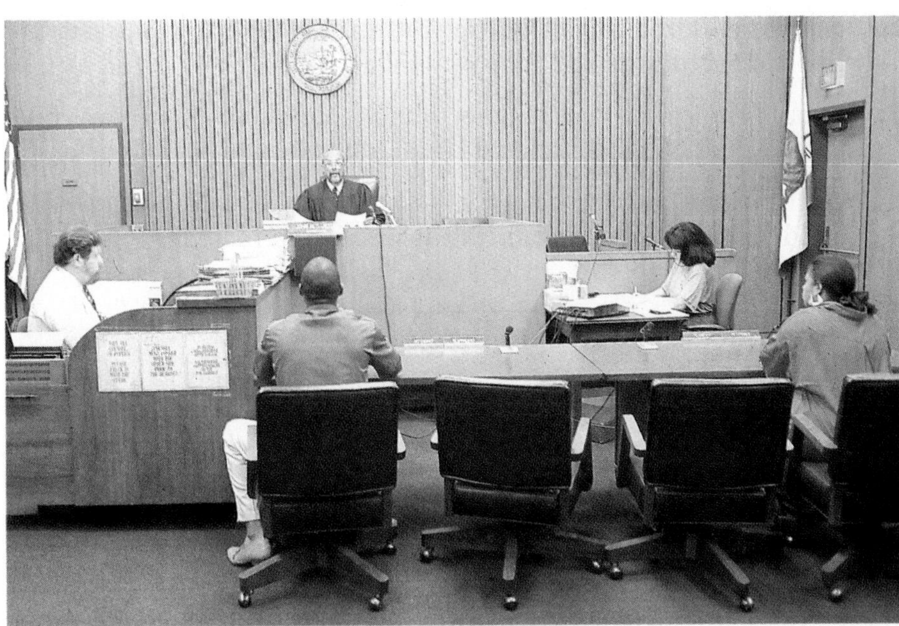

Why do you think decisions regarding custody issues are among the most difficult a judge must make?

If parents cannot agree on custody or the court does not approve their agreement, the decision is made by the court. Traditionally, the law presumed that young children were better off with their mothers. This presumption was called the **tender years doctrine**. Today, all states treat men and women equally in custody disputes.

To determine custody, courts now ask what is in the best interest of the child. This is often difficult to determine. Courts look at factors such as the youth's actions in the home, school, and community; the emotional and economic stability of the parents; and each parent's religion. Courts also consider which parent has stronger bonds with the child and which has been the primary care provider. Courts often listen to the children's desires, especially if they are over a certain age (in some states, 12). To help with this decision, judges often order a social service agency to study the parents and children. The results of this study are used as the basis for a custody recommendation.

Increased mobility and high divorce rates, along with an increase in the number of grandparents who provide care for their grandchildren, have created a new legal term: *grandparents' rights*. Today, most states have laws permitting grandparents to sue for the privilege of visiting their grandchildren after the parents have divorced or separated.

PROBLEM 31

a. Should a child's wishes be considered in determining custody? Does it make a difference if a child is 4 years old? 12? 16?

b. Should children have their own attorneys or other representatives in custody cases? Why or why not?

c. Should the courts be the ones to make decisions regarding child custody? If not, who might be better able to make such decisions?

d. Assume that you have been asked to draw up a list of rights for children in divorce actions. What would you include?

PROBLEM 32

Eleanor, aged six, is the subject of a custody dispute between her divorcing parents. For the past year, she has been living in the family home, and her parents have taken equal turns living there. Both parents work and Eleanor's mother earns $5,000 per year more than her father. Eleanor's father will live in the house after the divorce. Her mother will live in a two-bedroom apartment on the other side of town. Her mother will share the apartment with a man she fell in love with before the separation. Eleanor's father blames this man for the marital breakup. Her mother blames the father's long working hours, which left him little time for his family. During the past year, Eleanor's father has been working fewer hours and spending more time with Eleanor.

a. If you were the judge in this case, to whom would you award custody of Eleanor? Why? What other information would you want to know?

b. Assume that you awarded custody to the mother. If Eleanor's mother became disabled and used a wheelchair to get around, should it make a difference in the custody arrangement?

Some custody disputes are so bitter that one parent takes the children from the other parent and hides them. This may involve simply taking the children and moving permanently to another state. Or the parent may have to move constantly to avoid being found. Hundreds, perhaps thousands, of parents have resorted to this illegal means of opposing a court's custody decision. Such abductions may account for the majority of children reported missing each year. The *Federal Parental Kidnapping Prevention Act of 1980* prevents parents who abduct their children from getting new custody orders in a different state. It also provides resources to help custodial parents locate their missing children.

The Hidden Child

Dr. Martin accused her ex-husband, Dr. Forest, of sexually abusing their daughter, Hilary. She claimed that the abuse had begun before their divorce and continued when Hilary was with her father for court-ordered visitation periods. For that reason, she said, she refused to allow any future visitation without supervision. After conducting hearings on the alleged abuse, the court ordered Dr. Martin to continue to allow Dr. Forest to have unsupervised visits with Hilary. In response, Dr. Martin hid Hilary with friends. The court found Dr. Martin guilty of civil contempt and ordered that she be jailed until she complied with the visitation order.

PROBLEM 33

a. Assume that the court's contempt order is appealed and that Dr. Martin has been in jail for 18 months. What arguments would you make on Dr. Martin's behalf? On Dr. Forest's behalf?

b. If you were the appellate judge, how would you rule? Why?

c. What else could the judge have done, besides jailing Dr. Martin? If Dr. Martin does not disclose Hilary's whereabouts, when (if ever) should the judge release her from jail?

Alimony, Property Division, and Child Support

Since the development of no-fault divorce, most divorce disputes center on two issues: children and economics. The major economic issues are alimony, child support, and property division. These issues are frequently negotiated between the parties, who then make a brief courtroom appearance to finalize the breakup.

Alimony is money paid to support an ex-wife or ex-husband after a divorce. It covers household and personal expenses, work-related costs, educational expenses, and recreation. Alimony has traditionally been paid by men to support their ex-wives. However, in 1980, the U.S. Supreme Court ruled that state laws restricting alimony to women are unconstitutional.

Alimony is based on need. As a result, alimony awards vary from case to case. When awarding alimony, courts consider the couple's

What property division issues will this family face if the couple divorce?

standard of living, the financial status of both husband and wife, and the wage-earning capacity of each spouse. Sometimes "rehabilitative alimony" is awarded to help one spouse regain or develop job skills needed for future employment.

Dividing the property owned by the couple is another important issue. It involves deciding who gets the house, the car, the furniture, the bank account, the life insurance, and so on. In all states, property owned by one spouse prior to the marriage belongs to that person after divorce. In community property states, all the property acquired during the marriage is divided in half. In other states, such property is divided based on what the court considers equitable, or fair.

Note that alimony and property division are separate concepts. Property includes all physical possessions that have been acquired by the family during the marriage. Alimony consists of future payments of support money after the end of the marriage.

Divorcing couples with children need an agreement and court order regarding child support. Both parents have a legal duty to support their children after divorce. The level of support is based on the parents' ability to pay and the amount necessary to cover the child's needs. Child support is usually paid until the child becomes an adult or is emancipated.

Census Bureau statistics show that most women suffer financial hardship as a result of divorce but most men experience financial improvement. The average income for families headed by single

The Medical School Degree

Roberto and Marta Flores sought a divorce to end their 11-year marriage. At first, the case seemed simple. The couple had little property to divide and, with California's no-fault divorce law, seemingly little to argue about. However, at the time of the divorce, Roberto argued that he deserved part of his ex-wife's income as a physician because he had worked to support the family (and pay some of her tuition) while she went to school to earn her medical degree.

Roberto claimed that he was entitled to a share of Marta's total projected lifetime income as a doctor. This is likely to amount to over $1 million dollars in 30 years of medical practice. She countered that he might be entitled to reimbursement for part of the *cost* of her education but not for the *value* of her degree.

To understand the difference, imagine that a couple buys a stock for $100 when they are first married and the stock is worth $1,000 when they divorce. Should the court give the ex-husband $50 or $500?

PROBLEM 34

a. What happened in this case? What is Roberto asking for?

b. What is fair reimbursement: the cost of Marta's education or the value in terms of her increased earnings? Explain your answer.

women is $16,932, whereas the figure for those headed by single men is $29,046. One-fifth of the children in the United States live with a single parent as a result of a divorce, almost all of them with their mothers. The Census Bureau estimates that only 51% of those mothers receive full child support payments from their ex-husbands. Another 25% receive nothing at all.

When one spouse fails to provide the agreed-upon financial support, the other may seek a court order requiring payment. However, support orders are difficult to enforce. To remedy this problem, the federal government passed the *Family Support Act of 1988*. The act requires states to have clear formulas for calculating child support and to expand their child support enforcement procedures and parent locating services. It allows child support payments to be deducted from a parent's salary and permits states to track parents by means of their Social Security numbers.

PROBLEM 35

Each of the following situations involves a divorce. Should either spouse pay alimony or child support? If so, which spouse should pay? How much should be paid, and for how long?

a. Miguel, a successful plumbing contractor, earns $50,000 per year. His wife, Carmen, stays home and takes care of their four children. When Miguel and Carmen divorce, the two older children—a junior in high school and a freshman in college—wish to stay with Miguel. The two younger children prefer to stay with Carmen.

b. Angela, a government social worker, divorces her husband, Leroy, an occasionally employed writer. He has been staying home, taking care of their two-year-old son. Angela's yearly salary is $33,000; Leroy has earned $3,000 in the past 12 months. The child will stay with his mother.

GOVERNMENT SUPPORT FOR NEEDY FAMILIES AND OTHERS

What can be done to assist children living in poverty?

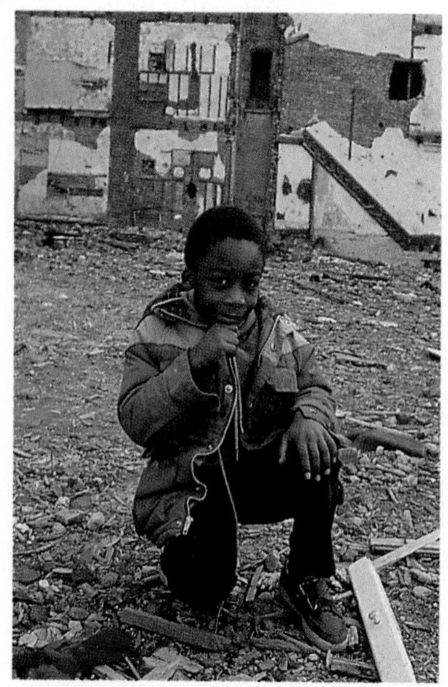

Since the Great Depression of the 1930s, the government has operated social programs to provide for needy families. This section discusses who benefits from these programs, how much individuals receive, and how government aid programs operate.

The U.S. government estimates that there are 34 million poor people in America. It defines poor people as those who live in households with less than a certain annual income. In 1992, that amount was $10,419 for a family of three. Many of these poor people are children. Approximately 20% of children were living in poverty during the 1980s. Estimates are that by the year 2000, nearly one out of four American children will be poor.

Federal, state, and local governments spend over $300 billion a year on social service programs. However, at least half of this money goes to people who are not poor through social insurance programs, such as Social Security, Medicare, and unemployment compensation. These programs provide benefits to people who are retired, disabled, or otherwise in need of assistance.

Programs designed to aid the poor include Aid to Families with Dependent Children (AFDC), food stamps, Medicaid, and public housing. How much a person receives under these programs depends on individual state laws. The federal government pays a minimum amount to the states and asks them to increase this with state funds. The state contributions vary. As a result, an unemployed person or someone receiving public assistance in one state may receive two or three times as much as a person in a similar situation in another state.

PROBLEM 36

a. What do you think are the causes of poverty in America? Can government programs help solve these problems? If so, how?

b. Should people receiving money under social programs receive the same amount no matter what state they live in? Why or why not?

Social Insurance Programs

Some government aid programs protect all Americans regardless of income. Most of these programs act like insurance policies whereby people receive benefits based on the amount of money they paid to the government when they were working.

What government programs assist older Americans?

Social Security When you apply for a job, the employer will ask for your Social Security number. This may seem unimportant now, but your Social Security number will be a valuable asset when you retire. Social Security works like an insurance policy. When you work, a percentage of your wages is deducted by your employer, who pays an equal amount to the federal government. Once you reach retirement age, you are entitled to benefits based on the amount paid into your account.

Almost all Americans—men, women, and children—have Social Security protection either as workers or as dependents of workers. The following list summarizes some of the major provisions of the Social Security law. For additional information, contact the nearest office of the U.S. Social Security Administration.

- **Retirement benefits.** Workers aged 62 or older may retire and receive a monthly Social Security check. A worker's spouse and children may also be eligible. The amount a person receives is a percentage of earnings. In 1993, a retiring worker could receive up to $1,128 monthly.

- **Disability benefits.** Workers who are blind, injured, or too ill to work can receive monthly checks if the disability is expected to last at least 12 months or to result in death. Spouses and children are also eligible.
- **Survivor's benefits.** When workers die, their families become eligible for payments. This is like a government life insurance policy.

To illustrate how Social Security works, consider the case of Mary Smith, aged 28, a single parent with two children. She works in a bakery for five years. Then she becomes very ill and stops working. After a required waiting period, Social Security will pay Mary and her children a monthly check until Mary is able to return to work. If Mary dies, Social Security will continue to pay each of her children until they reach 18 or until they reach 22 if they are full-time students.

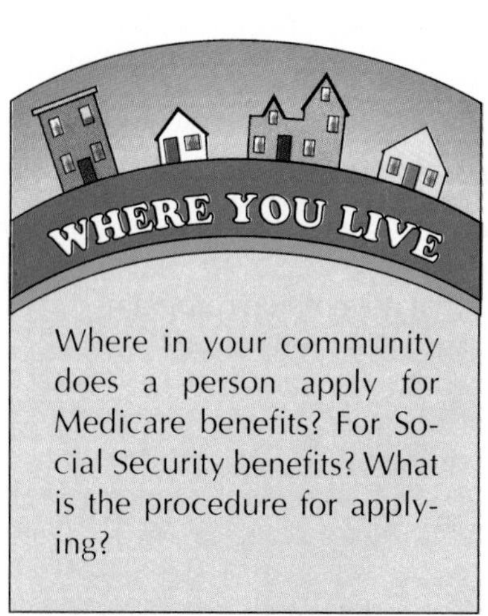

Where in your community does a person apply for Medicare benefits? For Social Security benefits? What is the procedure for applying?

Medicare Medicare is a federal health insurance program for people aged 65 or older. It also aids people of any age with permanent kidney failure, as well as certain disabled people. Medicare has two parts: hospital insurance and medical insurance. Hospital insurance helps pay for major hospital expenses and certain follow-up care. Medical insurance helps pay for physician's fees and other medical expenses. Local Social Security Administration offices take applications for Medicare, assist people in filing claims, and provide information about the program.

During the early 1990s, politicians and the public debated the need to reform the health care system. Some people proposed a national health insurance program that would provide coverage for all Americans. Supporters of this plan pointed to countries, such as Canada and Sweden, that currently have some form of universal medical coverage. Critics, however, emphasized the costs involved and voiced opposition to the larger government role in private health care.

Programs to Aid the Poor

Government welfare programs are designed to provide all persons with a certain minimum standard of financial support, often called a "safety net." Welfare programs exist at the federal, state, and local levels, and these programs help people who qualify for aid on the basis of need. The programs discussed below provide cash benefits, food stamps, medical care, and housing.

Supplemental Security Income The federal Supplemental Security Income (SSI) program provides money for needy aged, blind, and disabled people. This federal program provides monthly benefits at a standard rate all over the country. States may add their own benefits to those of the federal government. To receive SSI benefits, a person must be aged 65 or older, be legally blind, or have a major disability that prevents employment for a year or more. Applications for SSI are handled by local Social Security offices.

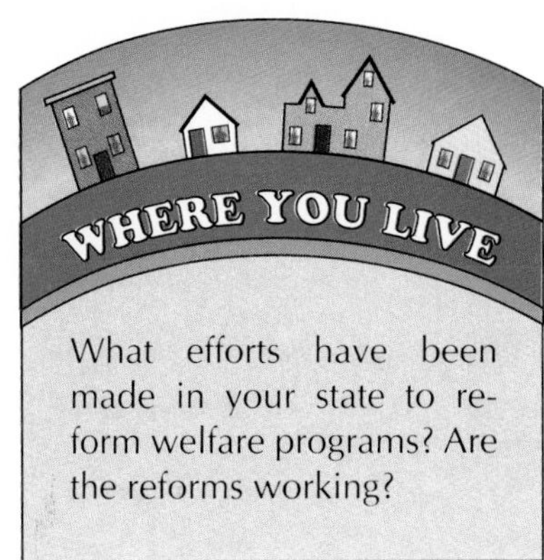

What efforts have been made in your state to reform welfare programs? Are the reforms working?

Aid to Families with Dependent Children (AFDC) AFDC—sometimes referred to as "welfare"—is a joint federal–state program that provides aid to needy families with dependent children. It is the primary source of support for 1 out of 15 Americans. Each state sets its own payment level. In 1992, for instance, payments for a family of three were $121 per month in Alabama and $694 per month in California. In every state, however, families with no other income remained below the poverty level after receiving both AFDC and food stamps.

Families receiving AFDC benefits have, on average, 1.9 children, about the same as the average for all American families. A child is considered dependent if one parent has died, has left home, or is physically or mentally unable to fulfill parental duties. The child must be under age 18 or under 21 and attending school regularly. Each state sets its own minimum income levels for eligibility, so eligibility requirements vary from state to state. AFDC usually goes to single-parent families, such as a mother with small children. However, families in which one parent is incapacitated may be eligible. In some states, a family may receive AFDC if a parent is unemployed and unable to find work.

What programs exist in your state to aid needy families? Are there any innovative programs in your state to deal with poverty? How much AFDC funding may a mother with three children receive in your state? What are the rules determining who is eligible for AFDC?

To receive AFDC benefits, the recipient can be required to make a reasonable effort to obtain a job. However, there are some exceptions. For example, the recipient is not required to work if the dependent child is under six or if the recipient is old or ill. Applications for AFDC are made at local offices of state social service agencies.

Welfare programs are controversial. Critics say that welfare discourages people from working, because welfare payments are reduced based on income received from employment. Others argue that it breaks up the family, because many states will not pay AFDC if the father lives in the home. Still others contend that the program costs too much. Although nearly everyone agrees that the present system needs improvement, welfare reform has been slow.

Some communities make direct payments of money, called general assistance, to poor people who are not covered by other programs or who receive inadequate assistance. Most states provide such money, but it is often limited to short-term emergencies.

PROBLEM 37

Discuss whether you approve or disapprove of the following aspects of AFDC.

a. Money is given to families under this program without the parent's being required to work.

b. The amount received varies substantially from state to state.

c. It is possible for parents to receive AFDC payments during the entire time they have a child under the age of 18.

d. Welfare payments are usually reduced dollar for dollar by the amount a recipient earns on a job.

PROBLEM 38

Some people propose abolishing the welfare system and replacing it with a program that would guarantee all Americans a certain minimum income. Do you favor or oppose this proposal? Explain your answer.

Medicaid Medicaid is a government program that provides private medical care to poor, elderly, and disabled people. It covers most common medical services, including hospital and outpatient care, nursing-home services, hearing aids, eyeglasses, prescription drugs, dental care, physicians' fees, medical supplies, and transportation to and from hospitals or doctors' offices.

Anyone receiving welfare (AFDC) is automatically eligible for Medicaid. Nevertheless, only about 62% of the children who are below the poverty level receive Medicaid benefits. More than 70% of Medicaid expenditures go to persons over age 65 or those who are blind or totally disabled. Elderly and disabled persons are eligible for Medicaid if they are U.S. citizens or legal aliens, live in the state where they apply, and have a low income. Application for Medicaid can be made at local social service offices.

Food Stamps People with incomes below a certain level may be eligible for food stamps. Food stamps are coupons of various denominations that can be exchanged like money for food at authorized stores. Food stamps can be denied to illegal aliens and to people who refuse

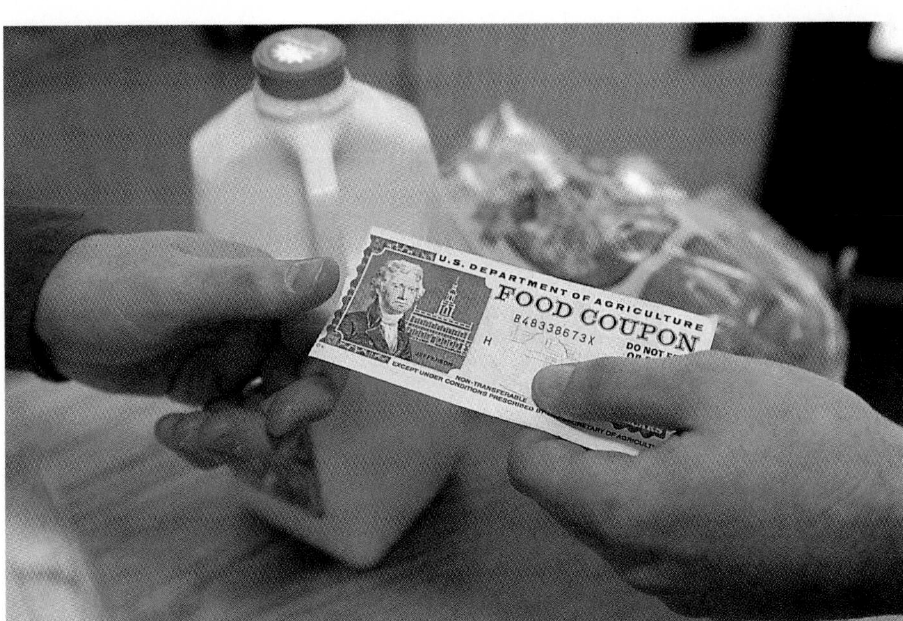

Do you approve or disapprove of the food stamp program? Give reasons.

to seek employment. The program is funded chiefly by federal money through the U.S. Department of Agriculture. It is administered under uniform national standards, so eligibility requirements and the amount a household can receive are the same in all states.

Housing Assistance and Employment Training Federal, state, and local governments have programs designed to provide poor people with housing assistance. These programs include government-operated housing projects, direct payments of rent money, low-interest loans, and insurance to help people buy homes. (See the section on housing for low- and moderate-income persons on page 417.)

In addition, there are programs to train people in skills necessary to obtain a job. Some programs also provide full-time, part-time, or summer jobs. Interested people should check with their state personnel, labor, or employment agency. The U.S. Department of Labor can also provide information on government programs in your area. (See Appendix F.)

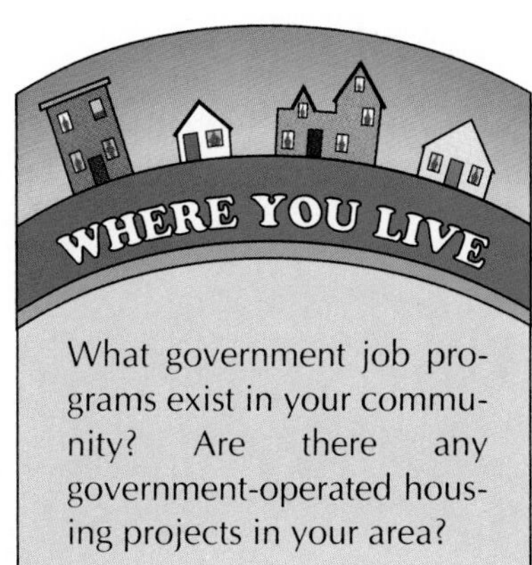

What government job programs exist in your community? Are there any government-operated housing projects in your area?

PROBLEM 39

The people in the following situations call a local government office and ask if they can receive aid. To what program or agency should each be referred?

a. Gerald retires at age 70 after 50 years as an employee of Banks & Company. He needs money for living and medical expenses.

b. Monique is pregnant. She quits her job, and the father runs off. She needs money for living and medical expenses.

c. Twana is laid off from work. Several weeks later, her husband is killed in a construction accident. She needs money for living expenses for herself and their child.

d. William and Mildred have four children and cannot afford to pay their bills for food, housing, clothing, and medical services.

e. José, 17, drops out of high school. He has little money and is having trouble finding a job.

f. James, 65, is in very poor health but cannot afford nursing-home care.

WILLS AND INHERITANCE

A **will** is a document that explains how a person wants his or her property distributed after death. Everyone who has any money or property should consider making a will. Even if you do not presently have much money or property, this may not be the case when you die. For example, if you die in an auto or other type of accident, those you name in your life insurance policy could receive a great deal of money.

If you die without a will, state law determines who receives your property. State law usually requires that a portion of the property go to your spouse if you are married. The remainder may go to your children, parents, grandchildren, or brothers and sisters, depending on state law. Having a will ensures that everything you own—your **estate**—goes to whomever you wish in the amounts you choose.

How old does a person have to be to write a will in your state? Is a person's will valid if it is written in his or her own handwriting? If someone dies without a will, who inherits his or her property?

In most states, persons cannot legally make wills until they reach the age of majority, 18 or 21. However, some states allow persons as young as 14 to make wills if they are married, emancipated, near death, or in other special circumstances. When minors die without a will, their property, such as money and clothes, goes to their parents or legal guardians, who decide what to do with it.

Wills prepared by lawyers are usually typewritten so they can be easily read. Approximately half the states, however, allow wills to be handwritten as long as they are written entirely in the handwriting of the person making the will. In some states, a person may even make a will orally during his or her final illness. Most states require two or three witnesses to validate a will.

Spouses are required by most states to provide for each other and for minor children in their wills. If a spouse or minor child is not list-

ed in the will, the state will usually require that he or she receive a **forced share** of the estate—usually one-third or one-half of the property. Once children become adults, their parents are not required to leave them anything. Sometimes disagreements take place, and children are **disinherited**—left out of their parents' wills.

A will should name an **executor** or **executrix**, who delivers the will to the court's register of wills for **probate** after a person dies. The probate process includes taking charge of the deceased person's property; keeping records; paying taxes; and with court approval, distributing the property to the persons named in the will, called **heirs**. This process can be slow and costly.

People can write wills on their own without hiring lawyers, and will-writing kits are available to help them do this. There are differing views on whether a person should consult a lawyer when writing a will. Those who favor using lawyers argue that people will make mistakes without attorneys to guide them through technical rules and complicated tax issues. Those favoring writing a will without a lawyer say the task is often simple and the required form can be found in inexpensive will-writing kits.

PROBLEM 40

a. Jacob, aged 60, owns a house, a car, and other property. He is married with two children, aged 28 and 25. He dies without a will. Who will inherit his property? In another case, who will inherit the property of Sabrina, who also dies without a will but is 16 years old and has beautiful clothes and a car she bought with money from her part-time job? Do you think Jacob's and Sabrina's property will be distributed in the best way? If not, how would you change the law governing distribution of property?

b. At what stage in your life would you consider writing a will? Explain. Would you hire a lawyer or try to write it on your own? Why?

Chapter 6

Housing Law

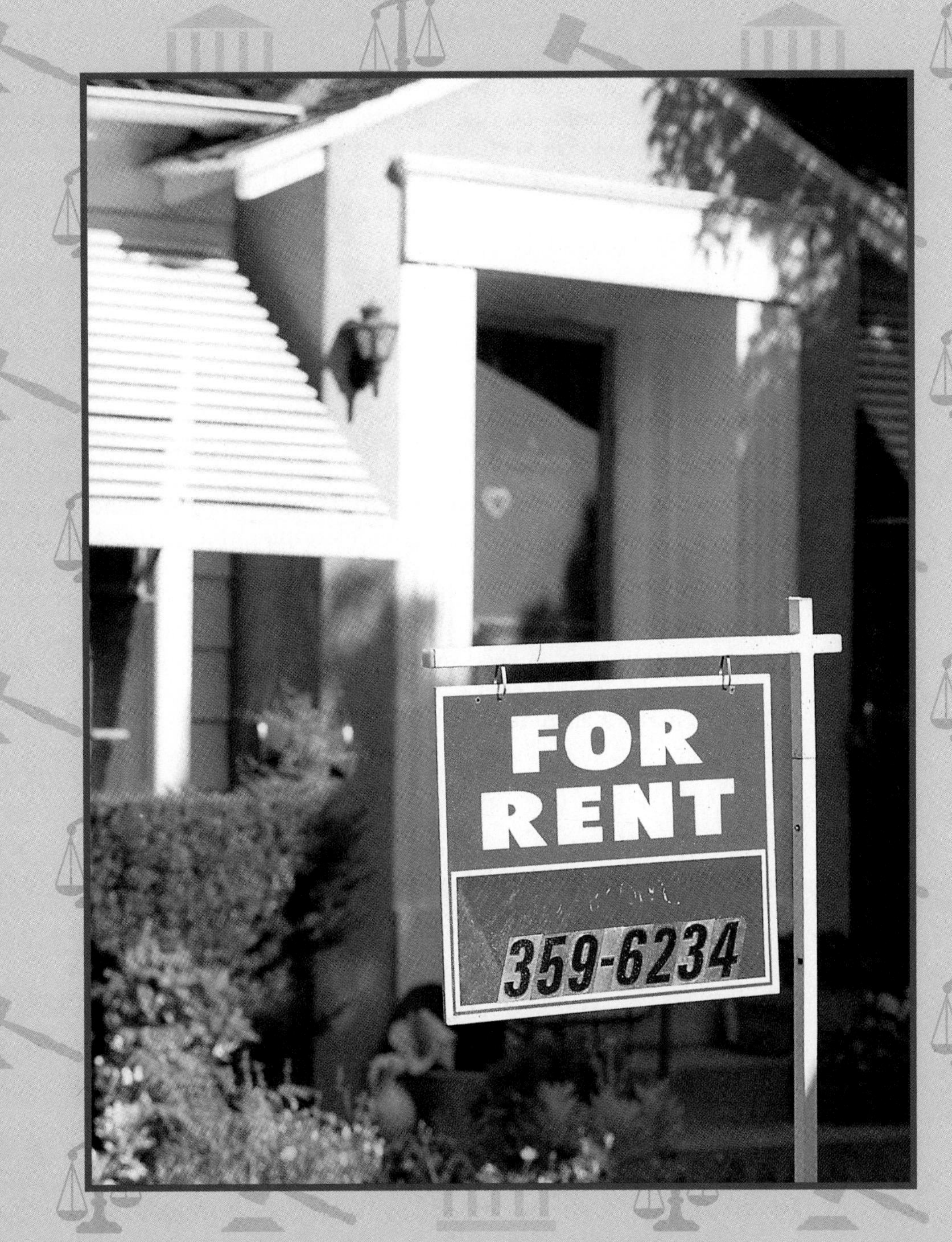

Whether you live in a farmhouse or a high rise, a mobile home or a suburban split-level, a condominium or a walk-up flat, you and your family probably use and pay for housing. Some families own their homes. Many others rent houses or apartments owned by someone else. Still others are homeless and in need of housing. Everyone needs to be aware of some of the legal issues and practical problems involving housing.

In this chapter, you will find information on the pros and cons of renting versus buying a home; where and how to find a place to live; and how local, state, and federal governments are involved in housing issues. You also will learn what to do if you are discriminated against in buying or renting a home and what to look for in a dwelling and a lease.

RENTING VERSUS BUYING

There are important differences between renting and buying a home. Those who rent **(tenants)** do not pay property taxes, and they can call on the owner of the property **(landlord)** to make major repairs. Depending on the arrangement with the owner, a renter may have to pay for utilities (for example, electricity, gas, and water). Since utility costs can be expensive, a prospective renter should consider them along with the rent. Before either renting or buying, you should find out what the average monthly utility bills were for the previous year. A good way to do this is to look at copies of recent bills. You also should check to see if the utility companies require tenants to make a cash deposit before receiving service.

What are the advantages of renting a house versus buying one?

A person buying a home will probably be required to make a cash **down payment** before moving in. The amount required can vary from no down payment, under certain government loan programs, to as much as 20 or 30% of the selling price. Most buyers arrange for a **mortgage** loan for the remainder of the cost of the house. For example, someone buying a house costing $100,000 might make a down payment of 20% ($20,000). The remaining $80,000 would be the mortgage amount, to be repaid in monthly payments over a number of years (30 years is common). If the homeowner fails to make the mortgage payments, the mortgage lender can take the house and sell it. The lender will then use the proceeds of the sale to satisfy the loan. In addition to the mortgage, homeowners must pay for utilities, property taxes, insurance, maintenance, and repairs. Unlike a renter, a homeowner will probably not have to pay utility deposits.

When considering the purchase of a home, many people think only of single-family houses, but condominiums, cooperatives, and mobile homes are other alternatives. **Condominiums** usually are units in multidwelling buildings. Each resident owns an individual unit, but the rest of the property—hallways, lobbies, elevators, grounds, and parking areas—is jointly owned by all residents, who pay a maintenance fee to take care of it. In a **cooperative**, each resident owns a share in a multidwelling building and has the right to occupy one unit. **Mobile homes** are factory-built houses that usually come equipped with furniture and appliances. An owner must rent or purchase land on which to put the mobile home, and many communities restrict the areas where mobile homes may be located.

Why might someone buy a mobile home?

Ideally, whether you are renting or buying, you should not have to spend more than 25% of your monthly take-home income for housing. Thus, if you take home $1,500 per month, your rent or mortgage payment should not exceed $375. However, the high cost of housing often drives people to spend up to 50% of their income for shelter. In an effort to help with this problem, many communities offer some form of financial assistance to low-income people. This assistance may include government-owned apartments for which rents are partially subsidized. (For more information on low-income housing, see page 417.)

PROBLEM 1

Fred and Jill, both 25 years old, have just married. They both have jobs paying about $22,000 a year. Each takes home $1,500 a month ($3,000 total). Between them they have about $8,000 in savings. They are trying to decide whether they should rent or buy a home. They visit a real estate agent and ask that she help them find a small, two-bedroom house.

a. Determine how much money the couple can afford to pay each month for housing and how much they have available for making a down payment.

b. Make a list of the features they might want in their home (type, location, price, convenience to schools and shopping, and the like).

c. Look in the classified section of your local newspaper at the houses to rent and the houses for sale to see what you can find that meets this description. Are there more listings for some locations than others? Does the cost of housing vary depending on its location? Why?

d. Select one house for sale and one for rent from those listed in your newspaper. List all the reasons the couple should buy the house offered for sale; then list all the reasons they should rent the one offered for lease. Decide what Fred and Jill should do.

HOUSING DISCRIMINATION

The federal *Fair Housing Act of 1968* forbids discrimination in the selling, leasing, or financing of housing based on the race, color, reli-

The Unwanted Tenant

Since the death of her husband, Mrs. Amy Weaver has operated a small, five-unit apartment house. She lives in one unit and makes a meager income by renting out the other four. She doesn't really dislike members of minority groups but knows that several of her regular tenants have threatened to move out if she rents to people in these groups. Anyway, she feels she has the right to do whatever she wants in her own building.

Wan Chai Rewkratrok, a new immigrant from Thailand, is looking for an apartment to rent. When a friend at work tells him about a vacancy at Mrs. Weaver's, he calls and makes an appointment to inspect the apartment. When Mr. Wan Chai arrives for the appointment, Mrs. Weaver takes one look at him and tells him the apartment has been rented. "After all," she says to herself, "it's my property, and no one has the right to tell me whom I must allow to live here."

PROBLEM 2

a. What happened in this case? Why did Mrs. Weaver refuse to rent the apartment to Mr. Wan Chai?

b. Do you think what Mrs. Weaver did was legal or illegal? Why?

c. Should the law allow landlords to rent to whomever they want?

d. Which do you think is more important: the right to control one's own property or the right to live where one chooses?

e. Is there anything Mr. Wan Chai can do? Explain.

gion, gender, or national origin of the applicant. The act was amended in 1988 to include persons with disabilities and families with children among the categories of people protected. The statute applies to the rental, sale, or financing of a privately owned house or a multidwelling building with four or more units. A presidential order prohibits similar forms of discrimination in federally owned, operated, or assisted housing, including public housing. Many states and cities also have antidiscrimination laws that may protect people not mentioned in the act.

What laws prohibit housing discrimination in your state or community? What state or local agencies enforce these laws and investigate complaints?

What is the purpose of this sign?

We Do Business in Accordance With the Federal Fair Housing Law

(Title VIII of the Civil Rights Act of 1968, as Amended by the Housing and Community Development Act of 1974)

IT IS ILLEGAL TO DISCRIMINATE AGAINST ANY PERSON BECAUSE OF RACE, COLOR, RELIGION, SEX, OR NATIONAL ORIGIN

- In the sale or rental of housing or residential lots
- In advertising the sale or rental of housing
- In the financing of housing
- In the provision of real estate brokerage services

Blockbusting is also illegal

An aggrieved person may file a complaint of a housing discrimination act with the:

U.S. DEPARTMENT OF HOUSING AND URBAN DEVELOPMENT
Assistant Secretary for Fair Housing and Equal Opportunity
Washington, D.C. 20410

Accordingly, a landlord may not discriminate against potential tenants because of a disability and must permit tenants with disabilities to reasonably modify a dwelling to accommodate their needs, at the tenants' expense. All new multifamily dwellings must be accessible to persons with disabilities.

A landlord also may not refuse to rent to a family because it has children under age 18. This is meant to end discrimination against families with children. In certain instances, landlords may still be able to exclude large families from homes that are clearly not large enough to provide them with adequate living space.

The 1988 amendments to the *Fair Housing Act* allow restriction of retirement housing to the elderly if certain criteria are met. Examples of such criteria include the existence of buildings in which all residents are over 62 years of age, or new housing in which over 80% of the units will be occupied by someone age 55 or older and in which specific facilities and services for the elderly will be provided. The act does not allow "adults only" housing except for the elderly.

Discrimination in housing can take many forms. For instance, a real estate agent can be guilty of **steering**. This means directing prospective buyers or renters to particular areas because of their race or some other factor. Some community groups employ "testers" to uncover steering practices. For example, prospective renters or

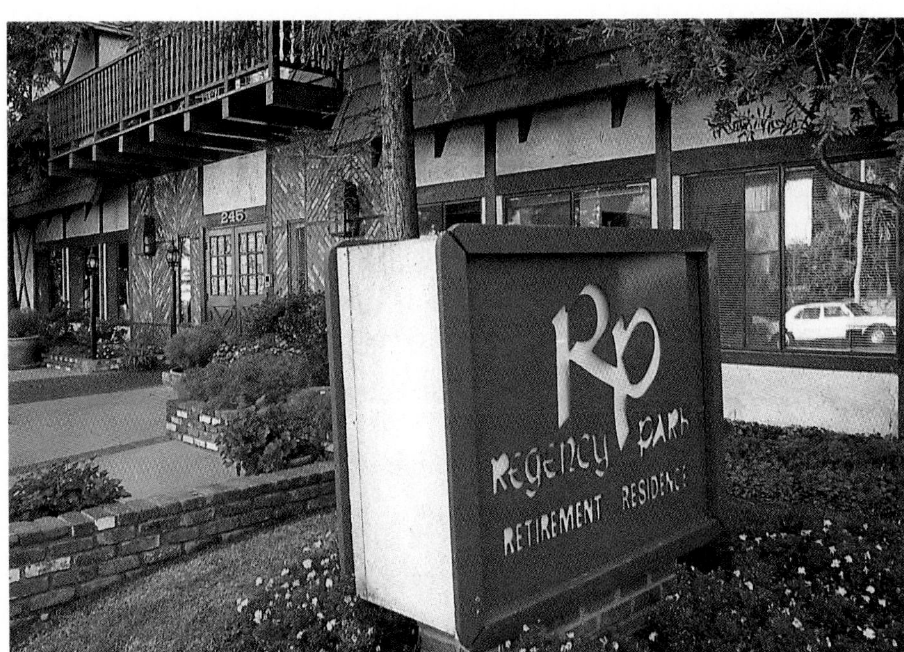

Why do some older people choose to live in retirement residences?

buyers of different races but similar qualifications may approach an agent. Those agents who show housing to one person, but tell the other that the same housing is unavailable, are guilty of steering.

Another type of housing discrimination is **redlining**. This is the refusal by a bank or other mortgage lender to make loans for the purchase of homes in certain neighborhoods. Congress passed the *Community Reinvestment Act of 1977* to stop lenders from routinely rejecting loan applications from people attempting to buy homes in poor and minority neighborhoods. Under the act, a bank cannot purchase another bank or otherwise expand its business unless it can prove that it makes a sufficient number of loans to fund low-income housing. As a result, banks now invest over $1 billion a year to finance such housing.

If you think you have been illegally discriminated against, you may file a complaint with a state or local agency that deals with housing discrimination or with the U.S. Department of Housing and Urban Development's (HUD's) Fair Housing Office (see Appendix F for the address). The state or local agency or HUD has the authority to investigate your complaint and either resolve the problem or bring a lawsuit on your behalf. You also may be able to file a lawsuit in court.

Choice of housing is sometimes unfairly limited by unlawful discrimination. For various reasons, some owners, real estate agents, and mortgage lenders prefer to sell or rent to certain types of people rather than to others.

Not all housing discrimination is illegal. For example, landlords and sellers may refuse to rent or sell to people who have poor credit ratings or whose income is not sufficient to meet the rent or mortgage payments. Other legitimate reasons for discriminating include poor rental references and unwillingness to follow reasonable rules (for example, "no pets").

Usually, a major consideration of those who sell or rent is whether the money owed them will be paid in full and on time. To help ensure that this will occur, they usually want to know the following information about a potential tenant or buyer:

- Does the person have a steady income that is likely to continue into the future?
- Is the income high enough to enable the person to pay for the housing?

The Annoying Ramp

Mrs. Clark uses a wheelchair. When she moved into one of the five apartments in her building, she notified the owner that she would need a ramp built near the front door so that she could leave the building and get to her car without assistance. The owner hired a worker to build the ramp, and Mrs. Clark paid for it. The ramp extends along the front walkway to the edge of the parking lot. There are two other entrances to the building.

Recently, other tenants have complained that the ramp is an eyesore and a nuisance. They must walk around it whenever they use the building's front entrance. The owner removed the ramp, telling Mrs. Clark that he was tired of receiving complaints. He also suggested that she move to another apartment building.

PROBLEM 3

a. Has the landlord discriminated against Mrs. Clark? If so, in what way?

b. Is this discrimination illegal?

c. Does the fact that other tenants dislike the ramp affect the legality of the discrimination? What if some tenants move out because of the ramp?

- Does the person have a record of paying off previous bills or loans?
- Will the person take good care of the property?

PROBLEM 4

Consider each of the following situations, and decide whether you think the action of the landlord, homeowner, lender, or sales agent is legal or illegal under the federal *Fair Housing Act*. If the action is legal, do you think the law should be changed to prohibit the action?

a. A real estate company runs a series of advertisements in a major newspaper featuring photographs that portray potential tenants as whites. The few African Americans who appear are janitors or door attendants.

b. A woman seeking a two-bedroom apartment is turned down by the landlord, who thinks the apartment is too small for her and her three children.

c. A landlord refuses to rent an apartment to two men who disclose they are gay and want to share a one-bedroom unit.

d. A homeowner refuses to sell to a Hispanic-American couple because he thinks the neighbors won't approve.

e. A woman is rejected for a mortgage by a bank officer who believes her divorce makes her a financial risk.

f. A zoning change to allow a group home for persons with disabilities is blocked by a neighborhood association of homeowners.

g. A landlord turns down a rental application from a man who is participating in a drug rehabilitation program, although the man says he no longer uses drugs.

h. A young musician is rejected as a tenant by a landlord who thinks the musician looks like a drug user and might make too much noise.

i. A credit unit official discourages an elderly man from buying a house because the official thinks the man won't live long enough to pay off the mortgage.

j. A landlord makes repeated suggestive sexual comments to a young female tenant, making it uncomfortable for her to live in the building.

k. The landlord of a ten-unit building turns down the rental application of a man suffering from acquired immune deficiency syndrome (AIDS).

Why might this woman be examining this shower?

ADVICE

What to Inspect Before Renting an Apartment

- What is the condition of the building?
- Are hallways, lobbies, and common areas clean and well lighted?
- Does the building have laundry facilities?
- Is there enough parking space?
- Are there any signs of insects or rodents?
- How are routine and emergency maintenance handled?
- Is storage and closet space adequate?
- Is the apartment soundproof?
- Are the plumbing, heating, and electrical fixtures in working order?
- Are kitchen appliances clean and in good condition?
- Is there any evidence of water stains or peeling paint on walls and ceilings?
- Does the building provide protection against burglars or uninvited guests?
- Is it likely to be too cold in winter or too hot in summer?
- Is the apartment furnished or unfurnished?
- Do windows and doors open easily?
- Are there any broken windows or screens?
- Are smoke detectors installed?
- Are fire extinguishers and safety exists available?
- Is the apartment big enough?

RENTING A HOME

Many people rent their homes. A renter (tenant) pays the owner (landlord) a certain amount of money in return for the right to live there for a period of time.

The landlord-tenant relationship is created by a type of contract called a lease or rental agreement. A lease sets out the amount of rent that must be paid and the length of time for which the dwelling may be rented. It also states the rights and duties of both landlord and tenant.

Before you rent an apartment or a house, you should do at least two things to protect your interests. First, completely inspect the dwelling to ensure that it meets your needs. Second, because most leases are written to the advantage of the landlord, carefully read the lease. If you don't understand or can't read the lease, get help from someone else before signing it.

PROBLEM 5

Assume that you are looking for a new apartment. You are married and have a two-year-old child and a small dog.

a. What things should you look for when inspecting an apartment? Make a checklist.

b. What questions would you ask the landlord?

The Lease

Once you've inspected a rental house or apartment, you'll probably be asked to fill out a **lease application**. This is a form that the landlord uses to determine whether you qualify for the rental. You will be asked for information such as your name, age, address, place of employment, source of income, and a list of previous residences. You will also be asked for credit references. Landlords use this information to determine your ability to pay the rent. If the landlord approves your lease application, you will then be asked to sign a lease.

A **lease** is a legal agreement or contract in which both the landlord and the tenant agree to certain things. A lease usually includes the date the tenant may move in, the amount of the rent, the dates on which the rent is to be paid, and the length or term of the lease. It also includes the amount of any security deposit; the conditions under which the rent may be raised; and the rules governing repairs, maintenance, and other conditions in the apartment.

Depending upon your particular situation, one type of lease may be better than another. For example, if you are planning to rent for only a short period, or if your job requires you to move on short notice, you might prefer a **month-to-month lease**. This type of lease usually enables you to leave after 30 days' notice. However, it has the disadvantage of allowing the landlord to raise the rent or evict you with just 30 days' notice, too.

Another type of lease allows a tenant to move in with the understanding that the lease is for an indefinite period. This arrangement is called a **tenancy at will**. It allows the tenant to leave or be told to leave at any time.

A lease for a fixed period of time—such as six months or a year—is called a **tenancy for years**. This type of lease generally prevents the landlord from raising the rent or evicting the tenant during the period of the lease. If you are planning to rent for a long period of time, this may be the best type of lease for you.

The Summer Rental

A college student goes to a resort town to work for the summer and agrees to rent an apartment from a landlord for three months. After a month, she moves to a cheaper apartment down the street. The landlord demands rent for the two remaining months, but the young woman claims she doesn't owe any money, because the lease was not in writing.

PROBLEM 6

a. Is the student obligated to pay the additional two months' rent? Would it make a difference if the landlord rented the apartment immediately after she moved out?

b. What should the woman have done when she found the cheaper apartment?

c. Role-play a phone call between the woman and the landlord after she finds the cheaper apartment and wishes to get the landlord's permission to move.

Written leases are generally difficult to read and understand. To protect yourself, be sure to read all clauses in your lease carefully before signing it. Never sign a lease unless all blank spaces are filled in or crossed out. If you're unsure of anything in the lease, ask to take it home and consult with representatives of tenant organizations, legal aid offices, private law firms, or others experienced with leases. Also make sure that any promises made by the landlord are written into the lease. For example, if the landlord promises to paint the apartment before you move in, get the promise in writing.

Leases for one year or more must be in writing to be enforceable in court. However, leases for less than one year do not have to be written to be legally effective. In such instances, an oral agreement may be binding. To avoid problems, you are *always* better off getting a written lease that is signed and dated by both you and the landlord. If there is only an oral agreement and problems arise, one of you may remember the terms of the agreement differently from the other.

Landlord-Tenant Negotiations

In many places, housing is in big demand and short supply. In that kind of market, landlords generally have the upper hand and can often tell tenants to "take it or leave it." Negotiating with a landlord about the rent and other lease terms can be difficult, but it is worth a try, particularly if you know your rights and know what you want in an apartment or house. If you do try negotiating with a landlord, it is best to be assertive, but tactful and polite. Landlords want to know you'll be a good tenant. But tenants expect something in return—namely, fair treatment and a clean, well-maintained place to live.

It may be possible to change parts of the lease. To strike a section from a lease, both the tenant and the landlord or rental agent should cross out the particular clause and put their initials next to the change. If anything is added to the lease, be sure the addition is written on all copies of the lease and is signed by both the landlord and the tenant.

RIGHTS AND DUTIES OF LANDLORDS AND TENANTS

Most landlords ask that you sign a standard form lease, because it is usually written to the landlord's advantage. Sometimes it may even contain clauses that are unenforceable in court. The lease reprinted in Figure 6.1 contains many provisions found in standard

What to Consider Before Renting

- In what kind of area do you wish to live?
- What are the costs, including rent, utilities, security deposit, and so on?
- What is the condition of the apartment or house? Will repairs be made by the landlord before you move in?
- How long will the lease last, and how can it be ended?
- Will the landlord make or pay for repairs that occur after you move in?
- What services (storage, trash removal, maintenance of yard, appliances, and the like) will the tenant receive?
- Are there any special rules (for example, no pets, or no parties)?
- Do you understand all the clauses in the lease? Are any of them illegal or difficult for you to accept?

LAW IN ACTION

Lease Negotiation

Read the following information. Then two people should role-play the landlords (the Randalls). Two others should role-play the tenants (the Monicos). Those role-playing the Monicos should inspect the apartment and ask the landlords all the questions a tenant should ask before deciding to rent an apartment. Those role-playing the Randalls should find out everything a landlord needs to know before renting to a tenant. The landlords should give a copy of the lease to the tenants. The tenants should discuss it and reach a decision on whether to sign it.

Mr. and Mrs. Randall own an apartment building in the city of Johnstown. They have a two-bedroom apartment for rent. They require all their tenants to sign a two-year lease (the same as the one printed in Figure 6.1) and pay a two-month security deposit. They don't allow pets in the building. The rent is $550 per month plus utilities, which average about $50 a month. The Randalls are eager to rent the apartment right away, because it has been empty for two weeks.

Mr. and Mrs. Monico have just moved to Johnstown, where they have new jobs. Mrs. Monico's job may last only one year, and they may then have to move back to Williamsport, a city 100 miles away. They have a three-year-old son and a dog. Based on their salaries, they wish to pay only $450 a month in rent and utilities. They want a nice neighborhood and are a little worried about the crime in Johnstown. They want an apartment right away, because Mrs. Monico starts work in three days. They see a notice advertising the Randalls' apartment. They don't know much about the neighborhood, but they decide to look at the apartment.

The apartment has two bedrooms, a living room, a dining area, and one bathroom with a tub but no shower. It is on the second floor and has a small balcony overlooking a parking lot. The paint is peeling in the larger bedroom, and a small window is broken in the bathroom. The kitchen has a new refrigerator and sink, but the stove is old and worn and has a missing handle. The front door and the door to the balcony have locks that could easily be opened by an intruder.

PROBLEM 7

After the role-play, answer the following questions:

a. Did the Monicos ask any questions about the neighborhood or building as a whole? Should they have?

b. What was decided regarding the amount of rent and other costs of the apartment? In reality, can tenants ever convince landlords to take less than they are asking?

c. In discussing the conditions in the apartment, did the tenants get the landlords to agree to any repairs?

d. Did the Monicos ask about such services as laundry, parking, and playgrounds? Should they have?

e. Are there any special rules in the lease that the Monicos didn't like? Did they ask the landlords to discuss these rules? If so, what was decided? Could the Monicos have done a better job in negotiating these rules?

f. Is it worthwhile for tenants to try to negotiate with landlords? Can tenants be hurt by doing this?

Figure 6.1 A Rental Agreement

RANDALL REAL ESTATE CO.
PROPERTY MANAGEMENT–INVESTMENT
PROPERTY–SALES–INSURANCE

THIS AGREEMENT, Made and executed this _____ day of _________A.D., 19___, by and between RANDALL REAL ESTATE COMPANY, hereinafter called the Landlord, and ______________________________ , hereinafter called the Tenant.

WITNESSETH, That Landlord does hereby let unto Tenant the premises known as Apartment No. 301, at 12 Marshall Street in Johnstown, for the term commencing on the ___day of _____________, 19___, and fully ending at midnight on the day of ____, 19___, at and for the total rental of _____________Dollars, the first installment payable on the execution of this agreement and the remaining installments payable in advance on the ___ day of each ensuing month, to and at the office of RANDALL REAL ESTATE COMPANY, 1000 Columbia Road, in Johnstown.

On the ___ day of _________, 19___, a sum of __________ shall become due and payable. This sum shall cover the period up to the day of ______________, 19___; thereafter, a sum of _________________shall be due and payable on the ___day of each month.

AND TENANT does hereby agree as follows:

1. Tenant will pay the rent at the time specified.
2. Tenant will pay all utility bills as they become due.
3. Tenant will use the premises for a dwelling and for no other purpose.
4. Tenant will not use said premises for any unlawful purpose, or in any noisy or rowdy manner, or in a way offensive to any other occupant of the building.
5. Tenant will not transfer or sublet the premises without the written consent of the Landlord.
6. Landlord shall have access to the premises at any time for the purpose of inspection, to make repairs the Landlord considers necessary, or to show the apartment to tenant applicants.
7. Tenant will give Landlord prompt notice of any defects or breakage in the structure, equipment, or fixtures of said premises.
8. Tenant will not make any alterations or additions to the structure, equipment, or fixtures of said premises without the written consent of the Landlord.
9. Tenant will pay a security deposit in the amount of $____________, which will be held by Landlord until expiration of this lease and refunded on the condition that said premises is returned in good condition, normal wear and tear excepted.
10. Tenant will not keep any pets, live animals, or birds of any description in said premises.
11. Landlord shall be under no liability to Tenant for any discontinuance of heat, hot water, or elevator service, and shall not be liable for damage to property of Tenant caused by rodents, rain, snow, defective plumbing, or any other source.
12. Should Tenant continue in possession after the end of the term herein with permission of Landlord, it is agreed that the tenancy thus created can be terminated by either party giving to the other party not less than Thirty (30) days' Written Notice.
13. Tenant shall be required to give the Landlord at least thirty (30) days notice, in writing, of his or her intention to vacate the premises at the expiration of this tenancy. If Tenant vacates the premises without first furnishing said notice, Tenant shall be liable to the Landlord for one month's rent.
14. Both Landlord and Tenant waive trial by jury in connection with any agreement contained in the rental agreement or any claim for damages arising out of the agreement or connected with this tenancy.
15. Landlord shall not be held liable for any injuries or damages to the Tenant or his or her guests, regardless of cause.
16. In the event of increases in real estate taxes, fuel charges, or sewer and water fees, Tenant agrees during the term of the lease to pay a proportionate share of such charges, fees, or increases.
17. Tenant confesses judgment and waives any and all rights to file a counterclaim, or a defense to any action filed by the Landlord against the Tenant and further agrees to pay attorney's fees and all other costs incurred by the Landlord in an action against the Tenant.
18. Tenant agrees to observe all such rules and regulations which the Landlord or his agents will make concerning the apartment building.

IN TESTIMONY WHEREOF, Landlord and Tenant have signed this Agreement the day and year first hereinbefore written.

____

Signed in the presence of ______________________

____

______________________ ______________________

____

form leases. Since landlord-tenant law differs from state to state, a few of that lease's clauses would be illegal in some states. You should inform yourself about the landlord-tenant laws in your state.

PROBLEM 8

a. What are the key provisions of the lease in Figure 6.1? Who is the landlord? Who pays the utilities? Is the tenant allowed to have a pet?

b. As a tenant, would you object to any of the provisions in this lease? If so, which ones?

c. As the landlord, are there any clauses you would add to the lease? If so, draft them.

The following pages provide information on several of the clauses from the lease reprinted in Figure 6.1. This material is designed to help you read and understand a lease and avoid problems. After a person signs a lease and moves into a rental home, both the landlord and the tenant take on certain rights and duties. Most of these are set out in the lease, but others exist regardless of whether they are stated there or not.

If the tenant violates a provision of the lease (for example, does not pay the rent), the landlord can go to court and attempt to have the tenant evicted. The tenant may be able to defend against the landlord in court and prevent the eviction.

Paying the Rent

Tenant will pay the rent at the time specified. (Clause 1)

A tenant's most important duty is paying the rent. Leases generally state the amount of rent to be paid and the dates on which it is due. Most leases require payment on the first day of each month. If you and the landlord agree to a date other than the first, be sure that it is written into the lease.

Historically, courts have required tenants to continue paying rent no matter what happened to the house or apartment. For example, if the apartment was damaged by fire, the tenant was still required to pay rent for the term of the lease. In recent years, courts and legislatures in most states have ruled that in situations in which a house or apartment is made unlivable by fire, landlord neglect, or other causes, the tenant cannot be forced to pay the rent. These situations are discussed more fully in the section on landlord-tenant problems. For now, keep in mind that tenants have a duty to pay the rent and that landlords generally have a right to evict tenants who don't pay it.

Rent Control Legislative Hearing

Suppose your city council is considering rent control. Housing costs have been rising steadily, and a law is proposed limiting rent increases to 5% a year for all rental properties. Read the following statements. Then conduct a hearing at a city council meeting in which each side—tenants and landlords—gets a chance to speak. The council members ask questions and then vote on the issue.

Representative of a tenant group: There is a severe shortage of apartments and rental homes in the area. As a result, landlords have been able to charge just about any rent they want. During the last two years, rents have risen an average of 15% a year. The housing shortage and rent increases particularly hurt low- and middle-income tenants, who are barely able to meet expenses and pay their rents. Only government control can stop the continued rapid rise in rents. Rent control should be passed by the legislature.

Representative of a landlord group: Rent control will mean more run-down housing, because area landlords won't be able to pay for repairs or improvements. Some landlords may be forced to sell or abandon their buildings, because operating them will be uneconomical. In addition, if landlords can't expect reasonable profits, they won't build new apartment buildings. An even greater shortage of rental units will result.

Landlords raise rents to meet the increased costs of heating fuel, electricity, taxes, and repairs. Also, landlords are in business to earn a profit and have a right to charge whatever they want. Besides, tenants can always move out and find another apartment if they think the rent is too high. Rent control would be a big mistake.

Raising the Rent

In the event of increases in real estate taxes, fuel charges, or sewer and water fees, Tenant agrees during the term of the lease to pay a proportionate share of such charges, fees, or increases. (Clause 16)

Generally, landlords cannot raise the rent during the term of a lease. When the term is over, the rent can normally be raised as much as the landlord wants. Some leases, however, include provisions (like Clause 16 in the sample lease) that allow for automatic increases during the term of the lease. Many landlords include such clauses to cover the rising costs of fuel and building maintenance. A lease with an escalation clause is obviously not favorable to a tenant.

Another factor that can affect whether the landlord may raise the rent is **rent control**. Many communities—especially large cities—have rent control laws, which put a limit on how much existing rents can be raised. Cities with rent control laws use various standards to control the rise in rents. Some places limit rent increases to a certain percentage each year. In other places, rent increases are tied to the cost of living or improvements in the building, or increases are allowed only when a new tenant moves in.

Rent control laws slow down the rising cost of housing. However, there are many arguments for and against rent control. Wherever it has been tried, it has been controversial.

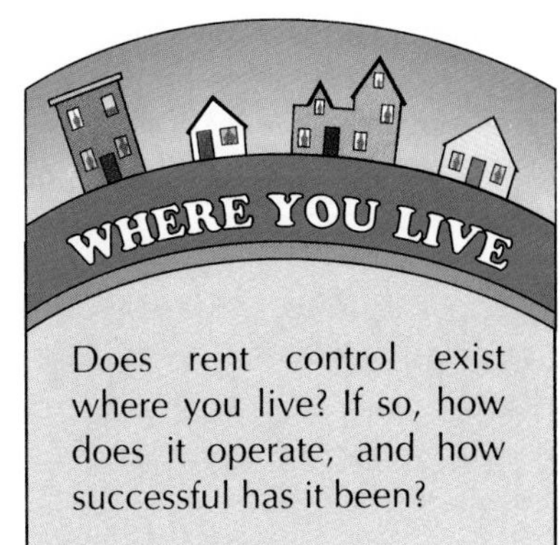

Does rent control exist where you live? If so, how does it operate, and how successful has it been?

Quiet Enjoyment

One of a tenant's most basic rights is the **right to quiet enjoyment** of the property. This simply means that a tenant has a right to

The Noisy Neighbor

Mike and Marcy O'Reilly sign a one-year lease, and they are pleased when they move into a beautiful old apartment building in their favorite part of town. However, soon after moving, they discover that the building is incredibly noisy and disorderly. During the first week, their next-door neighbor throws several wild parties, keeping the O'Reillys up all night. They also discover that when their neighbor isn't having parties, he is receiving visitors at all hours of the day. These visits are almost always accompanied by loud music, shouting, and constant coming and going. The partying often spills into the halls, and the O'Reillys are frequently hassled by the visitors.

The O'Reillys complain to the landlord on a dozen occasions, but the late-night parties and noisy visitors continue. Finally, the O'Reillys decide they have had enough, and they move out. The landlord then sues the O'Reillys, claiming they owe her 11 months' rent. Will the O'Reillys have to pay?

Can a tenant play a musical instrument without violating the rights of other tenants?

use and enjoy the property without being disturbed by the landlord or other tenants. Of course, there is always some noise involved in living in a building with other people. Nevertheless, each tenant should be able to live in relative peace.

Tenants have a right to quiet enjoyment even if it is not stated in the lease, and landlords have a duty to ensure that no tenant unreasonably disturbs the other people in the building. A tenant annoyed by noisy or otherwise bothersome neighbors should send a written complaint to the landlord and keep a copy of it.

Upkeep and Repairs

> *Landlord shall be under no liability to Tenant for any discontinuance of heat, hot water, or elevator service, and shall not be liable for damage to property of Tenant caused by rodents, rain, snow, defective plumbing, or any other source.* (Clause 11)

What is your state's law regarding repairs and the warranty of habitability?

Traditionally, landlords did not have a duty to maintain the premises or make repairs to a rented house or apartment. In the few places where this is still true, tenants have to make all repairs that are needed to keep the property in its original condition.

Clause 11 from the sample lease states that the tenant must continue to pay the rent whether or not the landlord provides a dwelling fit to live in. In some states, this provision is unenforceable. Today, most states require the landlord to keep the house or apartment in a condition fit to live in.

Many state courts and legislatures have said that a **warranty of habitability** is implied in every lease. This means that the landlord promises to provide a place fit for human habitation. This promise is said to exist whether or not it is written into the lease. Thus, if major repairs are needed—the furnace breaks down, the roof leaks, or the apartment is overrun by insects or rodents—the landlord has a duty to correct the problems.

PROBLEM 9

a. If you were a landlord, what repairs and maintenance would you expect the tenant to perform? Make a list and explain it.

b. If you were a tenant, what repairs and maintenance would you expect the landlord to perform? Make a list and explain it.

c. Role-play the following situation, with one person playing the tenant and another, the landlord.

The tenant has serious infestations of roaches and mice in his or her apartment. The tenant also feels that the walls should be repainted, because the children have made them dirty over the seven months that they have lived there. The tenant meets with the landlord to complain.

In performing the role-play, consider the following questions:

1. How should the tenant present his or her rights?
2. How should the landlord respond when the tenant complains?
3. Should the landlord agree to correct the problems?
4. Would it be better for the tenant to complain by writing a letter to the landlord?

Besides the warranty of habitability, many communities also have **housing codes**. These codes set minimum standards for repairs and living conditions within rental houses or apartments. Landlords are required to meet the standards of the housing code, and they may lose their license to rent if the standards are not maintained. Housing codes differ from area to area, but in most places, tenants have the right to call in a government housing inspector to examine their apartment for code violations.

Is there a housing code in your community? If so, what does it cover? Who enforces it?

Although most places hold landlords responsible for major repairs, remember that the landlord's duty to make repairs differs from place to place and from lease to lease. It is always best to have the respon-

Sample Housing Code

The following are examples of provisions included in a typical housing code.

Maintenance and Repair

- Floors and walls shall be free of holes, cracks, splinters, or peeling paint.
- Windows and doors shall be weatherproof, easily operable, free of broken glass, and equipped with workable locks.
- Stairs and walkways shall be in good repair, clean, and free of safety hazards or loose railings.
- Roof shall be free of leaks.

Cleanliness and Sanitation

- Each unit shall be generally free of rodents and insects. Common areas shall be free of dirt, litter, trash, water, or other unsanitary matter.

Use and Occupancy

- Each unit shall have a minimum of 120 square feet of livable floor space per occupant.
- Each bedroom shall have a minimum of 50 square feet of floor space per occupant.
- Each unit shall have a private bathroom.
- Each common area shall be accessible without going through another apartment.

Facilities and Utilities

- Sinks, lavatories, and bathing facilities shall be in working order.
- Every room shall have a minimum of two electrical outlets and no exposed wiring.
- Water, electricity, gas, heating, and sewer services shall be in good operating condition.
- Halls, stairways, and common areas shall be adequately lighted.
- The building shall be free of fire hazards and secure from intruders or uninvited visitors.

sibility for repairs spelled out in the lease. Also, remember that tenants have a duty to notify the landlord when repairs are needed. If someone is injured as a result of an unsafe or defective condition, the landlord cannot be held liable unless he or she knew or should have known that the condition existed.

What is the law in your community regarding the steps a landlord must take to evict a tenant accused of committing a crime on the rental premises? What steps must be taken if the tenant is in public housing?

Use of the Property

> *Tenant will use the premises for a dwelling and for no other purpose.* (Clause 3)

Tenants pay for the right to use a landlord's property. As a general rule, tenants may use the property only for the purposes stated in the

The Unsavory Visitors

Mr. and Mrs. Larkin were excited about the birth of their first child. On the day they returned home with the new baby, the Larkins' friends gathered at their apartment to greet them. The Larkins did not notice that two of their friends had some cocaine and took it into the back bedroom. However, their landlord, who was present for the occasion, did notice. A week later, the Larkins received a notice that they were being evicted for allowing drug use in their apartment.

PROBLEM 10

a. Does the law allow the Larkins to be evicted for what their friends did in their apartment? Should the law allow this?

b. Does the Larkins' ignorance of their friends' possession and use of cocaine affect your answer to Question a?

c. After the Larkins receive the landlord's notice that she intends to evict them, are there any steps they can take to prevent her from doing so?

d. Should the government assist private landlords in identifying possible drug users and sellers and in evicting them? What are the arguments for and against doing this?

Is the landlord or the tenant responsible for making these repairs?

lease. For example, if you rented a house as a residence, you would not be allowed to use it as a restaurant or a dry cleaning business.

Most leases contain clauses that permit eviction if the landlord reasonably believes that the tenants have committed crimes or allowed the commission of crimes on the rented premises. Even if the lease does not contain a clause banning criminal activity, the landlord may be able to have the tenants evicted. Judges frequently will enforce such requests from landlords.

A lease may specify the names, ages, and number of people who will live on the premises. Although having occasional guests will not violate such a lease, there can be problems if there is a change in the number of people permanently occupying the premises, as happens after the birth or adoption of a child.

Although tenants have a right to use the rental property, they also have a duty to take care of the property and return it to the landlord in the same general condition in which it was rented. Tenants generally are responsible for the upkeep of the premises, including routine cleaning and minor repairs. Major repairs and upkeep of common areas, such as apartment hallways, normally are the responsibility of the landlord. However, the landlord and tenant may make different arrangements if they mutually agree to do so.

Tenants are not responsible for damages that result from normal wear and tear or ordinary use of the property. For example, tenants are not liable for worn spots in the carpet caused by ordinary foot traffic. In contrast, damages caused by a tenant's misuse or neglect are known as **waste**. The landlord can force the tenant to pay for such repairs. Moreover, tenants have a duty to let the landlord know when major repairs are needed and to take reasonable steps to prevent unnecessary waste or damage.

Security Deposits

> *Tenant will pay a security deposit in the amount of $__________, which will be held by Landlord until expiration of this lease and refunded on the condition that said premises is returned in good condition, normal wear and tear excepted.* (Clause 9)

WHERE YOU LIVE

What is the law in your area regarding security deposits? Is there a limit on the amount that can be required? Does the landlord have to pay interest on the security deposit?

In most places, landlords have the right to ask for a **security deposit**. This deposit is an amount of money—usually one month's rent—that is kept by the landlord to ensure that the tenant takes care of the apartment or house and abides by the terms of the lease. If the tenant damages the landlord's property, the landlord may keep the security deposit (or a part of it) to pay for the damage. Also, if the tenant does not pay all the rent, the landlord may be able to keep the security deposit to cover the portion of the rent still owed.

Some states put a limit on the amount of the security deposit. Some also require landlords to pay tenants interest on the money and return it within a specified time after the end of the lease. When a landlord requires a security deposit, the tenant should always get a receipt and should keep it until the deposit is returned. The tenant may also ask that the money be placed in an interest-paying bank account.

Whether damages to the landlord's property are determined to result from normal wear and tear or from tenant neglect depends on all the facts. To protect yourself, make a list of all defects and damages that exist at the time you move in. Keep a copy of the list, and give another copy to the landlord.

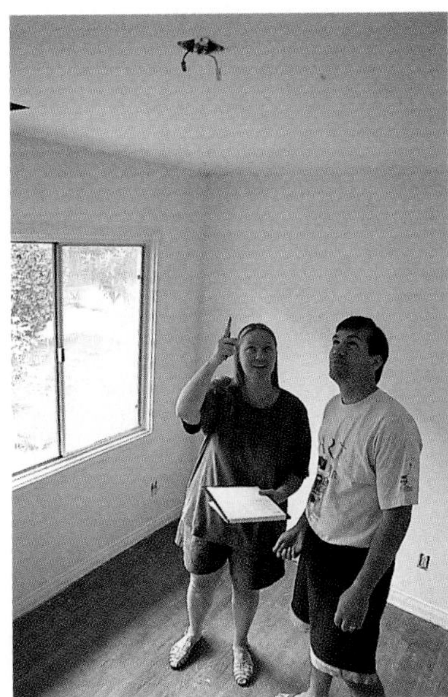

What can a landlord do if a ceiling lighting fixture is missing after a tenant moves out?

When moving out, you should inspect the apartment or house again and make a list of any damages. Sometimes an inspection with both the landlord and the tenant present can help avoid any disagreements. Bringing a friend along as a witness can also be helpful in case you have a dispute with the landlord. If there are no damages, the landlord should return your money. If the landlord withholds part or all of the money, you can demand a written statement itemizing the cost of any repairs. If the landlord keeps the security deposit and you disagree with the reasons for not returning it, you have a right to sue for the money in small claims court.

Finally, tenants generally have no right to make any changes in the structure or character of the property without the permission of the landlord. Even if the landlord agrees to changes or improvements, the improvement becomes the property of the landlord if it cannot be removed without serious damage to the premises. For example, if you build new cabinets in the kitchen, they become a **fixture** of the property and cannot be removed at the end of the lease. Fixtures are items attached to the property in such a way that their removal would damage the property. As noted, fixtures belong to the owner of the property.

PROBLEM 11

In each of the following situations, the tenant is moving out, and the landlord wants to keep part of the tenant's security deposit. Decide who should pay for the damages involved in each case.

a. The tenant moves without cleaning the apartment. The landlord is forced to remove trash, clean the walls and floors, wash the windows, and clean out the oven and refrigerator.

b. The toilet overflows in the apartment upstairs from that of the tenant moving out. The water leaks through the floor, ruining the ceiling and carpet in the apartment below.

Security Deposits

- Before signing the lease, inspect the apartment, and make a list of all defects or damages.
- Give a copy of the list to the landlord, and keep a copy for yourself.
- Always get a receipt.
- Ask to be paid interest on your money. In many places, you are entitled to this.
- Before moving out, inspect the apartment and make a list of all damages.
- Clean the apartment. Repair any damage for which you are responsible, and remove trash so you won't be charged for cleaning.
- Have a friend go through the apartment with you in case you later need a witness.

c. The tenant's pet stains the carpet. The lease allowed the tenant to have a pet.

d. The stove stops working, and the repairer says that it has simply worn out. The tenant is a cookware salesperson who has held many cooking demonstrations in the apartment.

e. The walls are faded and need repainting.

f. The roof leaks and ruins the hardwood floors. The tenant never told the landlord about the leak.

g. The tenants panel the recreation room of their apartment, build kitchen cabinets, and install drapes and two air-conditioning units. When they move, they remove all of their improvements and keep them.

Responsibility for Injuries in the Building

Landlord shall not be held liable for any injuries or damages to the Tenant or his or her guests, regardless of cause. (Clause 15)

Many standard form leases contain clauses stating that the tenant cannot hold the landlord responsible for damages or personal injuries that result from the landlord's negligence. For example, the lease may say that the tenant can't sue the landlord if the tenant is injured because of a broken guardrail that the landlord should have repaired.

This type of clause is known as a **waiver of tort liability**. Under this provision, the tenant agrees to **waive** (give up) the usual right to hold the landlord responsible for personal injuries. Most courts will not uphold such a clause. Therefore, if you or your guest is injured as a result of a landlord's negligence, you can usually recover damages no matter what the lease says. However, you are always better off getting a lease without this type of clause, because, if possible, you want to avoid going to court. Also, a few courts still enforce these clauses. (See also Chapter 3 for a discussion of these issues.)

Landlord Access and Inspection

Landlord shall have access to the premises at any time for the purpose of inspection, to make repairs the Landlord considers necessary, or to show the apartment to tenant applicants. (Clause 6)

The Dormitory Rape

One Saturday night, Audrie was asleep in her college dormitory room. Her roommate was away for the weekend. There was a guard at the front door to the dormitory, and all the students were supposed to use that door to enter and leave the building after dark. Earlier in the evening, someone had gone out a side door and failed to shut it securely, but no guard ever checked it that night. Audrie was awakened after midnight by a strange man in her room, who then raped and beat her. Although she later notified the police, they never found the man.

PROBLEM 12

a. Should the college have a responsibility to provide security for dormitory residents? If so, did the college provide adequate security in this instance?

b. What other measures might the college have taken to ensure the security of the dormitory residents?

Can tenants sue landlords for injuries or damage to property in your state? Will courts enforce a waiver of tort liability clause in the lease?

Most leases give landlords and their agents the right to enter the premises to make repairs, collect the rent, or enforce other provisions of the lease. This provision is called a **right of entry or access clause**. Taken literally, this provision would allow the landlord to enter your apartment any time, day or night, without your permission.

However, the law in almost every state requires that visits by the landlord be at a reasonable time. Moreover, without your permission, landlords do not have the right to enter your apartment or house simply to snoop around or check on your housekeeping.

Rules and Regulations

Tenant agrees to observe all such rules and regulations which the Landlord or his agents will make concerning the apartment building. (Clause 18)

Some leases require tenants to obey all present and future rules that landlords make concerning the apartment. In most cases these rules are quite reasonable, but in some cases they aren't. Typical examples include rules against having pets; rules against keeping bicycles or other items in the halls; and rules concerning visitors, cooking, storage, children, building security, and hanging pictures on the walls.

It is important to read all the rules and regulations before you move into a building. This is because you may lose your security deposit or be evicted for violating the apartment rules. If you are going to sign a lease that requires you to obey all rules—even those made in the future—it is best to have the lease state, "The tenant agrees to follow all reasonable rules and regulations."

PROBLEM 13

a. Suppose you own a three-bedroom house that you wish to rent. Make a list of all the rules and regulations you would want for your house.

b. Suppose you are a tenant seeking to rent the house in Question a. Which rules would you consider reasonable, and which would you consider unreasonable?

c. If tenants don't like some of the landlord's rules, what should they do?

Sublease of a House or Apartment

Tenant will not transfer or sublet the premises without the written consent of the Landlord. (Clause 5)

Clause 5 is a **sublease clause**. It requires you to obtain the landlord's permission before subleasing the apartment or house. A sublease takes place when the tenant allows someone else to live on the premises and pay all or part of the rent.

For example, suppose you sign a one-year lease on a small house. After six months, you find a larger house and want to move. If the landlord agrees, a sublease clause would allow you to rent the small house to someone else for the remainder of the lease. In a sublease situation, the original lease remains in effect, so if the new tenant fails to pay the rent, you are still responsible.

To avoid continued responsibility under the lease, a tenant can seek a **release**. If the landlord gives a release, the tenant is excused from all duties related to the apartment or house and the lease.

Landlords do not have to agree to tenants' requests to sublease. Therefore, you are better off with a lease that says, "The landlord agrees not to withhold consent unreasonably." This way, you would be able to sublease except when the landlord could give a good reason for refusing. Remember, even if your lease lets you sublet, you are still responsible for paying the rent to the landlord if the person to whom you sublet does not pay.

PROBLEM 14

a. Why do most leases require the tenant to get the landlord's permission before subleasing an apartment?

b. Assume the lease requires the tenant to get the landlord's permission before subletting. José, the tenant, leaves town and lets his friend William take over the lease, but William never pays the rent. Does José still owe the landlord the rent?

LANDLORD-TENANT PROBLEMS

Landlords and tenants don't always live up to their responsibilities. Even after a thorough inspection of the apartment or house and a careful reading of the lease, problems may arise. When either the landlord or the tenant fails to fulfill the conditions of the lease, there is a violation or breach of the lease. Some breaches of a lease are minor and easily corrected. Other breaches of a lease are more serious and may result in an end to the lease, eviction, or other court action.

If the tenant is at fault, the landlord has certain remedies that can be used to solve the problem. These include evicting the tenant or bringing a suit to correct the problem. If it is the landlord who causes the problem, tenants also have certain things they can do.

What Tenants Can Do When Things Go Wrong

Some tenants think that once they move into an apartment or house, there is not much they can do if things go wrong. Although this may once have been the case, in most states this is no longer true. Tenants now have many rights. When problems arise, tenants may take many actions:

- Complain to the landlord
- Complain to government agencies
- Organize a tenants' group

What can a tenant do if a lamp doesn't work because of an electrical problem?

- Withhold rent
- Sue the landlord
- Move out

Complaining to the Landlord If you have a repair problem in your apartment or house, the first thing you should do is tell the landlord, rental agent, or building manager. Landlords usually have a duty to make repairs, but only if a tenant has notified them of the need to do so. After making your oral complaint, write a letter to the landlord, again stating what repairs need to be made. Keep a copy of the letter.

Complaining to Government Agencies Most local governments have agencies to handle tenant complaints and housing problems. Most communities also have housing codes that set minimum standards for repairs, services, and living conditions in an apartment or rental house. Tenants may report unsafe or unsanitary conditions to the agency that enforces the housing code.

When you complain to the government agency that enforces the housing code, request a housing inspection. Get the name of the inspector who comes, and request a copy of the report. If the inspector finds code violations in the rental unit, the landlord usually will be ordered to correct them. Landlords who fail to make ordered repairs usually can be fined or have their licenses to rent revoked. In extreme cases, the authorities might order a building vacated and have it demolished.

Tenant Organizing If conditions in one tenant's apartment are bad, similar conditions may exist in apartments throughout the building. When this is the case, tenants might consider forming an organization to seek solutions to their common problems. For assistance, a tenants' organization can contact the local legal aid office.

Is there an agency in your area that handles tenant complaints? Does it enforce a housing code? If so, how effective is the agency?

Rent Withholding States that recognize the warranty of habitability also give tenants the right to withhold their rent if the landlord won't make repairs. This means not paying part or all of the rent until the landlord makes certain repairs or meets other tenant demands. Obviously, if several tenants in a building have similar problems and withhold rent as a group, this will have an economic effect on the landlord and is more likely to bring results.

Refusing to pay rent because of needed repairs is sometimes referred to as a rent strike. *Some states allow tenants to withhold rent when needed repairs are not made by the landlord. However, this is a serious step that could lead to eviction, so tenants should always talk with a lawyer before withholding rent.*

Another type of rent withholding may take place in states where the law allows tenants to make repairs themselves and then deduct the bill from the rent. Laws vary on when and how this may be done, but generally it is permitted only if the landlord has been given adequate notice of the repairs and has not made them. In most cases, tenants cannot withhold rent unless the repairs are of a serious nature, and most places restrict the amount that can be withheld.

Tenants who consider withholding rent should follow certain basic procedures. First, they should have a housing inspector check the building for code violations. Second, they should send the landlord a letter by registered mail announcing that they intend to withhold rent unless repairs are made by a certain date. Third, if repairs are not made by the date set, the rent money should be placed in a special, separate bank account called an **escrow** account. In some states, the rent must be paid directly to the court.

If rent is being withheld, the landlord may decide to give in or may try to evict the tenant for not paying the rent. If the landlord tries to evict the tenant, the tenant can go to court and tell the judge about the needed repairs. The housing inspector's report, copies of letters to the landlord, and photographs of the apartment or house will all help to prove the tenant's case. Once again, remember that rent withholding is illegal in some states, so be sure to check your state law before taking this action.

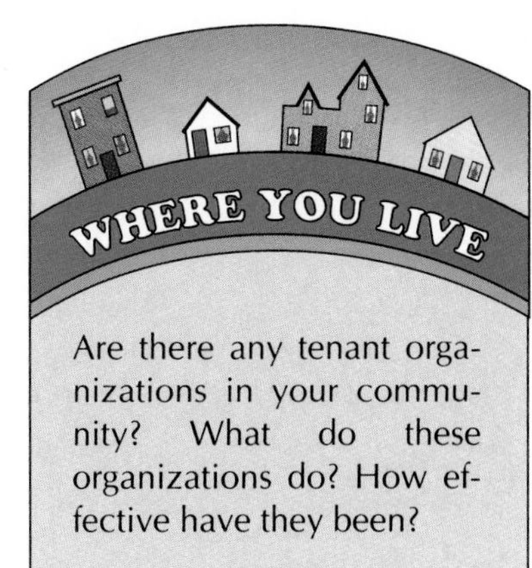

Are there any tenant organizations in your community? What do these organizations do? How effective have they been?

Does the law in your community allow tenants to make repairs and deduct the cost from rent?

PROBLEM 15

The following law is proposed in your state: "Tenants may withhold rent whenever the landlord does not make repairs within two weeks of being notified that such repairs are needed."

a. Take a landlord's point of view, and list all the arguments against the law.

b. Take a tenant's point of view, and list all the arguments in favor of the law.

c. If you were a member of the state legislature, would you vote for or against this law? Why? Would you change the law in any way? If so, how?

Suing the Landlord In most places, if the landlord breaks the lease, the tenant may sue the landlord in court. In this kind of lawsuit, the tenant may ask the court to order that repairs be made or that part of rent previously paid to the landlord be returned to the tenant. If tenants have made repairs themselves, it may also be possible to ask the court to order the landlord to pay them back. This kind of case may be costly in time and money. However, most places have small claims courts or landlord-tenant commissions that make the process easier and less expensive.

Moving Out A final remedy available to tenants is moving out. When a tenant ignores the lease and moves out, this is known as **abandonment**. If this happens, the landlord may sue for the remainder of the rent owed under the lease.

In extreme cases, however, tenants may legally break the lease and move without the landlord's permission. **Constructive eviction** occurs when the property is so run-down that it is unlivable, or when the landlord has denied the tenant his or her right to quiet enjoyment. Most states consider constructive eviction a valid reason for abandonment. A few do not, however, so be sure to check your state law and talk with a lawyer before taking this action.

PROBLEM 16

Mr. and Mrs. Walker rented a one-bedroom apartment for $250 a month from Mr. Martinez. It was run-down, but they couldn't find anything else for the price. Two weeks after they moved in, the heat went out on a cold night, and the Walkers were forced to stay with relatives for several days. The Walkers also discovered that the roof leaked when it rained, the apartment was overrun by roaches, and the toilet continually overflowed.

a. If you were the Walkers, what would you do? Which of the possible tenant actions would provide the best solution for their problem? Why?

b. If you were the landlord, what would you do if the Walkers took each of the possible actions listed in this section?

c. Role-play a telephone call from the Walkers to Mr. Martinez.

d. Assume that the Walkers withheld one month's rent, and the landlord brought the case to court. If you were the judge, what would you do?

What Landlords Can Do When Things Go Wrong

While tenants sometimes have problems with landlords, there are also times when tenants don't live up to their responsibilities. If a tenant breaks apartment rules or fails to fulfill conditions in the lease, the landlord has a number of remedies. These include ending the lease and eviction through court action.

Ending the Lease Landlords and tenants sometimes come into conflict at the end of a lease. In most places, unless there is a clause that automatically continues the lease, or the landlord agrees to a new lease, the tenant must move out when the term of the lease is over. If a tenant refuses to move at the end of the lease, the landlord has three choices. First, the landlord can go to court and ask to have the tenant evicted. That is, the landlord can take legal action to have the tenant forced off the property. Second, the landlord can let the tenant stay in the apartment as a **holdover tenant**. In many states, if a tenant stays on after the lease is over, the landlord has the right to hold the tenant to a new lease identical to the one just ended. Third, a tenant who stays on beyond the end of the lease becomes a tenant at will in some states. This means that either the landlord or the tenant can end the lease with whatever notice the law requires—typically, 30 days.

Tenants who are moving should always give the landlord adequate notice in a letter and should keep a copy. If there is a month-to-month lease, the landlord should be notified that the tenant intends to move 30 days before the rent is next due. If the lease is for a fixed period, such as one year, the notice should be given at least 30 days before the end of the term.

A common problem arises when a tenant seeks to leave before the end of the lease. If this happens, it is always best to talk with the landlord and try to get a release. A landlord and tenant can always end a lease by mutual agreement, and in many cases this is what occurs.

A tenant who moves out before the end of a lease is still responsible for the rent owed. The landlord may keep any security deposit and also sue the tenant for all rent still owed until the end of the lease.

One way the tenant can be released from the lease is by subletting to another tenant. Usually this can only be done with the landlord's permission. In most places, if a tenant moves out before the lease is over, the landlord is required to try to rent to someone else. The rent the original tenant owes is then reduced by the rent the landlord receives from a new tenant.

PROBLEM 17

a. Wendy signs a two-year lease for $200 a month. After six months, she decides to get married and wants to break the lease. How much rent does she still owe? Is there anything she can do to break the lease?

Is there a landlord-tenant court in your community? If so, where is it located, and what procedures does it follow? Is there a legal aid or legal services office in your area that represents tenants?

b. Wu signs a one-year lease at $300 a month for an apartment near his college. Before he moves in, he gives the landlord a $300 security deposit. After six months, he decides to move back to campus and just packs up and leaves. What can the landlord do?

Eviction Eviction is the legal process of having a tenant removed from the property. Many situations give a landlord the right to evict a tenant. The most common reason for eviction is a tenant's failure to pay the rent. However, any serious breach of the lease can give the landlord cause for eviction.

A landlord may not physically throw a tenant out but must usually file a case in court. In some places, this occurs in the regular civil court system. In others, evictions are handled by special housing courts or landlord-tenant commissions.

If you receive a court notice that your landlord intends to evict you, respond to it promptly. Be sure to show up at your eviction hearing. You may have a defense to the landlord's claim. If you do not show up, the court may enter a judgment in favor of the landlord. This may lead to your eviction. In many places, landlord-tenant cases are heard within a few days or weeks after they are filed. You also should speak to your landlord, since the two of you may be able to resolve your problems without going to court.

Landlords sometimes try to evict tenants who complain or otherwise organize against the landlord. Called **retaliatory eviction**, this action is illegal in most states.

What is the law in your state regarding retaliatory evictions?

Edwards v. Cooper

Ms. Edwards rented a house from Mr. Cooper on a month-to-month basis. Shortly after moving in, she called the city housing inspector and reported a number of unsanitary conditions. When an inspector came in to investigate, he found more than 40 housing code violations. The landlord was ordered to correct them.

Instead of making the repairs, Mr. Cooper notified Ms. Edwards that he was ending the lease and that she must move within 30 days. She went to court, claiming that she was being evicted as revenge for her report of the code violations. She said that the First Amendment to the U.S. Constitution gives citizens the right to petition the government and that Mr. Cooper was interfering with this right.

Mr. Cooper claimed his actions were legal. He said a month-to-month lease can be legally ended merely by giving the tenant a proper 30 days' notice, without stating any reasons for the action.

PROBLEM 18

a. What happened in this case? Why did Mr. Cooper try to evict Ms. Edwards?

b. Do you think Mr. Cooper's action is legal or illegal? Explain.

c. What rights and interests are in conflict in this case?

d. Should landlords be able to evict tenants in cases like this? List all the arguments in favor of Mr. Cooper and all those in favor of Ms. Edwards.

e. If tenants have housing code violations or other problems in their apartment or house, what can they do?

HOUSING FOR LOW- AND MODERATE-INCOME PEOPLE

A 1988 report found that nearly one-half of low-income families in the United States paid more than 50% of their income for rent. At the same time, the number of low-cost housing units available has been decreasing, and a nationwide critical housing shortage is predicted to occur by the year 2003. The lack of affordable housing in many communities has resulted in homelessness for many people.

A number of federal, state, and local government programs have been designed to provide opportunities for low-income people to rent apartments or houses. These programs include the provision of government-owned public housing, funds for rent subsidies to landlords or directly to tenants, and tax benefits or other incentives to owners or developers of housing for low-income people.

Many people are critical of the government's involvement in housing assistance to low-income people. Some note that crime rates often are higher in neighborhoods containing public housing. Low-income people, they argue, don't take proper care of their housing and simply create their own problems. Taxpayers, they say, should not have to pay for those problems.

If these buildings were all public housing for low income people, what problems would you foresee occurring?

Other people argue that it is often local governments that don't take proper care of low-income housing. People with limited incomes, they point out, are unable to make costly repairs. Some studies have shown that attractive, well-maintained public housing is less likely to be vandalized than run-down housing. Community, religious, and other public interest groups, as well as some local governments, are experimenting with new ways of providing low-income people with the means of owning and maintaining their own housing. Such projects, many suggest, will result in a higher quality of living for the entire community.

To obtain information about government housing assistance in your community, go to your local housing, social welfare, or human resources agency. Agency personnel can give advice on where and how to apply for housing aid. Free counseling and advice on housing is also provided by local offices of the U.S. Department of Housing and Urban Development.

Government agencies have detailed rules—based primarily on family income—for determining who is eligible for government-sponsored housing aid. As noted above, even people who qualify may not be able to acquire housing and will find themselves on a waiting list. If a housing agency decides that you do not meet the qualifications, you may be able to appeal that decision. You should first ask the agency for a personal interview or hearing to discuss your situation. If that is unsuccessful, contact a legal aid office for help in making a further appeal.

In recent years it has become more and more difficult for people to purchase homes. Due to higher housing prices and high interest rates, many people have been turned down for loans. Federal, state, and local governments have programs to encourage lenders to make loans to first-time buyers and others who might not otherwise qualify. These programs often insure the loans so that if the purchasers cannot make the payments, the government will do so for them. The loans are issued by the Federal Housing Administration (FHA) and are called *FHA-insured loans*. At the end of 1988, FHA insurance in force totaled about $296 billion for 6.5 million homeowners. FHA loans often permit smaller down payments, thus allowing some people who do not have cash for a standard-sized down payment to purchase their own homes.

What types of housing for low-income people exist in your community? Where are the housing units located? What efforts, if any, are made in your community to increase the supply of low-income housing? Are the efforts sufficient to meet the need?

PROBLEM 19

Assume that you are in charge of a program to expand housing for the poor in a middle-sized city. Four proposals have been made:

1. Private landlords would receive direct payments of money each month to subsidize a portion of the rent for low-income tenants.
2. Tenants would receive a government-issued voucher each month for a sum of money they could give to any landlord to help pay the rent.
3. Landlords would receive funds to rehabilitate run-down buildings if they promised to lease to low-income tenants at reduced rents.
4. Low-income tenants would be given funds to assist in buying and managing buildings that are presently owned by private landlords.

a. What are the advantages and disadvantages of each proposal? Which of the proposals do you feel would best meet the needs of low-income tenants? Why?

b. Should the government increase funding for rental housing for the poor, or should it devote most of its efforts to helping middle-class people buy homes?

One of the biggest problems with public housing is where to locate it. Many people do not want it in their neighborhoods. Major battles over this issue are often waged before local legislatures and administrative agencies or in the courts.

The Town Divided Against Itself

A town is divided by a major road. Whites traditionally have lived east of the road, while African Americans and Hispanic Americans have lived to the west. More than 90% of the public housing in the town lies west of the road.

Many of the town's eastern residents moved there to escape the drugs and poverty they had encountered in a larger city nearby. They fear that having public housing projects in their part of town would create the same problems with drugs and crime they wanted to leave behind.

However, the U.S. Department of Justice accused the town of intentionally promoting racial discrimination in its schools by refusing to build low-income housing in white neighborhoods. It sued the town, claiming that it used its housing policies to segregate its neighborhood schools along racial lines.

PROBLEM 20

a. How could placing public housing projects in particular neighborhoods lead to racial segregation of the schools?

b. Should a city have the legal right to confine public housing to particular neighborhoods? Give your reasons.

c. Assume that you are a member of the town council. The federal court has ruled that your town is guilty of racial discrimination for placing most of its public housing west of the road. What actions should the town council now take?

d. Assume that you are the judge in this case and have decided that the town's placement of public housing has racially segregated the schools. What orders could you give the town to help solve this problem?

THE PROBLEM OF HOMELESSNESS

Homelessness means lack of a fixed residence. The homeless live in public or private shelters, in emergency temporary housing (arranged by social service agencies), and in abandoned buildings, as well as on the street, in parks, in transportation terminals (bus stations, subway stations, and so on), and in automobiles. The exact number of homeless people in America is not known. Estimates range from 500,000 to three million. What is known is that the number of homeless people has increased greatly in recent years.

According to a 1988 survey by the U.S. Department of Housing and Urban Development, the largest group of homeless people is made up of single males (45%). Approximately one-third (34%) of the homeless are mentally ill, and one-fifth (21%) are victims of domestic violence. Most surveys indicate that families make up the fastest-growing group of homeless people.

In addition to those officially homeless according to various surveys, there are also many "hidden" homeless people. These people shift from one dwelling to another, moving in temporarily with friends or family and only occasionally visiting shelters.

Most housing experts agree that the leading cause of homelessness is the lack of affordable housing. There has been a reduction in available housing for both low-income families and single people. Other factors cited as contributing to the problem are lack of job opportunities, increasing rents and evictions, cutbacks in federal housing and other poverty programs, greater drug use, and the release of many people from mental hospitals under a recent policy of treating more of the mentally ill in the community. (This policy is called **deinstitutionalization.**)

Is homelessness a serious problem in your community? How many single individuals and how many people in families are estimated to be homeless? What emergency shelters exist to help these people? Are there programs to help the homeless obtain permanent housing? What are the rules to determine who is eligible for these programs?

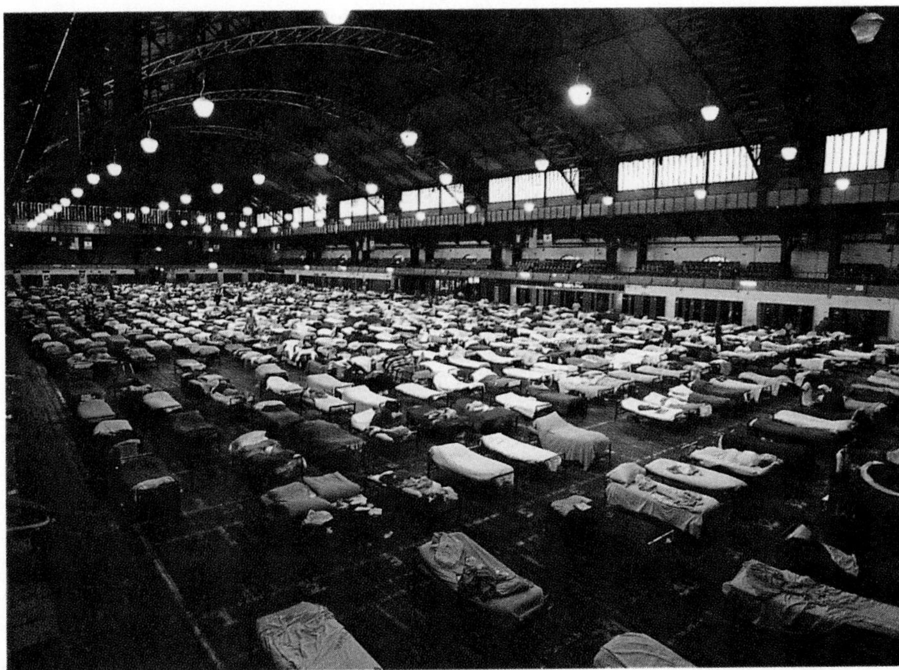

What housing, if any, should the government be required to provide for homeless people?

What are the causes of homelessness in the United States?

Besides the lack of adequate shelter, homeless people have many other problems. Some need treatment for their mental illness or addiction to drugs or alcohol. Many find it difficult to receive government benefits or send their children to school because they lack a permanent address. Children who do attend school often find themselves ridiculed by other children because they live in a shelter. Many of the homeless are in need of food, medical care, education, and job assistance.

There are an estimated half million homeless children nationally. Social services agencies report that teenagers are the most difficult group to help. Many local governments have failed to provide adequate support for runaway and poor teenagers. The difficulty lies in placing the teenagers; often there are insufficient foster care placements for them. Frequently, teenagers are rotated through the shelter system, or they are left to survive on the streets.

The federal government, as well as some state and local governments, has been pressured by advocates for the homeless and others to do more to address these problems. More shelters have been set up in some communities, and public and private efforts have increased. Congress passed laws that gave the federal Department of Housing and Urban Development funds for cities to build emergency shelters and increase social services. The *Stewart B. McKinney Homeless Assistance Act of 1987* has provided some funding for shelters, permanent housing, job training programs, education, and health care. Some people criticize the amount of funding as inadequate to meet the enormous need.

The *McKinney Act* also required the federal government to turn over surplus (that is, unused) government property for use by the homeless. Some people criticize the government for not moving faster to implement this provision or to renovate abandoned buildings that exist in many cities. Others say it is improper for the federal government to try to solve the homeless problem. They argue that this should be addressed either by state or local government or by private charities. Still others argue that being homeless is the individual's own responsibility and that there are jobs available for those willing to work.

PROBLEM 21

Thomas, who has been the night manager at a motel for the past five years, has a drinking problem. This contributed to difficulties in his marriage, which ended a year ago in divorce. The motel closed due to lack of business, and Thomas lost his job. Thomas, who had lived at the motel since his divorce, is now homeless and unable to make car or child support payments. His relatives refuse to help, because they blame him for the failure of his marriage. He begins to drink more and live on the street, asking passersby for money.

a. Why is Thomas living on the street? Is it his fault that he does not have a home? What could he have done to prevent this from occurring?

b. If you were passing Thomas and he asked you for money, would you give any to him? Why or why not? Should it be against the law for Thomas to ask passersby for money? Explain your answer.

c. Should Thomas be allowed to spend the night on sidewalks, streets, or beaches, or in parks, subway and bus stations, or other public places?

d. Should the government take some action to help Thomas? If so, what should it do? If not, why not?

An important legal issue that has risen relating to the homeless is whether there is, or should be, a "right to shelter" for all Americans. Although courts have not ruled that the U.S. Constitution includes this right, a few state constitutions and state laws have been interpreted to guarantee it. Advocates for the homeless would like to see the right to shelter adopted in more places. Opponents, however, do not see this as the proper role for government.

The Homeless Family

Stanley and Nora Johnson and their two children lost their apartment when Stanley became ill and they were not able to pay the rent. After spending several nights sleeping at various friends' and relatives' homes, they went to the city's emergency shelter. Workers at the shelter told them that they had no room for a family, just space for single men. Following conversations with several government social workers, the Johnsons received a voucher to pay for the rental of an apartment or hotel room. After several days of searching, all they found was an unfurnished room. They did not have any chairs or a bed on which they or their children could sleep.

The Johnsons and several other families in similar situations have sued the city. They claim that under their state's constitution, they are entitled to adequate shelter. A room without a bed, they say, is not adequate shelter. The state's constitution reads:

The aid, care, and support of the needy are public concerns and shall be provided by the state and by each of its municipalities, and in such manner and by such means as the legislature may from time to time determine.

The Johnsons are asking the court to issue an order requiring the city to provide adequate shelter to all persons needing it, including families.

PROBLEM 22

a. What arguments can you make on the Johnsons' behalf? On behalf of the city?

b. Assume that you are the judge in this case. Will you grant the Johnsons the order? Give your reasons.

c. Assume that you decide to grant the Johnsons' request. What, specifically, will you order the city to do?

d. Assume that a "right to adequate shelter" amendment to the U.S. Constitution has been proposed. What are the arguments for and against such an amendment? Do you support this amendment? Explain.

e. Would establishing a "right to adequate shelter" clause in the Constitution solve the problem of providing long-term housing to homeless people? What are possible solutions to this problem? Which of the solutions would be most successful? Why?

ZONING

In the United States, zoning is the principal type of land-use regulation. It is done by the local government, which derives the legal authority to zone from the powers of the state. Zoning may be used to promote health, safety, morals, or the general welfare of the community.

Squatters in South Africa

For over 40 years, the South African government has been dominated by white Africans chosen through elections in which black Africans were not allowed to vote. This government designated where people of various races were allowed to live, through a system known as apartheid. Under this system, white people, who make up less than 15% of the population, own 87% of the land; black people, who make up over 85% of the population, are made to live on about 13% of the land.

Many black people cannot find jobs near their designated living areas. Consequently, many of them live in squatter camps of makeshift houses that are made from corrugated iron, cardboard, or whatever material they can find. Millions of people lack formal housing.

In recent years, many black squatters have decided to camp on unused land near some nice suburbs where white people live. The white people complain that these camps lower their property values, create unsanitary conditions (many have no running water or toilets), and increase the crime rate. They have asked the government to move the squatters elsewhere.

PROBLEM 23

a. Should the government force the squatters to move out? If so, to what type of area should they be relocated? Would it be better to move the squatters into the cities, where they might have to live on the streets or in shelters, or should they be moved to other unoccupied rural areas?

b. If the squatters are allowed to stay, what should the government do regarding their housing, living conditions, and schools? How should any improvements be paid for?

c. Would your answers to the above questions change if the squatters had occupied farmland owned by wealthy white farmers?

Assume the whites had worked hard to farm the land but had also benefitted over the years through laws passed by the white government. (For example, they had received subsidies for growing certain crops.)

d. Is the situation in South Africa similar to any in American history regarding Native Americans, African Americans, or other groups? What are the similarities and differences? How has the U.S. government acted toward these people? Should it have acted differently?

e. Does this type of problem exist in other countries? If so, how have these countries addressed the problem?

In use zoning, perhaps the most important type of zoning, the community is divided into districts in which only certain uses are permitted. For example, residential apartments may not be allowed in an area zoned for factories.

Zoning can be used to exclude certain groups and to prevent property from being used in specific ways in a given part of a community.

Should zoning allow this company to be located in this area?

For example, the residents might pass a zoning law to keep public housing developments out of their neighborhood because they do not want their property values to go down. However, this might exclude people who earn lower incomes or belong to certain racial or ethnic groups from living in that neighborhood.

To challenge a zoning law effectively, one must show that the law has a negative impact on certain groups (such as minorities) or restricts the exercise of a constitutional right (such as freedom of religion). Otherwise, if the zoning law can be shown to be reasonably related to protection of the general welfare, it will be considered valid.

PROBLEM 24

Discuss whether the following laws or policies would be a proper use of the government's zoning authority.

a. A law forbids more than four unrelated adults from living together in a residential university neighborhood.

b. A tenants' group lobbies for legislation that would prevent the city from constructing emergency homeless shelters near the tenants' high-rent apartment buildings.

c. Because of health concerns, the residents of a town want to close down an AIDS hospice in a residential neighborhood.

d. A city zoning law prohibits churches from operating in residential neighborhoods.

Chapter 7

Individual Rights and Liberties

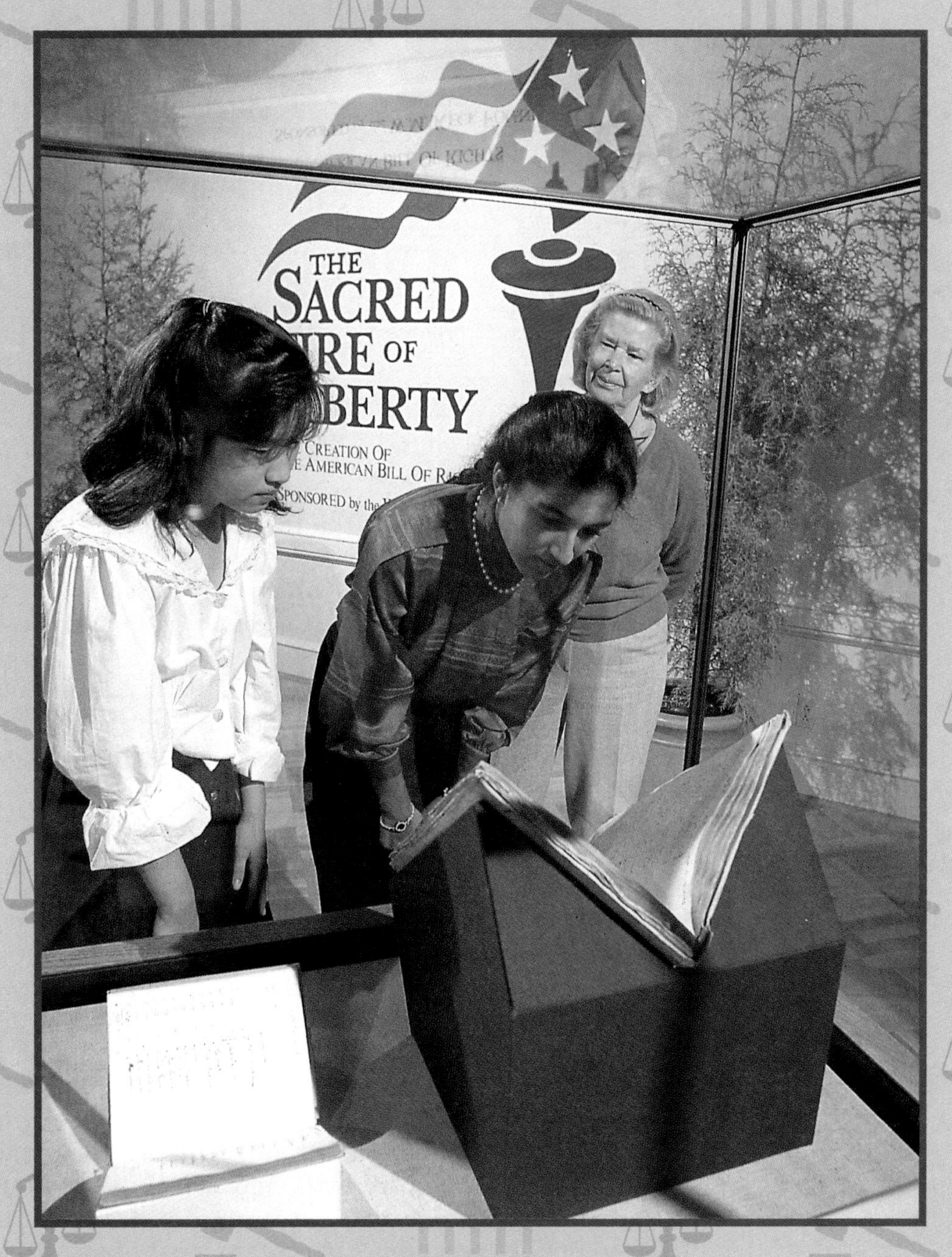

By what process can the United States Constitution be amended?

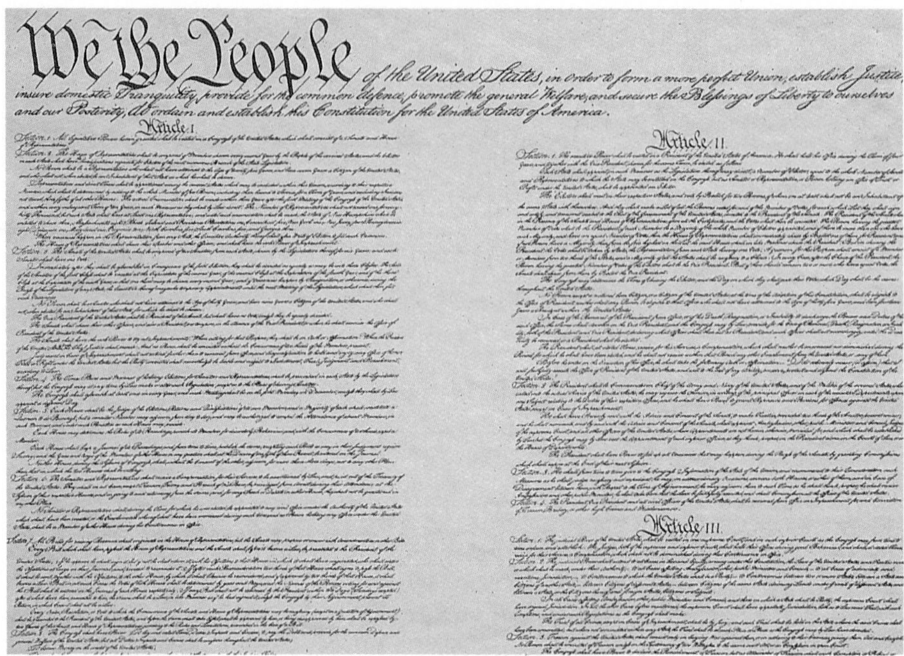
We the People of the United States, in order to form a more perfect Union, establish Justice, insure domestic Tranquility, provide for the common defence, promote the general Welfare, and secure the Blessings of Liberty to ourselves and our Posterity, do ordain and establish this Constitution for the United States of America.

Article I

Article II

Article III

The U.S. Constitution is the framework of our government. It establishes the executive, legislative, and judicial branches. It is also the supreme law of the land, which all public officials are bound by oath to enforce. Moreover, the Constitution guarantees each American certain basic rights.

One remarkable feature of our Constitution is its endurance. It is the oldest written national constitution in use in the world. Another remarkable feature of the Constitution is its ability to adapt itself to changing conditions.

The founders of our nation knew that the Constitution might have to be changed. Therefore, they provided two methods of proposing **amendments** (additions to the Constitution): by a two-thirds vote of both houses of Congress or by a national convention called by Congress at the request of the legislatures in two-thirds of the states. Once proposed, an amendment does not take effect unless it is ratified either by the legislatures in three-fourths of the states or by special ratifying conventions in three-fourths of the states.

The original Constitution, adopted in 1787, contained only a few provisions guaranteeing individual rights. However, citizens pressured their leaders to add a Bill of Rights. In response, the first 10 amendments were adopted by Congress in 1791 and quickly ratified by the states.

These first 10 amendments contain most of our basic rights. The First Amendment protects the freedoms of religion, speech, press, assembly, and petition. The Second Amendment protects the right of the people to bear arms. The Third Amendment protects against the quartering of soldiers in private homes, and the Fourth Amendment protects against unreasonable searches and seizures.

The Fifth Amendment provides a right to due process of law and gives rights to accused people, including protection against self-incrimination. The Sixth Amendment provides the rights to a lawyer, an impartial jury, and a speedy trial in criminal cases.

The Seventh Amendment provides for jury trials in civil cases. The Eighth Amendment bars cruel and unusual punishment and excessive bail or fines. The Ninth Amendment declares that the rights spelled out in the Constitution are not all the rights that people have. Finally, the 10th Amendment reserves to the states and the people any powers not belonging to the federal government. (The full text of all 27 amendments can be found in Appendix A.)

The Bill of Rights was designed to protect Americans against the power of the *federal* government. Nothing in the Constitution specifically requires *state* governments to abide by the Bill of Rights. But in interpreting the 14th Amendment, passed after the Civil War, the Supreme Court has extended most Bill of Rights protections to the states.

In addition to the Bill of Rights, later amendments provide other important rights. The 13th Amendment forbids slavery and outlaws involuntary servitude, except as a punishment for crime. The 14th Amendment requires equal protection of the laws for all citizens. It also provides that no state can deprive any citizen of "life, liberty, or property without due process of law."

Several amendments protect and broaden the right to vote. The 15th Amendment forbids denying the right to vote based on race or color. The 19th Amendment gives women the right to vote. The 24th Amendment gives citizens of Washington, D.C., the right to vote in presidential elections, and the 26th Amendment gives all people 18 years of age or older the right to vote.

PROBLEM 1

a. Do we have any important rights not listed in the Bill of Rights? If so, what are they? Make a list.

b. Over the years, a number of new constitutional amendments have been suggested or proposed. Do you think we need any new amendments to the Constitution? If so, what amendments do you propose, and why?

c. The following are some of our most basic and important rights. Based on your opinion, rank these rights in order from the most important to the least important. Explain your rankings.

1. Right to privacy
2. Right to a jury trial
3. Right to freedom of religion
4. Right to travel freely
5. Right to freedom of speech
6. Right to be free from self-incrimination
7. Right to bear arms
8. Right to freedom of the press
9. Right to be free from cruel and unusual punishment
10. Right to legal counsel
11. Right to assemble peacefully
12. Right to vote

To understand constitutional law, you should keep three basic ideas in mind. First, the rights guaranteed in the Constitution are not, and cannot be, absolute. The totally free exercise of certain rights would, in some instances, restrict the rights of others. The courts have designed several "tests" to determine how cases should be decided. These tests are needed because the language of the Constitution is typically brief and often written in general terms. The words are not self-explanatory.

Why does the Constitution protect a citizen's right to boycott?

In this chapter you will study many of the tests developed by the justices of the U.S. Supreme Court. These tests are not like those you have taken in school. Instead, they are rules that the Supreme Court requires courts to use to analyze similar issues that arise in later cases.

For example, suppose someone, as a joke, yells "Fire!" in a crowded theater. The exact words protecting freedom of speech are: "Congress shall make no law . . . abridging the freedom of speech . . ." Do these words adequately explain whether the police can arrest the person for shouting "Fire!" falsely?

To analyze our "Fire!" in a crowded theater case, the courts might use the *balancing test*. This means they would weigh the danger to the public of shouting "Fire!" falsely in a crowded theater against the benefit of an individual's right to freedom of speech. In balancing one interest against the other, a court would probably decide that protection of the public is more important and restrict the speech of the person yelling "Fire!" We know this from analyzing the case using the balancing test, but we might not have been able to determine it simply from reading the language of the First Amendment.

The second idea basic to understanding constitutional law is that the Constitution usually prohibits Congress or the states from taking away basic rights. Although the Constitution protects citizens from certain actions by the government, its protection usually does not extend to situations that are purely private in nature. This means that actions by private citizens, businesses, or organizations are generally not covered by the Constitution. For example, the Fourth Amendment protects against unreasonable searches and seizures by the government. It does not protect against searches and seizures by private individuals. Therefore, if a neighbor comes into your house and seizes your television, this act does *not* violate the Constitution. It may, however, constitute the crime of larceny. As you will see later in this chapter, many private actions, though not unconstitutional, have been made unlawful by congressional action.

Third, remember that enforcing your rights can be time-consuming and expensive. Before trying to enforce a right, you should be aware of the time and money involved. You should then weigh these costs against the importance of the right. However, remember that you can do many things to protect your rights. Therefore, if you think you are correct, don't give up.

This chapter focuses on freedom of speech and expression; freedom of the press; freedom of association; freedom of assembly; freedom of religion; and the rights to privacy, due process, and equal protection. Because of the importance of the U.S. Constitution, we sometimes assume that it contains all our rights. However, many basic rights are also protected by state constitutions, as well as by laws passed by the U.S. Congress and state and local legislatures.

The U.S. Constitution does provide a so-called constitutional floor. The government—federal, state, or local—cannot take away the basic rights protected by the federal Constitution. However, governments can grant citizens greater rights than those found in the U.S. Constitution. Federal courts, for example, have not interpreted the Constitution's equal protection clause to provide homosexuals with the same degree of protection from discrimination by state laws as African Americans. Some state and local governments, however, have laws and regulations forbidding discrimination based on sexual orientation. They are protecting more rights than those found in the U.S. Constitution.

The individual rights discussed in this chapter can also be called human rights. The world community has adopted a "Universal Declaration of Human Rights," as well as a number of covenants and other international documents whereby countries promise to work to protect these rights. Most of the human rights included in the U.S. Bill of Rights can be classified as political or civil rights. However, there are other rights, classified as social and economic rights, which are not included in the U.S. Constitution. These include the right to

Can this woman publicly express an opinion that criticizes the local government?

an adequate standard of living, housing, adequate health care, and education.

Some people criticize the United States for being a leader in political and civil rights while ignoring the need for social and economic rights. Others say that such rights are not enforceable and that the government can attempt to provide them, but should make them goals rather than enforceable rights.

The final section of this chapter deals with rights and responsibilities in the workplace. The federal Constitution has a limited effect in the workplace, because most employees work for private employers and not for the government. However, state and federal lawmakers have passed many important laws that spell out rights and responsibilities of employers and employees.

PROBLEM 2

a. What is meant by the statement, "Rights are not absolute"? Give an example of a right that is not absolute, and explain why this is so.

b. How does the U.S. Supreme Court use tests? What test does the Court use when determining whether the state can use a confession obtained by police from an accused person?

c. Name three different sources for information about specific rights in your state.

d. Do you think the United States emphasizes political and civil rights too much? Should it put more emphasis on social and economic rights?

FREEDOM OF SPEECH

Congress shall make no law . . . abridging the freedom of speech, or of the press; or the right of the people peaceably to assemble, and to petition the Government for a redress of grievances.

—First Amendment

Freedom of speech guarantees the right to communicate information and ideas. It protects all forms of communication: speeches, books, art, newspapers, television, radio, and other media. The Constitution protects not only the person *making* the communication but also the person *receiving* it. Therefore, the First Amendment includes a right to hear, see, read, and in general be exposed to different points of view.

How does the First Amendment protect people who hold and express opinions that are unpopular with the majority?

Freedom of speech is not absolute and was not intended to be. However, the expression of an opinion or point of view is usually protected under the First Amendment, even if most people disagree with the speaker's message. Remember that the First Amendment was designed to ensure a free marketplace of ideas—even unpopular ideas. Freedom of speech protects everyone, even people who criticize the government or express unconventional views.

The First Amendment enables citizens to express and obtain a diversity of opinions. It helps us make political decisions and communicate these to our government. In short, the First Amendment is the heart of an open, democratic society.

Conflicts involving freedom of expression are among the most difficult ones that courts are asked to resolve. Free speech cases frequently involve a clash of fundamental values. For example, how should the law respond to a speaker who makes an unpopular statement to which the listeners react violently? Should police arrest the speaker or try to control the crowd? Courts must balance the need for peace and public order against the fundamental right to express one's point of view.

PROBLEM 3

a. A Supreme Court justice once wrote that the most important value of free expression is "not free thought for those who agree with us, but freedom for the thought we hate." What did the justice mean by this? Do you agree or disagree?

b. Can you think of any public statements or expressions of public opinion that made you angry? How did you feel about protecting the speaker's right to freedom of expression? What is the value of hearing opinions you dislike? What is the danger of suppressing unpopular thought?

The language of the First Amendment appears absolute ("Congress shall make no law"). However, freedom of speech is at times limited by government action. To understand these limits, you should be familiar with exceptions to the rule that protects all expression. These exceptions include obscenity, defamation, commercial speech, and fighting words. They will be discussed in more detail in the following sections. Governments can also regulate speech using clear, specific rules limiting the time, place, and manner of the speech.

Vagueness and Overbreadth

The Cross-Burning Law

In the late 1980s many states and localities passed laws against hate crimes. These laws defined types of acts that constituted hate crimes and provided criminal penalties for them. St. Paul, Minnesota, was one of many cities to pass such a law. This city's ordinance read as follows:

> Whoever places on public or private property a symbol . . . or graffiti, including but not limited to a burning cross or Nazi swastika, which one knows or has reasonable grounds to know arouses anger, alarm, or resentment in others on the basis of race, color, creed, religion, or gender, commits disorderly conduct and shall be guilty of a misdemeanor.

Russell and Laura Jones and their five children were an African-American family who had just moved into a white St. Paul neighborhood. Late one night they were awakened by noise outside their bedroom window. When they parted the curtains, they saw a cross burning on their front lawn. St. Paul police arrested a white 18-year-old factory worker. He was prosecuted and convicted under the local ordinance described above.

PROBLEM 4

a. What happened in this case? Why was the 18-year-old prosecuted?

b. Could the state have prosecuted the defendant using some other law or ordinance? If so, which ones? Why do you think it used the hate crimes ordinance?

c. On appeal, what legal arguments can the defendant raise? What legal arguments can the state make?

d. When interviewed by a national newspaper, the lawyer for the defendant said, "Everybody's gotten real thin-skinned lately, and I'm defending the right to express yourself in that kind of climate. . . . With an ordinance like this, you open up a doctrine that swallows the First Amendment." What did the lawyer mean by these comments? Do you agree or disagree with them? Give your reasons.

e. How should this case be decided? Give your reasons.

f. Assume that the ordinance is upheld. Could a man in St. Paul be prosecuted for wearing a sexist T-shirt, based on the language of the ordinance? Could a Native American family in St. Paul have a visitor from Washington, D.C., arrested because the visitor's car had a Washington Redskins bumper sticker? What steps can government take to prevent hateful speech?

Courts have ruled that laws governing free speech must be clear and specific. This is so that a reasonable person can understand what expression is prohibited. Laws also need to be clear so they can be enforced in a nondiscriminatory way. Laws governing free speech that are not clear and specific can be struck down by courts on grounds of **vagueness**.

In addition, laws that regulate free speech must be narrowly drafted to prohibit only as much as is necessary to achieve the government's goals. Laws that unnecessarily prohibit too much expression can be struck down by courts on grounds of **overbreadth**. In specific cases, courts may strike down vague or overbroad statutes, even if the expression in question could have been prohibited under a clearer, more narrowly drafted law.

Besides rules against vagueness and overbreadth, some actions that may not appear to be speech are sometimes given First Amendment protection. Foremost among these is symbolic speech.

Symbolic Speech

Expression may be symbolic, as well as verbal. **Symbolic speech** is conduct that expresses an idea. Although speech is commonly thought of as verbal expression, we are all aware of nonverbal communication. Sit-ins, flag waving, demonstrations, and wearing armbands or protest buttons are examples of symbolic speech. While most forms of conduct could be said to express ideas in some way, only some conduct is protected as symbolic speech. In analyzing such cases, the courts ask whether the speaker intended to convey a particular message and whether it is likely that the message was understood by those who viewed it.

In order to convince a court that symbolic conduct should be punished and not protected as speech, the government must show it has an important reason. However, the reason cannot be that the government disapproves of the message conveyed by the symbolic conduct.

In a case from the Vietnam War era, a protestor violated a federal law by burning his draft card on the steps of a government building to demonstrate his opposition to that war. It was clear that he intended to convey a particular message and that his audience understood the message. The U.S. Supreme Court found that the government had an interest in running a smooth system of drafting men into the army. The Court said that burning draft cards would interfere with the government's ability to operate this system. In upholding his conviction and the law on which the conviction was based, the Court said that Congress was punishing the protestor's conduct, not the message he was trying to convey.

What message are these famous film stars communicating by wearing ribbons that call attention to AIDS?

The Flag Burning

While the Republican National Convention was taking place in Dallas in 1984, Gregory Lee Johnson participated in a political demonstration. Demonstrators marched through Dallas streets, stopping at several locations to stage "die-ins" intended to dramatize their opposition to nuclear weapons. One demonstrator took an American flag from a flagpole and gave it to Johnson.

The demonstration ended in front of the Dallas City Hall, where Johnson unfurled the American flag, doused it with kerosene, and set it on fire. While the flag burned, protestors chanted, "America, the red, white, and blue, we spit on you." There were no injuries or threats of injury during the demonstration.

Of the 100 demonstrators, only Johnson was arrested. He was charged under a Texas criminal statute that prohibited desecration of a venerated object (including monuments, places of worship or burial, or a state or national flag) "in a way that the actor knows will seriously offend one or more persons likely to observe or discover his action."

At Johnson's trial, several witnesses testified that they had been seriously offended by the flag burning. He was convicted, sentenced to one year in jail, and fined $2,000. The case was appealed to the U.S. Supreme Court.

PROBLEM 5

Assume you are a justice on the U.S. Supreme Court. Study the two opinions that follow, decide which you would vote for, and give the reasons for your decision.

Opinion A

Johnson argues that his burning of the flag should be protected as symbolic speech under the First Amendment. The First Amendment literally protects speech itself. However, this Court has long recognized that First Amendment protection does not end with the spoken or written word. While we have rejected the idea that virtually all conduct can be labelled speech and protected by the First Amendment, we have recognized conduct as symbolic speech when the actor intended to convey a particular message and there was a great likelihood that those viewing the conduct would understand the message.

In this case, Johnson's conduct is similar to conduct protected as symbolic speech in our earlier cases. However, the First Amendment does not provide an absolute protection for speech. This Court will analyze the Texas law, along with the facts of the case, to determine whether the state's interest is sufficient to justify punishing Johnson's action.

In earlier cases we upheld the conviction of a protestor who burned his draft card. We reached that decision because the government had an important interest in requiring that everyone aged 18 and older carry a draft card. In that case we did not punish the protestor's speech, but rather his illegal act (burning his draft card). However, we have held that freedom of speech was violated when individuals were arrested for displaying a flag with a peace symbol constructed of masking tape and for wearing pants with a small flag sewn into the seat.

In the Johnson case the state argues that it has two important interests: preventing a breach of the peace and preserving the flag as a symbol of nationhood and national unity. The first interest is not involved in this case because there was no breach of the peace or even a threat of such a breach.

The state's other argument—the preservation of the flag as a symbol of nationhood and national unity—misses the major point of this Court's earlier First Amendment decisions: the government may not prohibit expression simply because society finds the ideas presented to be offensive or disagreeable. Johnson was prosecuted for burning the flag to express an idea—his dissatisfaction with the country's policies. His conviction must be reversed because his act deserves First Amendment protection as symbolic speech. The government has not provided sufficient justification for punishing his speech.

Opinion B

For more than 200 years the American flag has occupied a unique position as the symbol of the nation. Regardless of their own political beliefs, millions of Americans have an almost mystical reverence for the flag. Both Congress and the states have enacted many laws prohibiting the misuse and mutilation of the American flag. With the exception of Alaska and Wyoming, all the states have specific laws prohibiting the burning of the flag. We do not believe that the federal law and the laws in 48 states that prohibit burning of the flag are in conflict with the First Amendment. While earlier cases have protected speech and even some symbolic speech related to the flag, none of our decisions has ever protected flag burning.

The First Amendment is designed to protect the expression of ideas. Indeed, Johnson could have denounced the flag in public or even burned it in private without violating the Texas law. In fact, other methods of protest were used and permitted at the demonstration. The Texas statute did not punish him for the ideas that he conveyed but rather for the conduct he used to convey his message. Requiring that Johnson use some method other than flag burning to convey his message places a very small burden on free expression.

We have never held that speech rights are absolute. If Johnson had chosen to spray-paint graffiti on the Washington Monument, there is no question that the government would have the power to punish him for doing so. The flag symbolizes more than national unity. It symbolizes to war veterans, for example, what they fought for and what many died for. It also symbolizes our shared values such as freedom, equal opportunity, and religious tolerance. If the great ideas behind our country are worth fighting for—and history demonstrates that they are—then the flag that uniquely symbolizes the power of those ideas is worth protecting from burning. The conviction should be affirmed.

Obscenity

The portrayal of sex in art, literature, and films is a troublesome topic in our society. The First Amendment guarantees freedom of expression. However, the government has the power to prohibit the distribution of obscene materials. In general terms, **obscenity** applies to anything that treats sex or nudity in an offensive or lewd manner or that exceeds recognized standards of decency.

As you might expect, courts have had difficulty developing a precise legal definition of obscenity. For example, in speaking about pornography, Justice Potter Stewart once said that he couldn't define it, "but I know it when I see it." In 1957, the Supreme Court ruled that obscenity is not protected by the Constitution. Later, in the 1973 case of *Miller v. California*, the Supreme Court set out the following three-part guideline for determining whether a work is obscene:

1. Would the average person applying contemporary community standards find that the material, taken as a whole, appeals to prurient interest (that is, an immoderate, unwholesome, or unusual interest in sex)?
2. Does the work depict or describe, in a patently offensive way, sexual conduct specifically outlawed by applicable state law?
3. Does the work, taken as a whole, lack serious literary, artistic, political, or scientific value?

Applying these standards, a medical textbook on anatomy is not obscene, because it has scientific value. But a sex magazine filled only with nude photos of persons committing illegal acts may be obscene, depending on the standards of the local community.

Recently, state and local governments have developed new strategies for dealing with pornography. Some communities have tried to ban all pornographic works that degrade or depict sexual violence against women. Such works, they argue, are a form of sex discrimination that may lead to actual violence or abuse against women. Other communities regulate adult bookstores and movie theaters through their zoning laws. Such laws restrict these stores and theaters to special zones or ban them from certain neighborhoods. Finally, many communities have passed laws outlawing child pornography and greatly restricting minors' access to sexually oriented material. The Supreme Court has held that laws against child pornography are constitutional, even when the laws ban material that is not technically obscene.

PROBLEM 6

a. Should the government be allowed to censor books, movies, or magazines? If so, what kind, and why?

b. Who should decide if a book or movie is obscene? What definition should be used?

c. Do you think books and movies that depict nude women and emphasize sex encourage violence against women? Should they be banned? Explain your answer.

Defamation

The First Amendment does not protect defamatory expression. **Defamation** is a false expression about a person that damages that person's reputation. When defamation is spoken, it is called **slander**. Written defamation is called **libel**. For example, assume a patient said that her doctor was careless and had caused the death of patients. If others heard this remark, the doctor could sue the patient for slander. If the patient had written the same thing in a letter, the suit would be libel. However, if a damaging statement—written or spoken—is proven to be true, the plaintiff cannot win in court.

The Supreme Court has special rules that make it difficult for public officials or public figures to win defamation suits. In the case of *The New York Times v. Sullivan*, for example, the Supreme Court ruled that, to win a defamation suit, public officials or public figures must prove that the defendant acted with "actual malice." Actual malice means that the defendant knew the statement was false *or* acted with reckless disregard as to whether the statement was true or not. For additional information on defamation lawsuits, see Chapter 3.

Commercial Speech

Another form of speech that is not fully protected by the Constitution is **commercial speech**. All forms of advertising are considered

Why is it so difficult for a public figure to win a defamation or libel suit?

In what ways can states regulate commercial speech?

commercial speech, as distinguished from individual speech. The Supreme Court has ruled that states may regulate and even ban commercial speech under certain circumstances. Specifically, states may prohibit deceptive or misleading advertisements. State and local governments may also place restrictions on the time, place, and manner of commercial speech. For example, cities can ban commercial billboards or restrict them to certain areas. However, cities cannot totally prohibit the dissemination of commercial information, and states cannot prevent abortion clinics from advertising in

The Lottery Advertisements

Gambling and lotteries are legal in some states. Virginia has a state lottery, while North Carolina prohibits gambling. A North Carolina radio station aired advertisements for the Virginia lottery. These ads were heard by listeners in both states. About 11% of the station's listeners were North Carolina residents.

The radio broadcasting company filed suit, asking a court to rule that the regulations prohibiting this type of advertising were unconstitutional. The radio station argued that forbidding it to air lottery advertisements was a violation of freedom of speech. The state argued that regulation of radio advertisements was allowed because commercial speech is given less protection under the Constitution.

The U.S. Supreme Court ruled that radio advertising for a legal state lottery could not be aired in a neighboring state where lotteries are illegal. In this case, the law forbidding the North Carolina station from broadcasting lottery advertisements was held constitutional.

PROBLEM 7

a. What is the law on gambling in your state? Does your state have a lottery?

b. Should the government be allowed to regulate gambling and gambling advertising? Give your reasons.

c. Based on this decision, would it be constitutional for a state to ban advertising for beer (alcohol) on television and radio stations throughout the state? Explain.

newspapers. Professional associations cannot totally prevent their members from advertising their services. For example, courts have struck down rules that prevented lawyers from advertising and other rules that kept pharmacies from advertising prescription drug prices.

Time, Place, and Manner Restrictions

Laws may regulate expression in one of two ways. Some laws regulate expression based on its content. These laws prescribe *what* a speaker is allowed to say. Other laws regulate the time, place, and manner of expression. These laws prescribe *when, where*, and *how* speech is allowed.

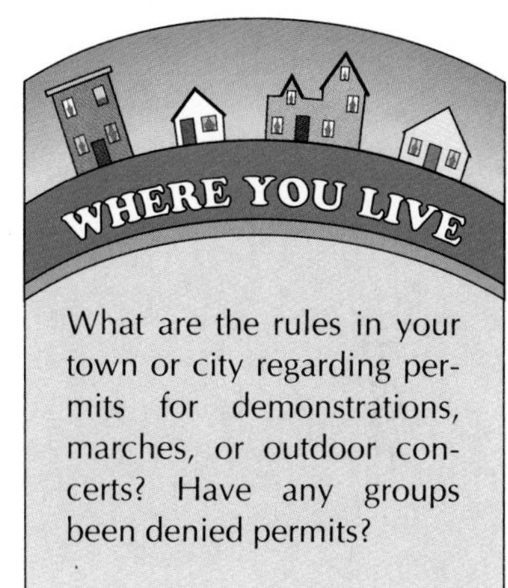

What are the rules in your town or city regarding permits for demonstrations, marches, or outdoor concerts? Have any groups been denied permits?

As a general rule, government cannot regulate the content of expression (except in special situations, such as obscenity, libel, or false advertising). However, it may make reasonable regulations governing the time, place, and manner of speech. For example, towns may require citizens to obtain permits to distribute handbills; use sound trucks; or stage protests in parks, on streets, or on other public property. Cities may regulate the time during which loudspeakers may be used, the places where political posters may be located, and the manner in which demonstrations may be conducted.

Courts analyze such regulations by first determining whether the site affected is a public forum, such as a street or park that is traditionally open to expression (or designated for this purpose), or whether the site is a nonpublic forum, such as a bus terminal or a school. If the site is a public forum, then the regulation will be overturned unless it serves an important government interest (for example, the government may prohibit loudspeakers from blaring in quiet hospital zones or keep marchers off busy main streets when commuters are driving to or from work). However, regulations for nonpublic forums are upheld if they are reasonable. For example, a school district could choose to limit the use of school buildings (a nonpublic forum) to educational purposes.

Why should governments be allowed to put time, place, and manner restrictions on speech?

Regulations for public and nonpublic forums must also be content neutral (that is, they cannot censor a particular point of view), and they cannot be vague or overbroad. The government cannot favor some ideas over others. In addition, the regulations must allow alternative means of communication.

Fighting Words, Offensive Speakers, and Hostile Audiences

In addition to obscenity, defamation, and commercial speech, there are a few additional situations in which the Constitution does

Parade Permit Fees

Forsyth County, Georgia, is a predominantly white rural area outside Atlanta. Historically, Forsyth County has had significant racial troubles. Following civil rights marches, Forsyth County enacted an ordinance that allowed a county administrator to use her discretion in determining what fee to charge for a parade permit, with a maximum of $1,000. The county administrator's determination of a fee took into consideration the potential expense required for security should the parade crowd become hostile to the marchers' speech.

The Nationalist Movement proposed to march in opposition to the holiday in honor of Martin Luther King, Jr. This organization was charged $100 for a parade permit. However, the fee was not paid. Instead, the Nationalist Movement wanted to march without any interference from the county.

The county argued that the ordinance and fee constituted a legitimate time-place-manner regulation based on a content-neutral determination of expenses that might be incurred. The Nationalist Movement argued that the ordinance and subsequent fee constituted a content-based regulation based on the organization's message.

PROBLEM 8

a. How should this case be decided? Give your reasons.

b. Why do you think courts generally approve of laws that regulate the time, place, and manner of expression but disapprove of laws that regulate the content of expression?

c. Which of the following laws regulate the content of expression, and which regulate the time, place, and manner of expression? Which, if any, violate the First Amendment?

1. A city ordinance prohibits posting signs on public property such as utility poles, traffic signs, and street lamps.
2. A regulation prohibits people from sleeping in federal parks, even though the sleeping is part of a demonstration.
3. A federal regulation prohibits public radio stations from airing editorials.
4. A town ordinance prohibits commercial billboards anywhere within the town limits.

5. A District of Columbia ordinance prohibits the display within 500 feet of a foreign embassy of any sign that tends to bring a foreign government into "public disrepute."
6. A town ordinance prohibits picketing outside abortion clinics.
7. A city ordinance prohibits political or religious organizations from passing out leaflets or asking for donations inside the airport terminal.

not protect the content of a person's speech. When a person speaks publicly, two elements are interacting: the speaker and the audience. Protection of a person's speech by the First Amendment depends on how these elements interact in different situations. There may be times when certain words may be protected and other times when the same words may not be protected because the surrounding situation has changed.

The First Amendment does not protect you if you use words that are so abusive or threatening that they amount to what the Court calls **fighting words**. These are words spoken face to face that are likely to cause an imminent breach of the peace between the speaker and the listener. Fighting words are like a verbal slap in the face. Such expression is more like an assault than information or opinion whose communication is safeguarded by the Constitution. For example, in 1942 a person was arrested for calling a city official a "goddamned racketeer" and a "damned Fascist." The person was convicted because his words were considered likely to cause an average person to fight and therefore would not be protected by the First Amendment.

In recent years there has been a growing effort to punish those who express views that many people believe are motivated by bigotry and racism. Sometimes this is done by putting pressure on organizations to fire employees who utter racial or ethnic slurs or other intolerant or insensitive remarks. A television network, for example, fired a sports commentator for making a racially insensitive statement on the air. In another case, law schools banned recruitment visits from a law firm after an attorney from that firm made a racial comment in a campus recruitment interview.

Some organizations and universities have adopted written policies or codes that prohibit certain types of racially or ethnically offensive speech. Some have criticized these policies as violating a person's

Should schools and universities be allowed to adopt policies that prohibit offensive or distasteful expression?

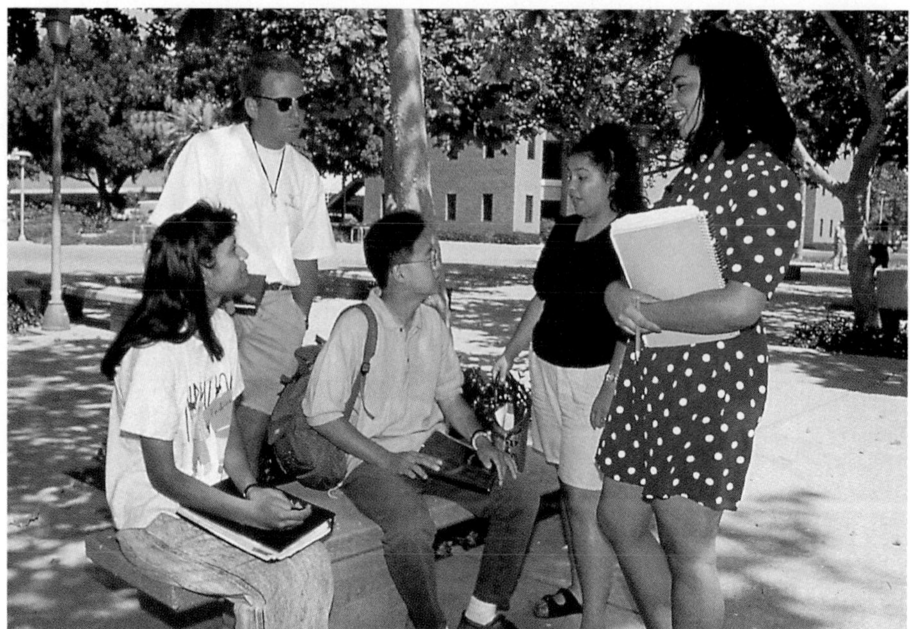

right to free speech and as being too vague to be enforceable. However, supporters argue that without the policies, verbal harassment of racial and religious groups would go unpunished. After the U.S. Supreme Court struck down the ordinance in the Case of the Cross-Burning Law (see page 437), the constitutionality of many policies was questioned. In response, many universities dropped or revised their policies against hateful, offensive speech. In addition, after the U.S. Supreme Court decision in the cross-burning case, many states and localities have dropped or revised their hate speech laws.

PROBLEM 9

A state university adopts the following policy: "A student or faculty member may be suspended or expelled for any behavior, verbal or physical, that stigmatizes an individual on the basis of race, ethnicity, religion, national origin, sex, sexual orientation, creed, ancestry, age, marital status, handicap, or Vietnam veteran status."

a. Decide whether the following actions violate the above policy. If they do, should the actor or actors be punished?

1. After writing a limerick for an assignment, a student reads it aloud in an English class. It makes fun of the reported homosexual acts of a politician.
2. A white student writes an article on race relations for the school newspaper. It points out that African Americans are

more likely than whites to become criminals in America, which is one reason why whites do not mix more with African Americans.

3. Two students on the football team get into a fight on the field during a practice session. One student calls the other a "dirty spik."
4. The athletic director schedules the varsity club's awards dinner on a Jewish holiday. Several Jewish athletes are unable to attend.
5. An African-American student hears that a group of Chinese students will not socialize with African Americans. She calls them "typical Chinese racists."
6. Wearing white robes and hoods, a white supremacist student group stages a silent march on campus.

b. What are the arguments for and against the above policy? Do you support or oppose it? Can it be rewritten for improvement? If so, how?

c. Should organizations like television and radio stations be regulated by laws, or should they have their own rules similar to the above university policy? Should other private businesses have similar rules? Give your reasons.

d. Think about how racial and ethnic slurs compare with fighting words. In what ways are they the same? How do they differ?

International Forum on Hate Speech

Individuals from many different countries have gathered to discuss whether all nations should enact criminal laws against hate speech. The following speakers give their views.

A German: "Because of the experience of our country under Hitler, we are very worried about how speech can be used to condemn and abuse millions of people. If there had been laws forbidding anti-Semitic speech, could the Holocaust have been prevented? Today, we see strong antiforeigner feeling in our country. We are thankful that we have 'incitement to hatred' laws and believe they are needed in all countries."

An American: "Our history includes a revolution that was at least partially a reaction to government censorship. We think it is dangerous to allow government to decide what speech will be allowed. It is true that racism is a serious problem in our country and that racist speech can have a very negative impact on the victims. However, it may be overly paternalistic to have the government try to protect people from such speech. Would it not be better to let the marketplace of ideas condemn the racists?"

An Israeli: "The continual conflict between Arabs and Jews in our region led the government to pass a criminal law governing incitement to racism. However, this law has done nothing but create the illusion of progress against racism. There have been few prosecutions, and the ones that have occurred have been against Arabs. While the law has value symbolically, it may be better not to have prosecutions, because these just give racists on both sides a platform from which to speak.

A South African: "I would think that my country, with so much ethnic and racial division, would seem a likely candidate for a law against hate speech. In fact, for many years there has been such a law, which prohibited "bringing any section of inhabitants of the country into ridicule or contempt." This law was used principally by the white government to prosecute blacks. But many in my country think that the violence can only be stopped if people aren't allowed to promote racial hatred. My view is that it is better to debate these ideas openly than to drive an evil view underground, where it may pick up more strength."

PROBLEM 10

a. Which of the speakers favor laws against hate speech? Why?

b. Which of the speakers oppose such laws? Why?

c. Do you think that the history of each speaker's country affects the viewpoints expressed? How?

d. What are the pros and cons of encouraging nations to enact their own criminal laws against hate speech? What is your position? Give your reasons.

The Offensive Speaker

In 1948, Father Terminiello arrived to make a speech at a Chicago auditorium. Outside the auditorium about 300 people were picketing his speech. Inside, Terminiello criticized Jews and African Americans, as well as the crowd outside. By the time his speech was finished, 1,500 people were gathered outside. A police line prevented the protestors from entering the building. However, the "howling mob" outside was throwing stones and bricks at the building, and the police were unable to maintain control. The crowd was also yelling at and harassing people who came to hear Terminiello speak.

Terminiello was arrested and charged under a statute that prohibited conduct "which stirs the public to anger, invites dispute, brings about a condition of unrest or creates a disturbance." The U.S. Supreme Court held that the statute was unconstitutional on grounds of vagueness and overbreadth. Terminiello's conviction was reversed.

PROBLEM 11

a. What happened in the Terminiello case? Why was Terminiello arrested?

b. Should the police have controlled the crowd instead of arresting Terminiello? Did the police violate Terminiello's First Amendment rights? Why or why not?

c. What did the U.S. Supreme Court decide in this case? Why?

d. Should people be prohibited from voicing unpopular views? Explain your answer.

In addition to analyzing face-to-face speech, the police must also decide how to handle the responses of a large audience to speech. Police action may depend on whether the audience is friendly or hostile toward the speaker.

In the Case of the Offensive Speaker, the police had to deal with an audience that disagreed with the speaker's message. The police must also deal with problems caused when the audience *agrees* with the message. For example, the government must decide how to deal with speakers who advocate illegal activities. Prior to the 1950s, the courts used the **clear and present danger** test. This test examined the circumstances under which a speech was made and determined whether a clear and present danger of unlawful action existed. The courts generally held that the unlawful action did not have to occur immediately after the speech (for example, when a speaker encourages the audience to overthrow the U.S. government). When there was a clear and present danger of unlawful activity, the government could punish the speaker.

The clear and present danger test was frequently used in political cases in which people advocated antigovernment positions. In 1919, the Supreme Court first discussed the clear and present danger test in two cases, affirming convictions under the Espionage Act of 1917. One case, *Schenk v. United States*, involved the mailing of leaflets stating that the military draft was unconstitutional. The other case, *Abrams v. United States*, involved the distribution of pamphlets criticizing U.S. actions toward the new Communist government in Russia.

In the early 1950s, the Supreme Court reflected the nation's concern with the Cold War and national security. In *Dennis v. United States*, decided in 1951, the defendants were convicted for attempting to organize the U.S. Communist party, whose goal was to overthrow the government. In *Dennis*, the Court used a **balancing test** that ignored the probability of the act. The Court balanced the right of the speaker against the harm the speaker proposed. When the speech advocated very dangerous acts, like overthrowing the government, the Court required less proof of clear and present danger.

In the late 1960s, however, the Supreme Court began using the **incitement test** for cases in which the speaker urged the audience to take unlawful action. This test allowed the government to punish advocacy only when it was directed toward inciting or producing immediate lawless action from the audience *and* when the advocacy was likely to produce such behavior. Unlike the clear and present danger test, the incitement test required the unlawful action to be likely to occur within a short period of time. Therefore, the incitement test gave speakers greater protection.

For example, if a speech causes members of an audience to talk to one another in disagreement, the speaker may not be arrested. However, if the speech urges the audience to throw objects at others and the audience begins to do this, the speaker may be arrested. In practice, the police may face a difficult dilemma in deciding whether to arrest an unpopular speaker or control a hostile audience.

FREEDOM OF THE PRESS

If it were left to me to decide whether we should have a government without a free press or a free press without a government, I would prefer the latter.

—Thomas Jefferson

The First Amendment guarantees freedom of the press. It protects us from government **censorship** of newspapers, magazines, books, radio, television, and film. Censorship occurs when the government examines publications and productions and prohibits the use of material it finds offensive. Traditionally, courts have protected the press from government censorship. For example, in 1966 the Supreme Court said that "justice cannot survive behind walls of silence." It said this to emphasize our system's distrust of secret trials. In addition to providing information about news events, the press subjects all of our political and legal institutions to public scrutiny and criticism.

The Constitution's framers provided the press with broad freedom. This freedom was considered necessary to the establishment of a strong, independent press. An independent press can provide citizens with a variety of information and opinions on matters of public importance. However, freedom of the press sometimes collides with other rights, such as a defendant's right to a fair trial or a citizen's right to privacy.

When should the government be allowed to prevent the press from publishing information?

Among the difficult questions government and the press have controlled are these: When can the government prevent the press from publishing information? When can the government keep the press from obtaining information? When can the government force the press to disclose information? Is freedom of the press limited in places such as schools or prisons?

Prohibiting Publication

The Gag Order

Six people were brutally murdered in their home in a small Nebraska town. The murders and the later arrest of a suspect received widespread news coverage. At a pretrial hearing, which was open to the public, the prosecutor introduced a confession and other evidence against the accused. Both the judge and the lawyers believed that publication of the information would make it impossible for the suspect to have a fair trial before an unbiased jury. As a result, the trial judge issued a gag order, which prohibited the news media from reporting the confession and any other evidence against the accused. Members of the news media then sued to have the order declared unconstitutional.

PROBLEM 12

a. What happened in this case? Why did the judge issue a gag order?

b. Should judges be able to close criminal trials to the press? If so, when and why?

c. Which is more important: the right to a fair trial or the right to freedom of the press? Explain your answer.

d. As a practical matter, how could the court protect the rights of the accused without infringing on the rights of the press?

In the Case of the Gag Order, the judge was concerned about the defendant's Sixth Amendment right to a fair trial. The reporters were concerned about their First Amendment right to freedom of the press.

This case presented a conflict between two important constitutional rights: free press and fair trial.

In 1976, the U.S. Supreme Court decided that the gag order was unconstitutional. The Court held that the trial judge should have taken less drastic steps to lessen the effects of the pretrial publicity. The Court suggested postponing the trial until a later date, moving the trial to another county, questioning potential jurors to screen out those with fixed opinions, and carefully instructing the jury to decide the case based only on the evidence introduced at the trial.

If the gag order had been approved, it would have amounted to a **prior restraint** (censorship before publication) on the press. Attempts to censor publications before they go to press are presumed unconstitutional by the courts. Prior restraint is only allowed if (1) publication would cause a certain, serious, and irreparable harm; (2) no lesser means would prevent the harm; and (3) the prior restraint would be effective in avoiding the harm.

Another example of a government attempt to impose censorship before publication took place in 1971, when a government employee gave top secret documents about the Vietnam War to several newspapers. The documents outlined America's past conduct of the war in Vietnam. The government sued to block publication of the so-called

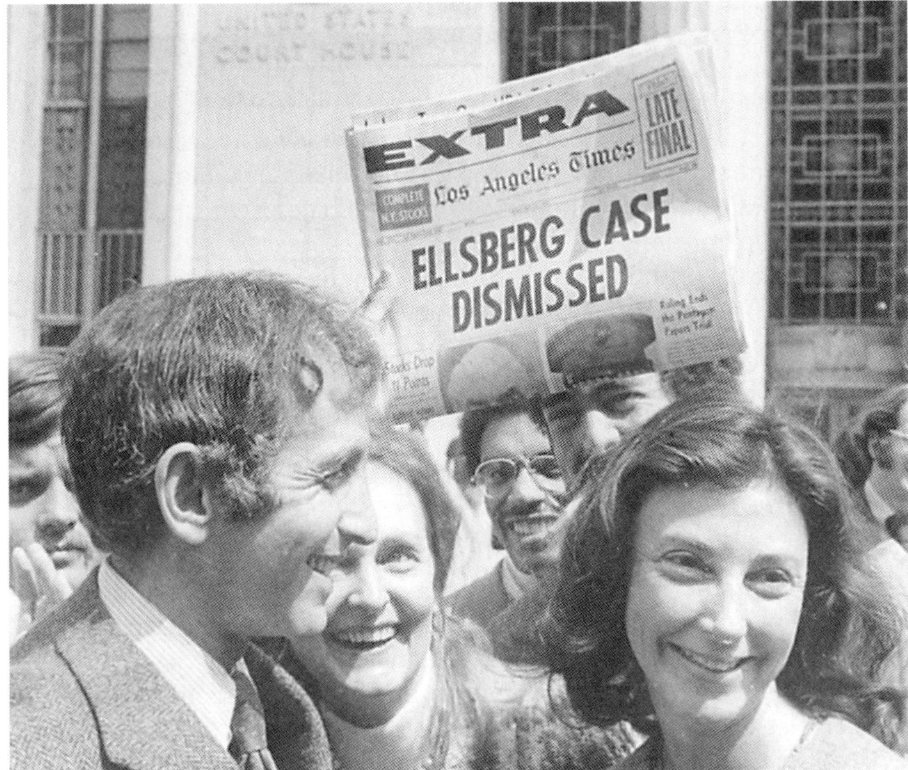

Daniel Ellsberg was accused of violating the law when he gave the "Pentagon Papers" to the press during the Vietnam War. Why does the Constitution protect whistle-blowers?

Pentagon Papers, but the Supreme Court refused to stop publication. It said that the documents, although perhaps embarrassing, would not cause "direct, immediate, and irreparable harm." However, if the documents had, for example, contained a secret plan of attack during a time of war, the Court might have blocked publication.

PROBLEM 13

A state law made it a crime to publish the name of any youth charged as a juvenile offender. A newspaper published an article containing the name of a juvenile charged with the murder of another youth. The newspaper learned the name of the arrested youth by listening to the police radio and by talking to several witnesses to the crime.

a. What is the state's interest in having and enforcing this law?

b. What is the newspaper's interest in publishing the juvenile's name?

c. How should the conflict be resolved?

Denying the Press Access to Information

Another way in which the government tries to control the press is by denying the public access to certain information. Some people argue that denying access to information does not violate the rights of the press. Others contend that freedom of the press implies a right to obtain information.

To protect the public's access to government information, Congress passed the *Freedom of Information Act* (FOIA) in 1966. This law requires federal agencies to release information in their files to the public. The law allows citizens to obtain government information and records unless the material falls into the category of a special exception. Exceptions include information affecting national defense or foreign policy, personnel and medical files, trade secrets, investigatory records, and other confidential information.

Does your state have a Freedom of Information Act? If so, what information is covered by the act? How can a citizen get information under the act?

The purpose of the law is to allow citizens to learn about the business of government. Federal agencies must respond to requests for information within 10 days. Agencies that refuse to release unprivileged information can be sued in federal court.

If you want to request information under the *Freedom of Information Act*, send a letter to the head of the agency or to the agency's FOIA officer. For a sample letter requesting information under the

Freedom of Information Act, see Figure 7.1. An agency's address can be found in the *United States Government Manual* or in Appendix F. Write "Freedom of Information Request" on the bottom left-hand corner of the envelope.

Identify the records you want as accurately as possible. Although you are not required to specify a document by name, your request must reasonably describe the information sought. The more specific and limited the request, the greater the likelihood that it will be processed without delay. You are not required to demonstrate a need or even a reason for wanting to see the information. However, you are more likely to receive the documents if you explain why you want them.

Some states have laws similar to the FOIA. These provide citizens with access to state agency files.

PROBLEM 14

Rumors about the federal prison had circulated for years. Former prisoners claimed that rape, suicide, murder, and mistreatment were all common occurrences. The warden denied the allegations but refused to provide any information about prison conditions.

A newspaper asked permission to inspect the prison and interview the prisoners, but the warden denied the request. The newspaper then asked the federal government for information about the prison. The newspaper asked for a list of inmates and for information about anyone who had died or been injured while in custody. The government refused to provide any information.

The newspaper then did two things. It filed suit seeking admission to the prison, and it filed a *Freedom of Information Act* request for information about the prison.

a. How would you decide this lawsuit?

b. What are the newspaper's rights under the *Freedom of Information Act*? How would you decide its request for information?

c. Draft a letter to the government (Federal Bureau of Prisons) seeking information under the FOIA.

Requiring the Press to Disclose Information

The government and the press also argue over the extent to which the First Amendment protects a reporter's sources of information. Reporters contend that requiring them to reveal their sources makes

Figure 7.1 Sample FOIA Letter

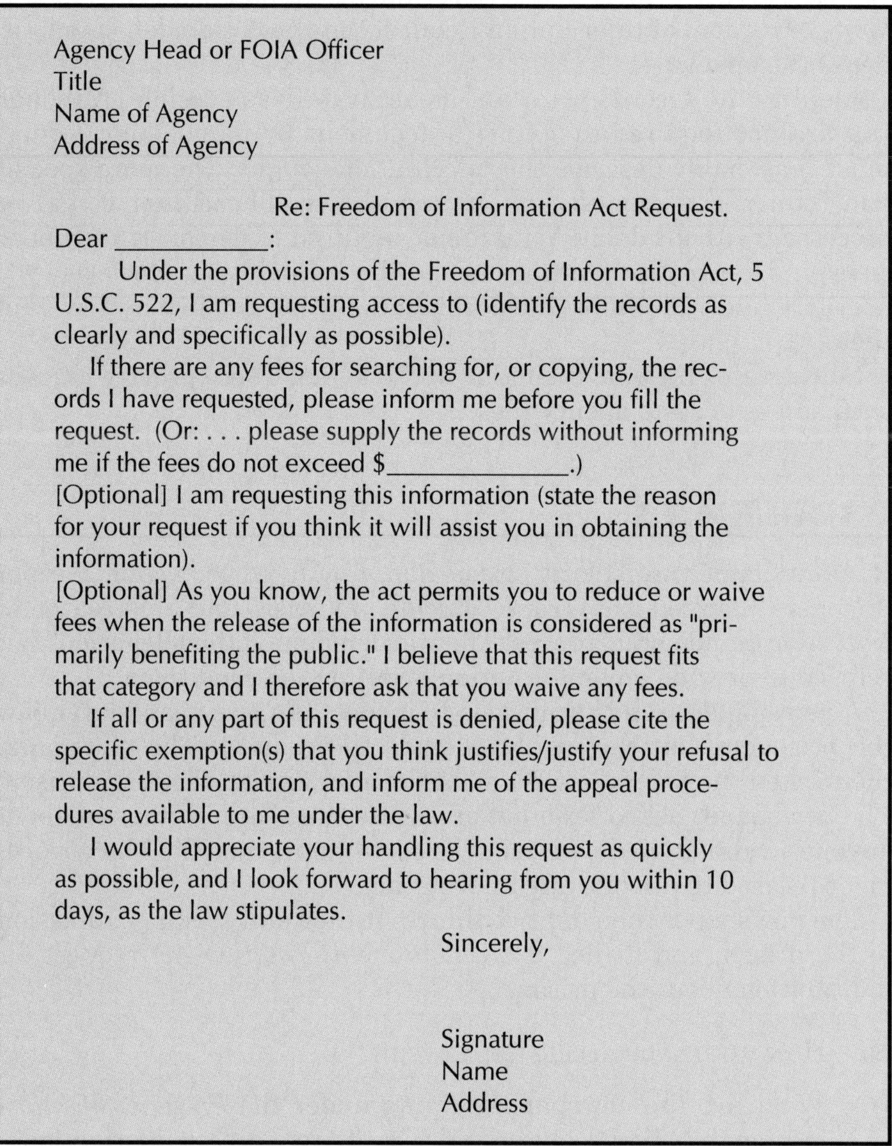

Agency Head or FOIA Officer
Title
Name of Agency
Address of Agency

Re: Freedom of Information Act Request.

Dear ___________:

Under the provisions of the Freedom of Information Act, 5 U.S.C. 522, I am requesting access to (identify the records as clearly and specifically as possible).

If there are any fees for searching for, or copying, the records I have requested, please inform me before you fill the request. (Or: . . . please supply the records without informing me if the fees do not exceed $_____________.)

[Optional] I am requesting this information (state the reason for your request if you think it will assist you in obtaining the information).

[Optional] As you know, the act permits you to reduce or waive fees when the release of the information is considered as "primarily benefiting the public." I believe that this request fits that category and I therefore ask that you waive any fees.

If all or any part of this request is denied, please cite the specific exemption(s) that you think justifies/justify your refusal to release the information, and inform me of the appeal procedures available to me under the law.

I would appreciate your handling this request as quickly as possible, and I look forward to hearing from you within 10 days, as the law stipulates.

Sincerely,

Signature
Name
Address

Source: House Committee on Government Operations, *A Citizen's Guide on How to Use the Freedom of Information Act and the Privacy Act Requesting Government Documents*, 95th Cong., 1st sess., 1977.

it more difficult to gather and publish information. When this problem arises, the freedom of the press often conflicts with other important rights.

FREEDOM OF ASSOCIATION AND FREEDOM OF ASSEMBLY

Two other rights protected by the First Amendment are freedom of association and freedom of assembly. Freedom of association means

The Shield Law

In 1976 the *New York Times* published a story suggesting that a doctor had murdered several patients. As a result, New Jersey authorities investigated the case and charged the doctor with murder.

Defense attorneys asked the *New York Times* to turn over the names of all persons who had been interviewed during the investigation and any other information it had. The defense contended that it could not properly prepare its case without this information. The *New York Times* and the reporter who conducted the investigation refused to turn over any information. They argued that the First Amendment and a New Jersey law that protected a reporter's sources of information allowed them to withhold any unpublished material in their possession.

PROBLEM 15

a. Should the judge allow the reporter to withhold the information sought by the defense attorney? Why or why not?

b. What rights are in conflict in this case?

that people have the right to associate with one another in order to join or form groups for political, economic, or religious purposes without undue government regulation. Freedom of association does not appear directly in the Constitution. Rather, it grows out of other constitutional rights.

Freedom of assembly means that citizens have the right to gather together peacefully to petition the government for some action or policy. Citizens exercise freedom of assembly rights in many ways. They write letters to government officials, they lobby in Congress or their state legislatures, and they march or demonstrate in the streets.

Like other rights, the freedom of assembly is not absolute. The government may make reasonable rules regarding the time, place, and manner of protests and demonstrations. Although the government can restrict protests to certain areas or to certain times of day, it cannot prohibit all protests. Furthermore, the government cannot regulate a protest based on what people plan to say.

Why does the U.S. Constitution protect our right to gather in a public place to express ourselves?

THE CASE OF . . .

The Teen Dance Hall

In order to protect teens from the potentially negative influence of certain young adults, the city of Dallas passed an ordinance requiring a special license to operate a dance hall for teens. City officials were worried that the young adults would involve the teens in drugs, alcohol, and juvenile crime. The license limited these dance halls to teens aged 14 to 18 (with exceptions in the law for parents, guardians, law enforcement officers, and dance hall staff) and limited the daily hours of operation from 1:00 P.M. to midnight when school was not in session.

The owner of the Twilight Skating Rink obtained this type of license for a teen dance hall. He used portable plastic cones to divide his rink into two areas: one for teen dancing and another for roller skating by people of all ages. A disc jockey provided the music, which could be heard in both parts of the arena. No alcohol was served.

After operating the teen dance hall for a time, the owner sued the city of Dallas, arguing that the licensing ordinance violated the Constitution by limiting the rights of people aged 14 to 18 to associate with people outside that age group.

The trial court upheld the ordinance, but a state appeals court reversed the age restriction. The appeals court held that the notion that a teen "might" associate with a young adult who would be a bad influence is not a good enough reason to limit the associational rights of all teen dancers.

The U.S. Supreme Court heard the case in 1989. In their decision, the justices reversed the state appeals court and held that the Dallas law did not violate the rights of teens. The justices said that the exact words "freedom of association" do not appear in the Constitution and that the Court had never recognized a general right of "social" association. However, in earlier cases the Court had upheld the right to associate in order to engage in other protected First Amendment activities, such as speech, assembly, petition to redress grievances, and the exercise of religion.

Teens at the dance hall were not exercising other First Amendment rights. Because the ordinance did not infringe on any fundamental right and was related to the city's legitimate goal of improving the welfare of teens, the Court found no violation of the Constitution.

PROBLEM 16

a. Why did the city pass the ordinance?

b. Why did the dance hall owner challenge it?

c. Do you agree or disagree with the Supreme Court's decision? Give your reasons.

PROBLEM 17

The American Nazi party planned a demonstration in the town of Skokie, Illinois. Most of Skokie's residents were Jewish, and many were survivors of Nazi concentration camps during World War II. Many others had lost relatives in the gas chambers. Because of this, many residents strongly opposed the Nazi demonstration in their town.

To prevent violence and property damage, the town passed a law that it hoped would keep the Nazis from demonstrating there. The law required anyone seeking a demonstration permit to obtain $300,000 in liability insurance. However, this requirement could be waived by the town. The law also banned distribution of material promoting racial or religious hatred and prohibited public demonstrations by people in military-style uniforms. The Nazis challenged the law as a violation of their First Amendment rights.

a. Why did Skokie's Jewish population feel so strongly about this demonstration?

b. Some people claimed that the purpose of the demonstration was to incite Skokie's Jews and to inflict emotional harm rather than to communicate ideas. Do you agree or disagree? Should the motive of the speaker influence whether a speech is protected by the Constitution?

c. Does the government have an obligation to protect the rights of Nazis and other unpopular groups, even if their philosophy would not permit free speech for others? Should Ku Klux Klan or Communist party rallies have the same protection?

d. How should this case be decided? In what ways, if any, should the town be able to regulate speech and assembly?

EXPRESSION IN SPECIAL PLACES

Schools, military bases, and prisons present special First Amendment problems. The rights of students, military personnel, or inmates often conflict with the rights of others or interfere with the need to preserve order. When this conflict occurs, courts must balance the competing interests in each case.

As a general rule, courts allow greater freedom of speech and assembly in public parks and on street corners than in schools, military bases, and prisons. Courts sometimes speak of these places where First Amendment rights are traditionally exercised as **public forums**. For the most part, courts find that schools, military bases, and prisons (and their publications) provide only a limited forum for the exercise of First Amendment freedoms. In these places, you can usually exercise your rights, but only as long as the expression does not interfere with the purpose of the facility.

The Student Armbands

Mary Beth Tinker and her brother John were opposed to the Vietnam War. They decided to wear black armbands to school as symbols of their objection. When school administrators learned of this, they adopted a policy of asking anyone wearing armbands to remove them. Students who refused would be suspended until they returned to school without the armbands.

The Tinkers and three other students wore black armbands to school. Although some students argued the Vietnam issue in the halls, no violence occurred. The five protesting students were suspended from school until they came back without their armbands.

Should wearing armbands be considered a form of free speech protected by the Constitution?

In *Tinker v. Des Moines School District* (1969), the U.S. Supreme Court decided that the right to freedom of expression "does not end at the schoolhouse door." The Court held that wearing armbands was a form of "symbolic speech" protected by the First Amendment. However, the Court also held that the students' right to free speech could be restricted when the school could show that the students' conduct would "materially and substantially disrupt" the educational process. For example, a student could probably not insist on giving an antiwar speech during a biology class. This type of disruption did not occur in reaction to the Tinkers' armbands, nor could it reasonably have been predicted, so their suspensions were unconstitutional.

Hazelwood v. Kuhlmeier

A high school principal deleted two pages from the year's final issue of the school newspaper because these pages contained one story on student experiences with pregnancy and another about the impact of divorce on students. The principal believed that the stories had been written in such a way that the privacy rights of some students might be violated. He also believed the topics might offend some of the younger students at the school.

The newspaper was written as part of the school's advanced journalism class. Following the school's regular practice, the journalism teacher had submitted the page proofs to the principal just before publication. The principal deleted the two pages on which the articles appeared. Those pages also contained several stories he did not object to. His reason for deleting the pages was that the school year was almost over, and he did not believe there would be enough time to rewrite the offensive stories.

The existing school board policy said, "School-sponsored student publications will not restrict free expression or diverse viewpoints within the rules of responsible journalism."

The student editors of the paper sued the principal and the school district, arguing that their First Amendment rights had been violated.

PROBLEM 18

a. What arguments can the students make?

b. What arguments can the principal make?

c. How is this case similar to *Tinker*? How is it different?

d. How should the court decide this case?

e. Did the principal violate the school's policy? Give your reasons.

f. Is a new policy needed for student publications? If so, draft one.

The *Tinker* case provides a standard the courts use to determine whether punishment of student speech by public school officials violates the First Amendment. While the *Tinker* case clearly involved expression not endorsed or sponsored by the school, in other cases the courts have been asked to determine the extent to which student speech can be controlled as part of school-sponsored activities. In these cases the courts must balance students' First Amendment rights against the schools' duty to determine the educational program.

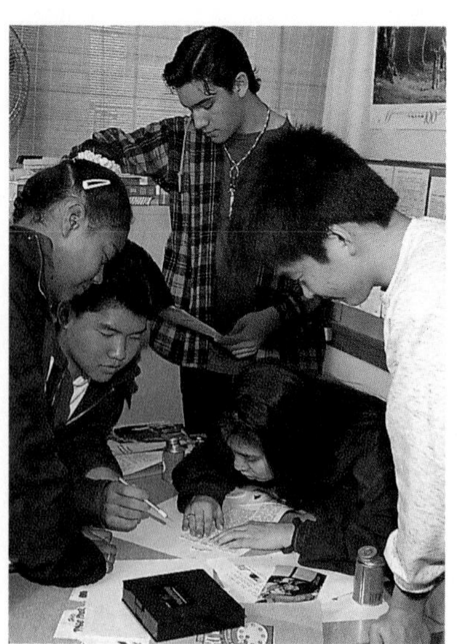

When can a principal remove an article from a school newspaper?

In *Hazelwood*, the U.S. Supreme Court ruled that school officials could have editorial control over a school-sponsored newspaper produced in a journalism class. The justices found that such a publication should not be treated as a public forum for young journalists. The reasons given for allowing this control are that (1) schools should not have to permit student speech that is inconsistent with their basic educational mission (for example, schools could refuse to sponsor student speeches advocating drug or alcohol use) and (2) schools should be allowed to control expression that students, parents, and others in the community might reasonably believe the school has endorsed (for example, students could be stopped from printing vulgar or lewd material in the school newspaper).

This decision gives educators editorial control over the style and substance of school-sponsored student speech if they can show their actions are reasonably related to legitimate educational concerns. Therefore, even with the greater editorial control allowed by the *Hazelwood* decision, a principal who opposes gun control, for example, cannot censor a student publication that fairly presents all points of view on that subject.

In addition to cases dealing directly with student speech and press rights, courts have had to consider whether student appearance (dress and grooming) is protected expression. In recent years students have worn shirts with messages promoting violence, gang membership, drug use, drinking, and sexism. Alarmed educators argue that these clothes transmit a message inconsistent with school and community values and that these messages can lead to school disruption, including violence. Parents also worry that their children may become targets for violence when wearing such clothing. Some principals have refused to allow students inside the school wearing such clothing. Some students argue that their choice of clothing and personal grooming is expression protected by the First Amendment.

PROBLEM 19

Based on the Supreme Court decisions in *Tinker* and *Hazelwood*, analyze each of the following cases. Give arguments both for permitting the expression and for supporting the school's need to regulate the expression. How should each case be decided?

a. At a schoolwide assembly before student council elections, a student makes a campaign speech for a friend. While not legally obscene, the speech has many sexual references and makes some students in the audience uncomfortable. Others applaud, jeer, and shout additional sexual references. The principal meets with the speaker after the assembly, and then suspends him for several days. The student sues the school for violating his free speech rights.

b. Students publish an "underground newspaper" off school premises that contains the results of best/worst teacher and best/worst class surveys. The principal does not allow distribution of the newspaper at school. The students sue the school for violating freedom of the press.

c. A major project of a high school drama class is the production of a spring musical. The musical is held on the last Thursday and Friday nights of May each year in the school auditorium. Tickets are sold at the school and at several locations in town to students, their parents, and others in the community. The students and their drama teacher select the musical *Hair*, which has several scenes with partially clothed actors and actresses. They begin rehearsals, print tickets, and start to publicize the performances in town. When the school board learns which play has been selected, it cancels the production. The students sue, alleging violation of their freedom of expression.

d. A few parents complain to the high school librarian that several of the school's library books contain negative stereotypes about women and certain racial and ethnic groups. The parents ask that the books be removed from the library. The principal agrees and removes the books, even though they are available in the town library. Other students and their parents sue the school for violating the rights of students who want access to those books.

e. Lakeside High School students operate a radio station each morning before school begins, playing music, reporting scores from athletic contests, and making other announcements in the student lounge. The faculty member responsible for supervising the student lounge believes that the lyrics of a popular song frequently played on the station are sexually suggestive. He complains to the principal, who removes the record from the radio station and tells the student disc jockeys that they must submit an upcoming music play list monthly for her approval. The student disc jockeys sue, alleging a violation of their rights.

f. At one school it is known that local gangs use the names and logos of professional sports teams. Gang-related shootings have occurred in the area. The principal bans the wearing of any clothing imprinted with the names and logos of any professional sports team. Students sue, arguing that this ban on clothing violates their freedom of expression.

Compared with prisons and the military, schools are relatively open institutions. Schools are supposed to prepare students for life in our constitutional democracy with its emphasis on individual freedom. By contrast, both prisons and the military closely regulate almost all aspects of life. Prisons, even more than the military, physically separate their members from society. In a 1987 case, the Supreme Court upheld a prison regulation generally prohibiting correspondence between inmates at different institutions. In 1976 the Court upheld a regulation on a large military base that completely prohibited political speeches or the distribution of campaign literature. These cases show that individual rights are often very limited when balanced against the special needs of the military and prisons for order and discipline.

FREEDOM OF RELIGION

Congress shall make no law respecting an establishment of religion, or prohibiting the free exercise thereof . . .

—First Amendment

The first 16 words of the First Amendment deal with freedom of religion. These words reflect the deep concern the founders of our nation had about the relationship between church and state, and about the right of individuals to practice their religion freely. Religious freedom is protected by two clauses in the amendment: the establishment clause and the free exercise clause.

The **establishment clause** forbids the government from setting up a state religion. It also prohibits the government from preferring one religion over another or from passing laws that aid or promote religion. The **free exercise clause** protects the right of individuals to worship or believe as they choose.

Why did America's founders believe it was so important to protect a person's right to religious freedom?

Taken together, the establishment and free exercise clauses prohibit the government from either endorsing religion or punishing religious belief or practice. Some people believe that the two clauses require the government to be neutral toward religion. This means that the government should not favor one religion over another or favor religion over nonreligion in its actions or its laws. Others believe that the First Amendment requires the government to accommodate religious belief and practice, as long as it does not establish a state religion.

Between 1791 and 1940 the U.S. Supreme Court heard only five cases dealing with church-state relations. Since then, the Court has heard more than 100 such cases, half of them since 1980.

America is a religious country, and many Americans are religious people. Many of our national traditions have religious overtones. For example, our money includes the words "In God We Trust." The Pledge of Allegiance contains references to God. And many state legislatures, Congress, and the Supreme Court begin their sessions with a brief prayer. Although these traditions are criticized by some people as violating the First Amendment, they have been upheld by the courts.

The Establishment Clause

The establishment clause in the First Amendment forbids both state and federal governments from setting up churches and from passing laws aiding one or all religions, or favoring one religion over another. In addition, the establishment clause forbids the government from passing laws barring or requiring citizen attendance at church or belief in any religious idea.

Thomas Jefferson once referred to the establishment clause as a "wall of separation between church and state." In America, there is a wall of separation, but it is not complete. Churches are indirectly aided by government in many ways. For example, churches do not have to pay real estate taxes, even though they receive government services such as police and fire protection.

Cases involving the establishment clause have been among the most controversial to reach the Supreme Court. In these cases, the justices pay particularly close attention to the facts before rendering their decisions. In recent years they have relied on several tests. One of these, the *endorsement test*, asks whether the challenged law or government action has either the purpose or the effect of endorsing religion in the eyes of members of the community. When using this test, the Court will analyze whether the government has sent a message to nonbelievers that they are outsiders and not full members of the political community. As the following case illustrates, the test is not always easy to apply.

The Holiday Displays

For many years the city of Pittsburgh located two holiday displays on public property in the downtown area. A crèche, which depicted the Christian nativity scene, was placed at the main staircase of the county courthouse. The crèche had been donated to the city by the Holy Name Society, a Roman Catholic group. The display's manager had at its crest an angel proclaiming *Gloria in Excelsis Deo*, meaning "Glory to God in the Highest."

The other holiday display was an 18-foot Hanukkah menorah (or candelabrum) that was placed next to the city's 45-foot-tall decorated Christmas tree, just outside the city-county building. At the foot of the Christmas tree was a sign with the mayor's name and the words "Salute to Liberty." The menorah, which was owned by a Jewish religious group, was stored, erected, and removed each year by the city.

Several residents sued the city, claiming that both displays violated the First Amendment's establishment clause.

The Supreme Court justices, disagreeing as to how the case should be decided, issued several written opinions. In the majority decision, the Court ruled that the display of the creche violated the establishment clause but that the display of the menorah and Christmas tree did not. The justices who signed this opinion emphasized that the words on the crèche endorsed a Christian belief and that nothing else in that scene detracted from the religious message. By contrast, the menorah, located in a "Salute to Liberty" display with a decorated Christmas tree, was a recognition of cultural diversity rather than a government endorsement of religion.

In an opinion concurring with part of the majority decision and dissenting in part, several of the justices argued that *neither* display violated the Constitution, because such passive and symbolic exhibits do not present a genuine risk of establishing religion. They said this was typical of the ways in which government has accommodated religion throughout the nation's history.

In another opinion concurring in part and dissenting in part, other justices wrote that *both* displays violated the establishment clause. For them, the fact that two religious traditions rather than one were endorsed at the city-county building did not make that display constitutional. These justices believed that the First Amendment should almost always prohibit the display of religious symbols on public property, regardless of the number of religions included.

PROBLEM 20

a. How did the Supreme Court rule in this case? What other points of view were put forth by the justices?

b. How would you have decided this case? Does either display convey the message that some citizens are religious outsiders in their own community? Give your reasons.

c. If you believe that both displays are permissible, would you allow the permanent display of a Christian cross or a Jewish star above a government building? Would it make a difference to you if you both were displayed?

d. If you believe that neither display is permissible, should the White House Christmas tree be prohibited? Should "In God We Trust" be removed from our coinage?

Do either or both of these displays on government property violate the First Amendment?

In addition to the endorsement test, the Supreme Court also uses the following three-part test from a case decided in 1971 to determine whether a government law or action meets the requirements of the establishment clause:

1. The challenged law or government action must have a secular (nonreligious) purpose.
2. The primary effect of the law or action must be to neither advance nor inhibit (hold back) religion.
3. The operation of the law or action must not foster excessive entanglement of government with religion.

Establishment clause cases are particularly controversial when they involve aid to parochial schools or prayer in public schools. Over the years, the Court has approved some forms of aid to parochial school students and their parents. For example, it has allowed states to provide bus transportation and loans of certain textbooks to parochial school students.

However, state and federal laws that provide financial aid directly to a religious institution or its instructors are less likely to be approved. For example, in 1985 the Supreme Court decided that Michigan could not pay public school teachers to teach after-school courses in parochial schools. Although the courses were nonreligious, the Court struck down the program because it provided direct aid to religious schools and had the effect of advancing religion.

Not all laws that provide financial aid to religious institutions are unconstitutional. The Court has upheld a federal law that funds construction of buildings and facilities at religious colleges, as long as the buildings are not used for religious purposes.

Although the topic continues to be very controversial, the Court has held that public school–sponsored prayer violates the establishment clause. Even *voluntary* school-sponsored prayer (or school-sponsored daily Bible reading or recitation of the Lord's Prayer) has been found to be unconstitutional.

The Rabbi's Invocation

For many years the Providence, Rhode Island, school committee and superintendent have permitted, but not directed, school principals to include invocations and benedictions in the graduation ceremonies of the city's public junior high schools. As a result, some public middle schools in Providence have included invocations and benedictions in their graduation ceremonies.

The invocations and benedictions are not written or delivered by public school employees, but by members of the clergy invited to participate in these ceremonies for that purpose. The schools provide the clergy with guidelines prepared by the National Conference of Christians and Jews. These guidelines stress inclusiveness and sensitivity in preparing nonreligious prayer for public, civic ceremonies. The clergy who have delivered these prayers in recent years at the graduations have included ministers of various Christian denominations, as well as rabbis.

Attendance at graduation ceremonies is voluntary, and parents and friends of the students are invited to attend. Middle school ceremonies are held at the schools.

Daniel Weisman's daughter, Deborah, graduated from Nathan Bishop Middle School, a public junior high school in Providence. Rabbi Leslie Gutterman, from a local synagogue in Providence, delivered the invocation and benediction at the ceremony. Both were consistent with the guidelines that had been sent to him by the school principal.

The Weismans filed a case in federal court contending that inviting religious leaders to provide the invocation and benediction at public school graduations violated the separation of church and state required by the First Amendment.

PROBLEM 21

a. What happened in this case? Why did the Weismans object to the rabbi's providing the invocation and benediction?

b. What arguments can the Weismans make?

c. What arguments can the school make?

d. Compare this case to the decisions of the U.S. Supreme Court that have found public school–sponsored school prayer to be unconstitutional. How is this case like the school prayer cases? How is it different?

e. How should this case be decided?

f. Assume that the Supreme Court finds that public school officials *cannot* invite religious leaders to offer invocations and benedictions at graduation ceremonies. Based on that precedent, could a student graduation speaker (for example, the valedictorian) include a prayer in his or her remarks? Could the school provide students with information about a community-based baccalaureate service for graduating seniors sponsored by local churches? Could the football team and coaches say a prayer before a game?

The Free Exercise Clause

The free exercise clause in the First Amendment protects the right of individuals to worship as they choose. However, when an individual's right to free exercise of religion conflicts with other important interests, the First Amendment claim does not always win. As a rule, religious *belief* is protected. *Actions* based on those beliefs may be restricted, however, if the actions violate an important government interest.

As long ago as 1878, the U.S. Supreme Court upheld the conviction of a Mormon man who had violated the criminal law against polygamy (having multiple spouses), even though his religion at that time encouraged this practice. In 1990, the Court upheld the drug conviction of a Native American man even though his religion specifically required the sacramental use of peyote, an illegal drug. The Supreme Court's rule is that a valid, neutral law (that is, a law that does not specifically target a religious belief or practice)—in this case, the state's drug laws—will be upheld even if it interferes with religious practice.

Should the state require Amish parents to send their children to a school that does not provide the religious education they believe necessary?

The Amish Children

Wisconsin had a law requiring all children to attend school until age 16. However, the Amish believe that children between the ages of 14 and 16 should devote that time to Bible study and to training at home in farm work. The Amish believe that high school is "too worldly for their children." State officials prosecuted several Amish parents for not sending their children to school. The parents defended their actions as an exercise of their religion.

Wisconsin v. Yoder reached the U.S. Supreme Court in 1972. The Court weighed the rights of the Amish to practice their religion against the state's interest in requiring school attendance. The Court held that the Amish people's right to free exercise of religion was more important than the two years of required schooling. Among the factors the Court considered was the tendency for Amish children to become employed, law-abiding citizens after completing their religious education.

Do you agree with this decision? Give your reasons.

PROBLEM 22

The following situations involve government action and religion. For each, determine whether the establishment clause, the free exercise clause, or both are involved. Then decide whether the government's action violates the First Amendment.

a. A state law disqualified members of the clergy from holding certain public offices.

b. A high school student who has been deaf since birth asks his school district to pay for a sign language interpreter to accompany him to classes at a local religious school. A federal law requires school districts to provide for the education of all children with disabilities. The school district (which had provided him with an interpreter while he attended the public school) refuses to pay.

c. A state law authorizes a one-minute period of silence in all public schools "for meditation or voluntary prayer."

d. A state law requires that the Ten Commandments be posted in each public school classroom.

e. A group of high school students applies to the school principal to form a prayer club. The group agrees to follow the rules required of student clubs, which meet twice a week at the beginning of the school day during an activity period. A faculty member volunteers to supervise the group. However, the principal refuses the group's request.

f. A state requires citizens applying for unemployment benefits to accept appropriate jobs that are available. A citizen is denied continued unemployment compensation because she refuses to accept a job that requires her to work on the day she celebrates her Sabbath.

g. A local school board adopts regulations that permit the after-hours use of school property for 10 specified purposes. Meetings for religious purposes are not allowed.

The establishment and free exercise clauses are closely related and often come into conflict. Ensuring that a law does not establish a religion can interfere with free exercise of religion. For example, consider aid to parochial schools. Does the *failure* to aid parochial schools deprive some people of the free exercise of their religion? Similarly, laws that protect free exercise may appear to establish a religion. For example, Sunday closing laws protect Sunday as a day when individuals can attend church. To people whose day of worship is not Sunday, however, these laws may appear to be an establishment of religion.

THE RIGHT TO PRIVACY

What laws in your state protect privacy? How are these laws enforced?

The makers of our Constitution . . . conferred, against the Government, the right to be let alone—the most comprehensive of rights and the right most valued by civilized men.

—*Olmstead v. United States* (1928), dissenting opinion

Today, Justice Louis D. Brandeis's words from the *Olmstead* case continue to have meaning in our daily lives. Although the words *right to privacy* or *right to be let alone* cannot be found anywhere in the federal Constitution, many citizens agree that **privacy** is a basic right that should be protected.

PROBLEM 23

a. What does privacy mean to you at home? At school? At work? On the phone? In other places?

b. How would you feel if someone listened in on your phone calls, opened your mail before you saw it, inspected your locker, or looked at your medical or tax records without your permission?

c. In what other ways can privacy be invaded? How can the law protect the right to privacy?

Since the mid-1960s, the Supreme Court has recognized a constitutional right to privacy. This right is protected both when citizens seek to be let alone (as in search and seizure cases) and when citizens want to make certain kinds of important decisions (such as marriage and family planning) free of government interference.

The Supreme Court has said that the Constitution creates "zones of privacy." The zones are derived from the freedoms of speech and association (First Amendment), the freedom from unreasonable search and seizure (Fourth Amendment), the right to remain silent (Fifth Amendment), the right to have one's home free of soldiers during peacetime (Third Amendment), and the unspecified rights kept by the people (Ninth Amendment). The right to privacy generally protects citizens from unreasonable interference by the government.

The right to privacy sometimes conflicts with important government interests. For example, the government may need information about individuals to solve a crime or to determine eligibility for government programs. In such cases, the government can regulate certain acts or activities, even though an individual's interest in privacy is affected. Deciding whether a constitutional right to privacy exists involves a careful weighing of competing private and government interests.

Surveys regularly show popular support for protecting privacy, and some states have passed new privacy laws or added a right to privacy to their state constitutions. However, there has been a movement among certain judges and legal scholars to limit privacy protections that are based on the federal Constitution. Those who favor such limitations believe that the "zones of privacy" discussed above are the creation of some justices who have gone too far in reading privacy rights into the Constitution. Others point to popular support for privacy, extensive state laws in this area, and the many U.S. Supreme Court decisions supporting privacy rights. They argue that privacy rights are settled law on which citizens have come to rely, and that these precedents should not be overruled.

In this section you will learn about privacy in a number of contexts: at home and at school, in gathering information, and in birth control and abortion. There is also information dealing with privacy on the job at the end of this chapter in the section on rights and responsibilities in the workplace.

PROBLEM 24

For each of the following situations, decide what rights or interests are in conflict and what arguments can be made for each side. Indicate whether you agree or disagree with the law or policy.

a. A public school requires students to obey a dress code and restricts the hair length of boys.

b. The government requires taxpayers to reveal the source of their income, even if it is from illegal activities.

c. A law forbids nude bathing anywhere at a community's beaches.

d. In a prison that has had several stabbings, inmates are strip-searched every day.

e. A state law requires motorcyclists to wear helmets.

f. The police place a small device in a phone that enables them to record all numbers dialed on that phone.

Privacy in the Home

There is a saying that a person's home is his or her castle. Historically, the law has recognized that people may reasonably expect considerable privacy in their homes. However, when police carry out valid search warrants, for example, the privacy of the home may be legally invaded.

In a 1986 case, the Supreme Court considered whether a state had the authority to prosecute consenting adult males for engaging in a sexual act in a bedroom of their own home. In a 5 to 4 decision, the Court held that there was no constitutionally protected right to engage in homosexual conduct. The Court found that outlawing homosexual conduct was deeply rooted in the nation's history and traditions. The dissenters, basing their reasoning on the Georgia case that follows, believed that the sexual practices of consenting adults in their own bedrooms should be fully protected under previous privacy decisions and the fundamental "right to be let alone" by the government.

Possessing Obscene Materials at Home

Georgia had a law prohibiting the possession of obscene or pornographic films. A man was arrested in his own home for violating this law. He said (and the state prosecutor did not challenge him) that he had the films for his own use and not for sale.

In this case, the Supreme Court recognized the right to possess obscene materials in one's own home for private use. The Court indicated that individuals have the right to think, observe, and read whatever they please, especially in their own homes.

PROBLEM 25

a. Do you agree or disagree with the Court's opinion?

b. Would you decide the case differently if the man had showed the obscene films to people outside his home? Would your decision be different if people had to pay to see the films? Why?

c. Assume a person is arrested for possessing a small amount of illegal marijuana in her home. Could she successfully argue, based on the prior case, that the law violates her right to privacy? How are the cases the same? How are they different?

Privacy at School

Courts generally limit students' right to privacy in schools. For example, most courts uphold searches of students' desks and lockers. The courts reason that lockers belong to the school and that students cannot reasonably expect privacy on school property. Likewise, the Supreme Court has upheld searches of students' belongings without

How do schools in your community notify people of their privacy rights? What written procedures have been developed to implement this law?

a warrant and without probable cause, as long as school officials have some reasonable suspicion of wrongdoing.

There is, however, a federal law that protects students' right to privacy. Known as the *Family Educational Rights and Privacy Act of 1974*, this law gives parents the right to inspect their children's school records. If parents find any inaccurate, misleading, or inappropriate information, they may insist on a written correction. The law also prohibits the release of school records without a parent's permission.

Students who reach age 18 or enroll in college have a right to see their own records. Requests to see school records must be honored within 45 days. Schools have a duty to inform parents and students of their rights under this law.

The Tenth-Grade Discipline Problem

Michon, age 17, is getting ready to apply to college. Before filling out her college recommendation, the guidance counselor reviews her school records and finds this note from her tenth-grade teacher: "Michon has a serious discipline problem. She can't control herself and will have problems succeeding in school because of this." Her counselor includes this remark on the college recommendation form.

PROBLEM 26

a. What, if anything, can Michon do about the comments on her recommendation form?

b. What are her rights under the *Family Educational Rights and Privacy Act*? What are her parents' rights?

Information Gathering and Privacy

Computers have changed the way we live, work, and play. Computers allow businesses and organizations to collect, store, and examine detailed information about individuals. Some organizations

What problems could arise now that computers allow for the collection and storage of detailed information about individuals?

sell the information collected to businesses or other organizations. Individuals are often unaware of this practice.

The federal government's computers contain enormous amounts of information. Today, there are more than 5,000 federal data banks. For example, the federal government requires banks to microfilm large checks passing through customer accounts. In fact, most banks keep copies of all checks written or deposited by their customers. This information can be useful when authorities investigate white-collar crime, but it may be unfairly damaging if it falls into the hands of other investigators.

Courts have held that the right to privacy does not protect checks or deposit slips. However, limited protection is provided by a federal law that requires customers to receive notice whenever a federal agent seeks a copy of their financial records from a bank, savings and loan association, or credit card company. Individuals can then ask a federal court to decide whether the government's request should be honored. However, the law does not protect against requests from state and local governments, private investigators, or credit bureaus to see a person's financial records.

Although laws such as the *Freedom of Information Act* encourage the government to release information to the public, another law has tightened control over federal records. *The Privacy Act of 1974* prevents the government from releasing information about an individual without that person's written consent. It protects medical, financial, criminal, and employment records from unauthorized dis-

The Candidate's Indiscretion

A married male state senator running for governor had a reputation for dating women in the state's capital city. The candidate's wife and two children lived in their hometown about 200 miles from the state capital. The members of the press who traveled with the senator on campaign trips noticed that his wife seldom came along and that he often dined late at night with one particular woman. The press decided to investigate further and discovered this woman leaving the candidate's house early one morning.

PROBLEM 27

a. Is it reasonable for the candidate to expect the reporters not to disclose this information? Give arguments on both sides of this issue.

b. How would you analyze the situation with respect to the candidate's privacy if the reporters also had information that the senator had used cocaine at a social gathering?

c. Some states have laws requiring that a candidate reveal the source and amount of all campaign contributions. Do these laws violate the privacy rights of the contributors?

closure. The law also entitles individuals (with some exceptions) to see information about themselves and to correct any mistakes. If your rights are violated under this law, you may sue for damages in federal court.

Birth Control and Abortion

Birth control and abortion continue to be controversial issues. In 1965, the U.S. Supreme Court struck down a state law that prohibited the possession of contraceptives by married couples. Later, the Supreme Court declared that a law prohibiting the sale of birth control devices to unmarried people was also unconstitutional. In both cases, the laws had violated the right to privacy.

The most recent issue to arise regarding birth control is condom distribution and Norplant counseling in schools. Some high schools already have condom-distribution programs in place. These programs may require attendance at lectures about HIV infections and AIDS, other sexually transmitted diseases (STDs), and other health issues. Some educators and parents view the condom-distribution programs as one way to slow the spread of AIDS.

Many parents and educators argue that discussing and dispensing birth control to youth will only promote sexual activity. Others say that we must provide our youth with accurate sex education and appropriate birth control at an early age. They argue that this will assist young people, who may already be sexually active, to be responsible and safe in their activities.

Another controversial contraceptive program in schools involves Norplant, a device consisting of six matchstick-sized capsules that are surgically implanted under the skin in the girl's arm. These capsules release a contraceptive over a five-year period. With Norplant, there is no problem of forgetting to use a contraceptive. Counseling about Norplant includes recommending the use of a condom to reduce the risk of AIDS and other STDs.

Some parents, educators, religious leaders, and others oppose the discussion and distribution of birth control in public schools. They believe that this topic is best handled through families, not schools. In many instances, they also believe that the correct message is **abstinence** (not having sex) rather than safe sex.

Both the condom-distribution and Norplant counseling programs aim at reducing teenage pregnancy. Although some teens faithfully use contraception, pregnancies still occur. Many girls then face the decision of whether to continue the pregnancy or to have an abortion.

Abortion availability and legislation have changed over time. In the early 1800s, abortion was legal in the United States prior to "quickening" (when the mother can first feel the fetus moving). By the late 1870s, attitudes changed, and almost every state had laws restricting abortions. Abortion activity went underground.

In the mid-1960s, people once again became vocal about the need for legalized abortion. People proposed many arguments on both sides, giving moral, religious, financial, political, and constitutional reasons.

Some people argue that abortion is wrong in all situations. These individuals believe that life begins at conception and must be protected from that moment on. Others argue that abortion is a constitutional right and a private matter to be decided by a woman. These individuals believe that a woman must be allowed to control her own

What is the law in your state regarding abortion? Who can get an abortion? Is permission required from one or both parents of a pregnant teenager or the father of the fetus? Have there been important court cases in your state regarding abortion?

body and not have it regulated by laws that work against her personal choices.

The U.S. Supreme Court and many state courts have struggled with these issues. In 1973, a landmark Supreme Court decision, *Roe v. Wade*, made abortion legal in certain circumstances. Based on a woman's constitutional right to privacy, *Roe* held that a woman had a fundamental, though not absolute, right to an abortion. This right was defined on a trimester basis. During the first trimester of pregnancy (the first three months), a woman could have an abortion on demand without interference from the state. During the second trimester of pregnancy (the second three months), the state could regulate abortions for safety but could not prohibit them entirely. During the third trimester of pregnancy (the last three months), the state could regulate or forbid all abortions except to save the life of the mother.

The 1973 *Roe* decision did not end the debate over abortion. In some ways, the decision intensified the debate. Since 1973, the Supreme Court has held that states could not give a husband veto power over his wife's decision to have an abortion. Parents of minor, unwed girls also could not have absolute veto power over abortion decisions. However, the Supreme Court has said that states may be able to require that pregnant unmarried minors obtain parental consent as long as the minor has the option to avoid this by going before the court to obtain permission from a judge.

Where do you stand on the abortion issue? Give reasons.

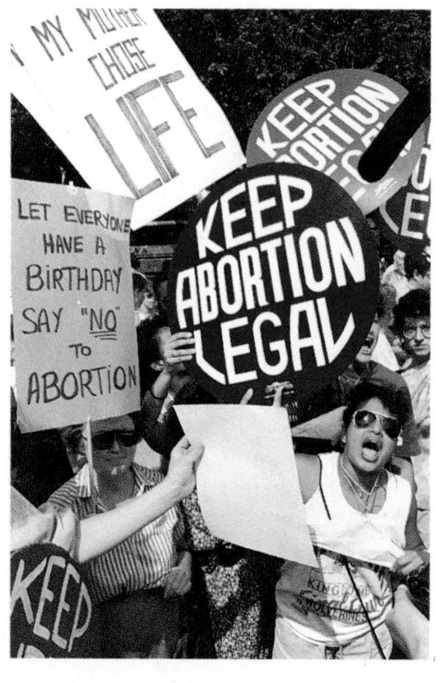

While never actually overturning *Roe v. Wade*, the Supreme Court has allowed states additional authority to limit the right to an abortion. In one case, the Court upheld a Missouri law that prohibited abortions in state hospitals. In this case, the Court also stated its dislike for the original *Roe* trimester system. The Court called this system "too rigid."

A woman's right to an abortion was further reduced by the use of a gag order put into effect by President Ronald Reagan and continued by President George Bush. The gag order prohibited abortion counseling at federally funded clinics. In this way, many women were not provided with information about the option of abortion and thus were not able to make informed decisions. However, within the first few days of his administration, President Bill Clinton lifted the gag order regarding abortion counseling.

Some people argue that the gag order on abortion counseling should remain in place. They believe that prohibiting the use of public funds and public facilities for abortion counseling and abortions will reduce the total number of abortions performed. Others argue that access to information about abortion, as well as government funding, will protect poor women from dangerous "back alley" abortions, which have caused serious injury and loss of life in the past. (See Appendix D for an "Abortion and the States" chart.)

PROBLEM 28

List the advantages and disadvantages of each of the following proposed government regulations. Give your reasons.

a. The father of the child must give his consent to the proposed abortion.

b. A pregnant minor must obtain permission from one or both of her parents prior to having an abortion.

c. A 24-hour waiting period is required between a woman's decision to have an abortion and the actual procedure.

d. Before having an abortion, a woman must hear a lecture on, and see photos of, aborted fetuses.

e. A woman who cannot afford to pay for an abortion may not obtain one free at a local public hospital.

f. A pregnant minor may obtain permission for an abortion from a judge instead of her parents.

g. Condoms are to be dispensed from the school health clinic in junior and senior high schools.

h. Norplant is to be made available to teenage girls upon request.

Abortion Law Challenges

In 1992 the U.S. Supreme Court decided the case of *Planned Parenthood of Southeastern Pennsylvania v. Casey*. As a result of that case, a woman continues to have a right to an abortion before the fetus is viable (before the fetus could live independently outside the mother's womb). After fetal viability, however, a state has increased power to restrict the availability of abortions. The state maintains the power to restrict some abortions because of its legitimate interests in protecting the health of the woman and the potential life of the fetus.

States can pass some laws that regulate abortion, but these laws cannot place a "substantial obstacle in the path of a woman seeking an abortion," the Court said in the *Casey* decision. However, the Court declined to define specifically what constitutes a substantial obstacle. This decision held that regulations were constitutional if they did not place an "undue burden" on obtaining an abortion. For example, the decision allowed a regulation that requires a woman to give "informed consent" at least 24 hours before the planned abortion.

The law regarding abortion and birth control is not settled. Congress and many state legislatures continue to consider these topics major political issues. Lobbyists on both sides of the issue work hard to present their positions to legislators.

Abortion policies also vary around the world. Some countries (Argentina, Brazil, and Egypt, for example) do not allow abortions for economic and social reasons, preservation of maternal mental health, or rape or incest. Canada, China, and Denmark permit abortions on demand. Cameroon allows abortions to preserve the physical health of the mother and for rape and incest, but not to preserve the mental health of the mother.

PROBLEM 29

a. What is the current legal status of abortion?

b. Should abortion be made illegal again? What are the arguments on both sides? How would you vote? Why?

c. Should abortion be regulated but not illegal? If so, in what ways?

DUE PROCESS

No person shall be . . . deprived of life, liberty, or property, without due process of law . . .

—Fifth Amendment

No State shall . . . deprive any person of life, liberty, or property, without due process of law . . .

—14th Amendment

The phrase **due process** embodies society's basic notions of legal fairness. The courts have looked at the due process language of the 5th and the 14th Amendments as providing two different types of protection. The first type is called **substantive due process**. When applying substantive due process, courts look at whether a law or government action infringes on a fundamental liberty.

During the first third of the 20th century, the U.S. Supreme Court used the due process clause to strike down social and economic legislation, such as child labor and minimum wage laws. Since the late 1930s, however, the courts have deferred much more to the legislative judgments of elected officials. It is common in current court opinions upholding economic regulations for judges to write that "we will not substitute our wisdom for that of the legislators."

During the 1960s, however, a new version of substantive due process emerged as the Supreme Court used it to protect certain fundamental personal rights *not* specifically protected in the Constitution. For example, the Court has said that the right of personal privacy is a part of the concept of liberty, protected by the 5th and 14th Amendments. Cases dealing with abortion, contraception use, and the rights to marry and have children, among others, are all based on this personal right to privacy, a right protected by substantive due process.

Most of the modern due process cases, however, deal with what is called **procedural due process** (fair, or due process, procedures). Due process procedures do not guarantee that the *result* of government action will always be to a citizen's liking. However, fair procedures do help prevent arbitrary, unreasonable decisions. Due process requirements vary depending on the situation. At a minimum, due process means that citizens must be given *notice* of what the government plans to do and have a *chance to comment* on the action.

How does a trial help to prevent arbitrary or unreasonable decisions?

Government takes many actions that may deprive people of life, liberty, or property. In each case, some form of due process is required. For example, a state might fire someone from a government job, revoke a prisoner's parole, or cut off someone's social security payments. Due process does not prohibit these actions, but it does require that certain procedures be followed before any action is taken.

You are probably familiar with some due process requirements from your knowledge of criminal law. For example, among the procedures that the government must use before sending someone to jail (thereby depriving the person of liberty) are notice of the charges, an opportunity to be heard at a trial, the assistance of a lawyer, and the right to appeal. (For additional information, see the materials on the criminal justice process in Chapter 2.)

If a person has a right to due process, the next issue is this: What process is due? Due process is a flexible concept. The procedures required in specific situations depend on several factors: (1) the seri-

Goss v. Lopez

In 1971 widespread student unrest took place in the Columbus, Ohio, public schools. Students who either participated in, or were present at, demonstrations held on school grounds were suspended. Many suspensions were for a period of 10 days. Students were not given a hearing before suspension, although at a later date some students and their parents were given informal conferences with the school principal. Ohio law provides free education to all children between the ages of 6 and 21. A number of students, through their parents, sued the board of education, claiming that their right to due process had been violated when they were suspended without a hearing.

In *Goss v. Lopez*, the Supreme Court decided that students who are suspended for 10 days or less are entitled to certain rights before their suspension. These rights include (1) oral or written notice of the charges, (2) an explanation (if students deny the charges) of the evidence against them, and (3) an opportunity for students to present their side of the story.

The Court stated that in an emergency, students could be sent home immediately and a hearing held at a later date. The Court did *not* give students a right to a lawyer, a right to cross-examine witnesses, a right to call witnesses, or a right to a hearing before an impartial person.

In *Goss*, the Court considered the due process interests of harm, cost, and risk. The Court ruled that reputations were harmed and educational opportunities were lost during the suspension; that an informal hearing would not be overly costly for the schools; and that while most disciplinary decisions were probably correct, an informal hearing would help reduce the risk of error.

PROBLEM 30

a. What happened in the *Goss* case? What rights did the Supreme Court say the students should be given prior to a brief suspension?

b. What rights might the students want that they did not receive in this case? What are the arguments for and against providing these additional rights?

c. Do you think this case was decided correctly? Give your reasons.

What due process procedures are followed by schools in your area before a student is suspended?

ousness of the harm that might be done to the citizen; (2) the cost to the government, in time and money, of carrying out the procedures; and (3) the risk of making an error without the procedures.

In addition to notice and an opportunity to be heard, due process may include a hearing before an impartial person, representation by an attorney, calling witnesses on one's behalf, cross-examination of witnesses, a written decision with reasons based on the evidence introduced, a transcript of the proceeding, and an opportunity to appeal the decision.

If you believe that the government has not followed fair procedures, you may want to consult an attorney. With the attorney's advice and assistance, you can file a complaint directly with the government agency. You may also be able to go to court and seek an order that the government follow due process in dealing with you.

Remember that when the U.S. Supreme Court decides a constitutional issue, it sets out the *minimum* protection required. No government can offer less. For example, a state could not decide to do away with the "notice" requirement in the *Goss* decision. However, government agencies can (and some do) offer greater due process protection than the Supreme Court requires.

The Unruly Daughter

Katherine Stone, age 17, was a junior at Northwest High School. As a sophomore, she had been a varsity cheerleader, a member of the school orchestra, and an honor roll student. During the summer between her sophomore and junior years, she began to stay out late and was never able to provide her parents with an adequate explanation of her whereabouts. Several times in August of that summer, she came home with the smell of alcohol on her breath. Her parents learned from several of her friends that she was going out with a 30-year-old man.

Once the fall semester began, she quit all her school activities, and her grades began to drop. Her parents and school counselor tried to speak with her about her behavior, but they were unsuccessful.

The Stones were afraid that Katherine would run away with her new boyfriend or get into serious trouble with either drugs or alcohol. Feeling desperate and believing that they had tried everything they could, they signed the papers needed to commit her to a state mental hospital for diagnosis and treatment. The director of the hospital assured the Stones that a psychiatrist from the department of social services would thoroughly examine Katherine to determine whether she should stay at the hospital. The psychiatrist diagnosed Katherine's behavior problem as "adolescent adjustment reaction" and recommended continued hospitalization.

Katherine acknowledges that she has a problem communicating with her parents but claims that she is not mentally ill. She wants to leave the hospital. Assume that she is able to make a phone call to a lawyer.

PROBLEM 31

a. What arguments can Katherine's attorney make to secure her release?

b. What arguments can the hospital's attorney make?

c. What rights or interests do the parents have in this case?

d. Can you think of any additional steps that could be taken before hospitalization to avoid making a mistake? Describe them.

e. If Katherine sues to be released from the hospital, how should this case be decided?

f. Would Katherine have any due process rights if her parents had committed her to a private hospital instead of a state hospital? Explain. Are there any legal arguments she might make instead of due process? If so, which ones? Would she win?

PROBLEM 32

For each of the following situations, decide whether the citizen has any interest at stake. If there is an interest, is it in life, liberty, or property? If you think there is an interest, what procedures do you think the government should follow to protect the citizen's rights?

a. City welfare officials believe a person is no longer eligible for welfare. They end payments without a hearing.

b. A defendant, convicted of first-degree murder, is sentenced to death. The state supreme court refuses to hear his appeal.

c. A student who is a discipline problem is paddled by the teacher. The student is not given a hearing before the paddling.

d. Federal officials plan to build a dam that will flood a privately owned farm. The farmer does not want to sell her land or move from her home. No hearing is held, but the farmer is offered the fair market value of her property.

e. A consumer misses two car payments in a row. The finance company takes the car back without notice or a hearing.

f. A student with emotional difficulties is expelled for constantly fighting with other students. The student is not given a hearing.

DISCRIMINATION (RIGHT TO EQUAL PROTECTION)

We hold these Truths to be self-evident, that all Men are created equal, that they are endowed by their Creator with certain inalienable rights . . .

—Declaration of Independence

No State shall . . . deny to any person within its jurisdiction the equal protection of the laws.

—14th Amendment

The promise of equality set out in the Declaration of Independence and the 14th Amendment is one of our nation's most ambitious ideals. But what does equality mean? Does it mean equal result, equal treatment, equal opportunity, or something else? Citizens claiming they have been denied equality have flooded the courts and legislatures in recent years. However, the government has found the promise of equality difficult to explain and enforce.

Over time, ideas about equality have changed. For many years, the courts held that equal protection did not mean that all persons had to have access to the same facilities, such as schools, restaurants, railroad cars, or public restrooms. Instead, the law allowed separate facilities for whites and African Americans as long as the facilities were equal. This was known as the separate but equal doctrine. In the 1954 case of *Brown v. Board of Education*, the Supreme Court ruled that separate schools were "inherently unequal." It then ordered the public schools integrated "with all deliberate speed." In the years following the *Brown* case, other court decisions and laws required the desegregation of all other public facilities.

Why did the Supreme Court believe that the "separate but equal" doctrine for public schools was unfair?

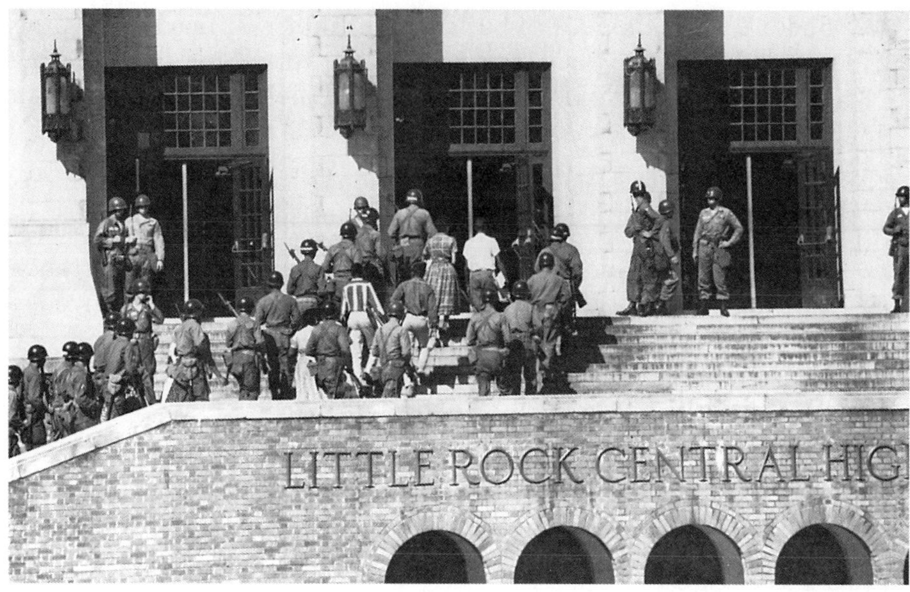

The *Brown* decision started a period of growing national awareness about discrimination. During the next 40 years, courts and legislatures confronted issues of discrimination based on race, **national origin** (the status of being born in another country), **alienage** (the status of being a foreign-born person and not yet a U.S. citizen), sex, age, disability, income, and **legitimacy** (whether or not a child is born to a married couple). Unquestionably, the civil rights movement improved the economic and social positions of millions of Americans. However, despite landmark Supreme Court decisions and numerous civil rights laws, equality remains an elusive goal rather than an accomplished fact. Today society faces the problem of overcoming past discrimination against minorities and women without causing reverse discrimination against others.

What Is Discrimination?

Many laws discriminate. They do this by classifying people into different groups. Discrimination is an unavoidable result of lawmaking. Not all types of discrimination are illegal. As long as classifications are reasonable, they usually do not violate the equal protection clause.

Everyone is familiar with laws that require a person to be a certain age to obtain a driver's license. These laws discriminate but are not unconstitutional. For example, in some states, people 16 or older qualify for a license; those under 16 do not. This classification is considered reasonable. However, what if the law required a person to be left-handed to get a license? Or what if whites but not African Americans, or Polish Americans but not Mexican Americans, could get a license? Would these laws be constitutional? How do they differ from the age requirement?

Does your state or local government have any laws against discrimination? What groups are protected by these laws? What state and local agencies are responsible for their enforcement?

PROBLEM 33

The following situations all involve some form of discrimination. Decide whether the discrimination is reasonable and should be permitted or is unreasonable and should be prohibited. Explain your reasons.

a. An airline requires pilots to retire at age 50.

b. A business refuses to hire a man with good typing skills for a secretary's position.

c. People who have AIDS cannot be hired as phone operators.

d. People under age 18 are not allowed into theaters showing X-rated movies.

e. A child with a disability is not permitted to play at a public playground.

f. In selecting applicants for government jobs, preference is given to veterans.

g. Girls are not allowed to try out for positions on an all-boy baseball team at a public high school.

h. Auto insurance rates are higher for young, unmarried drivers.

i. Gay men and lesbians are not allowed to serve in the military.

The 14th Amendment provides that no state shall deny to any person the equal protection of the law. To determine whether a law or government practice meets the equal protection standard, courts use three different tests, depending upon the type of discrimination involved.

The Rational Basis Test In most discrimination cases that come to court, judges use the rational basis test. Using this test, judges will uphold the law or practice in question if it has a rational basis. A rational basis exists when there is a logical relationship between the classification and the purpose of the law.

For example, states require their citizens to be a certain age before they can marry. These laws discriminate against people below a certain age. However, is the discrimination unconstitutional? The reason for such a law is to ensure that young people are capable of accepting the responsibilities of marriage. In general, people become more responsible as they get older, so there is a rational relationship between the classification and the purpose of the law. For the most part, courts uphold government laws and practices that are judged according to the rational basis test.

The Strict Scrutiny Test Certain laws and practices discriminate based on race; national origin; alienage; or some fundamental right set out in the Constitution, such as freedom of religion. In these cases, the courts use a test called strict scrutiny. Judges applying strict scrutiny will find the law or practice unconstitutional *unless* the state can show it serves a compelling (very important) interest that requires the classification. Strict scrutiny is used to protect our most precious freedoms, and the challenger in these cases is often successful.

For example, a town in Florida passed a local ordinance that outlawed ritual animal sacrifices by the members of a particular religion. When the law was challenged, the Supreme Court used the strict scrutiny test. Although the government does have a compelling interest in sanitation and avoiding undue cruelty to animals, those interests had to be dealt with through laws applied fairly to everyone in the community, not simply by targeting the religious practices of one group. The Court determined that the ordinance was unconstitutional.

The Substantial Relationship Test In sex discrimination cases, the Supreme Court uses the substantial relationship test. In these cases, there must be a close connection (not just a rational relationship) between the law or practice and its purpose. In addition, laws that classify based on sex must serve an important government purpose.

For example, a state law prohibited beer sales to males aged 18 to 20 but not to females, because more males had been arrested for drunk driving. Although this law served an important government purpose (reducing drunk driving), it was ruled unconstitutional. The Court held that there was not a close connection between the classification and the purpose, because females were legally free to buy beer and give it to 18- to 20-year-old males.

Equal protection cases are complicated and controversial. Some people have argued, for example, that when the 14th Amendment was ratified in 1868, Congress intended it to protect only against racial discrimination. Others argue that it was intended to protect only African Americans, not other racial minorities or whites, against racial discrimination. Still others contend that the amendment embodies our national commitment to the fundamental value of equality, and that *all* unfair forms of government discrimination should be prohibited by the equal protection clause.

Other Sources of Equality Protection In addition to Supreme Court decisions interpreting the 14th Amendment, citizens have other legal protections of their equality rights. There are many federal civil rights laws, as well as court decisions interpreting these statutes. Similarly, there are numerous state and local antidiscrimination laws and trial and appellate court decisions interpreting them.

In studying discrimination, you will encounter some specific instances in which various civil rights laws collide with one another. For example, do some affirmative action laws protecting minorities actually discriminate against whites? Can the state require a private club to accept members of other races or the opposite sex without interfering with the existing members' freedom of association or their privacy?

Discrimination Based on Race, National Origin, and Alienage

Most Americans believe that racial discrimination is both morally and legally wrong. Today, almost no one defends segregated public facilities or the operation of separate public school systems for African-American and white children. Nevertheless, discrimination is still a problem.

Americans are still coming to grips with their history of race discrimination in light of the Constitution's guarantee of equal protection. Today, the government faces the dilemma of helping those exposed to racial injustice while avoiding discrimination against others. The following questions focus our attention on the troubling issue of how to use just means to rid society of injustice: Does providing greater opportunities for some who have historically been denied equal protection result in fewer opportunities for others? Do discrimination laws originally passed to protect minorities protect the majority as well? Must the disadvantaged be treated differently in order to be treated equally?

Today, discrimination is usually more subtle than in the past. Moreover, reasonable people sometimes disagree as to what constitutes discrimination. For example, a town denied a request to rezone land to build townhouses for low- and moderate-income tenants. The town had mostly detached single-family houses, and almost all the town's residents were white. The Supreme Court upheld the zoning law because the Court found no *intent* to discriminate. However,

Conflict at Windsor Beach

Thousands of African-American college students are planning their fourth annual fraternity party weekend at Windsor Beach. As the event has grown in size over the years, there have been some complaints from residents about noise and minor vandalism. Town officials decide to deny requests from the students for use of the civic center for a concert, and the chamber of commerce advertises in the newspapers of African-American colleges in the area, discouraging students from coming to Windsor Beach for that weekend.

Many of the students are angered by the ads and by what they believe are the racist attitudes of the townspeople, most of whom are white. They believe that Windsor Beach would treat a group of white college students differently.

More than 100,000 African-American students come to Windsor Beach despite the warnings. The town council passes a midnight curfew law and issues written rules prohibiting behavior such as drinking in the street, excessive noise, and street gatherings. Late one night during the weekend, large numbers of students mill about on downtown streets, and some confrontations with police take place. There are incidents of vandalism and looting, arrests, and some injuries to both police and college students.

PROBLEM 34

a. Why did the townspeople want to prohibit the party weekend? Were their reasons valid?

b. Why were the students angered by the actions of the townspeople? Were their reasons valid?

c. How might this problem have been avoided or resolved differently?

d. Does this incident illustrate the state of race relations in America today? Explain.

when a school system redrew school attendance lines to keep African-American and white children from attending the same schools, the Court found that this action violated the 14th Amendment.

Reasonable people also sometimes disagree as to what constitutes a fair and effective **remedy** for discrimination. Controversy has often surrounded efforts to desegregate public schools and to eliminate unlawful discrimination in the workplace.

Public school segregation was declared unconstitutional in the *Brown* case. In theory, the schools were opened to students of all races. In many instances, however, segregation continued. Many methods were used to desegregate the schools, including allowing students to attend any school they desired, redrawing neighborhood school boundary lines, transferring teachers, and developing magnet schools with special programs to attract a racially mixed student population.

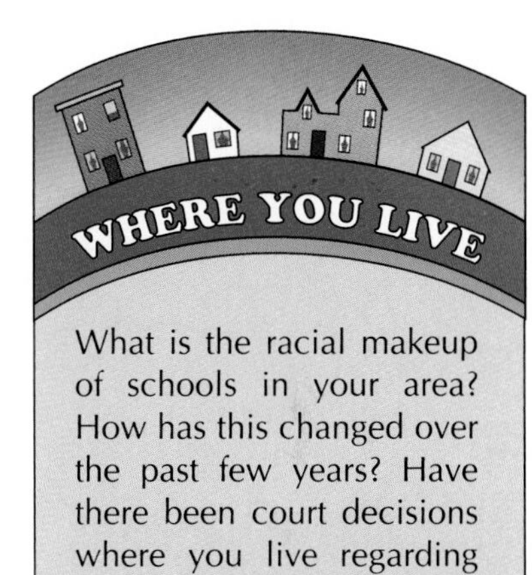

What is the racial makeup of schools in your area? How has this changed over the past few years? Have there been court decisions where you live regarding school desegregation? Has busing been ordered? If so, has it worked?

Perhaps the most controversial method of school desegregation is busing. Busing as a means of transporting children to school has a long history. Today, millions of children ride buses to and from school. However, controversy arose in 1971 when the Supreme Court first required busing as a means of achieving school integration.

Supporters of busing claim that requiring racially balanced schools can help provide equal educational opportunity and quality education for both African-American and white children They also argue that busing, which was once used to support segregation by transporting students to separate African-American and white schools, is an appropriate remedy. Opponents of busing contend that neighborhood schools are better, because children will be in school

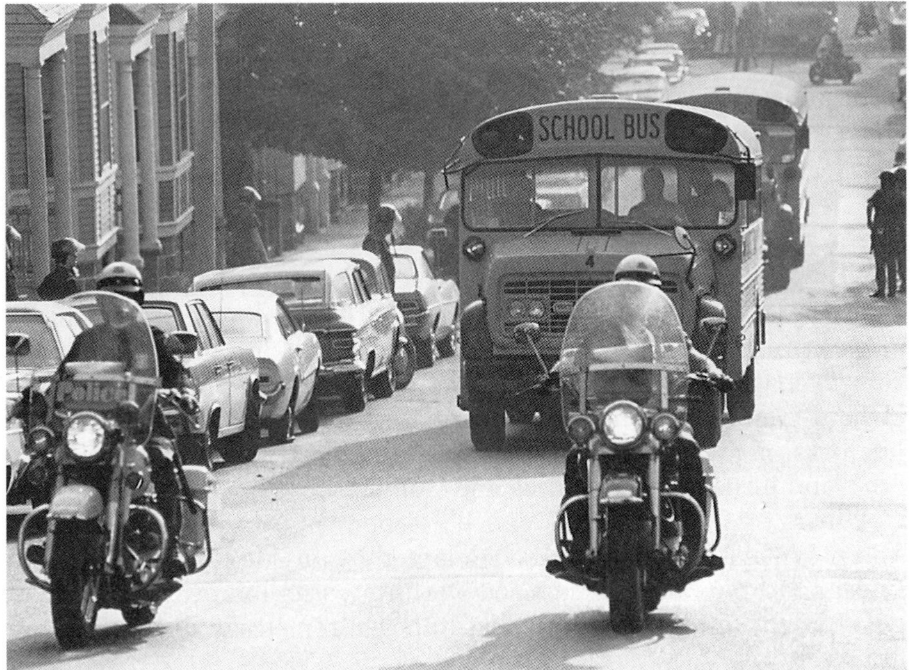

Is it important to have racially balanced schools?

with their friends and will be closer to home in case of an emergency. Critics also maintain that court-ordered busing has caused whites to flee city schools, resulting in even more segregation.

Recently, the Supreme Court has issued decisions that make it easier for school districts to stop court-ordered busing. The Court emphasized that desegregation orders are only meant to be temporary and can end once the prior segregation has been remedied. This means that a desegregation order can be stopped even if a racial imbalance still exists. For example, in a 1992 case, the Court allowed a Georgia school district to end busing because the prior segregation was remedied and the current racial imbalance resulted from a population change (more minorities than whites moved into the area).

Many feel that discrimination exists between the rich and poor school districts in a state. Many school districts depend on local taxes for money. Thus, the wealthier areas are able to provide more support to their school districts. Some states are considering "share the wealth" plans that require the richer districts to give tax money to the poorer districts. Supporters argue that this plan will equalize education between the wealthy and poor districts. Critics argue that the plan is unfair and that money will not automatically solve the school's educational problems.

PROBLEM 35

a. Why do so many public schools continue to have a racially imbalanced student population?

b. Should the government take steps to bring about greater integration of public schools? If so, what should the government do? If not, why not?

Affirmative action is another remedy for dealing with the effects of discrimination. Affirmative action means taking positive steps to remedy past discrimination in employment and education. It goes beyond merely stopping or avoiding discrimination. For example, a business might take affirmative action by starting a program to recruit and hire more minorities and women.

Affirmative action plans can be either voluntary or mandatory. Voluntary plans are those freely adopted by an employer or university. Mandatory plans are imposed by the government as a condition of government funding or as a court-imposed remedy in discrimination cases.

Affirmative action programs are sometimes controversial. Supporters of affirmative action say that preferential admissions and hiring policies are needed to overcome the effects of past discrimination. Opponents of affirmative action say that it is a form of reverse discrimination. They argue that race and sex should not be used as a basis for classification, because special treatment for some means discrimination against others.

Can a white male be the victim of discrimination?

Several methods are used to increase the number of minorities admitted to educational programs and hired for jobs. These methods include **quotas** (which require a specific number of minorities at a certain position), **goals**, **preferences** (which are given to minority applicants), and **set-asides** (percentages of contract money available that are reserved for minority companies). These methods have been the source of considerable controversy. In this debate, each side claims that its position is fair.

The affirmative action issue was presented to the Supreme Court in the case of. *The University of California v. Bakke* (1978). In this case, the medical school of the University of California at Davis had decided that the best way to increase minority enrollment was to give certain advantages to minority applicants. Each entering class reserved 16 of 100 places for minority applicants. Allan Bakke, a 33-year-old white engineer, was twice denied admission to the medical school. He claimed that without the special admissions program, he would have been admitted, because his grades and test scores were higher than those of the minority students. Bakke sued the university, saying that the affirmative action program denied him equal protection of the laws.

The Supreme Court held the medical school's special admissions program unconstitutional and ordered Bakke admitted to the university. However, the decision left many questions unanswered. The Court seemed to say that racial quotas were illegal but that race could be considered as one of the factors in the admissions decision as long as schools sought to obtain a diverse student body. Before long, the issue of affirmative action was again before the Court.

THE CASE OF . . .

The Voluntary Affirmative Action Program

Brian Weber was a white employee at the Kaiser Aluminum factory in a small Louisiana town. After five years at the plant, Weber applied for a position in a training program for skilled workers. He was turned down even though he had more seniority (more years of experience at this job) than some of those selected.

Weber was not selected because Kaiser Aluminum had an affirmative action program designed to increase the number of African Americans in skilled positions. To do this, Kaiser and the local union had agreed to give 50% of the training positions to African Americans and 50% to whites. Kaiser believed that this was necessary because although nearly 40% of the local work force was African American, fewer than 2% of the company's skilled employees were African Americans.

Weber believed this plan was unfair. He said it discriminated against him because of his race. Weber sued the company, relying on *Title VII* of the *Civil Rights Act of 1964*, which makes it illegal for employers to discriminate on the basis of race.

PROBLEM 36

a. What happened in this case? Why was Brian Weber denied admission to the training program?

b. Should schools or businesses ever be allowed to use race as a factor in decision making? If so, when and why? If not, why not?

c. What values are in conflict in this case? In the *Bakke* case?

d. What is the purpose of affirmative action programs? How do these programs affect society?

e. Do you think statistical underrepresentation of a group in school or business proves discrimination?

In 1979, Brian Weber lost his case. The Supreme Court found that *Title VII* had been passed to improve employment opportunities for minorities and that it did not prohibit a voluntary affirmative action plan designed to end racial imbalance.

During the 1980s the Supreme Court made several decisions that made it harder for minorities to challenge discriminatory practices. In other decisions, the Court made it easier for nonminorities to challenge affirmative action policies. For example, a 1989 case involved a city's policy of setting aside 30% of its government construction contracts for minority-owned businesses. The Court said it was wrong for the city to do this unless there was convincing evidence from the past that the employers or unions actually excluded minorities from local industry.

Why had the Court changed its mind about discrimination cases?

Most people point to the change in the composition of the Court. In the mid-1980s, President Reagan was able to appoint several justices who had more conservative views. Some people saw the Court's rulings as important to balance the rights of nonminorities. Other people criticized the Court for taking away too many benefits gained from the civil rights struggle. However, a majority of the U.S. Congress felt the courts had gone too far in cutting back on civil rights. In response to the criticism, Congress reversed many of the decisions of the late 1980s in the *Civil Rights Act of 1991*.

When we think about the civil rights struggle, we mostly remember cases in which African Americans brought lawsuits to end discriminatory practices. During the middle of the 20th century, the National Association for the Advancement of Colored People (NAACP) and other organizations developed careful strategies for bringing important cases before the U.S. Supreme Court. Also during this time, however, groups representing Latino and Asian plaintiffs brought significant cases in federal courts. While some of these cases dealt with racial discrimination, others analyzed discrimination based on national origin or alienage.

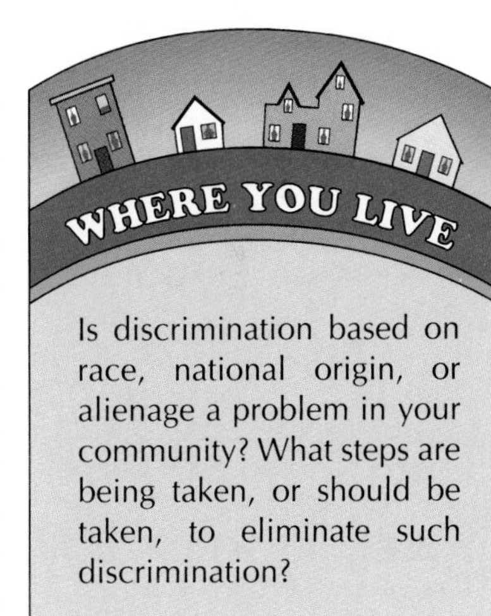

Is discrimination based on race, national origin, or alienage a problem in your community? What steps are being taken, or should be taken, to eliminate such discrimination?

For the most part, the courts have not favored government laws and policies that discriminate based on national origin and alienage. The basic problem with these laws and policies is that they treat people as members of a group, rather than consider their individual abilities and needs. For example, courts have struck down laws prohibiting aliens (non-citizens) from becoming lawyers or engineers. State laws excluding aliens from all government jobs have also been

Can Congress deport aliens who engage in unlawful activities?

Educating the Children of Undocumented Aliens

According to state law, local school districts receive no money for educating children not legally admitted into the United States. The same law also authorizes local school districts to deny enrollment to such children. A child of parents not legally admitted to the United States is excluded from his local school and brings suit against the state. He claims that the law has denied him equal protection.

Read the two opinions below, and decide which should be the decision of the U.S. Supreme Court. Give your reasons.

Opinion A

The Fourteenth Amendment says that "No state shall . . . deny to any person within its jurisdiction the equal protection of the laws." This should be applied literally to all persons, even the children of undocumented aliens. While our past decisions have allowed states to treat undocumented aliens differently from legally admitted aliens, the idea of punishing innocent children for the misconduct of their parents does not fit with our basic idea of fairness. Although there is no federal constitutional right to an education, we recognize that economic opportunity is severely limited for those unable to obtain one. This law unconstitutionally places a lifetime hardship on the children of undocumented aliens.

Opinion B

Undocumented aliens, as opposed to legal aliens, are not a group receiving special judicial protection according to our past decisions, and this Court has never held that education is a fundamental right. Therefore, when we look at this new law, we should not be tempted to substitute our wisdom for that of the representatives elected by the state's citizens. Our precedents require only that state laws not violate the Constitution. In this case the law must have a rational basis. It is certainly not irrational for the state to conclude, as it apparently has, that it does not have the responsibility to provide benefits for persons whose presence in this country is illegal. The state law in question is constitutional. The children of undocumented aliens need to address their problem to their state legislature.

held unconstitutional, although citizenship may be required for some jobs.

In distributing government benefits, state laws that deny welfare benefits to all aliens are unconstitutional. However, Congress's power to exclude some aliens (those living here less than five years) from Medicare has been upheld.

Sex Discrimination

Equality of rights shall not be denied or abridged by the United States or by any state on account of sex.

—Proposed Equal Rights Amendment

The movement to secure equal rights for women has a long history. From the nation's earliest days, women protested against unequal treatment. The first women's rights convention was held in 1848 in Seneca Falls, New York. It set out a list of demands for political, social, and economic equality. The most controversial issue to come out of the Seneca Falls convention was women's demand for the right to vote. Over 70 years later, women finally won full voting rights in 1920 with the ratification of the 19th Amendment.

Although women have made many gains, the U.S. Supreme Court was slow to recognize sex discrimination as a problem. Even after passage of the 19th Amendment, it took another 50 years for the Court to find a government policy based on sex to be unconstitutional.

For many years women fought to get the *Equal Rights Amendment (ERA)* passed. The ERA would have prohibited federal, state, and local governments from passing discriminatory laws or enforcing laws unequally based on sex. In 1982 the ERA failed to become federal law when the ratification deadline passed while the vote was still three states short of the 38 total needed. However, although there is no federal ERA, at least 16 states have equal rights provisions in their state constitutions.

Does your state have an equal rights act? What state and local laws protect against sex discrimination where you live? What agencies enforce these laws?

Activity over the ERA has become less vocal. However, the Supreme Court and Congress continue to handle sex discrimination issues. For example, in 1963 Congress passed the *Equal Pay Act*, which made it illegal to pay women less money than men for doing the same job. However, today women as a whole still earn considerably less than men. One year later, Congress passed the *Civil Rights Act of 1964* (see Appendix C for a summary of this and other civil rights laws). *Title VII* of the *Civil Rights Law* prohibits discrimination against women and minorities in all forms of employment: hiring, firing, working conditions, and promotion.

The Fetal Protection Policy

In 1990 the Supreme Court heard the case of *UAW v. Johnson Controls*, which dealt with an employer's fetal protection policy that restricted women from particular job positions based on fertility. Johnson Controls, Inc., manufactured automobile batteries. This process included exposure to lead. Johnson Controls modified its employment policy to deny all women of childbearing years access to certain jobs because of lead exposure and the potential harm this exposure might cause to a fetus. Johnson Controls allowed women access to these positions if they could provide medical documentation of their sterility.

The Supreme Court unanimously held unlawful employer "fetal protection" policies that are used to keep women out of particular, potentially hazardous jobs. The Johnson Controls policy discriminated on the basis of gender when it excluded only women who could bear children, despite the similar health risks to men.

The careers of women who work in a corporate setting are often limited by the "glass ceiling." The glass ceiling refers to barriers—actions, beliefs, and attitudes—that prevent qualified women and minorities from advancing in the corporate world.

PROBLEM 37

Ms. Weeks, a telephone company employee, applies for the job of electrician. This position sometimes requires lifting items weighing about 30 pounds. The company gives the job to a man with less seniority. In her rejection letter, Ms. Weeks is told that the company has decided not to assign a woman to the job of electrician.

a. Why did the company decide not to assign a woman to this job?

b. Was the company's decision fair?

c. Is Ms. Weeks protected by the law? If so, by what law?

d. Are there any jobs women should not have? Are there any jobs men should not have? Explain your answers.

For many, efforts to narrow the pay gap now center on the concept of **comparable worth**. This means that women in traditionally female jobs (such as secretaries and nurses) would be paid the same as men in traditionally male jobs (such as truck drivers and construction workers) when the two kinds of work are deemed to require comparable skills, effort, and responsibility.

Women or men who think they have been discriminated against because of their sex can contact the U.S. Equal Employment Opportunity Commission or state or local anti-discrimination agencies.

PROBLEM 38

a. What does comparable worth mean? Should occupations dominated by women pay the same as occupations dominated by men? Can totally different jobs—such as those of secretaries and construction workers—really be compared?

b. Have you ever been the victim of sex discrimination? If so, what happened? What can you do if you are discriminated against because of your sex at school or at work?

PROBLEM 39

Based on your knowledge of sex discrimination law, analyze each of the following situations and decide whether illegal sex discrimination is present. Give reasons for your decisions.

a. A state-supported nursing school does not accept applications from men.

b. A man applies for a job as a used-car salesperson, but the woman who owns the business does not hire him. The reason she gives is that "he is not good-looking enough to entice the young women who come here looking for a car to buy one."

c. A state government provides three months of paid leave to women who become mothers. Paid disability leave for men who become fathers is limited to four weeks.

d. A state-supported military academy has had a tradition for over a century of admitting men only.

e. Women in the military are not allowed to fight alongside men in the front line of battle.

One type of sex discrimination that has been the subject of increased attention in recent years is **sexual harassment**. The federal Equal Employment Opportunity Commission (EEOC) has defined this as "unwelcome sexual advances, requests for favors, and other verbal or physical conduct of a sexual nature which takes place in the workplace." In one type of sexual harassment, a male supervisor leads a female employee to believe she will lose her job if she does not submit to his sexual advances. Or a promotion is offered in exchange for sexual favors. This is called **quid pro quo** (literally, "this for that") sexual harassment.

The Obnoxious Remarks

Theresa Harris worked as a manager at Forklift Systems. The president of the company, Charles Hardy, made comments to Harris on the job like, "You're a dumb-ass woman," and "Let's go to the Holiday Inn to negotiate your raise." These comments were made to Harris in the presence of other employees. In addition, Hardy asked Harris to retrieve coins from his front pants pockets and made sexual comments about her clothes.

At a private meeting, Harris complained to Hardy about his behavior. At that meeting he apologized, said he had only been joking, and promised to stop the behavior. But when the obnoxious comments continued, Harris quit her job.

Harris filed a lawsuit under *Title VII* of the *Civil Rights Act of 1964*, claiming sexual harassment. At the trial, other female employees testified that they were not offended by Hardy's comments and considered them to be jokes. Harris testified that the comments upset her so much that she began drinking heavily and had to quit her job.

The trial judge concluded that, while Hardy's behavior was annoying and insensitive, it did not create a hostile, abusive environment nor did it interfere with Harris' work performance. The court believed that the conduct offended Harris and that it would offend a reasonable woman in the same position as Harris. The court found, however, that the conduct was not so severe as to seriously affect her psychological well-being. Therefore, the court decided that Harris could not win her lawsuit. The court of appeals upheld the trial court's decision, and Harris appealed to the U.S. Supreme Court.

In a unanimous decision, the U.S. Supreme Court established a new standard for deciding sexual harassment cases. The Court stated that *Title VII* is violated when a hostile or abusive work environment has been created. The victim must only show that he or she was offended by the conduct in question and that a reasonable person would find the conduct abusive as well. Thus, Harris did not have to show harm to her psychological well-being in order to win her sexual harassment suit.

The Court found it difficult to say exactly what conduct would be considered abusive or hostile. Instead, courts must look at all the circumstances surrounding the offensive conduct: How often did it occur? How severe was it? Did it unreasonably interfere with the victim's work performance? Was the victim physically threatened or humiliated? No single factor is required to make a case for a hostile or abusive environment. While the mere utterance of an offensive remark certainly does not violate the law, according to Justice Sandra Day O'Connor's opinion, "Title VII comes into play before the harassing conduct leads to a nervous breakdown."

PROBLEM 40

a. What was the standard decided by the U.S. Supreme Court in the *Harris* case? How does this differ from the standard used by the trial court when it first heard the case?

b. Assume the *Harris* case is tried again, this time using the standard announced by the U.S. Supreme Court. As Harris' attorney, what arguments would you make on her behalf? As Hardy's attorney, what arguments would you make on his behalf? If you were the trial judge, would you find sexual harassment in this case? Explain your reasons.

c. Why is sexual harassment considered a form of sex discrimination? How is it related to *Title VII*'s goal of equal opportunity?

d. What steps should companies take to deal with the issue of sexual harassment in the workplace? What steps should an employee take if he or she has been a victim of sexual harassment?

e. Refer to the steps in a typical mediation session in Chapter 1. Assume that Forklift Systems had a mediation program for dealing with employee complaints. Roleplay the mediation between Harris and Hardy. Be sure to produce a written agreement that both parties sign. What are the advantages and disadvantages of mediation in situations involving sexual harassment?

The courts have also held that constant vulgar comments, unwelcome physical touching, or other sexual conduct affecting an employee's working conditions constitute sexual harassment. This is called **hostile environment** sexual harassment. When a hostile or offensive work environment exists, there is no need to show that the employee was in danger of losing his or her job or of being denied a promotion.

Surveys show a high incidence of sexual harassment in the workplace. A majority of women surveyed indicated that they had been the victims of sexual harassment. Men are victims less frequently.

Sexual harassment does not occur only in the workplace. Many types of sexual harassment occur in schools as well. There may be harassment from a teacher against a student, a student against a teacher, or harassment from one student against another. Studies indicate that a high percentage of both girls and boys are subject to sexual harassment in the school setting.

Many instances of sexual harassment go unreported because of embarrassment or fear of retaliation. It is illegal for a supervisor to take punitive action against an employee because the worker complains of sexual harassment. Many employers now have established policies making it clear that sexual harassment will not be tolerated and providing procedures for filing complaints. An employee can always file a complaint with the EEOC or a similar state agency or file a sex discrimination case in state or federal court. According to EEOC guidelines, employers can be held liable for sexual harassment they knew of or should have known of.

There may be more than one way to handle a sexual harassment situation. It may be possible, for example, to use mediation to manage the conflict. In mediation, an impartial third party assists individuals in discussing and resolving their problems. (See the section on mediation in Chapter 1.)

PROBLEM 41

Which of the following situations, taken alone, constitute sexual harassment? Why or why not? How should each situation be handled?

a. William and Ella are police officers who share the same patrol car. He is the senior officer in charge of the patrol. One night he tells her he is attracted to her and would like to start dating her after work.

b. Lois is one of a few female welders. Her male co-workers repeatedly displayed graphic photographs and drawings of nude women and also made derogatory sexual comments to her.

Figure 7.2 A Statement of Federal Employment Discrimination Law

Equal Employment Opportunity is THE LAW

Employers Holding Federal Contracts or Subcontracts

Applicants to and employees of companies with a Federal government contract or subcontract are protected under the following Federal authorities:

RACE, COLOR, RELIGION, SEX, NATIONAL ORIGIN

Executive Order 11246, as amended, prohibits job discrimination on the basis of race, color, religion, sex or national origin, and requires affirmative action to ensure equality of opportunity in all aspects of employment.

INDIVIDUALS WITH HANDICAPS

Section 503 of the Rehabilitation Act of 1973, as amended, prohibits job discrimination because of handicap and requires affirmative action to employ and advance in employment qualified individuals with handicaps who, with reasonable accommodation, can perform the essential functions of a job.

VIETNAM ERA AND SPECIAL DISABLED VETERANS

38 U.S.C. 4212 of the Vietnam Era Veterans Readjustment Assistance Act of 1974 prohibits job discrimination and requires affirmative action to employ and advance in employment qualified Vietnam era veterans and qualified special disabled veterans.

Any person who believes a contractor has violated its nondiscrimination or affirmative action obligations under the authorities above should contact immediately:

The Office of Federal Contract Compliance Programs (OFCCP), Employment Standards Administration, U.S. Department of Labor, 200 Constitution Avenue, N.W., Washington, D.C. 20210 or call (202) 523-9368, or an OFCCP regional or district office, listed in most telephone directories under U.S. Government, Department of

Private Employment, State and Local Governments, Educational Institutions

Applicants to and employees of most private employers, state and local governments, educational institutions, employment agencies and labor organizations are protected under the following Federal laws:

RACE, COLOR, RELIGION, SEX, NATIONAL ORIGIN

Title VII of the Civil Rights Act of 1964, as amended, prohibits discrimination in hiring, promotion, discharge, pay, fringe benefits, job training, classification, referral, and other aspects of employment, on the basis of race, color, religion, sex or national origin.

DISABILITY

The Americans with Disabilities Act of 1990, as amended, protects qualified applicants and employees with disabilities from discrimination in hiring, promotion, discharge, pay, job training, fringe benefits, classification, referral, and other aspects of employment on the basis of disability. The law also requires that covered entities provide qualified applicants and employees with disabilities with reasonable accommodations that do not impose undue hardship.

AGE

The Age Discrimination in Employment Act of 1967, as amended, protects applicants and employees 40 years of age or older from discrimination on the basis of age in hiring, promotion, discharge, compensation, terms, conditions or privileges of employment.

SEX (WAGES)

In addition to sex discrimination prohibited by Title VII of the Civil Rights Act (see above), the Equal Pay Act of 1963, as amended, prohibits sex discrimination in payment of wages to women and men performing substantially equal work in the same establishment.

Retaliation against a person who files a charge of discrimination, participates in an investigation, or opposes an unlawful employment practice is prohibited by all of these Federal laws.

If you believe that you have been discriminated against under any of the above laws, you immediately should contact:

The U.S. Equal Employment Opportunity Commission (EEOC), 1801 L Street, N.W., Washington, D.C. 20507 or an EEOC field office by calling toll free (800) 669-4000. For individuals with hearing impairments, EEOC's toll free TDD number is (800) 800-3302.

Programs or Activities Receiving Federal Financial Assistance

RACE, COLOR, NATIONAL ORIGIN, SEX

In addition to the protection of Title VII of the Civil Rights Act of 1964, Title VI of the Civil Rights Act prohibits discrimination on the basis of race, color or national origin in programs or activities receiving Federal financial assistance. Employment discrimination is covered by Title VI if the primary objective of the financial assistance is provision of employment, or where employment discrimination causes or may cause discrimination in providing services under such programs. Title IX of the Education Amendments of 1972 prohibits employment discrimination on the basis of sex in educational programs or activities which receive Federal assistance.

INDIVIDUALS WITH HANDICAPS

Section 504 of the Rehabilitation Act of 1973, as amended, prohibits employment discrimination on the basis of handicap in any program or activity which receives Federal financial assistance. Discrimination is prohibited in all aspects of employment against handicapped persons who, with reasonable accommodation, can perform the essential functions of a job.

If you believe you have been discriminated against in a program of any institution which receives Federal assistance, you should contact immediately the Federal agency providing such assistance.

Should the law protect women working in traditionally male job settings from sexual harassment?

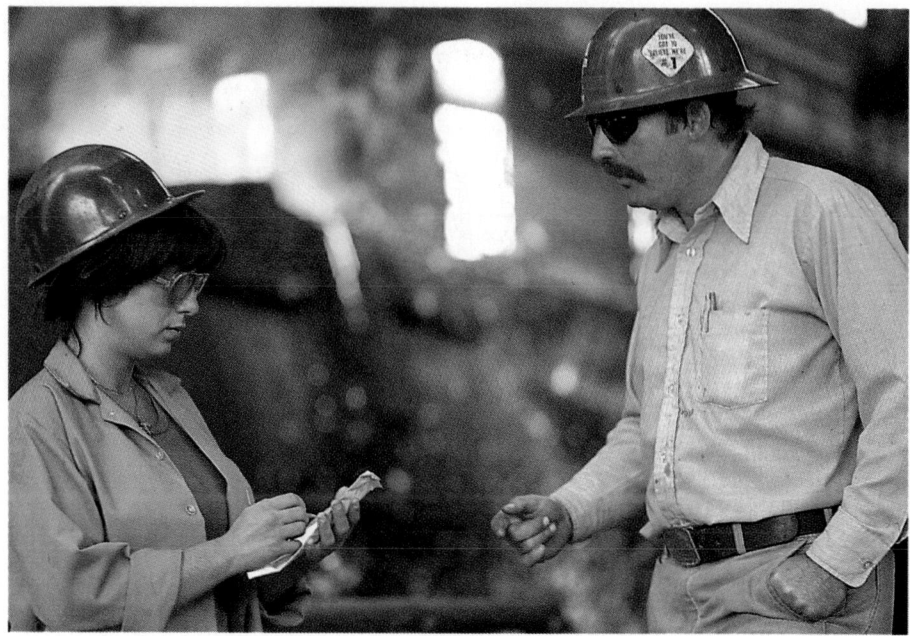

c. Pasquale likes to make sexual comments to Sylvia, who works with him on a construction crew. Sylvia says she hates his remarks and responds with similar comments only to get back at him for embarrassing her.

d. Maria supervises five computer programmers, including Victor and four women. She often puts her arm on his shoulder when she is supervising him and calls him "honey." She invites Victor, but never the other women, to lunch.

e. A gay male supervisor tells a new male employee, "We only hired you because you are nice to look at."

f. A male high-school teacher hugs a female student after she receives high college entrance exam scores. He tells her she has everything going for her, "including smarts and an attractive physique."

g. A female professor testifies before a government committee that her former male boss frequently made sexual remarks to her and asked her out on dates.

h. A female high-school student tells a boy in school that he has "nice buns."

In 1972 Congress acted to end sex discrimination in education. *Title IX* of the *Education Act of 1972* prohibits sex discrimination in most school activities, including curriculum, faculty hiring, and student athletic programs.

Title IX's impact on school athletes has been particularly controversial. The law requires equal opportunity in athletic programs. This means that sports programs must effectively accommodate the interests and abilities of both sexes. For example, assume a school has a men's basketball team and that it also has a number of women interested in playing basketball. The law requires the school to either establish a women's basketball team or allow women to try out for the men's team. Moreover, if a separate women's team is established, the school cannot discriminate against the women by providing inferior facilities or equipment.

If only one woman is interested in baseball (or any other *noncontact* sport for which a men's team exists), the school must allow her to try out for the men's team. In *contact* sports, however, such as football or wrestling, schools can limit teams to members of one sex. Although athletic opportunities must be equal, the law does not require that total expenditures on men's and women's sports be equal.

If a school violates *Title IX*, the government or the person discriminated against can go to court. *Title IX* also allows the federal government to cut off financial aid to schools that discriminate on the basis of sex.

PROBLEM 42

Title IX states: "No person in the United States shall, on the basis of sex, be excluded from participation in, be denied the benefits of, or be subjected to discrimination under any education program or activity receiving federal financial assistance."

Which, if any, of the following situations do you believe are in violation of *Title IX*? Assume each school receives federal funds.

a. The music department at the state college has two glee clubs, one for men and the other for women.

b. A school establishes a women's baseball team, which receives used equipment from the men's team.

c. A high-school grooming code requires that men's hair not reach the shirt collar, but women's hair length is not regulated.

d. A U.S. history textbook does not include important contributions made by American women.

e. A small public high school competes in volleyball and has a team of only female students. A male student wants to play interscholastic volleyball.

f. An eighth-grade curriculum offers shop for boys and home economics for girls.

g. A large state university has established separate teams for women in all noncontact sports and has provided them with equivalent equipment. Twice as many males as females participate in the school's interscholastic programs, and 85% of the school's athletic scholarship funds go to males.

Age Discrimination

Mario Campisi, age 55, worked for the same company for 20 years. His boss said that Mario was an excellent worker, but that he wanted to bring in someone younger. According to his boss, Mario had two choices: take a new, lower-paying job or quit.

Can older workers be fired or given a lower-paying position because of age? No! Age discrimination is against the law.

The *Age Discrimination in Employment Act* protects workers aged 40 or older. It forbids discrimination in hiring, firing, paying, promoting, and other aspects of employment. The law applies to private employers of 20 or more people, labor unions, government agencies, and employment agencies.

Can you identify jobs in which an employer might be justified in refusing to hire an applicant over 40 years of age?

The Forced Retirement

Massachusetts required state police officers to retire at age 50. The law was designed to ensure that police officers were physically fit. The state police department required complete physical examinations every two years until an officer reached age 40. Then it required exams every year until the officer reached age 50, the mandatory retirement age. Officer Murgia passed all examinations and was in excellent health when the state police retired him on his 50th birthday. Murgia sued the state police, arguing that the mandatory retirement age denied him equal protection. Should the 14th Amendment protect Officer Murgia in this case?

In deciding Officer Murgia's case, the Supreme Court said, "Drawing lines that create distinctions is . . . a legislative task and an unavoidable one. Perfection in making the classification is neither possible or necessary. Such action by a legislature is presumed to be valid." Although Officer Murgia was in good health, the Court accepted the fact that physical fitness generally declines with age. Therefore, it was rational to draw a line at some age, and the Court upheld this law.

The law has several important exceptions. It does not apply if age is a bona fide job qualification. This means there must be a real and valid reason to consider age. For example, an older person could be refused a youthful role in a movie. The law also does not apply if an employment decision is made for a good reason other than age. For example, an older employee could be fired for misconduct. If you think you've been discriminated against because of age, you can file a complaint with the Equal Employment Opportunity Commission.

Age discrimination is not limited to older people. Many laws and practices discriminate against youth. For example, restrictions on voting, running for public office, making a will, driving, and drinking are generally upheld by the courts.

Although the courts have not used the equal protection clause to protect the rights of youth, some state and local legislatures have passed laws or regulations forbidding age discrimination. In addition, the 26th Amendment gives 18-year-olds the right to vote in federal and state elections.

Why did Congress and a majority of the states feel it was important to give 18-year-olds the right to vote?

The Age Restriction

The owner of a convenience store that has had many instances of shoplifting decides that keeping youngsters out of the store will reduce his problems. The few shoplifters he has caught have been minority youths. He posts a large sign on the front door that reads as follows: "Customers below the age of 18 allowed only if accompanied by an adult." The owner tends to enforce this rule only against minority youths.

Should his policy be considered unlawful? Give your reasons.

Discrimination Based on Disability

No otherwise qualified individual with a disability . . . shall, solely by reason of his disability, be excluded from participation in, be denied the benefit of, or be subjected to discrimination under any program or activity receiving Federal financial assistance.

—Rehabilitation Act of 1973

It is the purpose of the Americans with Disabilities Act to provide a clear and comprehensive national mandate for the elimination of discrimination against individuals with disabilities.

—Americans with Disabilities Act (1990)

Approximately 43 million Americans have a mental or physical disability. Many people with disabilities regularly suffer discrimination in different areas of daily life. Discrimination often exists because of prejudice, ignorance, or fear. For example, society may ignore or separate people who are different, believing it may not be appropriate or possible for people with disabilities to participate in certain activities. In addition, other people may not be comfortable seeing people with disabilities participating in society.

Since the 1970s, a number of laws have been passed to prohibit discrimination against people with disabilities. These laws requiring consideration of a person's special needs involve such issues as education, employment, building design, and transportation.

The *Rehabilitation Act of 1973* prohibits discrimination by the federal government, federal contractors, and recipients of federal financial assistance. This act bans discrimination in employment and requires employers who receive federal benefits to set up programs to assist people with disabilities. Discrimination against people with disabilities is also prohibited in services, programs, or activities provided by all state and local governments.

Education is another area in which the law provides protection to people with disabilities. Historically, millions of children were excluded from public schools because of mental or physical disabilities. However, in 1975 Congress passed the *Education for All Handicapped Children Act*. This law, now known as the *Individuals with Disabilities Education Act* (IDEA), requires states to provide a free and appropriate education to children with special needs.

The Student with a Disability

Amy Rowley, who is deaf, was placed in kindergarten and first-grade classes with children who hear without assistance. She attended special speech therapy and tutoring sessions in addition to her required classes and also wore a special hearing aid provided by the school. Amy received passing grades in all her classes. Her parents believed that she would gain much more from her education if she had an interpreter, and they asked the school district to provide one. They contended that Amy understood only about 60% of what was said in class and that she would understand everything with an interpreter. The school district denied the Rowleys' request, calling it unnecessary and an undue financial burden.

The Rowleys sued the school district under the federal *Education for All Handicapped Children Act*. This law entitled exceptional children to "a free and appropriate education." The case was eventually appealed to the U.S. Supreme Court. The Court held that under this law, the schools were required to provide "specialized instruction and related services which are individually designed to provide an educational benefit to the handicapped child." The school is not required, however, to provide a program that will maximize the child's potential. With this language, the Court approved the program the school district was offering to Amy.

Do you agree with the Court's decision? Give your reasons.

In 1990 the *Americans with Disabilities Act (ADA)* was passed to provide much broader protection against discrimination. Many people consider this the most important federal civil rights legislation since the *Civil Rights Act of 1964*. Now many more entities and businesses are prohibited from discriminating against people with dis-

How does federal law protect those with hearing impairments against discrimination?

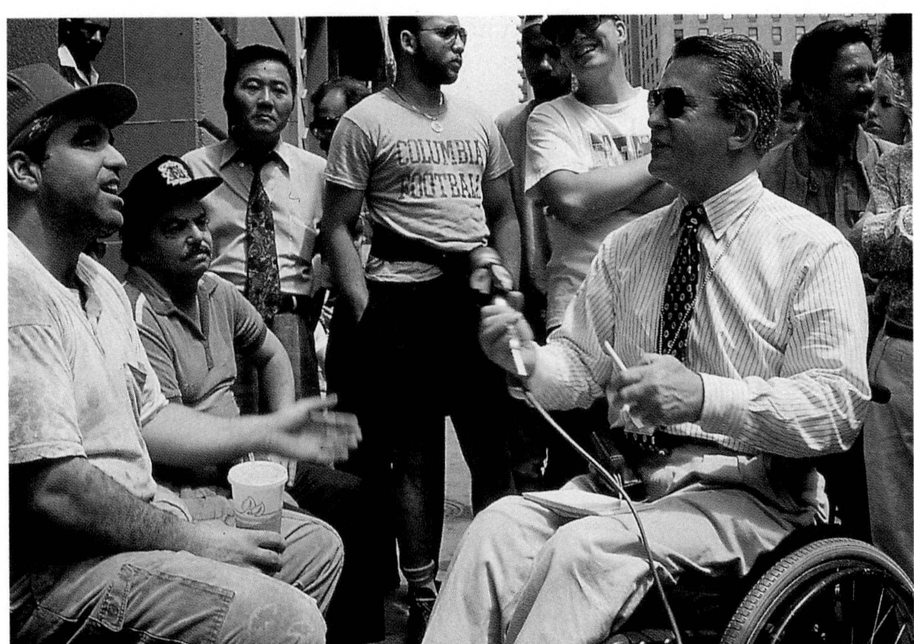

What is the primary purpose of the ADA?

abilities. This includes businesses in the private sector, public accommodations, services provided by state and local governments, transportation, and telecommunications.

The ADA defines a person with a disability as someone with "a mental or physical impairment that substantially limits one or more of the major life activities of a person; a record of such an impairment; or being regarded as having such an impairment." It is important to note that the ADA does not list the specific diseases and impairments that come under the definition of disability. This was done because a specific disease (such as diabetes) or a specific impairment (such as a hearing loss) may not be disabling for one person but may be severely disabling for another person.

People with AIDS and HIV infection, however, are protected under the ADA. Alcoholics who are in treatment or rehabilitated are also protected under the ADA, as well as rehabilitated drug users and drug users in treatment.

The primary purpose of the ADA is to assist in bringing people with disabilities into the economic and social mainstream of society. For most Americans, a fundamental aspect of life is employment. However, many people with disabilities have been denied the opportunity to participate fully in an employment situation, thus denying them full access to economic involvement in society. For this reason, a major portion of the ADA deals with employment.

A "qualified individual with a disability" is entitled to "reasonable accommodations" in order to overcome existing barriers. Some examples of reasonable accommodations include making facilities accessible for workers with mobility difficulties; modifying examinations and training materials, such as providing these items in large print; providing qualified readers or interpreters; and providing reserved parking. What constitutes a reasonable accommodation will be different for each person.

An employer is not required to make an accommodation if doing so would cause the employer an undue hardship. However, an undue hardship must be "excessively costly"—not just inconvenient—and one that would "fundamentally alter" the business. An employer is not required to make changes ahead of time for any or all possible disabilities. A person with a disability must request an accommodation. In addition, an employer may not ask questions about a particular disability until after a job offer has been made. An employer, however, may ask if the person will be able to handle tasks that are essential to the job.

Finally, other federal, state, and local laws also assist people with disabilities. *The Architectural Barriers Act of 1968* requires that all public buildings be made accessible. Restrooms, elevators, drinking fountains, meeting rooms, and public telephones must be designed to accommodate people with disabilities. Similarly, many local laws require wheelchair ramps, braille signs for the blind, designated parking spaces, and other special accommodations for people with disabilities.

People with physical and mental disabilities now have many rights. However, some problems and conflicts still remain. For example, people who use wheelchairs need curb ramps, but people who

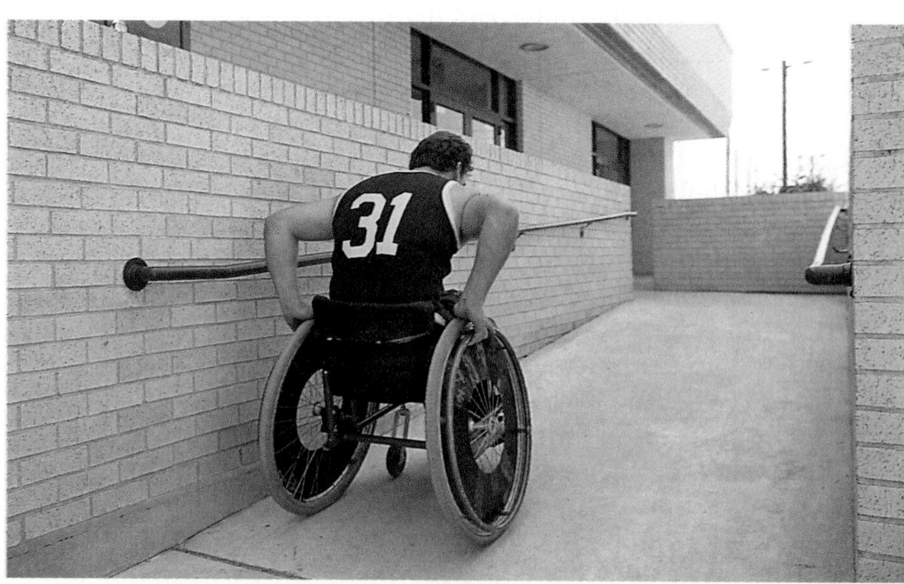

What steps should building owners take to ensure that their buildings are accessible to wheelchairs?

are blind and use canes need curb markers to warn them where sidewalks end.

PROBLEM 43

Evaluate each of the following examples, and then answer these questions: Does the person have a disability? If so, describe the disability. Is there discrimination based on disability? Should an accommodation be provided? Explain.

a. A high-school student who uses a wheelchair needs a ramp installed to reach the stage during graduation. The principal says the diploma can be awarded down in front of the stage.

b. A 28-year-old woman who is HIV-positive cannot find a dentist in her area who will see her.

c. A Little League baseball coach who uses a wheelchair is told that for safety reasons he can no longer coach from the playing field. He may now coach only from the dugout.

d. A 59-year-old executive director is fired from her job after her superiors learn she has brain cancer.

e. A woman who is qualified to be a school lunchroom aide, but is overweight, is denied the position because of her weight.

f. A man with only one hand is a major league baseball pitcher.

The Fire Fighter with HIV

John Doe wanted to be a fire fighter. He applied for a position as a fire fighter and passed all the written and physical examination requirements. Following testing, the city sent him a letter of appointment stating his salary and the date on which to report to work. However, prior to his starting work, the city learned John Doe was HIV-positive. The city then decided he was no longer qualified to be a fire fighter and told him not to report for work. John Doe sued to get his job as a fire fighter.

How should this case be decided? Give your reasons.

State and Local Laws Against Discrimination

When the Supreme Court makes a decision regarding the Constitution, it determines the *minimum* protection that governments must extend to their citizens. However, governments may offer greater protection than what the Court says the Constitution requires.

For example, the *Civil Rights Act of 1968* prohibits discrimination in the rental or sale of property on the basis of race, color, religion, or national origin. Although this law provides important protections, it does not forbid discrimination against homosexuals, single people, or

Actions to Take If Your Rights Are Violated

No single procedure can be followed for all situations in which your rights have been violated. You should know that civil rights are protected by laws at both the state and federal levels. Federal law sometimes requires that you first try to solve your problem on a state or local level. Also, some civil rights laws have specific time limits for filing a case. Don't delay if you believe that some action should be taken. If you decide to act, you may wish to consider the following options:

- Protest in some way—either verbally, by letter, or by demonstration.
- Contact an attorney who may be able to negotiate a settlement or file a case for you.
- Contact a private organization with an interest in your type of problem (for example, the ACLU for First Amendment problems or the NAACP for race discrimination). See Appendix F for a list of other organizations.
- Contact a state or local agency with the legal authority to help (for example, a state fair-employment commission or a local human rights agency).
- Contact a federal agency with the legal authority to help. Although many federal agencies are based in Washington, D.C., most have regional offices and field offices in larger cities throughout the country. Look in the telephone directory under "U.S. Government."
- Contact the U.S. Commission on Civil Rights (see Appendix F for an address) for general information on where to look for help, or if your complaint goes unanswered.

those whose income is from alimony or welfare. To protect these and other individuals, some state and local governments have passed their own discrimination laws. These laws, which extend the protections offered by federal law, may cover discrimination based on one or more of the following characteristics:

- Age (young or old)
- Marital status
- Personal appearance
- Source of income
- Sexual orientation
- Family responsibility (having children)
- Physical handicap
- Matriculation (status of being a student)
- Political affiliation

Some places have commissions that receive, investigate, and resolve complaints based on violations of these laws.

In recent years there has been an increase in civil rights activity in state courts. This activity has made state and local laws and state supreme court decisions particularly important for those who claim to have been victims of unlawful discrimination. For example, several cities and states have enacted **domestic partnership** laws, which allow an employee's heterosexual or homosexual live-in partner to receive the same employment and health benefits a spouse would receive.

Should there be laws that protect individuals based on sexual preference?

Although no federal laws protect homosexuals against discrimination, there has been an increase in the number of state and local laws that provide such protection. In New York, for example, the legal definition of *family* was modified by the state's highest court to allow one man to continue living in a rent-controlled apartment after his male partner died. However, there has also been a backlash against expanding gay and lesbian rights, and initiatives have been passed in some states that prevent gay and lesbian rights legislation from being enacted.

Other controversial questions that often arise under state and local laws against discrimination involve private clubs that limit their membership based on race, sex, religion, or ethnic background. Small, selective, distinctly private clubs have generally been able to

The Gay Student Club and the Religious University

A large university affiliated with the Catholic church set aside some funds from tuition to support registered student clubs. A group of gay students applied to become a club at the university and was turned down. The reason given was that the religious teachings of the institution did not approve of homosexuality. Local law where the university was situated protected individuals against discrimination based on sexual preference. The students sued the university.

PROBLEM 44

a. What arguments can the students make?

b. What arguments can the university make?

c. How should this case be resolved? Give your reasons.

d. Would your answer to Question c be different if a state university had been involved?

e. Should there be a national law that protects individuals against discrimination based on sexual preference, or should the development of policy in this area be left to state and local governments? Give your reasons.

decide who their members will be without violating antidiscrimination laws. For example, prohibiting a church's youth group from requiring that its members be of the same religion might interfere with the basic purpose of the club. However, larger private clubs that regularly serve meals and rent out their facilities to nonmembers for business purposes have usually been deemed by the courts to have lost their "distinctly private" nature.

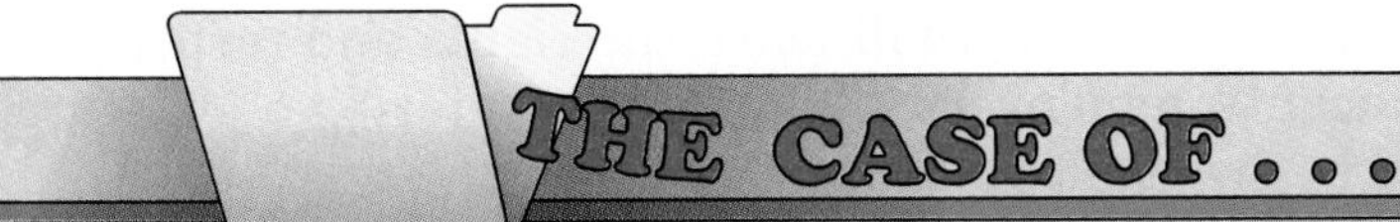

The Discriminating Country Club

An expensive and very selective country club limits its membership to men. The club has as its stated purposes "male camaraderie and the playing of golf." The club does not rent out its facilities and does not allow any formal business meetings. A law in the state where the club is located has given all country clubs a significant property tax break in exchange for preserving their lands as open spaces.

State officials argue that this club should not receive the tax break because it discriminates based on sex, and the state should not provide support for such an organization. The golf club's officers contend that the state is trying to force the club's members to give up their privacy and associational rights. If the case goes to court and the club loses, it will either have to accept women as members or pay additional annual property taxes of more than $300,000.

PROBLEM 45

a. What are the arguments for and against allowing the club to receive the property tax break?

b. How should this case be decided? Give reasons for your answer.

c. When individuals form private groups or clubs, what criteria do they usually set up for membership? Why?

d. Should any clubs be able to discriminate based on race, sex, religion, or ethnic background? If so, which ones?

e. Draft a law that explains clearly when a club should be considered distinctly private and allowed to discriminate in selecting its members.

RIGHTS AND RESPONSIBILITIES IN THE WORKPLACE

Without a job all there is to life is boredom and insecurity.

—John Lennon of the Beatles

In this chapter you have studied how the Bill of Rights and other important civil rights laws apply at home, at school, and on the street. Another important set of federal and state laws governs the workplace. In this section you will learn the rights and responsibilities of job applicants, employers, and employees during a job search, on the job, and in the event of job loss.

Looking for a Job

When looking for a job, you should keep a number of legal and practical considerations in mind. Important issues may arise during job interviews or when job applicants are tested.

The Job Interview Once you have obtained an appointment for an interview, it is important to be prepared for it. How you dress, act, and otherwise present yourself at this interview may determine whether you get the job. The interview is also a chance for you to learn as much as you can about the position and the organization so you can decide whether you really want to work there.

Employers ask many questions during job interviews to help them decide whether to hire applicants. Based on employment discrimination laws discussed earlier in this chapter and generally accepted employment practices, employers should not raise issues in job interviews that may infringe on an applicant's privacy or that could be viewed as evidence of illegal discrimination. Examples include inappropriate references to a person's sex, race, national origin, religion, disability, marital status, or personal practices outside the workplace. It is appropriate, however, for employers to ask applicants to identify their race, sex, or national origin for statistical purposes.

In pre-employment discussions, an employer may not ask about a person's disability. An employer is allowed, however, to ask questions related to a person's *ability* to perform a particular task or assignment. The ADA does not require employers to hire a person with a disability who is not qualified for the position. The ADA, however, states that it is illegal to discriminate against a "qualified individual with a disability."

An inappropriate question does not necessarily constitute discrimination. To charge an employer with discrimination, it must be proven that the job was actually denied for unlawful reasons. For example, it may be inappropriate to ask a female applicant for a secretarial position whether she is married. However, the question would not constitute discrimination if she were denied the job because of poor word-processing skills.

Employers may raise issues such as race, sex, and age in a work-related context. For example, white applicants for a job requiring frequent contact with African Americans may be asked about their work history relating to other races. The law will require the employer to show that the race, sex, or age discrimination is based on a **bona fide occupational qualification (BFOQ)**, which means a qualification that is reasonably necessary for performance of the job. Turning down a male actor for a female role would be another example of reasonably necessary discrimination.

All employers must verify whether job applicants are U.S. citizens or have employment authorization. The *Immigration Reform and Control Act of 1986* made it unlawful for employers knowingly to hire or continue to employ persons without work authorization. Such employers are subject to fines under this law.

Whether employers have the right to ask questions about prior arrests and convictions is not as clear. Some states have laws barring employers from turning down applicants because of prior arrests, while others allow this practice. In a number of states, ex-felons are barred from being hired as police or corrections officers or are denied the right to apply for barber or taxi driver licenses. Some federal courts have declared it illegal to have a blanket rule prohibiting employment of ex-felons without regard to the job or the nature of the offense.

Employers may inquire about the age of young applicants to determine whether they are old enough to work, to find out how long they have been working, or to help decide their probable level of maturity. Some states require permits or "working papers" before young people can be hired. Those between the ages of 12 and 14 may obtain permits in certain states to work during holidays and vacations. Older people are protected against discrimination based on age by the *Age Discrimination in Employment Act* (see page 510). Asking older people for their age may be evidence of unlawful discrimination unless there is another valid reason for not hiring them.

PROBLEM 46

Jill Johnson, age 21, is applying for a job as an assistant hotel manager for a company that operates a chain of hotels throughout the country. She has scheduled a job interview with William Marconi, the regional manager of the company.

a. During the interview, Marconi asks Johnson the following questions. Which questions may be illegal? Legal but inappropriate? Legal and appropriate? Give reasons for each answer.

1. How old are you?
2. Why do you want this job?
3. Are you an American citizen?
4. Do you plan to get married and have children in the near future?
5. Are you willing to move to another area of the country?
6. Have you ever been arrested?
7. How tall are you? How much do you weigh?
8. Have you ever worked with Hispanic Americans? Do you speak Spanish?
9. Do you have a good credit rating?
10. Will you have dinner with me tonight?
11. Have you ever been treated for any mental problems?
12. Have you ever had, or been treated for, any of the following conditions? (Johnson is given a checklist of diseases and conditions.)
13. Why do you use a guide dog? An interpreter?

b. Role-play the interview, and have Johnson decide whether and how to answer each question. How did she answer or respond to any improper or illegal questions? How should she have answered each question? Should any of her answers have changed if she wanted the job? If so, which answers? How should these answers have changed?

c. If someone is asked an improper or illegal question in an interview and later is denied the job, can he or she file a lawsuit claiming discrimination?

What does the law in your state say about permitting lie detector, drug, or aptitude testing of job applicants?

Testing Job Applicants A controversial legal issue often arising in the job application process is whether applicants can be required to take psychological, lie detector, or drug tests. Some claim that such tests are an invasion of privacy and question the tests' accuracy. Others argue that employers should have a right to find out everything they can before hiring employees who might steal or otherwise harm their businesses.

Aptitude, personality, or psychological tests that can be shown to relate to an applicant's ability to do the job are allowed. However, such tests have been successfully challenged when they have been shown to be inaccurate or inappropriate for measuring a person's ability to succeed in the job, or when they were actually used to discriminate based on such factors as race, sex, age, or national origin.

Many employers argue that lie detector tests, called **polygraph tests**, are necessary to verify information on job applications and resumes, as well as to prevent the hiring of dishonest employees. A number of states have passed laws restricting the use of lie detectors. In 1988 Congress passed the *Polygraph Protection Act*, which makes it illegal for almost all employers to use such tests to select job applicants. This law does not cover security guards and federal, state, and local government employees, who still may have to take these tests.

Why do many employers use aptitude tests to screen potential employees?

Employers may test applicants to determine whether they are qualified for the job. However, there are two restrictions on testing. First, a test can't be used if it screens out people with disabilities unless the tested activity is specifically job related. Second, tests must be given in a manner that does not use the impaired skill of a disabled person unless that is what the test was specifically designed to measure. For example, in a job that requires fast typing skills, an employer is not required to provide alternate testing for a person with cerebral palsy whose manual motor skills may be limited. In addition, some states have laws regulating the use of AIDS testing for hiring purposes. People with HIV infections and AIDS are protected under the ADA as individuals with disabilities.

To reduce the hiring of workers who use drugs and alcohol, many people advocate drug testing of some or all job applicants. As a result, pre-employment drug testing has been increasing in recent years. Generally, private corporations have been allowed to require drug testing. However, some states have recently passed laws prohibiting such testing or requiring that employers have reasonable grounds for suspicion before testing takes place. For many years the federal government has used drug testing on applicants for military, law enforcement, and certain other positions.

PROBLEM 47

Manuel has decided to apply for the following jobs. If you were the employer for each job, would you ask Manuel to take a lie detector, drug, or aptitude test? If you were Manuel, would you object to taking any of these tests? Should the law allow these tests for these particular jobs?

a. Cashier in a grocery store

b. FBI agent

c. Construction worker

d. Secretary for the county government

e. Taxi driver

PROBLEM 48

a. What are the arguments for and against allowing private employers to require lie detector testing of job applicants? Which position do you agree with, and why? What should the law be regarding such testing? Explain your position.

b. The mayor of your town proposes a new ordinance that will require all applicants for town jobs to submit to drug testing. As a member of the city council, will you support this legislation? Give reasons for your position. Will you support the proposal if it only covers police officers, fire fighters, and ambulance drivers? Why or why not? Should the test also cover the use of alcohol and tobacco? If so, why?

What are the advantages and disadvantages of working in a fast food restaurant?

Should children be allowed to work during school hours or on school nights?

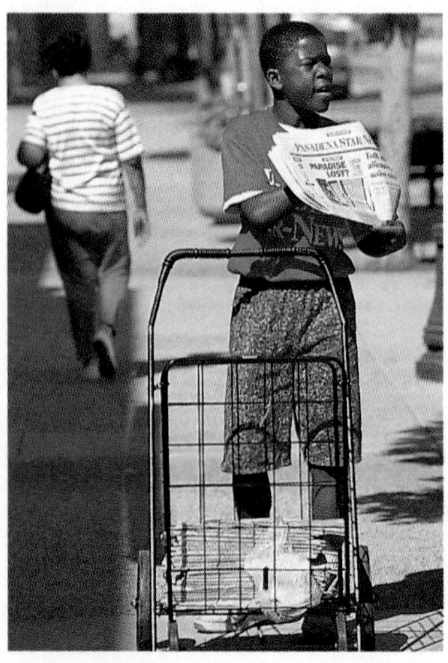

Conditions on the Job

Once on the job, you will find that various local, state, and federal laws apply in the workplace. These laws deal with wages and hours, taxes and benefits, social security, unions, health and safety, and privacy issues.

Wages and Hours The vast majority of workers in the United States are covered by the *Fair Labor Standards Act*, which requires that a minimum hourly wage be paid to all employees. In 1989 Congress changed the federal minimum wage (then \$3.35 per hour), providing for an increase to \$3.80 in 1990 and \$4.25 in 1991. In addition, this law allows employers to pay a lower "training wage" for up to 90 days to certain workers under age 20. Some states have their own laws that set a minimum wage based on the type of job.

Certain jobs are not covered by the *Fair Labor Standards Act*, and some jobs are designated under federal or state law as having lower minimum wages. These include newspaper delivery and part-time retail, service, or agricultural jobs held by full-time students. Some jobs can pay less than the minimum wage if the workers actually receive tips to make up the difference.

The federal law also requires employers to pay overtime wages at a rate of 1½ times the regular hourly pay when employees work more than 40 hours per week. For example, an employee who receives $5.00 per hour but works 50 hours in a week must receive $7.50 per hour for the 10 extra hours. Overtime pay rules do not apply to certain types of employees, including professionals who receive fixed salaries and those who work for commissions (for example, some salespeople).

Each state has its own laws concerning the employment of minors. These laws regulate how many hours a youth may work per day and per, week, the minimum age (usually 15 or 16), which hours of the day they cannot work (for example, school hours), whether work permits are required, and what types of jobs minors are prohibited from holding (for example, dangerous activities or selling alcohol).

Employees sometimes have their wages reduced for reasons such as showing up late, leaving early, or not working while on the work premises. If workers believe they have been treated unfairly in such cases, they may be able to file a complaint or even sue their employer. Such a problem may occur, for example, when an employee who operates a cash register has less money in the register at the end of the shift than receipts indicate should be there. Whether the employer can reduce the employee's wages may depend on the employment contract.

How to Complain about Wage and Hour Problems

- Employees who think their employer may not be paying them a fair wage should contact the Wage and Hour Division of the U.S. Department of Labor or their state or local government employment agency.
- If there is a union, it will have an established grievance procedure that must be followed.
- A complaint can be made to the union or to the appropriate government agency if an employer lays off or fires an employee who has complained about a wage and hour problem.
- Employees can also file a case directly in court to enforce wage and hour laws or agreements with their employers.

PROBLEM 49

a. Should all workers be covered by a minimum wage? Why? Some people favor a lower minimum wage for young people than for adults. What are the advantages and disadvantages of this proposal? Do you support it? Why or why not?

b. As a fast-food cook who is paid $4.50 an hour, you hear that another cook at your restaurant, who is a good friend of the manager, is making $5.50 an hour. Also, last week you worked 42 hours and were paid your regular hourly wage ($4.50 × 42 = $189). What actions, if any, will you take to handle these problems?

c. Vana works as a waitress in a restaurant and is given her own cash bank from which to make change for her customers. At the end of her shift, she is $10 short based on her receipts. Should she have to pay this money to the restaurant owner?

Taxes and Benefits Employers must withhold federal and state taxes from the paychecks of most employees. These taxes are used to

Contact your state or local government employment agency to learn about the laws in your area governing young people in the workplace. What kinds of jobs may they hold at different ages, and what minimum wages apply to them? Where can you complain if you believe your employer is not following the wage and hour laws?

provide government services, such as education, law enforcement, trash collection, and road building and maintenance. The law requires employers to provide workers with a W-2 form showing their earnings and the amounts withheld each year by January 31 of the following year. By April 15 of each year, most workers must file state, federal, and sometimes local tax returns based on the information reported on the W-2 form. Depending on the total income for the year, amounts withheld by the employer, and other factors, a worker may either receive a refund from the government or have to pay an additional amount.

Other items employers may decide to provide to employees free of charge or at reduced cost are called **fringe benefits**. These benefits include life, health, or disability insurance; pension plans; education and training; sick leave, vacations, holidays, and breaks; parking; meals; and severance pay in case of job loss. In recent years a growing number of employers have begun to offer maternity and paternity leave to parents following the birth of a child. In 1993 Congress passed the *Family and Medical Leave Act* (FMLA). This act requires employers with over 50 employees to grant up to 12 weeks' leave (usually unpaid) within a 12-month period to people who want to care for newborn babies, newly adopted children, or ailing relatives. Individual state laws may provide additional benefits. Employees may also bargain individually or collectively to include these fringe benefits as part of an employment contract.

Social Security Social security is the federal program that pays retirement, disability, or death benefits to eligible workers, their families, or both. Payroll deductions help to fund this program. The amount deducted is a percentage of an employee's salary. Beginning in 1994, employers pay a social security tax of 6.2% on each employee's salary up to $60,600 each year. The employer also pays a Medicare tax of 1.45% of each employee's salary (regardless of the amount).

PROBLEM 50

a. Kim, age 22, has just graduated from college and is going to work for a computer company. Kim is single and would like to return to school someday to acquire a master's degree in business. What company fringe benefits will most interest Kim? Why?

b. The JKR Corporation has 40 employees (25 men and 15 women). The company gives women 10 days of paid maternity leave when they give birth but does not offer a similar benefit to men who become fathers. Ralph, whose wife just had a baby, asks Frank, the president of JKR, for paid paternity leave. Role-play this meeting. What reasons can Ralph present to support his request? What pros and cons might Frank consider in making his decision? If you were Frank, would you change JKR's policy? Explain why or why not.

c. Willie, age 18 and single, just graduated from high school and plans to work for several years to save money for college. He applies for a job delivering pizzas that requires him to wear a uniform. What fringe benefits might he want the company to provide? Why?

Unions When someone begins a job, it is important to find out whether the company has a **union**. A union is an association of workers that seeks to secure favorable wages, improve working conditions and hours, and resolve grievances with employers. It is estimated that 20% of American workers belong to unions. A union can be established only by an election in which more than 50% of the company's workers vote for it. Unions, which have been protected by federal law since 1935, are governed today principally by a federal law, the *National Labor Relations Act*. This law is administered by the National Labor Relations Board, a federal agency.

The primary purpose of a union is to bargain as a group with an employer. Those who favor unions claim they accomplish much more

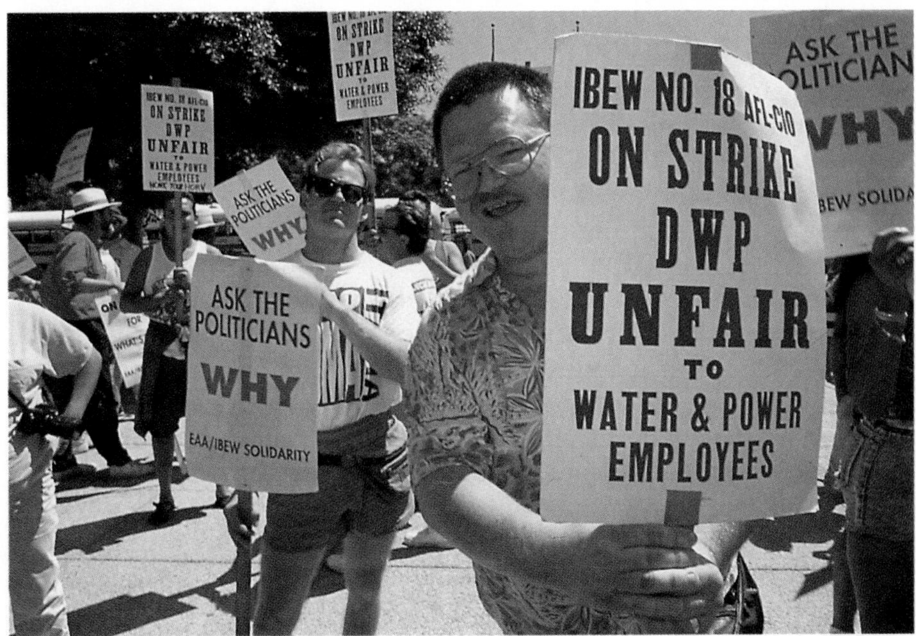

What role do unions play in protecting and ensuring workers' rights?

for workers, through collective bargaining, than individual employees are likely to achieve. **Collective bargaining** is the process of settling labor disputes through negotiations between the employer and representatives of the employees. Union supporters cite higher wages, greater fringe benefits, and better working conditions as results of union activity. Those who criticize unions say they are costly, unnecessary, and disruptive. The critics believe the higher wages have produced higher prices and fewer jobs for American workers. Some U.S. companies have begun to manufacture goods in other countries with lower labor costs. In addition, foreign companies are sometimes able to produce items that can be sold at prices lower than those charged for similar items made in America.

A union contract is an employment contract negotiated between the owners of a company and the union representatives. The wages and benefits that union members receive are based on agreements written into the union contract. Although employees can never be required to join a union, in most states a union contract can require everyone who works for a company to pay union dues and fees. This is based on the argument that the union is the sole bargaining agent for the workers, and all must pay for the work done on their behalf. However, this is not the case in 20 **right-to-work states**, where it is illegal under state law to require workers to join unions *or* pay dues as a condition of employment. These states are Alabama, Arizona, Arkansas, Florida, Georgia, Iowa, Kansas, Louisiana, Mississippi, Nebraska, Nevada, North Carolina, North Dakota, South Carolina, South Dakota, Tennessee, Texas, Utah, Virginia, and Wyoming.

A branch of law known as labor relations determines how employees, unions, and employers may operate. Employees have the right to join and/or support a union, as well as the right not to engage in union activities. Unions have the right to take certain actions, such as organizing **strikes** (work stoppages) and **picketing** (public demonstrations) to publicize a dispute. They also can conduct group protests of hazardous and dangerous working conditions. However, unions may not organize work slowdowns, refusals to perform valid and safe work assignments, or violence or destruction of company property.

Neither employers nor unions are allowed to engage in acts that are classified as **unfair labor practices**. Examples of unfair practices by employers include firing a worker for trying to organize a union, questioning union members about their activities, and spying on union meetings. Refusing to bargain with a recognized union or to reinstate workers who take part in a legal strike are other examples.

Unions commit unfair labor practices when they threaten workers to get them to join the union or to take part in a strike. A mass picketing action that makes it impossible for a nonstriking worker to enter the workplace is also an unfair practice. In addition, the use of violence during a strike is prohibited.

Two different types of strikes exist. An **economic strike** is based on economic factors, such as wage demands. An **unfair labor practice strike** is based on claims of unfair labor practices. A worker who takes part in an unfair labor practice strike must be reinstated following the strike. Workers will not automatically get their jobs back after an economic strike during which the jobs of striking workers have been given to other employees. In this case, worker reinstatement may depend on the union contract and other factors.

The National Labor Relations Board (NLRB) considers charges of unfair labor practices filed by either unions or employers. After investigating a claim, the NLRB decides whether the case should be prosecuted or dismissed. A case that is prosecuted will receive a formal hearing before an administrative law judge.

Federal employees and some state and local government employees have the right to belong to unions, but they generally are not allowed to strike. The rights of federal employees are governed by the *Federal Labor Relations Act*. The rights of state and local public employees are established by state laws. State labor laws may also include special rules regarding the rights of private sector employees, unions, strikes, and other labor issues.

PROBLEM 51

a. Why might some workers want to have a union in an auto manufacturing plant? Why might other workers in the plant prefer not to have a union? What information can you acquire to help you decide whether to support the formation of a union in an auto plant?

b. What is a right-to-work state? What are the arguments for and against a right-to-work law? Do you support or oppose such laws? Explain.

c. If city sanitation workers have had the same low salaries for five years and the city refuses to increase them, should the workers have the right to strike? Give reasons for your decision. If a public strike is illegal in their state, what else can the workers do to try to increase their wages?

d. Should any public employees be allowed to strike? Is your answer different for police officers, fire fighters, school teachers, government clerks, or maintenance workers at city hall? Explain.

PROBLEM 52

Taki works as a desk clerk at a local hotel. He is a member of a union that is about to go on strike. Examine the following actions or situations, and determine whether they are legal or illegal.

a. Before the strike begins, workers start to perform their job duties very slowly.

b. The union contract has a "no strike" clause.

c. When Taki comes to work one day, he finds that a strike has been called, and there is a union picket line. Taki refuses to cross it.

d. The employer locks the door of the hotel during the strike, but the striking workers break it down.

e. Several employees tell Taki he may get hurt if he refuses to go on strike.

f. The strike demands are for better health insurance and more vacation days. Taki goes on strike and is not offered his job back after the strike.

How does the Occupational Safety and Health Administration help to promote a safe and healthy work environment?

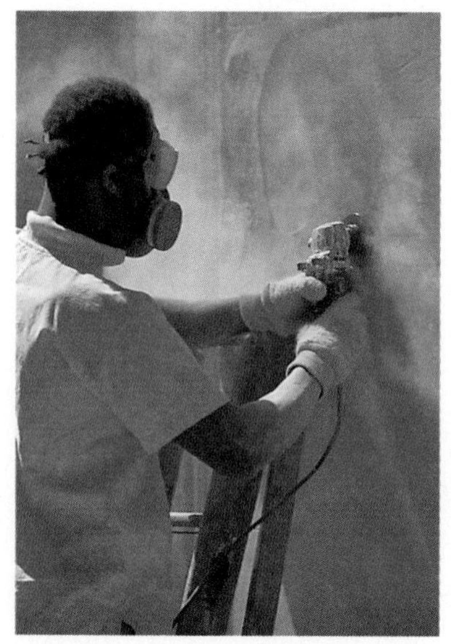

Health and Safety in the Workplace A government study estimated that there were more than 14,000 work-related deaths and 2.2 million injuries on the job in 1970. Many people became alarmed at the number of deaths and illnesses caused by the effects of lead and mercury poisoning, asbestos materials, cotton dust, pesticides, new toxic substances, and new technologies. As a result, Congress passed the *Occupational Safety and Health Act* in 1970. This law requires that employers provide safe and healthy working conditions for all workers. Self-employed people and members of a farmer's family are not covered. The law also does not cover state and local government employees, who usually receive protection under other laws. Many states have additional laws and standards to protect the health and safety of workers.

The 1970 act established a federal agency, the Occupational Safety and Health Administration (OSHA), to issue safety regulations and standards that industries must follow. The act requires employers to keep records of all job-related illnesses and injuries among their workers. Workers may file complaints against their employers without making the workers' names known to employers. If an employer discovers who complained, it may not take any disciplinary action against the employee. If agency inspections show that health or safety hazards exist, citations can be issued requiring employers to take corrective action.

The Collapsed Building

In 1986 a building under construction in Bridgeport, Connecticut, collapsed and killed 28 workers. A federal investigation showed that unsafe working conditions and practices caused the disaster. The construction site had been inspected once by OSHA six months before the accident because there had been a complaint. After the accident, OSHA issued fines of $5.1 million against three construction companies. What could be done to prevent this type of accident?

The Case of the Collapsed Building illustrates a number of problems with the government's attempts to reduce health and safety problems in the workplace. Some people say that OSHA does not administer the regulations properly. Other say that some people in business do not follow the standards. Most agree that OSHA has too few inspectors and that it would take millions of additional dollars to do the job right.

To enforce the regulations, OSHA conducts on-site inspections, orders changes, and sometimes fines employers. For example, a large defense contractor was fined $1.5 million for willfully failing to record 251 employee illnesses and injuries and failing to tell workers in 88 instances that they were working with hazardous materials. OSHA also issues safety and health standards that industries must follow.

Standards have been issued for the use of such items as hand tools, power presses, electrical wiring, ladders, hazardous gases, and chemicals. OSHA does not assist workers in filing lawsuits and collecting money damages from employers. Generally, individuals may only receive compensation from their employers for injuries under the workers' compensation system. However, an injured worker may be able to sue a negligent co-worker for tort damages.

Some people criticize OSHA for overregulating businesses and industries and requiring companies to spend large sums of money to comply with unnecessary standards. OSHA has also been criticized for expending too much effort on concerns about accidents while neglecting the health issues that lead to many work-related illnesses and deaths. Examples of such illnesses include lung cancer resulting from asbestos exposure, "black lung" disease among coal miners, and "brown lung" disease in textile workers exposed to cotton dust.

In 1981, there were 5.4 million workplace injuries and illnesses. By 1991, that number had increased to 6.4 million, costing employers and companies an estimated $83 billion per year.

PROBLEM 53

a. What is the purpose of OSHA, and how does it work? Some individuals say that people are safer in the workplace than in their cars. Do you think this is true? If so, is OSHA needed, or is it an example of overregulation by the government?

b. Jack works in a factory where there are strong fumes in the air. He and other workers cough a lot on the job. Jack complains to OSHA. He is laid off by the factory manager, who says the company has lost money due to the cost of controlling the fumes as ordered by OSHA. What actions can Jack take?

c. If workers have complained and reasonably believe that performing their duties exposes them to serious injury or possible death, can they refuse to work? What if their supervisor disagrees and orders them to work anyway? Can they lose pay or have an official reprimand placed in their personnel files? Does your answer change according to whether the danger is long term (such as the possibility of contracting lung disease from pollution) or short term (falling from an unsafe ladder, for example)?

d. Should corporate executives who willfully or recklessly violate safety and health standards be prosecuted criminally for their actions? If convicted of a crime, should they be fined or sent to jail? If so, under what circumstances? What is the best way to motivate an employer to provide a safe workplace?

In recent years, increasing numbers of workers have complained about health and safety conditions. These complaints include concerns about toxic substances within the workplace and about hearing damage caused by noisy office equipment. The prolonged use of computer keyboards and monitors has also resulted in various

How can long hours at a computer harm your health?

health hazards, including eyestrain, neck and back pain, and wrist injuries.

In response to workers' concerns, the federal government and many state governments have enacted community "right-to-know" laws. These laws require employers using certain hazardous materials to inform their employees about the accident and health hazards of chemicals in the workplace and to train them to minimize problems. Information about the materials and emergency response plans must be made available to employees and local officials. In addition, many employers have training programs to inform employees of possible health hazards from assembly line work or exposure to computer monitors.

Many people also view cigarette smoke in the workplace as a serious health hazard. As a result, some states and cities have prohibited smoking inside office buildings or restricted smoking to certain areas of the workplace.

Privacy at Work The right to privacy is often referred to as "the right to be let alone." This means that individuals should be able to determine how much of their personal lives they wish to share with others. Many people say privacy is not possible at work, because an employer has an interest in monitoring, supervising, and evaluating employees' work to ensure that employees do their jobs properly. However, many employees believe that they do not give up all rights to privacy when they take a job.

The Smoking Insurance Agent

Arnold is an insurance agent who works in a separate office with glass partitions that do not reach all the way to the ceiling. There are 20 other agents with similar offices in the area around his. Arnold says he must smoke because it is a habit he cannot break and it reduces the stress caused by his job. Sam, who occupies the office next to Arnold, claims that Arnold's smoking is unhealthy for him and everyone else in the office. He asks the office manager to issue a no-smoking rule for the entire office.

PROBLEM 54

a. If you were the office manager, what would you do?

b. Does your answer change if Sam is allergic to smoke?

c. Role-play a mediation session (see Chapter 1, page 44) in which the office manager meets with Arnold and Sam and attempts to help them come to an agreement regarding Arnold's smoking.

d. Should there be a law prohibiting smoking in offices? If so, what should be included in the law?

Those who work for the federal and some state governments generally have greater privacy rights than those who work for private employers. For example, the *Federal Privacy Act of 1974* gives federal government employees the right to be told what is in their personnel files, to correct an error in those files, and to limit access to them. Some states provide similar protections for state government employees, but only a few states do so for private employees. However, union contracts often provide some privacy rights.

Employee privacy rights have also become an issue in connection with certain programs that employers have undertaken to reduce workplace crime. In an effort to cut down on theft by employees, many employers hire private security guards to watch workers, and some use video monitoring as well. The courts have generally allowed employers to take such actions. They have also approved searches of employees' desks and of employees as they arrive at work and depart, based on the rationale that employers have the right to search their premises for business purposes. If an employer or security guard goes too far and detains employees against their will without good reason, the workers may have a tort claim for false imprisonment. Evidence of illegal activity found as a result of such searches can usually be used in court because the Fourth Amendment's exclusionary rule only prohibits the use in court of the fruits of unreasonable searches by the government.

Wiretapping without a warrant is prohibited by federal law, but the courts have allowed telephone monitoring of employees by employers on extension phones. Employers also have other methods of monitoring how much work an employee performs. For example, some firms use computers to determine how much typing each secretary does per day. Employers are also allowed to read electronic mail (E-mail) sent between company employees. Electronic mail is messages that employees can send to one another through their work computers. Employers argue that such monitoring is necessary to make sure employees are doing their jobs properly. Others claim that monitoring should be illegal and that it creates a negative work atmosphere.

Employers can also generally regulate how employees dress on the job unless such regulation is a cover-up for some form of illegal discrimination based on race, sex, national origin, or religion. Uniforms, if appropriate to the job, and a neat appearance can be required. This may even include rules regarding length of hair, wearing a beard or moustache, and other modes of dress. In recent years, as styles have changed, many employers have relaxed such rules.

PROBLEM 55

Decide whether the law should protect the employee's right to privacy in each of the following situations. Explain your answers.

a. Judy, who works for a cement company, has applied for a new job with a construction firm. The manager of the construction firm calls the cement company's president, who reads the contents of Judy's personnel file over the phone, including many negative comments about her work and personality.

b. Lionel, an African-American salesperson in a store mostly frequented by white people, begins to wear his hair in dreadlocks. His supervisor says Lionel will hurt business if he wears his hair that way and sends him home.

c. Jasper is missing some expensive jewelry from his store. He asks the police to come to the store and search the handbags of the three saleswomen who work for him.

d. Barnes, who owns a painting company, suspects Jenny, one of his painters, of not working very hard when he is not around. Without informing Jenny, he offers $20 to Sally, another of his painters, to spy on Jenny when he is not present and tell him how hard she works.

e. To reduce theft in his factory, Jay installs one-way mirrors that enable supervisors to watch employees.

f. Timi owns a business and begins monitoring the electronic mail between her employees. She fires Hugo after discovering he has sent messages to other employees criticizing Timi and mentioning that he suspects her of stealing money.

One of the most controversial issues involving privacy in the workplace is the drug testing of employees. Recently, more private employees have begun to test their workers for drugs. These private testing programs are generally legal, unless they are conducted in a state with a strong privacy law or privacy protection in the state constitution. Some unions have been able to curtail drug testing through collective bargaining. Rulings under the *National Labor Relations Act* have held that companies must comply with union requests to negotiate about drug testing.

In 1989 the U.S. Supreme Court addressed the drug-testing issue when it decided that blood and urine testing of railroad employees by the federal government after an accident was not a violation of the Fourth Amendment. This case made many references to public safety concerns regarding train accidents. Decisions in future cases will have to determine whether random drug testing of government employees will be allowed or whether some reasonable suspicion of the employees involved or some special public safety interest relating to the jobs involved will be required.

Testing Customs Agents for Drugs

U.S. Customs agents work along the country's borders and at air-

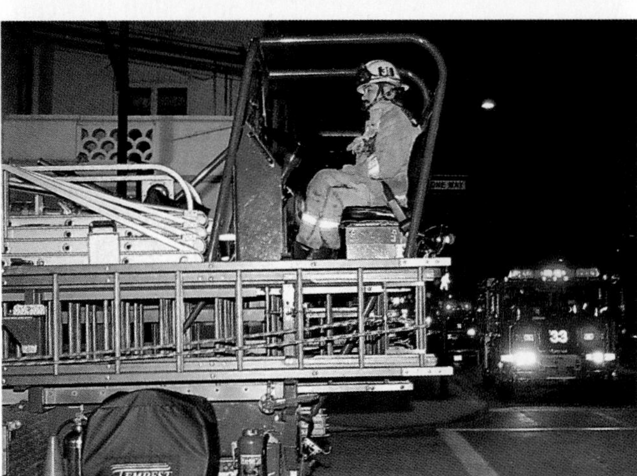

Should the government or a private employer always have a reasonable suspicion of drug use before administering a drug test?

ports. One of their duties is to stem the tide of drugs being smuggled into the United States. The customs commissioner establishes a drug-testing program for all employees who apply for promotion to "sensitive positions." In such positions, employees (1) stop shipments of drugs, (2) carry firearms, or (3) handle classified information. Employees who fail the required urinalysis test are fired, but the results are not turned over to law enforcement officials. Under this program, five customs employees out of 3,600 test positive for drugs. The customs agents' union files a lawsuit challenging the drug-testing program.

PROBLEM 56

a. What are the arguments in favor of the drug-testing

program?

b. What are the arguments against it?

c. If you were the judge in the case, how would you rule, and why?

Losing a Job

Few things disturb people more than the thought of losing their jobs. Job loss can occur through firing for cause or, in some cases, for no reason at all. Workers also lose their jobs through layoffs, which may be the result of poor management by the employer or problems beyond the employer's control.

The fear of unemployment and the resulting loss of income needed to support workers and their families is indeed a serious matter. The law provides some protection from job loss and some assistance for workers who have lost their jobs.

Employment Contracts Most jobs are based on oral or written contracts between employees who promise to perform certain duties and employers who promise to pay them and provide benefits for doing so. Most employment agreements with private employers are referred to as **employment-at-will** contracts. Under this doctrine, the employees can quit any time they wish, and the employer can discharge them any time it wishes for any reason or for no reason at all. This is not true for government jobs, which often must follow specific standards and procedures in order to discharge an employee. It is also not true for some private employers that have negotiated contracts with unions or with nonunion employees providing some rights before job termination (for example, 30-day notice of termination).

In some written employment contracts, the employee must give the employer notice before resigning. If the failure to do so causes the employer to lose money, the employee may be liable.

People differ on whether it is better to have the at-will approach to employment, in which the employer has great freedom to discharge employees, or whether the law should provide greater protection for workers, as it does in a number of other countries. Those in favor of keeping the at-will system argue that it gives businesses the freedom they need to achieve economic success and that restricting them would be inefficient and less profitable. They insist that employers must be able to get rid of workers who do not show up, are constantly late, do not follow the rules, or just cannot perform their jobs. They

Should employers be able to discharge employees without a contract for any reason or no reason at all?

say the government is not as efficient as private business at least partly because of restrictions on discharging employees.

Others call at-will employment very unfair, arguing that workers are often discharged without a good business reason or as a cover-up for illegal discrimination. They argue that workers should be discharged only for a good reason, such as inability to do the job.

In recent years, courts and state legislatures have begun to carve out exceptions to the at-will doctrine by placing more restrictions on the employer's ability to discharge employees. Referring to employee handbooks or other personnel policies stating, for example, that "employees may only be fired for just cause," certain courts have forced employers to reinstate persons fired for no apparent reason or to provide just cause before firing. Other courts have said that there is an implied duty to treat the other party to a contract fairly and in good faith. For example, one state court would not allow an employer to end the employment contract of a salesperson in order to avoid paying him commissions he had already earned. The court held that the employer was not treating the worker fairly under his employment contract.

When a Firing May Be Illegal As noted earlier, federal law provides that employees may not be discharged from their jobs based on race, sex, color, national origin, religion, age (if 40 or older), or physical handicap. Federal law also prohibits discharge because of membership in a union or union activity. Some state laws go further and

The Shoe Store Firing

Mr. Larry works as a salesperson at a shoe store in a mall. He has no written employment contract or employee handbook, and there is no union at the store. Recently, Mr. Larry was fired by the owner, Mrs. Hinoshita, without a stated reason. Mr. Larry and others who work there are sure Mr. Larry was fired because he often argued with Mrs. Hinoshita over the way the shoes were arranged in the storeroom, which shifts he worked, breaks, and other issues. The other salespeople in the store believe that Mrs. Hinoshita is a difficult supervisor and that Mr. Larry was a little outspoken, but they do not think he should have been fired. Mrs. Hinoshita thinks Mr. Larry was more trouble than he was worth and was not a very good salesperson. She also thinks that because it is her store, she should not have to give reasons for firing him.

PROBLEM 57

a. Does Mr. Larry have an employment at-will contract? If so, how does this affect his being fired by Mrs. Hinoshita without a stated reason?

b. Should the law allow at-will employment contracts? What are the arguments for and against them?

c. Role-play a meeting between Mrs. Hinoshita and the other shoe salespeople who want Mr. Larry reinstated in his job and an employee handbook specifying the circumstances under which an employee can be fired. What was the outcome of the meeting? If you were Mrs. Hinoshita, what would you do when confronted with the complaining salespeople? Why?

d. Assume Mrs. Hinoshita agrees to issue an employee handbook listing the reasons for which an employee can be fired. Draft such a list. Are those fair to Mrs. Hinoshita? Are they fair to the employees? How would you modify them to make them fairer?

e. If the employees and Mrs. Hinoshita disagreed on the acceptable reasons for firing people, what other process might be used to come to an agreement both sides can live with? Should Mrs. Hinoshita care whether the other employees support her firing decisions or think her rules are unfair? Explain.

prohibit discrimination because of marital status, AIDS, and sexual orientation.

Courts have also held that discharges were unlawful when they determined that the employer's action worked against a public policy. In one example, an employee was threatened with job loss when he refused to lie before a grand jury as ordered by his supervisor. In another case, an employee called for jury duty was told by his supervisor not to serve.

Closely related to the public policy exception are the laws that protect **whistle-blowing**. This occurs when an employee "blows the whistle" on, or reports, an employer to the authorities for illegal acts. Some federal laws specifically protect this type of conduct. These include the *Fair Labor Standards Act*, *Title VII* of the *Civil Rights Act of 1964*, and the *Occupational Safety and Health Act*, all of which protect employees from being fired for complaints about unfair labor practices, sex discrimination, and unsafe or hazardous conditions. Some states also have laws that forbid the firing of whistle-blowers.

Whistle-blowing might also take the form of telling someone other than the government about a problem. For example, a court ordered the reinstatement of a bank employee who was fired for telling bank vice-presidents that the institution was illegally overcharging customers. Whistle-blowing raises the conflict between employees' duty of loyalty to their employer and their obligation to act ethically and legally. In situations not involving whistle-blowing, loyalty is expected of employees, and they can be fired for disloyal actions such as selling a company's trade secrets to a competing firm.

Employees must be careful when they complain to someone on the outside. For example, employees who call a newspaper to complain that their employer is breaking the law can be fired if they are acting unreasonably (that is, if the report is based on hearsay and no effort has been made to confirm its accuracy). Workers who complain are required to act reasonably and in good faith. If they do not, the courts are likely to let the firing stand.

PROBLEM 58

Assume that the following situations occur at companies with handbooks stating that "any employee may be fired at any time for just cause." These events occur in a state that has recognized such handbooks as implied terms of employment contracts. If employees are fired for the following reasons, which firings should the court allow, and which do you think should be declared illegal?

a. Warren is more than 30 minutes late for work two or three times a week and has been warned three times about it.

b. Michael, the owner of the restaurant at which Leona works, has instructed her not to ring up every check on the cash register so he can avoid paying the full sales tax. She refuses to follow his instructions.

c. Pierre has an alcohol problem that makes it difficult for him to work most days after lunch.

d. While working on a computer, Naomi accidently destroys an important company file. She has been warned about the importance of this file and has destroyed files before.

e. Winston and Nigel's inability to get along is harming company operations. After starting a fist fight with Winston, Nigel is fired. Winston does not lose his job.

f. The ice cream company that Chome works for produces one flavor that is a big seller. He gives the recipe to his friend, who works at another ice cream company.

g. D'Angelo, a government scientist, gives a newspaper reporter classified information showing that a recently issued report to Congress contains false statements.

Procedures Before Job Loss If someone is about to lose a job, it is necessary to determine whether the employer must first follow due process procedures. Should employees receive notice of the complaints against them and a hearing or at least some opportunity to defend themselves before being fired? In the case of government employees, the U.S. Constitution, the state constitution, or state law will usually require that certain procedures be followed. This may not be required in private employment unless it appears in a union contract, employee handbook, or elsewhere.

Sometimes employees are not fired but are laid off. This often occurs when a company is in trouble financially or experiences a temporary lag in business. After some time, the laid-off workers may get their jobs back. Depending on the company's policies or the employment contracts, the workers may have rights to health insurance or other benefits during the layoff.

In recent years, a number of large factory closings have put many employees out of work. To protect such workers, Congress passed a law requiring that factories with more than 100 employees warn their workers at least 60 days in advance of an impending plant closing or large-scale layoff. If employers fail to provide such warnings, they may be liable for fines, back pay, and benefits. Notice is not required under some emergency and other special circumstances.

Employees who have been fired or laid off may be eligible for **severance** pay. This is pay for the loss of their jobs and for time they are not going to work. The amount is determined either by the employer or an employment contract. Although such employees may be eligible for unemployment compensation, it may not begin for a period of time and may not provide sufficient financial support while they look for other jobs.

PROBLEM 59

a. Assume you work for a computer software company. One morning the boss says, "I am sorry, but we have information that you use drugs and even bought some at work one day. We are going to have to let you go. The company has a clearly stated rule against drugs in the workplace." What procedures would you insist on before you were fired? If the employer refused to provide these procedures, what would you do?

b. If your employer is in financial trouble and going out of business, what are the arguments for and against requiring the owner to give you notice and severance pay? Which point of view do you agree with, and why?

c. Can you think of any jobs in which the employee should be required to give the employer notice of an intent to leave the job? If so, which ones, and why should such notice be required? Should there be a penalty if the worker fails to do this? If so, what should the penalty be?

If You Lose Your Job All states have a system of unemployment compensation (also called unemployment insurance) that protects you if you lose your job through no fault of your own. This system allows you to collect payments from the government while you look for another job. The pay will not be as much as you were earning while you were working, and it will not last forever—typically, payments are for up to 26 weeks, although they may continue for longer periods in some states. Congress also has the power to extend unemployment benefits for up to 20 additional weeks. However, the money may keep you from using up your savings or going into debt during the period of unemployment. The unemployment payments come from payroll taxes collected from employers by the federal and state governments.

What steps should be taken to help decrease or eliminate unemployment?

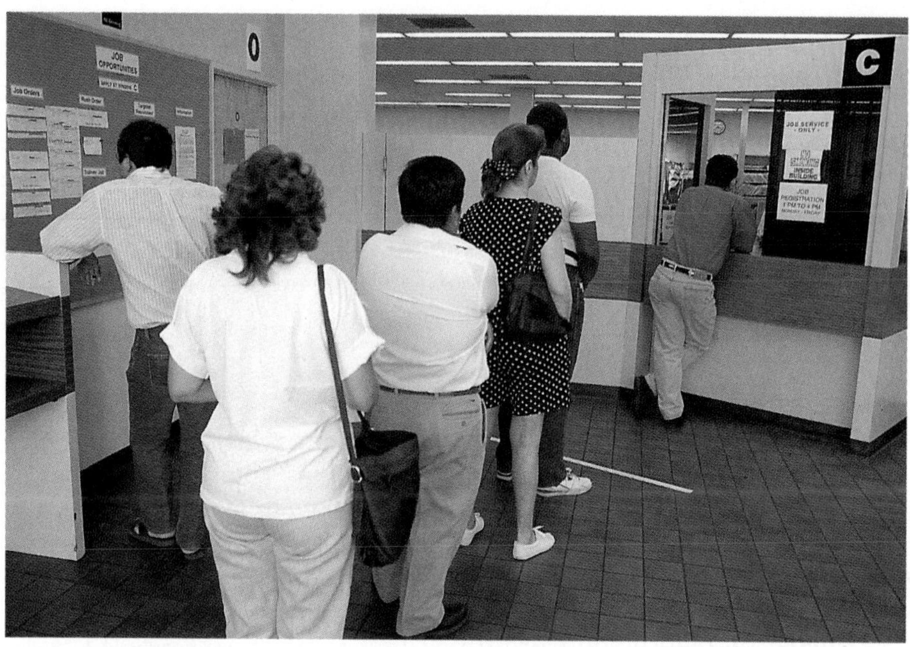

Where is the office at which people can apply for unemployment compensation in your area? What are the rules that determine whether people are eligible? How much can they receive each week? For how many weeks can unemployment benefits be paid?

Some people do not qualify for unemployment compensation. For example, someone who can't work due to an on-the-job injury is eligible for workers' compensation (see page 207) but probably not for unemployment benefits. To qualify for unemployment benefits, you must have worked for 20 to 40 weeks during the 12 months prior to your unemployment and earn a certain amount of wages, depending on the state.

Someone who was fired for misconduct is not eligible. An intentional action against the employer's interest would be considered misconduct. For example, theft would clearly constitute misconduct, whereas an error in filling out a form would not. Generally, a single incident would probably not be misconduct, but repeated incidents after being warned might make an employee ineligible for unemployment compensation. An employee fired for poor performance, such as slow typing, may still be able to obtain unemployment compensation. However, a typist who keeps showing up late after being warned would probably be ruled ineligible because of misconduct.

People who quit voluntarily will usually not be eligible for unemployment benefits unless they can show that the situation at work was unbearable. For example, a person who opposed war as part of his religion and who quit after being transferred to a job producing tanks was allowed to collect unemployment compensation. Someone who is physically unable to do a job can also quit and retain eligibility for benefits.

To apply for unemployment compensation, a person must file an application form with the state agency that handles these claims. It is important to do this immediately after being discharged or quitting, because it may take a while to process the application. Agency staff must investigate the applications, and hearings are sometimes held when employers protest the claims. Employers may protest the payment of unemployment benefits to a former employee because it sometimes results in higher payroll taxes for the employer in the future. In other instances employers may wish to deny the benefits to the fired employee because of that person's misconduct on the job.

PROBLEM 60

Assume that the following employees lose their jobs for the stated reasons. Should they be eligible to receive unemployment compensation? Explain.

a. Eric is injured on the job and is unable to return to work.

b. Mary dislikes her boss and says she will no longer do any work he assigns. She is fired.

c. A fellow employee offers Bert some marijuana. He is caught smoking it in the men's room and is fired.

d. Sybil stays home from work several times to care for her sick children. Her boss fires her, saying he needs someone he can count on.

e. When business declines, a company closes the plant where Alonzo works. The company offers him a job at its other plant, which is 1½ hours away by car. Alonzo turns down the new job because he doesn't want to drive that far.

APPENDIX A

The Constitution of the United States*

PREAMBLE

We the People of the United States, in Order to form a more perfect Union, establish Justice, insure domestic Tranquility, provide for the common defence, promote the general Welfare, and secure the Blessings of Liberty to ourselves and our Posterity, do ordain and establish this Constitution for the United States of America.

ARTICLE I

Section 1. All legislative Powers herein granted shall be vested in a Congress of the United States, which shall consist of a Senate and House of Representatives.

Section 2. The House of Representatives shall be composed of Members chosen every second Year by the People of the several States, and the Electors in each State shall have the Qualifications requisite for Electors of the most numerous Branch of the State Legislature.

No Person shall be a Representative who shall not have attained to the Age of twenty five Years, and been seven Years a citizen of the United States, and who shall not, when elected, be an Inhabitant of that State in which he shall be chosen.

[Representatives and direct Taxes shall be apportioned among the several States which may be included within this Union, according to their respective Numbers, which shall be determined by adding to the whole Number of free Persons, including those bound to Service for a Term of Years, and excluding Indians not taxed, three fifths of all other Persons.][1] The actual Enumeration shall be made within three Years after the first Meeting of the Congress of the United States, and within every subsequent Term of ten Years, in such Manner as they shall by Law direct. The Number of Representatives shall not exceed one for every thirty Thousand, but each State shall have at Least one Representative; and until such enumeration shall be made, the State of New Hampshire shall be entitled to chuse three, Massachusetts eight, Rhode Island and Providence Plantations one, Connecticut five, New York six, New Jersey four, Pennsylvania eight, Delaware one, Maryland six, Virginia ten, North Carolina five, South Carolina five, and Georgia three.

When vacancies happen in the Representation from any State, the Executive Authority thereof shall issue Writs of Election to fill such Vacancies.

The House of Representatives shall chuse their Speaker and other Officers; and shall have the sole Power of Impeachment.

Section 3. The Senate of the United States shall be composed of two Senators from each State, [chosen by the Legislature thereof,][2] for six Years; and each Senator shall have one Vote.

Immediately after they shall be assembled in Consequence of the first Election, they shall be divided as equally as may be into three Classes. The Seats of the Senators of the first Class shall be va-

* The Constitution and all amendments are shown in their original form. Parts that have been amended or superseded are bracketed and explained in the footnotes.

[1] Modified by the Fourteenth and Sixteenth Amendments.

[2] Superseded by the Seventeenth Amendment.

cated at the Expiration of the second Year, of the second Class at the Expiration of the fourth Year, and of the third Class at the Expiration of the sixth Year, so that one third may be chosen every second Year; [and if Vacancies happen by Resignation, or otherwise, during the Recess of the Legislature of any State, the Executive thereof may make temporary Appointments until the next Meeting of the Legislature, which shall then fill such Vacancies][3].

No Person shall be a Senator who shall not have attained to the Age of thirty Years, and been nine Years a Citizen of the United States, and who shall not, when elected, be an Inhabitant of that State for which he shall be chosen.

The Vice President of the United States shall be President of the Senate, but shall have no Vote, unless they be equally divided.

The Senate shall chuse their other Officers, and also a President pro tempore, in the Absence of the Vice President, or when he shall exercise the Office of President of the United States.

The Senate shall have the sole Power to try all Impeachments. When sitting for that Purpose, they shall be on Oath or Affirmation. When the President of the United States is tried, the Chief Justice shall preside: And no Person shall be convicted without the Concurrence of two thirds of the Members present.

Judgment in Cases of Impeachment shall not extend further than to removal from Office, and disqualification to hold and enjoy any Office of honor, Trust, or Profit under the United States: but the Party convicted shall nevertheless be liable and subject to Indictment, Trial, Judgment, and Punishment, according to Law.

Section 4. The Times, Places and Manner of holding Elections for Senators and Representatives, shall be prescribed in each State by the Legislature thereof; but the Congress may at any time by Law make or alter such Regulations, except as to the Places of chusing Senators.

The Congress shall assemble at least once in every Year, and such Meeting shall [be on the first Monday in December,][4] unless they shall by Law appoint a different Day.

Section 5. Each House shall be the Judge of the Elections, Returns, and Qualifications of its own Members, and a Majority of each shall constitute a Quorum to do Business; but a smaller Number may adjourn from day to day, and may be authorized to compel the Attendance of absent Members, in such Manner, and under such Penalties as each House may provide.

Each House may determine the Rules of its Proceedings, punish its Members for disorderly Behavior, and, with the Concurrence of two thirds, expel a Member.

Each House shall keep a Journal of its Proceedings, and from time to time publish the same, excepting such Parts as may in their Judgment require Secrecy; and the Yeas and Nays of the Members of either House on any question shall, at the Desire of one fifth of those Present, be entered on the Journal.

Neither House, during the Session of Congress, shall, without the Consent of the other, adjourn for more than three days, nor to any other Place than that in which the two Houses shall be sitting.

Section 6. The Senators and Representatives shall receive a Compensation for their Services, to be ascertained by Law, and paid out of the Treasury of the United States. They shall in all Cases, except Treason, Felony and Breach of the Peace, be privileged from Arrest during their Attendance at the Session of their respective Houses, and in going to and returning from the same; and for any Speech or Debate in either House, they shall not be questioned in any other Place.

No Senator or Representative shall, during the Time for which he was elected, be appointed to any civil Office under the Authority of the United States, which shall have been created, or the Emoluments whereof shall have been increased during such time; and no Person holding any Office under the United States, shall be a Member of either House during his Continuance in Office.

Section 7. All Bills for raising Revenue shall originate in the House of Representatives; but the Senate may propose or concur with Amendments as on other Bills.

Every Bill which shall have passed the House of Representatives and the Senate shall, before it become a Law, be presented to the President of the

[3] Modified by the Seventeenth Amendment
[4] Superseded by the Twentieth Amendment.

United States; If he approve he shall sign it, but if not he shall return it, with his Objections to that House in which it shall have originated, who shall enter the Objections at large on their Journal, and proceed to reconsider it. If after such Reconsideration two thirds of that House shall agree to pass the Bill, it shall be sent, together with the Objections, to the other House, by which it shall likewise be reconsidered, and if approved by two thirds of that House, it shall become a Law. But in all such Cases the Votes of both Houses shall be determined by Yeas and Nays, and the Names of the Persons voting for and against the Bill shall be entered on the Journal of each House respectively. If any Bill shall not be returned by the President within ten Days (Sundays excepted) after it shall have been presented to him, the Same shall be a Law, in like Manner as if he had signed it, unless the Congress by their Adjournment prevent its Return in which Case it shall not be a Law.

Every Order, Resolution, or Vote, to which the Concurrence of the Senate and House of Representatives may be necessary (except on a question of Adjournment) shall be presented to the President of the United States; and before the Same shall take Effect, shall be approved by him, or being disapproved by him, shall be repassed by two thirds of the Senate and House of Representatives, according to the Rules and Limitations prescribed in the Case of a Bill.

Section 8. The Congress shall have Power To lay and collect Taxes, Duties, Imposts and Excises, to pay the Debts and provide for the common Defence and general Welfare of the United States; but all Duties, Imposts and Excises shall be uniform throughout the United States;

To borrow Money on the credit of the United States;

To regulate Commerce with foreign Nations, and among the several States, and with the Indian Tribes;

To establish an uniform Rule of Naturalization, and uniform Laws on the subject of Bankruptcies throughout the United States;

To coin Money, regulate the Value thereof, and of foreign Coin, and fix the Standard of Weights and Measures;

To provide for the Punishment of counterfeiting the Securities and current Coin of the United States;

To establish Post Offices and post Roads;

To promote the Progress of Science and useful Arts, by securing for limited Times to Authors and Inventors the exclusive Right to their respective Writings and Discoveries;

To constitute Tribunals inferior to the supreme Court;

To define and punish Piracies and Felonies committed on the high Seas, and Offenses against the Law of Nations;

To declare War, grant Letters of Marque and Reprisal, and make Rules concerning Captures on Land and Water;

To raise and support Armies, but no Appropriation of Money to that Use shall be for a longer Term than two Years;

To provide and maintain a Navy;

To make Rules for the Government and Regulation of the land and naval Forces;

To provide for calling forth the Militia to execute the Laws of the Union, suppress Insurrections and repel Invasions;

To provide for organizing, arming, and disciplining, the Militia, and for governing such Part of them as may be employed in the Service of the United States, reserving to the States respectively, the Appointment of the Officers, and the Authority of training the Militia according to the discipline prescribed by Congress;

To exercise exclusive Legislation in all Cases whatsoever, over such District (not exceeding ten Miles square) as may, by Cession of particular States, and the Acceptance of Congress, become the Seat of the Government of the United States, and to exercise like Authority over all Places purchased by the Consent of the Legislature of the State in which the Same shall be, for the Erection of Forts, Magazines, Arsenals, dock-Yards, and other needful Buildings;—And

To make all Laws which shall be necessary and proper for carrying into Execution the foregoing Powers, and all other Powers vested by this Constitution in the Government of the United States, or in any Department or Officer thereof.

Section 9. The Migration or Importation of such Persons as any of the States now existing shall think proper to admit, shall not be prohibited by the Congress prior to the Year one thousand eight hundred and eight, but a Tax or duty may be imposed on such Importation, not exceeding ten dollars for each Person.

The privilege of the Writ of Habeas Corpus shall not be suspended, unless when in Cases of Rebellion or Invasion the public Safety may require it.

No Bill of Attainder or ex post facto Law shall be passed.

[No Capitation, or other direct, Tax shall be laid, unless in Proportion to the Census or Enumeration herein before directed to be taken.][5]

No Tax or Duty shall be laid on Articles exported from any State.

No Preference shall be given by any Regulation of Commerce or Revenue to the Ports of one State over those of another; nor shall Vessels bound to, or from, one State be obliged to enter, clear, or pay Duties in another.

No Money shall be drawn from the Treasury, but in Consequence of Appropriations made by Law; and a regular Statement and Account of the Receipts and Expenditures of all public Money shall be published from time to time.

No Title of Nobility shall be granted by the United States: And no Person holding any Office of Profit or Trust under them, shall, without the Consent of the Congress, accept of any present, Emolument, Office, or Title, or any kind whatever, from any King, Prince, or foreign State.

Section 10. No State shall enter into any Treaty, Alliance, or Confederation; grant Letters of Marque and Reprisal; coin Money; emit Bills of Credit; make any Thing but gold and silver Coin a Tender in Payment of Debts; pass any Bill of Attainder, ex post facto Law, or Law impairing the Obligation of Contracts, or grant any Title of Nobility.

No State shall, without the Consent of the Congress, lay any Imposts or Duties on Imports or Exports, except what may be absolutely necessary for executing it's inspection Laws: and the net Produce of all Duties and Imposts, laid by any State on Imports or Exports, shall be for the Use of the Treasury of the United States; and all such Laws shall be subject to the Revision and Controul of the Congress.

No State shall, without the Consent of Congress, lay any Duty of Tonnage, keep Troops, or Ships of War in time of Peace, enter into any Agreement or Compact with another State, or with a foreign Power, or engage in War, unless actually invaded, or in such imminent Danger as will not admit of delay.

ARTICLE II

Section 1. The executive Power shall be vested in a President of the United States of America. He shall hold his Office during the Term of four Years, and, together with the Vice President, chosen for the same Term, be elected, as follows:

Each State shall appoint, in such Manner as the Legislature thereof may direct, a Number of Electors, equal to the whole Number of Senators and Representatives to which the State may be entitled in the Congress; but no Senator or Representative, or Person holding an Office of Trust or Profit under the United States, shall be appointed an Elector.

[The Electors shall meet in their respective States, and vote by Ballot for two Persons, of whom one at least shall not be an Inhabitant of the same State with themselves. And they shall make a List of all the Persons voted for, and of the Number of Votes for each; which List they shall sign and certify, and transmit sealed to the Seat of the Government of the United States, directed to the President of the Senate. The President of the Senate shall, in the Presence of the Senate and House of Representatives, open all the Certificates, and the Votes shall then be counted. The Person having the greatest Number of Votes shall be the President, if such Number be a Majority of the whole Number of Electors appointed; and if there be more than one who have such Majority, and have an equal Number of Votes, then the House of Representatives shall immediately chuse by Ballot one of them for President; and if no Person have a Majority, then from the five highest on the List the said House shall in like Manner chuse the President. But in chusing the President, the Votes shall be taken by States, the Representation from each State having one Vote; A quorum for this Purpose shall consist of a Member or Members from two thirds of the States, and a Majority of all the States shall be necessary to a Choice. In every Case, after the Choice of the Presi-

[5] Modified by the Sixteenth Amendment

dent, the Person having the greater Number of Votes of the Electors shall be the Vice President. But if there should remain two or more who have equal Votes, the Senate shall chuse from them by Ballot the Vice President.][6]

The Congress may determine the Time of chusing the Electors, and the Day on which they shall give their Votes; which Day shall be the same throughout the United States.

No person except a natural born Citizen, or a Citizen of the United States, at the time of the Adoption of this Constitution, shall be eligible to the Office of President; neither shall any Person be eligible to that Office who shall not have attained to the Age of thirty five Years, and been fourteen Years a Resident within the United States.

[In Case of the Removal of the President from Office, or of his Death, Resignation or Inability to discharge the Powers and Duties of the said Office, the same shall devolve on the Vice President, and the Congress may by Law provide for the Case of Removal, Death, Resignation or Inability, both of the President and Vice President, declaring what Officer shall then act as President, and such Officer shall act accordingly, until the Disability be removed, or a President shall be elected.][7]

The President shall, at stated Times, receive for his Services, a Compensation, which shall neither be increased nor diminished during the Period for which he shall have been elected, and he shall not receive within that Period any other Emolument from the United States, or any of them.

Before he enter on the Execution of his Office, he shall take the following Oath or Affirmation: "I do solemnly swear (or affirm) that I will faithfully execute the Office of President of the United States, and will to the best of my Ability, preserve, protect and defend the Constitution of the United States."

Section 2. The President shall be Commander in Chief of the Army and Navy of the United States, and of the Militia of the several States, when called into the actual Service of the United States; he may require the Opinion, in writing, of the principal Officer in each of the executive Departments, upon any Subject relating to the Duties of their respective Offices, and he shall have Power to grant Reprieves and Pardons for Offenses against the United States, except in Cases of Impeachment.

He shall have Power, by and with the Advice and Consent of the Senate to make Treaties, provided two thirds of the Senators present concur; and he shall nominate, and by and with the Advice and Consent of the Senate, shall appoint Ambassadors, other public Ministers and Consuls, Judges of the supreme Court, and all other Officers of the United States, whose Appointments are not herein otherwise provided for, and which shall be established by Law; but the Congress may by Law vest the Appointment of such inferior Officers, as they think proper, in the President alone, in the Courts of Law, or in the Heads of Departments.

The President shall have Power to fill up all Vacancies that may happen during the Recess of the Senate, by granting Commissions which shall expire at the End of their next Session.

Section 3. He shall from time to time give to the Congress Information of the State of the Union, and recommend to their Consideration such Measures as he shall judge necessary and expedient; he may, on extraordinary Occasions, convene both Houses, or either of them, and in Case of Disagreement between them, with Respect to the Time of Adjournment, he may adjourn them to such Time as he shall think proper; he shall receive Ambassadors and other public Ministers; he shall take Care that the Laws be faithfully executed, and shall Commission all the Officers of the United States.

Section 4. The President, Vice President and all civil Officers of the United States, shall be removed from Office on Impeachment for, and Conviction of, Treason, Bribery, or other high Crimes and Misdemeanors.

ARTICLE III

Section 1. The judicial Power of the United States, shall be vested in one supreme Court, and in such inferior Courts as the Congress may from time to time ordain and establish. The Judges, both of the supreme and inferior Courts, shall hold their Offices during good Behaviour, and shall, at stated Times, receive for their Services a Compensation, which shall not be diminished during their Continuance in Office.

[6] Superseded by the Twelfth Amendment.

[7] Modified by the Twenty-fifth Amendment.

Section 2. The judicial Power shall extend to all Cases, in Law and Equity, arising under this Constitution, the Laws of the United States, and Treaties made, or which shall be made, under their Authority;—to all Cases affecting Ambassadors, other public Ministers and Consuls;—to all Cases of admiralty and maritime Jurisdiction;—to Controversies to which the United States shall be a Party;—to Controversies between two or more States;—[between a State and Citizens of another State;][8] between Citizens of different States;—between Citizens of the same State claiming Lands under Grants of different States, and between a State, or the Citizens thereof, and foreign States, Citizens or Subjects.

In all Cases affecting Ambassadors, other public Ministers and Consuls, and those in which a State shall be a Party, the supreme Court shall have original Jurisdiction. In all the other Cases before mentioned, the supreme Court shall have appellate Jurisdiction, both as to Law and Fact, with such Exceptions, and under such Regulations as the Congress shall make.

The Trial of all Crimes, except in Cases of Impeachment, shall be by Jury; and such Trial shall be held in the State where the said Crimes shall have been committed; but when not committed within any State, the Trial shall be at such Place or Places as the Congress may by Law have directed.

Section 3. Treason against the United States, shall consist only in levying War against them, or, in adhering to their Enemies, giving them Aid and Comfort. No person shall be convicted of Treason unless on the Testimony of two Witnesses to the same overt Act, or on Confession in open Court.

The Congress shall have Power to declare the Punishment of Treason, but no Attainder of Treason shall work Corruption of Blood, or Forfeiture except during the Life of the Person attainted.

ARTICLE IV

Section 1. Full Faith and Credit shall be given in each State to the public Acts, Records, and judicial Proceedings of every other State. And the Congress may by general Laws prescribe the Manner in which such Acts, Records and Proceedings shall be proved, and the Effect thereof.

Section 2. The Citizens of each State shall be entitled to all Privileges and Immunities of Citizens in the several States.

A Person charged in any State with Treason, Felony, or other Crime, who shall flee from Justice, and be found in another State, shall on Demand of the executive Authority of the State from which he fled, be delivered up, to be removed to the State having Jurisdiction of the Crime.

[No Person held to Service or Labour in one State, under the Laws thereof, escaping into another, shall, in Consequence of any Law or Regulation therein, be discharged from such Service or Labour, but shall be delivered up on Claim of the Party to whom such Service or Labour may be due.][9]

Section 3. New States may be admitted by the Congress into this Union; but no new State shall be formed or erected within the Jurisdiction of any other State; nor any State be formed by the Junction of two or more States, or Parts of States, without the Consent of the Legislatures of the States concerned as well as of the Congress.

The Congress shall have Power to dispose of and make all needful Rules and Regulations respecting the Territory or other Property belonging to the United States; and nothing in this Constitution shall be so construed as to Prejudice any Claims of the United States, or of any particular State.

Section 4. The United States shall guarantee to every State in this Union a Republican Form of Government, and shall protect each of them against Invasion; and on Application of the Legislature, or of the Executive (when the Legislature cannot be convened) against domestic Violence.

ARTICLE V

The Congress, whenever two thirds of both Houses shall deem it necessary, shall propose Amendments to this Constitution, or, on the Application of the Legislatures of two thirds of the several States, shall call a Convention for proposing Amendments, which, in either Case, shall be valid to all Intents and Purposes, as part of this Constitution, when ratified by the Legislatures of three fourths of the several States, or by Conventions in three fourths thereof, as the one or the other Mode of Ratification may be proposed by the Congress; Provided that no

[8] Modified by the Eleventh Amendment.

[9] Superseded by the Thirteenth Amendment.

Amendment which may be made prior to the Year One thousand eight hundred and eight shall in any Manner affect the first and fourth Clauses in the Ninth Section of the first Article; and that no State, without its Consent, shall be deprived of its equal Suffrage in the Senate.

ARTICLE VI

All Debts contracted and Engagements entered into, before the Adoption of this Constitution shall be as valid against the United States under this Constitution, as under the Confederation.

This Constitution, and the Laws of the United States which shall be made in Pursuance thereof; and all Treaties made, or which shall be made, under the Authority of the United States, shall be the supreme Law of the Land; and the Judges in every State shall be bound thereby, any Thing in the Constitution or Laws of any State to the Contrary notwithstanding.

The Senators and Representatives before mentioned, and the Members of the several State Legislatures, and all executive and judicial Officers, both of the United States and of the several States, shall be bound by Oath or Affirmation, to support this Constitution; but no religious Test shall ever be required as a Qualification to any Office or public Trust under the United States.

ARTICLE VII

The Ratification of the Conventions of nine States shall be sufficient for the Establishment of this Constitution between the States so ratifying the Same.

AMENDMENT I [1791][10]

Congress shall make no law respecting an establishment of religion, or prohibiting the free exercise thereof; or abridging the freedom of speech, or of the press; or the right of the people peaceably to assemble, and to petition the Government for a redress of grievances.

[10] The first ten amendments were passed by Congress September 25, 1789. They were ratified by three-fourths of the states December 15, 1791.

AMENDMENT II [1791]

A well regulated Militia, being necessary to the security of a free State, the right of the people to keep and bear Arms, shall not be infringed.

AMENDMENT III [1791]

No Soldier shall, in time of peace be quartered in any house, without the consent of the Owner, nor in time of war, but in a manner to be prescribed by law.

AMENDMENT IV [1791]

The right of the people to be secure in their persons, houses, papers, and effects, against unreasonable searches and seizures, shall not be violated, and no Warrants shall issue, but upon probable cause, supported by Oath or affirmation, and particularly describing the place to be searched, and the persons or things to be seized.

AMENDMENT V [1791]

No person shall be held to answer for a capital, or otherwise infamous crime, unless on a presentment or indictment of a Grand Jury, except in cases arising in the land or naval forces, or in the Militia, when in actual service in time of War or public danger; nor shall any person be subject for the same offence to be twice put in jeopardy of life or limb; nor shall be compelled in any criminal case to be a witness against himself, nor be deprived of life, liberty, or property, without due process of law; nor shall private property be taken for public use, without just compensation.

AMENDMENT VI [1791]

In all criminal prosecutions, the accused shall enjoy the right to a speedy and public trial, by an impartial jury of the State and district wherein the crime shall have been committed, which district shall have been previously ascertained by law, and to be informed of the nature and cause of the accusation; to be confronted with the witnesses against him; to have compulsory process for obtaining witnesses in his favor, and to have the Assistance of Counsel for his defence.

AMENDMENT VII [1791]

In Suits at common law, where the value in controversy shall exceed twenty dollars, the right of trial by a jury shall be preserved, and no fact tried by jury, shall be otherwise re-examined in any Court of the United States, than according to the rules of the common law.

AMENDMENT VIII [1791]

Excessive bail shall not be required, nor excessive fines imposed, nor cruel and unusual punishments inflicted.

AMENDMENT IX [1791]

The enumeration in the Constitution, of certain rights, shall not be construed to deny or disparage others retained by the people.

AMENDMENT X [1791]

The powers not delegated to the United States by the Constitution, nor prohibited by it to the States, are reserved to the States respectively, or to the people.

AMENDMENT XI [1798][11]

The Judicial power of the United States shall not be construed to extend to any suit in law or equity, commenced or prosecuted against one of the United States by Citizens of another State, or by Citizens or Subjects of any Foreign State.

AMENDMENT XII [1804]

The Electors shall meet in their respective states, and vote by ballot for President and Vice-President, one of whom, at least, shall not be an inhabitant of the same state with themselves; they shall name in their ballots the person voted for as President, and in distinct ballots the person voted for as Vice-President, and they shall make distinct lists of all persons voted for as President, and of all persons voted for as Vice-President, and of the number of votes for each, which lists they shall sign and certify, and transmit sealed to the seat of the government of the United States, directed to the President of the Senate;—The President of the Senate shall, in the presence of the Senate and House of Representatives, open all the certificates and the votes shall then be counted;—The person having the greatest number of votes for President, shall be the President, if such number be a majority of the whole number Electors appointed; and if no person have such majority, then from the persons having the highest numbers not exceeding three on the list of those voted for as President, the House of Representatives shall choose immediately, by ballot, the President. But in choosing the President, the votes shall be taken by states, the representation from each state having one vote; a quorum for this purpose shall consist of a member or members from two-thirds of the states, and a majority of all states shall be necessary to a choice. [And if the House of Representatives shall not choose a President whenever the right of choice shall devolve upon them, before the fourth day of March next following, then the Vice-President shall act as President, as in the case of the death or other constitutional disability of the President.][12]—The person having the greatest number of votes as Vice-President, shall be the Vice-President, if such number be a majority of the whole number of Electors appointed, and if no person have a majority, then from the two highest numbers on the list, the Senate shall choose the Vice-President; a quorum for the purpose shall consist of two-thirds of the whole number of Senators, and a majority of the whole number shall be necessary to a choice. But no person constitutionally ineligible to the office of President shall be eligible to that of Vice-President of the United States.

AMENDMENT XII [1865]

Section 1. Neither slavery nor involuntary servitude, except as a punishment for crime whereof the party shall have been duly convicted, shall exist within the United States, or any place subject to their jurisdiction.

Section 2. Congress shall have power to enforce this article by appropriate legislation.

AMENDMENT XIV [1868]

Section 1. All persons born or naturalized in the United States, and subject to the jurisdiction thereof, are citizens of the United States and of the State wherein they reside. No State shall make or enforce any law which shall abridge the privileges or immunities of citizens of the United States; nor shall any State deprive any person of life, liberty, or property, without due process of law; nor deny to any person within its jurisdiction the equal protection of the laws.

Section 2. Representatives shall be apportioned among the several States according to their respective numbers, counting the whole number of persons in each State, excluding Indians not taxed. But

[11] Date of ratification appears in brackets following each amendment.

[12] Superseded by the Twentieth Amendment.

when the right to vote at any election for the choice of electors for President and Vice President of the United States, Representatives in Congress, the Executive and Judicial officers of a State, or the members of the Legislature thereof, is denied to any of the male inhabitants of such State, being twenty-one years of age, and citizens of the United States, or in any way abridged, except for participation in rebellion, or other crime, the basis of representation therein shall be reduced in the proportion which the number of such male citizens shall bear to the whole number of male citizens twenty-one years of age in such State.

Section 3. No person shall be a Senator or Representative in Congress, or elector of President and Vice President, or hold any office, civil or military, under the United States, or under any State, who having previously taken an oath, as a member of Congress, or as an officer of the United States, or as a member of any State legislature, or as an executive or judicial officer of any State, to support the Constitution of the United States, shall have engaged in insurrection or rebellion against the same, or given aid or comfort to the enemies thereof. But Congress may by a vote of two-thirds of each House, remove such disability.

Section 4. The validity of the public debt of the United States, authorized by law, including debts incurred for payment of pensions and bounties for services in suppressing insurrection or rebellion, shall not be questioned. But neither the United States nor any State shall assume or pay any debt or obligation incurred in aid of insurrection or rebellion against the United States, or any claim for the loss or emancipation of any slave; but all such debts, obligations and claims shall be held illegal and void.

Section 5. The Congress shall have power to enforce, by appropriate legislation, the provisions of this article.

AMENDMENT XV [1870]

Section 1. The right of citizens of the United States to vote shall not be denied or abridged by the United States or by any State on account of race, color, or previous condition of servitude.

Section 2. The Congress shall have power to enforce this article by appropriate legislation.

AMENDMENT XVI [1913]

The Congress shall have power to lay and collect taxes on incomes, from whatever source derived, without apportionment among the several States, and without regard to any census or enumeration.

AMENDMENT XVII [1913]

[1] The Senate of the United States shall be composed of two Senators from each State, elected by the people thereof, for six years; and each Senator shall have one vote. The electors in each State shall have the qualifications requisite for electors of the most numerous branch of the State legislatures.

[2] When vacancies happen in the representation of any State in the Senate, the executive authority of such State shall issue writs of election to fill such vacancies: *Provided*, That the legislature of any State may empower the executive thereof to make temporary appointments until the people fill the vacancies by election as the legislature may direct.

[3] This amendment shall not be so construed as to affect the election or term of any Senator chosen before it becomes valid as part of the Constitution.

AMENDMENT XVIII [1919][13]

Section 1. After one year from the ratification of this article the manufacture, sale, or transportation of intoxicating liquors within, the importation thereof into, or the exportation thereof from the United States and all territory subject to the jurisdiction thereof for beverage purposes is hereby prohibited.

Section 2. The Congress and the several States shall have concurrent power to enforce this article by appropriate legislation.

Section 3. This article shall be inoperative unless it shall have been ratified as an amendment to the Constitution by the legislatures of the several States, as provided in the Constitution, within seven years from the date of the submission hereof to the States by the Congress.

AMENDMENT XIX [1920]

[1] The right of citizens of the United States to vote shall not be denied or abridged by the United States or by any State on account of sex.

[2] Congress shall have power to enforce this article by appropriate legislation.

[13] Repealed by the Twenty-first Amendment.

AMENDMENT XX [1933]

Section 1. The terms of the President and Vice President shall end at noon on the 20th day of January, and the terms of Senators and Representatives at noon on the 3d day of January, of the years in which such terms would have ended if this article had not been ratified; and the terms of their successors shall then begin.

Section 2. The Congress shall assemble at least once in every year, and such meeting shall begin at noon on the 3d day of January, unless they shall by law appoint a different day.

Section 3. If, at the time fixed for the beginning of the term of the President, the President elect shall have died, the Vice President elect shall become President. If a President shall not have been chosen before the time fixed for the beginning of his term, or if the President elect shall have failed to qualify, then the Vice President elect shall act as President until a President shall have qualified; and the Congress may by law provide for the case wherein neither a President elect nor a Vice President elect shall have qualified, declaring who shall then act as President, or the manner in which one who is to act shall be selected, and such person shall act accordingly until a President or Vice President shall have qualified.

Section 4. The Congress may by law provide for the case of the death of any of the persons from whom the House of Representatives may choose a President whenever the right of choice shall have devolved upon them, and for the case of the death of any of the persons from whom the Senate may choose a Vice President whenever the right of choice shall have devolved upon them.

Section 5. Sections 1 and 2 shall take effect on the 15th day of October following the ratification of this article.

Section 6. This article shall be inoperative unless it shall have been ratified as an amendment to the Constitution by the legislatures of three-fourths of the several States within seven years from the date of its submission.

AMENDMENT XXI [1933]

Section 1. The eighteenth article of amendment to the Constitution of the United States is hereby repealed.

Section 2. The transportation or importation into any State, Territory, or possession of the United States for delivery or use therein of intoxicating liquors, in violation of the laws thereof, is hereby prohibited.

Section 3. This article shall be inoperative unless it shall have been ratified as an amendment to the Constitution by conventions in the several States, as provided in the Constitution, within seven years from the date of the submission hereof to the States by the Congress.

AMENDMENT XXII [1951]

Section 1. No person shall be elected to the office of the President more than twice, and no person who has held the office of President, or acted as President, for more than two years of a term to which some other person was elected President shall be elected to the office of President more than once. But this Article shall not apply to any person holding the office of President when this Article was proposed by the Congress, and shall not prevent any person who may be holding the office of President, or acting as President, during the term within which this Article becomes operative from holding the office of President or acting as President during the remainder of such term.

Section 2. This article shall be inoperative unless it shall have been ratified as an amendment to the Constitution by the legislatures of three-fourths of the several States within seven years from the date of its submission to the States by the Congress.

AMENDMENT XXIII [1961]

Section 1. The District constituting the seat of Government of the United States shall appoint in such manner as the Congress may direct:

A number of electors of President and Vice President equal to the whole number of Senators and Representatives in Congress to which the District would be entitled if it were a State, but in no event more than the least populous state; they shall be in addition to those appointed by the states, but they shall be considered, for the purposes of the election of President and Vice President, to be electors appointed by a state; and they shall meet in the District and perform such duties as provided by the twelfth article of amendment.

Section 2. The Congress shall have power to enforce this article by appropriate legislation.

AMENDMENT XXIV [1964]

Section 1. The right of citizens of the United States to vote in any primary or other election for President or Vice President, for electors for President or Vice President, or for Senator or Representative in Congress, shall not be denied or abridged by the United States, or any State by reason of failure to pay any poll tax or other tax.

Section 2. The Congress shall have power to enforce this article by appropriate legislation.

AMENDMENT XXV [1967]

Section 1. In case of the removal of the President from office or of his death or resignation, the Vice President shall become President.

Section 2. Whenever there is a vacancy in the office of the Vice President, the President shall nominate a Vice President who shall take office upon confirmation by a majority vote of both Houses of Congress.

Section 3. Whenever the President transmits to the President pro tempore of the Senate and the Speaker of the House of Representatives his written declaration that he is unable to discharge the powers and duties of his office, and until he transmits to them a written declaration to the contrary, such powers and duties shall be discharged by the Vice President as Acting President.

Section 4. Whenever the Vice President and a majority of either the principal officers of the executive departments or of such other body as Congress may by law provide, transmit to the President pro tempore of the Senate and the Speaker of the House of Representatives their written declaration that the President is unable to discharge the powers and duties of his office, the Vice President shall immediately assume the powers and duties of the office as Acting President.

Thereafter, when the President transmits to the President pro tempore of the Senate and the Speaker of the House of Representatives his written declaration that no inability exists, he shall resume the powers and duties of his office unless the Vice President and a majority of either the principal officers of the executive department or of such other body as Congress may by law provide, transmit within four days to the President pro tempore of the Senate and the Speaker of the House of Representatives their written declaration that the President is unable to discharge the powers and duties of his office. Thereupon Congress shall decide the issue, assembling within forty-eight hours for that purpose if not in session. If the Congress, within twenty-one days after receipt of the latter written declaration, or, if Congress is not in session, within twenty-one days after Congress is required to assemble, determines by two-thirds vote of both Houses that the President is unable to discharge the powers and duties of his office, the Vice President shall continue to discharge the same as Acting President; otherwise, the President shall resume the powers and duties of his office.

AMENDMENT XXVI [1971]

Section 1. The right of citizens of the United States, who are eighteen years of age or older, to vote shall not be denied or abridged by the United States or by any State on account of age.

Section 2. The Congress shall have power to enforce this article by appropriate legislation.

AMENDMENT XXVII [1992]

No law, varying the compensation for the services of the Senators and Representatives, shall take effect, until an election of Representatives shall have intervened.

APPENDIX B

The Universal Declaration of Human Rights (1948)

PLAIN LANGUAGE VERSION*

ARTICLE 1

When children are born, they are free and each should be treated in the same way. They have reason and conscience and should act towards one another in a friendly manner.

ARTICLE 2

Everyone can claim the following rights, despite

- a different sex
- a different skin colour
- speaking a different language
- thinking different things
- believing in another religion
- owning more or less
- being born in another social group
- coming from another country.

It also makes no difference whether the country you live in is independent or not.

ARTICLE 3

You have the right to live, and to live in freedom and safety.

ARTICLE 4

Nobody has the right to treat you as his or her slave and you should not make anyone your slave.

ORIGINAL TEXT

ARTICLE 1

All human beings are born free and equal in dignity and rights. They are endowed with reason and conscience and should act towards one another in a spirit of brotherhood.

ARTICLE 2

Everyone is entitled to all the rights and freedoms set forth in this Declaration, without distinction of any kind, such as race, colour, sex, language, religion, political or other opinion, national or social origin, property, birth or other status.

Furthermore, no distinction shall be made on the basis of the political, jurisdictional or international status of the country or territory to which a person belongs, whether it be independent, trust, non-self-governing or under any other limitation of sovereignty.

ARTICLE 3

Everyone has the right to life, liberty and security of person.

ARTICLE 4

No one shall be held in slavery or servitude; slavery and the slave trade shall be prohibited in all their forms.

* The plain language version is only given as a guide. This version is based in part on the translation of a text, prepared in 1978 for the World Association for the School as an Instrument of Peace, by a Research Group of the University of Geneva, under the responsibility of Prof. I Massarenu. In preparing the translation, the Group used a basic vocabulary of 2,500 words in use in the French-speaking part of Switzerland.

PLAIN LANGUAGE VERSION

ARTICLE 5

Nobody has the right to torture you.

ARTICLE 6

You should be legally protected in the same way everywhere, and like everyone else.

ARTICLE 7

The law is the same for everyone; it should be applied in the same way to all.

ARTICLE 8

You should be able to ask for legal help when the rights your country grants you are not respected.

ARTICLE 9

Nobody has the right to put you in prison, to keep you there, or to send you away from your country unjustly, or without a good cause.

ARTICLE 10

If you must go on trial this should be done in public. The people who try you should not let themselves be influenced by others.

ARTICLE 11

You should be considered innocent until it can be proved that you are guilty. If you are accused of a crime, you should always have the right to defend yourself. Nobody has the right to condemn you and punish you for something you have not done.

ORIGINAL TEXT

ARTICLE 5

No one shall be subjected to torture or to cruel, inhuman or degrading treatment or punishment.

ARTICLE 6

Everyone has the right to recognition everywhere as a person before the law.

ARTICLE 7

All are equal before the law and are entitled without any discrimination to equal protection of the law. All are entitled to equal protection against any discrimination in violation of this Declaration and against any incitement to such discrimination.

ARTICLE 8

Everyone has the right to an effective remedy by the competent national tribunals for acts violating the fundamental rights granted him by the constitution or by law.

ARTICLE 9

No one shall be subjected to arbitrary arrest, detention or exile.

ARTICLE 10

Everyone is entitled in full equality to a fair and public hearing by an independent and impartial tribunal, in the determination of his rights and obligations and of any criminal charge against him.

ARTICLE 11

1. Everyone charged with a penal offence has the right to be presumed innocent until proved guilty according to law in a public trial at which he has had all the guarantees necessary for his defence.
2. No one shall be held guilty of any penal offence on account of any act or omission which did not constitute a penal offence, under national or international law, at the time when it was committed. Nor shall a heavier penalty be imposed than the one that was applicable at the time the penal offence was committed.

PLAIN LANGUAGE VERSION

ARTICLE 12

You have the right to ask to be protected if someone tries to harm your good name, enter your house, open your letters, or bother you or your family without a good reason.

ARTICLE 13

You have the right to come and go as you wish within your country. You have the right to leave your country to go to another one; and you should be able to return to your country if you want.

ARTICLE 14

If someone hurts you, you have the right to go to another country and ask it to protect you.

You lose this right if you have killed someone and if you, yourself, do not respect what is written here.

ARTICLE 15

You have the right to belong to a country and nobody can prevent you, without a good reason, from belonging to another country if you wish.

ARTICLE 16

As soon as a person is legally entitled, he or she has the right to marry and have a family. In doing this, neither the colour of your skin, the country you come from nor your religion should be impediments. Men and women have the same rights when they are married and also when they are separated.

Nobody should force a person to marry.

The government of your country should protect your family and its members.

ARTICLE 17

You have the right to own things and nobody has the right to take these from you without a good reason.

ORIGINAL TEXT

ARTICLE 12

No one shall be subjected to arbitrary interference with his privacy, family, home or correspondence, nor to attacks upon his honour and reputation. Everyone has the right to the protection of the law against such interference or attacks.

ARTICLE 13

1. Everyone has the right to freedom of movement and residence within the borders of each State.
2. Everyone has the right to leave any country including his own, and to return to his country.

ARTICLE 14

1. Everyone has the right to seek and enjoy in other countries asylum from persecution.
2. This right may not be invoked in the case of prosecutions genuinely arising from non-political crimes or from acts contrary to the purposes and principles of the United Nations.

ARTICLE 15

1. Everyone has the right to a nationality.
2. No one shall be arbitrarily deprived of his nationality nor denied the right to change his nationality.

ARTICLE 16

1. Men and women of full age, without any limitation due to race, nationality or religion, have the right to marry and to found a family. They are entitled to equal rights as to marriage, during marriage and at its dissolution.
2. Marriage shall be entered into only with the free and full consent of the intending spouses.
3. The family is the natural and fundamental group unit of society and is entitled to protection by society and the State.

ARTICLE 17

1. Everyone has the right to own property alone as well as in association with others.
2. No one shall be arbitrarily deprived of his property.

PLAIN LANGUAGE VERSION

ARTICLE 18

You have the right to profess your religion freely, to change it, and to practice it either on your own or with other people.

ARTICLE 19

You have the right to think what you want, to say what you like, and nobody should forbid you from doing so.

You should be able to share your ideas also–with people from any other country.

ARTICLE 20

You have the right to organize peaceful meetings or to take part in meetings in a peaceful way. It is wrong to force someone to belong to a group.

ARTICLE 21

You have the right to take part in your country's political affairs either by belonging to the government yourself or by choosing politicians who have the same ideas as you.

Governments should be voted for regularly and voting should be secret. You should get a vote and all votes should be equal. You also have the same right to join the public service as anyone else.

ARTICLE 22

The society in which you live should help you to develop and to make the most of all the advantages (culture, work, social and welfare) which are offered to you and to all the men and women in your country.

ORIGINAL TEXT

ARTICLE 18

Everyone has the right to freedom of thought, conscience and religion; this right includes freedom to change his religion or belief, and freedom, either alone or in community with others and in public or private, to manifest his religion or belief in teaching, practice, worship and observance.

ARTICLE 19

Everyone has the right to freedom of opinion and expression; this right includes freedom to hold opinions without interference and to seek, receive and impart information and ideas through any media and regardless of frontiers.

ARTICLE 20

1. Everyone has the right to freedom of peaceful assembly and association.
2. No one may be compelled to belong to an association.

ARTICLE 21

1. Everyone has the right to take part in the government of his country, directly or through freely chosen representatives.
2. Everyone has the right of equal access to public service in his country.
3. The will of the people shall be the basis of the authority of government; this will shall be expressed in periodic and genuine elections which shall be by universal and equal suffrage and shall be held by secret vote or by equivalent free voting procedures.

ARTICLE 22

Everyone, as a member of society, has the right to social security and is entitled to realization, through national effort and international co-operation and in accordance with the organization and resources of each State, of the economic, social and cultural rights indispensable for his dignity and the free development of his personality.

PLAIN LANGUAGE VERSION

ARTICLE 23

You have the right to work, to be free to choose your work, to get a salary which allows you to live and support your family. If a man and a woman do the same work, they should get the same pay. All people who work have the right to join together to defend their interests.

ARTICLE 24

Each work day should not be too long, since everyone has the right to rest and should be able to take regular paid holidays.

ARTICLE 25

You have the right to have whatever you need so that you and your family do not fall ill; go hungry; have clothes and a house; and are helped if you are out of work. If you are ill, if you are old, if your wife or husband is dead, or if you do not earn a living for any other reason you cannot help. The mother who is going to have a baby, and her baby should get special help. All children have the same rights, whether or not the mother is married.

ARTICLE 26

You have the right to go to school and everyone should go to school. Primary schooling should be free. You should be able to learn a profession or continue your studies as far as you wish. At school, you should be able to develop all your talents and you should be taught to get on with others, whatever their race, religion or the country they come from. Your parents have the right to choose how and what you will be taught at school.

ORIGINAL TEXT

ARTICLE 23

1. Everyone has the right to work, to free choice of employment, to just and favourable conditions of work and to protection against unemployment.
2. Everyone, without any discrimination, has the right to equal pay for equal work.
3. Everyone who works has the right to just and favourable remuneration ensuring for himself and his family an existence worthy of human dignity, and supplemented, if necessary, by other means of social protection.
4. Everyone has the right to form and to join trade unions for the protection of his interests.

ARTICLE 24

Everyone has the right to rest and leisure, including reasonable limitation of working hours and periodic holidays with pay.

ARTICLE 25

1. Everyone has the right to a standard of living adequate for the health and well-being of himself and of his family, including food, clothing, housing and medical care and necessary social services, and the right to security in the event of unemployment, sickness, disability, widowhood, old age or other lack of livelihood in circumstances beyond his control.
2. Motherhood and childhood are entitled to special care and assistance. All children, whether born in or out of wedlock, shall enjoy the same social protection.

ARTICLE 26

1. Everyone has the right to education. Education shall be free, at least in the elementary and fundamental stages. Elementary education shall be compulsory. Technical and professional education shall be made generally available and higher education shall be equally accessible to all on the basis of merit.

PLAIN LANGUAGE VERSION

ARTICLE 27

You have the right to share in your community's arts and sciences, and any good they do. Your works as an artist, a writer, or a scientist should be protected, and you should be able to benefit from them.

ARTICLE 28

So that your rights will be respected, there must be an "order" which can protect them. This "order" should be local and worldwide.

ARTICLE 29

You have duties towards the community within which your personality can only fully develop. The law should guarantee human rights. It should allow everyone to respect others and to be respected.

ARTICLE 30

In all parts of the world, no society, no human being, should take it upon her or himself to act in such a way as to destroy the rights which you have just been reading about.

ORIGINAL TEXT

2. Education shall be directed to the full development of the human personality and to the strengthening of respect for human rights and fundamental freedoms. It shall promote understanding, tolerance and friendship among all nations, racial or religious groups, and shall further the activities of the United Nations for the maintenance of peace.
3. Parents have a prior right to choose the kind of education that shall be given to their children.

ARTICLE 27

1. Everyone has the right freely to participate in the cultural life of the community, to enjoy the arts and to share in scientific advancement and its benefits.
2. Everyone has the right to the protection of the moral and material interests resulting from any scientific, literary or artistic production of which he is the author.

ARTICLE 28

Everyone is entitled to a social and international order in which the rights and freedoms set forth in this Declaration can be fully realized.

ARTICLE 29

1. Everyone has duties to the community in which alone the free and full development of his personality is possible.
2. In the exercise of his rights and freedoms, everyone shall be subject only to such limitation as are determined by law solely for the purpose of securing due recognition and respect for the rights and freedoms of others and of meeting the just requirements of morality, public order and the general welfare in a democratic society.
3. These rights and freedoms may in no case be exercised contrary to the purposes and principles of the United Nations.

ARTICLE 30

Nothing in this Declaration may be interpreted as implying for any State, group or person any right to engage in any activity or to perform any act aimed at the destruction of any of the rights and freedoms set forth herein.

APPENDIX C

Major Federal Civil Rights Laws

Equal Pay Act of 1963

- Requires equal pay for equal work, regardless of sex.
- Requires that equal work be determined by equal skill, effort, and responsibility under similar working conditions at the same place of employment.
- Requires equal pay when equal work is involved even if different job titles are assigned.

(Enforced by the Equal Employment Opportunity Commission and private lawsuit.)

Civil Rights Act of 1964 (amended in 1972)

- Prohibits discrimination based on race, color, religion, or national origin in public accommodations (for example, hotels, restaurants, movie theaters, sports arenas). It does not apply to private clubs closed to the public.
- Prohibits discrimination in employment based on race, color, sex, religion, or national origin by businesses with more than 15 employees or by labor unions. (This section is commonly referred to as *Title VII.*)
- Prohibits discrimination based on race, color, religion, sex, or national origin by state and local governments and public educational institutions.
- Prohibits discrimination based on race, color, national origin, or sex in any program or activity receiving federal financial assistance. It authorizes ending federal funding when this ban is violated.
- Permits employment discrimination based on religion, sex, or national origin if it is a necessary qualification for the job.

(Enforced by the U.S. Equal Employment Opportunity Commission and private lawsuit.)

Voting Rights Act of 1965 (amended in 1970, 1975, and 1982)

- Bans literacy and "good character" tests as requirements for voting.
- Requires bilingual election materials for most voters who don't speak English.
- Reduces residency requirements for voting in federal elections.
- Establishes criminal penalties for harassing voters or interfering with voting rights.

(Enforced by the U.S. Department of Justice and private lawsuit.)

Age Discrimination in Employment Act of 1967 (amended in 1978)

- Prohibits arbitrary age discrimination in employment by employers of 20 or more persons, employment agencies, labor organizations with 25 or more members, and federal, state, and local governments.
- Protects people aged 40 and older.
- Permits discrimination where age is a necessary qualification for the job.

(Enforced by the U.S. Equal Employment Opportunity Commission, a similar state agency, and private lawsuit.)

Civil Rights Act of 1968 (amended in 1988 and 1992)

- Prohibits discrimination based on race, color, religion or national origin in the sale, rental, or financing of most housing.

(Enforced by the U.S. Department of Justice, the U.S. Department of Housing and Urban Development, and private lawsuit.)

Title IX of the *Education Act Amendments of 1972*

- Prohibits discrimination against students and others on the basis of sex by educational institutions receiving federal funding.
- Prohibits sex discrimination in a number of areas, including student and faculty recruitment, admissions, financial aid, facilities, and employment.
- Requires that school athletic programs effectively accommodate the interest and abilities of members of both sexes; equal total expenditure on men's and women's sports is not required.
- Does not cover sex stereotyping in textbooks and other curricular materials.

(Enforced by the U.S. Department of Education's Office of Civil Rights.)

Rehabilitation Act of 1973

- Prohibits government employers and private employers receiving government assistance from discriminating on the basis of physical handicap.
- Requires companies that do business with the government to undertake affirmative action to provide jobs for the handicapped.
- Prohibits activities and programs receiving federal funds from excluding otherwise qualified handicapped people from participation or benefits.

(Enforced by lawsuit in federal court and, in some cases, state or local human rights or fair employment practices commissions.)

Americans with Disabilities Act of 1990 (ADA)

- Prohibits discrimination against individuals with disabilities.
- Prohibits discrimination in employment. This covers such things as the application process, testing, hiring, evaluation, assignments, training, promotion, termination, compensation, leave, and benefits. (*Title I*)
- Prohibits discrimination in public services. This title covers state and local government services and all services, programs, and activities provided or made available by these governments. This includes entities such as state metro rail systems and AMTRAK. (*Title II*)
- Prohibits discrimination in public accommodations and services operated by private entities. This includes entities such as private taxi companies, schools, restaurants, hotels, and grocery stores. (*Title III*)
- Prohibits discrimination in telecommunications. This covers relay services for hearing-impaired and speech-impaired individuals, and closed-captioning of public service announcements. (*Title IV*)
- Prohibits discrimination in such activities as construction, prohibits retaliation and coercion, and regulates the Architectural and Transportation Barriers Compliance Board. (*Title V*)

(Enforced by various methods including administrative complaint to a specific federal agency or private lawsuit.)

Civil Rights Act of 1991

- Addresses discrimination in the workplace.
- Addresses discrimination at any point in the employment relationship, including private and governmental discrimination.
- Allows individuals who prove intentional employment discrimination on the basis of sex, disability, or religion to collect compensatory and punitive damages.
- Creates a limit on damages.

(Enforced by private lawsuit.)

Individuals with Disabilities Education Act of 1991 (IDEA)

- Guarantees a "free appropriate public education" for all children with disabilities.

- Entitles each child with a disability to free special services, including medical services necessary to secure an appropriate education.
- Requires schools to develop an "individualized education program" (IEP) for each child with a disability.
- Requires parental approval of "individualized education programs" (IEP) and all changes in plan or placement.
- Includes learning disabilities, behavioral disorders, and mental and physical impairments within the definition of "disability."

(Enforced by private lawsuit and state and federal departments of education.)

APPENDIX D

Charts of State Laws

VOTER REGISTRATION INFORMATION

State or other jurisdiction	*Mail registration allowed for all voters*	*Closing date for registration before general election (days)*	*Persons eligible for absentee registration (a)*	*Automatic cancellation of registration for failure to vote for ______ years*
Alabama	. . .	10	M/O	4
Alaska	*	30	(b)	2
Arizona	*	29	D,O	1 general election
Arkansas	. . .	20	B,D,S,T	4
California	*	29	(b)	—
Colorado	. . .	25	D,T	2 general elections
Connecticut	*	21 (c)	(b)	—
Delaware	*	3rd Sat. in Oct. (c)	(b)	4
Florida	. . .	30	B,D,E,R,S,T	5 (d)
Georgia	. . .	30	P	3
Hawaii	*	30	(e)	2 elections
Idaho	. . .	17/10 (f)	T	4
Illinois	. . .	29	M/O	6 (d)
Indiana	*	29	B,D,S,T	4
Iowa	*	10	(b)	2
Kansas	*	14	(b)	2 general elections
Kentucky	*	28	(b)	—
Louisiana	. . .	24	D	—
Maine	*	Election day	(b)	—
Maryland	*	29	(b)	5
Massachusetts	. . .	28	D	—
Michigan	. . .	30	D,T	5
Minnesota	*	Election day (g)	(b)	4
Mississippi	*	30	M/O	4
Missouri	. . .	20	B,D,E,R,S,T	—
Montana	*	30	(b)	1 presidential election
Nebraska	*	(h)	(b)	—
Nevada	*	30	M/O	1 general election
New Hampshire	. . .	10	B,D,E,R,S,T	3 elections
New Jersey	*	29	(b)	4
New Mexico	. . .	28	T	8
New York	*	25	(b)	2 general elections
North Carolina	. . .	21 (i)	M/O	2 presidential elections
North Dakota			(j)	
Ohio	*	30	(b)	4
Oklahoma	. . .	10	M/O	8
Oregon	*	20	(b)	2 general elections
Pennsylvania	*	30	(b)	2
Rhode Island	. . .	30	D	5
South Carolina	*	30	(b)	2 general elections
South Dakota	. . .	15	B,D,E	4
Tennessee	*	30	(b)	4
Texas	*	30	(b)	—
Utah	*	5 (k)	(b)	4
Vermont	*	17	(e)	—
Virginia	. . .	30 (l)	T	4
Washington	. . .	30	M/O	2 (m)
West Virginia	*	30	(b)	(n)
Wisconsin	*	Election day (k)	(b)	4
Wyoming	. . .	(g)	B,D,E,R,S,T	1 general election
Dist. of Columbia	*	30	(b)	2
American Samoa	*	30	M/O	2 general elections
Guam	*	10	(b)	1 general election
Puerto Rico	. . .	50	(b)	1 general election
U.S. Virgin Islands	. . .	30	(o)	2 general elections

Key:
* — Mail registration allowed
. . . — Mail registration not allowed
— — No automatic cancellation

(a) In this column: B—Absent on business; C—Senior citizen; D—Disabled persons; E—Not absent, but prevented by employment from registering; M/O—No absentee registration except military and overseas citizens as required by federal law; O—Out of state; P—Out of precinct; R—Absent for religious reasons; S—Students; T—Temporarily out of jurisdiction.
(b) All voters. See column on mail registration.
(c) Closing date differs for primary election. In Connecticut, 1 day; Delaware, 21 days.
(d) In Florida, registration is suspended for failure to vote after two years and cancelled after five years. In Illinois, suspended after four years and cancelled after six years.
(e) Anyone unable to register in person.
(f) With precinct registrar, 17 days before; with county clerk, 10 days.
(g) Minnesota, 21 days or election day; Wyoming, 30 days or primary election day.
(h) 2nd Friday before election day.
(i) Business days.
(j) No voter registration.
(k) By mail: Utah, 20 days; Wisconsin, 13 days.
(l) Six-13 days for special elections.
(m) Four years if person voted in presidential election.
(n) Two general elections and two primary elections.
(o) No one is eligible to register absentee.

Source: *The Book of the States, 1992-1993* (Lexington, Kentucky: Council of State Governments, 1993), p. 279.

MINIMUM AGE FOR SPECIFIED ACTIVITIES

State or other jurisdiction	*Age of majority* (a)	*Minimum age for marriage with consent* (b)		*Minimum age for making a will*	*Minimum age for buying alcohol*	*Minimum age for serving on a jury*	*Minimum age for leaving school* (c)
		Male	*Female*				
Alabama..........................	19	14 (d)	14 (d)	19	21	19	16
Alaska.............................	18	16 (e)	16 (e)	18	21	18	16
Arizona...........................	18	16 (e)	16 (e)	18	21	18	16
Arkansas.........................	18	17 (f)	16 (f)	18	21	18	18
California........................	18	(g)	(g)	18 (h)	21	18	16
Colorado..........................	18	16 (e)	16 (e)	18	21	18	16
Connecticut......................	18	16 (e)	16 (e)	18	21	18	16
Delaware..........................	18	18 (f)	16 (f)	18	21	18	16
Florida............................	18	16 (d,f)	16 (d,f)	18	21	18	16
Georgia...........................	18	(g)	(g)	18	21	18	16
Hawaii............................	18	16 (i)	16 (i)	18	21	18	18
Idaho..............................	18	16 (e)	16 (e)	18 (h)	21	18	16
Illinois.............................	18	16	16	18	21	18	16
Indiana............................	18	17 (f)	17 (f)	18	21	18	16 (j)
Iowa................................	18	18 (e)	18 (e)	18	21	18	16
Kansas............................	18	18 (e)	18 (e)	18	21	18	16
Kentucky.........................	18	18 (e,f)	18 (e,f)	18	21	18	16 (j)
Louisiana........................	18	18 (e)		18 (h)	21	18	17
Maine..............................	18	16 (e)	16 (e)	18	21	18	17
Maryland.........................	18	16 (f,k)	16 (f,k)	18	21	18	16
Massachusetts.................	18	16 (i)	16	18	21	18	16
Michigan..........................	18	16 (f,i)	16 (f)	18	21	18	16
Minnesota........................	18	16 (e)	16 (e)	18	21	18	16 (l)
Mississippi.......................	18	(g)	(g)	18	21	21	14
Missouri..........................	18	15 (i), 18 (e)	15 (i), 18 (e)	18	21	21	16
Montana..........................	18	16	16	18	21	18	16 (m)
Nebraska..........................	19	17	17	18	21	19	16
Nevada............................	18	16 (e)	16 (e)	18	21	18	17
New Hampshire..............	18	14 (n)	13 (n)	18	21	18	16
New Jersey.....................	18	16 (e, f)		18	21	18	16
New Mexico...................	18	16 (i)	16 (i)	18	21	18	18
New York......................	18	14 (n)	14 (n)	18	21	18	16 (o)
North Carolina................	18	16 (f,p)	16 (f,p)	18	21	18	16
North Dakota..................	18	16	16	18	21	18	16
Ohio................................	18	18 (e,f)	16 (e,f)	18	21	18	18
Oklahoma.......................	18	16 (f)	16 (f)	18	21	18	18
Oregon............................	18	17	17	18	21	18	18
Pennsylvania...................	21	16 (i)	16 (i)	18	21	18	17
Rhode Island...................	18	18 (i)	16 (i)	18	21	18	16
South Carolina................	18	16 (f)	14 (f)	18	21	18	17
South Dakota..................	18	16 (f)	16 (f)	18	21	18	16 (m)
Tennessee.......................	18	16 (i)	16 (i)	18	21	18	17
Texas..............................	18	14 (n)	14 (n)	18 (h)	21	18	17
Utah................................	18	14	14	18	21	18	18
Vermont..........................	18	16 (e)	16 (e)	18	21	18	16
Virginia...........................	18	16 (d,f)	16 (d,f)	18	21	18	18
Washington.....................	18	17 (i)	17 (i)	18	21	18	18
West Virginia..................	18	18 (f)	18 (f)	18	21	18	16
Wisconsin.......................	18	16	16	18	21	18	18
Wyoming.........................	19	16 (i)	16 (i)	19	21	18	16
Dist. of Columbia...........	18	16 (d)	16 (d)	18	21	18	17

Sources: Distilled Spirits Council of the United States, Inc.; Education Commission of the States; National Center for State Courts.

(a) Generally, the age at which an individual has legal control over own actions and business (e.g., ability to contract) except as otherwise provided by statute. In many states, age of majority is arrived at upon marriage if minimum legal marrying age is lower than prescribed age of majority.

(b) With parental consent. Minimum age for marrying without consent is 18 years in all states, except Georgia (16 years) and Mississippi (17 years for males, 15 years for females; notice to parents necessary if under 21).

(c) Without graduating.

(d) Parental consent not required if minor was previously married.

(e) Younger persons may marry with parental consent and/or permission of judge. In Connecticut, judicial consent.

(f) Younger persons may obtain license in case of pregnancy or birth of child.

(g) No age limits.

(h) Age may be lower for a minor who is living apart from parents or legal guardians and managing own financial affairs, or who has contracted a lawful marriage.

(i) Younger persons may obtain license in special circumstances.

(j) In Indiana, effective with the 1992-93 school year, students between 16 and 18 must submit to an exit interview and have written parental approval before leaving school. In Kentucky, must have parental signature for leaving school between 16 and 18.

(k) If under 16, proof of age and the consent of parents in person is required. If a parent is ill, an affidavit by the incapacitated parent and a physician's affidavit to that effect required.

(l) Age 18, year 2000.

(m) Or completion of eighth grade, whichever is earlier.

(n) Parental consent and/or permission of judge required. In Texas, below age of consent, need parental consent and permission of judge.

(o) Age 17 in New York City and Buffalo.

(p) Unless parties are 18 or over, female is pregnant, or applicants are the parents of a living child born out of wedlock.

Source: *The Book of the States, 1992-1993* (Lexington, Kentucky: Council of State Governments, 1993), p. 518.

MOTOR VEHICLE LAWS (AS OF 1991)

State or other jurisdiction	Minimum age for driver's license (a): Regular	Learner's	Restrictive	Liability laws (b)	Vehicle inspection (c)	Transfer of plates to new owner	Child restraints mandatory for passengers under ____ years (d)	Mandatory seat belt law (e)
Alabama	16	15 (f)	14 (g)	S	(h)	*	6	...
Alaska	16	14 (i)	14 (i)	S	spot	*	7	*
Arizona	18	15+7 mo. (f,i)	16 (i)	C	(j)	*	5	*
Arkansas	16	(f)	14 (i,k)	S,NF	*	...	6	...
California	18	15 (k,l)	16 (l)	(m)	(j)	*	5 (n)	* (o)
Colorado	21	15+6 mo. (f,p)	16 (i)	S,NF	(j)	...	4 (n)	*
Connecticut	18	(q)	16 (l)	S,NF	*	...	4	*
Delaware	18	15+10 mo. (f,k,l)	16 (l)	S,NF	*	*	5 (n)	...
Florida	16	(f)	15 (i)	(r)	(j)	...	6	*
Georgia	21	15	16 (i)	C	(j)	*	4	*
Hawaii	18	(f)	15 (i)	S,NF	*	*	4	*
Idaho	16	(f)	14 (l)	S,C	...	...	4	*
Illinois	18	(f)	16 (i,l)	S	(s)	...	5	*
Indiana	18	15 (k,l,p)	16+1 mo. (i,l)	S,C	(j)	...	5	*
Iowa	18	14 (l)	16 (l)	S	spot	...	3	*
Kansas	16		14 (k)	NF,UM	spot	...	4	*
Kentucky	18	(f)	16 (i)	C,NF	...	*	(n)	...
Louisiana	17		15 (i,t)	C	*	*	5	*
Maine	17	(f,k,)	16 (l)	S	*	...	5	(o)
Maryland	18	15+9 mo. (f,k)	16 (i,l,t)	NF	(u)	...	5	*
Massachusetts	18	16 (f)	16+6 mo. (i,l,t)	C,NF	*	...	5	(o)
Michigan	18	(f)	16 (i,l,v)	C,NF	spot	...	4	*
Minnesota	18	(f)	16 (l)	NF	spot (h)	*	4	* (o)
Mississippi	15	(f)		S,F	*	...	2	*
Missouri	16		15 (p)	C	*	...	4	*
Montana	18	(f)	15 (i,l)	C	...	...	4 (n)	*
Nebraska	16	15 (f,k)	(v)	F	...	...	4 (n)	...
Nevada	18	15+6 mo.	16 (i)	F,C	(u)	...	5	* (o)
New Hampshire	18	(q)	16 (l)	S,F	*	...	12	...
New Jersey	17	(k)	(v)	S,NF,UJ	*	...	5	* (o)
New Mexico	16	15 (k)	15 (i,l)	S,UM	...	...	11	*
New York	18	(f,k)	16 (i,t)	S,C,NF	*	...	4	* (o)
North Carolina	18	15 (k,l)		S,C	*	...	7	*
North Dakota	16	(f)	14 (l)	S,NF,UM,UJ	spot	*	6	...
Ohio	18 (w)	(k)	(v)	S,C	(j)	...	4 (n)	*
Oklahoma	16	(p)	15+6 mo. (l)	S,C	*	*	6	*
Oregon	16	15 (f)	(v)	F,C,NF	spot (j)	*	16	* (o)
Pennsylvania	18	(f,k)	16 (i,t)	C	* (j)	...	4	*
Rhode Island	18	(f)	16 (l)	S	*	...	14	...
South Carolina	16	15 (k)	15	C,NF,UM	*	...	6	* (o)
South Dakota	16	14 (k)	14 (t)	F,UM	...	*	5	...
Tennessee	16	15		S,F	(h)	...	4	*
Texas	18	15 (k,p)	16 (l,v)	S,F,C,UM	*	*	2	*
Utah	16 (l)	(f)		S,NF	*	...	8	*
Vermont	18	15 (k)	16 (k)	S	*	...	5	(o)
Virginia	18	15+8 mo. (f,i,k)	16 (i,l)	S	*	...	5	*
Washington	18	15 (f,p)	16 (l)	S,F	(j)	*	5	* (o)
West Virginia	18	(f)	16 (i)	S,C	*	...	9	...
Wisconsin	18	(f)	16 (l)	S	spot	...	4	* (o)
Wyoming	18	15 (k)	16 (i)	S,C	...	...	3	*
Dist. of Columbia	18	(f)	16 (i)	NF	*	...	7	* (o)
American Samoa	18	(f,k)	16 (i,l)	C	*	*	...	...
Guam	18	15 (i,k)	16 (i)	S	*	...	12	*
Puerto Rico	18	(f)	16 (i)	(x)	*	*	...	*
U.S. Virgin Islands	18		16 (l)	C	*	*	...	...

See source, key, and footnotes on next page.

MOTOR VEHICLE LAWS (AS OF 1991) — Continued

Source: American Automobile Association, *Digest of Motor Laws* (1991).
Note: All jurisdictions except Guam have chemical test laws for intoxication. All except the District of Columbia have an implied consent provision. (Colorado has expressed consent law.)
Key:
* — Provision.
. . . — No provision.
(a) See Table 8.16, "Motor Vehicle Operators and Chauffeurs Licenses 1990" for additional information on driver licenses.
(b) All jurisdictions except Colorado, Hawaii, District of Columbia, American Samoa, Guam, Puerto Rico and the U.S. Virgin Islands have a non-resident service of process law. Alabama, Arkansas, California, Georgia, Illinois (applicable to hitchhikers only), New Mexico, Oregon, Texas, Utah, Virginia, Wyoming and the U.S. Virgin Islands each have a guest suit law.
In this column only: S — "Security-type" financial responsibility law (following accident report, each driver/owner of the vehicles involved must show ability to pay damages which may be charged in subsequent legal actions arising from accident); F — "Future-proof type" financial responsibility law (persons who have been convicted of certain serious traffic offenses or who have failed to pay a judgment against them for damages arising from an accident must make a similar showing of financial responsibility); C — "Compulsory insurance" law (motorists must show proof of financial responsibility — liability insurance — usually as a condition of vehicle registration); NF — "No-fault insurance" law (vehicle owner looks to own insurance company for reimbursement for accident damages, rather than having to prove in court that the other party was responsible); UJ — "Unsatisfied judgment funds" law (state-operated funds financed with fees from motorists unable to provide evidence of insurance or from assessments levied on auto insurance companies to cover pedestrians and others who do not have no-fault insurance); UM — "Uninsured motorist" law (insurance companies must offer coverage against potential damage by uninsured motorists).
(c) "Spot" indicates spot check, usually for reasonable cause, or random roadside inspection for defective or missing equipment.
(d) The type of child restraint (safety seat or seat belt) required may differ depending upon the age of the child.
(e) These states have enacted mandatory seat belt legislation. Unless otherwise specified, legislation covers driver and front-seat passengers.
(f) Permit required. In Arkansas, for 30 days prior to taking driving test. In Delaware, for up to two months prior to 16th birthday. In Michigan, for 30 days prior to application for first license. In Minnesota, not required if driver can pass road test. In Oregon, not required if applicant can already drive.
(g) Restricted to mopeds.
(h) Cities have authority to maintain inspection stations. In Alabama, state troopers also authorized to inspect at their discretion.
(i) Guardian or parental consent required.
(j) Emission inspections. In Arizona, Colorado, Florida, Georgia, Indiana, Ohio, Pennsylvania and Washington, mandatory annual emission inspections in certain counties. In California, biennial inspections are required in portions of counties which do not meet federal clean air standards. In Oregon, biennial inspections in Portland metro area and Jackson County. In Washington, also other checks (e.g., out-of-state vehicles, salvaged).
(k) Driver must be accompanied by licensed operator. In California and Vermont (learner's permit), a licensed operator 25 years or older. In Kansas, may drive to school or work without licensed operator. In Maine, New York, Texas, Vermont (restrictive license), Virginia and Wyoming, a licensed operator 18 years or older. In Maryland, individual 21 years or older, licensed to drive vehicle of that class, and licensed for 3 or more years. In Nebraska, a licensed operator 19 years or older. In New Jersey, an individual licensed for same classification as the learner's permit. In Pennsylvania, a licensed operator 18 years or older, licensed in same or equivalent class as learner. In South Carolina, a licensed operator 21 years or older. In American Samoa, must be accompanied by parent, legal guardian, or safety instructor. In Guam, must be accompanied by parent or legal guardian.
(l) Must have successfully completed approved driver education course.
(m) Financial responsibility required of every driver/owner of motor vehicle at all times.
(n) Other restrictions. In California, Colorado, Montana, Nebraska and Ohio, age restriction or child under 40 pounds. In Delaware, age restriction and under 40 pounds. In Kentucky, 40 inches in height or under.
(o) Covers other passengers in vehicle. California, Nevada, Oregon, South Carolina, Washington, Wisconsin and District of Columbia, all passengers. Maine, passengers between 4 and 15 years. Massachusetts, passengers between 5 and 12 years. In Minnesota, driver, front-seat passengers, and anyone under 11. New Jersey, driver responsible for all passengers between 5 and 18 years. New York, all back-seat occupants under 10 years and over 4 years, as well as all front-seat occupants. In Vermont, required for passengers age 5 through 12.
(p) Must be enrolled in driver education course. In Colorado, if not in such course, wait until 15 + 9 mo.; in Washington, 15 + 6 mo.
(q) Required for motorcyclists only. In New Hampshire, otherwise, unlicensed persons who are being taught to drive must be accompanied by licensed operator 25 years or older.
(r) Proof of personal injury protection is required. In event of an accident in which operator is charged with a moving violation, the operator must prove liability insurance in force on date of accident.
(s) Trucks, buses and trailers only. Required for vehicle owners in certain counties.
(t) Driving hours restricted. In Louisiana, drivers under 17 not permitted to operate vehicles between hours of 11 p.m. and 5 a.m. Monday through Thursday; between midnight and 5 a.m. Friday through Sunday. In Maryland, drivers prohibited from driving between midnight and 5 a.m. unless accompanied by licensed driver 21 years or older. In Massachusetts, drivers prohibited from driving between 1 a.m. and 4 a.m., unless accompanied by parent or legal guardian. In New York, drivers 16-17 years old are restricted from driving between 8 p.m. and 5 a.m. (may not drive in New York City at any time). In Pennsylvania, drivers prohibited from driving between midnight and 5 a.m., unless accompanied by parent or spouse 18 years or older or in possession of employer's affidavit. In South Dakota, drivers not permitted to operate vehicle between 8 p.m. and 6 a.m., unless accompanied by licensed driver in front seat.
(u) Mandatory inspection only under certain circumstances. In Maryland, all used cars upon resale or transfer. In Nevada, used cars registered to new owner and emissions test for first-time registration in Clark and Washoe counties.
(v) License will be granted at lower age under special conditions. In Michigan (extenuating circumstances), 14. In Nebraska (school permit), 14. In New Jersey (agriculture pursuit), 16. In Ohio (proof of hardship), 14. In Oregon (special conditions), 14. In Texas (proof of hardship), 15.
(w) Probationary license issued to persons 16-18 upon completion of approved driver education course.
(x) Has financial responsibility law; details not available.

Source: *The Book of the States, 1992-1993* (Lexington, Kentucky: Council of State Governments, 1993), p. 538.

MARRIAGE LAWS

States	Age with parental consent		Age without consent		Physical exam & blood test for male and female			
					Maximum period between exam and license	Scope of medical exam	Waiting period	
	male	female	male	female			Before license	After license
Alabama*	14a	14a	18	18	---	b	---	s
Alaska	16z	16z	18	18	---	b	3 da., w	---
Arizona	16z	16z	18	18	---	---	---	---
Arkansas	17c	16c	18	18	---	---	v	---
California	aa	aa	18	18	30 da., w	zz	---	h
Colorado*	16z	16z	18	18	---	bb	---	s
Connecticut	16z	16z	18	18	---	bb	4 da., w	ttt
Delaware	18c	16c	18	18	---	---	---	e, s
Florida	16a,c	16a,c	18	18	---	b	3 da.	s
Georgia*	aa	aa	18	18	---	b	3 da., g	s*
Hawaii	16d	16d	18	18	---	b	---	---
Idaho*	16z	16z	18	18	---	bb	---	---
Illinois	16	16	18	18	30 da.	b, n	---	ee
Indiana	17c	17c	18	18	---	bb	72 hrs.	t
Iowa*	18z	18z	18	18	---	---	3 da., v	tt
Kansas*[y]	18z	18z	18	18	---	---	3 da., w	---
Kentucky	18c,z	18c,z	18	18	---	---	---	---
Louisiana	18z	18z	18	18	10 da.	b	72 hrs., w	---
Maine	16z	16z	18	18	---	---	3 da., v, w	h
Maryland	16c,f	16c,f	18	18	---	---	48 hrs., w	ff
Massachusetts	14j	12j	18	18	60 da.	bb	3 da., v	---
Michigan	16c,d	16c	18	18	30 da.	b	3 da.,w	---
Minnesota	16z	16z	18	18	---	---	5 da.,w	---
Mississippi	17	15	21	21	30 da.	b	3 da., w	---
Missouri	15d, 18z	15d, 18z	18	18	---	---	---	---
Montana*[yy]	16	16	18	18	---	b	---	ff
Nebraska[yy]	17	17	19	19	---	bb	---	---
Nevada	16z	16z	18	18	---	---	---	---
New Hampshire	14j	13j	18	18	---	l, zz	3 da., v	h
New Jersey	16z,c	16z,c	18	18	30 da.	b	72 hrs., w	s
New Mexico[y]	16d	16d	18	18	30 da.	b	---	---
New York	14j	14j	18	18	---	nn*	---	24 hrs., w, t
North Carolina	16c,g	16c,g	18	18	---	m	---	---
North Dakota	16	16	18	18	---	---	---	t
Ohio*	18c,z	16c,z	18	18	30 da.	b	5 da., w	t
Oklahoma*	16c	16c	18	18	30 da., w	b	---	s
Oregon	17	17	18	18	---	---	3 da., w	---
Pennsylvania*	16d	16d	18	18	30 da.	b	3 da., w	t
Puerto Rico[y]	18c,d,z	16c,d,z	21	21	---	b	---	---
Rhode Island*	18d	16d	18	18	---	bb	---	---
South Carolina*	16c	14c	18	18	---	---	1 da.	---
South Dakota	16c	16c	18	18	---	---	---	tt
Tennessee	16d	16d	18	18	---	---	3 da., cc	s
Texas*[y]	14j,k	14j,k	18	18	---	---	---	s
Utah*	14	14	18x	18x	30 da.	b	---	s
Vermont	16z	16z	18	18	30 da.	b	1 da., w	---
Virginia	16a,c	16a,c	18	18	---	b	---	t
Washington	17d	17d	18	18	---	bbb	3 da.	t
West Virginia	18c	18c	18	18	---	b	3 da., w	---
Wisconsin	16d	16d	18	18	---	b	5 da., w	s
Wyoming	16d	16d	18	18	---	bb	---	---
Dist. of Columbia*	16a	16a	18	18	30 da.	b	3 da., w	---

Source: Gary N. Skoloff, Skoloff & Wolfe, Livingston, N.J.; as of May 1, 1993.

* Indicates 1987 common-law marriage recognized; in many states, such marriages are only recognized if entered in many years before.

(a) Parental consent not required if minor was previously married. (aa) No age limits. (b) Venereal diseases. (bb) Venereal diseases and Rubella (for females). In Colorado and Wyoming, Rubella for female under 45 and Rh type. (bbb) No medical exam required; however, applicants must file affidavit showing non-affliction of contagious venereal disease. (c) Younger parties may obtain license in case of pregnancy or birth of child. (cc) Unless parties are over 18 years of age. (d) Younger parties may obtain license in special circumstances. (e) Residents before expiration of 24-hour waiting period; non-residents formerly residents, before expiration of 96-hour waiting period; others 96 hours. (ee) License effective 1 day after issuance, unless court orders otherwise, valid for 60 days only. (f) If parties are at least 16 years of age, proof of age and the consent of parents in person is required. If a parent is ill, an affidavit by the incapacitated parent and a physicians's affidavit to that effect required. (ff) License valid for 180 days only. (f) Unless parties are 18 years of age or more, or female is pregnant, or applicants are the parents of a living child born out of wedlock. (h) License valid for 90 days only. (i) Parental consent and/or permission of judge required. (k) Below age of consent parties need parental consent and permission of judge. (l) With each certificate issued to couples, a list of family planning agencies and services available to them is provided. (m) Mental incompetence, infectious tuberculosis, vaginal diseases and Rubella (certain counties only). (n) Venereal diseases; test for sickle cell anemia given at request of examining physician. (nn) Tests for sickle cell anemia may be required for certain applicants. Marriage prohibited unless it is established that procreation is not possible. (s) License valid for 30 days only. (t) License valid for 60 days only. (tt) License valid for 20 days only. (ttt) License valid for 65 days. (v) Parties must file notice of intention to marry with local clerk. (w) Waiting period may be avoided. (x) Authorizes counties to provide for rermarital counseling as a requisite to issuance of license to persons under 19 and persons previously divorced. (y) Marriages by proxy are valid. (yy) Proxy marriages are valid under certain conditions. (z) Younger parties may marry with parental consent and/or permission of judge. In Connecticut, judicial approval. (zz) Required offer of HIV test, and/or must be provided with information on AIDS.

Source: *The World Almanac and Book of Facts, 1993* (New York, New York: Pharos Books, 1993), p. 398.

DIVORCE LAWS

Some grounds for absolute divorce

	Residence	Adultery	Cruelty	Desertion	Alcoholism	Impotency	Non-support	Insanity	Pregnancy at marriage	Bigamy	Separation	Felony conviction or imprisonment	Drug addiction	Fraud, force, duress
Alabama	6 mos.*	Yes	Phys. only	1 yr.	Yes	Yes*	2 yrs.	5 yrs.	Yes	A	2 yrs.*	2 yrs.*	Yes	A
Alaska	*	Yes	Yes	1 yr.	1 yr.	Yes	No	18 mos.	No	A	No	Yes	Yes	A
Arizona	90 da.	No	No	No	No	No	No	No	No	No	No	No	No	No
Arkansas	60 da.	Yes	Yes	No	1 yr.	Yes	Yes	3 yrs.	No	No	18 mos.	Yes	No	A
California	6 mos.	No	No	No	No	A	No	Yes, A	No	A	No	No	No	A
Colorado	90 da.	No	No	No	No	No	No	No	No	A	No	No	No	A
Connecticut	1 yr.*	Yes	Yes	1 yr.	Yes	No	No	5 yrs.	No	A	18 mos.*	life*	No	Yes
Delaware	6 mos.	Yes	Yes	Yes	Yes	A	No	A	No	Yes	6 mos.	Yes	Yes	A
Florida	6 mos.	No	No	No	No	No	No	3 yrs.	No	No	No	No	No	No
Georgia	6 mos.	Yes	Yes	1 yr.	Yes	Yes	No	2 yrs.	Yes	A	No	Yes*	Yes	Yes
Hawaii	6 mos.*	No	No	No	No	No	No	A	No	A	2 yrs.*	No	No	A
Idaho	6 wks.	Yes	Yes	Yes	Yes	A	Yes	3 yrs.	Yes	A	5 yrs.	Yes	No	A
Illinois	90 da.	Yes	Yes	1 yr.	2 yrs.	Yes	No	No	No	Yes	2 yrs.*	Yes	2 yrs.	No
Indiana	6 mos.*	No	No	No	No	Yes	No	2 yrs.	No	A	No	Yes	No	A
Iowa	1 yr.*	No	No	No	No	A	No	A	No	A	No	No	No	No
Kansas	60 da.	No	No	No	No	No	Yes	2 yrs.	A	A	No	No	No	A
Kentucky	180 da.	No	No	No	No	A	No	No	No	A	No	No	No	A
Louisiana	1 yr.*	Yes	No	No	No	No	No	No	No	A	6 mos.	Yes*	No	A
Maine	6 mos.*	Yes	Yes	3 yrs.	Yes	Yes	Yes	A	No	A	No	No	Yes	No
Maryland	1 yr.*	Yes	Yes	1 yr.*	No	No	No	3 yrs.	No	A	1 yr.*	1 yr.*	No	No
Massachusetts	1 yr.*	Yes	Yes	1 yr.	Yes	Yes	Yes	No	No	A	No	5 yrs.	Yes	No
Michigan	180 da.	No	No	No	No	No	No	No	No	No	No	No	No	A
Minnesota	180 da.	No	No	No	No	No	No	No	No	No	No	No	No	A
Mississippi	6 mos.	Yes	Yes	1 yr.	Yes	Yes	No	3 yrs.	Yes	Yes	No	Yes*	Yes	A
Missouri	90 da.	No	No	No	No	No	No	No	No	No	No	No	No	A
Montana	90 da.	No	No	No	No	A	No	No	No	No	180 da.*	No	No	A
Nebraska	1 yr.*	No	No	No	No	A	No	No	No	A	No	No	No	A
Nevada	6 wks.	No	No	No	No	No	No	2 yrs.	No	A	1 yr.	No	No	A
New Hampshire	1 yr.*	Yes	Yes	2 yrs.	2 yrs.	Yes	2 rs.	No	No	A	Yes	1 yr.*	No	No
New Jersey	1 yr.*	Yes	Yes	1 yr.	1 yr.	A	No	2 yrs.	No	A	18 mos.	18 mos.	1 yr.	A
New Mexico	6 mos.	Yes	Yes	Yes*	No	No	No	No	No	No	No	No	No	No
New York	1 yr.*	Yes	Yes	1 yr.	No	No	No	No	No	A	1 yr.	3 yrs.	No	A
North Carolina	6 mos.	No	No	No	No	A	No	3 yrs.	No	A	1 yr.	No	No	No
North Dakota	6 mos.	Yes	Yes	1 yr.	1 yr.	A	1 yr.	5 yrs.*	No	A	No	Yes	1 yr.	A
Ohio	6 mos.	Yes	Yes	1 yr.	Yes	Yes	Yes	No	No	Yes, A	1 yr.	Yes	No	Yes, A
Oklahoma	6 mos.	Yes	Yes	1 yr.	Yes	Yes	Yes	5 yrs.	Yes	Yes	No	Yes	No	Yes
Oregon	6 mos.*	No	No	No	No	No	No	No	No	No	No	No	No	A
Pennsylvania	6 mos.	Yes	Yes	1 yr.	No	No	No	18 mos.*	No	Yes	2 yrs.*	Yes	No	No
Rhode Island	1 yr.	Yes	Yes	5 yrs.*	Yes	Yes	1 yr.	No	No	Yes	3 yrs.	Yes	Yes	No
South Carolina	1 yr.*	Yes	Phys. only	1 yr.	Yes	No	No	No	No	No	1 yr.	No	Yes	No
South Dakota	none*	Yes	Yes	1 yr.	1 yr.	A	1 yr.	5 yrs.	No	A	No	Yes	No	A*
Tennessee	6 mos.*	Yes	Yes	1 yr.	Yes	Yes	Yes	No	Yes	Yes	2 yrs.	Yes	Yes	A
Texas	6 mos.*	Yes	Yes	1 yr.	*	A	No	3 yrs.	No	No	3 yrs.	1 yr.	No	No
Utah	3 mos.*	Yes	Yes	1 yr.	Yes	Yes	Yes	Yes	No	A	3 yrs.*	Yes	No	No
Vermont	6 mos.*	Yes	Yes	7 yrs.*	No	No	Yes	5 yrs.	No	A	6 mos.	3 yrs.	No	A
Virginia	6 mos.*	Yes	Yes*	1 yr.	No	A	No	No	A	A	1 yr.*	1 yr.*	No	A
Washington	bona fide res.	No	No	No	No	No	No	No	No	No	No	No	No	No
West Virginia	1 yr.*	Yes	Yes	6 mos.	Yes	A	No	3 yrs.	A	A	1 yr.	Yes	Yes	No
Wisconsin	6 mos.	No	No	No	No	A	No	No	No	A	1 yr.	No	No	A
Wyoming	60 da.*	No	No	No	No	No	No	2 yrs.	No	A	No	No	No	No
Dist. of Columbia	6 mos.	No	No	No	No	A	No	A*	No	A	6 mos-1 yr.	No	No	A
Puerto Rico	1 yr.	Yes	Yes	1 yr.	Yes	Yes	No	Yes	No	A	2 yrs.	Yes*	Yes	No

Source: Gary N. Skoloff, Skoloff & Wolfe, Livingston, N.J.; as of May 1, 1993. Important: almost all states also have other laws, as well as qualifications of the laws shown above and proposed divorce-reform laws, pending. It would be wise to consult a lawyer in conjunction with the use of this chart.

(*) Indicates qualification–check local statutes; (A) Indicates grounds for annulment.

Source: *The World Almanac and Book of Facts, 1993* (New York, New York: Pharos Books, 1993), p. 399.

STATE DEATH PENALTY (AS OF DECEMBER, 1990)

State or other jurisdiction	*Capital offenses*	*Minimum age*	*Persons on death row*	*Method of execution*
Alabama	Murder during kidnaping, robbery, rape, sodomy, burglary, sexual assault, or arson; murder of peace officer, correctional officer, or public official; murder while under a life sentence; murder for pecuniary gain or contract; aircraft piracy; murder by a defendant with a previous murder conviction; murder of a witness to a crime.	None	117	Electrocution
Alaska	. . .			
Arizona	First-degree murder.	None	91	Lethal gas
Arkansas	Felony murder; arson causing death; intentional murder of a law enforcement officer; murder of prison, jail, court or correctional personnel, or military personnel acting in line of duty; multiple murders; intentional murder of public officeholder or candidate; intentional murder while under life sentence; contract murder.	14	33	Lethal injection or electrocution (a)
California	Treason; aggravated assault by a prisoner serving a life term; first-degree murder with special circumstances; train wrecking; perjury causing execution.	18	280	Lethal gas
Colorado	First-degree murder; kidnaping with death of victim; felony murder.	18	3	Lethal injection
Connecticut	Murder of a public safety or correctional officer; murder for pecuniary gain; murder in the course of a felony; murder by a defendant with a previous conviction for intentional murder; murder while under a life sentence; murder during a kidnaping; illegal sale of cocaine, methadone, or heroin to a person who dies from using these drugs; murder during first-degree sexual assault; multiple murders.	18	2	Electrocution
Delaware	First-degree murder with aggravating circumstances.	None	6	Lethal injection
Florida	First-degree murder.	None	299	Electrocution
Georgia	Murder; kidnaping with bodily injury when the victim dies; aircraft hijacking; treason; kidnaping for ransom when the victim dies.	17	98	Electrocution
Hawaii	. . .			
Idaho	First-degree murder; aggravated kidnaping.	None	19	Lethal injection or firing squad
Illinois	Murder accompanied by at least one of 10 aggravating factors.	18	128	Lethal injection
Indiana	Murder with 12 aggravating circumstances	16	48	Electrocution
Iowa	. . .			
Kansas	. . .			
Kentucky	Aggravated murder; kidnaping when victim is killed	16	26	Electrocution
Louisiana	First-degree murder; treason	16	31	Lethal injection (b)
Maine	. . .			
Maryland	First-degree murder, either premeditated or during the commission of a felony.	18	19	Lethal gas
Massachusetts	. . .			
Michigan	. . .			
Minnesota	. . .			

See source, key, and footnotes at end of table.

STATE DEATH PENALTY — Continued (AS OF DECEMBER, 1990)

State or other jurisdiction	*Capital offenses*	*Minimum age*	*Persons on death row*	*Method of execution*
Mississippi	Capital murder includes murder of a peace officer or correctional officer, murder while under a life sentence, murder by bomb or explosive, contract murder, murder committed during specific felonies (rape, burglary, kidnaping, arson, robbery, sexual battery, unnatural intercourse with a child, nonconsensual unnatural intercourse), and murder of an elected officer; capital rape is the forcible rape of a child under 14 years by a person 18 years or older; aircraft piracy.	16 (c)	47	Lethal injection (d)
Missouri	First-degree murder.	14	72	Lethal injection or lethal gas
Montana	Deliberate homicide; aggravated kidnaping when victim or rescuer dies; attempted deliberate homicide, aggravated assault, or aggravated kidnaping by a state prison inmate with a prior conviction for deliberate homicide or who has been previously declared a persistent felony offender.	(e)	6	Lethal injection or hanging
Nebraska	First-degree murder.	None (f)	11	Electrocution
Nevada	First-degree murder.	16	57	Lethal injection
New Hampshire	Contract murder; murder of a law enforcement officer; murder of a kidnap victim; killing another after being sentenced to life imprisonment without parole.	17	0	Lethal injection or hanging (g)
New Jersey	Purposeful or knowing murder; contract murder.	18	10	Lethal injection
New Mexico	First-degree murder; felony murder with aggravating circumstances.	18	1	Lethal injection
New York	. . .			
North Carolina	First-degree murder.	(h)	84	Lethal injection or lethal gas
North Dakota	. . .			
Ohio	Assassination; contract murder; murder during escape; murder while in a correctional facility; murder after conviction for a prior purposeful killing or prior attempted murder; murder of a peace officer; murder arising from specified felonies (rape, kidnaping, arson, robbery, burglary); murder of a witness to prevent testimony in a criminal proceeding or in retaliation.	18	105	Electrocution
Oklahoma	Murder with malice aforethought; murder arising from specified felonies (forcible rape, robbery with a dangerous weapon, kidnaping, escape from lawful custody, first-degree burglary, arson); murder when the victim is a child who has been injured, tortured or maimed.	16	118	Lethal injection
Oregon	Aggravated murder.	18	10	Lethal injection
Pennsylvania	First-degree murder.	None	121	Lethal injection
Rhode Island	. . .			
South Carolina	Murder with statutory aggravating circumstances.	None	42	Electrocution
South Dakota	First-degree murder; kidnaping with gross permanent physical injury inflicted on the victim; felony murder.	(i)	0	Lethal injection
Tennessee	First-degree murder.	18	84	Electrocution

See source, key, and footnotes at end of table.

STATE DEATH PENALTY — Continued (AS OF DECEMBER, 1990)

State or other jurisdiction	*Capital offenses*	*Minimum age*	*Persons on death row*	*Method of execution*
Texas	Murder of a public safety officer, fire fighter, or correctional employee; murder during the commission of specified felonies (kidnaping, burglary, robbery, aggravated rape, arson); murder for remuneration; multiple murders; murder during prison escape; murder by a state prison inmate.	17	320	Lethal injection
Utah	First-degree murder.	16	11	Lethal injection or firing squad
Vermont	. . .			
Virginia	Murder during the commission or attempts to commit specified felonies (abduction, armed robbery, rape); contract murder; murder by a prisoner while in custody; murder of a law enforcement officer; multiple murders; murder of a child under 12 years old during an abduction; murder arising from drug violations.	15	45	Electrocution
Washington	Aggravated first-degree premeditated murder.	None	10	Lethal injection or hanging
West Virginia	. . .			
Wisconsin	. . .			
Wyoming	First-degree murder including felony murder.	16	2	Lethal injection
Dist. of Columbia	. . .			

Source: U.S. Department of Justice, Bureau of Justice Statistics, *Capital Punishment, 1990* (September 1991).

Key:

. . . — No capital punishment statute

(a) State authorizes lethal injection for those whose capital offense occurred after 7/4/83; for those whose offense occurred before that date, the condemned prisoner may select lethal injection or electrocution.

(b) State authorizes all sentences imposed on or after 1/1/91 to be carried out by lethal injection; sentences of those imposed prior to that date will be carried out by electrocution.

(c) Minimim age defined by statute is 13, but effective age is 16, based on state attorney general's interpretation of U.S. Supreme Court decisions.

(d) State authorizes lethal injection for those convicted after 7/1/83; execution of those convicted prior

(e) Youths as young as 12 may be tried as adults, but age less than 18 is a mitigating factor.

(f) Age can be a statutory mitigating factor.

(g) State authorizes hanging only if lethal injection cannot be given.

(h) Age required is 17 unless the murderer was incarcerated for murder when a subsequent murder occurred; then the age may be 14.

(i) Age 10, but only after a transfer hearing to try a juvenile as an adult.

Source: *The Book of the States, 1992-1993* (Lexington, Kentucky: Council of State Governments, 1993), pp. 549-551.

COUNTRIES WHOSE LAWS DO NOT PROVIDE FOR THE DEATH PENALTY FOR ANY CRIME

Country	*Date of abolition*	*Date of last execution*
Australia	1985	1967
Austria	1968	1950
Cape Verde	1981	1835
Colombia	1910	1909
Costa Rica	1877	
Denmark	1978	1950
Dominican Republic	1966	
Ecuador	1906	
Finland	1972	1944
France	1981	1977
German Democratic Republic	1987	
Germany (Federal Republic)	1949	1949
Haiti	1987	1972*
Honduras	1956	1940
Iceland	1928	1830
Kiribati		**
Liechtenstein	1987	1785
Luxembourg	1979	1949
Marshall Islands		**
Micronesia (Federated States)		**
Monaco	1962	1847
Netherlands	1982	1952
Nicaragua	1979	1930
Norway	1979	1948
Panama		1903*
Philippines	1987	1976
Portugal	1976	1849*
San Marino	1865	1468*
Solomon Islands		**
Sweden	1972	1910
Tuvalu		**
Uruguay	1907	
Vanuatu		**
Vatican City State	1969	
Venezuela	1863	

Total: 35 countries

Key:

• Date of last known execution

** No executions since independence

Note: The date given for abolition is the date when the decision to abolish the death penalty was taken, unless that decision only came into effect years later, in which case the latter date is given.

Source: *When the State Kills . . . The Death Penalty: A Human Rights Issue* (New York, New York: Amnesty International U.S.A., 1989), pp. 259-260.

TRENDS IN STATE PRISON POPULATION (1989-90)

State or other jurisdiction	Total population			Population by maximum length of sentence: More than a year				Year or less and unsentenced		
	1990 (a)	1989	Percentage change	1990 (a)	1989	Percentage change	Incarceration rate 1990 (b)	1990 (a)	1989	Percentage change
United States	771,243	712,557	8.2	739,763	680,955	8.6	293	31,480	31,602	-0.4
Alabama	15,665	13,907	12.6	15,365	13,575	13.2	370	300	332	-9.6
Alaska	2,622	2,744	-4.4	1,851	1,908	-3.0	348	771	836	-7.8
Arizona	14,261	13,251	7.6	13,781	12,726	8.3	375	480	525	-8.6
Arkansas	6,766	6,409	5.6	6,718	6,306	6.5	277	48	103	-53.4
California	97,309	87,297	11.5	94,122	84,338	11.6	311	3,187	2,959	7.7
Colorado	7,018	6,908	1.6	7,018 (c)	6,908 (c)	1.6	209	(c)	(c)	ND
Connecticut	10,500	9,301	12.9	7,771	6,309	23.2	238	2,729	2,992	-8.8
Delaware	3,506	3,458	1.4	2,231	2,284	-2.3	321	1,275	1,174	8.6
Florida	44,387	39,999	11.0	44,387	39,996	11.1	336	0	33	ND
Georgia	22,345	20,885	7.0	21,605	19,619	10.1	327	740	1,266	-41.5
Hawaii	2,533	2,464	2.8	1,708	1,752	-2.5	150	825	712	15.9
Idaho	2,074	1,850	12.1	2,074	1,850	12.1	201	0	0	ND
Illinois	27,516	24,712	11.3	27,516 (c)	24,712 (c)	11.3	234	(c)	(c)	ND
Indiana	12,732	12,341	3.2	12,615	12,220	3.2	223	117	121	-3.3
Iowa	3,967	3,584	10.7	3,967	3,584	10.7	139	0	0	ND
Kansas	5,777	5,616	2.9	5,777	5,616	2.9	227	0	0	ND
Kentucky	9,023	8,289	8.9	9,023	8,289	8.9	241	0	0	ND
Louisiana	18,599	17,257	7.8	18,599	17,257	7.8	427	0	0	ND
Maine	1,523	1,455	4.7	1,480	1,432	3.4	118	43	23	87.0
Maryland	17,798	16,514	7.8	16,684	15,378	8.5	347	1,114	1,136	-1.9
Massachusetts	8,273	7,524	10.0	7,899	7,268	8.7	132	374	256	46.1
Michigan	14,267	31,639	8.3	34,267	31,639	8.3	366	0	0	ND
Minnesota	3,176	3,103	2.4	3,176	3,103	2.4	72	0	0	ND
Mississippi	8,375	7,911	5.9	8,179	7,700	6.2	311	196	211	-7.1
Missouri	14,919	13,921	7.2	14,919	13,921	7.2	287	0	0	ND
Montana	1,425	1,328	7.3	1,409	1,328	6.1	174	16	0	ND
Nebraska	2,403	2,393	0.4	2,286	2,278	0.4	140	117	115	1.7
Nevada	5,322	5,112	4.1	5,322	5,112	4.1	144	0	0	ND
New Hampshire	1,342	1,166	15.1	1,342	1,166	15.1	117	0	0	ND
New Jersey	21,128	19,439	8.7	21,128	19,439	8.7	271	0	0	ND
New Mexico	2,961	2,934	1.0	2,879	2,759	4.3	184	82	175	-53.1
New York	54,895	51,227	7.2	54,895	51,227	7.2	304	0	0	ND
North Carolina	18,412	17,454	5.5	17,713	16,628	6.5	264	699	826	-15.4
North Dakota	483	451	7.1	435	404	7.7	67	48	47	2.1
Ohio	31,855	30,538	4.3	31,855 (c)	30,538 (c)	4.3	289	(c)	(c)	ND
Oklahoma	12,322	11,608	6.2	12,322 (c)	11,608 (c)	6.2	383	(c)	(c)	ND
Oregon	6,436	6,744	-4.6	6,436	6,744	-4.6	221	0	0	ND
Pennsylvania	22,290	20,469	8.9	22,281	20,458	8.9	183	9	11	-18.2
Rhode Island	2,394	2,479	-3.4	1,585	1,469	7.9	157	809	1,010	-19.9
South Carolina	17,319	15,720	10.2	16,208	14,808	9.5	451	1,111	912	21.8
South Dakota	1,345	1,252	7.4	1,345	1,252	7.4	187	0	0	ND
Tennessee	10,388	10,630	-2.3	10,388 (c)	10,630 (c)	-2.3	207	(c)	(c)	ND
Texas	50,042	44,022	13.7	50,042	14,022	13.7	290	0	0	ND
Utah	2,503	2,394	4.6	2,482	2,368	4.8	143	21	26	-19.2
Vermont	1,049	905	15.9	681	626	8.8	117	368	279	31.9
Virginia	17,319	16,477	5.1	17,124	16,273	5.2	274	195	204	-4.4
Washington	7,995	6,928	15.4	7,995	6,928	15.4	162	0	0	ND
West Virginia	1,565	1,536	1.9	1,565	1,536	1.9	85	0	0	ND
Wisconsin	7,362	6,788	8.5	7,335	6,775	8.3	149	27	13	107.7
Wyoming	1,110	1,016	9.3	1,110	1,016	9.3	237	0	0	ND
Dist. of Columbia	9,121	10,039	-9.1	6,660	6,735	-1.1	1,125	2,461	3,304	-25.5

Source: U. S. Department of Justice, Bureau of Justice Statistics, *Prisoners in 1990* (May 1991).
Key:
ND—Not defined
(a) Advance count of prisoners is conducted immediately after calendar year ends.
(b) The number of prisoners sentenced to more than one year per 100,000 resident population on December 31, 1990.
(c) Population counts include an undetermined number of inmates with a sentence of one year or less.

Source: *The Book of the States, 1992-1993* (Lexington, Kentucky: Council of State Governments, 1993), p. 543.

ADULTS ON PROBATION (1990)

State or other jurisdiction	Probation population 1/1/90	1990		Probation population 12/31/90	Percent change in probation population during 1990	Probation population (a)	
		Entries	*Exits*			*Under intensive supervision*	*Under electronic monitoring*
Alabama	25,519	14,251	12,084	27,686	8.5	705	91
Alaska	3,335	1,993	1,729	3,599	7.9	0	0
Arizona	27,340	11,978	8,921	30,397	11.2	2,232	127
Arkansas (b)	15,552	3,531	3,100	15,983	2.8	0	0
California (c)	284,437	173,883	152,620 (d)	305,700	7.5	DK	DK
Colorado (c)	28,037	22,310	19,236	31,111	11.0	1,015	248
Connecticut	42,842	28,738	24,940	46,640	8.9	160	6
Delaware (b)	9,701	6,393	3,871	12,223	26.0	951	93
Florida (c)	192,731	266,244	248,194	210,781	9.4	11,215	1312
Georgia	125,147	76,042 (e)	66,349 (e)	134,840	7.7	2,820	0
Hawaii	10,960	6,442	5,735	11,667	6.5	22	6
Idaho	4,025	2,024	1,672	4,337	8.7	141	0
Illinois	93,944	58,870	57,115	95,699	1.9	660	DK
Indiana (c)	61,177	65,388	58,482 (f)	68,683	12.3	111	983
Iowa (b)	13,722	346	173	13,895	1.3	DK	DK
Kansas	21,675	12,683	12,175	22,183	2.3	(g)	(g)
Kentucky	8,062	3,030	3,610 (h)	7,482	-7.2	506	0
Louisiana	32,295	13,310	15,414	30,191	-6.5	50	6
Maine	6,851	4,698	4,000	7,549	10.2	95	10
Maryland	84,456	44,435	45,993 (i)	82,898	-1.8	151	0
Massachusetts (c)	88,529	44,486	60,556	72,459	-18 .2	0	0
Michigan (b)	122,459	100,151	89,171	133,439	9.0	1,128	1801
Minnesota	58,648	31,394	30,719	59,323	1.2	(g)	(g)
Mississippi (c)	7,333	3,138	2,250	8,221	12.1	244	0
Missouri (b, c)	44,158	25,000 (j)	26,836	42,322	-4.2	460	96
Montana	3,459	1,873	1,280	4,052	17.1	35	19
Nebraska	12,627	17,767	15,740	14,654	16.1	45	45
Nevada (b)	7,065	3,518	2,883	7,700	9.0	718	25
New Hampshire	2,991	1,775	1,620	3,146	5.2	25	10
New Jersey	64,398	33,540	25,597	72,341	12.3	572	263
New Mexico (c)	5,660	9,650	9,016 (k)	6,294	11.2	270	135
New York	136,686	47,656	39,076	145,266	6.3	3,400	DK
North Carolina	72,325	41,981	36,477	77,829	7.6	1,452	704
North Dakota	1,644	523	436	1,731	5.3	(g)	(g)
Ohio	78,299	59,049 (l)	53,968 (l)	83,380	6.5	2,341	358
Oklahoma (m)	24,240	12,565	12,394	24,411	0.7	(g)	(g)
Oregon (n)	31,878	15,742	9,989	37,631	18.0	1,033	380
Pennsylvania	89,491	46,111	38,275	97,327	8.8	10,400	200
Rhode Island	12,231	9,294	6,159	15,366	25.6	0	0
South Carolina	31,623	14,405	13,741	32,287	2.1	1,824	0
South Dakota (o)	2,757	3,995	3,592	3,160	14.6	50	0
Tennessee	30,906	21,925	20,112	32,719	5.9	735	280
Texas (p)	291,156	151,767	134,566	308,357	5.9	7,124	463
Utah	5,524	3,596	3,290 (q)	5,830	5.5	140	0
Vermont	5,399	3,144	2,631	5,912	9.5	230	0
Virginia (c)	19,085	11,951	9,733 (r)	21,303	11.6	327	0
Washington	74,918	54,791	44,892	84,817	13.2	1,996	50
West Virginia (b)	4,646	2,360 (s)	1,947	5,059	8.9	(g)	(g)
Wisconsin (c)	27,284	17,806	15,720	29,370	7.6	222	55
Wyoming	3,060	1,557	1,637 (t)	2,980	-2.6	17	17
Dist. of Columbia	10,132	8,070	8,460	9,742	-3.8	100	0

Source: U. S. Department of Justice, Bureau of Justice Statistics, *Probation and Parole 1990* (November 1991).

Key:

DK—Number not known

(a) Estimated number. Counts of persons under intensive supervision reported by some states include persons under electronic monitoring. Some states were unable to provide separate counts of probation and parole populations under intensive supervision (see also Table 8.23, "Adults on Parole").

(b) State estimated all or portion of data. Michigan and Nevada estimated entries and exits.

(c) State omitted absconders from their Jan. 1 and Dec. 31, 1990 counts.

(d) Exits include 13,496 transfers of jurisdiction, deaths or loss of jurisdiction.

(e) Enties include 1,945 abandonment and bastardy cases, and interstate compact cases. Exits include 3,621 abandonment and bastardy cases, special termination, and trasferred out-of-state cases. All data exclude probationers who have been sent to another state for supervision and include probationers that state supervises for other states.

(f) Exits include 1,435 intrastate transfers and 575 interstate transfers.

(g) State reported either not having persons under intensive supervision and electronic monitoring or not knowing their numbers.

(h) Exits include 13 dismissed cases.

(i) Exits include 4,875 unsatisfactory closings.

(j) Entries include 118 diversion cases without sentence.

(k) Exits include 1,108 closed semi-active cases and interarea transfers.

(l) Entries and exits include persons transferred between state and county probation agencies.

(m) Data do not include probationers with weekend incarcerations.

(n) Data do not include 6,209 probationers supervised by county agencies.

(o) All data are midyear 1990 counts.

(p) All data are for August 1990.

(q) Exits include 207 revocations and discharges and six reversals of court orders.

(r) Exits include revocations, out-of-state cases terminated and cases closed administratively.

(s) Entries include 50 reinstatements.

(t) Exits include 221 bench warrants, relief of responsibility and interstate transfers.

Source: *The Book of the States, 1992-1993* (Lexington, Kentucky: Council of State Governments, 1993), p. 546.

ABORTION AND THE STATES (1991–92)

State	Governor	Senate	House	Number of abortions	Number of providers	Type of regulations in place
Alabama	N	N	N	18,220	20	A, B(2), F(1), M+, V
Alaska	N	Y	Y	2,390	12	A, F(2)
Arizona	Y	Y	N	23,070	29	A, B(2)-, F(1), M-, P
Arkansas	Y	C	N	6,250	10	B(2)-, F(1), M+
California	Y	Y	Y	311,720	608	B(2)-, F(2), M-
Colorado	Y	Y	Y	18,740	61	B(2)-, F(1), S-, M
Connecticut	Y	Y	Y	23,630	43	B-, F(2), L(2), M-
Delaware	Y	C	Y	5,710	17	A-, B(2)-, F(1), M-, W-
Florida	Y	Y	Y	82,850	143	A-, B-, F(1), I, S-
Georgia	Y	Y	Y	36,720	55	B-, F(1), M+
Hawaii	Y	Y	Y	11,170	53	F(2)
Idaho	N	Y	N	1,920	9	A, B -, I, M
Illinois	Y	C	C	72,570	52	B, F(I), L(1), M-, S-
Indiana	Y	C	N	15,760	24	A, B-, F(1), M+, W
Iowa	N	C	Y	9,420	16	B
Kansas	N	Y	Y	11,440	19	B(2)-, F(1)
Kentucky	Y	N	N	11,520	9	A-, B-, F-, L(1), M-, P-, S-, W-
Louisiana	N	N	N	17,340	13	A, B(1)-, F(1), L(1), M+, P, V
Maine	Y	Y	Y	4,620	21	A, B, F(1), M+, W-
Maryland	Y	Y	Y	32,670	53	A-, B(2)-, F(2), M-, W-
Massachusetts	Y	Y	Y	43,720	64	A-, B(2)-, F(1), M+, W-
Michigan	N	N	N	63,410	78	B(2)-, M+
Minnesota	Y	N	N	18,580	13	A, B, F(1), M+
Mississippi	N	N	N	5,120	5	A-, B(2)-, F(1), M-, W-
Missouri	N	N	N	19,490	20	A, B, F(1), M+, P, S-, V, W-
Montana	N	Y	Y	3,050	13	A, B, F(1), M, I, S-
Nebraska[a]	N	N	N	6,490	9	A, B, M+, W
Nevada	N	C	N	10,190	20	A, B-, F(1), L(2), M-
New Hampshire	N	Y	Y	4,710	15	B(2)-, F(1)
New Jersey	Y	N	N	63,900	89	F(2)
New Mexico	Y	Y	Y	6,810	24	A-, B(2)-, F(1), M, S-, W-
New York	Y	Y	Y	183,980	305	B(2), F(2)
North Carolina	Y	Y	Y	39,720	97	B(2), F(2)
North Dakota	Y	N	N	2,230	3	A, B(1)-, F(1), P, M+, S-
Ohio	N	N	N	53,400	53	A-, F(1), M+, W-
Oklahoma	Y	C	N	12,120	13	B(2)-, F(1)
Oregon	Y	Y	Y	15,960	45	F(2)
Pennsylvania	N	N	N	51,830	90	A, B(2)-, M, P, S-, W
Rhode Island	Y	N	C	7,190	6	A-, B(1)-, F(1), M+, S-
South Carolina	N	C	C	14,160	15	B(1)-, F(1), M+, S-
South Dakota	N	C	N	900	1	A-, B(1)-, F(1), L(1), M-, W-
Tennessee	Y	C	N	22,090	41	A, B, F(1), M-, W-
Texas	Y	C	C	100,690	91	B(2)-, F(1)
Utah	N	N	N	5,030	8	A, B(1), F(1), M+, S-
Vermont	Y	Y	Y	3,580	16	B(2)-, F(2)
Virginia	Y	C	Y	35,420	73	A, B-
Washington	Y	Y	Y	31,220	68	F(2), L (2)
West Virginia	N	N	N	3,270	6	B(2)-, F(2), M+
Wisconsin	N	N	N	18,040	17	A, B(2)-, M, W-
Wyoming	N	C	Y	600	7	B-, M+
Total abortions				1,555,630		
Total providers					2,552	
Total Y	29	20	24			
Total N	21	17	21			
Total C		4	4			

Source: Compiled from The National Abortion Rights Action League Foundation, *Who Decides? A State-by-State Review of Abortion Rights,* 3d ed. (Washington, D.C.: NARAL, 1992). Data on the number of abortions performed comes from M. Hall, "In the States: Abortion Laws State by State," *USA Today,* 30 June 1992, 8A.

Key:

N = Opposes abortion or wants restrictions Y = Supports abortion rights C = Too close to call

a. Nebraska's one-house legislature opposes abortion

A = Abortion counseling requirement

B(1) = Abortion banned after viability or similar restriction, but may allow for certain exceptions as in cases of rape; passed after *Roe*

B(2) = Abortion banned after viability or similar restriction, but may allow for certain exceptions as in cases of rape; passed before *Roe,* and though unenforced, still on the books

F(1) = Prohibits Medicaid funding for abortions

F(2) = Provides funding for most abortions

I = Informed consent required

L(1) = Legislative declaration that if *Roe* is overturned, abortion will be prohibited

L(2) = Legislative declaration that if *Roe* is overturned, right to obtain an abortion will be guaranteed under state law

M = Parental notification and/or consent requirements

M+ = Parental notification and/or consent requirements enforced

P = Prohibits use of public facilities for abortions

S = Spousal notification and/or consent requirement

W = Waiting period required

V = Requires doctors to perform fetal viability tests before performing an abortion

- = Provisions ruled unconstitutional by state or federal courts

Source: Barbara Hinkson Craig and David M. O'Brien, *Abortion and American Politics* (Chatham House Publishers, Inc., 1993), pp. 351-353.

APPENDIX E

Careers in the Law

This appendix describes some legal careers. The information is based on the U.S. Department of Labor's *Occupational Outlook Handbook*. This book is an excellent resource for locating basic information on all types of careers. Updated annually, the *Occupational Outlook Handbook* contains information for each major profession on the nature of the work, working conditions, qualifications and training, job outlook, earnings, and related occupations, as well as additional sources of information. The *Occupational Outlook Handbook* is usually available in school and public libraries.

Salaries for some legal careers are listed below. These are *average starting salaries*. Salaries for all legal careers can differ widely depending on the geographic location, the type of business, and the experience and education of the candidate.

Attorney	$30,000–47,000
Corrections Officer	$18,400–23,800
Court Reporter	$20,000–25,000
Forensic Scientist	$19,200–31,200
Judge	$40,000–75,000
Legal Assistant (Paralegal)	$14,400–21,000
Legal Secretary	$14,400–20,000
Local Law Enforcement Officer	
Police Officer, Deputy Sheriff	$22,000–24,000
Probation or Parole Officer	$18,000–26,000
U.S. Government Law Enforcement Officer	
Alcohol, Tobacco, and Firearms (ATF) Agent	$22,000
Drug Enforcement Agency (DEA) Agent	$22,000
Federal Bureau of Investigation (FBI) Agent	$30,600
Internal Revenue Service (IRS) Agent	$22,000
Secret Service Agent	$22,000
Deputy U.S. Marshal	$22,000

ATTORNEY

Job Description

Attorneys, or lawyers, who practice law do two major things. First, they advise individuals and organizations about ways of preventing legal problems by informing them of their legal rights and responsibilities. Second, lawyers provide counsel if their clients do get into legal difficulty. In providing these services, attorneys do legal research, prepare documents, write briefs, interview parties and witnesses to legal problems, and advocate their clients' cases both in and out of court. (However, while many people think of lawyers in terms of trials, few licensed attorneys are trial lawyers.)

Most lawyers are employed in private practice, although many work for government agencies and corporations. Some have general law practices, which involve matters such as writing wills and contracts. Others specialize in one or two legal areas, such as criminal law, labor law, property law, family law, contract law, environmental law, international law, or tax law. Still others work with legal services programs representing poor people.

A small number of lawyers are judges, while some attorneys also use their legal knowledge to teach classes in law schools and colleges. In addition, a significant number of individuals in public life at the local, state, and federal levels are attorneys.

Education

To become a licensed attorney, one must attend four years of college and receive a bachelor's degree and then attend a three-year college of law approved by the American Bar Association. Years ago, some studied law by working with certified lawyers instead of attending law school. Today, this is extremely rare.

Each attorney candidate must also pass all parts of the bar exam in the state in which he or she wishes to establish a practice. Finally, except in Indiana, Iowa, Louisiana, and Washington, an attorney candidate must pass what is called the multistate bar examination.

College classes helpful in preparation for the practice of law include writing, speech, drama, foreign languages, logic, computers, philosophy, history, government, mathematics, business, and accounting, as well as others.

Special Skills

The practice of law is an especially demanding profession. Among the essential skills a person must bring to the profession is an ability to work efficiently under pressure while relating in a positive manner to people. An attorney must be a good listener as well as a good communicator. Attorneys must be able to think and write precisely and logically and must be able to give clear, concise directions to clients and co-workers. They must also be able to meet strict deadlines and maintain the confidentiality of clients' communications.

Salary and Benefits

The starting salary and benefits for an attorney differ widely depending on the location of the practice and the size and type of the law firm. Small-town attorneys beginning their own practice may take in less than $25,000 and may have to pay for their own medical insurance, retirement, and business expenses. Most starting salaries are larger, however. In 1990, the average salary for beginning attorneys working in government averaged nearly $30,000 per year, while beginning attorneys engaged with private firms averaged about $47,000. These attorneys had virtually no overhead and had some benefits paid for by their employers. First-year attorneys for large corporate law firms in large urban areas may make as much as $85,000 and have medical benefits and retirement packages paid for completely by their firms. Partners in large law firms can make very substantial salaries.

Working Conditions

Lawyers do their work in offices, libraries, and courts of law. They may also visit businesses, government offices, prisons, and homes in the process of doing work for their clients.

The pressures of developing a practice are great in this profession. There is a tremendous amount of paperwork. Documents must be finished in time to meet deadlines. Many lawyers work more than 40 hours a week. In fact, it is not unusual for attorneys to put in 50-, 60-, and even 70-hour weeks in order to complete their work.

Outlook

There are many lawyers — over 630,000 — in the United States today. Attaining a position in a law firm is extremely competitive, and getting a job as an attorney in some areas of the country may be difficult. Nevertheless, projections from the *Occupational Outlook Handbook* of the U.S. Department of Labor indicate that there will be an increasing need for lawyers through the year 2005, so job opportunities in the field remain good.

For More Information

Information Services
American Bar Association
750 North Lake Shore Drive
Chicago, IL 60611

Association of American Law Schools
One Dupont Circle NW, Suite 370

Washington, D.C. 20036

CORRECTIONS OFFICER

Job Description

Corrections officers, also known as prison guards, are responsible for maintaining the security of the prison or correctional facility where they work. These officers supervise prisoners as the prisoners work, eat, sleep, attend educational classes, or participate in recreation. They operate electronic security systems. Corrections officers are also responsible for the security of the prison when the prisoners receive visitors and when the prisoners travel to and from the correctional facility.

Education

The hiring requirements for corrections officers are not as extensive as for other careers in the legal field. All that is required in many areas is a high-school diploma or a GED. Once hired, corrections officers may participate in training programs that prepare them for their duties.

Special Skills

Corrections officers need strong observational skills to help detect changes in prisoners' behavior that might affect the security of the prison. It also helps to have good interpersonal skills in order to reduce tension among the many different personalities found in the prison population.

Salary and Benefits

Most corrections officers work for governmental agencies responsible for operating jails and prisons. However, some now work for private companies that have received contracts from the government to operate correctional facilities. Most government employers provide health and retirement benefits. According to a 1990 survey, starting pay at the state level averaged nearly $18,400 per year, while average earnings were about $23,000. Beginning pay for federal officers was slightly higher — about $18,900 — and average pay was about $23,800.

Working Conditions

Correctional officers generally work 40-hour weeks, although they may be required to work off-hour shifts. They work both indoors and outdoors in correctional facilities, depending on the job requirements. The work of a corrections officer may be stressful and even dangerous because of problems involved in dealing with inmates.

Outlook

Approximately 230,000 people work as correctional officers in prisons across the country. With 10 to 20% of corrections officers leaving their jobs each year and the number of prisons and jails increasing, the outlook for employment of corrections officers through 2005 remains strong.

For More Information

The American Correctional Association
8025 Laurel Lakes Ct.
Laurel, MD 20707

American Jail Association
P.O. Box 2158
Hagerstown, MD 21742

COURT REPORTER

Job Description

A court reporter keeps the record of the court proceedings. This means that the reporter takes down every "official" word said in court. Court reporters often take down what is said at speeds of up to 200 words per minute.

The trial court record is the basis of all appeals to appellate courts. Lawyers making appeals base their arguments on exactly what has been stated in the trial court. Appeals court justices write their opinions based on the transcripts of the trial courts as well as what has been argued on appeal. Thus, the accurate work of court reporters is vital to an effective judicial system.

Court reporters also take down depositions, interrogatories, and other parts of pretrial proceedings. They are often called upon to take down what is said at public hearings as well.

Education

To become a court reporter, one must attend court-reporting school or a similar program given by a community college or university. The duration of these programs varies from two to four years, depending on the type of degree or certificate offered.

In a court-reporting program, students learn court-reporting language and develop skill in using the court-reporting machine, or stenotype. Classes in various types of law, English, keyboarding, computers, and medical terminology form the core of the curriculum.

Special Skills

Persons who wish to attend court-reporting school should have an excellent command of the English language, good hearing, and extremely strong typing and keyboarding skills. They must be good listeners since they must sit and concentrate for long periods of time.

Salary and Benefits

Court reporters can work for the courts, freelance for different businesses, or do both. Starting salaries for this position are generally between $20,000 and $25,000 per year. Most employers offer medical insurance and a retirement package. Because this position is vital and requires great skill, the amount of money a court reporter earns can increase sharply as he or she becomes more proficient. It is not unusual for court reporters to earn at least $50,000 annually after five years.

Working Conditions

Most court reporters who work for courts follow the schedule of the court. This means most work 40-hour weeks, unless deadlines require that court transcripts be ready at a certain time. In this case, the court reporter must work overtime to get the work done.

Court reporters may work anywhere an official record is needed for a meeting or conference. They work in courts, law offices, businesses, or public buildings such as town halls and legislatures.

Outlook

With the rising number of civil and criminal cases, the outlook for employment for court reporters is good. Although technological breakthroughs, such as voice-activated transcription equipment, may eventually cut down on the need for court reporters, the job outlook through the year 2005 is bright.

For More Information

National Court Reporters Association
8224 Old Courthouse Road
Vienna, VA 22182

FORENSIC SCIENTIST

Job Description

Forensic scientists collect and analyze evidence found at crime scenes. Specifically, they analyze blood, saliva, semen, drugs, fingerprints, and firearms and perform reconstructions on skeletal bones. Forensic scientists also confer with law enforcement personnel and attorneys on evidence collection, preserve evidence, write reports, and testify in court. The scientific analysis of evidence often proves critical in determining the innocence or guilt of a person accused of a crime. Thus, forensic scientists play a vital role in the criminal justice process.

Education

Entry-level jobs in forensic science require a four-year degree in one of the following: biology, chemistry, physics, microbiology, genetics, or medical technology. Communication arts and law classes are considered helpful. Some crime labs also require laboratory experience.

Special Skills

A forensic scientist works with many different kinds of people, often under stressful circumstances. Thus, it is essential for a person in this field to have good "people" skills. Because forensic scientists must complete many reports and make court appearances, it is also important for them to be capable writers and good speakers. Finally, forensic scientists must be able to manipulate tiny bits of evidence under a microscope. Thus, excellent hand–eye coordination is considered essential.

Salary and Benefits

Forensic scientists generally work for state or federal crime laboratories. Because these positions are found primarily in government, some medical and retirement benefits are paid.

At the state level, beginning forensic scientists are paid about $1,600 per month. Those who start with laboratory experience may receive as much as $2,600 per month. Depending on the state, experienced workers may eventually earn between $35,000 and $45,000 per year. Federal salaries are usually higher.

Working Conditions

As employees of the government, forensic scientists generally work 40-hour weeks. However, because of increasing caseloads and the need to meet deadlines, forensic scientists may often work extra hours.

Forensic scientists work primarily in the crime lab. However, they also go to the scene of the crime to examine and secure evidence, and they testify in court.

Outlook

Good forensic scientists are always in demand. However, because of pressures to reduce government funding, beginning positions are usually limited, and there is a good deal of competition for them. Thus, the job outlook in this area is, at best, fair.

For More Information

American Academy of Forensic Scientists
P.O. Box 669
410 North 21st St., Suite 203
Colorado Springs, CO 80901

JUDGE

Job Description

Judges interpret laws to resolve disputes between conflicting parties. There are two basic types of judges: trial judges and appellate judges.

Trial judges rule on pretrial motions, conduct pretrial hearings between parties to resolve points of conflict between the parties, and thereby make for more efficient trials. At trial, trial judges rule on points of law. In bench trials, they are also called upon to render a verdict.

Appellate judges review possible errors of law made by trial judges and write decisions, which then become part of common law, or judge-made law.

In addition, some judges, called administrative judges or hearing officers, are employed by administrative agencies to make decisions about conflicts involving the rules and regulations of particular government agencies.

Education

Judges must have graduated from a law school accredited by the American Bar Association and must have passed the state's bar examination. This means that judges have had a minimum of seven years of education beyond high school. In addition, because most judges are appointed or elected to their positions, several years of establishing a reputation as a successful practitioner of law is considered essential.

The competition is usually great for judicial positions. Depending on the type of position, a committee of the local, state, or national bar association is asked to review the record of lawyer applicants and then make a recommendation to a public official, who makes the appointment. In some areas, political parties select candidates for judgeships. These individuals campaign on a particular platform and convince the voters to elect them to office.

(An exception to these requirements exists. The office of justice of the peace, which has some judicial responsibilities, need not be held by a lawyer in some states.)

Special Skills

Judges must be both very knowledgeable about the law and highly skilled in legal research. They must be excellent listeners and must have the ability to quickly analyze areas of dispute between opposing parties. Judges must have high ethical standards. They must also be able to write well and give precise instructions to all parties in the courtroom. Above all, they must be able to make sound decisions.

Salary and Benefits

The amount of money a judge makes depends on the type and location of the court where the judge presides. In 1991, federal trial court judges averaged over $125,000 a year, while federal appellate judges earned about $132,000. State trial court judges averaged about $77,500, with salaries ranging from $55,000 to $100,000. State appellate court salaries averaged over $85,000. Judges in state and federal systems have most of their medical and retirement benefits paid for by the court system.

Working Conditions

Judges work primarily in courtrooms, in law libraries, and in their chambers. Like the attorneys who practice in their courtrooms, judges often work much longer than 40 hours a week. In fact, because of the increasing amount of litigation, it is not unusual for judges to work 50 hours or more each week. The caseloads of trial judges in large urban areas have grown substantially over the last few decades. Consequently, the responsibilities are enormous, and the stress faced by judges in these areas is very great.

Outlook

Currently, there are about 46,000 judges in the United States. Although caseloads keep climbing, the amount of money available to hire new judges has not been increasing as fast. There is always a long list of candidates waiting to fill openings; so the competition for positions will remain great.

For More Information

Information Services
American Bar Association
750 North Lake Shore Drive
Chicago, IL 60611

Dean, National Judicial College
Judicial College Building
University of Nevada – Reno
Reno, NV 89557

LEGAL ASSISTANT (PARALEGAL)

Job Description

Legal assistants, or paralegals, work under the supervision of licensed attorneys. They provide support services by drafting documents, interviewing clients, reviewing and updating files, doing legal research, assisting in the writing of legal briefs, and preparing trial notebooks.

Education

Legal assistants have traditionally received their training "on the job," but many receive training today from specialized legal assistant programs at community colleges, business schools, and universities. These programs range from several months to four years in length and usually involve a combination of specific legal classes, related electives, and general college requirements.

Although national certification is generally not a job requirement, the Certifying Board of Legal Assistants of the National Association of Legal Assistants has developed a two-day examination for those who are interested in receiving a certificate.

Special Skills

Legal assistants must prepare documents under the same time constraints as their supervising attorneys. For this reason, legal assistants need to be able to write logically and precisely. Because they are often called on to interview clients, paralegals must also be excellent listeners and be able to relate to people from many different backgrounds. Knowledge of a foreign language can be useful. Legal assistants must be able to maintain a client's confidentiality. Proficiency in word processing and legal research is also important in providing the legal assistant with the ability to assist attorneys.

Salary and Benefits

Salary and benefits for paralegals range widely, depending on the type of law office, the location, and the job responsibilities. In smaller towns and in smaller firms, legal assistants may start at salaries ranging from $1,200 to $1,500 per month. However, most make somewhat more money. In 1991, the paralegals hired by the federal government averaged between $17,000 and $21,000 per year, depending on their experience and their training. In addition, according to a survey by the National Association of Legal Assistants, paralegals had an average salary of nearly $25,000 in 1991. Although the majority of employers contribute to medical and retirement benefits, the amount of the contribution differs among employers.

Working Conditions

Like attorneys, paralegals do most of their work at desks in offices or libraries. They may also be called on to interview clients at homes and businesses and to assist attorneys in the courtroom. They generally work 40-hour weeks but may be called on to put in extra hours to meet various deadlines.

Outlook

Statistics from the *Occupational Outlook Handbook* indicate that the career of legal assistant is among the fastest growing in the United States. Currently, there are over 90,000 legal assistants. Competition for positions is increasing. However, the job outlook for paralegals coming out of formal training programs seems excellent.

For More Information

Standing Committee on Legal Assistants
American Bar Association
750 North Lake Shore Drive
Chicago, IL 60611

National Association of Legal Assistants, Inc.
1601 South Main St., Suite 300
Tulsa, OK 74119

LEGAL SECRETARY

Job Description

Legal secretaries apply traditional secretarial skills to specialized legal work. Secretarial duties often differ from attorney to attorney. However, generally, legal secretaries prepare legal documents for attorneys and their clients. They also set up appointments, maintain the court calendar, handle client billing, manage client and office files, do general word processing, handle receptionist and telephone duties, and make travel arrangements for their employers. Under the supervision of a managing partner, some legal secretaries handle bookkeeping, perform office management tasks such as payroll and billing, maintain checkbooks and office accounts, and oversee other staff personnel.

Education

Traditionally, secretaries were prepared for their work by taking a variety of typing/keyboarding, business, and law classes in high school. They were then given more specialized training by their attorney-employers. This path is still often taken by aspiring legal secretaries. However, the complexities of legal practices now demand that secretaries come to the job with skills in many other areas. Thus, many legal secretaries attend one- or two-year programs at community colleges with an emphasis on office practices, shorthand, keyboarding, business machines, computer use, word processing, legal terminology, and law.

The Certifying Board of the National Association of Legal Secretaries gives a test to certify a legal secretary with three years' experience as a Professional Legal Secretary.

Special Skills

Legal secretaries need to be able to take dictation and to type and keyboard accurately and quickly. They must be able to deal with clients from many different backgrounds. They must have strong communication skills and a good command of the English language. They must also be able to work under pressure and maintain client confidentiality. Knowledge of a foreign language can be exceptionally helpful in some locations.

Salary and Benefits

The starting salary for legal secretaries varies widely depending on the the location, the size of the law firm, and the amount of responsibility. Beginning salaries for some secretaries in small firms can be as low as $1,200 per month. In larger areas, beginning salaries average between $18,000 and $20,000 per year. The average salary for all secretaries in 1990 was about $24,000, with some experienced legal secretaries/office managers earning $40,000 or more. Medical and retirement benefits vary widely from firm to firm.

Working Conditions

Legal secretaries work primarily in law offices and work approximately 40-hour weeks. Given the demanding and diverse nature of law practices, legal secretaries often juggle many different functions in the office while trying to meet court deadlines. Legal secretaries must be able to deal with stressful situations on a daily basis.

Outlook

Jobs for legal secretaries should continue to grow as fast as or faster than other types of jobs through the year 2005. Although many traditional secretarial functions are being done by computers or other machines, increases in the volume of legal paperwork should allow for continuing growth in this area.

For More Information

National Association of Legal Secretaries
(International)
2250 East 73rd St., Suite 550
Tulsa, OK 74136

LOCAL LAW ENFORCEMENT OFFICERS: POLICE OFFICER, SHERIFF'S DEPUTY

Job Description

Police officers and sheriff's deputies help enforce the law. They are a community's primary defense against criminals. These law enforcement officials investigate crimes, gather and secure evidence to help prosecute criminals, make arrests, write detailed reports, assist citizens with specific emergencies, and testify in court.

Police officers work primarily in cities or towns, while the jurisdiction of deputies extends primarily to rural areas outside of cities where no police department exists. In larger cities, police work can be quite specialized, with officers specifically assigned to areas such as homicide, rape, or traffic. In smaller towns and in rural areas, where the incidence of crime and the number of law enforcement personnel are much lower, a police officer or sheriff's deputy often becomes a "jack of all trades," responding to a variety of emergencies.

Education

The education necessary to become a police officer or sheriff's deputy varies from area to area. In some larger areas, a four-year degree in criminal justice is required. In some small towns, only a high-school education is necessary. Increasingly, most areas are requiring some formal training — often a two-year associate degree. Classes taken often involve the study of criminal law, the criminal justice system, criminal investigation, corrections, community relations, and administration. Once hired, a law enforcement officer usually receives additional training at a state or federal law enforcement academy.

Special Skills

A law enforcement officer must have excellent communication skills. He or she must be able to speak clearly at the scene of a major accident and be able to write precise, understandable reports that can be explained in court. The officer must also be a good listener and decision maker and be able to use good judgement in stressful, dangerous situations. A background in foreign languages, accounting, business practices, and computers can be helpful. Finally, law enforcement officers must be able to pass physical examinations involving agility, vision, and strength.

Salary and Benefits

A 1990 survey by the International City Management Association indicated that most police officers' salaries start somewhere between $22,000 and $23,000. In some locales, beginning salaries are as low as $17,000. The average salary within six years is about $29,000. Most departments provide medical and life insurance benefits, and many offer 20-year retirement plans.

Working Conditions

The duties of a police officer or sheriff's deputy may take that officer anywhere within his or her jurisdiction. This means an officer may patrol a regular beat, visit businesses, courts, and jails, assist at community functions, and write reports at the office. Police generally work 40-hour weeks but are sometimes called on to put in overtime.

The job of a law enforcement official can be quite stressful. Sometimes the work can be physically taxing. In large municipal areas, danger is ever present on some beats. Even in the smallest town, an officer must live with the threat of unexpected violence.

Outlook

With increasing crime, the job outlook for sheriff's deputies and police officers is excellent. However, any forecast must take into account the budget limitations that have beset government at every level.

For More Information

International Association of Chiefs of Police
515 N. Washington St.
Alexandria, VA 22314

National Sheriffs Association
1450 Duke St.
Alexandria, VA 22314

PROBATION OR PAROLE OFFICER

Job Description

Probation and parole officers supervise two types of people: offenders placed on probation (people who fulfill the terms of court-ordered sentences) and parolees (people who are released from prison to fulfill parole-board-ordered sentences). In fulfilling these duties, these officers ensure the public safety while working to help rehabilitate their clients.

Serving as links to a variety of social services, probation and parole officers try to help their clients secure the education, counseling, jobs, and housing necessary to become fully rehabilitated. They also write presentence reports for judges. Based on the officers' investigative work on the offenders' backgrounds, these reports provide judges with important information necessary to make an appropriate sentence for each offender. Probation and parole officers testify at pretrial and parole board hearings to help explain these reports. In addition, they are responsible for investigating any violations of court-ordered sentences.

Education

Generally, at the state level, probation and parole officers must complete a four-year degree program in a social science area such as sociology, criminal justice, psychology, or correctional counseling. Classes in writing and other communication arts, as well as in law, are considered helpful. At the federal level, the officer must also have had at least two years of work experience in the field.

Special Skills

Probation and parole officers must possess excellent communication skills in order to write precise presentence reports and be able to defend them in court. They must also be able to relate to people from a variety of legal professions, as well as clients with different backgrounds. In addition, probation and parole officers must be able to deal with the stress that comes with large caseloads.

Salary and Benefits

Starting salaries at the state level vary from $18,000 to $22,000. Federal starting salaries average about $26,000. Both state and federal governments provide some health and retirement benefits.

Working Conditions

Probation and parole officers work in offices, courts, jails, and prisons. The nature of their work often takes them to both the places of business and the residences of their clients. These officers usually work a 40-hour week but may be called on to work overtime to investigate their clients and to meet court-ordered deadlines.

Outlook

The job outlook in this area is fair. The number of defendants is growing. In some areas, the budgets for probation and parole officers are growing along with the number of prisoners. However, because of budget problems, it is more common for probation and parole officers to have more clients than for government to hire more officers.

For More Information

American Probation and Parole Association
P.O. Box 51017
Salt Lake City, UT 84152

National Association of Social Workers
7981 Eastern Ave.
Silver Spring, MD 20910

U.S. GOVERNMENT LAW ENFORCEMENT OFFICER

Job Description

The duties of law enforcement officers working for the U.S. government are similar in many respects to those of local police officers. These officers help their respective federal agencies enforce the law. In the process of doing that, they investigate crimes, help preserve evidence, write reports for government prosecutors, apprehend fugitives, and testify in court.

However, the work of U.S. law enforcement officers differs from traditional law enforcement in that their authority in dealing with federal crimes extends throughout the United States and in that their work often relates to specialized types of crimes. Also, with the exception of the officers of the U.S. Marshal Service, the federal law enforcement officers discussed in this section are officially designated as "special agents."

Alcohol, Tobacco, and Firearms (ATF) Agent ATF agents work for the U.S. Treasury Department. These agents enforce U.S. laws pertaining to the sale and possession of alcohol, tobacco, and firearms. They participate in investigations that involve conducting surveillance, making raids, interviewing suspects and witnesses, making arrests, obtaining search warrants, and searching for physical evidence. ATF agents work closely with other federal, state, and local law enforcement agencies and provide assistance in the fight against crime and violence. ATF agents also review all evidence at the conclusion of an investigation and prepare case reports that aid the U.S. attorney in trial preparation.

Drug Enforcement Agency (DEA) Agent DEA agents work under the authority of the U.S. Department of Justice in enforcing the federal *Controlled Substance Act.* Agents are involved in the following: carrying out surveillance of criminals; infiltrating illicit drug channels; identifying and apprehending drug traffickers; confiscating illegal drug supplies; arresting drug law violators; collecting and preparing evidence; writing detailed reports; and coordinating activities with local, state, federal, and foreign governments to prevent the flow of illegal drugs to and through the United States.

Federal Bureau of Investigation (FBI) Agent FBI agents work under the authority of the U.S. Department of Justice and deal with investigation and apprehension of federal fugitives, investigation of civil rights violations, and investigation of organized crime, white-collar crime, foreign counterintelligence, sabotage, espionage, terrorism, and kidnapping. FBI agents coordinate their activities closely with the U.S. attorney in their jurisdiction.

Internal Revenue Service (IRS) Agent IRS agents work for the U.S. Treasury Department. Their duties involve investigating people for tax violations, money laundering, computer fraud, and illegal tax shelters. In fulfilling these duties, the agents interview witnesses and principals, write reports for trial preparation, and participate in surveillance, undercover activities, and searches and seizures.

Secret Service Agent Secret Service agents work for the U.S. Treasury Department. Their primary responsibility is to protect the president and vice president of the United States and their immediate families. Secret Service agents also protect past presidents of the United States, foreign heads of state, and official representatives of the United States performing special missions abroad. In addition, Secret Service agents are responsible for investigating currency counterfeiting and various types of fraud and forgery that violate federal laws.

Deputy U.S. Marshal Every deputy U.S. marshal works under the authority of a U.S. marshal. There are 94 U.S. marshals, each appointed to manage a particular district. Service is under the jurisdiction of the U.S. Department of Justice.

Deputy U.S. marshals are involved in conducting fugitive investigations, protecting U.S. courts, protecting federal witnesses, seizing and managing assets acquired from criminal activities, providing prisoner custody and transportation, and providing law enforcement support in national emergencies.

Education

FBI Agent People can enter the FBI in one of five areas with the following qualifications:

Law

J.D. degree from an accredited resident law school.

Accounting

B.S. degree with a major in accounting and eligibility to take the CPA examination.

Engineering / Science

B.S. degree in engineering, computer science, or one of the physical sciences. Additional experience may be required.

Language

B.S. or B.A. degree in any discipline and proficiency in Spanish, Russian, Arabic, Chinese, or another language that meets the needs of the FBI.

ATF, DEA, IRS, and Secret Service Agents and Deputy U.S. Marshal Entry requirements for these careers generally include a four-year college degree and, with the exception of IRS agents, some law enforcement experience. Those preparing to become IRS agents should emphasize accounting and business while in college.

Backgrounds in foreign languages, computers, and business are extremely helpful on the job.

Additional training is provided at one of the federal law enforcement academies for each entering agent.

Special Skills

All federal law enforcement officers must pass rigorous physical, vision, and medical examinations in order to be hired. They must be able to maintain the confidentiality of their work and relate effectively to people from different backgrounds. Like local and state law enforcement personnel, agents must be able to listen carefully, speak articulately, write proficiently, and exercise good judgment in dangerous situations.

Salary and Benefits

FBI agents are hired at a salary of about $30,600 per year. However, beginning agents often make more money because of the large amount of overtime necessary for the job. Additionally, within a few years, FBI agents progress up the government pay scale to salaries above $50,000. Other agents generally enter the salary schedule at about $22,000. However, within five years, agents can be earning over $45,000. Medical and retirement benefits are provided for all U.S. government law enforcement employees.

Working Conditions

Law enforcement agents at the federal level work in offices and courtrooms but may travel extensively to do their jobs. They often put in a lot of overtime. The potential for physical danger always exists. Thus, special agents carry weapons and must be ready to use them.

Outlook

The job demand for federal law enforcement officers through the year 2005 should increase as fast as the demand for other legal occupations because of the increase in crime. However, the availability of jobs could be limited by the government's budget limitations.

For More Information

ATF Agent

Bureau of Alcohol, Tobacco, and Firearms
Personnel Division
1200 Pennsylvania Ave., N.W.
Washington, D.C. 20226

DEA Agent

DEA Headquarters
Attn: Special Agent Recruiting Unit
1405 I Street, N.W.
Washington, D.C. 20537

FBI Agent

Federal Bureau of Investigation
Attn: Applicant Unit
Department of Justice
10th and Pennsylvania Ave., N.W.
Washington, D.C. 20535

IRS Agent

Internal Revenue Service
Department of the Treasury
Division of Criminal Investigation
1111 Constitution Ave., N.W.
Washington, D.C. 20224

Secret Service Agent

United States Secret Service
Personnel Division
1800 G Street, N.W.
Washington, D.C. 20223

Deputy U.S. Marshal

U.S. Marshal Service
Office of Policy and Communications
600 Army Navy Drive
Arlington, VA 22202-4210

APPENDIX F

Organizations to Know

I. U.S. GOVERNMENT

Executive Office of the President
The White House
1600 Pennsylvania Avenue, N.W.
Washington, D.C. 20500
(202) 456-1414

Office of the Vice President
Executive Office Building
17th Street & Pennsylvania Avenue, N.W.
Washington, D.C. 20501
(202) 456-2326

Executive Departments

Department of Agriculture
14th Street & Independence Avenue, S.W.
Washington, D.C. 20250
(202) 720-4623
Responsible for U.S. agricultural policy. Regulates and expands markets for agricultural products. Directs food and nutrition services, including food stamp program. Inspects, grades, and safeguards quality of food products. Involved in rural development, forest management, and water and soil conservation.

Department of Commerce
14th Street & Constitution Avenue, N.W.
Washington, D.C. 20230
(202) 482-2000
Concerned with economic development and technological advancement. Provides assistance and information to business and industry. Assists development of the U.S. merchant marine and the growth of minority businesses. Provides social, economic, and scientific data to business and government. Conducts the U.S. census. Promotes travel to the United States by foreign tourists, and assists development of economically deprived areas throughout the country.

Department of Defense
The Pentagon
Washington, D.C. 20301
(703) 545-6700
Provides for the common defense of the United States.

Department of Education
400 Maryland Avenue, S.W.
Washington, D.C. 20202
(202) 401-5986
Administers federal aid programs for all aspects of education, including preschool through college; adult, vocational, and bilingual education; public libraries; and education for the handicapped.

Department of Energy
1000 Independence Avenue, S.W.
Washington, D.C. 20585
(202) 586-5000
Has responsibility for energy development and conservation policies. Conducts research on new energy sources and advises the government on energy matters.

Department of Health and Human Services
200 Independence Avenue, S.W.
Washington, D.C. 20201
(202) 690-6343

Administers federal programs involving all aspects of public health and human services, including medical research, health care financing, mental health and disease control, alcohol and drug abuse, health services, social security, and public welfare. Operates a hotline offering civil rights information, as well as one for runaways.

Department of Housing and Urban Development
451 7th Street, S.W.
Washington, D.C. 20410
(202) 708-1112

Has responsibility for programs concerned with housing and community development. Administers programs involving urban planning, mortgage insurance, rent subsidies, home building, and neighborhood rehabilitation and preservation. Operates a hotline that handles discrimination complaints.

Department of the Interior
1849 C Street, N.W.
Washington, D.C. 20240
(202) 208-3100

Has responsibility for management and conservation of most publicly owned lands and natural resources. Operates and preserves national parks and historical places, protects fish and wildlife, conserves and develops mineral resources, and is responsible for outdoor recreation and Indian and territorial affairs.

Department of Justice
10th Street & Constitution Avenue, N.W.
Washington, D.C. 20530
(202) 514-2000

Has responsibility for enforcing federal laws, representing the government in federal cases, and interpreting laws under which other departments act. Has divisions involved in antitrust, civil rights, natural resources, and tax law. Special bureaus include the FBI, Bureau of Prisons, Immigration and Naturalization Service, U.S. Marshals, Law Enforcement Assistance Administration, National Institute of Justice, Drug Enforcement Administration, Office for Victims of Crime, Office of Juvenile Justice and Delinquency Prevention, Bureau of Justice Statistics, and Bureau of Justice Assistance.

Department of Labor
200 Constitution Avenue, N.W.
Washington, D.C. 20210
(202) 219-6666

Has responsibility for all aspects of labor and employment, including wages, hours, safety and health conditions, job training, pensions and benefits, collective bargaining, and union/management relations.

Department of State
2201 C Street, N.W.
Washington, D.C. 20520
(202) 647-4000

Is the primary source of foreign affairs information for the U.S. government. Provides much of the national security and economic facts available to the government and most of the data on the internal politics of foreign countries.

Department of Transportation
400 7th Street, S.W.
Washington, D.C. 20590
(202) 366-4000

Responsible for U.S. transportation policy. Provides funds for highway planning and construction and urban mass transit. Assists and regulates railroads, airlines, ports, waterways, and highway safety.

Department of the Treasury
1500 Pennsylvania Avenue, N.W.
Washington, D.C. 20220
(202) 622-2000

Responsible for U.S. tax and money policies. Designs and prints coins, stamps, and currency. Collects federal taxes via the Internal Revenue Service. Oversees the Secret Service, the Customs Service, and the Bureau of Alcohol, Tobacco, and Firearms.

Department of Veterans Affairs
810 Vermont Avenue, N.W.
Washington, D.C. 20420
(202) 233-4000

Administers veterans' benefit programs, including disability compensation, pensions, education, home loans, insurance, vocational rehabilitation, medical care, and burial benefits.

*Legislative Branch**

U.S. House of Representatives
The Capitol
Washington, D.C. 20515
(202) 224-3121

* A good source for information about a specific bill or law is the congressional committee that drafted the bill or has authority for overseeing the law's implementation.

To contact a member of the House of Representatives, write to the address provided.

U.S. Senate
The Capitol
Washington, D.C. 20510
(202) 224-3121
To contact a member of the Senate, write to the address provided.

Judicial Branch

Supreme Court of the United States
#1 First Street, N.E.
Washington, D.C. 20543
(202) 479-3211
Copies of recently decided cases can be obtained by contacting the clerk of the court at the address provided.

Federal Agencies and Offices

ACTION
1100 Vermont Ave., N.W.
Washington, D.C. 20525
(202) 606-5245
The federal domestic volunteer agency. Oversees six volunteer programs operated in the United States: VISTA, Foster Grandparent Program, Senior Companion Program, Retired Senior Volunteer Program, Student Community Service Project, and ACTION Drug Alliance.

Commission on Civil Rights
624 9th Street, N.W.
Washington, D.C. 20425
(202) 376-8312
Encourages equal opportunity for minority groups and women. Conducts studies and makes recommendations regarding discrimination. Serves as a clearinghouse for civil rights information. Investigates complaints of denial of voting rights.

Consumer Product Safety Commission
5401 Westbard Avenue
Bethesda, MD
(800) 638-2772 Consumer Hotline
(800) 492-6600 in Maryland
Establishes and enforces product safety standards, studies causes and prevention of product-related injuries, and conducts surveillance and enforcement programs.

Environmental Protection Agency
401 M Street, S.W.
Washington, D.C. 20460
(202) 260-2090
Responsible for policies and laws that protect the environment, including regulations aimed at land, water, air, and noise pollution, solid waste disposal, pesticides, and other hazardous materials.

Equal Employment Opportunity Commission
1801 L Street, N.W.
Washington, D.C., 20507
(202) 663-4264
To file a charge:
1400 L Street, N.W.
Washington, D.C. 20005
Handles complaints regarding job discrimination based on race, color, religion, sex, national origin, age, and disability. Has power to conduct investigations and bring court actions where necessary.

Federal Communications Commission
1919 M Street, N.W.
Washington, D.C. 20554
(202) 632-7000
Regulates communications media, including radio, television, cable, and satellite. Investigates complaints regarding radio or television broadcasting.

Federal Election Commission
999 E Street, N.W.
Washington, D.C. 20463
(202) 219-3440
Administers and enforces provisions of the *Federal Election Campaign Act*. The act requires the disclosure of sources and uses of campaign money for any federal office, limits the amount of individual contributions, and provides for public financing of presidential elections.

Federal Information Center
P.O. Box 600
Cumberland, MD 21502
(301) 722-9098
Division of the General Services Administration that provides assistance to citizens lost in the maze of federal programs and services by directing them

to the proper offices for help with their problems. Maintains regional offices in addition to the District of Columbia office.

Federal Judicial Center
1 Columbus Circle, N.E.
Washington, D.C. 20002
(202) 273-4000

The federal courts' agency for research and continuing education. Conducts and promotes research on federal court organization, operations, and history, and develops recommendations about the operation and study of the federal courts. Also promotes orientation and continuing education for federal judges and court employees.

Federal Labor Relations Authority
607 14th Street, N.W.
Washington, D.C. 20424
(202) 482-8500

Administers the laws that protect the right of federal employees to bargain through labor organizations. Resolves labor disputes between federal agencies and unions that represent federal employees. Cases include unfair labor practices, exceptions to arbitration awards, negotiability appeals, and representation petitions.

Federal Mediation and Conciliation Service
2100 K Street, N.W.
Washington, D.C. 20427
(202) 653-5300

Provides mediation assistance and arbitration referrals in labor disputes. Also provides mediation training in other areas.

Federal Reserve System, Board of Governors
20th & C Streets, N.W.
Washington, D.C. 20551
(202) 452-3000

Serves as the central bank of the United States. Sets banking policies and regulates the availability of money.

Federal Trade Commission
6th Street & Pennsylvania Avenue, N.W.
Washington, D.C. 20580
(202) 326-2000

Responsible for keeping competition among U.S. businesses both free and fair. Will investigate complaints of deceptive or unfair practices involving price fixing, advertising, packaging, labeling or credit.

Interstate Commerce Commission
12th Street & Constitution Avenue, N.W.
Washington, D.C. 20423
(202) 275-7119

Regulates interstate commerce. The Office of Consumer Affairs, which appears in this listing, handles consumer complaints involving interstate moving companies, buses, trains, and small shipments.

National Labor Relations Board
1717 Pennsylvania Avenue, N.W.
Washington, D.C. 20570
(202) 254-8064

An independent federal agency that investigates, prosecutes and remedies unfair labor practices by employers and labor unions. Conducts secret ballot elections among workers to determine whether they wish to be represented by a labor union.

National Transportation Safety Board
490 L'Enfant Plaza, East
Washington, D.C. 20594
(202) 382-6600

Independent federal agency that investigates accidents and makes recommendations to avoid reoccurrences; works in all modes of transportation including aviation, railway, highway, pipeline, and marine.

Nuclear Regulatory Commission
11555 Rockville Pike
Rockville, MD 20852
(310) 504-2240

Regulates commercial uses of nuclear energy. Responsibilities include licensing, inspection, and enforcement.

Occupational Safety and Health Administration
200 Constitution Avenue, N.W.
Washington, D.C. 20210
(202) 523-9361

Division of the Department of Labor that sets policy, develops programs, and investigates complaints regarding occupational safety and health hazards.

Office on Consumer Affairs
1620 L Street, N.W.
Suite 700
Washington, D.C. 20036
(202) 634-9610
(202) 634-4310 (consumer inquiries)

Set up by the president to be the consumer's "voice" in Washington. Provides consumer information, advises on consumer policies and programs, conducts consumer education, and will advise citizens where and how to file consumer complaints. Publishes *Consumer Resource Handbook*, which is available from the Consumer Information Center.

Postal Service
475 L'Enfant Plaza West, S.W.
Washington, D.C. 20260
(202) 268-2020
Provides mail processing and delivery services to individuals and businesses throughout the United States. (The Consumer Protection Office handles consumer complaints, enforces law to prevent receipt of unwanted mail, and investigates postal fraud and lost mail.)

Small Business Administration
409 3rd Street, S.W.
Washington, D.C. 20416
(202) 205-6600
Provides information and assistance to small businesses on problems of marketing, accounting, product analysis, production methods, and research and development. Runs many financial assistance programs to small businesses.

II. PRIVATE AGENCIES AND ORGANIZATIONS

Academy of Family Mediators
P.O. Box 10501
Eugene, OR 97440
(503) 345-1205
Advocates mediation as an alternative to litigation in domestic affairs matters. Provides a referral service.

AFL-CIO (American Federation of Labor—Congress of Industrial Organizations)
815 16th Street, N.W.
Washington, D.C. 20006
(202) 637-5000
Voluntary coalition of unions that represents labor interests in legislative and judicial contexts. Formulates policy on worker-related issues.

American Arbitration Association
140 West 51st Street
New York, NY 10020
(212) 484-4000
Provides dispute resolution services, training, and technical assistance through its headquarters and regional offices.

American Association for Marriage and Family Therapy
1100 17th Street, N.W.
10th Floor
Washington, D.C. 20036
1-800-374-2638
A membership association of therapists that will provide referral lists. The Commission for Marriage and Family Therapy Education accredits marriage and family therapy programs.

American Bar Association
750 N. Lakeshore Drive
Chicago, IL 60611
(312) 988-5000
Professional organization of lawyers that provides services and information to state and local bar associations. Serves as a resource on most law-related topics. Acts as a national spokesperson for the legal profession. Establishes standards for lawyers and courts and accredits law schools.

American Civil Liberties Union (ACLU)
132 W. 43rd Street
New York, NY 10036
(212) 944-9800
Nonprofit organization supporting civil liberties through lobbying and trying test cases in court.

American Conservative Union
38 Ivy Street, S.E.
Washington, D.C. 20003
(202) 546-6555
A conservative lobbying and educational group. Puts out a yearly rating on members of Congress on their "conservativeness," hosts the Conservative Political Action Convention, and puts out various conservative publications.

American Jewish Congress
15 East 84th Street
New York, NY 10028
(212) 879-4500
Advocacy body interested in protecting constitutional and civil rights.

American Tort Reform Association
1212 New York Avenue, N.W., Suite 515
Washington, D.C. 20005
National advocate of lawsuit reform. Mission is to bring greater efficiency, fairness, and predictability to the civil justice system through public education and legislation.

Center for Dispute Settlement
1666 Connecticut Avenue, N.W., Suite 501
Washington, D.C. 20009
(202) 265-9572
Designs and assesses nontraditional methods of dispute resolution.

Center for Law and Education
955 Massachusetts Avenue
Cambridge, MA 02139
(617) 876-6611
Helps legal services programs in local communities on issues concerning law and education.

Center for Law and Social Policy
1616 P Street, N.W., Suite 150
Washington, D.C. 20036
(202) 328-5140
National public interest organization addressing the problems of low-income families and the legal needs of the poor through policy advocacy, education, research, and legal representation.

Center for Study of Responsive Law
P.O. Box 19367
Washington, D.C. 20036
(202) 387-8030
Information center for a variety of topics of public interest law, including environmental protection, banking and insurance regulation, and workplace safety and health.

Chamber of Commerce of the United States
1615 H Street, N.W.
Washington, D.C. 20062
(202) 659-6000
Federation of businesses, chambers of commerce, American chambers of commerce overseas, and trade and professional associations. The Chamber is America's principal advocate for the American business community.

Children's Defense Fund
122 C Street, N.W.
Washington, D.C. 20001
(202) 628-8787
Concerned with long-range and systematic advocacy on behalf of the nation's children in the areas of education; child care, health, and welfare; and family support services.

Citizens' Commission on Civil Rights
2000 M Street, N.W.
Washington, D.C. 20036
(202) 659-5565
Assists civil rights groups and monitors government compliance with civil rights laws. They do not take individual cases.

Citizens' Committee for the Right to Keep and Bear Arms
600 Pennsylvania Avenue, S.E., Suite 205
Washington, D.C. 20003
(202) 543-3363
Study and advisory body dealing with gun owners' rights. Is also a grass-roots lobbying organization.

Common Cause
2030 M Street, N.W.
Washington, D.C. 20036
(202) 833-1200
A national citizens' lobby devoted to making government at national and state levels more open and accountable to citizens.

Consumer Federation of America
1424 16th Street, N.W., Suite 604
Washington, D.C. 20036
(202) 387-6121
Federation of national, regional, state, and local consumer groups. Helps consumer groups organize and act; lobbies on proposed consumer legislation and publicizes important issues.

Consumer Information Center
Pueblo, CO 81002
(719) 948-3334
Publishes a catalog of free and low-cost federal publications for consumers. Arm of the General Services Administration.

Consumers Union
2001 S Street, N.W., Suite 520
Washington, D.C. 20009
(202) 462-6262
Nonprofit organization providing information, education, and counseling about consumer goods and services and the management of a family income. Tests, rates, and reports on competing brands of

products, and publishes reports in monthly *Consumer Reports* magazine.

Cooperative Housing Foundation
1010 Wayne Drive
Suite 240
Silver Spring, MD 20910
(301) 587-4700
Interested in improving the quality of housing and urban development, especially for people of modest income, through the encouragement of cooperative housing. Offers training and technical assistance to low-income families in developing countries.

Council of Better Business Bureaus
4200 Wilson Boulevard, Suite 800
Arlington, VA 22203
(703) 276-0100
Supported by membership of private businesses and local Better Business Bureaus in the United States and Canada. Local bureaus provide company reliability reports, handle consumer complaints, and provide mediation and arbitration services.

Environmental Defense Fund
257 Park Avenue South
New York, NY 10010
(212) 505-2100
Citizens interest group that links science, economics and law to create innovative, economically cost-effective, and viable solutions to today's environmental problems.

Handgun Control
1225 Eye Street, N.W., Suite 1100
Washington, D.C. 20005
(202) 898-0792
Advocacy group that supports gun control through lobbying and acts as a clearinghouse for information on handgun control issues.

Help Abolish Legal Tyranny—An Organization for Legal Reform (HALT)
1319 F Street, N.W., Suite 300
Washington, D.C. 20004
(202) 347-9600
Educates the public about the legal system. Studies and promotes mediation services as an alternative.

Institute for Local Self-Reliance
2425 18th Street, N.W.
Washington, D.C. 20009-2096
(202) 232-4108
Tries to teach communities the tools of economic self reliance through environmental conservation and environmentally sound behaviors. Provides technical assistance to those concerned with issues of local initiation and independence.

Lawyers Committee for Civil Rights Under Law
1400 I Street, N.W., Suite 400
Washington, D.C. 20005
(202) 371-1212
Operates through local committees of private lawyers in 10 cities to provide legal assistance to poor and minority groups.

Lawyers for Civil Justice
1225 19th Street, N.W., Suite 470
Washington, D.C. 20036
(202) 429-0045
Attorneys' coalition working for tort reform.

Leadership Conference on Civil Rights
1629 K Street, N.W., Suite 1010
Washington, D.C. 20006
(202) 466-3311
Coalition of civil rights interest groups working for enforcement and enactment of social welfare laws. Clearinghouse for information on related legislation.

League of Women Voters
1730 M Street, N.W., 10th Floor
Washington, D.C. 20036
(202) 429-1965
Nonpartisan, political organization that encourages the informed and active participation of citizens in government and influences public policy through education and advocacy. Works for voter registration and turnout and encourages media to extract the truth from candidates.

Major Appliance Consumer Action Panel
Complaint Exchange
20 North Wacker Drive, Suite 1500
Chicago, IL 60606
(312) 984-5858 (Call collect)
Helps mediate unresolved consumer complaints involving major appliances once the consumer has already contacted the dealer and manufacturer.

Mexican American Legal Defense and Educational Fund
634 S. Spring Street
Los Angeles, CA 90014
(213) 629-2512
Concerned with protecting the constitutional rights of Latinos and supporting the education of Latino-American lawyers.

Migrant Legal Action Program
2001 S Street, N.W., Suite 310
Washington, D.C. 20009
(202) 462-7744
Provides civil legal representation for migrant and seasonal farmworkers. Farmworker clients must meet Legal Services Corporation guidelines, which include poverty, to be eligible for representation. Staff has both English and Spanish language capabilities.

Mothers Against Drunk Driving (MADD)
511 East John Carpenter Freeway
Suite 700
Irving, TX 75062-8187
1-800-GET-MADD
National organization with over 400 chapters. Advocates tougher laws against drunk driving. Mission is to stop drunk driving and to support the victims of this violent crime.

National Abortion Rights Action League (NARAL)
1156 15th Street, N.W.
Washington, D.C. 20005
(202) 973-3000
Initiates and coordinates political, social, and legal action of individuals and groups concerned with maintaining abortion rights. Conducts research and maintains speakers' bureau.

National Association for the Advancement of Colored People (NAACP)
4805 Mount Hope Drive
Baltimore, MD 21215
(410) 358-8900
Citizens' interest group seeking elimination of racial segregation and discrimination through legal, legislative, citizen action, and educational programs.

National Association for Mediation in Education
425 Amity Street
University of Massachusetts
Amherst, MA 01002
(413) 545-2462
Provides a clearinghouse of information on mediation in education. Helps develop school mediation programs.

National Association of Attorneys General
444 N. Capital Street, N.W., Suite 339
Washington, D.C. 20001
(202) 434-8000
Has committees on many legal topics. Issues newsletters and publications.

National Association of Housing and Redevelopment Officials
1320 18th Street, N.W., Suite 500
Washington, D.C. 20036
(202) 429-2960
Organization that represents local housing authorities, community development agencies, and individual professionals in the field of housing. Works to provide safe, decent, and affordable housing for low- and moderate-income persons. Provides information in the areas of housing, community development and redevelopment in federal policy, legislation, regulation, and funding.

National Bar Association
1225 11th Street, N.W.
Washington, D.C. 20001
(202) 842-3900
Organization of mainly minority lawyers and other legal professionals. Active in legal education projects.

National Center for State Courts
300 Newport Avenue
Williamsburg, VA 23185
(804) 253-2000
Committed to modernizing court operations and improving justice at the state and local levels throughout the country. Provides information, research training, and technical assistance on court topics.

National Center for Youth Law
1663 Mission Street, 5th Floor
San Francisco, CA 94103
(415) 543-3307
Part of the national system of legal services for the poor. Provides specialized assistance to attorneys and others who work on behalf of poor children.

National Center of Law and the Deaf
Gallaudet University
800 Florida Avenue, N.E.
Washington, D.C. 20002
(202) 651-5373

Provides legal assistance to deaf and hearing-impaired individuals in various civil matters, including landlord/tenant disputes, public benefits, consumer problems, and discrimination. Does not handle personal injury, bankruptcy, wills, or domestic relations cases.

National Clients Council
2617 Martha Street
Philadelphia, PA 19125
(215) 686-2913

Provides advocacy of clients' interests and concerns in legal services programs and trains clients to participate in the planning and execution of these programs. Affiliated with the American Bar Association.

National Coalition Against Domestic Violence
P.O. Box 18749
Denver, CO 80218-0749
(303) 839-1852

Assists victims of domestic violence. Monitors related legislation and provides educational services.

Coalition to Stop Gun Violence
100 Maryland Avenue, N.E.
Washington, D.C. 20002
(202) 544-7190

Information resource for groups interested in banning handguns.

National Committee for Prevention of Child Abuse
332 S. Michigan Avenue, Suite 1600
Chicago, IL 60604
(312) 663-3520

Resource and advocacy group. Operates a crisis intervention hotline.

National Council on Family Relations
3989 Central Avenue, N.E., Suite 550
Minneapolis, MN 55421
(612) 781-9331

Nonpartisan membership organization devoted to research and dissemination of information on families, marriage and family life.

National Crime Prevention Council
1700 K Street, N.W., 2nd Floor
Washington, D.C. 20006
(202) 466-6272

Provides a clearinghouse of information and materials on crime prevention activities and programs. Also provides technical assistance and training in this area.

National Foundation for Consumer Credit
8611 2nd Avenue, Suite 100
Silver Spring, MD 20910
1-800-388-2227

Sponsors nationwide free or low-cost counseling program to consumers in credit difficulty and provides an educational program for families.

National Housing Law Project
2201 Broadway, Suite 815
Oakland, CA 94612
(510) 251-9400

Publishes information on housing.

National Institute for Dispute Resolution
1901 L Street, N.W., Suite 600
Washington, D.C. 20036
(202) 466-4764

Promotes conflict resolution processes and their use, and works on innovative approaches to avoid future conflict. Provides information and technical assistance for use of dispute resolution processes.

National Insurance Consumer Organization
121 N. Payne Street
Alexandria, VA 22314
(703) 549-8050

Studies insurance marketing and pricing practices and educates the public about buying insurance. Active in the tort reform movement.

National Legal Aid and Defender Association
1625 K Street, N.W.
Washington, D.C. 20006
(202) 452-0620

Association of local organizations and individuals that provide legal services to the poor. Publishes a directory of legal aid and defender facilities.

National Legal Center for the Public Interest
1000 16th Street, N.W., Suite 301
Washington, D.C. 20036
(202) 296-1683

Resource center on issues relating to the public interest. Desires to foster knowledge of the administration of justice in a society committed to the rights of individuals, free enterprise, private ownership of property, balanced use of private and public resources, limited governments, and a fair and efficient judiciary.

National Network of Runaway and Youth Services
1318 F Street, N.W.
Washington, D.C. 20004
(202) 783-7949
Provides information and services targeted toward runaway, at-risk, and homeless young people.

National Office for Social Responsibility
222 S. Washington Street
Alexandria, VA 22314
(703) 549-5305
Educates public and private agencies about the juvenile justice system and youth employment programs.

National Organization for the Reform of Marijuana Laws (NORML)
1001 Connecticut Avenue, N.W.
Suite 119
Washington, D.C. 20036
(202) 483-5500
Clearinghouse on marijuana laws. Supports legalization of the drug for personal use.

National Organization for Victim Assistance
1757 Park Road, N.W.
Washington, D.C. 20010
(202) 232-6682
Provides information and technical assistance on victim assistance programs. Counsels victims and makes referrals to counseling programs.

National Organization for Women
1000 16th Street, N.W.
Suite 700
Washington, D.C. 20036
(202) 331-0066
Takes action to bring women into full participation in the mainstream of American society so they can assume all its privileges and responsibilities in full, equal partnership with men.

National Pro-Family Coalition
717 2nd Street, N.E.
Washington, D.C. 20002
(202) 546-3003
Coalition supporting antiabortion and antipornography laws.

National Resource Center for Consumers of Legal Services
1444 I Street, N.W., 8th Floor
Washington, D.C. 20005
(202) 842-3503
Publishes a biweekly newsletter reviewing developments in the field of legal services. Serves as a clearinghouse for information on legal services.

National Rifle Association of America (NRA)
1600 Rhode Island Avenue, N.W.
Washington, D.C. 20036
(202) 828-6000
Supports firearms laws that enable persons to own guns for sport and recreational shooting.

National Right to Life Committee
419 7th Street, N.W., Suite 500
Washington, D.C. 20004
(202) 626-8800
Lobbies for constitutional amendments against abortion. Operates an information clearinghouse and speakers bureau.

National Runaway Switchboard
3080 N. Lincoln Avenue
Chicago, IL 60657
(800) 621-4000
A 24-hour, toll-free national switchboard for runaways and their families. Provides information on shelters and counseling services. Offers to relay messages confidentially.

National Trust for Historic Preservation
1785 Massachusetts Avenue, N.W.
Washington, D.C. 20036
(202) 673-4000
Nonprofit organization created to help protect the built environment and our cultural heritage. Offers advice on preservation problems; works with individuals, preservation groups, and public agencies to help them plan and carry out preservation programs; sponsors educational programs; issues publications; and owns and operates historical museums.

National Urban League
111 14th Street, N.W.
Washington, D.C. 20005
(202) 898-1604
Nonprofit charitable and educational social services organization working to secure equal opportunity for African Americans and other minorities.

Concerned with all issues that affect its constituency. Publishes information booklets supplying research data on the economic gap between black and white Americans.

National Women's Health Network
1111 14th Street, N.W.
Suite 600
Washington, D.C. 20005
(202) 347-1140

Nonprofit organization which monitors legislation, lobbies, and educates people on women's health care issues. Seeks to protect women's health rights.

National Women's Law Center
1616 P Street, N.W., Suite 100
Washington, D.C. 20036
(202) 328-5160

Works to protect women's rights. Focuses on issues such as health and reproductive rights, education, employment, income security, and family support. Has multiple strategies for change, including advocacy, public education, and litigation.

Native American Rights Fund
1506 Broadway
Boulder, CO 80302
(303) 447-8760

Represents Native-American individuals and tribes in legal matters of national significance and publishes a quarterly account of its activities. Deals with large-scale cases.

Pacific Legal Foundation
2700 Gateway Oaks Drive, Suite 200
Sacramento, CA 95833
(916) 641-8888

Represents the economic, social, and environmental interests of the public in court while emphasizing private property rights, freedom from excessive government regulation, free enterprise, balanced environmental policy, and nonwasteful, productive, and fiscally sound government.

Public Citizen Organization
2000 P Street, N.W.
Washington, D.C. 20036
(202) 833-3000

Nonprofit consumer advocacy organization, founded in 1971 by Ralph Nader, has five divisions: 1) Congress Watch—research and lobbying for corporate and government responsibility; 2) Health Research Group—concerned with health care delivery, safe medications and medical devices, and occupational health and safety; 3) Litigation Group—public interest law firm emphasizing open government and effective government regulations; 4) Critical Mass Energy Project—opposes nuclear fuels and promotes safe, sustainable energy use; and 5) Buyers Up—home heating oil buying group.

Puerto Rican Legal Defense and Education Fund
99 Hudson Street
New York, NY 10013
(212) 219-3360

Provides legal services and educational assistance for Puerto Rican and other Hispanic communities.

Rand Corporation
P.O. Box 2138
Santa Monica, CA 90407-2138
(310) 393-0411

Think tank that assesses practices in both the civil and criminal justice systems. Publishes studies widely used by groups both for and against tort reform.

Rural Coalition
2001 S Street, N.W.
Washington, D.C. 20009
(202) 483-1500

Coalition of groups working to develop public policy favorable to rural interests. Studies a broad range of issues.

Southern Poverty Law Center
P.O. Box 548
Montgomery, Al 36101
(205) 264-0286

Seeks, through legal precedents it helps to establish, to protect and guarantee the legal and civil rights of the poor population in the United States. Publishes bi-monthly reports.

State Justice Institute
1650 King Street, Suite 600
Alexandria, VA 22314
(703) 684-6100

Established by Congress to improve judicial administration in the state courts.

Trial Lawyers for Public Justice
1717 Massachusetts Ave., N.W.
Washington, D.C. 20036
(202) 797-8600

A public interest law firm founded in 1982 that specializes in precedent-setting litigation in the areas of toxic torts, environmental protection, consumer rights, worker safety, civil rights and liberties, and access to the courts.

United States Public Interest Research Group (USPIRG)
215 Pennsylvania Avenue, S.E.
Washington, D.C. 20003
(202) 546-9707

Advocacy group that studies consumer and environmental issues, educates the public on findings, and urges appropriate legislative action.

Women's Legal Defense Fund, Incorporated
1875 Connecticut Avenue, N.W., Suite 710
Washington, D.C. 20009
(202) 986-2600

Established for the purpose of fighting sex discrimination. Works for equal opportunity, reproductive freedom, quality health care, and economic security for women. Works with Congress, the media, and at the state level to advance public policy for women and their families.

APPENDIX G

Glossary

A

abandonment desertion of people or things.

abortion a premature end to a pregnancy. Can result from a medical procedure performed in the early stages of pregnancy or as in a miscarriage, when the fetus leaves the womb before it can survive on its own.

abstinence not having sexual intercourse.

acceleration clause a provision in a contract that makes the entire debt due if a payment is not made on time or if some other condition is not met.

acceptance the act of agreeing to an offer and becoming bound to the terms of a contract.

accessory a person who helps commit a crime. An **accessory before the fact** is one who encourages, orders, or helps plan a crime. An **accessory after the fact** is someone who, knowing a crime has been committed, helps conceal the crime or the criminal.

accomplice someone who voluntarily helps another person commit a crime.

acquaintance rape sexual assault by someone known to the victim, such as a date or neighbor.

act (1) something done voluntarily that may have legal consequences; (2) a written law that has been passed by Congress.

adjudicatory hearing the procedure used to determine the facts in a juvenile case; similar to an adult trial, but generally closed to the public.

administrator someone appointed by the court to supervise the distribution of another person's property after his or her death.

admissible said of evidence that can be used or introduced in a trial or other court proceeding.

adoption the legal process of taking a child of other parents as one's own.

adultery voluntary sexual intercourse between a married person and someone other than his or her spouse.

adversary system the judicial system used in the United States. It allows opposing parties to present their legal conflicts before an impartial judge and jury.

advocacy supporting or arguing for a cause.

advocate a person who speaks for the cause of another or on behalf of someone or something.

affidavit a written statement sworn to or made under oath before someone authorized to administer an oath.

affirmative action steps taken by an organization to remedy past discrimination in hiring, promotion, education, etc.; for example, by recruiting minorities and women.

aftercare the equivalent of parole in the juvenile justice system. A juvenile is supervised and assisted by a parole officer or social worker.

agency an administrative division of a government set up to carry out certain laws.

age of majority the age (usually 18 or 21) at which a person becomes an adult, as specified by state law, and acquires both the rights and the responsibilities of adulthood.

aggravating factors factors that might increase the seriousness of an offense. The presence of these factors may be considered by the judge and jury.

alibi a Latin word meaning "elsewhere," an excuse or plea that a person was somewhere else at the time a crime was committed.

alienage the status of being a person born in a foreign country who has not qualified for U.S. citizenship.

alimony a court-ordered allowance a husband or wife (or an ex-husband/ex-wife) pays to his or her spouse after a legal separation, a divorce, or while the case is being decided.

allegation an accusation that has not been proven.

amendment one of the provisions of the U.S. Constitution enacted after the original Constitution became law.

annual percentage rate (APR) the interest rate paid per year on borrowed money.

annulment a court order that declares a marriage never existed.

answer a defendant's response to a complaint, made in a written statement and filed with the court.

appeal to take a case to a higher court for a rehearing.

appeals court a court in which appeals from trial court decisions are heard.

arbitration a way of settling a dispute without going to trial. The people who disagree select an impartial person to settle the argument. If the arbitration is binding, the decision must be followed by all parties.

arraignment a court session at which a defendant is charged and enters a plea. For a misdemeanor this is also the defendant's initial appearance, at which the judge informs him or her of the charges and sets the bail.

arrest to take a person suspected of a crime into custody.

arson the deliberate and malicious burning of property.

assault to attempt to hurt someone (physically) in a way that makes the victim feel immediately threatened. There is no need for physical contact. If the victim feels that he or she will be hurt, there has been an assault. In some states, assault is combined with battery. *See also* battery

assumption of the risk a legal defense to a negligence tort, whereby the individual is considered to have voluntarily accepted a known risk of danger.

attachment the act of taking a debtor's property or money to satisfy a debt, by court approval.

attempt an effort to commit a crime that goes beyond mere preparation but does not result in the commission of the crime.

attractive nuisance doctrine that says if a person keeps something on his or her premises that is likely to attract children, the person must take reasonable steps to protect children against dangers that it might cause.

B

bail money or property put up by the accused or his or her agent to allow release from jail before trial. The purpose of bail is to assure the court that the defendant will return for trial. If the defendant is present for trial, the money or property is returned.

bait and switch a deceptive sales technique in which customers are "baited" into a store by an ad promising an item at a low price and then "switched" to a more expensive item.

balancing test a method by which courts determine whether free expression should be allowed. Using this test, judges balance an individual's interest in free expression against the government's interest in prohibiting that expression. Courts also use this test in other types of cases by balancing the interests in conflict.

balloon payment the last payment of a loan, which is much higher than any of the regular monthly payments.

bankruptcy the procedure under the *Federal Bankruptcy Act* by which a person is relieved of all debts once he or she has placed all property and money in a court's care.

bar association an organization of lawyers.

battery any intentional, unlawful physical contact inflicted on one person by another without consent. In some states, this is combined with assault. *See also* assault.

bequeathal the act of giving anything by a will; for example, giving your body to a medical institution.

beyond a reasonable doubt the level of proof required to convict a person of a crime. It does not mean "convinced 100 percent," but does mean there are no reasonable doubts as to guilt.

bigamy the crime of being married to more than one person at a time.

bill (1) a draft of a proposed law being considered by a legislature; (2) a written statement of money owed.

bill consolidation a form of credit in which the lender combines all of a person's debts into a single monthly payment. In effect, this is a refinancing of a person's existing debts, often with an additional interest charge.

Bill of Rights the first ten amendments (additions or changes) to the Constitution, which guarantee basic rights to all United States citizens. *See* Appendix A.

black market adoption a form of adoption, illegal in many states, that bypasses licensed adoption agencies by using a go-between to negotiate between the expectant mother and the adopting parent(s).

bona fide occupational qualification (BFOQ) a reasonable employment requirement. It is reasonable because a person must meet this requirement in order to perform the job. For example, good vision is a BFOQ for a bus driver; the race or national origin of a bus driver is not a BFOQ.

bond a mandatory insurance agreement or obligation. A bail bond is the money a defendant pays to secure release from jail before the trial.

booking the formal process of making a police record of an arrest.

breach the violation of a law, duty, or other form of obligation, either by engaging in an action or failing to act.

burden of proof in a criminal or civil case, the requirement that to win a point or have an issue decided in one party's favor, that party must show that most of the evidence is on his or her side. "Most of the evidence" does not just mean the amount of evidence. It also means that evidence is more believable and important.

burglary breaking and entering a building with the intention of committing a felony.

burial the act of placing the dead in a grave, underground or above ground.

business necessity the legally acceptable reason for employee selection requirements. A business must show it can operate well only if these selection requirements are met by employees.

C

capital offense an offense that may be punishable by death or life imprisonment.

capital punishment the death penalty.

causation the reason an event occurs; that which produces an effect.

cause in fact one of the things the plaintiff must prove to win a negligence suit. To do this, the plaintiff must prove he or she would not have been harmed if the defendant had not acted wrongfully.

caveat emptor Latin phrase meaning "let the buyer beware."

cease and desist order an order given by an administrative agency or a judge to stop some illegal or deceptive activity.

censorship (1) the denial of freedom of speech or freedom of the press; (2) the process of examining publications or films for material that the government considers harmful or objectionable.

charge (1) the formal accusation of a crime; (2) a type of credit in which payment is made over a period of time.

checks and balances a division of power among the three government branches. To prevent an abuse of power, each branch can check (or limit) the power of another.

child abuse neglect or mistreatment of children.

child snatching the act by a divorced or separated parent of taking his or her child away from the parent with custody and fleeing to another state.

child support money for a child's life necessities that must be provided by the child's parents.

civil action a lawsuit brought by one or more individuals against another person, a business, or the government.

civil law all law that does not involve criminal matters. Civil law usually deals with private rights of individuals, groups, or businesses.

class action a lawsuit brought by one or more persons on behalf of a larger group.

clause a paragraph, sentence, or phrase in a legal document, such as a contract, lease, or will.

clear and present danger test test formerly used by courts to look at what was happening when a speech was made. The court decides whether, at the time of the speech, the danger of unlawful action was obvious.

closing statement at the end of a trial, the comments a lawyer makes to summarize the evidence presented.

codicil an addition to a will made after the will is drawn up.

coercion the act of forcing a person to act against his or her free will.

cohabitation agreement a written or oral contract outlining how unmarried couples want to deal with their money, property, or responsibilities during and after their relationship.

collateral money or property given as security in case a person is unable to repay a debt.

collective bargaining a required procedure in the National Labor Relations Act providing that under certain circumstances, employers must bargain with official union representatives about wages, hours, and other work conditions.

collision coverage insurance that pays for damage caused by an automobile collision.

commercial speech speech that is directed at buying or selling of goods and services. The law treats commercial speech differently from political speech and other forms of expression.

common law a system in which court decisions establish legal principles and rules of law.

common law marriage a marriage created without legal ceremony by a couple living together and publicly presenting themselves as husband and wife.

community property property acquired during a marriage that is owned by both husband and wife, regardless of who earned it or paid for it.

comparable worth a legal theory that women in traditionally female jobs should be paid the same as men in traditionally male jobs when the two kinds of work involve a similar level of skill, effort, and responsibility.

comparative negligence in a tort suit, a finding that the plaintiff was partly at fault and, therefore, does not deserve full compensation for his or her injuries. It is based on percentages. For instance, if 40% of the accident was the plaintiff's fault, the plaintiff's damages are reduced by 40%.

comparison shopping considering several products and their prices before deciding which purchase best meets one's needs.

compensatory damages in a civil case, money the law requires a defendant to pay a winning plaintiff. It is to make up for the harm that the defendant caused the plaintiff. This harm can be financial (for example, lost wages, medical expenses, etc.), physical (for example, past, present, and future pain and suffering), and, in some jurisdictions, mental (fright and shock, anxiety, etc.).

complaint the first legal document filed in a civil lawsuit. It includes a statement of the wrong or harm done to the plaintiff by the defendant and a request for a specific remedy from the court. A complaint in a criminal case is a sworn statement regarding the defendant's actions that constitute the crime charged.

comprehensive coverage the portion of an insurance policy that protects an individual against automobile damages or losses. It does not cover damages and losses caused by collisions. It does cover damages and losses caused by such things as fire, vandalism, or theft.

computer crime the unauthorized access to someone else's computer system.

concurring opinion a judicial opinion that agrees with the result, though not necessarily the reasoning, expressed in another judicial opinion.

condominiums property characterized by individual ownership of living units and shared ownership of common areas.

confession an accused person's voluntary admission of wrongdoing.

confession of judgment a lease provision in which the tenant agrees in advance to let the landlord decide without challenge if the tenant has been at fault in any disagreement.

consent decree a voluntary agreement to stop a practice that is claimed to be illegal.

consideration something of value offered or received, constituting the main reason for making a contract.

conspiracy an agreement between two or more persons to commit a crime along with an act done to begin the crime.

constituents those entitled to vote for a representative from a district.

constructive eviction a situation in which a landlord fails to maintain housing in a livable condition. As a result of this condition, the tenant may leave such housing before the end of the lease without owing any additional rent.

consumer anyone who buys or uses a product or service.

consumer protection laws statutes that protect consumers by prohibiting unfair or misleading trade practices; setting standards for quality, safety, and reliability of many goods and services; and establishing agencies to enforce consumer laws and help consumers.

contempt of court any act to embarrass, hinder, or obstruct the court in the administration of justice.

content neutral the concept that the government cannot favor some ideas over others when regulating or restricting freedom of expression.

contested divorce a divorce in which the parties disagree over the ending of the marriage itself or over issues such as custody or the division of property.

contingency fee the fee paid to an attorney based on a percentage of the sum awarded in a lawsuit.

contraband any items that are illegal to possess.

contraceptives any of a number of devices that reduce the chance of conceiving a child.

contract a legally enforceable agreement between two or more people to do a certain thing in exchange for payment in some form.

contributing to the delinquency of a minor the act of aiding or encouraging improper conduct of a minor.

contributory negligence a defense to a negligence tort, in which a plaintiff cannot recover any damages from a defendant because the plaintiff's failure to be careful contributed to the injury.

conversion the unlawful taking or damaging of someone else's property. It is so serious that the property cannot be returned to the rightful owner. The court forces the defendant to buy the plaintiff's property.

convict (1) a person who has been found guilty of a crime and is now in prison; (2) to find a person guilty of a crime or wrongdoing.

cooperative property owned by a group of people. Together these people own the entire premises and make the rules governing it. Depending on the type of cooperative, individuals in the group may occupy specified units or the entire premises for a specified time.

corrective advertising a remedy imposed by the Federal Trade Commission requiring that any false claim in an advertisement be corrected in future ads.

cosign to sign a legal document, guaranteeing to pay off the debt or contract if the original signer defaults.

counterclaim a claim made by a defendant against the plaintiff in a civil lawsuit.

credit (1) a deduction from what is owed; (2) purchasing goods with delayed payment, as with a credit card; (3) money that is loaned.

creditor a person who provides credit, loans money, or delivers goods or services before payment is made.

cremation using fire, the act of reducing a dead body to ashes.

crime an act or failure to act that violates a law for which a penalty (usually a fine, jail, or probation) is set by the state.

criminal a person who is judged guilty of committing a crime.

criminal fraud knowingly misstating or misrepresenting an important fact, with the intent to harm another person.

criminal homicide the killing of another person intentionally and with malice.

criminal justice process the system by which government enforces criminal law. It includes everything from the arrest of an individual to the individual's release from control by the state.

criminal law the branch of law dealing with crimes and their punishment.

cross examination during a hearing or trial, the questioning of the opposing side's witnesses.

custody the care and keeping of something or someone, such as a child.

D

damages (1) the injuries or losses suffered by one person due to the fault of another; (2) money asked for or paid by a court order for the injuries or losses suffered.

death certificate a legal document that certifies the date and place of a person's death.

death penalty a sentence to death for commission of a serious crime, such as murder.

debtor a person who owes money or buys on credit.

deceased dead; a dead person.

decree an official decision of a court setting out the facts found in a case and what the legal results are. It orders that the court's decision (for example, a divorce decree) be carried out.

deductible a paragraph in an insurance policy stating that before the insurer will pay for a loss, the insured must pay a certain amount, called a deductible. For instance, if the deductible on a policy is $50, and an accident results in repairs costing $150, the insured pays the first $50 and the insurer pays the remaining $100.

deep pockets a description of the person or organization, among many possible defendants, best able to pay damages and therefore most likely to be sued in a tort case.

defamation written or spoken expression about a person that is false and damages that person's reputation.

default failure to fulfill a legal obligation, such as making a loan payment or appearing in court on a specified date and time.

default judgment a ruling against a party to a lawsuit who fails to take a required step (for example, failing to file a paper on time).

defendant the person against whom a claim is made. In a civil suit the defendant is the person being sued; in a criminal case the defendant is the person charged with committing a crime.

defense a denial, answer, or plea disputing the correctness of the charges against a defendant.

deinstitutionalization a policy of releasing many mentally ill patients from mental hospitals into the community.

deliberate to consider carefully, discuss, and work toward forming an opinion or making a decision.

delinquent a child who has committed an act that, if committed by an adult, would be a crime under federal, state, or local law.

delinquent offender a minor who has committed an offense ordinarily punishable by criminal processes. Such offenders are usually processed through the juvenile justice system.

desegregation the removal of barriers based on racist concepts.

desertion abandoning one's spouse with no intention of returning or of reassuming the duties of marriage. Desertion is usually a ground for divorce.

deterrence a reason for punishment. It is the belief that punishment will discourage the offender from committing future crimes and will serve as an example to keep other people from committing crimes.

directed verdict a verdict in a criminal case entered by the judge when the prosecution has not presented enough evidence to show that the defendant committed the crime.

direct examination the questioning of a witness by the side calling the witness to the stand.

disability a physical or mental handicap.

disbar to take away an attorney's license to practice law because of illegal or unethical conduct.

disclaimer a clause or statement that rejects liability for anything not expressly promised.

discovery the pretrial process of exchanging information between the opposing sides.

discrimination generally, choosing or selecting. In law, it may be the decision to treat or categorize persons based on race, color, creed, sex, or other characteristics rather than on individual merit. Also, the denial of equal protection of the law.

disinherit to leave someone, usually a close relative, out of one's will.

disposition the final settlement or result of a case.

dispositional hearing the procedure in which a judge decides what type of punishment or sentence a juvenile offender should receive.

dissenting opinion in a trial or appeal, the written opinion of a minority of judges who disagree with the decision of the majority.

divorce the ending of a marriage by court order.

DNA fingerprinting a method of testing blood for genes that link a specific parent and child.

domestic partnership laws laws that allow an employee's heterosexual or homosexual live-in partner to receive the same employment and health benefits a spouse would receive.

down payment the cash that must be paid initially when something is bought by installments.

drunk driving the operation of a motor vehicle while intoxicated (overcome by alcohol to the point of losing control over one's conscious faculties). A drunk person's blood-alcohol concentration is above a predefined level, usually 0.10 percent.

due process the idea stated in the Fifth and Fourteenth Amendments that every person involved in a legal dispute is entitled to a fair hearing or trial. The requirements of due process vary with the situation, but they basically require that no law or government procedure be arbitrary or unfair.

duress unlawful pressure on a person to do something that he or she would not otherwise do. Duress may be a defense to a criminal charge.

E

economic strike the slowing down, stopping, or disrupting of work by employees in order to gain higher wages.

egg shell skull a negligence rule in which damages are awarded based on the notion that even if the victim is extremely or unusually vulnerable to injury, the defendant must still pay for the total injury.

elements the conditions that make an act unlawful.

emancipation the voluntary surrender by parents of the care, control, and earnings of a minor. A minor becomes emancipated upon reaching legal adulthood, or before that time if legally married or self-supporting.

embalming treating a dead body with chemicals to preserve it.

embezzlement the taking of money or property by a person who has been entrusted with it, for example a bank teller or a company accountant.

employment-at-will contract a work agreement in which the employee can quit at any time, and the employer can fire the employee for any reason or no reason at all.

entrapment an act by law enforcement officials to persuade a person to commit a crime that the person would not otherwise have committed. If proven, entrapment is a valid defense to a criminal charge.

equal protection a constitutional requirement of the Fourteenth Amendment that protects individuals against unlawful discrimination by government.

Equal Rights Amendment a proposed amendment to the U.S. Constitution. It was not ratified by enough states, so it was not added. If ratified, it would have prevented gender discrimination (i.e., the denial of rights based on sex).

equitable just, fair, and right for a particular situation.

error of law a mistake made by a judge in legal procedures or rulings during a trial that may allow the case to be appealed.

escrow money or property that a neutral party, such as a bank, holds for someone until that person fulfills some obligation or requirement.

establishment clause part of the U.S. Constitution that prohibits government from establishing a church or preferring one religion over another.

estate an individual's personal property, including money, stocks, and all belongings.

euthanasia an act of mercy killing in instances where individuals are terminally sick or injured.

eviction the action by a landlord of removing a tenant from a rental unit.

exclusionary rule a legal rule that does not allow the use of illegally obtained evidence against the defendant at trial.

exclusive remedy the only solution, or compensation, available to a plaintiff in a particular legal situation.

executive branch the administrative branch of a government. It carries out (enforces) the laws. This branch includes a chief executive (for example, the president), executive offices, and agencies.

executor, executrix the person named in a will as responsible for carrying out its terms and paying all debts, taxes, and funeral expenses of the deceased.

ex post facto law a law that attempts to make criminal an act that was not a crime at the time it was committed. Such a law is prohibited by the Constitution.

express warranty a statement of fact or a demonstration concerning the quality or performance of goods offered for sale.

extortion taking property illegally by force or threats of harm (for example, blackmail).

F

false imprisonment the intentional or wrongful confinement of another person against his or her will.

false pretenses premeditated and calculated lies about facts or situations intended to cheat a person out of money or property.

family car doctrine a legal rule stating that the owner of a car will be liable for damage done by a family member driving the owner's car.

family immunity laws common law doctrine that prevents husbands and wives or children and parents from suing one another for damages.

family mediator a professional who works directly with a divorcing couple, helping them preserve their relationship for the future. To save time and money, this person helps the couple reach some agreements out of court.

family responsibility laws laws that require children to care for their parents in their old age.

federalism the division of powers between the states and the federal government.

felon a person serving a sentence for a felony.

felony a serious criminal offense punishable by a prison sentence of more than one year.

fighting words a legal term applying to words that are so abusive that they are likely to cause a fight between the speaker and the person spoken to.

finance charge additional money owed to a creditor in exchange for the privilege of borrowing money.

fine a monetary penalty imposed upon someone convicted of an offense.

fixture (1) anything attached to land or a building; (2) those things that, once attached, may not be removed by a tenant.

food stamps coupons given to people with incomes below a certain level. The coupons can be exchanged like money for food at authorized stores.

forced share the portion of an estate, usually one-third or one-half of the property, that must go to a spouse or minor child who is not listed in a will.

foreclosure a proceeding in which a bank or other lender takes a house and sells it if a person fails to make mortgage payments.

foreseeable harm an injury a person could reasonably predict. For instance, a person who leaves a banana peel on the floor could reasonably predict that someone might slip on the peel, fall, and break a bone. If this happens, the broken bone is a foreseeable harm.

forgery the act of making a fake document or altering a real one with the intent to commit fraud.

foster home the residence or home of people who take in a child.

foster parents a couple or family who take in and care for a child who is without parents or who has been removed from the custody of his or her parents.

fraud any deception, lie, or dishonest statement made to cheat someone.

free exercise clause part of the U.S. Constitution that protects individuals' right to worship as they choose.

fringe benefits items provided by employers to their employees free of charge or at reduced cost.

funeral services ceremonies held for a dead person before the burial.

G

garnishment the legally authorized process of taking a person's money, generally by taking part of the person's wages in order to pay creditors.

goals selection by a business or educational institution of a fair number of minority applicants.

grand jury a group of 12 to 23 people who hear preliminary evidence to decide if there is sufficient reason to formally charge a person with a crime.

grandparents' rights laws permitting grandparents to sue for the privilege of visiting their grandchildren after the parents are divorced or separated.

grounds the basis or foundation for some action; legal reasons for filing a lawsuit.

guardian ad litem a guardian appointed to prosecute or defend a suit on behalf of a minor or other party unable to represent him- or herself.

guilty but mentally ill a verdict that allows convicted criminal defendants to be sent to a hospital and later transferred to a prison after recovery from mental illness.

H

heirs people who inherit property and/or money from a person who dies.

holdover tenants tenants who are allowed to remain on the property after the lease expires.

home confinement the type of sentence in which the defendant must serve the term at home and usually can leave only for essential purposes, such as work or school.

homicide the killing of another person. Homicide can be criminal, noncriminal, or negligent. *See also* manslaughter and murder.

homosexuality sexual and emotional preference for a person of the same sex.

housing codes the municipal ordinances that regulate standards of safety and upkeep for buildings.

human rights basic privileges a person has as a human being.

hung jury the situation in which a jury cannot reach a unanimous decision.

I

immunity freedom from; protection from some action, such as being sued.

impair to damage or make worse.

implied consent (1) an unwritten agreement to submit to forms of interrogations or searches in exchange for certain privileges, such as driving or flying; (2) a defense frequently used in rape cases. The defense is that the victim agreed to sexual intercourse, because she did not take steps to oppose the defendant's advances.

implied warranty the unwritten standard of quality the law requires of products offered for sale.

imprisonment confinement, usually in jail or prison. *See also* false imprisonment.

incapacitation a theory of sentencing that stresses keeping a convicted criminal locked up to protect society.

incest sexual relations between people who are closely related to each other.

incitement test a method used by the courts to determine whether to restrict expression based on its potential for immediate lawlessness.

indeterminate term a sentence that does not set the exact period of time to be served, but provides maximum and minimum time limits.

indictment a grand jury's formal charge or accusation of criminal action.

infancy the legal status of a person considered not yet legally responsible for his or her activities; the time before which a person becomes entitled to the legal rights normally held by citizens.

infliction of mental distress an intentional tort in which a defendant engaged in an action that caused foreseeable emotional harm to the plaintiff.

informal separation occurs when a married couple lives apart without a formal legal agreement.

information a prosecuting attorney's formal accusation of the defendant for supposedly committing a crime.

inheritance property received from a dead person either by intestacy laws or from a will.

initial hearing a preliminary examination of the validity of a youth's arrest, during which the state must prove that an offense was committed and there is reasonable cause to believe the youth committed it. Decisions are made about further detention and legal representation, and a date is set for a hearing on the facts.

initiatives the procedures by which voters can propose a law and submit it to the electorate or the legislature for approval.

injunction a court order requiring a person to do or refrain from doing a particular act.

inmate a person deprived of liberty by a government due to conviction for a crime; a prisoner.

inquisitional system a European method for handling disputes in which the judge plays an active role in gathering and presenting evidence and questioning witnesses.

insanity defense defense raised by a criminal defendant stating that because of mental disease or defect, the defendant should not be held responsible for the crime committed.

insurance a contract in which one party pays money and the other party promises to reimburse the first party for specified types of losses if they occur.

intake in informal process in which court officials or social workers decide if a complaint against a juvenile should be referred to juvenile court.

intent determination to achieve a particular end by a particular means.

intentional torts actions taken to deliberately harm another person or his or her property; intentional wrongs.

intentional wrongs *See* intentional torts.

interest money paid for the use of someone's money; the cost of borrowing money. Money put in a savings account earns interest, while borrowing money costs interest.

interrogation the questioning of a witness or suspected criminal.

intestate having died without a will.

intoxication state of drunkenness or similar condition created by use of drugs or alcohol.

J

jail a place of short-term confinement for persons convicted of misdemeanors or awaiting trial.

joint custody a custody arrangement in which divorced or separated parents have an equal right to make important decisions concerning their children.

joint property property owned by two or more people.

judgment a court's decision in a case.

judicial branch the portion of government that interprets laws and resolves legal questions.

judicial integrity as used in discussing search and seizure, this is an argument for the use of the exclusionary rule, which emphasizes that the courts should not permit lawbreaking by the police.

judicial review the process by which courts decide whether the laws passed by Congress or state legislatures are constitutional.

jurisprudence the study of law and legal philosophy.

jury in a legal proceeding, a body of men and women selected to examine certain facts and determine truth.

juvenile a person not yet considered an adult for the purposes of determining either criminal or civil liability; a minor.

L

labor relations law the branch of law that determines how unions and employers may operate.

landlord (1) the property owner who leases or rents space; (2) the company or person who manages the property for the owner.

larceny the unlawful taking of another's property with the intent to steal it. Grand larceny, a felony, is the theft of anything above a certain value (often $100). Petty larceny, a misdemeanor, is the theft of anything below a certain value (often $100).

lease a contract between a landlord and a tenant for the use of property for a specified length of time at a specified cost.

lease application a form the landlord uses to determine whether someone qualifies for a rental.

legal cause a wrongful act that causes foreseeable harm for which there may be legal liability.

legal defense a legally recognized excuse for a defendant's actions, such as implied consent, privilege, and self defense, which may remove liability for certain offenses.

legal malpractice the type of lawsuit brought against a lawyer for loss to his or her client caused by the lawyer's failure to meet acceptable standards of practice for the legal profession.

legal separation a situation in which the two spouses are separated but still maintain some marital obligations.

legislation laws or statutes that have been enacted by a legislature.

legislative branch the portion of government that passes the laws.

legislative intent what the lawmakers who passed a law wanted the law to mean. Finding this meaning is necessary so judges can correctly interpret laws (i.e., statutes).

legitimacy the legal status of a child born to a married couple.

legitimate lawful or legal; a child born to a married couple is called legitimate.

liability legal responsibility; the obligation to do or not do something. The defendant in a torts case incurs liability for failing to use reasonable care, resulting in harm to the plaintiff.

liability insurance the type of coverage or insurance that pays for injuries to other people or damage to property if the individual insured is responsible for an accident.

libel a written expression about a person that is false and damages that person's reputation.

lien a creditor's claim on property until a debt is paid.

limited government a basic principle of our constitutional system. It limits government to powers provided to it by the people.

litigator an attorney; a lawyer; a barrister.

living will a document that specifies whether a person wants to continue living if, with no hope of recovery, he or she is being kept alive by artificial means.

loan sharking lending money at high, often illegal, interest rates.

lobbying influencing or persuading legislators to take action to introduce a bill or vote a certain way on a proposed law.

M

malice ill will; intentionally harming someone.

malpractice failure to meet acceptable standards of practice in any professional or official position; often the basis for lawsuits by clients or patients against their attorney or doctor.

mandatory sentencing laws that require courts to sentence convicted criminals to certain prison terms.

manslaughter the killing of a person without malice or premeditation, but during the commission of an illegal act. Manslaughter can be either voluntary, when intentional but not premeditated, resulting from the heat of passion or the diminished mental capacity of the killer; or involuntary, when unintentional but done during an unlawful act of a lesser nature. *See also* homicide and murder.

marriage the legal union of a man and woman in wedlock.

marriage counselor a trained person who helps couples settle their marital problems.

maternity leave a temporary absence from work given to women when they give birth.

mausoleum Greek word for a large tomb; usually a building with a place for burying the dead above ground.

mediation the act or process of resolving a dispute between two or more parties.

Medicaid a government program that provides medical care to poor people.

medical coverage when dealing with insurance, that which covers an individual's own medical expenses resulting from accidents.

Medicare the federal health insurance program for people aged 65 and older.

memorial services after the burial, services commemorating the life of the deceased.

minor a child; a person under the legal age of adulthood (usually 18 or 21).

Miranda warnings rights that a person must be told when arrested or taken into custody by police or other officials. These include the right to remain silent, to contact a lawyer, and to have a free lawyer if the person arrested cannot afford one.

misdemeanor a criminal offense, less serious than a felony, punishable by a prison sentence of one year or less.

mitigating factors factors that may lessen the seriousness of an offense. The presence of these factors may be considered by the judge or jury.

mobile home a movable, factory-built house that usually comes with furniture and appliances.

month-to-month lease a lease enabling the tenant to leave with 30 days' notice and the landlord to raise the rent or evict the tenant with 30 days' notice.

mortgage a loan in which land or buildings are put up as security.

motion for change of venue a request to change the location of a trial to avoid community hostility, for the convenience of a witness, or for other reasons.

motion for continuance a request to postpone a lawsuit to gain more time to prepare the case.

motion for discovery of evidence a request by the defendant to examine, before trial, certain evidence possessed by the prosecution.

motions requests made by one party to a lawsuit that a judge take specific action or make a decision.

motion to suppress evidence a motion filed by a criminal defense attorney, asking the court to exclude any evidence that was illegally obtained from the attorney's client.

motive the reason a person commits a crime.

murder the unlawful killing of a person with malice aforethought. Murder in the first degree is planned in advance and done with malice or during the commission of a dangerous felony. Murder in the second degree does not require malice or premeditation but is the result of a desire to inflict bodily harm. It is done without excuse, and is therefore more serious than manslaughter. *See also* manslaughter and homicide.

mutual agreement agreement by the parties to the exact terms of a contract, either by signing the contract or by beginning to carry it out.

N

national origin country where one was born or from which one's ancestors came.

necessities those things that parents have a legal obligation to provide their children and that one spouse has the responsibility to provide the other. These usually include food, clothing, housing, and medical care.

necessity a defense that presents a just or lawful reason for the defendant's conduct.

neglect the failure to properly feed, clothe, shelter, educate, or tend to the medical needs of a child.

negligence the failure to exercise a reasonable amount of care in either doing or not doing something, resulting in harm or injury.

negotiation the process of discussing an issue to reach a settlement or agreement.

no-fault divorce a divorce in which neither party is charged with any wrongdoing. The marriage is ended on the grounds that there are irreconcilable differences (i.e., basic disagreements), causing the marriage to break down.

no-fault insurance a form of automobile or accident insurance in which each person's insurance company pays a certain share of damages, regardless of fault.

nolo contendere Latin phrase meaning "no contest." A defendant's plea to criminal charges that does not admit guilt but also does not contest the charges. It is equivalent to a guilty plea, but it cannot be used as evidence in a later civil trial for damages based on the same facts.

nominal damages symbolic compensation to show that a claim is justified, whereby the plaintiff can recover limited damages even if she or he is unable to prove economic harm.

nonbinding arbitration a method in which disputants agree to have a third party listen to arguments from both sides and make a decision that is not final (i.e., either party may still take other steps to settle the dispute).

notice a written statement intended to inform a person of some proceeding in which his or her interests are involved.

nuisance unreasonable interference with the use and enjoyment of one's property, usually repeated or continued for prolonged periods of time.

O

obscenity a general term applying to anything that is immoral, indecent, or lewd.

offer a definite proposal by one person to another to make a deal or contract.

ombudsperson a person who has the power to investigate reported complaints and help achieve fair settlements.

opening statement at the start of a trial, one side's explanation of what it expects to prove and how it intends to prove it.

ordinance a county or city law.

overbreadth the term used to describe portions of statutes that attempt to punish or prohibit conduct protected by the Constitution.

overt open; clear (for example, an overt act in criminal law is more than mere preparation to do something; it is at least the first step of actually attempting the crime.)

P

palimony name given to support payment made by one unmarried cohabitant to another after the couple split up.

parens patriae the doctrine under which the court protects the interests of a juvenile.

parental responsibility laws statutes in which parents are held responsible and may be prosecuted for crimes committed by their children.

parochial school a school supported and controlled by a church.

parole release from prison before the full sentence has been served, granted at the discretion of a parole board.

partial emancipation the legal doctrine that allows minors to keep and spend their own earnings.

parties the people directly concerned with or taking part in any legal matter.

paternity leave a temporary absence from work for men to care for their infants.

paternity suit a lawsuit brought by a woman against a man she claims is the father of her child. If a paternity suit is proven, the man is legally responsible for contributing to the support of the child.

peace bond a sum of money deposited with the court to guarantee good behavior for a period of time.

penal institution a prison or jail.

peremptory challenge part of the pretrial jury selection. This allows each side to dismiss a certain number of possible jurors without giving any reason. There is one exception: peremptory challenges cannot be used to discriminate based on race.

personal property property or belongings that can be moved, such as cars, clothing, furniture, and appliances.

personal recognizance a release from legal custody based on a defendant's promise to return to court. An alternative to cash bail, this practice is used if the judge decides that the defendant is likely to show up for trial.

petition (1) to file charges in a juvenile court proceeding; (2) a request to a court or public official.

physical incapacity the inability of a spouse to engage in sexual intercourse. This may be grounds for annulment.

picketing a gathering of individuals in a public place to express their opposition to certain views or practices.

plaintiff in a civil case, the injured party who brings an action against the alleged wrongdoer.

plea bargaining negotiations in a criminal case between a prosecutor and a defendant and the defendant's attorney. If the defendant agrees to plead guilty, the prosecutor charges the defendant with a less serious crime generally leading to a lighter sentence.

polygamy the practice of having more than one spouse at the same time. Polygamy is illegal in the United States.

polygraph a lie detector instrument.

precedent court decisions on legal questions that guide future cases with similar questions.

preferences a method used to increase the number of minorities admitted to educational programs and hired for jobs. It involves giving some advantage to minority applicants.

preliminary hearing pretrial proceeding at which the prosecutor must prove that a crime was committed and establish the probable guilt of the defendant. If the evidence presented does not show probable guilt, the judge may dismiss the case.

premiums in insurance, payments made for coverage.

prenuptial agreement an agreement between a man and woman prior to marriage. It often includes provisions for the disposal of property in the event of separation, divorce, or death.

preponderance of the evidence in most civil suits, the standard of proof used. To win, a party must provide more evidence than the other side. "More evidence" does not just mean the amount of evidence. It also means that evidence is more believable and important.

presentence report a probation officer's written report that gives the sentencing judge information about the defendant's background and prospects for rehabilitation.

presentment the initial appearance of defendants in felony cases. At that time they are informed of the charges against them and advised of their rights.

pretrial motion a document by which a party asks the judge to make a decision before the trial begins.

preventive detention holding a person against his or her will because of the likelihood that the individual will commit a crime.

principal (1) the person who actually commits a crime; (2) the amount of money borrowed or loaned. This amount does not include interest.

prior restraint any effort to censor a publication before it goes to press.

prison a place of confinement for criminals who are serving long-term sentences.

privacy the state of being left alone.

privilege an advantage, or not having to perform duties that others must perform. Also, a duty not to give information because of some special, confidential relationship.

privilege against self-incrimination the rule that suspects have a right to remain silent and cannot be forced to testify against themselves.

probable cause a reasonable belief, known personally or through reliable sources, that a person has committed a crime.

probate the process of proving to a court that a will is genuine; distributing the property according to the terms of the will.

probation a system of supervised freedom, usually under a probation officer, for persons convicted of a criminal offense. Typically, the probationer must agree to certain conditions such as getting a job, avoiding drugs, and not traveling outside a limited area.

procedural due process a citizen's right to fair access to the courts and to fair treatment in those courts. Generally, a right to fair treatment when government action affects a person's interests.

product liability the legal responsibility of manufacturers and sellers for injuries caused by defective products they produce or sell.

pro se Latin term meaning "for oneself," "on one's own behalf," typically used to describe a person who represents him- or herself in court.

prosecution (1) the process of suing a person in a civil case or of bringing a person to trial on criminal charges; (2) the side bringing a case against another party.

prosecutor the government's attorney in a criminal case.

prostitution the act of performing sexual acts for money.

protective order in family law, a court order directing one spouse not to abuse the other spouse or the children. The penalty for violating a protective order is jail.

proximate cause in negligence law, the legal cause of the harm. This concept limits damages the defendant must pay. It covers only harms that are reasonably predictable consequences of the defendant's wrongful acts. *See also*, foreseeable harm.

public forums places, such as parks or streets, where First Amendment expression rights are traditionally exercised.

public hearings proceedings that are open to the public. During these proceedings, evidence is considered and then a decision is reached based on this evidence.

puffing an exaggerated statement as to the desirability of a product or service.

punitive damages awards in excess of the proven economic loss. In a tort action, they are paid to the victim to punish the defendant and to warn others not to engage in such conduct.

Q

qualified immunity a limited protection from lawsuits, unless the individual knew or should have known that his or her acts violated the legal rights of another person.

quotas a system that requires a certain number of minority applicants be selected for educational programs or jobs.

R

rape unlawful sexual intercourse. It is committed when one party forces another party to have sexual intercourse. It implies resistance and lack of consent.

ratify to confirm a previous act done by you or another person.

real property land and all items attached to it, such as houses and crops.

reasonable person standard the idealized standard of how a community expects its members to act. It is based on how much care a person of ordinary prudence would exercise in a particular situation.

rebuttal argument the presentation of facts to a court, demonstrating that the testimony of a witness or evidence presented by the opposing party is not true.

recall the removal of an elected official from office by a vote of the people.

receiving stolen property receiving or buying property that is known or reasonably believed to be stolen.

redlining a discriminatory procedure in which certain geographical areas in a community are designated by a bank as ineligible for mortgage loans.

referenda procedures in which issues are voted on directly by the citizens rather than by their representatives in government.

regulation a rule made by a government agency.

rehabilitate to attempt to change or reform a convicted person so that he or she will not commit another criminal act.

rehabilitation the process through which a convicted person is changed or reformed, so as not to commit another criminal act.

rehabilitative alimony after a divorce, money awarded a spouse to regain or develop job skills.

release (1) the giving up of a claim or right by a person; (2) a landlord's act of excusing a tenant from all duties related to the apartment and the lease.

remedy what is done to compensate for an injury or to enforce some right.

removal for cause part of the jury selection process. It permits removal of any juror who does not appear capable of rendering a fair and impartial verdict.

rent control a law that limits how much existing rents can be raised.

rent withholding the right of tenants in some states not to pay part or all of the rent until the landlord makes certain repairs or meets other tenant demands.

repossession the taking back by a lender of a debtor's property because the debtor failed to repay a debt.

rescission the act of canceling a contract and treating it as if it never existed.

restitution the act of restoring something to its owner; the act of making good for loss or damage; repaying or refunding illegally obtained money.

retainer a down payment by which a client hires an attorney to act in his or her behalf.

retaliatory eviction a landlord's illegal action of evicting a tenant because the tenant complained about the building or otherwise took action against the landlord.

retribution punishment given as a kind of revenge for wrongdoing.

revoke to take back or cancel.

right of entry or access the part of a lease that allows a landlord and his or her agents to enter a tenant's premises to make repairs, collect the rent, or enforce other provisions of the lease.

right to die the right of hopelessly ill (or comatose) patients not to be kept alive by artificial or extraordinary means.

right to quiet enjoyment a tenant's right to use and enjoy the property without being disturbed by the landlord or other tenants.

right-to-work states states in which it is illegal to require workers to join unions or pay dues as a condition of employment.

robbery the unlawful taking of property from a person's immediate possession by force or threat of force.

S

sales contract a contract, constituting the seller's offer, that includes all the major terms of a sale and becomes enforceable when the buyer agrees to and signs it.

search warrant an order issued by a magistrate, giving police the power to enter a building to search for and seize items related to a crime.

secular nonreligious.

secured credit the act of putting up some kind of property as a protection in the event a debt is not repaid.

security deposit refundable money that a landlord requires a tenant to pay before moving in; used to cover any damages, cleaning costs, or unpaid rent, if such fees arise.

segregation the unconstitutional practice of separating persons in housing, education, public facilities, and other ways based on their race, color, nationality, or other arbitrary categorization.

self-defense the right to defend oneself with whatever force is reasonably necessary against an actual or reasonably perceived threat of personal harm.

self-incrimination giving evidence and answering questions that would tend to subject one to criminal prosecution.

separate but equal doctrine the rule, now unconstitutional, that allowed facilities to be racially segregated as long as they were basically equal.

separate property a system under which property owned by either spouse before the marriage remains that person's property throughout the marriage, and any property acquired during the marriage belongs to the person who acquired it.

separation agreement a written document that lists the continuing legal rights and duties of each spouse when a couple separates, including alimony, child custody, support, and division of property.

separation of powers the division of power among the separate branches of government (executive, legislative and judicial).

set-asides certain amounts of available money saved for minority companies (i.e., companies owned by members of minority groups).

settlement a mutual agreement between two sides in a lawsuit, made before the case goes to trial, that settles or ends the dispute.

severance pay money paid to employees who have been dismissed (generally through no fault of their own) to compensate for the time they are not going to work because of the job loss.

sexual harassment unwelcome sexual advances, requests for sexual favors, and other verbal or physical conduct of a sexual nature that occurs in the workplace.

shoplifting a form of larceny in which items are taken from a store without payment or the intention to pay.

slander spoken expression about a person that is false and damages that person's reputation.

small claims court a court that handles civil claims for small amounts of money. People usually represent themselves rather than hire an attorney.

solicitation the act of requesting or strongly urging someone to do something. If the request is to do something illegal, solicitation is considered a crime.

specific performance a remedy available in civil court that orders the breaching party to do exactly what he or she promised under the contract.

speculation the process of buying property at a low price, holding it for a short period of time, and then selling it for a large profit.

spouse abuse the criminal act by one spouse of beating or physically assaulting the other.

status offenders youths who are charged with the status of being beyond the control of their legal guardians, habitually disobedient, truant from school, or of committing other acts that would not be crimes if committed by an adult.

status offenses illegal acts that can only be committed by juveniles (for example, truancy or running away from home).

statutes laws enacted by legislatures.

statutory rape the act of unlawful sexual intercourse by a male with a female who is under the age of consent, even if she is a willing and voluntary participant in the sexual act.

steering a discriminatory practice on the part of real estate agents that directs buyers or renters to particular areas because of their race or for other unlawful reasons.

stop and frisk to "pat down" or search someone who the police believe is acting suspiciously.

strict liability the legal responsibility for damage or injury even if you are not at fault.

strike the act in which employees stop, slow down, or disrupt work to win demands from an employer.

sublease clause the part of most standard leases that requires the tenant to obtain the landlord's permission before allowing someone else to live on the premises and pay all or part of the rent.

subpoena a court order to appear in court on a specified date and time.

substance a chemical, often mind-altering, that people abuse, such as alcohol, drugs, and tobacco.

substance abuse the harmful overuse of chemicals, such as drugs or alcohol.

substantive due process used by courts to protect a person's basic freedom. Courts do this by making sure that government does not violate basic constitutional rights.

suicide the deliberate taking of one's own life.

suit a lawsuit or civil action in court.

summons a legal notice informing a person of a lawsuit and telling that person when and where to go to court.

supremacy clause the provision in Article VI of the Constitution stating that U.S. laws and treaties must be followed even if state and local laws disagree with the Constitution and these treaties.

surrogate parent a woman who agrees to be artificially inseminated with the sperm of the husband of a couple desiring a child.

suspended sentence a sentence issued by the court but not actually served. The individual is usually released with no conditions attached.

symbolic speech conduct that expresses an idea (for example, flag-waving).

T

tenancy at will a situation in which a tenant remains on rented property beyond the end of the lease. In this situation, either the landlord or the tenant can end the lease with whatever notice the law requires.

tenancy for years refers to any lease for a fixed period of time. The lease specifies that the tenant may live on the property for a single definite period of time.

tenant a person who rents property.

testify to give evidence under oath.

throw-aways children, usually older teenagers, whose parents have refused to continue to care for them.

tort a breach of some obligation causing harm or injury to someone. A civil wrong, such as negligence or libel.

tort action a civil lawsuit for damages.

tort reform the movement that focuses on changing the process of settling tort claims. It emphasizes methods other than going to court or establishes limitations on how much money the winning party may receive.

treason the offense whereby a U.S. citizen attempts by overt acts to overthrow or seriously harm the U.S. government.

trespass the unexcused intrusion on, or improper use of, property belonging to another person. This can be the basis of an intentional tort.

trial courts courts that listen to testimony, consider evidence, and decide the facts in a disputed situation.

truant a pupil who stays away from school without permission.

trust handing over property or money to one person, to be held for the benefit of another person.

U

unconscionable (1) unfair, harsh, oppressive; (2) a sales practice or term in a contract that is so unfair that a judge will not permit it.

uncontested divorce a divorce in which the parties agree to the grounds and terms of the settlement.

unconstitutional conflicting with some provision of the constitution.

undertaking putting up bond or stocks as security against theft. An executor of an estate is often named in a will and specifically exempted from putting up bond or undertaking.

unemployment compensation the government system that protects employees who are not at fault for losing their jobs, by providing them with payments while they look for other jobs.

unfair labor practices the failure on the part of an employer or a union to abide by the regulations of the National Labor Relations Act.

unfair labor practices strike the slowing down, stopping, or disrupting of work by employees due to employer violations of the National Labor Relations Act.

uninsured motorist coverage insurance that protects drivers from those with no insurance or inadequate insurance.

union an association of workers that seeks to secure favorable wages, improve working conditions and hours, and resolve grievances with employers.

unsecured credit credit based only on a promise to repay in the future.

U.S. Constitution the written document that contains the fundamental laws of the nation and the principles of a free, representative democracy.

usury the act of charging interest for various types of credit at rates higher than the state's legal limit.

uttering offering to someone as genuine a document known to be a fake.

V

vagueness indefiniteness, uncertainty, imprecision.

vandalism the deliberate destruction or defacement of property.

variable interest rate a percentage of the money borrowed. It tells the extra amount a person must pay for borrowing money. The rate can change (i.e., go up or down), usually within certain limits, depending on the economy.

verdict a jury's decision on a case.

vetoed prohibited; in government, the veto is the power of a chief executive to prevent enactment of a bill (i.e., to prevent the bill from becoming a law). An executive may exercise a pocket veto by refusing to sign a bill, which will automatically become a law after a certain period of time.

visitation rights a noncustodial parent's privilege to visit his or her children. It is given in a separation or divorce situation.

void not valid or legally binding; canceled.

voir dire the process in which opposing lawyers question prospective jurors to get as favorable or as fair a jury as possible.

voluntary separation act of a married couple informally agreeing to live apart.

W

waive to give up some right, privilege, or benefit voluntarily.

waiver of tort liability a lease clause in which the tenant agrees to give up the usual right to hold the landlord responsible for personal injuries.

warrant a paper signed by a judge authorizing some action, such as an arrest or a search and seizure.

warranty a guarantee or promise made by a seller or manufacturer concerning the quality or performance of goods offered for sale.

warranty of fitness for a particular purpose a seller's promise that the item sold will meet the buyer's stated purpose. The promise is not spoken or written by the seller but is implied by law.

warranty of habitability implied or unwritten obligation of a landlord to provide a unit that is fit to live in.

warranty of merchantability an implied promise that the item sold is of at least average quality for that type of item.

warranty of title the seller's promise that he or she owns and may transmit title to the item being offered for sale.

waste damages caused by a tenant's misuse or neglect of property. The landlord can force the tenant to make repairs or can sue for damages.

whistle blower an employee who tells the authorities about his or her employer's illegal acts.

will a legal document that states what a person wants done with his or her belongings after death.

workers' compensation system a system of compensating employees who are injured on the job. These benefits are paid no matter who caused the accident.

work release the type of sentence in which a defendant is allowed to work in the community but is required to return to prison at night or on weekends.

writ a judge's order, or authorization, that something be done.

wrongful act an unreasonable behavior that violates an individual's duty to others.

Index

National Advisory Committee

Chairperson:
Mark Gelber
New York, NY

Aggie Alvez
Montgomery County Public Schools
Rockville, MD

Judy Areen
Georgetown University Law Center
Washington, D.C.

Robert B. Barnett
Williams & Connolly
Washington, D.C.

Stuart Bindeman
Commercial Investors, Inc.
Bethesda, MD

John Buchanan, Jr.
Council for the Advancement of Citizenship
Bethesda, MD

Anthony Carroll
Pagonis & Donnelly
Washington, D.C.

David Copenhaver
Ameritech Enhanced Business Services
Indianapolis, IN

Joseph Eldridge
Lawyers Committee for Human Rights
Washington, D.C.

Richard J. Gable
National Center for Juvenile Justice
Pittsburgh, PA

Elliott Hall
Ford Motor Company
Washington, D.C.

Charles Kolb
United Way of America
Alexandria, VA

Judge David B. Mitchell
Circuit Court for Baltimore
Baltimore, MD

Charles Mwalimu
Silver Spring, MD

Stuart G. Newman
Miami, FL

Theodore A. Pinnock
Attorney at Law
San Diego, CA

Judge William Pryor
D.C. Superior Court
Washington, D.C.

Dr. Scott Satterlund
UGLETI
Marquette, MI

Steve Shapiro
Germantown, MD

Monte Shepler
Consortium of Universities of the Washington Metropolitan Area
Washington, D.C.

Linda Start
Michigan LRE Project
Waterford, MI

Jerrol Tostrud
West Publishing Company
St. Paul, MN

Elvin Tyrone
Texas Education Agency
Austin, TX

Fay Williams
Attorney at Law
Indianapolis, IN

Howard Zipser
Rosenman & Colin
New York, NY

Photo Credits

©Ira Wyman/Sygma; **45 (left)** ©Don Milici; **45 (right)** ©Gilles Bassignac/Gamma Liaison; **50** ©Don Milici; **52** ©Don Milici; **56** ©Don Milici; **59** ©Don Milici; **60** ©Don Milici; **64** ©J. Patrick Forden/Sygma; **65 (top)** ©Don Milici; **65 (bottom)** ©Don Milici; **68** ©Jeff Dunas/Sygma; **70** ©Don Milici; **71** ©Don Milici; **72** ©Don Milici; **74** ©Don Milici; **75** ©Don Milici; **80** ©J.L. Atlan/Sygma; **82** ©Mary Kate Denny/PhotoEdit; **83** ©David Young-Wolff/PhotoEdit; **88** ©Don Milici; **91** ©Ellis Herwig/Stock, Boston, Inc.; **93** ©Don Milici; **94 (top)** ©C. Simonpietri/Sygma; **94 (bottom)** ©Don Milici; **98** ©Tony Freeman/PhotoEdit; **100** ©Don Milici; **102** ©D&I MacDonald/PhotoEdit; **103** ©Don Milici; **104** ©Don Milici; **107 (left)** ©Tony Savino/Sygma; **107 (right)** ©James Prince/Photo Researchers, Inc.; **108 (top)** ©Don Milici; **108 (bottom)** ©Don Milici; **109** ©Don Milici; **116** ©Don Milici; **121** ©Don Milici; **126** ©Don Milici; **132** ©Don Milici; **133** ©Don Milici; **135 (top left)** ©Don Milici; **135 (top right)** ©Don Milici; **135 (bottom left)** ©Don Milici; **135 (bottom right)** ©Don Milici; **137** ©Don Milici; **142** ©Don Milici; **150** ©Don Milici; **151** ©AP/Wide World Photos, Inc.; **154** ©AP/Wide World Photos, Inc.; **157** ©Bob Daemmrich/Stock, Boston, Inc.; **161** ©William Campbell/Sygma; **164** ©Fabricius/Stock, Boston, Inc.; **166 (left)** ©AP/Wide World Photos, Inc.; **166 (right)** ©AP/Wide World Photos, Inc.; **172** ©Rhoda Sidney/PhotoEdit; **176** ©William Snyder/Gamma Liaison; **180** ©Billy E. Barnes/Stock, Boston, Inc.; **181** ©Bob Daemmrich, Stock Boston, Inc.; **182** Bob Daemmrich/Stock, Boston, Inc.; **185** ©Don Milici; **186** ©Don Milici; **188** ©Jeff Persans/Stock, Boston, Inc.; **190** ©Stacy Pick/Stock, Boston, Inc.; **191** ©Don Milici; **192** ©Don Milici; **195** ©Richard Pasley/Stock, Boston, Inc.; **196** ©Don Milici; **198** ©Don Milici; **201** ©Don Milici; **205** ©Don Milici; **208** ©Don Milici; **211** ©David Young-Wolff/PhotoEdit; **214** ©Don Milici; **218** ©Don Milici; **219** ©Don Milici; **220** ©Don Milici; **224** ©Don Milici; **227** ©The Bettmann Archive; **229** ©Don Milici; **231** ©Tony Freeman/PhotoEdit; **232** ©Don Milici; **233** ©UPI/Bettmann; **234** ©Don Milici; **236** ©Ira Wyman/Sygma; **237** ©E. Adams/Sygma; **238** ©Don Milici; **241** ©Don Milici; **242** ©Don Milici; **246** ©Don Milici; **249** ©Don Milici; **250** ©Don Milici; **252** ©Don Milici; **253** ©Don Milici; **257 (top)** ©Don Milici; **257 (bottom)** ©Don Milici; **260** ©Don Milici; **264** ©Don Milici; **268** ©Don Milici; **270** ©Don Milici; **273** ©Don Milici; **276** ©Don Milici; **281** ©Don Milici; **283** ©Don Milici; **285** ©Don Milici; **287** ©Don Milici; **296** ©Robert A. Isaacs/Photo Researchers, Inc.; **298** ©Don Milici; **303** ©Don Milici; **308** ©Don Milici; **310** ©Don Milici; **314** ©Bachmann/Photo Researchers, Inc.; **318** ©Don Milici; **319** ©Don Milici; **320** ©Don Milici; **321 (top left)** ©Charles Gupton/Stock, Boston, Inc.; **321 (top right)** ©Tony Freeman/PhotoEdit; **321 (bottom left)** ©Myrleen Ferguson/PhotoEdit; **321 (bottom right)** ©Don Milici; **322** ©Don Milici; **325** ©Don Milici; **326** ©Don Milici; **334** ©David Young-Wolff/PhotoEdit; **336** ©Michael Newman/PhotoEdit; **340** ©Don Milici; **342** ©Peter Menzel/Stock, Boston, Inc.; **343** ©Don Milici; **345** ©Don Milici; **347** ©Robert Brenner/PhotoEdit; **350 (top)** ©Don Milici; **350 (bottom)** ©Mark C. Burnett/PhotoEdit; **354** ©Tony Freeman/PhotoEdit; **358** ©Don Milici; **361** ©Don Milici; **363** ©Michael Newman/PhotoEdit; **365** ©Don Milici; **369** ©Don Milici; **372** ©Don Milici; **374** ©Joseph Sohm/Stock, Boston, Inc.; **375** ©Don Milici; **379** ©Brooks Draft/Sygma; **381** ©Stock, Boston, Inc.; **383** ©Don Milici; **384 (left)** ©Don Milici; **384 (right)** ©Don Milici; **385** ©Don Milici; **389** ©Don Milici; **392** ©Don Milici; **402** ©Don Milici; **406** ©Don Milici; **407** ©Don Milici; **412** ©Don Milici; **418** ©C. Vergara/Photo Researchers, Inc.; **421** ©Patrick Forestier/Sygma; **422** ©O. Franken/Sygma; **426** ©Don Milici; **429** ©Don Milici; **430** ©Joseph Sohm/Stock, Boston, Inc.; **432** ©AP/Wide World Photos; **434** ©Bob Daemmrich/Stock, Boston, Inc.; **435** ©William Campbell/Sygma; **439** ©Frank Trapper/Sygma; **443** ©Don Milici; **444** ©Don Milici; **445** ©Don Milici; **448** ©Michael Newman/PhotoEdit; **453** ©Don Milici; **455** ©UPI/Bettmann Newsphotos; **459** ©David Young-Wolff/PhotoEdit; **464** ©Don Milici; **467** ©Don Milici; **469 (top)** ©Sue Klemens/Stock, Boston, Inc.; **469 (bottom)** ©Merkel/Gamma Liaison; **472** ©J.L. Atlan/Sygma; **479** ©PhotoEdit; **482** ©Reuters/Bettmann Newsphotos; **485** ©Don Milici; **490** ©UPI/Bettmann; **495** ©UPI/Bettmann; **497** ©Sygma; **499** ©Don Milici; **508** ©Cary Wolinsky/Stock, Boston, Inc.; **510** ©Don Milici; **512** ©Don Milici; **514** ©Ellis Herwig/Stock, Boston, Inc.; **515** ©Robert Brenner/PhotoEdit; **516** ©Bob Daemmrich/Stock, Boston, Inc.; **519** ©Jeffrey Markowitz/Sygma; **525** ©Don Milici; **526 (top)** ©Don Milici; **526 (bottom)** ©Don Milici; **529** ©Don Milici; **532** ©Frank Siteman/Stock, Boston, Inc.; **535** ©Don Milici; **539 (top left)** ©Don Milici; **539 (top right)** ©Tony Freeman/PhotoEdit; **539 (bottom left)** ©Don Milici; **539 (bottom right)** ©Don Milici; **541** ©Don Milici; **546** ©Don Milici.